# *The Batsford*
# DICTIONARY
# OF DRAMA

Acting is like holding a bird in the hand:
if you close your hand too tightly, the bird
will be killed; if you open it too much the
bird will fly away.

MICHEL SAINT-DENIS


Writing for the theatre is a peculiar
business. It involves a craft you have to
learn and a talent you must possess.
Neither is common and both are essential.

GOETHE


Everything that is of importance to the
writing of a play must be said at least three
times. The first time one half of the
audience will understand it, the second
time the other half, only on the third
occasion may we be sure that everybody
understands, except for deaf persons and
certain critics.

BENEVENTE


The drama's laws the drama's patrons give
And we that live to please must please to
live.

DR JOHNSON

# The Batsford
# DICTIONARY
# OF DRAMA

**Terry Hodgson**

B.T. BATSFORD · LONDON

# To Nadine

© Terry Hodgson 1988

First published in 1988

All rights reserved. No part of this publication
may be reproduced, in any form or by any means,
without permission from the Publisher

Typeset by Progress Filmsetting, London
and printed in Great Britain by
Billings Ltd, Worcester
Published by B.T. Batsford Ltd
4 Fitzhardinge Street, London W1H 0AH

British Library Cataloguing in Publication Data

Hodgson, Terry
The Batsford Dictionary of Drama
1. Drama——Dictionaries
I. Title
809.2′003′21          PN1625

ISBN 0-7134-4693-5
ISBN 0-7134-4694-3 Pbk

# *Preface*

The main intention of *The Batsford Dictionary of Drama* is to provide useful working definitions of terms used in the theatre and by theatre critics. It does not aim to provide exhaustive information about dramatists, plays, theatre companies and theatre buildings. Excellent reference books, such as the *Oxford Companion to the Theatre* and the smaller *Concise Oxford Companion* already answer such a need. The information and the examples provided here are rather meant to support the practical, critical and theoretical entries.

The idea of a dictionary which combines the definition of practical and critical terms springs from two beliefs: first, that there is too great a divide between those who work in the theatre, and those who teach, write about and study drama in schools and universities; and secondly, that drama is best studied by combining discussion of dramatic texts with practical involvement in aspects of performance, through acting, designing, directing or workshop activity. Some of the entries, it is hoped, benefit from the author's involvement, over a number of years, with professional actors and workshop groups, as well as with groups of students and theatre-goers both inside and outside universities.

The *Dictionary* is aimed therefore at students, theatre-goers, amateur and professional performers and the common reader in the hope that each will find something of interest when consulting it for their own immediate concerns. It is also hoped that the system of cross-referencing (by asterisks* and by explicit references in small capitals: 'see THEATRE OF CRUELTY') will encourage an interest in aspects of drama which may seem less immediate, and that the book may in some way contribute to the bridging of a regrettable gap between the practical theatre and those who read and write about drama.

Dictionaries of the theatre have tended to be either practical or academic and this book endeavours to bring the two together. It tries to avoid jargon, to be as clear as possible within necessary word-limits and to illustrate more abstruse points with interesting examples from plays likely to be widely known, since reference to the unknown is often tedious. Should the examples be unfamiliar, however, it is hoped that enough information is given to tempt the reader to read, see, direct or perform in the plays mentioned.

A handbook written by one person has advantages and limitations. It offers more coherence than a compendium but necessarily contains gaps in practical and reading experience; references to more specialist books afford some remedy to this. Individual entries are cross-referenced to expand their necessary brevity, but continual consultation of dates of plays and authors is avoided by including references under each entry. For similar reasons certain standard books on or by major theorists like Stanislavski are frequently listed.

The idea of including an exhaustive discussion of the major ideas of the main theorists was first contemplated, then rejected, when it was realized this would lead to repetition of material contained in separate entries referring to terms they frequently employ. To help the reader gain a fuller impression of individual theorists, however, entry references are given under their names.

Dates of publishers before 1900 are omitted as being of little use. Sometimes one part of speech cross-refers to another: *rehearse to *rehearsal, *raked to *rake, *naturalistic to *naturalism, for example. To include various parts of speech as a title for each entry would have proved cumbersome and did not seem necessary.

I would like to thank colleagues and friends inside and outside Sussex University for reading through sections of the manuscript and making suggestions from their own particular expertise in music, literature, film, television, acting, stage direction and design. They include Bernard Gallagher, Michael Hall, Geoffrey Hemstedt, Carol Lorac, Gough Quinn, Cliff Skeet, Sylvia Vickers and Professor Cedric Watts. I would also like to thank Arnold Hare for recommending the idea of the book, Tony Seward for fertile suggestions and congenial company and my wife and daughters for typing, proof-reading and general support over the period of writing.

# A

**Abbey Theatre**, see IRISH LITERARY THEATRE.
ROBINSON, L., *Ireland's Abbey Theatre*, Sidgwick, 1951.

**Above**. *Stage direction indicating that an actor performs *upstage of another. See CROSS ABOVE and CROSS BELOW.

**Abstraction**. Term used by the tragic actress Sarah Siddons (1755–1831) to define her practice of 'abstracting' or isolating individual traits of a character. This apparently resulted in a *stylized performance in which emotional range was subordinate to a single dominant emotional impression.

**Absurd**, see THEATRE OF THE ABSURD. A concept associated with *existentialism, both Christian and atheist. It is found in Søren Kierkegaard's famous declaration: '*Credo quia absurdum est*' ('I believe because it is absurd'). It is frequent in the philosophical writings of J.-P. Sartre (1905–80) and given particular attention in Albert Camus's *Myth of Sisyphus* (1942). The term became popular in the 1960s with the publication in 1961 of Martin Esslin's *The Theatre of the Absurd*, and it was applied to such dramatists as Beckett (1906–  ), Adamov (1908–70), and Ionesco (1912–  ).

**Academic drama**, see SCHOOL DRAMA; JESUIT DRAMA.

**Accident**, see CHANCE.

**Acoustics**. The way sound behaves in a particular *space. Theatres and concert halls have varying acoustics. Angles and curvatures of walls and ceiling may, for example, 'trap' the sound and create 'dead areas'. Professional performers must try to compensate for this through *voice projection. There are special problems with *thrust stages and *theatre in the round since actors can never address the whole of the audience directly and frequently speak with their backs to a section of it.

**Act**. Section of a play containing an important development in the overall action. The convention whereby a play was given a five-act structure derives from the division of Greek tragedy into *epeisodia divided by *choruses, from Horace's critical precepts in *Ars Poetica* and the commentary of Donatus on Terence (*c.*190–159 B.C.). It was established as a rule by *neo-classical theorists in France and introduced to England by Ben Jonson (1572–1637). The five-act division of *Elizabethan and *Jacobean plays, including Shakespeare's, was imposed by later editors, and does not always correspond to the natural movements of these plays. In modern productions of Shakespeare a single interval is often all that is taken. Moreover, this may occur in the middle of the act.

The act divisions became more obvious as the practice of dropping a *curtain between acts developed in the eighteenth century. In the nineteenth century the careful build-up towards *climax and curtain can be seen in *farce, *melodrama and the plays of the *naturalist movement. The number of acts, however, varied. The *well-made play normally employed three acts. Ibsen (1828–1906) used three-, four-, and five-act structures. Chekhov (1860–1904) generally used four, though he also wrote a number of single-act farces.

Both Ibsen and Chekhov had a musical sense of dramatic structure and gave each act an individual rhythm, mood and atmosphere. Chekhov's *The Cherry Orchard* (1904) has a first act consisting of an early morning arrival in which excitement and tiredness compete. It is followed by a slow 'movement', set late in a summer's day, in which characters make unhurried and infrequent *entrances and *exits, and fill the time with seemingly desultory talk. The third and fourth acts, too, have their own musical quality. Anxiety about the sale of the cherry orchard mingles with the sound of dancing to an orchestra. The play progresses from May to October. It reaches a climax as the cherry orchard is sold. Then comes the final act with its sad departure, lightened by the hope of the younger generation and darkened again by the sad abandonment of the old Feers.

The subtlety of Chekhov's technique demonstrates how musical a play can be. In his drama, an act, with its variations of pace and rhythm, resembles a movement in a symphony, as well as being a stage in plot development.

In the twentieth century there has been a general movement towards the division of a play into *scenes or *tableaux separated by *blackouts, or, as in Brecht's *epic theatre, by *song.

**Act-drop**. A painted cloth dropped between *acts in the later eighteenth century. It is to be distinguished from the *curtain which opened and closed the play.

**Acting**. The *imitation by one person of another person or creature, quality or object. The process is complex. Theorists and practitioners differ widely in their analysis of it, particularly when dealing with the question of how far an actor may (or should) lose his own identity or take on another. One school emphasizes that acting is a craft. The actor must achieve full technical control of *voice and body. He must learn the art of *gesture and physical expression. He must learn by detached observation how to simulate people widely different from himself in age, class, nationality or temperament. Diderot's *Paradox of Acting* (1773–8) is the classic expression of this viewpoint: 'Actors impress the public, not when they are furious, but when they play fury well.' The actor 'must have in himself an unmoved and disinterested spectator'. In other words, an actor must remain detached from the part he plays in order to communicate his *role. This view is *classical and also post-*romantic. Brecht (1898–1956) takes a similar view (based in part on his admiration of the technical prowess of *Chinese theatre). For him the actor must remain detached. He may even, as actor, seem to comment sardonically on the character he is representing.

There is another tradition, however, which is expressed most cogently by Stanislavski in *An Actor Prepares* (1936), which has had a very strong impact on western acting methods, in particular on the so-called *'method' actors. This *naturalistic school stresses the psychological and imaginative exploration of *character rather than the development of physical skills and technique. The emphasis is on playing from the heart rather than from the head, on working from the 'inside', on emotional content, rather than the 'outside' or containing form.

It is apparent that acting may tend to either of these extremes, but in practice it combines both. Acting is a craft. It is also an art. Control is necessary, but so, paradoxically, is loss of control, if by that we mean loss of a sense of self. The degree to which control is retained or lost will vary with the kind of performance given. More stylized, caricatural and comic forms require acting closer to the ideas of Diderot and Brecht. More naturalistic plays, with fuller psychological exploration (as generally in *tragedy), benefit from the methods of Stanislavski. Acting remains, however, a highly artificial process. Any performer who allows personal emotion to drown the 'unmoved . . . and disinterested spectator' is likely to lose an audience's sympathy. On the other hand, the calculating technician is never likely to gain it fully.

The two attitudes may be compared to the nature of *simile; in one the actor emphasizes 'vehicle'; in the other, he emphasizes 'tenor'. One emphasizes form and the other content. Form and content, however, are never fully separable and certain practition-ers and theorists, such as Michel Saint-Denis, and indeed Brecht and Stanislavski themselves, have sought a cogent integration of the two.

Saint-Denis, speaking from fifty years' experience of the theatre, compares acting to holding a bird in the hand: 'if you close your hand too tightly, the bird will be killed; if you open it too much the bird will fly away.'

ARCHER, W., *Masks or Faces*, intro. by Lee Strasberg, Hill and Wang, NY, 1957.

COLE, T. and CHINOY, H.C., *Actors on Acting*, Crown, NY, 4th edition, 1974.

DIDEROT, D., *The Paradox of Acting*, 1773–8.

SAINT-DENIS, M., *Training for the Theatre*, Theatre Arts, NY/ Heinemann, London, 1982.

**Action**. This word is used in different ways: (a) to mean *narrative, *story or *fable; (b) to mean the embodiment of the fable, i.e. what happens on stage — the enacted events of the story and not the events reported to have happened before, after, or between the *acts of a play. Thus when a *messenger comes on stage it is his *speech which forms part of the action, not the events he describes. In this sense the action is the way a dramatist organizes his chosen fable and causes it to move through *time. This gives rise to various kinds of action: rising and falling action (growing and declining in intensity), enacted or reported action, interior (mental) or exterior (physical) action, primary and secondary action (*main and *sub-plot), group and individual action, and 'closed' (*fourth wall) or 'open' (recognizing the audience) action. The word may also refer to violent stage activity, but should not exclude reflective and quiet moments, such as Hamlet's *soliloquy. It would be difficult to consider 'To be or not to be' as external to the dramatic action. Action can also take place in a character's mind.

Aristotle, of course, in the seventh chapter of the *Poetics*, makes crucial use of the term: '. . . tragedy is an *imitation of a whole and complete *action* of some amplitude . . . Now a whole is that which has a *beginning, a *middle and an *end . . .' Aristotle here seems to be using the word to mean the *original story* from which the play was taken, but subsequent comments in the ninth and tenth chapters suggest that he is considering both the pattern of the original material and the organization of the play itself.

A further point to consider is how the action embodies an *ideology. How are the events of the action linked with each other? Why do things happen as they do? How far do the gods, fate, nature, destiny, economics, class-structure or personal choice affect the train of events? These are questions which plays ask, and to which they sometimes suggest, or covertly assume, answers.

**Activity/Inactivity**. A play, according to Aristotle, is based on *action, but the action of a play may consist, at least in part, of inactivity. Action involves calculation of effect and consideration of consequences. Moreover the static contemplation of action may take up much of a play. Not only *Hamlet* (1601) but Chekhov's *The Cherry Orchard* (1904) and the whole of Beckett's *oeuvre* are in certain ways static. In each, characters contemplate action but do not act. The plays remain, however, dramatic since the physical inactivity provokes intense mental and emotional reactions. The characters consider what they should or may do, or what they have or should have done. Even if the characters do not consider such questions, the audience often does. Providing the audience is stimulated it does not matter if there is no apparent stage activity. Stillness on stage may be intensely dramatic.

**Actor, Actress**. Performer of *roles in the theatre. Successful actors need many qualities including energy, a relaxed physical *presence, a good *voice, an expressive countenance, toughness and dedication, and perhaps also a gift which enables them to assimilate other kinds of personality — a gift allied to what Keats called *negative capability.

**Actor/audience relationship**. A relationship determined by: (a) the expectations of an audience; (b) the *conventions of the play; (c) the qualities of the actor, and (d) the nature of the theatrical *space.

An easy, and perhaps slack, relationship may exist when the conventions of a play are entirely what an audience expects. On the other hand, a fertile unease may issue from challenging an audience's expectations. This is potentially a source of *surprise and *tension, and occurs whenever an important new dramatist arrives, be it Ibsen or Chekhov, Beckett or Brecht. Arguably, all successful drama must challenge expectations to some degree.

The performance and quality of an actor is of course very important. The actor may speak to an audience directly in *soliloquy or *aside; alternatively, he or she may seem to ignore it completely from behind the *proscenium arch. It is the skill, confidence and *presence of the actor that establishes a necessary complicity, and for this the shape of the theatre building is important. Thus Glenda Jackson (1936–   ), who played Nina in O'Neill's *Strange Interlude* (1928) in New York and London, explained how both the theatre space and different audiences affected her: 'A wider proscenium arch changed my relationship with the audience . . . In London you could play the whole house on about three angles, but here [in New York] you almost have to 'use a spray-gun technique.' She added that the audiences were different too. In New York the 'laughs' were longer: 'Americans carry on so much more. They like to laugh sometimes to a near hysterical degree. So you have to allow for that in your *timing.'

**Actor manager**. An actor who is also a theatre manager. The term suggests a line of important theatrical figures stretching from Sir William Davenant (1606–68) and David Garrick (1717–79) to Sir Henry Irving (1838–1905). According to Colley Cibber (1671–

1757) the early duties of the actor manager were onerous, see *Apology for the Life of Mr Colley Cibber, Comedian* (1740). The manager had to:

1. attend rehearsals 'or else every Rehearsal would be a rude meeting of Mirth and Jollity!'
2. attend every play.
3. attend readings of every new play 'often as painfully tedious as the getting rid of the Authors of such plays must be disagreeable.'
4. order all new 'cloaths'.
5. 'direct and oversee Painters, Machinists, Musicians, Singers, Dancers.'
6. 'have an eye upon the Doorkeepers, Under-servants and Officers that without such Care are too often apt to defraud us.'

**Actor *and* Player.** The French make a distinction between the two words 'acteur' and 'comédien' and the words actor and player sometimes translate this sense. Louis Jouvet (1887–1951) speaks of the player who identifies naturally and fully with his part and the actor who 'keeps it at a distance' ('tient son rôle à distance'). The distinction, however, between the English words is not so precise. 'Player' is an old-fashioned word for actor and once had a pejorative sense suggesting a person of lower social status. Otherwise the two terms are used interchangeably.

**Actors' Studio.** Training school and theatre founded in New York in 1947 by Lee Strasberg (1901–82), Elia Kazan (1909–85) and Cheryl Crawford (1902– ). It was based on Stanislavskian principles, aiming to develop the emotional and imaginative resources of the actors by use of *improvisation techniques in a training system which was soon widely known as the *'method'. HETHMON, R.H. (ed.), *Strasberg at the Actors' Studio*, Jonathan Cape, 1966.

**Act-tunes.** Music played between the acts of *Elizabethan plays; developed during the *Restoration period by composers such as Henry Purcell (1658–95) who were commissioned to write it.

**Adaptation.** The alteration of a text by cutting words and characters, or by adding material and remodelling the *action. An adaptation generally responds to theatre conditions, such as the taste of the audience, the theatre's budget and the requirements of censorship. The *translation of plays from one language and culture to another also entails adaptation. Sewell Collins, an expert in the practice of adapting French *farce and *melodrama, asserted for example that French plays needed to be 'sprinkled with metaphorical holy water, till they be fit for the chaste world outside France.' This process he also called 'dry-cleaning', though he warns against cleansing a play too far. Only an *appearance* of purity is required. An adapter is a 'pure-minded sprinkler'. Collins here distinguishes between adaptation and adoption. An *adopter* takes something and makes it his own, whilst the *adapter* 'takes another fellow's work and makes it nobody's'.

The distinction is worth remembering. Drama from Aeschylus to Brecht has been a process of adopting *myth or folk-tale or history or other men's work. One is reminded of Brecht's comment that a writer is a thief, not a borrower. He makes other people's property his own, and it is not always evident where it came from. He adapts material to new theatrical conditions and adopts it by shaping it to his own individual needs and purposes.

An adaptation is also a term used for a *revival, played in modern dress.

**Ad lib**. From the Latin, *ad libitum*: 'at one's pleasure' or 'as much as one likes'. An 'ad lib' is an improvised remark. Used as a verb it describes the process of covering breaks in continuity when lines are forgotten and an actor *'dries' in performance. Ad libbing requires quick wits and confidence, and it can 'throw' other actors who are less nimble or relaxed. Sometimes ad libs can rival or better the original script, and one or two gifted actors or comedians, such as the late A.E. Matthews (1869–1960) or 'Matty' as he was universally known, made a consistent practice of it. At other times it may show, as Hamlet says, 'a pitiful ambition in the fool that uses it'.

**Advertisement curtain**. Drop curtain formerly used in smaller theatres to advertise the wares of local tradesmen.

**Afterpiece**. A kind of condensed comedy, developing out of the *jig or *pantomime and played after the main play of the evening at London theatres in the eighteenth century. One of its functions was to entertain latecomers, who were admitted at reduced prices. Another was to provide light relief after a heavier drama and in this it recalls the use of the *satyr play in Greek classical drama.

**Agit-prop**. Propaganda theatre deriving its name from the Department of Agitation and Propaganda, formed in the Soviet Union in 1920 as a section of the Communist Party's Central Committee secretariat. Its fundamental aim is to promote the party line.
CLAWS, J.C., *Communist Propaganda Techniques*, Methuen, 1964.

**Agon**. (a) The argument of the third of the four sections into which, according to the rules of classical *rhetoric, a speech should be divided; (b) the conflict between enemies at the heart of a play, especially in Aristophanes (c.448—c.380 B.C.); (c) a Greek and Roman public festival, such as the athletic games at Olympia. In Athens, the dramatic festivals in honour of *Dionysos were also *agones*.

T.S. Eliot wrote an interesting short verse drama called *Sweeney Agonistes*, an 'Aristophanic melodrama', followed by a '*Fragment of an Agon*' (1925). In these works he begins his experiments with forms of drama, especially Greek, which unobtrusively underlie his later plays.

**Alazon**. One of the main character types of the comic tradition — the cowardly braggart. He is found in Plautus (c.254–184 B.C.) as the *Miles Gloriosus* (c.202 B.C.). He is there in the first known English comedy, Udall's *Ralph Roister Doister* (c.1534), in Shakespeare's Parolles and Armado and Falstaff, in Jonson's Bobadill (*Everyman in his Humour*) (1598), in Farquhar's Captain Brazen (*The Recruiting Officer*), and elsewhere.

The type is of perennial interest, perhaps because he is dual (and thus less 'flat'). He wears a *mask of courage, but his fears often overcome his *pride and the mask falls. He thus invites us to feel satisfaction at seeing vanity brought low. And yet he may gain the *sympathy of all who know the need to mask their private fears. He stands for ourselves and the *personae we adopt to control the world outside. He may also stand for those who pretend to control the world, and whom we would enjoy seeing humbled. See EIRON.

**Alienation effect**. Translation of German '*verfremdungseffekt*'. A term popularized by Bertolt Brecht (1898–1956), sometimes translated as *estrangement. Brecht defines the term often and it always implies a switch of *viewpoint. Alienation occurs when we see 'a schoolmaster hounded out by bailiffs', or when we see 'a mother as a man's wife', or when we imagine how an eskimo might consider a car — as 'an aeroplane without wings'. Each of these examples involves seeing with someone else's eyes, so that the familiar becomes strange.

This 'making strange' is, of course, an intrinsic part of the dramatic process. Brecht systematizes it. Thus in *Galileo* (1937–9) we see the *hero through the eyes of different characters, and he is often unheroic. He is cowardly, courageous, greedy, slippery, clever, contemptible, human. Each scene shows him in different ways, alienating us from our previous view. The effect, Brecht hoped, is that an audience will think about the *situations which provoke such varied behaviour, and especially about Galileo's responsibilities as man and scientist. To this end he employed a further alienation effect — a *backdrop showing a mushroom cloud. The *anachronism invites us to see Galileo's age in the light of our own.

Brecht employed other techniques of alienation. Songs cut across the *action; words are projected on screens; *scenes are compared and contrasted with each other; characters respond differently in similar situations. All these techniques surprise the spectator into thought. When Kattrin in *Mother Courage* (1941) bangs a drum as an army approaches the sleeping town, while the peasants choose to pray, we compare and criticize, and we also sympathize. Alienation does not mean the elimination of feeling. It aims to complicate feeling by eliminating single viewpoints and preventing simple processes of *identification. In short, it is another name for elements of *surprise which have existed in drama from the Greeks to Chekhov. Brecht brings these together to help construct his 'new' *epic theatre.

BRECHT, B., *Brecht on Theatre*, trs. J. Willett, Methuen, 1964; *Messingkauf Dialogues*, trs. J. Willett, Methuen, 1965.

**Allegory**. From the Greek for 'speaking otherwise'. Literary term for a story in prose or verse whose characters and events stand for something else. The general practice since the seventeenth century has been to use it as a comic and ironic form which can manipulate the reader's responses. Thus *Absalom and Achitophel* (1681) by John Dryden, Swift's *Gulliver's Travels* (1726) or George Orwell's *Animal Farm* (1945) arouse *sympathy or dislike for characters in the surface story. The parallels are then made clear, so that a reader's sympathy is enlisted for a particular religious, political or other viewpoint (generally by making the opposition ridiculous or distasteful). Swift's Lilliputians, including Flimnap (Sir Robert Walpole) their Prime Minister, behave like children so that the reader mocks them. Then, in the kingdom of Brobdingnag, Gulliver himself becomes a childish Lilliputian, and finds himself mocked along with the reader. In a simpler but similar way Orwell conditions our response to the Russian Revolution in his allegorical *fable, *Animal Farm*. He creates sympathies and antagonisms in the surface story and then makes the parallels clear. The repugnant pig, Napoleon, 'is' Stalin, Snowball 'is' Trotski, and so on.

This kind of allegory has come into theatrical use in the twentieth century, especially in political and religious drama. One of the best examples is J.-P. Sartre's *The Flies* (1942) which uses as surface story the myth of Orestes returning to Argos to kill his mother Clytemnestra and her lover Aegisthus with the aid of his sister Electra. Played before an audience in Paris in World War II, the play made its appeal through its hidden parallels: for Argos read Paris, for Orestes read 'Free French', for Electra read the Resistance Movement, for Clytemnestra, the collaborating Vichy government, for Aegisthus, the occupying Nazi power. Such parallels were for French ears only. An invitation to join the Resistance had to be hidden in allegory, so that its existence could be denied. In a more general way, Brecht's *Galileo* (1937–9) is an allegory about the political and social responsibility of nuclear scientists in the twentieth century.

T.S. Eliot (1889–1965) uses allegory in a different manner to create a sense that we live on more than one plane of existence. Thus in *The Cocktail Party* (1949) the psychiatrist, Harcourt-Reilly, and his assistants, Alex and Julia, exist both on a *naturalist and *symbolic level. They are apparently 'ordinary' characters at the beginning of the play, but then move from a psychological to a theological level and become a kind of Trinity of guardian angels. (The problem for Eliot is that our feelings for these characters on the surface level are not easily transferred to a religious plane. The allegory is not fully convincing.)

Allegory, then, is a kind of extended *simile, with a surface story which is the 'vehicle', carrying the 'tenor' of the intended parallel. It is used to reinforce moral, religious and political attitudes, or to effect a conversion. Earlier forms of allegory precede the *Enlightenment. They reflect a world which was seen as consisting of *correspondences between different and parallel planes. The microcosm or 'little world' of man paralleled the 'great world' or macrocosm of the state. Reason, will and appetite in the individual corresponded to the legislature, executive and consumer in the political body. The four *humours of the human body paralleled the four elements of the world itself. This led naturally to allegorical expression, as did the notion that time moved in cycles. In history, especially Biblical history, there was *repetition or equivalence. The Promised Land corresponded to the Kingdom of God; the Crossing of the Red Sea to Christian baptism; Moses paralleled Christ, and so on. Inevitably then, allegory was built into the *mystery cycles which expressed this sense of history. The *morality plays which developed out of them also presented the spectators with an allegory of their own condition, seen as a journey or a battle in which man walked towards salvation or damnation with Angels and Devils, Virtues and Vices, competing for his soul. Such allegory differs perhaps from the modern ironic form in the seriousness with which the surface vehicle is taken. *Animal Farm* is an obvious fiction, while the story of Noah was not so considered.

The seriousness of the medieval allegory is still to be found in the literary journeys which link *Everyman* (1509–19) with *Pilgrim's Progress* (1676–84), the travels of Kafka's heroes and the parallel episodes of Joyce's *Ulysses* (1922). Everyman lies behind Joseph K and Leopold Bloom. We might add that Gulliver and Pilgrim and the animals of Orwell share with K and Bloom and Everyman a naivety which allows us to link them, and which is a source of different kinds of *irony.

In twentieth-century drama the allegorical mode is found

particularly in *expressionist drama and the so-called *theatre of the absurd. Such forms embody qualities resembling *dream (which Freud considered a kind of allegory containing 'latent' meanings behind the 'manifest'). Strindberg's late plays, including *The Dream Play* (1902) and *Ghost Sonata* (1907) may be seen as both psychological and religious allegories.

Samuel Beckett uses the allegorical form differently. His strange plays invite interpretation as allegory but mock the allegorizer who attempts to pin meanings on them. Like a Kafka story, *Waiting for Godot* (1953) makes us ask whether the allegory is not in our own minds. The same is true of Pinter's *The Caretaker* (1960). Terence Rattigan is reputed to have told Pinter that it was 'about the Old and New Testament'. 'It's not, you know,' said Pinter, 'It's about a tramp and two brothers.'

Pinter's reply indicates that 'allegorizing' is an escape from the responsibility of responding to the surface story. In drama, since the characters perform as full human beings on the stage, allegory tends to escape the writer's control. If, as has been said, allegory is a 'form of rhetoric used by people who know all the answers, to enlighten those who might neglect to ask the questions' it can take its revenge on the former as well as the latter.

MACQUEEN, J., *Allegory*, Methuen, 1970.

**Alternative theatre**. A phrase coined to define the great variety of *theatre in education, *performance art, *political, *feminist and other *fringe groups, which have flourished outside the *West End and *Off Off Broadway since the 1960s. According to Sandy Craig, alternative theatre contains 'an explosive mixture of socialism, song, satire, community expression, twilight entropy and apocalyptic dada'. Disciples assert the need for a real alternative to the established theatre, whose power to absorb, and soften opposition to entrenched attitudes, they greatly suspect. In Britain gifted writers such as John Arden (1930–  ) and John McGrath (1935–  ) have opted to work 'outside'. In the United States the *Living Theatre and the *Open Theatre are among many groups which may be so described.

ANSORGE, P., *Disrupting the Spectacle*, Pitman, 1975.
CRAIG, S. (ed.), *Dreams and Deconstructions*, Amber Lane Press, 1980.
SHANK, T., *American Alternative Theatre*, Macmillan, 1982.

**Amateur theatre**. Theatre in which staff and performers are unpaid. It is often used as a pejorative term to imply 'poorly done', or 'inexperienced and self-indulgent'. Standards, however, in such organizations as the *Little Theatres can often be surprisingly high. Amateur actors can achieve powerful and convincing performances, especially in the hands of experienced *directors, and it is well known that some film directors, such as Robert

Bresson, prefer to use them. Even so, especially in large-cast productions, lack of professional training and inexperience is always likely to show. Amateur drama, however, is arguably for the benefit of the performer as much as the audience, and one should remember that drama was originally performed neither for money nor applause. Early seasonal and *folk drama, both secular and ecclesiastical, was amateur, and the existence of large numbers of amateur theatrical groups in a culture is surely a sign of health.
COTES, P., *A Handbook for the Amateur Theatre*, Oldbourne, 1957.
RENDLE, A., *Everyman and his Theatre*, Pitman, 1968.

**Ambiguity**. Double meaning. William Empson, in his important book *Seven Types of Ambiguity* (1930) defined the term as 'any verbal nuance, however slight, which gives room for alternative reactions to the same piece of language'.

In drama we speak of ambiguous characters, motivation, relationships and situations. Each of these gives room for alternative reactions in an audience, and each is highly dramatic, since it leaves an audience in *suspense. Such ambiguities need not be verbal, though they often are. They may arise out of a *facial expression, a *gesture, or another form of *theatre language. Sometimes a character within the play becomes conscious of these different ambiguities, and this may heighten the suspense. (One need only cite *Hamlet*.)

Ambiguity in dramatic *dialogue is a source of the *comic, as where remarks made to one character are taken in a sense opposite to that intended, or where two characters mistakenly assume that the pronoun 'he' refers to the same person. Alan Ayckbourn's plays, for example, are full of such ambiguities.

Ambiguity of meaning is also closely related to a tragic sense of the world. Consider, for instance, Shakespeare's pun at the end of *King Lear*:

> . . . he hates him
> That would, upon the rack of this tough world
> Stretch him out *longer*.

The double meanings here, unlike comic ambiguities which rely on a disparity between the meanings, are sombrely appropriate. It would be torture for Lear to remain longer in the world. As in comedy, however, the verbal ambiguity seems to refer to incongruities and absurdities beyond the merely verbal. For a study of narrative ambiguity see:
RASTIER, F., 'Les niveaux d'ambiguité des structures narratives', in *Semiotica III*, 4, 1971.

**Ambivalence**. Psychoanalytic term, frequently used in literary and dramatic criticism. It defines a state in which contradictory and interdependent feelings, such as love and hate, are focused on the same person or object, perhaps a father, mother, child or sexual partner. It is often loosely used to mean 'mixed feelings', but feelings can be mixed without being ambivalent. That is to say, they may be based on a clear un-neurotic recognition of the strengths and weaknesses of another person. Ambivalence is a product of neurotic conflict, i.e. repression, or a refusal to recognize the source of emotion.

The term is of particular importance for those who would apply Freud's views to the theory of drama. It appears that ambivalence is most clearly observed in states of obsessional neurosis, i.e. in neuroses which express themselves in physical *play and compulsive *rituals. If the writing of drama is considered a form of compulsive play, then this may explain something about the dynamic core of the dramatic conflict. Sophocles's *Oedipus Rex* (c.430 B.C.) Ibsen's *Rosmersholm* (1886) and *Hedda Gabler* (1890), Shakespeare's *Hamlet* (1601) and Euripides's *Hippolytus* (428 B.C.) are instances of plays which seem to have 'ambivalent' cores. How far, however, the writer is projecting ambivalent personal feelings, in such characters as Oedipus or Hamlet, Phaedra or Rebecca West, is a matter for speculation. See DREAM; UNCONSCIOUS.

**Anachronism**. Introduction of an inappropriate detail, or element from a different period in time, into a drama. An example is Shakespeare's mention of billiards in the early Egyptian scene in *Antony and Cleopatra* (1606–7).

Anachronism may be a sign of carelessness or hasty writing. It may be an attempt to give a contemporary vividness to a historical play. It may also indicate that a dramatist is not concerned with the accurate representation of period *costume or *set. The regard for strict historical accuracy only grew in the nineteenth century. In previous centuries, and especially in the *Elizabethan and *medieval drama, anachronistic contemporary *costume was commonplace. In the *mystery plays, Noah's ark was probably a boat of medieval design.

In recent times, too, with the cinema's greater capacity to create historically accurate drama, playwrights have begun to experiment with anachronism in interesting ways. Caryl Churchill, for example, in her play *Top Girls* (1984), engages in a common discussion characters who lived centuries apart: Pope Joan, Florence Nightingale, a Japanese concubine, and a modern business woman. The method aims to reveal points of difference and similarity in the situations of women in the past and in the present. It resembles in its distancing effect the methods of Brecht, who uses anachronism to set the past off against the present. His play *Galileo* (1937–9), for example, was seen against a *backdrop showing a mushroom cloud.

Anachronism is thus not only verbal, but also involves costume and set. It may also be used deliberately to compare past with present.

**Anagnorisis**. Aristotle's term in the *Poetics* for 'the movement from ignorance to awareness'. It generally refers to the state of mind of a *character rather than to the audience, since the audience is generally aware of the imminence of disclosure. See DISCLOSURE; RECOGNITION.

**Anger**. Primary emotion which demands sudden and violent expression or discharge in words and action. It is different from hatred, with which it is often confused, in that it is of much briefer duration and openly expressed, whereas hatred is a sentiment that is frequently hidden. In Shakespeare's *Othello*, Iago feels hate throughout the play, but arguably only feels anger at the end when he loses control of his wife Emilia. He then loses control of himself: 'Fie your sword upon a woman . . .'. See WRATH.

**Angry Young Man**. Term applied in the 1950s to a type of literary and dramatic character of whom Jimmy Porter in John Osborne's *Look Back in Anger* (1956) is the most famous and important. The violence of his invective, especially against apathy and complacency in the well-bred middle class, enraged an older generation while it seemed to express the feelings of a younger generation which had grown up during the war and in 'austerity England'.

The angry reaction to Osborne's work, its consequent publicity and commercial success, were important in that the *Royal Court was able to support generations of playwrights, including John Arden (1930–   ) and Edward Bond (1935–   ), enabling them to gain experience and find new forms of dramatic expression, despite financial losses.

ALLSOP, K., *The Angry Decade*, Owen, London, 1958.
ARMSTRONG, W., *Experimental Drama*, Bell, London, 1963, Ch. 1.
TAYLOR, J.R., *The Angry Theatre*, Hill and Wang, 1969.

**Anguish**. See ABSURD; EXISTENTIALISM.

**Antagonist**. The character who opposes the *protagonist, e.g. Creon in Sophocles's *Antigone* (c.441 B.C.), Iago in *Othello* (1604), the *villain in *melodrama. Drama, of course, has traditionally been built around strong pairs of opposing figures — tyrants and rebels, kings and usurpers, husbands and wives, the old and the young — and it seems a general characteristic of drama that oppositions and tensions which the novel shows *within* character (so that the character is his own antagonist) are presented *between* characters. However, drama need not be so. The plays of Chekhov (1860–1904), with their absence of the heroic and villainous, and their greater concern with venial than with deadly sin, are a general exception. No antagonist prevents Chekhov's three sisters going to Moscow, but rather a pervasive social and psychological condition. Instead of the opposition of *wills which occurs in the drama of his contemporaries Ibsen and Strindberg, we get in Chekhov a sapping of will-power, and as a result a very different and 'undramatic' drama.

**Antepirrema.** The final and counter movement to the *epirrema in the *parabasis of the Greek *old comedy.

**Anti-Aristotelian.** Brecht's term for his *epic theatre which aims not to 'purge' the spectators and reconcile them to a human situation, but to expose the contradictions of the world and to encourage men to change it. Brecht thus attacks Aristotle's doctrines of *catharsis (purgation) and of dramatic *unity, (the idea that a play should have a *beginning, middle and end). He deliberately wrote *episodic plays, despite Aristotle's dictum that 'of simple fables, those whose action is episodic are the worst'. The real object of his attack, however, was the kind of drama which encouraged thoughtless *identification with a character's suffering, and uncritical acceptance of the fate he undergoes. This would be far too simple a description of Greek tragedy, where (as Brecht knew) debate between contradictory viewpoints is an essential part of the dramatic process. Brecht may have described *Oedipus Rex* (which Aristotle takes as his ideal model) as 'a striptease show, in which the audience become little Oedipuses shouting "take it off, take it off"', but his comments were deliberately and humorously provocative. His aim was not to describe with scholarly accuracy, but to make people think for themselves about *ideology and political structure, as well as the function of drama.

ARISTOTLE, *Poetics*, trs. L. Potts, Cambridge University Press, 1953.
BRECHT, B., *Brecht on Theatre*, trs. J. Willett, Methuen, 1964.

**Anti-climax.** Bathos; a sudden diffusion of *tension as an *action appears about to reach a *climax. The process may be deliberate, as is frequently the case in comedy, when the writer or performer invites an audience to take something seriously and then reaches an unexpected and ridiculous conclusion. A joke is often a deliberate anti-climax. *Postponement may also be related to it, as in the 'gravedigger scenes' in *Hamlet*, where the tension is for a time lowered, only to be heightened later. Tension in the case of postponement, however, is not entirely diffused, whereas anti-climax is often accidental. The audience is removed from the play-world because some technical failure in the staging, acting or writing abruptly interrupts a state of *suspension of disbelief.

**Anti-hero**. A central character who reverses a reader's or spectator's conventional expectations of a *hero. He often parodies the social group or literary norm to which he ostensibly belongs. The term seems closely associated with the 'picaresque' and 'comic-epic' literary traditions, where heroes often exist *between* social groups, behaving in ways which mock the conventional ideal of a hero (i.e. as handsome, strong, courageous, honourable). Examples include Don Quixote and Sancho Panza, Tristram Shandy and Falstaff (another landless knight), as well as lower-class 'heroes' in recent fiction and drama in the picaresque and comic traditions, such as Beckett's tramps or Hašek's *Good Soldier Schweik* and Brecht's appropriation of him.

Anti-heroes tend to be misfits, failures and drop-outs. What they embody causes us to reconsider the basis (generally social) of our conception of heroism. Like Osborne's Jimmy Porter, they constitute an attack on those who belong to the established social order and accept its moral conventions. The attack on convention, however, may be *through* the character, rather than *by* the character. Unlike Jimmy Porter, a Schweik slavishly follows the rules, thereby rendering them ridiculous. See ANGRY YOUNG MAN.

**Anti-masque**. A brief *masque, invented by Ben Jonson in about 1609. It contained comic and *grotesque characters which contrasted with the *allegorical or mythical characters in the stately main masque which followed.

Shakespeare used a similar counterpointing of grotesque and harmonious elements in the famous pastoral scene (Act IV, scene iv) of *The Winter's Tale* (1610) by introducing a dance of centaurs. WELSFORD, E., *The Court Masque*, Cambridge University Press, 1927.

**Antistrophe**. Greek for 'turning round', the choral song and the movement of the Greek *chorus, which counters the *strophe and precedes the *epode.

**Anti-theatre**. Term coined to describe the *theatre of the absurd. It has also been applied since the 1950s to any play which seemed to defy the 'normal' and generally naturalistic expectations of an audience, by rejecting illusion and *identification, and employing apparently illogical *action and *dialogue. The *happening and *epic theatre have also been described as anti-theatrical.

**Antithesis**. A form of balanced *contrast effected by setting words and ideas in opposition to one another. It is especially found in the comic tradition of *wit, from Shakespeare through the eighteenth-century *comedy of manners to Shaw (1856–1950) and Wilde (1854–1900). A good example is the famous observation in Wilde's *The Importance of Being Earnest* (1895): 'All women become like their mothers. That's their tragedy. No man does. That's his.' The aesthetic balance of antithesis often carries a conviction that the statement does not fully warrant.

Its appeal in comedy often seems to lie in the expression of incongruous ideas or specious logic. Thus Malvolio's 'Not black in my mind, though yellow in my legs' (*Twelfth Night*), or Lady Bracknell's 'People either know everything or they know nothing, Mr Worthing. Which do you know?' Balanced expression (and especially rhyme) give a well-turned antithesis a spurious truthfulness, and the clash between polished style and fallacious content often provokes laughter.

Some antitheses, of course, are more serious. But there, too, verbal polish seems to add extra conviction to the argument. The oppositions seem to reinforce one another, and the able rhetorician knows how to handle the conviction they carry. Thus Mark Antony in Shakespeare's *Julius Caesar*:

> But yesterday, the word of Caesar might
> Have stood against the World: Now lies he there,
> And none so poor to do him reverence . . . (III.ii.124–6)

**Antode**. Lyrical response by half the *chorus in Greek *old comedy to the ode sung by the other half.

**Antoine, André** (1858–1943). French director and actor, founder of the *Théâtre Libre in Paris in 1887 where he developed a new style of *naturalist acting based on the observation of everyday behaviour:

> It is the environment which determines the characters, not the movement of the characters which determines the environment.

See: FREE THEATRES; NATURALISM; FOURTH WALL.
ANTOINE, A., *Le Théâtre*, 2 vols., Editions de France, 1932.

**Apocalyptic drama**. Drama which embodies a sense of the world's imminent end. In the past, the feeling no doubt derived from the experience of natural disasters and a consequent belief in God's or the gods' capacity to destroy the world. Nowadays the invention of the atom and hydrogen bombs has extended the possibility of destruction to man's self-destruction. Such apocalyptic feelings also invoke, as Harry Levin has pointed out, the idealized *pastoral places, millennial and utopian, which precede the cataclysms of the past and follow those of the future. The Fall and Doomsday divide us from our ideal states. Thus the term recalls the Doomsday episodes of the medieval cycles of *mystery plays. The influence of these, of Old Testament prophecy and examples of destruction (the Flood, Sodom and Gomorrah), together with the chiliasm of much medieval sermonizing, had its influence on *Jacobean drama. The works of Webster (*c*.1578–*c*.1632) and Tourneur (*c*.1575–1626), as well as Shakespeare's *King Lear* (1605) and *Macbeth* (1606), were written at a time when comets and eclipses seemed to betoken disaster, and are pervaded by a sense of doom. Macbeth's reference to 'heaven's cherubim horsed upon the sightless couriers of the air' relates to the apocalyptic *Book of Revelations*. Lear's 'universe' is also apocalyptic, though the concept of entropy, of a wearing-down process ('the great world itself shall so wear out to nought'), is also invoked.

In the twentieth century, the First World War seemed to engender a sense of an imminent ending which can be felt in the novels of Lawrence, and in German *expressionist drama. The war seemed to confirm *Marxist predictions that capitalism would lead states to mutual destruction, and in political drama, from Brecht's parodistic *Rise and Fall of the City of Mahagonny* (1930) to Edward Bond's visions of violence and breakdown, Marxist predictions have remained strong. The H-bomb and the Second World War have intensified the feeling. Writers who grew up during the 'Cold War', such as Harold Pinter (1930– ) and Edward Bond (1935– ), carry a sense of danger in their writing. In a different way, Samuel Beckett records in *Endgame* (1956) a final running-down after some unspecified cataclysm. There is no utopia in Beckett's world. Nor, it must be said, is there one to be found in our modern political drama.

KERMODE, F., *The Sense of an Ending*, Oxford University Press, 1966.

**Apollonian**. See DIONYSIAC.

**Appia, Adolphe** (1862–1928). Swiss scenic designer, who sought to coordinate *space, *movement, *music and *light in non-*naturalistic stagings much influenced by Wagnerian opera:

> Only light and music can express the inner nature of all appearance.

See LIVING LIGHT; GESAMTKUNSTWERK; SYNAESTHESIA.

APPIA, A., *Die Musik und die Inscenierung* (1899); *La Mise-en-scène du drame wagnérien*, L'Oeuvre d'art vivant (1921).

**Apron stage**. The *thrust stage associated with the *Elizabethan playhouse.

**Aquatic drama**. A form of popular spectacle associated with the nineteenth-century *circus. The arena was flooded and representations of, for example, Nelson's sea-battles took place. Such spectacles have also occurred in the twentieth century. The Battle of the River Plate was enacted in 1940 in the Tower Circus, Blackpool, with scale models of the warships. It had, no doubt, the same patriotic appeal.

**Archetypal patterns**. Jungian term for certain patterns or structures to be found perennially in the various art forms. Jung would have claimed that these are related to organizing principles in the natural world and in the human mind. In art they express themselves as *plot structures, or *characters, or in the poetic texture of a play or novel. A basic pattern might be the quaternary or four-fold structure found in nature as the four seasons, the four elements or the four points of the compass; in man it appears as the four stages of life, the four humours, the division of the psyche into ego and self, and shadow and animus/anima.

To take an example from drama, Shakespeare's *Macbeth* (1606) lends itself to Jungian analysis. It has strong oppositions between 'conscious' and *'unconscious' elements; between male and female principles *within* Macbeth and Lady Macbeth, ('bring forth men-children only . . .'); between hero and 'anima' figures (Macbeth and the three witches). The play also has a powerful symbolic texture, and patterns form around the references to children, clothes and horses. Macbeth, it may be urged, kills the child in himself, and the horses, representing unconscious forces (which have both positive and negative potential) relate to the same self-destruction: 'Tis said they eat each other'. The analysis could continue.

Jungian analysis was popular 50 years ago, but is no longer so highly regarded. What is disputed is not so much the *existence* of such patterns, which are especially obvious in folk-tale and *folk-drama, but the *explanation* for the organizing principle behind them. *Marxist critics, for instance, resist the emphasis on *universals and stress social and historical causes. Others feel that an emphasis on general patterns neglects the *individual* qualities of a work. Nevertheless, the question of how drama or literature or art express and relate to *dream, to *myth and to the 'unconscious' continues to be a rich source of speculation. The Jungian theory of archetypes attracts those who feel that rationalist explanations do not sufficiently account for the strange power that such works as Shakespeare's *Macbeth*, Euripides's *Hippolytus* and *Bacchae*, Aeschylus's *Oresteia* and Dostoevsky's *The Possessed* (1872) seem to contain.

BODKIN, M., *Archetypal Patterns in Poetry*, Vintage, 1958.
FRYE, N., *Anatomy of Criticism*, Princeton University Press, 1957.
JUNG, C.G., *The Collected Works*, Vol. 9, Parts I and II, Aion, 1952.
Part I: *The Archetypes and the Collective Unconscious*; Part II: *Researches into the Phenomenology of the Self*.

**Archon**. Magistrate in charge of the annual dramatic festivals in Greece. One of his tasks was to select plays from the manuscripts submitted by aspiring competitors.

**Area**. See STAGE; SPACE.

**Arena stage**. A *thrust or *open stage such as at the Chichester Festival Theatre, where the audience sits on three sides. In America, the term implies *theatre in the round. See STAGE.
JOSEPH, S., *New Theatre Forms*, Pitman Theatre Arts, NY, 1968.

**Aristotle** (384-322 B.C.). Greek philosopher whose short analysis of *tragedy became the foundation of dramatic theory. It contains the most famous, fertile and intriguing of all observations on *tragedy:

> Through *pity and *fear effecting the *catharsis or purgation of the emotions.

See: ACTION; ANAGNORISIS; BEGINNING; MIDDLE AND END; CHORUS; DITHYRAMB; HAMARTIA; MIMESIS; MYTHOS; PERIPETEIA; UNITY.
BUTCHER, S.H., *Aristotle's Theory of Fine Art*, Macmillan, 1902.
POTTS, L.J. (ed.), *Aristotle on the Art of Fiction*, Cambridge University Press, 1953.

**Arlecchino**. Original of *Harlequin in the *Commedia dell'Arte. See: HERRICK, M.T., *Italian Comedy in the Renaissance*, Illinois University Press, 1960.

**Artaud, Antonin** (1896–1948). French actor, director and theorist; the influential advocate of the *theatre of cruelty.

> It is through the skin that metaphysics should be made to reenter our minds.

> The theatre has been created to teach us that the sky can fall on our heads.

See: CRUELTY; PLAGUE.
ARTAUD, A., *Le Théâtre et son Double*, (1938).

**Artistic director**. Person in a theatre with overall responsibility for such matters as programme selection, appointment of *directors, casting of plays and quality of performance.

**Arts Council for Great Britain**. Body responsible for encouraging the development of the fine arts. It receives a grant-in-aid from the Treasury and allocates funds to such theatre companies as the *National, *Royal Shakespeare, *Royal Court and various fringe groups. In times of economic stringency its mediating position becomes difficult, and arguments over the way it divides grant, and its independence or otherwise of the government, are apt to create rancour. The importance, however, of twentieth-century subsidized theatre, and the drama it has produced, argues a strong need for subsidy and for such a body as this. Lord Keynes was primarily responsible for establishing it over the years 1940–6. The American equivalent, the *National Endowment for the Arts, was created by Congress in 1965 and in part modelled on the New York State Council for the Arts established in 1960. See: AMERICAN ASSEMBLY, Columbia View, *The Performing Arts and American Society*, Prentice Hall, 1978.

**Aside**. A remark addressed in mid-scene by an actor to the audience, presumed by convention to be inaudible to those on stage. It has various functions. It may convey simple information. It also lets the audience see the intentions, thoughts and decisions of a character, and establishes a kind of complicity between character and audience. The character appeals to the audience's awareness that a *game is being played. In *melodrama the aside has a more complex function, since it is usually the *villain who twirls a conspiratorial moustache, *provoking* the audience rather than enlisting sympathy. In a more subtle way, the aside may be used *within* the play when a character addresses an aside to another character on stage. This may be presumed inaudible to some characters, but not to others. Some of Hamlet's provocative sexual innuendo in the 'play-scene' is presumably meant to be overheard, but he speaks in the knowledge that other characters on stage must pretend *not* to hear. This is a very subtle use of the convention.

The aside, of course, as can be seen from a study of the evolution of Ibsen's *naturalistic drama, was eliminated from the dialogue because it broke the illusion of a *fourth wall. In other kinds of theatre it developed into *soliloquy, conveying thought and reflection, as in *Elizabethan drama or in O'Neill's *Strange Interlude* (1928).
PFISTER, M., *Das Drama*, Fink Verlag, Munich, 1977.

**As if**. In 1876, Hans Vaihinger put forward the suggestion that we react to art as if (*'als ob'*) it were real. The phrase is more strongly associated, however, with the *'magic if' of Stanislavski (1863–1938) who invited actors to improvise scenes which did not exist within the play *as if* their characters had a full existence outside it. The actor in rehearsal *improvises what *might have happened*. He becomes an imaginative creator as well as an interpreter, and provides himself with a memory and an exterior world which he can bring onto the stage with him, thus making the play more 'real'. See SUSPENSION OF DISBELIEF.
STANISLAVSKI, C., *Creating a Role*, Methuen, 1961.

**Asphaleian system**. An early twentieth-century stage system enabling sections of the stage to be separately tilted, raised and lowered by hydraulic pistons.

**Association**. See CONNOTATION; DENOTATION.

**Atellan farces**. Roman plays performed in Atella in south-east Italy, probably on market days. They were improvised rustic *farces with a small *cast who wore *masks and *costume to indicate their stock roles of clown and boaster (bucco); *fool (Maccus); old miser (Pappus); glutton (Manducus); and clever hunchback (Dossenus). The *atellannae* are in the clowning tradition which links Greek comedy, the fourth-century B.C. *phlyakes* and the Italian *Commedia dell'Arte*. A few titles — *The Farmer, The She-Goat, The Woodpile*, and *The Vine-Gatherers* — survive. Their *scenarios were developed into plays by Pomponius and Novius in the first century B.C.

**Attitude**. A held *gesture or position indicating a character's relationship to other characters and his response to a dramatic situation. The attitude may be unconscious or deliberately struck, as in a *freeze. In Brecht's plays the attitude or *Gestus* generally emphasizes the character's social situation. More generally, an attitude can mean the view an *actor, *director or *designer takes towards a *role or play.

**Audience**. Group of spectators. They are usually fused into a group by interest in a common spectacle, which moves through *time at the same speed for each spectator, in a *space which all share. An audience 'speaks' to actors, by its stillness, its concentration, its applause, its voices of disapproval, its restlessness and the relation of different sections, *stalls, circle or *gallery, to one another. Sometimes an audience may be divided against itself by the use of material which has a different appeal to different parts of the house. Piscator (1893–1966), for instance, sought to provoke audiences in this way. The audience is thus part of a transaction, the *actor/audience relationship, and influences a performance by its reactions, and its acceptance or otherwise of the theatrical conventions being used or broken.
STYAN, J.L., *Drama Stage and Audience*, Cambridge University Press, 1975.

**Audition**. Test of an actor's fitness for a forthcoming *role. Physical appearance, and the way an actor may perform alongside other members of the cast, as well as talent, experience and technical skill are important considerations.

**Auditorium**. *Audience's theatre *space. In London the ground floor, or *pit, had no seats till after 1660, when long benches were installed. In Paris the audience at the Comédie Française also had to stand — until 1782, when benches were provided.
Growing commercial pressures encouraged the transformation of the pit into orchestra stalls; the stage was drawn back to increase

room for seating; the boxes round the rear of the theatre were lifted to form balconies so that a 'pit' could be extended underneath; the balconies were subsequently extended upwards to increase seating capacity.

The effect of this on performance depended on the *acoustics of the individual house. The creation of a *space in which the actor had to cater for distant, and possibly 'dead', areas, as well as for front-row customers who paid high prices, could cause problems. The performers could seem to be 'over-acting' to those who were close, and 'under-acting' to those far away. This problem does not exist in theatres where the audience sits within the same band of proximity (as in a shallow ampitheatre).

Different kinds of drama produce different responses in the different spaces in which they are performed. An audience may sit entirely around, or in various arcs or blocks, in front of, or on both sides of a dramatic performance. (See STAGE.) The audience may be above, on the same level, or below; it may be large or small; in a larger or smaller space; or it may be a single person in a small room, in front of a TV screen.

The nature of the space for which a play is written can affect the structure of the play, its length, size of *cast, style and general appeal.

BURRIS-MEYER, H. and COLE, E., *Theatres and Auditoriums*, 2nd edition, Reinhold, NY, 1965.

**Authenticity**. Existential concept implying a state of mind which refuses to take refuge in 'bad faith' (comforting and protective beliefs). The plays of J.-P. Sartre (1905–1980), notably *The Flies* (1942) and *In Camera* (1944), are much concerned with this state. See EXISTENTIAL DRAMA.

**Autoclesis**. Rhetorical trick whereby a topic is introduced by a character under the guise of not wishing to speak of it: 'I will not mention . . .'. In this way Mark Antony introduces the subject of Caesar's will in Act III of Shakespeare's *Julius Caesar* (1599):

> Let but the commons hear this testament
> Which pardon me I do not mean to read —
> And they would go and kiss dead Caesar's wounds. (III.ii.137–9)

*Auto Sacramental*. Spanish religious drama involving a procession through the streets, the placing of the Blessed Sacrament on the church altar, the performance of a play for the clergy and town council, a religious service and a dance within the church. Plays of this kind, as written by Lope de Vega (1562–1635) and Calderón (1600–1681), developed out of the counter-reformation, and expressed the central beliefs of the Catholic church in the form of *allegory. The staging was rich, with musical accompaniment.

SHERGOLD, N.D., *A History of the Spanish Stage*, Oxford University Press, 1967.

**Avant-garde**. The forerunners of social and cultural change. In drama this is usually marked by *originality of *form and the overturning of conventional expectations.

# B

**Backcloth.** A painted cloth or 'backdrop', hung upstage to supply a scenic background. It was formerly used in *Restoration drama, together with *wings, to give the effect of *perspective. Since the *box-set superseded it in the nineteenth century it has been used mainly in *opera, *ballet, and *pantomime.

**Backdrop.** See BACKCLOTH.

**Backing flat.** A *flat, placed behind the doors and windows of a *box-set to sustain the illusion that they open upon a real world.

**Back-lighting.** *Lighting from behind the subject, so that it appears in silhouette to an audience or camera.

**Back projection.** The projection of photographs or moving *film onto a *backcloth or backdrop. The technique can work to create greater *realism, or as an *alienation device which contrasts ironically with stage action. It may also illustrate the general theme of a play, or even act as a flashback device, when, for example, a character is recalling a scene in memory. Its theatrical potential can be seen from the work of Erwin Piscator (1893–1966) in Germany during the Weimar Republic. The plans of Walter Gropius for his *totaltheater should be examined in this regard. A system of back projection was to enclose the whole *auditorium.

**Backstage.** Area behind the stage in a theatre, containing the *wings, dressing rooms, *scene-dock, etc. It is not to be confused with the *upstage area, which is the rear section of the stage.

**Ballad opera.** An eighteenth-century form, of which John Gay's *The Beggar's Opera* (1728) is the most famous example. It parodied Italian *grand opera, and its lower-class content, popular tunes, and strongly satirical tone reappeared in the 1920s in Brecht and Weill's *Threepenny Opera* (1928) and *The Rise and Fall of the City of Mahagonny* (1930).

Henry Fielding's use of the form to attack the government drove the Prime Minister, Robert Walpole, to impose stage *censorship in England by means of the 1737 *Licensing Act.

EMPSON, W.H., *Some Versions of Pastoral*, Chatto and Windus, 1936, Ch. 6.

**Ballet**. A *dance performance employing a set of very specific physical movements and postures. Its use of individual and choral expression, of spectacular *costume and *mise en scène, and above all of a narrative story-line, make it, despite its lack of *dialogue, a highly stylized form of drama. *Greek tragedy was in part balletic, since the *chorus danced.

**Barker**. Colourful, persuasive and vociferous character whose job is to entice customers into the fairground show. He has no doubt existed ever since the first *travelling players began to seek a living.

**Barnstormer**. An actor of rough style and extravagant *gesture who performed with his travelling company in barns and suchlike places in the nineteenth century.

**Baroque**. Important seventeenth-century movement in the arts. Baroque theatre was lavish and aristocratic and developed in the European court theatres out of a desire to fuse spectacular *perspective effects with novel operatic forms in new and impressive theatre buildings. For a detailed illustrated commentary, see: NICOLL, A., *The Development of the Theatre*, Harrap, 1927, pp.103–95.

**Barrel system**. An early method of moving scenery. Ropes were attached to barrels of varying diameter or a single shaft. When rotated they allowed synchronized *scene-changes.

**Bathos**. A literary effect, either accidental or deliberate, occasioned by a sudden deflation of a reader's expectations. The term *anti-climax is stronger and is more commonly used when referring to drama.

**Batten**. A piece of wood or length of pipe which gives rigidity to a *flat, or to a series of flats. It can also mean a pipe length used to fly a row of lights, *scenery or a *curtain.

**Bauhaus**. Famous school of art, architecture and design which engaged in experimental stage work and scenic design under Oskar Schlemmer. See also TOTALTHEATER.
SCHLEMMER, O., *et al*. *The Theatre of the Bauhaus*, Wesleyan University Press, 1961.

**Beginning, middle and end**. From the famous phrase in Aristotle's *Poetics*:

> Now a whole is that which has a beginning, a middle, and an end. A beginning is that which does not necessarily follow anything else, but which leads naturally to another event or development; an end is the opposite, that which itself naturally (i.e. either of necessity or most

commonly) follows something else, but nothing else comes after it; and a middle is that which itself follows something else and is followed by another thing.

It is likely that Aristotle had in mind the three-fold movement through *time of the natural world, in which living *forms — animals, plants and human beings — are born, mature to reproduce, and die. If drama is *mimetic, it must copy these natural patterns, in which the various parts combine in one whole. Aristotle's remarks argue for a *unity towards which art should aspire — a principle which has only recently been challenged, by Bertolt Brecht, amongst others. See MIDDLE; END; INDUCTION; PROLOGUE; ANTI-ARISTOTELIAN.

**Below**. Downstage of, as in *cross below*. The term derives from the period of *raked stages.

**Benefit**. A special theatrical performance, similar to modern benefit matches for sportsmen, in which the proceeds were given to an actor or other person deemed to deserve, or be in urgent need of, the money. The practice became common in the eighteenth century and died out later in the nineteenth century. There is an account of a benefit in Dickens's *Nicholas Nickleby* (1838–9).
TROUBRIDGE, SIR ST VINCENT, *The Benefit System in the British Theatre*, Society for Theatre Research, 1967.

**Bergson, Henri** (1859–1941). French philosopher, much concerned with the nature of creative expression. His importance in drama is as a theorist of *comedy.

> The writer asks himself every moment whether it will be indeed given to him to see it through. He gives thanks to Fortune for each partial success, as a maker of puns might thank words placed upon his path for having lent themselves to his game.

According to Bergson, to study comic form is to study 'the illusion of a machine working on the inside of a person'. See: CHANCE; FARCE; LAUGHTER; COMEDY.
BERGSON, H., *Le Rire* (1900).

**Berliner Ensemble**. Company established by Bertolt Brecht in 1947 at the Schiffbauerdamm Theater in East Berlin. There he trained his actors and directed the major plays he had written during his exile. The visits of the Ensemble to Paris in 1955, and to London just after Brecht's death in 1956, had a powerful impact on French and British theatrical production. The *structures of Brecht's plays, and the methods of acting and production he had evolved, strongly affected a new generation of writers seeking ways of politicizing the theatre and its audiences. See EPIC THEATRE.

**Bespeak performance**. A practice whereby a wealthy patron of a company chose a play from their *repertory and for its performance purchased large numbers of tickets to be re-sold or distributed free. The proceeds would be divided between members of the troupe.

TROUBRIDGE, SIR ST VINCENT, *The Benefit System in the British Theatre*, Society of Theatre Research, 1967.

**Besserungstück**. Morally improving German *Volkstück*.

**Bible-history**. Modern term for a *mystery play.

**Bienséances, Les**. French literary rules of *decorum which required literary or dramatic characters to behave outwardly in accordance with social rank and to observe aesthetic and psychological consistency. They owned much to Nicholas Boileau (1636–1711) the literary arbiter of his time.

BOILEAU, N., *Art Poétique* (1674).

**Big Close-up (BCU)**. Television term for a close shot of the face, not the ordinary *close-up of head and shoulders.

**Biomechanics**. Developed by Vsevolod Meyerhold in 1922, this was a way of using physical activity to arouse the emotions, in a basic system of exercises for the training of actors. 'Only via the sports arena can we approach the theatrical arena'; 'we need not ecstasy, but excitation, based firmly on the physical premise', he declared.

Meyerhold's theory seems to have been founded on his reading of Coquelin's *L'Art et le Comédien* (1880) or *L'Art du Comédien* (1886) combined with a study of the *Commedia dell'Arte* and of the theatres of the east, seen through his own experience of *mime. It assumes an actor capable of what Meyerhold calls 'reflex excitability'. Excitability he defines as: 'the ability to realize in feelings, movements and words a task which is prescribed externally'. The crucial word here is 'externally'. It may be compared with Stanislavski's internal and psychological, rather than physiological approach. Biomechanics thus works, according to a common distinction among actors, 'from the outside inwards', rather than 'from the inside outwards.'

Meyerhold goes on to define an 'acting cycle' which accompanies 'manifestations of excitability'. In this cycle there are three stages, which he calls 'Intention'. 'Realization' and 'Reaction'. During the first stage, the actor intellectually assimilates a task, 'prescribed externally by the dramatist, the director, or the initiative of the performer'. Then follows 'a cycle of volitional, mimetic and vocal reflexes' which consistute the 'realization'. Finally there is the 'reaction', which is a preparation for a new acting cycle, and involves 'the attenuation of the volitional reflex'.

This description seems mechanistic, and indeed biomechanics was seen as a response to the machine age. It provided a basis for the systemized forms of physical training which were incorporated into the curricula of Soviet schools. The theories of William James (the 'James/Lange theory' (1890)), which suggested that an emotion was not the cause but the result of a physical sensation (prompted by an external stimulus) gave biomechanics academic and theoretical respectability.

The theory worked in practice, and Meyerhold evolved a series of exercises, '*études*' and pantomimes, as part of his training programme. One of these exercises, the 'firing of the bow', developed into the *étude* called 'The Hunt'. However, theory is generally a simplification of practice, and it is likely that physical activity and emotion are related to each other in more complex forms of reaction and counter-reaction. Stanislavski and Meyerhold, as their mutual respect would seem to indicate, were not so far apart as their theories suggest.

BRAUN, E. (ed.), *Meyerhold on Theatre*, Methuen/Hill and Wang, 1969, Part 5.

**Biorama**. A stage on which two sets could be loaded, and a *scene-change effected, by revolving the stage through the sector of an arc. Used in Paris in 1822.

**Black comedy**. A form of comedy which extracts laughter from *chance, *cruelty, suffering and death, that is, from the material of *tragedy. Tragedy, however, keeps a full sense of the individual suffering it deals with, and holds at bay the dissociative and defensive process of laughter. If you take away a sense of the reality of Ophelia she becomes just another waiting gentlewoman, and the Gravedigger merely jokes about her death. If the pile of corpses grows too high, or the actors lack the power to sustain the fullness of the characters, the implicit horror of a story can dispel seriousness. In one way this form of laughter is natural. No one can sustain a full sense of the pain of the world. Laughter is a sign of healthy unawareness. The Gravedigger distances the horror of his trade and has in this way our sympathy. The humour of his scenes in *Hamlet*, though set in a graveyard, is thus not entirely 'black'. The situation and characters are too sane.

Black comedy seems to arise from exaggeration, from *carica-. ture and *repetition, which gives an edge of insanity to the proceedings. In Ionesco's *Amédée or How to Get Rid of it* (1954), a corpse distresses a couple by growing until it fills their apartment. In Ionesco's other plays, names, objects, animals and killers proliferate in a nightmare world where death looms large. When the characters attempt to normalize the situation we seek distance in laughter.

Black comedy, prominent in the *theatre of the absurd and in *existential writers from Dostoievski (1821–81) to Kafka (1883–1924) and Beckett (1906–    ), has its antecedents in *Jacobean tragi-comedy, and in medieval forms of the *grotesque. We might also speculate on the absence of human fullness, and the elements of cruelty and sadism in Shakespeare's Iago, which prompt him to attempt, though he fails, to make a black comedy out of *Othello*.

STYAN, J.L., *The Dark Comedy*, Cambridge University Press, 2nd edition, 1967.

**Blackfriars**. Indoor theatre built in the Parliament Chamber of the Blackfriars' Priory in the old City of London. It was the second theatre to be used on the site and was designed by James Burbage with a *tiring house, actors' gallery, a low stage with three entrances, and spectator galleries round three sides of a *pit filled with seats. It was used by the *King's Men from 1608 until the closing of the theatres in 1642, having previously been leased to the *Children of the Chapel Royal. It has been argued that the established tradition of music and spectacle at the theatre encouraged Shakespeare to develop these elements in such late plays as *Cymbeline* (1609), *The Winter's Tale* (1610) and *The Tempest* (1611). See PRIVATE THEATRES.

HOSLEY, R., 'The Playhouses and the Stage', in *A New Companion to Shakespeare Studies*, edited by K. Muir and S. Schoenbaum, Cambridge University Press, 1971.

**Blackout**. An eclipse of stage lighting between scenes which enables actors to exit and enter before the spectators' eyes re-adjust. It is more rapid than a *curtain but it can be used to suggest a time lapse and/or change of location, especially on an *open stage. Pinter makes pointed and comic use of a blackout in his *naturalist play *The Caretaker* (1960) when one character (Mick) needs to use the light plug to work the Electrolux and the consequent darkness provokes fear in another character (Davies).

**Black Theatre**. A theatrical movement which developed under the influence of the Black Power movement in the 1960s. It sought first to give a voice to black Americans and to establish a separate theatre for purely black audiences. The success of *A Raisin in the Sun* (1959) by Lorraine Hansberry provided a base for the movement. Leroi Jones (1934–    ) and James Baldwin (1924–87) have been the most successful of its exponents. Its influence has extended beyond America into former British and French colonies.

*Drama Revue*, Black Theatre Issue, December 1972, pp.3–61.

**Blank verse**. Unrhymed iambic pentameters — the poetic line introduced, in about 1540, in the Earl of Surrey's translation of Virgil's *Aeneid*. Its flexibility made it the medium of the Elizabethan and Jacobean dramatists. It could be used for colloquial speech, public *rhetoric, and intense personal emotion. T.S. Eliot (1888–1965) sought to emulate this flexibility in his blank verse experiments with *poetic drama in *The Family Reunion* (1939) and *The Cocktail Party* (1949).

**Blocking**. The process of deciding in *rehearsal the most effective points in the *dialogue at which characters should sit, stand, or move, so as to form the most effective stage positions and *groupings. Ideally, the blocking should emerge with the actor's conception of his character. It is important for an actor to be at home with his moves so that they look natural to the audience. A *director who simply 'issues' moves without giving the actors time to feel they are 'right' can cause problems. Actors may even *'dry' if they feel dialogue and movement are at odds with one another. Unfortunately, shortage of rehearsal time, or a director's lack of confidence, can often result in awkward movement. Few directors have the time, confidence, and expertise of Stanislavski, who recommended, in *Creating a Role*, that actors should postpone not only learning, but even reading their lines, until the play's general pattern of movement had been worked out by a process of *improvisation. Only then should the dialogue be (gradually) assimilated to the stage activity.

**Blood-tub**. The lowest kind of *gaff; a badly equipped theatre in the poorest quarters of London and the larger provincial cities. They provided, in the nineteenth century, a heavy diet of *melodrama.

**Blue**. A plain sky *border.

**Boards**. Colloquial term for the stage, as in the phrase 'tread the boards'. The boards forming the stage floor generally run towards the audience, across joists which lie parallel to the *proscenium arch. When the boards were cut to allow for *traps, especially on old *raked stages, a complicated system of strengthening was employed.

**Boat-truck**. A platform on wheels, used for the quick setting-up and shifting of *scenery.

**Body language**. Physical postures and movements which, often unconsciously, reveal a person's thoughts, feelings and attitudes. The position of hands and feet, the tilt of the head, the set of the

backbone, and so on, constitute *signs, which a spectator inter-
prets. Thus, in the theatre, body language is a form of *theatre
language. In *naturalistic acting, body language appears less
conscious and emphatic, since the actor's movements tend to
emerge 'naturally' from *dialogue and situation. More stylized and
less verbal forms of acting, such as *mime, are often comic. The
actor deliberately draws attention to a movement or pose by
exaggerating or prolonging it. The continuity of natural movement is broken up into a series of 'gestic' statements. See FOCUS and
GESTUS.

ARGYLE, M., and TROWER, P., *Person to Person, Ways of Communicating*,
Multimedia Publications Inc., Holland, 1979.

**Booked flat**. Two *flats hinged together.

**Book-holder (book-keeper)**. The man responsible, in the *Elizabethan and *Jacobean public theatres, both for seeing that
players were ready to come in on *cue, and for having *properties
ready when they were needed. He stood in the *tiring house and
was generally helped by several assistants or *stagekeepers.

1  *Itinerant players on booth or platform stage*

**Booth-stage**. A transportable stage, used by travelling actors in the
Middle Ages, consisting of a simple wooden platform with curtains
along one side, through which *exits and *entrances could be
made. The audience thus stood on three sides, as round the
Elizabethan *apron stage. Actors may, on occasions, have used the
space around the stage as well as on it, access being gained by
ladder, or from beneath the stage, through drapes which hung
around it.

SOUTHERN, R., *The Seven Ages of the Theatre*, 2nd edition, Faber,
1964; *The Staging of Plays before Shakespeare*, Faber, 1973.

**Border**. Narrow strip of material, attached to a *batten and suspended over a scene to conceal the *flies and the tops of scenes. Borders may represent clouds, limbs of trees, ceilings, skies etc. Attached at either end may be *tails or *legs, hanging down to the stage and functioning as *wings. (See Ill.13, p.166.)

The borders allow for batten or border lights to shine between them from above to illuminate the stage area. With the development of better *lighting and demands for stage realism, the *ceiling piece took the place of borders in the *naturalistic theatre.

**Border light**. American name for a *light batten.

**Boulevard theatre**. Translation of '*théâtre de boulevard*', a generally pejorative term for drama aiming at commercial success in the theatres of the Paris boulevards.

HOBSON, SIR H., *French Theatre Since 1830*, Calder, 1978/Riverrun 1979.

**Bourgeois drama**. General term for a number of different kinds of drama which present, examine or reflect the experience and psychology of a middle-class audience. The term does not cover theatre with a general social appeal, such as the *Elizabethan, or with an aristocratic appeal, such as earlier *Restoration plays, or with a working-class appeal such as much itinerant *fringe theatre, or nineteenth-century *melodrama. Nor should it be applied to plays reflecting working-class experience, such as those of John Osborne (1929– ) or Arnold Wesker (1932– ) who raised such a furore in the 1950s because the experience and attitudes they presented were so different from the expectations of London 'bourgeois' theatre audiences.

There are, however, problems in the fuller definition of the term. Plays may be considered 'bourgeois' in four ways: (a) in *content* (Ibsen dramatizing the experience of a middle-class family), or (b) in *form*, because they employ the dramatic structures the middle-class expects and responds to. (The *well-made play may contain a plot which reflects an (unconscious) bourgeois *ideology, since it shows events working the way the audience *wants* them to work.) See SOCIAL TRAGEDY and SOCIALIST REALISM. (c) A play may be bourgeois in *audience appeal*. This can mean any play which is successful in an 'established' theatre, including subsidized theatres such as the *National or Royal Shakespeare. Finally, (d) it may be bourgeois in *attitude*, i.e. the writer's views and feelings coincide with his audience's, which may as a category overlap with (a), (b), and (c).

Obviously, these categories lead to problems. A play may be 'bourgeois' in *content*, but not in *attitude*, because the bourgeois content is parodied, as, for instance, in Ibsen's *Pillars of Society*

(1877). It may be bourgeois in *form*, but not *content*, as has been claimed is the case with Osborne and Wesker, who do not break out of conventional, and hence 'bourgeois', forms. Or a play may be non-bourgeois in both content and form (Beckett's tramps and his anti-theatrical structures) and yet remain bourgeois in attitude and effect). J.-P. Sartre (1905–80) has suggested this is the case with *Waiting for Godot* (1953) whose conclusion that nothing can really be changed is what, he says, the class in power wishes to hear. Finally plays may be 'anti-bourgeois', in content, form and attitude, but yet, because they are put on in a theatre which caters for a middle-class audience, or on television, or in a subsidized theatre, they are labelled 'bourgeois' (like recent *fringe dramatists successful in establishment theatres).

The term, if it is to be used at all, needs very careful handling. The attitudes to which a writer gives convincing dramatic embodiment conflict with each other, and challenge the audience. Characters, plays and audiences are rarely fully explicable in class terms. (One of Brecht's points in the *Messingkauf Dialogues* is that there exists a tension between the individual and his class, for 'class attributes do not entirely explain a person'.) Indeed, one suspects that all plays, to be successful, need elements of subversion — certainly if Freud's theory of *laughter is relevant to commercial *farce.

On the whole it is best to use the term 'bourgeois' to describe theatre which presented the experience of the class which became dominant during the eighteenth and nineteenth centuries. During this time the middle-class family in the private room became the gradual focus of attention, perhaps first in Lillo's *London Merchant* (1731), then in eighteenth-century *sentimental comedy, and later in the *naturalist movement.

WILLIAMS, R., *The Long Revolution*, Pelican, 1965, pp.271–300.

**Bowdlerize**. To edit out passages which offend the proprieties — after Thomas Bowdler, who edited *The Family Shakespeare* in 1818 so that it 'could be read by a gentleman in the company of ladies'.

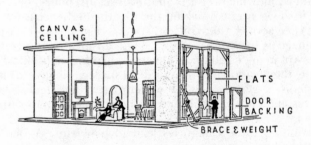

**2** *Box set*

**Box-set**. An arrangement of linked *flats and *ceiling cloths which create on stage the illusion of a room. It has doors and windows which can be opened and entered, with *reveals and *returns which strengthen the illusion. Hinges, cleats and sill-irons lend the necessary rigidity, and the furnishings, of course, are of appropriate style and period.

No one knows when the box-set first replaced *wings. The Mannheim Court Theatre folded back wings as early as 1804, and the plays of Diderot (1713–84) and Beaumarchais (1732–99) must have been enclosed on occasions, since Goethe attacked them for the practice. 'Such a set,' he said, 'could give pleasure only to the uneducated, who confused a work of art with a work of nature.' Madam Vestris (1797–1856) used a box-set in November 1832, and two years later Planché (1796–1880), seems to have used a ceiling instead of hanging *borders. In 1842, Madame Vestris staged Boucicault's *London Assurance* with highly realistic fittings and furniture, and the box-set was inevitably taken up by the *naturalist theatre, as appropriate for so-called *bourgeois plays, dealing with private family life, rather than public life in public places.

The cumbersome nature of the box-set meant that *scene-changing was slow, and this interfered with the *rhythm and *pace of performance. In the interests of speed, new methods were found. The stage was divided into sections which could be lowered to bring up scenery from the basement. This, however, meant costly machinery, and plays using the box-set had to limit their changes of location. Other restrictions were imposed by the need for *dialogue and *costume which were appropriate to the time and place.

Attempts have been made, of course, to transcend the restrictions of *realism. Chekhov (1860–1904) and Ibsen (1828–1906), for example, are expert at suggesting the existence of places beyond the limits of set — a railway station miles away, a village in the distance or a dark attic upstage which the audience never sees. More recently the 'stage room' has been made more directly symbolic of a human situation. Pinter (1930–    ) does this in most of his early plays, as did Sartre in *In Camera* (1944). Pinter asks whether, when there is a knock on the door, we let the person in, and if so, what happens next. Who stays and who leaves? And why? Sartre's rooms enclose characters who 'freely' imprison themselves. So, too, in a more *grotesque way, do Beckett's characters, though the freedom is even more questionable. His set for *Endgame* (1956) seems symbolic of the inside of a head, employing a circular box-set, obviously artificial, with two windows serving as eyes on the outside world. One of the characters, Hamm, insists on sitting exactly at the centre of it.

**Boy bishop**. The boy chosen to ride on a donkey at the head of the medieval processions which formed an important part of the New Year revels called the *Feast of Fools.

CHAMBERS, E.K., *The Medieval Stage*, Vol. I, Oxford University Press, 1903, pp.336–72.

**Boy companies**. Elizabethan troupes consisting of boy players from the royal choirs, who acted at court and at *Blackfriars. The Children of the Chapel and the Children of Paul's performed plays by John Lyly (*c*.1554–1606), Ben Jonson (1572–1637) and others, and achieved high popularity, threatening, on the evidence of Shakespeare's *Hamlet* Act II, to 'carry it away' in competition with the men's companies.

CHAMBERS, E.K., *The Elizabethan Stage*, Vol. II, Oxford University Press, 1923.

**Brace**. A support which holds a *flat upright, consisting of a metal rod anchoring it to the stage, or of a hinged wooden frame, called a 'French brace'.

**Braggadocio**. Either (a) empty boasting, or (b) the *Alazon or braggart, a comic character *stereotype.

**Bread and Puppet Theatre**. Company founded in New York in 1961 by Peter Schumann (1934–    ). It has a strong mythical and folk basis and specializes in elaborate visual theatre using *mime, *masks and huge puppets representing animals and supernatural beings. It generally operates outside established theatres and aims to create a sense of community and celebration. The bread of the company's title refers to Schumann's practice of sharing bread between actors and spectators.

SHANK, T., *American Alternative Theatre*, Macmillan, 1982, pp.103–11.

**Brecht, Bertolt** (1898–1956). Dramatist, director and major theorist who combined Marxist political theory with a theory of acting and a theory of dramatic structure to create new dramatic forms out of traditional patterns. Careful study of the Greeks, of Shakespeare, and of *medieval and *oriental theatre lay behind his plays:

> When a family is ruined I don't seek the reason in an inexorable fate, in hereditary weakness or special characteristics but try to establish how it could have been avoided by human action.

See: ACTING; ALIENATION; ANACHRONISM; ANTI-ARISTOTELIAN; CABARET; CATHARSIS; CHARACTER; COMEDY; DIALECTIC; EPIC THEATRE; FATE; GESTUS; MONTAGE; PARABLE PLAY.

BRECHT, B., *Kleines Organon für das Theater* (1949); *Dialoge aus dem Messingkauf* (1964); *Brecht on Theatre*, edited by J. Willett, Hill and Wang, 1964.

**Breeches part**. Young romantic male *role, played by a woman. A famous example in *Restoration comedy is Sir Harry Wildair in Farquhar's *The Constant Couple* (1699), notably played by Peg Woffington in 1740. Famous actresses from Nell Gwynn (1650–87) and Mrs Bracegirdle (c.1673–1748), to Madame Vestris (1797–1856) and Sarah Bernhardt (1845–1923) played these parts with great success. The *principal boy in *pantomime developed out of Madame Vestris's performances.

**Bridge**. Device for lifting heavy scenery from below stage to stage level.

**Brighella**. Sly and mendacious comic *zany; a *stereotype servant figure in the *Commedia dell'Arte*. Marivaux (1688–1763) and Beaumarchais (1732–99) created figures, notably Figaro in *Le Barbier de Séville* (1772), who seem to derive from him.

**Bristle trap**. A *trap consisting of a hole covered over by bristles through which sudden and alarming appearances can be made — such as that of the Demon King in *pantomime.

**Broadway**. Street running north and south through New York City. It gives its name to New York's entertainment industry and its big commercial theatres. It developed rapidly after the *Theatrical Syndicate took control in 1896, doubling the number of theatres in the years leading up to the Wall Street Crash of 1929. After World War I, Eugene O'Neill's *Emperor Jones* (1920) and *Anna Christie* (1921) came to Broadway from George Cook's Provincetown Players. They initiated O'Neill's varied and brilliant series of New York productions and led into a period of spectacular stage design. The intense commercialism of Broadway, however, engendered a conservatism dedicated to profit and to giving the public what it wanted. This discouraged innovations in dramatic form (see OFF BROADWAY). *Musical comedy became a dominant genre and immense risks were (and are) taken to secure colossal profits. Eight million people saw the 'hit' musical *Oklahoma* (1943) during its fifteen-year run. Recent musical successes on Broadway have included a number of British productions.

**Brook, Peter** (1925– ). Major English and European director associated with the *Royal Shakespeare Company and the International Centre of Theatre Research in Paris. He says:

> The time-honoured forms have shrivelled and died in front of us.
> From the zero you get to the infinite.

See: DEADLY THEATRE; HOLY THEATRE; IMMEDIACY; ROUGH THEATRE.
BROOK, P., *The Empty Space*, McGibbon and Kee, 1968.

**Buffoon**. A professional *clown, *fool or *jester. The word derives
from the Italian '*burla*' or jest, and is associated with '*buffare*' (to
puff). The word thus suggests a 'windbag', like the word 'fool'
which derives from the Latin for a bellows ('*follis*').

The word 'buffoonery', too, is worthy of note. T.S. Eliot made a
famous observation on Hamlet's 'antick disposition' (see *Selected
Essays*, 1919, p.146). He argues that Hamlet's play with words, and
his levity, are 'a form of emotional relief. In the character, Hamlet,
it is the buffoonery of an emotion which can find no outlet in
action; in the dramatist it is the buffoonery of an emotion which he
cannot express in art.' These challenging remarks lead to speculation about the links between art, madness and the nature of *play.

**Build**. To build is to increase in dramatic intensity; to move
towards a *climax.

**Built stuff**. General name for specially constructed three-
dimensional stage objects, such as steps, *rostra, columns and trees.

***Burla***. The longer comic episode, as compared with the briefer
*lazzo, in the *Commedia dell'Arte.

**Burlesque**. From the Italian '*burlesco*', stage entertainment. An
exaggerated *satire of a writer, style, fashion, form or convention.
Among the most famous in the language is the scene in
Shakespeare's *A Midsummer Night's Dream* (1595) in which the 'rude
mechanicals' play the Pyramus and Thisbe story. Buckingham's *The
Rehearsal* (1671) is an attack on John Dryden and other contempor-
aries. Sheridan's *The Critic* (1779) pillories, among others, Richard
Cumberland in the figure of Sir Fretful Plagiary.

Like *allegory, burlesque makes its appeal to a contemporary
audience, conscious of references to local events, well-known
people, and fashions in language or clothes. As with allegory,
succeeding generations find particular references increasingly
difficult to identify. *Revivals of burlesques are thus uncommon,
though some, like *The Critic*, retain audience appeal, because the
human types and situation continue to be recognizable. In *A
Midsummer Night's Dream*, of course, the burlesque is part of a more
complex structure, in which the audience not only watches a play,
but watches a stage audience watching burlesque. Shakespeare sets
burlesque, as a *play within a play, against other dramatic forms, so
that it becomes itself subject to scrutiny, thus ensuring a more
universal appeal. The clown, Bottom, of course, would alone
ensure the play's survival.

Burlesque has been said to be 'the treatment of low material in a high style', as compared with *travesty, 'the treatment of high material in a low style'. If this is true, the *Second Shepherd's Play* in the Wakefield *mystery cycle (which burlesques the Christmas story of the Three Shepherds) is more accurately a travesty. The term 'burlesque' however, is often used for both.

Burlesque is also the name of a specific type of American *variety performance, created by Michael Leavitt (1843–1935) in about 1868. This had a small amount of contemporary *parody but mainly consisted of chorus numbers in the opening and concluding stages, with musical and acrobatic turns in the centre and a suggestive erotic dance, the 'hootchy-kootchy' (origin unknown), as finale.

CLINTON-BADDELEY, V.C., *The Burlesque Tradition in the English Theatre after 1660*, Methuen, 1952.

TRUSSLER, S. (ed.), *Burlesque Plays of the Eighteenth Century*, Oxford University Press, 1969.

**Burletta**. An eighteenth-century entertainment, produced at *minor theatres, and defined legally as any three-act play with more than five songs. It was invented in order to circumvent the *Licensing Laws of 1737, as the use of song allowed its perform-ance in the smaller unlicensed theatres.

**Burnt cork**. Material used by *'nigger minstrels', or the *villain in *melodrama, to blacken the face. See ROLE REVERSAL.

**Business**. Stage activity, often involving clever play with *props, which actor or director introduce into a play to strengthen dramatic impact. It needs careful handling, since it can call attention to itself, or to the skills of the actor, to the detriment of the general performance.

**Busker**. Itinerant entertainer.

**Buskin**. Name for a boot, reaching to calf or knee, worn by actors, especially of *tragedy, in the Elizabethan period. The term 'busker' is derived from it. See COTHURNUS.

# C

**Cabaret**. In the seventeenth century the word meant a drinking shop. It came to refer to entertainment supplied during meals in restaurants, or accompanied by drinks in night-clubs, and developed strongly during World War I when many conventional theatres had to close by 10 p.m. After the war, when *censorship of scripts was lifted, Berlin, Munich and the big German cities all had their cabarets. The dadaists and futurists were attracted to the form. The *Cabaret Voltaire* in Zurich became a focal point for *dada in neutral Switzerland. The form also had a strong influence on German theatre. In 1919 Max Reinhardt brought back his *Schall und Rauch* cabaret to cellar rooms beneath the Grosses Schauspielhaus in Berlin. Cabaret's absence of formality, its *music hall format, its exploitation of *zany elements in colloquial speech, its *grotesque quality, its possibilities as a vehicle for social and political satire (demonstrated by such performers as Karl Valentin) – these appealed to Bertolt Brecht (1898–1956) and he appropriated them. 'This new kind of theatre has the original form of "Gestik"; it has humour, imagination and wisdom', he said.

RITCHIE, J.M., 'Brecht and Cabaret', in *Brecht in Perspective*, edited by
G. Bartram and A.E. Waine, Longman, 1982.

**Caesura**. A pause in the verse line. Thus in:

> Beseech/you sir,/be merr/y;//you/have cause.
> So have/we all,/of joy;//for our/escape
> Is much/beyond/our loss.//Our hint/of woe
> Is comm/on;//ev/ery day some sailor's wife,
> The mast/ers of/some mer/chant,//and/the merchant
> Have just/this theme/of woe.// (*The Tempest* II.i.1.1–6)

The caesura // usually accompanies a strong pause. It occurs frequently after the third foot, as in the first three lines of the extract above. Sometimes it occurs in the middle of a foot, as in lines four and five. Its variable position indicates the way *Elizabethan and *Jacobean dramatists adapted the *blank verse iambic pentameter to the rhythms and sentence patterns of colloquial speech, whilst retaining, as in the example, a powerful rhythmical beat.

**Call-board**. Board on which notices such as rehearsal schedules are posted. It is usually situated near the stage door.

**Call doors**. Nineteenth-century name for *proscenium doors. They were used only for actors acknowledging applause at the end of the play.

**Canon**. The books of the Bible which are recognized as authentic. By extension it came to mean an author's recognized works, especially the thirty-seven plays of Shakespeare. Hence 'canonical', belonging to the canon.

*Capa y espada*. *Comedias de Capa y Espada*. See CLOAK AND SWORD PLAYS.

**3** *The* capitano (*by* Abraham Bosse)

*Capitano*. The *stereotype cowardly soldier in the *Commedia dell'Arte*. The type derives from Plautus's *Miles Gloriosus* (c.202 B.C.). Shakespeare's Pistol in *Henry IV* and *V* (1597–9) and Parolles in *All's Well that Ends Well* (1602–3) are obviously related.

The continuing appeal of such a character may lie in his duality. He has his private fear, yet he puts on a bold public front. He is both *Everyman and a representative of those who would pretend to power. We sympathize and understand, yet at the same time mock. We recognize the need to cover weakness, and we rejoice at the fall of the bully. Our *laughter perhaps celebrates the mastery of *fear.

**Caricature**. Comic exaggeration. A pictorial term suggesting distortion of a physical feature: a long nose, shaggy eyebrows, pendulous ears, a large belly, thin legs. It mocks particular individuals and physical types. It also mocks mental characteristics: envy, complacency, avarice, and so on, by picking out the postures, facial expressions or other physical characteristics associated with the vice.

In a newspaper cartoon, or a Hogarth picture, the figure caricatured does not move. It cannot answer for itself. But when such caricatural figures are transported into drama they cease to have such a flat two-dimensional form. Cyrano de Bergerac's nose and Falstaff's belly belong to creatures who live and change. They may even develop a consciousness of their own caricatural potential. Falstaff deliberately caricatures himself. He also caricatures others and defeats those who would reduce him to a simple fixed figure.

Other dramatic characters, like Molière's miser in *L'Avare*, or the hypochondriac in *Le Malade Imaginaire* (1673), are closer to the simple caricature, since they lack such self-awareness. Even so, the actor's physical embodiment of such a character will endow it with a life which complicates our response and our *laughter. See STEREOTYPE.

**Carnivalesque**. A term associated with the Russian *formalist critic, M. Bakhtin, whose influential book *The World of Rabelais* argues for the importance of a dramatic folk *tradition which scholars using written soures have tended to ignore. The carnivalesque, he argues, embodies a set of attitudes which, in their celebration of life and mockery of death, in their emphasis on the body rather than the soul, countered the ecclesiastical and aristocratic traditions. Its *grotesque inversions expressed themselves in physical activity and speech, rather than in writing. Such a tradition lies behind Rabelais (*c*.1494–*c*.1553). It is oral, secular, comic and dramatic. It leads through Erasmus's *In Praise of Folly* (1511) to Shakespeare's *fools, to Sterne's *Tristram Shandy* (1759–67) and the *circus clown.

**Carnival play**. A *one-act play performed at Shrovetide in the fifteenth and sixteenth centuries. The tradition was very strong in Germany, where it was called the *Fastnachtspiel*. It resembled the more elaborate French *sotie*. See CARNIVALESQUE.

**Caroline theatre**. Drama written during the reign of Charles I, and before the closure of the theatres in 1642. It is regarded as a transition between *Jacobean and *Restoration drama. As represented by the work of James Shirley (1596–1666) and Richard Brome (c.1590–1652/3), it anticipates the *comedy of manners and *heroic tragedy.

**Carpenter**. Important stage technician. The 'master carpenter' builds the *sets; the 'stage carpenter' sets them.

**Carpenter's scene**. A scene played *downstage before a *curtain, to allow elaborate scenery to be set up behind it for the following scene. Used especially in *pantomime and in productions with a heavy emphasis on spectacle.

**Carpet cut**. A long slot in the stage behind the *proscenium arch. Floor coverings are tucked into it to ensure the actors do not trip in performance.

**Carriage and frame**. Another term for *chariot and pole.

**Cast**. The list of actors playing *roles in a particular play. The size of a cast will vary from play to play and will be selected for different reasons. Professional managers may wish to save on salaries and will thus prefer plays with a small cast. Amateur companies or schools may prefer to involve as many people as possible. They will then choose plays with a huge cast, such as Peter Terson's *Zigger-Zagger* (1967), written for the National Youth Theatre. Alternatively, an amateur company may have few good actors available, so that a small cast play is preferred. The proportion of parts allocated to men and women is also an important consideration. In the theatre, male actors have a greater variety of parts. Recently, *feminist groups have been concerned to rectify the imbalance by writing and producing plays with mainly female casts.

**Casting**. The selection of actors to play particular parts. This generally involves an *audition to decide the range of talent available, and which actors will work best together. *Voice, stature, *range, age and general physical 'rightness' are all, of course, important. One should remember, however, that 'type-casting' can encourage laziness. As Meyerhold (1874–1940) remarks: 'In order to spur an actor into action you sometimes need to set him a paradoxical task.' Brecht (1898–1956) also tells us that apparent 'miscasting' can stretch an actor and obtain an unusual performance.

The dangers of type-casting are evident in *TV drama where actors are known and well-established. Well-known faces and familiar personalities can make too frequent an appearance and insufficient effort may be taken to involve the large pool of unrecognized acting talent which exists. Casting is a process of fitting actors to plays. It is also possible to fit plays to actors. One may select, adapt, and even write plays to suit an acting troupe. The emergence of large numbers of *fringe companies has encouraged this practice, which is not, of course, new. Ingmar Bergman in his films, Bertolt Brecht and no doubt Shakespeare himself were aware of the talents and capacities of their fellow-players. Where writers work closely with *repertory companies, or with particular actors, the casting is apt to be an integral part of the writing.

**Catastrophe**. The final movement of *tragedy, usually involving the death of the *protagonist and/or *antagonist, when the audience is confronted with events both feared and (possibly) desired.

**Catharsis**. A Greek medical term meaning 'purgation', used by Aristotle to define the effect of *tragedy upon the spectator: 'through *pity and *fear effecting the catharsis or purgation of the emotions.' There is no further definition in the incomplete text of the *Poetics*, but Book VIII of his *Politics* suggests that drama shares with music the capacity to carry people out of themselves, as if by divine possession, and then to restore them as if they had taken a purge.

How this might be true has been endlessly debated. Freytag, in *Teknik des Dramas* (1857) argues that after the final curtain the spectator 'feels an intensification of vital power, his eye sparkles, his step is elastic, every movement is firm and free. His agitation has been succeeded by a feeling of joyful safety.' In other words, the spectator is released from his involvement with the sufferings of the tragic hero and he realizes he is safe.

This explanation may be amplified by what T.R. Henn called the 'Reduction to Scale Theory'. This argues that the tragic spectator recognizes the petty nature of his own troubles compared with the magnitude of the sufferings undergone in the tragedy. In this sense tragedy effects a reduction of self-absorption and self-pity, which may be considered a form of moral purification.

Other theorists focus on the emotions of pity and fear, arguing that tragedy brings these into balance. Pity is an emotion which moves us towards the sufferer. Fear, on the other hand, is an impulse to retreat. Catharsis arises out of the indulgence of these two opposite impulses and the two are brought into balance. In this way tragedy is a kind of ritual inoculation against the thing we fear.

Further theories argue that tragedy indulges our desire to see men suffer, especially men of power and authority. There is thus an element of sadism or 'Schadenfreude', born out of resentment at the trammels of existence and the limits of individual freedom within social power structures. Such a view emphasizes that tragedies have a *sacrifice at their centre, a *scapegoat, like Oedipus, who takes the sins of a community upon himself.

A less sombre view argues that catharsis arises out of the recognition that all who suffer are human, even the great who are brought low. The tragic effect involves a sense of kinship.

Such arguments as the above have much in common with Freudian theory and practice. The recognition of unconscious impulses, of neuroses which threaten balance, is an essential part of the 'cure' which psychotherapy aims to effect. Aristotle's comments in the *Politics*, where he refers to emotions being purged 'orgiasti-cally', seem to support the idea of a breakdown of identity, an irruption of unconscious impulses which is part of the process of restoration to selfhood. Psychotherapy, in its attempt to break down the patient's fears, encouraging expression and acceptance of what is repressed, seems to be relevant here.

There is a further point to be made about the need for *repetition of tragic experience which seems connected with the repeated need to *play. Freud, in his early work with Breuer, had emphasized that playing allows the child to act out situations with confuse and disturb him. This enactment was itself, he thought, of lasting cathartic or therapeutic value (though later he came to feel it was insufficient). The repetition, he postulated in 1922, was striving for mastery of the experience, though the need for repetition indicated a continuing failure to master the situation. Catharsis, or purging, however, was the aim of play.

The theory suggests that in the play (*Hamlet* perhaps) which a person is prepared to witness again and again, the spectator finds a situation he or she must struggle to master. Full mastery, or full catharsis, is never entirely achieved and we must endeavour again and again to control such problematical material as exists within us, or the play contains. Diderot in *Paradoxe sur le Comédien* (1773–8) says something similar when he declares that there are citizens 'who leave their vices at the entrance to the theatre, only to pick them up again on leaving.' Tragedy, like other forms of confessional, may degenerate into a technique which allows one to go on sinning and this recalls the opposition of Marxists, including Brecht, to a theatre which purges the individual and allows society to continue being unjust. (See ANTI-ARISTOTELIAN.)

No doubt there are degrees of truth in all the above theories. The degree of validity will vary from play to play, and from spectator to spectator. This is one reason why the question of catharsis has proved disturbing, resistant and fascinating for so long and why it may be regarded as the most fertile and enigmatic of all dramatic principles. For a summary of the different views see:

HENN, T.R., *The Harvest of Tragedy*, Methuen, London, 1956, Ch. 1.
HOUSE, H., HARDIE, C. (eds) *Aristotle's Poetics*, Hart Davis, 1956.
WODKE, F., 'Katharsis', in *Reallexikon*, 1955.

**Catwalk**. A narrow bridge, suspended in the *flies and running across the stage from one *fly floor to another. It enables stage hands to reach scenery and overhead *lighting.

**Causality**. The process whereby events determine one another. Earlier causal explanations tended to be superstitious or religious. It was supposed that events in the cosmos were controlled by spirits, demons or gods. *Fate and *destiny are later and more abstract concepts. History became a kind of causal god in Hegel's philosophy, and Marx introduced the concept of 'dialectical materialism' which defined as economic the dominant causal processes in the world.

Such explanations may be inventions, or discoveries, or a mixture of both. Man may invent a god, or a concept, to give himself the illusion that he understands the processes of life. Yet he also readily discards explanations which do not tally with a new and enlarged view of the way that natural and social worlds behave. Thus the discoveries of Copernicus and Galileo, of Darwin and Freud, Marx and Einstein have forced men to adapt and change their explanations of natural and social causality. Such changes have been reflected in drama.

Powerful drama tends to occur at moments when one system of explanation is being challenged by another. The conflict may be seen in fifth-century *classical Greek drama, in English *renaissance drama, in nineteenth-century naturalism, and elsewhere. In each of these dramatic forms conflicts of causality occur, and are presented either in theological terms, as a collision between 'new' and 'old' gods (Aeschylus's *Oresteia*), or as a collision between a theology and a character asserting his or her freedom (as often in *Jacobean drama), or as a collision between individual aspirations to freedom and a psychological and inherited determinism (as often in Ibsen) or as a conflict between individual and public opinion as again in Ibsen. See SOCIAL TRAGEDY.

Recently, the question of *chance or accident, challenging the more comforting belief that causal systems operate in the world, has manifested itself in the *theatre of the absurd. This was also present in earlier forms of tragic writing, and probably in *farce, from very early days.

One may say with some truth that drama arises out of tensions between causal belief systems; or between any such system and the sense of individual choice and responsibility; or between either of these and the operation of chance. Drama asks the question 'Why?' and it embodies tensions between some of the answers.

**Cavalier drama**. A type of court play of the 1630s, written by James Shirley (1596–1666), Sir John Suckling (1609–41) and Thomas Killigrew (1612–83).

**Ceiling cloth**. A stretched canvas closing in the top of a *box-set.

**Ceiling piece**. Scenery suspended from the *flies to give the appearance of a ceiling. It replaced the hanging *borders whereby ceilings had previously been represented. Its introduction was hastened by improvements in *lighting which did away with the need for the overhead lights which had formerly shone down between the borders.

**Cellar**. The space under the stage, into which scenery may in some theatres be lowered, and where machinery for *scene-changes, *traps etc. is housed.

**C.E.M.A.** Council for the Encouragement of Music and Arts; a body founded in 1940 and the forerunner of the *Arts Council of Great Britain.

**Censorship**. The United States has not distinguished between literary and theatrical censorship, but a system of political control has existed in the English theatre since the appointment of a *Master of the Revels, in the time of Henry VII. The Lord Chamberlain later assumed responsibility for suppressing heresy and sedition in theatre texts, and for preventing forms of misbehaviour at performances. Successive Licensing Acts, the first under James I, then in 1713 and 1737, together with the Theatres Act of 1843, reinforced his power, which included the issuing of licences for halls and theatres, and giving permission for the performance of new plays. (See PATENT THEATRES.)

The 1968 Theatre Act abolished the Lord Chamberlain's right of censorship of texts, which had restricted political and religious comment, the use of 'obscene' language, and certain forms of behaviour on stage, including nudity. Such powers had, of course, already called into existence strategies to avoid them, such as the inclusion of songs, and the reduction in the number of *acts, which blurred the distinction between *legitimate and *illegitimate theatre.

Forms of control still exist. Prosecutions under the 1959 Obscene Publications Act are still possible, as the *National Theatre production of Howard Brenton's *The Romans in Britain* (1980) showed, but this can only take place *after* performance. Power of censorship has passed from the Lord Chamberlain's office; it still exists more subtly in the minds of the 'controllers', the radio, TV and theatre administrators, who wonder whether they can risk public displeasure and possible prosecution. It is a form of censorship which must exist in the minds of writers and directors too.

FINDLATER, R., *Banned*, Macgibbon and Kee, 1967.

FOWELL, F., and PALMER, F., *Censorship in England*, Palmer, 1913, Blom, NY, 1969.

**Centre 42**. An organization founded by Arnold Wesker in 1962, to encourage working-class interest in the theatre. From 1964 it was associated with the Roundhouse in Chalk Farm, London, until it collapsed through debt and lack of sufficient support from the trade unions which Wesker had hoped to interest.

**Centres Dramatiques**. Centres founded since World War II to encourage the development of the French theatre outside Paris. The best known is probably the Théâtre de la Cité, founded by Roger Planchon at Villeurbanne, near Lyons, in 1957.

**Centre stage (C.S.)** The position in the middle of the stage. The strongest position in *fourth wall drama. See *DOWNSTAGE; *UPSTAGE.

**Chamberlain's Men**. Lord Chamberlain's Men, Shakespeare's company, the most famous and successful of the *Elizabethan period. It took this title in 1594 and performed in James Burbage's 'The Theatre' until the construction of the *Globe on the south bank of the Thames in 1599. When James I became their patron in 1603, the company became known as the King's Men, and as such continued to flourish until the closure of the theatres under the Commonweath in 1642. For a detailed summary of playing conditions in this period see:

GURR, A., *The Shakespearean Stage*, Cambridge University Press, 1970.

**Chance**. Accident; a causeless occurrence; the random element in life which cannot be accounted for.

The idea of chance is disturbing and its existence may be denied by minds which see life as a pattern determined by God, or fate, or any other *causal principle. It is also disturbing for those who believe in free will and the possibility of individual mastery over what happens in the world. Chance challenges the idea of control.

In different ways, however, the principle has been incorporated into scientific and philosophical theory. Darwin's theory of 'natural selection', for example, Bergson's 'creative evolution', Planck's 'quantum theory' and Heisenberg's 'uncertainty principle' all deal with ideas of randomness and unpredictability.

In so far as drama strives to be *mimetic, chance must be one of its concerns, and not only as a subject for discussion, but as a structural principle. Indeed chance seems to operate in the act of composition itself. Arbitrary relationships between apparently unrelated things, or accidental linguistic juxtapositions, often prompt new ideas.

We also have the long dramatic and tragic tradition in which chance is seen as intervening in the conflict between *causality and *freedom, and cause and cause. Thomas Hardy's dramatic novels are obviously relevant to this. (Why did Tess's letter, when slipped under Angel Clare's door, also go under the carpet?) Shakespeare's plays also handle chance. Heroes at the height of the tragedy question the purposive nature of existence. Is life 'a tale full of sound and fury/Signifying nothing', as it seems to Macbeth? Are we at the mercy of sadistic gods who 'kill us for their sport', as it seems to Gloucester in *King Lear* (1605)? (Gloucester still seeks the cause which Macbeth denies.) And what is the function of accident in the *plot of *Othello*, where the chance dropping of a handkerchief brings about a *catastrophe which chance could be easily have prevented?

In *comedy as well as tragedy, chance appears. It occurs in the 'wood outside Athens' in *A Midsummer Night's Dream* (1595). Even Oberon and Puck can make mistakes. Chance meetings, the wrong Athenian in the right place, and Puck's logic and Oberon's purpose are overthrown. In the wood, chance, for a while, reigns. Accidental encounters, in *space and *time (as in the theories of Darwin and Bergson) prove fruitful or destructive. Shakespeare, of course, *patterns* his events to give the appearance of chance, and the effect of the play is perhaps to reconcile us to the chances and changes of existence. The *laughter, however, which the play provokes may acknowledge the existence of an arbitrary element in life and art which we normally prefer to deny.

*Tragi-comedy is also relevant here. Plays of the *absurd, for example, like the novels of Franz Kafka (1883–1924), mock and question our need for purposive wholes and our unease when the idea of chance threatens both life and artistic form.

Purposive wholes, like Shakespeare's *Macbeth* (1606), do not affirm their hero's momentary perception of chaos. The structure offers the possibility of order though the accidental also remains as perceived possibility. The *paradox is at the heart of the relationship between tragedy and comedy.

STRINDBERG, A., *The Role of Chance in Artistic Creation*, (1894).

**Character**. A part in a play, i.e. a number of lines ascribed to a particular name, or function, or quality which an actor must embody.

A character generally has an individual name: Oedipus, Mrs Malaprop, Professor Higgins, and so on. Sometimes a character is defined as a function: Doctor, Student, Fool, Nurse; or as a moral quality: Sin, Greed, Honour, Pride; or as a supernatural being: Ariel, Athena, Aphrodite; or as a process: Time in *The Winter's Tale* (1610). It may also be an animal: Fox, Lion, or Pantomime Horse, or even an inanimate object such as Wall in the play within *A Midsummer Night's Dream* (1595).

Characters, however, are generally representations of human beings and the more 'rounded' the treatment, the more difficult it is to see a character as a fixed entity. We tend to think of characters as separable from the pattern of events in *plot and *story which surrounds them. They assume a life outside the play and this leads each of us to vary in our perception of a character since we each discover or invent different elements in the life of that character which is 'hidden'. Our perceptions of character also vary because every time an actor performs a *role, his or her physique, *voice, face and personality create the character anew. In a similar way the actor when he reads a dramatic text may recreate (and extend) a character. The spectator of a play must take, on the whole, what is given by the actor. But he or she, too, may build on and extend the actor's performance. In short, a character is a *transaction* whose reality emerges from the relationship between author's text, actor's embodiment, and audience recognition. To consider Hamlet's childhood, or his student days in Wittenberg in more detail than the play supplies, is to invent. And how far our inventions coincide with Shakespeare's original vision we shall never know. Characters are incomplete, and thus they invite us to complete them.

To act 'in character' is the normal aim of an actor. He seeks to discover, and part invent, the character behind the words on the page. Having done so the character can then seem on stage to invent the dialogue out of which the *characterization has come. Sometimes this takes a great deal of *rehearsal time and no actor is ever fully in character. Some part of the actor's mind is always conscious of stage conditions, adjusting to them as he or she performs.

*Naturalist drama disguises the actor behind the character and pretends the two are inseparable. Brecht, however, in his *epic drama, encourages an audience to recognize the actor/character duality so that the actor may 'comment' on the character he is playing. *Stand-up comedians frequently do this in their sketches, and Brecht adopts the process as an *alienation device. He shows characters who, within the play, are forced to pretend not to be themselves. Shen Te, in Brecht's *The Good Woman of Setzuan* (1938–41) is a 'good' character who is forced to adopt a *mask and pretend to be her ruthless cousin Shui Ta. The actor plays 'in' character for Shen Te, and 'out of' character for Shui Ta. The acting is thus both naturalistic and epic. The actor acts a character and then acts an actor. Brecht's theatre is a critique of the reasons why human beings are often forced by their social and economic situation to act out of character.

Brecht's theatre is not unique. Many characters, like Hamlet, act a number of different parts, behaving in different ways with different people. Such roles ask the question: what is it to be 'in character'? Characters can don *masks as well as actors, and plays can take their own processes as subject matter.

To be 'in character' therefore, is too simple a phrase for a complex process. Character, as Pirandello (1867–1936) suggested in his novel, can be *One Thing, Nothing, and a Hundred Thousand Things* (1927). A character may seem to be whole; it may seem to be a series of masks; it may also be what other characters and the audience make of it. For a discussion of this see the scenes between the Father and the Daughter in Pirandello's *Six Characters in Search of an Author* (1921) where the Daughter accuses the Father of wearing a mask and the Father contests the simplicity of her view. Sometimes, the play seems to say, it is 'in character' to be out of it. See PERSONA.

STANISLAVSKI, C., *Building a Character*, Theatre Arts, NY, 1949.

**Characterization**. The process whereby an *actor creates a *character, and the methods used by actor and writer to communicate this to an audience. These include: (a) the selection of name, (b) the quality and style of the *dialogue, (c) the *presence and performance of the actor, (d) the use of direct address such as *aside or *soliloquy, and (e) the discussion of the character by other characters.

**Chariot and pole**. A device for scene-changing, developed by Torelli (1608–78), whereby all the *wings were attached to trolleys under the stage, and a system of pulleys allowed them to be moved simultaneously. The purpose was twofold: to increase the speed of *scene-changes and to create, at the same time, a spectacular stage effect.

**Chester cycle**. One of the four extant cycles of *mystery plays, each of which is given the name of the town in which it was performed during the *medieval and *Tudor periods. Ralph Higden is thought to have been the writer.

CLOPPER, L.M., 'The Rogers' description of the Chester Plays', in *Leeds Studies in English 7*, 1974, pp.63–94.

SALTER, F.M., *Medieval Drama in Chester*, Toronto University Press, 1955.

**Children of Paul's; Children of the Chapel**. Names of *boy companies, founded during the later sixteenth century.

CHAMBERS, E.K., *The Elizabethan Stage*, Vol. II, Oxford University Press, 1923.

**Chinese classical theatre**. Very highly formalized drama which developed over a thousand years until it reached its mature state, the *Peking Opera of the nineteenth century. It was performed on a square platform resembling the Elizabethan *apron stage, with its two doors in the back wall, roof canopy supported by columns, dressing room behind and audience on three sides. Further similarities can be found in the use of simple *properties, rich *costume, all-male *casts, and little *scenery. The use of music, song, *dance, acrobatics and *mime, however, as well as *dialogue, all performed within a variable scenario, gives it more resemblance to the *Commedia dell'Arte.

SCOTT, A.C., An Introduction to the Chinese Theatre, Theatre Arts, NY, 1959.

**Chlamys**. A short cloak, flung across the left shoulder and worn with a brightly coloured robe. The *costume for gods and *heroes in ancient *Greek tragedy.

**Choice**. See CAUSALITY; SITUATION; WILL.

**Choregus**. The wealthy citizen chosen by lot to pay the costs of the *chorus at the Athenian *tragedy or *dythyrambic competitions.

**Chorus**. A group of performers, or single actor, with a *narrative function, also participating in the action of the play.

According to Aristotle, *Greek tragedy originated in the *dithyramb chorus, and *medieval religous drama probably emerged from the choral singing of the *liturgy, when priest or choir began to *imitate the episode narrated. (See QUEM QUAERITIS.)

The role of chorus was very important in Aeschylus (525–456 B.C.) and early *tragedy. The choral group, usually twelve in number, performed in the *orchestra. Their song, *dance, and group narration must have filled the large amphitheatres with sound and movement, easing the task of the individual actors on stage in the *epeisodia. They often repeat and reinforce the words of the *protagonist, and comment on situation and character for the audience's benefit. Thus they describe Cassandra in The Oresteia:

> She's in a trance, about to prophesy.
> Even in bondage her gift doesn't die.

When Cassandra speaks they voice the response of ordinary people:

> Now it's got worse. I can make no sense
> Of these dense riddles that grow more dense.

In this, the chorus are the audience's representatives. They emphasize the limitations of conventional wisdom, and project the audience's likely response. In a species of *dramatic irony the audience sees its own ignorance objectified.

Schiller (1759–1805) took a different view. In his preface to *The Fiancée of Messina* (1803), which was noted for the beauty of its choruses, Schiller sees them as a source of wisdom: 'The chorus leaves the narrow circle of the action to dwell on the past and the future, on ancient times and on peoples, on humanity in general, to draw out the great lessons of life.' The chorus was thus a distancing device, a kind of 'wall', rather than the audience's representative: 'a living wall by which tragedy surrounds itself to prepare its ideal ground and poetic liberty'. In *The Birth of Tragedy* (1872) Nietzsche binds these two views together. He argues that the chorus is both a wall and a bridge. It invites the audience in, and it keeps them out. It emphasizes the alien and extraordinary nature of the events witnessed. At the same time it brings the audience, albeit unwillingly, into the arena.

The chorus, for Nietzsche, was the core of tragedy, and when it disappeared, tragedy disappeared too. The chorus balanced the actors. It represented the *dionysiac element, whereas the separate actors represented an 'individuating principle' which he called the *apollonian. Music and dance in the orchestra were set against the dramatic speech of individual actors on a scenic stage. Physical and rhythmical appeal is set against intellectual discrimination. Both were necessary to tragedy.

Perhaps we may say that the chorus makes its musical appeal and the actors make us aware of the chorus's limitations. Cassandra's prophecy is beyond the chorus's understanding. The audience is caught up in the rhythms of dance and song. At the same time it sees the dancers from the outside. This is one way in which the chorus is both bridge and wall, although not quite in the manner that Schiller meant.

Whatever the truth of this, it is certain that the chorus is central to a discussion of drama. *Medieval drama seems to have arisen out of choral singing. In *morality plays the chorus was individualized as various Virtues and Vices. Vestiges remain in the *Elizabethan drama, not only in the obvious *prologues and *epilogues, or in characters such as *Time in Shakespeare's *The Winter's Tale* (1610) but also in the echoing of events and characters in the *sub-plot.

In *opera and *oratorio, of course, the chorus persists, and attempts have been made, particularly by religious dramatists, to re-use the old Greek and medieval patterns. T.S. Elliot's *Murder in the Cathedral* (1935) is a well-known example of this.

The functions of the chorus are various therefore. It represents an audience view; it makes the audience aware of the passage of time and the context of the play; it involves and it distances, it warns, supplicates and counsels; above all it constitutes a powerful communal appeal, expressed at its height in music and dance, which may absorb the spectator, as Wagner said, 'like lamplight into daylight'. See ORIGINS OF DRAMA.

**Christmas drama**. Plays relating the Biblical events of Christmas and Epiphany: the Journey of the Magi; the Three Shepherds; the Birth of Christ; Herod and the Massacre of the Innocents: the Flight into Egypt. These stories probably existed as independent plays before being incorporated into the *mystery cycles which narrated the whole story of the Bible.

**Chronicle play**. An earlier and more loosely organized form of *history play. In England, John Bale's *Kynge Johan* (1538) is generally considered to be the first, followed by Sackville and Norton's *Gorboduc* (1561), and others which reinforced and fed on a growing Tudor nationalism.

In the 1590s, after the defeat of the Spanish Armada, eighty or so chronicle and history plays were written, including those of Shakespeare, the favourite source materials of which were the chronicle narratives of Hall and Holinshed.

The chronicle play provides a basis for the long tradition of historical drama which moves from Shakespeare to Goethe (1749–1832) and Schiller (1759–1805), to Scandinavian national Romantic drama in Ibsen (1828–1906) and Bjørnson (1832–1910), and to twentieth-century *political drama from Brecht (1898–1956) to, say, Howard Brenton (1942–   ) and Trevor Griffiths (1935–   ).

SCHELLING, F.E., *The English Chronicle Play*, Macmillan, 1902.
TILLYARD, E.M.W., *Shakespeare's History Plays*, Chatto and Windus, 1944.

**Chronology**. Time sequence. A play normally works chronologically, presenting events in the order they occur in life and forming a *causal pattern which Aristotle defines as a *beginning, middle and end. Interruptions of dramatic time sequence are rarer than in a novel. This is probably because drama is a medium of visible action, moving through *time at a pace the whole audience must follow together. The causal and temporal relationships between events must be made very clear and to break chronology is to risk incomprehension. In addition, flashbacks often require very speedy changes of scene, *costume and *make-up. The resources of theatres do not often allow many of these. Unlike *film it cannot edit out the time taken in building scenes or faces.

There are, however, occasions when a play breaks chronology. *Double plots involve setting in sequence events which happen simultaneously. To present two events on stage at once involves complex and costly 'split' staging, and causes problems of dramatic *focus. Thus plays, like novels, *cross-cut to keep up the general continuity. This is the rule in *Jacobean drama, where *sub-plots and double plots are commonplace.

Flashback is notably employed in the plays of J.B. Priestley (1894–1984). *Time and the Conways* (1937) shows the end at the beginning, thereby sacrificing elements of narrative *suspense to provide the audience with an ironic awareness gained from knowing where the drama leads.

J.-P. Sartre (1905–1980) introduces flashbacks which represent a character's remembered experiences. They occur in the middle of *In Camera* (1944) and *Altona* (1960). Changes in *lighting and acting style help render this convincing.

Chronology is also sometimes broken in attempts to render *dream material. Strindberg's *Dream Play* (1902) and *Ghost Sonata* (1907) are examples. Characters who share the stage represent different points in time, perhaps the same person at different stages in life, or images from the past. In these plays an expectation of chronology is frustrated. The dramatist creates, on stage, a state of consciousness rather than a set of external events.

Harold Pinter, in *Landscape* and *Silence* (both 1969), achieves a 'stream of consciousness' effect which is normally the province of the novel. Characters are absorbed in the reconstruction of the past and the effect is similar to dream.

Beckett's plays retain chronology. Act II of *Waiting for Godot* (1953) begins with the *stage direction: 'Same time, same place, next day'. They mock *repetitions of habit and all attempts to defeat the passage of time. Chronology is the subject of Beckett's plays, even though the movement is slowed to almost a dream stasis.

Shakespeare's late plays work differently. *Cymbeline* (*c.*1609), *The Winter's Tale* (1610) and *The Tempest* (1611) contain dream-like reversals of time, and apparent miracles restore the dead to life. In these plays the miracle is incorporated into a chronological fiction. The defeat of time requires the enactment of time's passage.

**Cinefication**. Term used by V. Meyerhold (1874–1940) to mean 'the equipping of the theatre with all the technical resources of the cinema.'

The cinema, during the silent film period, offered a level of spectacle with which the theatre could not compete. D.W. Griffiths's *Birth of a Nation* (1915) and von Stroheim's *Greed* (1923) employed exterior locations and mass casts in a form of *realism which demonstrated the artificiality of the theatre's attempts at it in, say, spectacular *melodrama. When sound arrived, the film medium challenged the theatre even more radically, and Meyerhold felt that the theatre should fight back, by using rapid *scene-changes, elaborate machinery, and 'kinetic' constructions in large cinema-like halls. 'The proletariat is not interested in

chamber theatres', he declared.
BRAUN, E. (ed.), *Meyerhold on Theatre*, Eyre Methuen, 1969.

**Cinema and theatre**. Each of these art forms has advantages which the other does not possess. The rise of cinema and the simultaneous decline of *sensation drama with its 'realistic' and spectacular effects indicate one of the advantages of cinema — it can represent the world more fully and completely, and can register a human face in much greater detail than is possible in the theatre.

It has other advantages. It can vary the distance between spectator and dramatic action by shifting quickly, or slowly, from *long-shot to *close-up, by *zooming in or out, or *cutting from one camera to another. This intensifies effects of *surprise, or *contrast, or *focus. It also makes the audience aware of 'subjective' *viewpoint. It shows a scene. It also suggests an invisible viewer who sits with the spectator but is not necessarily him. Thus in Kozintsev's film of *Hamlet* (1964) a number of 'crane shots' place the audience in the position of the Ghost. Camera viewpoint is a subtle instrument whereby to play on the emotions of the spectator.

*Film can thus 'transport' the spectator from one room, or house, or country to another, in a fraction of a second. Theatre, on the other hand, must allow time for *scene-changes, or create the scene verbally, as Shakespeare often does. Film also has greater subtlety of *sound and musical effect.

What the theatre has is human presence. The actor is alive on stage whereas only an image is present on screen, and this image addresses a single viewer. The collective appeal is absent. The cinema is a realistic artifice; the theatre an artificial reality. Some such formula is needed to define the way live performance can create an involvement which the cinema lacks.
SARTRE, J.-P., 'Myth and Reality in the Theatre', in *Politics and Literature*, Calder and Boyars, 1966, pp.37–67.

**Circle of attention**. According to Stanislavski, the actor needs to establish a 'circle' around himself, within which he can isolate himself from any distractions, such as coughing or movement in the audience, so as to achieve full *concentration on his role. This circle can be very narrow, and may be created by the actor's focusing on a single object. If this is, say, a dagger, he fills his mind with a sense of its weight, colour, size, shape, age and so on, to the exclusion of all else. This done, the character may then widen the circle by considering the object's function within the play (to kill, for example).

If the actor creates a full imaginative reality within this circle, the audience will believe in the play. Should an actor begin to lose a sense of this reality, he has a safe area to retreat to, where he may

recover it.
STANISLAVSKI, C., *An Actor Prepares*, Theatre Arts, NY, 1936.

**Circus**. A form of popular entertainment which takes place in a circular *arena. In Rome the name implied chariot races and gladiatorial combat. The modern circus grew out of the Italian scenic theatres, where aquatic and equestrian shows were staged. This practice encouraged the building of both permanent and temporary structures, to contain exhibitions of skill on horseback, animal-training, and athletic and acrobatic feats. The *clown, whose skills both reinforced and parodied the acts he followed and preceded, became a permanent feature. His more obvious function was to provide continuity whilst apparatus was being set up for the next turn and to involve the audience, especially the children, in the performance.

*Aquatic drama became the rage in Paris circuses in the early nineteenth century, and aquatic displays still form the *climax of some circus performances, especially in permanent buildings, such as the Blackpool Tower Circus.

**City comedy**. General name for the varied Jacobean urban comedy, represented, say, by Thomas Middleton's *A Chaste Maid in Cheapside* (1611) and Ben Jonson's *Bartholomew Fair* (1614). See NEW COMEDY.
GIBBONS, B., *Jacobean City Comedy*, Methuen, 1980.

**City Dionysia**. The religious festivities, known as the 'Great' Dionysia, celebrating the god Dionysos, and held in ancient Athens for a week in late March and early April. During this time trade was suspended and offices closed. Outsiders flocked in to witness celebrations which were primarily given over to the performance of *tragedy in the Theatre of Dionysos on the south-east slope of the acropolis. A procession on the first day, led by the high priest on a float resembling a ship, seems to have been followed by festive dance and games. *Dithyrambic contests were then succeeded by performances of the plays chosen to compete for the annual prizes.

**Civic theatres**. Theatres which have developed in British towns and cities since World War II. They are supported by the local authority out of public rates, and are normally administered by a trust, though sometimes the local authority runs them directly. Two of the best known are the Nottingham Playhouse and the Belgrade Theatre, Coventry. These, with others, have provided a strong stimulus to the development of serious drama outside London since the late 1950s.

**Claque**. A group specially hired to applaud a theatre performance.

**Classical drama**. (a) Ancient Greek and Roman drama; (b) *neo-classical drama.

Generally, the term implies a drama which lays emphasis on rigour and control and abides by strict rules such as the *unities. It suggests objectivity, austerity, economy, balance and the absence of self-indulgence or farcical and *grotesque elements. Physical violence occurs 'off' and is reported by *messenger. Eating and drinking does not take place on stage.

Goethe (1749–1832), who declared 'classicism is health, romanticism disease' and F. von Schlegel (1767–1845) who contrasted the term with *romanticism in *Das Athenaum* (1798), encouraged the polarization of the term. (See ROMANTIC DRAMA.) For an elegant expression of *neo-classical principles, see N.D. Boileau's four-canto poem, *Art Poétique* (1674). For ancient and modern views see:

ARISTOTLE, *Poetics*, (*c*.344 B.C.)

ARNOLD, M., 'The Study of Poetry', in *Essays in Criticism, Second Series*, (1888).

ELIOT, T.S., '"Romantic" and "Classic"', in *After Strange Gods*, Faber, 1934; *What is a Classic?*, Faber, 1945.

HORACE, *Ars Poetica* (*c*.14 B.C.).

**Climax**. From the Greek meaning 'ladder'. The highest point of *tension in a *scene, *act, or play.

**Cloak and sword plays**. Seventeenth-century Spanish plays in the *romantic tradition, in which characters conceal their identity with cloaks, entangle each other in complicated plots, and use their swords to fight the duels which ensue. Their influence can be seen in the work of the French dramatist, Pierre Corneille (1606–1684).

**Closed form**. Form of drama which answers the audience's expectations that solutions will be provided to the problems posed. 'No one likes to be left with a mystery' says a character in Eliot's *The Cocktail Party* (1949). Dramatists have traditionally striven for coherent form and this has been taken as *mimesis, an imitation of life. *Tragedy, however, has always reminded us that life may not be coherent and that not all questions can be answered. Chekhov, too, declared, 'it is not my task to answer', and *open forms of theatre, *epic and *absurdist, have since put the onus on their audiences to provide solutions to an unresolved situation. Both Brecht's *Good Woman of Setzuan* (1938–41) and Beckett's *Waiting for Godot* (1953) in very different ways reject the closed form. Recent literary theory, too, has argued that the form which presents an audience with a closed and organized pattern is not mimetic or representative of 'life', but merely a fulfilment of its own needs. As Jacques Derrida puts it: 'To think of representation is to think of tragedy, not as a representation of fate, but as the fate of

representation'. See BEGINNING, MIDDLE and END.
DERRIDA, J., *L'Ecriture et la Différence*, Seuil, Paris, 1967.

**Closet drama**. (a) Drama written to be read in the study like a novel; (b) drama meant for reading aloud, rather than performance; (c) drama more suitable for reading, whatever the original intention.

Intentions are difficult to determine, but the rhetorical plays of Seneca (*c*.4 B.C.–A.D. 65) probably belong to the second category, as may Milton's *Samson Agonistes* (published in 1671) and Hardy's *The Dynasts* (1904–08). The many dramatic attempts of the *Romantic poets, of which Byron's *Manfred* (1817) and Shelley's *The Cenci* (1819) are best known, are often considered closet drama in the last sense of the term.

**Close-up**. Camera shot which focuses on close detail, as compared with the *long shot, which gives a general view. The close-up can reveal significant movements: a hand going into a pocket, a door-knob turning. It can thus heighten *suspense. It may also create feelings of *strangeness through close focusing on the familiar object. The film director has an advantage here over his stage counterpart who cannot control an audience in this way and must find other forms of *focus.

The close-up is probably most frequently used to show subtle details of human expression in a more intimate manner than can be seen in the theatre. Acting performances for the camera need to take this into account. A raised eyebrow scarcely perceptible in the *gallery can seem comic and melodramatic in a close-up on television.

**Cloth**. A general name for pieces of reinforced canvas, used for different purposes in the decoration of a stage. See CEILING CLOTH; CUT-CLOTH; GAUZE-CLOTH; STAGE-CLOTH.

**Cloud border**. Term for a *border shaped like a cloud to disguise the top of a *set. These could be hung in clusters from the *flies, so that as the *wings were slid on and off at *scene-changes, the borders could be raised and lowered.

**Clouding**. Early form of *cloud border, such as might have been used in the *court masques of Inigo Jones (1573–1642).

**Clown**. Modern *circus entertainer whose traits were developed in *pantomime performances by Joseph Grimaldi (1778–1837), from a long tradition of popular clowning which goes back through Shakespeare's clowns to the medieval *Vice figure.

The circus clown's characteristics are his *grotesque appearance, huge feet, painted face, ludicrous clothing, his taste for buckets of water and custard pies, his propensity for pratfalls and liability to all kinds of accident, his child-like innocence and good humour, and his capacity to get the better of authority, whether in the person of the ring-master, or of a companion 'white' clown. All of these relate him to other varieties of *fool figure, such as *Harlequin, *Kasperle and *Petrushka, and raise interesting questions about the nature of *laughter and *comedy.

WILLSON DISHER, M., *Clowns and Pantomimes*, London, 1925.

**Code**. Term from semiotics, meaning a system or *convention of signals, shared by the sender and receiver of a *message. Morse and semaphore are obvious codes in this sense.

In literature and in drama the codes are far more complex. They are not fixed and absolute, like morse, and the stricter formal conventions such as the *fourth wall mingle with linguistic, psychological and cultural codes. In the words of R. Barthes: 'Alongside each utterance, one might say that off-stage voices can be heard: they are the codes.' Thus an author and/or character speaks. The words appear personal but they simultaneously express and appeal to opinions or attitudes created by parents, family, and the general culture. The receivers, that is, the readers, listeners, or audience, respond in varying degrees to the whispered codes.

In the theatre, codes are contained in more than words. A tone of voice, style of costume, a gait or posture, gesture or facial expression, all imply codes which affect the way this kind of *theatre language is received. And, of course, the codes change as a culture changes, so that in the interpretation of dramatic and other art, a recognition of old codes mingles with the new. How far the codes are implicit or explicit, how far consciously acknowledged by sender or receiver, will vary with each.

BARTHES, R., *S/Z*, Seuil, Paris, 1970/ Cape, NY, 1975.
ELAM, K., *The Semiotics of Theatre and Drama*, Methuen, 1980.

**Cofradia**. Company of *travelling players in sixteenth- and seventeenth-century Spain. They performed in the *corrales, or three-sided courtyards, out of which the permanent Spanish theatres developed.

RENNERT, H.A., *The Spanish Stage in the time of Lope de Vega*, NY, 1909.
WILSON, E.M., and MOIR, D., *A Literary History of Spain: The Golden Age. Drama 1492–1700*, NY, 1971.

**Collage**. Art form which calls attention to the material out of which it is made. Collage rebels against the use of a single material. A picture is formed of old newspapers and pieces of cloth, as well as oil-paint. Picasso made a pair of bicycle handlebars into a bull's horns, demonstrating the skill of the artist, and the artificiality of the artistic process.

The theatrical equivalent is a play composed of borrowed *dialogue, *quotations, and theatrical and scenic styles. In this sense Shakespeare, as well as Brecht (1898–1956) and Ionesco (1912–   ), used collage techniques.

**Colour**. An important form of *theatre language. Colour communicates emotion through a combination of visual impact and symbolic association. Single colours such as blue, red, green, white, and black may suggest, rather obviously, peace, danger, jealousy, innocence and death. In a less simple way, colours which are 'echoed' may indicate relationships between characters, or between character and setting. Combinations of colours, too, may make a harmonious appeal, or they may deliberately clash. In such ways, colour in *scenery, *costume and *lighting clarifies dramatic pattern and sharpens *tension. It may also create a dominant feeling and *atmosphere which will vary according to the choices of *designer and *director for each individual production. Colour can *select* and accentuate certain aspects of a play: a 'silver' or 'blue' *Twelfth Night*, a black or red *Duchess of Malfi* and so on.

**Columbine**. Maid-servant of the *Commedia dell'Arte* who became the daughter of *Pantaloon in the English *Harlequinade. Her contest with her father is characteristic of the long tradition of *new comedy, and her relationship with Harlequin, suggested by a subtle blending of costume, raises interesting questions of overlapping male and female identity.

**Combat music**. A kind of musical accompaniment, played during the fight scenes of Victorian *melodrama.

**Comédie-ballet**. A form of drama developed by Molière, in which he interwove balletic interludes with the action of a play, in order to cater for the court and public interest in spectacular productions. *Le Malade Imaginaire* (1673) is a well-known example.

**Comédie; Comédien**. French terms meaning 'play' and 'player', rather than the apparent English equivalents, *comedy and *comedian.

**Comédie Française**. French National Theatre founded by Louis XIV, in 1680, by combining the players of the Hôtel de Bourgogne with those of the Marais theatre, who had already amalgamated with the troupe of Molière on Molière's death in 1673. The company changed theatres twice in the eighteenth century, split at the Revolution, and lost its monopoly. Since 1803 it has remained at the Palais Royal. It runs on a *repertory principle, with the advantages and limitations of state subsidy.

**Comédie Italienne**. The successors of the *Commedia dell'Arte* in Paris, and predecessors of the Opéra Comique. The company acted under this name from 1680 to 1801. They were thus to be distinguished from the *Comédie Française, also founded in 1680, who acted entirely in French. They offended Louis XIV and were banished in 1697, returning in 1715, after his death, to develop a new style of performance and stage the plays of Marivaux. Later, the new *opéra bouffe* attracted them and they devoted themselves to musical drama before amalgamating with a rival company to form the French Comic Opera.

**Comédie larmoyante**. Tearful comedy. A French mode akin to English *sentimental comedy. It was established in Paris by De la Chaussée with *False Antipathy* in 1733, and flourished until the mid-century when it began to be assimilated into other forms, notably the early *realism of Denis Diderot (1713–84). It aimed at *pathos, and appealed to a new middle-class theatre audience in France, England, Holland and Italy.

**4** *Comedy seems to have been an ever-popular dramatic form. (After a Greek vase drawing)*

**Comedy**. A broad category of drama ranging from 'low' forms such as *slapstick and *farce, through *satire, *parody, and *burlesque to *comedy of manners and forms bordering on *tragedy such as *black comedy and *tragi-comedy.

Despite its emphasis on *chance and *accident, which brings it into close relationship with tragedy, and despite the connection between *laughter and *cruelty, which provokes such statements as

Ionesco's *'le comique est tragique'*, comedy has normally been considered the opposite of tragedy. A separate comic tradition is seen as running from the Greek *\*komos* to the Old Comedy of Aristophanes (*c.*448–*c.*380 B.C.), to the *new comedy of Menander (*c.*342–*c.*292 B.C.), thence into the Roman comedy of Plautus (*c.*254–184 B.C.) and Terence (*c.*190–59 B.C.) and on to the fusion of *classical and *popular comic traditions in the drama of the *Renaissance. Lines of influence stretch from the *Commedia dell'Arte* into Molière (1622–73), through the eighteenth-century *comedy of manners into French nineteenth-century farce and popular commercial entertainment in the twentieth century. Similarly, influences can be traced from Shakespeare (1564–1616) and Jonson (1572–1637) through Congreve (1670–1720) and Sheridan (1751–1816) into *sentimental comedy and *melodrama. The process is complex, and nowhere more so than in the fusion of traditions in Shakespeare.

Comic theory, however, has normally agreed on the common characteristics of comedy: it concerns ordinary, humble or private people; it uses a humble rather than an elevated style; and it moves towards a happy ending. Emphasis on its moral value is seen in the work of Renaissance theorists such as Sir Philip Sidney (1554–86). His *Defence of Poetry* (1595) sees the purpose of comedy as the exposure of evil: 'In the actions of our life, who seeth not the filthiness of evil wanteth a great foil to perceive the beauty of vertue.'

More recent theorists, notably Henri Bergson (1851–1941) and Sigmund Freud (1856–1939), have developed important psychological theories of comedy. Bergson's 'superiority theory' argues that comedy mocks those whose behaviour has become fixed and obsessive. It attacks characters possessed by avarice or pride or sloth, and other vices. *Laughter arises out of a perception of 'the mechanical encrusted upon the living'. Comedy is thus on the side of life, for it mocks those who think in slogans and who are reduced to *stereotypes by habitual and repeated gesture and action. Freud's 'relief theory', on the other hand, argues that joking and comedy issue from the anarchic unconscious mind. Comedy expresses what the civilized self would prefer not to hear; hence the emphasis on sex, racism, and other disturbing subjects in comedy. Each of these theories lays emphasis on the need to see life as a whole, and perhaps in this lies the possibility of reconciliation between them. Comedy may be, according to both Bergson and Freud, a source of health.

A third, 'incongruity', theory, associated with Immanuel Kant (1724–1804), argues that comedy and laughter arise when two lines of logic conflict with one another. Laughter is 'an affect arising from the sudden coming to nothing of a strained expectation'. One or more of these three theories seems always to apply to any form of comedy.

The playing of comedy is difficult. It requires expert delivery, very fast *cueing, control of *gesture and extreme professionalism. In comedy the audience seems especially aware of the manner of delivery. The artificiality of comic situations and the stereotyping of characters distance the audience, and dramatic *tension derives in great degree from an awareness of the skill involved (like watching a tightrope walker). Any *fluff or lapse can destroy it. Comedy therefore demands rapid reactions. It also mocks slow ones. Indeed the *contrast between the rapid and the slow thinkers among comic characters is often extreme. Comedy thrives on effects of contrast.

Political writers have made important use of comedy. The *alienation or *V effects of Bertolt Brecht (1898–1956) are, he tells us, 'ein altes Kunstmittel; bekannt aus der Komödie' (an ancient artistic means, well-known in comedy). If comedy involves 'distanzgefühl' (distancing), then comedy can encourage audiences to think and make rational judgements. Although much comedy relies on standard formulae – the old popular comedy, according to Brecht, was one in which 'the bad get punished, the good get married, the industrious inherit, and the lazy face the consequences' — it can be put to good use. The anti-authoritarianism of comedy, its concern with human wholeness and its exposure of logical incongruities can all be used to express a strong sense of social injustice. The anarchic tendencies of comedy, however, are not always easy to harness. (See LAUGHTER and SATIRE.) Trevor Griffiths's play *Comedians* (1974) embodies and analyses different forms of the comedy/audience relationship.

BERGSON, H., *Laughter*, Garden City, NY, Doubleday, 1956.

FREUD, S., *Jokes and their Relation to the Unconscious*, Pelican Books, 1976.

LAUTER, P., (ed.), *Theories of Comedy*, Doubleday, 1964.

MIKAIL, E.H., *Comedy and Tragedy: A Bibliography of Critical Studies*, Whiston, NY, 1972.

**Comedy of humours**. Form of comedy developed by Ben Jonson (1572/3–1637) in his early plays, *Everyman in his Humour* (1598) and *Everyman out of his Humour* (1599). These were ostensibly based on the medieval theory that human temperaments were created by the dominance of one of four bodily fluids: choler, blood, phlegm, and black bile, each of which released 'spirits' which rose to the brain and affected a person's behaviour. The characters of Jonson, however, are traditional comic types, such as the jealous husband (Kitely), the boastful soldier (Bobadill), the young wife (Celia), the tricky servant (Brainworm), the *jester (Buffone), the miser (Sordido), the affected courtier (Fastidious Brisk), and the Malcontent (Macilente). They cannot be divided into four simple humours; the types are too varied. The search for a *cure* for an over-riding humour demands of the characters a capacity for self-recognition which goes beyond a determinist theory. (See the opening debate in the second play between Asper (Jonson) and the two moral commentators, Mitis and Cordatus.)

In later Jonson, e.g. in *Bartholomew Fair* (1614) or *Volpone* (1606), the matter is further complicated. The humour becomes an attitude which the character half chooses in order to protect himself from the world. Character thus becomes partly a question of choice, partly a question of social rather than physiological determinism.

The consideration of a character's freedom is a strong element in the development of the comedy of humours during the *Restoration period. There we find characters *affecting* attitudes which are not 'natural' to them. An 'Affection', as Congreve (1670–1729) reminds us, is not a humour, though when habitually assumed it may come to resemble a 'natural' character trait. A *mask may be freely assumed or socially necessary. It is not to be explained in physiological terms since the character may discard the mask, and an audience may be warned not to assume it. At this point, the comedy of humours fuses with the *comedy of manners, which is concerned with appropriate and inappropriate social responses. Jonson's comedy anticipates this, but is more sombre. His 'humourous' characters are a threat not only to themselves, but to those around them and dependent upon them. The question of their cure becomes a serious and general concern.

BURTON, R., *Anatomy of Melancholy* (1621).

DESSEN, A.C., *Jonson's Moral Comedy*, Northwestern University Press, 1971.

**Comedy of manners**. Form of *Restoration comedy deriving from Italian *mime, the plays of Molière, and observation of the mores of upper-class London. (See especially the plays of Sir George Etherege, c.1634–91.) Comedy of manners is particularly concerned with forms of behaviour and speech which are socially approved. At its most subtle, it examines the validity of the surfaces behind which characters seek security and social acceptance. Thus Congreve (1670–1729), in *The Way of the World* (1700), examines the quality of feeling which underlies *wit and the handling of language. This form of comedy appeals to an audience well aware of the discrepancies between public reputation and private reality. Its dramatic energy, indeed, often depends on the spectator's ironic awareness of a character's ignorance of this discrepancy. The same is true of Sheridan's later comedy of manners, *School for Scandal* (1777), in which the *plot in great part depends on Sir Peter Teazle's ignorance of the nature of Joseph Surface. The manners and language of Joseph and his brother Charles blind Sir Peter to their 'real' bad and good nature, as does the behaviour of his wife. When Charles, the 'plain dealer' pulls down the screen in the famous 'screen scene', the social façade begins to crack.

Sheridan and Congreve, like Shakespeare in *As You Like It* (1599), to which *The Way of the World* makes reference, are concerned with good nature. In this way they arguably rise above the limits of a *genre which implies at times that all standards are matters of social convention. See SENTIMENTAL COMEDY.

**Comic man/Comic woman.** Actors in the Victorian *stock company who took the comic roles.

*Commedia dell'Arte.* Improvised comedy performed by various troupes of highly professional Italian actors who toured Europe in the sixteenth and seventeenth centuries. The troupe varied between ten and twenty in number and their plays were based on a set of widely known *type characters operating within a varying scenario to which the actors brought a repertoire of jokes, acrobatic feats, set speeches and comic *business. Each actor would specialize in a particular role — the aged, avaricious and amorous *Pantaloon, the fat and pedantic black-clad *Doctor, the vainglorious and cowardly Spanish *Captain with the bristling mustachios, the shy and acrobatic servant *Arlecchino, the deceitful, crooked-nosed,

5 *Two* Commedia dell'Arte *characters (etching by Jacques Callot). Note the stage in the background*

artistic *Brighella, the young, unmasked, handsome *Lovers, and a variety of *Zanni or servant figures, instantly recognizable to the audience. The plot, location, sequence of entrances and the characters sharing the stage varied from performance to perform- ance as can be deduced from the '*canovacci*' or synopses which were pinned backstage. Presumably much dialogue was improvised, though no doubt actors had set pieces to fall back on. We have only the *canovacci*, a number of illustrations and the testimony of a few spectators to witness the immense appeal of a theatre whose influence was felt perhaps more than we know by the Elizabethans, and was certainly very strong in Paris where the troupes settled. Here, Molière, and later Marivaux, developed their work. In Italy, Goldoni (1709–93) and Gozzi (1720–1806) also assimilated and adapted their style and structures. Today, modern Italian troupes, such as the Tag Teatro of Venice, give formidably professional acrobatic song, dance and spoken performances with *Commedia dell'Arte* characters, in what must be a close approximation to their style. Recent emphasis on the value of *improvisation has meant a resurgence of interest in the *Commedia dell'Arte*.

DUCHARTE, P.-L., *The Italian Comedy: the improvisation, scenarios, lives, attributes, portraits and masks of the illustrious characters of the* Commedia dell'Arte, Harrap, 1929.

HERRICK, M.T., *Italian Comedy in the Renaissance*, Illinois University Press, 1960.

OREGLIA, G., *The Commedia dell'Arte*, Methuen, 1968.

NICOLL, A., *The World of Harlequin: A critical study of the Commedia dell'Arte*, Cambridge University Press, 1963.

**Commedia erudita**. 'Learned comedy'. The written comedy of Italy in the early sixteenth century, as compared with the improvised *Commedia dell'Arte*. A realistic and sardonic form of comedy, best represented perhaps by *La Mandragola* (*c.*1518) by Machiavelli and *I Suppositi* (1509) by Ariosto. It derived from the Roman *farce of Terence (*c.*190 or *c.*180–159 B.C.) and Plautus (*c.*254–184 B.C.).

**Commitment**. The acceptance of an ideology. A term associated in particular with a group of French writers, headed by Jean-Paul Sartre (1905–80), who were deeply marked by their experience of war. This, together with a reading of Marx, convinced them of the political nature of most forms of writing and the economic processes of production on which they depend. Thus Sartre, in *What is Literature?* (*Qu'est-ce que la Littérature?*, 1948), argues that writers of value commit themselves to the cause of the less fortunate and oppressed, even if it means working against or subverting the system of aristocratic (or state) patronage, or the paying middle-class audience or reading public. The writer, in the interest of freedom, may thus need to betray the power structure within which he works. Writers who flatter and reflect the opinions of the power groups which hold the purse-strings, and even those apparently uncommitted, conspire consciously or unconsciously to maintain the status quo (and their own income). This view is especially relevant to dramatists, intimately involved as they are with the economic means of production, needing both to entertain a public and please a commercial producer.

Sartre's trenchant arguments cannot easily be dismissed. Much great drama has been political. It is evident that Greek drama, like Sophocles's *Antigone* (*c*.441 B.C.) for instance, is concerned with choice, and the approval or disapproval of acts of political rebellion. Medieval religious drama had the obvious political and religious function of reinforcing institutional orthodoxies, and in different ways writers have sacrificed or maintained their integrity in their difficult relations with aristocratic audiences in *Restoration drama, or with the audience in the nineteenth-century *penny gaffs, or with the twentieth-century *West End or *Broadway public.

Drama is full of moral conflict. Important drama often confronts such conflicts, and presents the problems of resolving them. This is true of Sartre's plays and those of Brecht (equally concerned with choices, possibilities and *ends and means). It is also true of the recent generation of British writers which includes Trevor Griffiths (1935– ) and Edward Bond (1935– ). The latter, in particular, confronts the problems of social violence and ends and means.

GRIFFITHS, T., *The Party*, Methuen, 1973.
SARTRE, J.-P., *What is Literature?* (1948), trs. B. Frechtman, Methuen, 1950; *Lucifer and the Lord*, (1951), trs. K. Black, Hamish Hamilton, 1952.

**Commonwealth Company**. An American company flourishing in the mid-nineteenth century and associated with the early American actor-managers Noah Ludlow (1795–1886) and Sol Smith (1801–69). To obtan the flavour of the social history of this period of theatre, see Ludlow's *Dramatic Life As I Found It* and Smith's *Theatrical Management in the West and South* (1868).

**Communication**. The transaction in the theatre between (a) actor and spectator, (b) character and spectator, (c) character and character, (d) actor and actor, and (e) spectator and spectator. More complex forms of communication involve the dramatist, *director and *designer in the various transactions.

**Communion**. A Stanislavskian principle. It refers to the state of receptivity and sensitivity actors must achieve, either alone or as a group, if they are to convey their characters and situations to an audience. On stage, each actor must achieve a state of direct communion with other actors, as also with himself, and with the *props he uses, before the audience will believe what it sees and hears. The problem is that the circumstances of performance are constantly changing. A changed inflexion, a hurried or lost line, a missed laugh, a late lighting *cue, an unexpected movement or facial expression, all threaten the actor's concentration, and he or she must be ready, in character, to respond instinctively to the change. For the means of achieving this intense state of concentration, see CIRCLE OF ATTENTION. The whole of Stanislavski's *system works to this end.

STANISLAVSKI, C., *An Actor Prepares*, Theatre Arts, NY, 1936, Ch. 10.

**Community theatre**. A kind of theatre which has developed in Britain since 1968. It is associated with socially dedicated *fringe groups who seek new audiences and new relationships in communities outside the established theatre. This they do not only by *portable productions, but sometimes by living in a new community, learning from it and then acting out its tensions and problems. In this way they aim to raise the quality of community life, especially in deprived areas, among racial minorities, or in, say, mental or other institutions.

In Britain certain schools of drama, such as Rose Bruford's, put special emphasis on work in community theatre. In America much community theatre is run by regional theatres.

CRAIG, S., (ed.), *Dreams and Deconstructions*, Amber Lane, 1980, Ch. 4.

**Compagnie des Quinze**. A group founded in 1930 by Michel Saint-Denis and based in great part on the important and influential practice of Jacques Copeau (1879–1949).

SAINT-DENIS M., *Training for the Theatre*, Heinemann, 1982, p.33.

**Complication**. (a) The moment of intensification of *suspense, or (b) a factor which increases suspense as a *plot develops. Some obstruction of the *will of the *hero and/or the promotion of an apparently minor character to a prominent role, are common methods of achieving this.

**Concentration**. An actor's capacity to exclude extraneous noise and movement and remain in *character. Stanislavski (1863–1938) advocated the creation of a *circle of attention and the development of a point of *focus, which may be an aspect of the self, or of another actor sharing the stage, or the *prop being used.

Much of an actor's physical and mental training, including rhythmic and breathing exercise, is aimed at increasing concentration.

**Condensation**. Freudian term for a process which 'condenses' two or more images into one composite image. Thus one person in a *dream may be a fusion of at least two people whom the dreamer knows in life.

Characters in a play may also be considered composites of people known in life, and the creation of dramatic character is arguably related to the dream process, though consciousness no doubt plays a greater part. See UNCONSCIOUS.

FREUD, S., *The Interpretation of Dreams*, (1900), Penguin Freud Library, 1976.

**Confidant**. A person in whom other people confide. Confidants are useful in a play, since they are a means whereby major characters can reveal themselves to the audience. Horatio performs such a function in *Hamlet*, and the *comedy of manners has many maids-in-waiting who do the same. The confidant may be considered a descendant of the *chorus since he or she often takes a moderate or community view and acts as *repoussoir* to the *hero. The confidant, however, can become as powerful a figure as Figaro in *The Barber of Seville* (1772) by Beaumarchais (1732–99).

**Confidenti**. An early company of the *Commedia dell'Arte* who toured in Italy and dispersed in 1621.

**Conflict**. An opposition which creates unease and demands *resolution. It may be in the character's mind; it may be between characters' *wills; or between a character and his family or social group; or between two or more families or social groups; or within the spectator's mind; or between sections of the audience; or between the audience and the character; between the character and the gods or some more abstract principle such as fate. There may even be conflict between the actor and his role.

Conflict is essential to drama. The stronger the conflict, the stronger the interest; the stronger the interest the stronger the need for the audience to resolve the conflict. In *Macbeth* (1606), for example, the spectator is introduced to the inner workings of a murderer's mind and a conflict is created between a desire to repudiate the murderer and an awareness of the murderer's humanity.

Through the processes of *empathy and *identification, and an appeal to moral judgement and condemnation, the conflicts on stage are internalized as audience response. Why such conflict should be sought, and enjoyed, is a matter of great interest and complexity. Witness Aristotle's famous concept of *catharsis.

**Confrèrie de la Passion**. A 'brotherhood' founded in 1402 for the performance of religious plays. It acquired a monopoly of acting in

Paris in 1518 and built the famous Hôtel de Bourgogne in 1548, later leasing it to touring companies.

**Connotation**. Ideas, feelings or images suggested by a word's core meaning, or *denotation. A writer may use connotation, particularly in poetry and *poetic drama, to set up very subtle patterns of verbal cross-reference resembling musical *leitmotifs, and build up an *atmosphere of great intensity. The word 'wheel', for instance, in Shakespeare's King Lear (1605), echoes through the play. 'Let go thy hold when a great wheel run downhill . . .' says the Fool, and the word, which of course suggests a turning motion, gathers the sensations of weight, power and loss of control. When the word is used again, as in Lear's

> I am bound upon a wheel of fire
> That mine own tears do scald like burning lead . . .

the connotation widens to include torture, a saint broken on a wheel, tears of physical and mental suffering, weight again (lead) and the extended implication of dross, and tears perhaps worth more than the person they weep for, as we may recall Lear saying. In this way the connotations of the word accumulate and intensify.

**Constructivism**. Soviet art movement of the 1920s, inspired by cubism, sculpture and the forms and processes of the industrial revolution. Leaning towards abstraction on the one hand, and towards social utility on the other, the movement had a strong impact on the practice of Meyerhold (1874–1940) including his use of *biomechanics for training his actors.

It also strongly influenced theatre and stage design. Tairov (1885–1950), for instance, used Vesnin's constructivist sets, and huge productions involving constructivist artists were mounted to celebrate and reconstruct the events of the Revolution.

Outside Russia, the movement was felt strongly in Weimar Germany, particularly in the ambitious productions of Piscator (1893–1966) and the staging of Bertolt Brecht's plays (1898–1956).
BRAUN, E., (ed.), Meyerhold on Theatre, Eyre Methuen, 1969.
GRAY, C., The Russian Experiment in Art (1863–1922), Thames and Hudson, 1971.

**Context**. (a) The verbal and/or theatrical setting which gives meaning to a word, *gesture or *movement, and (b) the social and cultural setting which gives meaning to a whole play. See CODE; CONVENTION.

**Continuity**. Stanislavski's term for the 'flow' connecting the separate and successive stage appearances which constitute an actor's *role. The actor achieves this by *improvisation, in *rehearsal, of reported or imagined events occurring both before the play begins, and between its scenes. He so endows his character with a life which continues off stage. This helps the actor discover a *superobjective and a *through-line.

Continuity of individual roles is a necessary preparation for the overall continuity of the play. At an early stage of rehearsal this is lacking, because the customary process involves working on one scene at a time. *Run-throughs then become necessary to allow individual actors, and the *cast as a whole, to relate the scenes to one another and thus find *pace and flow.

The problem in *film is greater. For logistic reasons — availability of studio space, or, for outdoor shots, the weather, season, time of day and so on — scenes are often shot out of chronological sequence. 'Continuity girls' are required to number the *takes, and actors must have a strong sense of their roles when late scenes are shot early.

**Contrast**. Drama thrives on effects of contrast. These are everywhere to be found. Characters differ in temperament, age, size, shape, *voice, gait, *posture, and so on. *Set and *lighting changes bring visual contrast. *Costume and colour may be highly contrasted, as may styles of *delivery and performance.

Contrasts can provide comic incongruity. They intensify *suspense; they provide variety and interest; they clarify theme and *conflict. A good *director constantly seeks contrasts.

FERNALD, J., *The Play Produced*, Kenyon-Deane, 1933, Chs. 3, 4, 5.

**Convention**. (a) a *code. A rule tacitly agreed between writer and reader, or writer, actor and audience. Thus the *fourth wall convention tacitly assumes the existence of an invisible wall between play and spectator. The *aside or *soliloquy is a contrary convention permitting direct audience address. There are conventions concerning the use of *colour, as in the *Peking Opera, or the use of verse forms, or the use of *space and the passage of *time. (b) The term may be used in a broader sense to mean a *set* of rules. These may be theatrical, literary or social: thus 'the *pastoral convention'. This usage generally emphasizes the artificiality of the mode. (c) It also means a set of hardened and limited attitudes and responses: 'Convention dictates that . . .'.

Drama and indeed all forms of communication need conventions in the first sense. Language itself depends on an arbitrary agreement as to what any combination of sounds represents. D-O-G only suggests the image of a dog to someone who has learned that particular convention of the English language. Similarly, a dramatist works with agreements about the meaning of particular gestures, movements, colours and so on. These can be very conventionalized or highly coded, as in forms of *oriental theatre.

A dramatist shares conventions with his audience. In the behaviour of characters there are social conventions of dress, speech and gesture which convince an audience of accurate representation and allow in *naturalist drama the *willing suspension of disbelief. Such conventions the writer or actor may, as in *travesty or *burlesque, attack. In this case some agreement about a valid standard must be established. Indeed the exposure of conventions, whether theatrical and formal, or social and ideological, leads to the creation of new forms and new views of 'reality'. When conventions come to seem 'natural' they need to be *foregrounded so as to reveal their artificiality.

**Copeau, Jacques** (1879–1947). Famous and influential French director of the Vieux Colombier theatre in Paris.

> Pour l'oeuvre nouvelle qu'on nous laisse un tréteau nu. [For the new work, give me a bare stage.]

> He renewed and transformed the architecture of the stage, stage design, directing and acting. (Michel Saint-Denis)

COPEAU, J., *Cahiers du Vieux Colombier*, 1920–1.

**Copyright**. The author's right to prevent others making unlawful copies of his work. As the law stands at present, permission must be obtained to perform an author's work for a period of fifty years after his death.

LEAPER, W.J., *Copyright and the Performing Arts*, Stevens, 1957.

**Cornish round**. Arenas in Cornwall surrounded by a circular bank which were used for the performance of medieval plays. *The Castle of Perseverance* (early fifteenth-century) has a ground plan which shows how these rounds were probably used, with scaffolds at the four points of the compass where God in the East, and World, Flesh, and the Devil at the other cardinal points (accompanied by appropriate Deadly Sins) fought a battle for Mankind's soul. (See Ill.28, p.394.)

WICKHAM, G., *Early English Stages*, Vol. 1, Routledge, 1959.

**corpse, to**. Of an actor; to lose concentration as a result of some blunder.

**Corpus Christi plays**. *Mystery cycles were often referred to as Corpus Christi plays, since they were performed at the feast of Corpus Christi from about 1318 until Queen Elizabeth I finally suppressed the festival in England on her accession in 1558. The 'Play called Corpus Christi' is in fact the sub-title of the *Ludus Coventriae* or Coventry play. The festival was instituted by Clement V in 1311 after Pope Urban IV had first proclaimed it in 1264. Its function was to celebrate the Eucharist and the doctrine of transubstantiation. Although Maundy Thursday was the most appropriate day to hold the feast, Urban IV selected the first Thursday after Trinity as a day when full attention could be given to such an important celebration. The grandiose forms of worship known as the mystery cycles grew out of this decision.

KOLVE, V.A., *The Play called Corpus Christi*, Stanford University Press, 1966.

**Corral(es)**. Spanish playhouses of the sixteenth and seventeenth centuries, so-called because they were made out of courtyards formed by the backs of houses. Travelling companies in the northern cities of Spain used them rather as Elizabethan companies used inn-yards. The erection of a broad stage, seats on three sides, canopies overhead, and the use of the house windows as boxes for privileged spectators, led to the establishment of permanent theatres strongly resembling those of the Elizabethans, but thirty years earlier. Valladolid had such a public theatre by 1554. Madrid had five *corrales* by about 1570.

SHERGOLD, N.D., *A History of the Spanish Stage*, Oxford University Press, 1967, pp.360–404.

**Correspondence**. A term particularly associated with the so-called 'Elizabethan world picture' and hence with the drama of Shakespeare's time. It implies a world of established relationships between man, state and nature. The 'microcosm' or little kingdom of man 'corresponded' to the natural cosmos and to the 'macrocosm' of the state. Man was made up of four humours as the world had four elements. He had seven apertures in his head as there were seven stars in the sky. The head had the kingship of the body as the king was head of state, and so on. Fundamentally the correspondences derive from Plato, who found parallels between the workings of the state and the psychology of the individual. The faculties of 'judgement' and 'will', for example, were equivalent to the legislature and executive.

Shakespeare in particular made use of this *mythology. The storm in Act III of *King Lear* 'corresponds' to the storm inside the king's head. (It begins as he feels his sanity depart.) The correspondences link the public, natural and private worlds of the play and imply a fundamental design or unity in the universe (which, characteristically, the 'new men' like Edmund challenge and mock). Such connections enable Shakespeare to create an intense and richly poetic world and move easily between psychological, political and religious planes. Poetic drama, with the rise of empirical science, and the acceptance of the Copernican system, inevitably weakened as its mythology was undermined. See *GREAT CHAIN OF BEING.

In the later nineteenth century, a similar idea arose with

*romanticism and the later *symbolist movement. Baudelaire's sonnet, *Correspondances*, is generally taken to convey this:

> La nature est un temple où de vivants piliers
> Laisse parfois sortir de confuses paroles . . .

The suggestion that nature allows confused words to emerge from her bosom from time to time is neo-platonic. It suggests a correspondence between this world and a reality beyond it which from time to time we sense. Plato's *Symposium* (371–67 B.C.), for example, speaks of human beauty, momentarily perceived in this life, as being a hint of a beauty beyond time in another world.

Such a belief reasserts the value of the *image, the *symbol, the *simile or *metaphor, i.e. of a verbal or visual process which catches likenesses or correspondences between two realities. (When the world we live in is seen as the only reality, images lose any religious function, and are seen as no more than decorative, as tended to happen in the Augustan period.)

The relevance of this to drama in the twentieth century may be seen in a number of ways, perhaps especially in the use of *allegory. Religious and poetic dramatists have attempted to create a dramatic structure which will 'echo' and give a sense of a transcendent world beyond the world of the play. T.S. Eliot uses for this purpose the patterns of old plays. Euripides's *Alcestis*, for example, lies behind *The Cocktail Party* (1949), and the story of Orestes behind *The Family Reunion* (1938). He also uses characters who operate on two planes, the 'natural' and the 'spiritual', such as the 'guardians' or Harcourt-Reilly, also in *The Cocktail Party*. The use of a heightened language to support these effects led to Eliot's adoption of a flexible *verse form.

Eliot thus tried to communicate to an audience a sense of interrelated or corresponding planes. Yeats had similar aims, using Irish mythology (in a more direct way) and *sub- and *parallel plots to create an echo effect, as the Jacobeans did. He also borrowed from the Japanese *Noh play, with its ghosts and its sense of a spirit world. His late plays, including *The Herne's Egg* (1938) and *Purgatory* (1938) infer the existence of some other world. His strange private mythology, expressed in *A Vision* (1925) describes the experience behind such a sense of correspondence.

As drama these attempts were perhaps not fully successful. In Eliot's case the difference between the actual and spiritual planes creates a feeling of incongruity and the points at which they correspond are unconvincing, as in the ritual in *The Cocktail Party*, where the doctor becomes priest. In Yeats's case, the myths he employed were perhaps too far from popular belief to allow him to build a national drama on them, as he had earlier wished.

In the twentieth century, *epic or comic epic has made great use of corresponding planes and has deliberately emphasized the incongruity between the *naturalist surface and a parallel myth. One thinks of the journeys of Leopold Bloom and Ulysses in Joyce's *Ulysses* (1922) which again leads one to consider the comic epic tradition and the epic nature of Brecht's *parable plays. In these, an audience is asked how the story 'corresponds' with contemporary reality — how Galileo's responsibilities as scientist correspond to those of Robert Oppenheimer or Klaus Fuchs. Here the emphasis is on the serious comparison of past and present in one world, and on one plane. The general sympathy of a twentieth-century audience would be with Brecht's refusal to split the world into different levels of reality, and the inquiry is meant to make us active and restless. In a world of change and not *repetition, the use of correspondence in dramatic art has also changed. See ALLEGORY.

TILLYARD, E.M.W., *The Elizabethan World Picture*, Chatto and Windus, 1943.

**Corsican trap**. A concealed slot across the width of the stage which permitted the entrance, up an inclined plane, of ghostly apparitions in Victorian theatres. It was first used in *The Corsican Brothers*, a *gothic melodrama adapted from the French by Boucicault (1820–90) in 1852. The effect was so eery and successful that the trap became standard equipment.

**Coryphaios**. The *chorus leader in the Greek *dithyramb.

**Costume**. Clothing which in some way changes the identity of the wearer. Clothes have a number of different functions. They are worn as protection from the cold, to attract the opposite sex, to enhance dignity and rank, to affirm loyalty to the wearer's social group, and so on. In this way costume extends and defines the individual who wears it.

Costume also *conceals* identity. From childhood onwards, it is donned to *disguise* personality and in a complex way find release in some game of pretence.

The varied functions of clothing, as livery, uniform or disguise overlap in drama. Costume in the theatre copies, or suggests, or symbolizes, or honours, the realities it imitates. It may suggest animal or primitive elements in man's nature (as in the Greek tragic *chorus or the plays of Aristophanes). Spectacular costume may enhance the prestige of a patron or producer, as in, say, court performances for Louis XIV. It may honour the supernatural (God and the angels in the *mystery cycles). It may procure anarchic relief for spectators and actors (through the Devil or Belial in the *moralities). It indicates a character's place of origin (as in the *Commedia dell'Arte*). It establishes a *typological role (the *jester or *fool, *pantaloon and so on). Costume may also attempt to recreate a historical period, but historical accuracy in costume was not sought in any scholarly sense until we find Diderot (1713–84) and Goethe (1749–1832) advocating it in the later eighteenth century.

The publication in 1834 of Planché's *History of British Costume* is generally taken as an important development in the presentation of all historical costume drama. Actors and directors, such as MacCready, Kemble and Madame Vestris, moved towards the accurate costuming of the *naturalistic *box-set. Costume, however, even naturalistic costume, has its *signs and *codes, and theatre costume retains its varied functions.

LAVER, J., *Costume in the Theatre*, Harrap, 1964.

**Cothurnus**. Usually taken to be a thick-soled boot or *buskin worn by Greek tragic actors. No certain proof of this practice exists before the *Hellenistic period.

**Counterpoint**. Musical term for a combination of instrumental or vocal melodies which form a coherent whole. It is often applied figuratively to a play whose *voices, *rhythms and *motifs cohere in a similar way. The musical orchestration of Chekhov's plays invites this metaphor.

**Counterweight house**. Theatre in which the stage *scenery is moved by counterweighted ropes and pulleys. Compare the *hemp house in which scenery is moved by hand from a *fly-floor.

***Coup de théâtre***. Sudden event which transforms the dramatic situation. The Greek **deus ex machina*, the descent of Jupiter in Shakespeare's *Cymbeline* (1609), the appearance of the king in Molière's *Tartuffe* (1664), Brecht's peasant rising from his death bed (when he hears that the war is over) in *Caucasian Chalk Circle* (1948), are all examples. Diderot contrasts the *coup de théâtre* with the *tableau or *freeze. The *coup de théâtre* produces surprise or amazement and resolves a *conflict. The freeze allows the audience to reflect on what is typical in the dramatic situation.

DIDEROT, D., *Réflections sur le fils naturel*, 1757.

**Court masque**. See MASQUE.

**Coventry cycle**. One of the four remaining full cycles of *mystery plays. It may also have been performed at Lincoln.

**Crab**. See TRACK.

**Craft cycle**. *Mystery play cycle, so called because the different episodes were performed by different crafts or guilds.

**Craig, Edward Gordon** (1872–1966). English scenic designer, son of Ellen Terry; editor of the theatre journal *The Mask*.

> Show them beauty, not speak in difficult sentences.
> I try to perceive things feelingly, not thinkingly . . . thinking comes afterwards . . .

See: ÜBERMARIONETTE.
CRAIG, E.G., *On the Art of the Theatre* (1905), Heinemann, 1958; *Craig on Theatre*, edited by J.M. Walton, Methuen, 1983.

**Creative if**. See MAGIC IF.

**Creative objective**. See SUPEROBJECTIVE. A Stanislavskian term for the ruling idea of a play towards which the *through-line tends. Each actor must find this objective, define it and aim at it in his own way.

**Creed play**. Fifteenth-century religious play. The concern of one such play from York was, according to the *prompt book, 'to defend the Article of the Catholic Faith'. Glynne Wickham suggests in *The Mediaeval Theatre* (see pp.115–16) that it must be connected with the *morality plays.

*Crepidata*. See FABULA.

**Crisis**. Strictly speaking, the moment of decision, as in a disease, when a change in the patient's state determines whether the patient will recover or succumb. So, late in a play, a turning-point is reached when doubts are resolved and the outcome determined. In this sense, the crisis occurs at the play's *climax. The word is also used for powerful moments in any individual *scene or *act.
    *Classical drama concentrates on these moments of crisis. *Naturalistic and *epic drama incorporate more daily activity and do not seek the same intensity.

**Crispin**. A clever servant figure deriving from the *Commedia dell'Arte* character Scaramuccia, prominent in French comedies of the seventeenth and eighteenth centuries.

**Critic**. Writer not beloved of men of the theatre. When Beckett's Gogo and Didi play at insulting one another the word 'critic' beats 'sewer-rat', 'curate' and 'cretin' and is the worst insult they can find. Some critics and reviewers have been respected, however. Kenneth Tynan became a *dramaturg at the *National Theatre and it is encouraging to hear Sir Michael Hordern say he has adapted acting performances, even if he has not changed them, as a result of reading the critics. The separation, however, between practical theatre and academic dramatic criticism is greatly to be regretted.

**Cross above**. To move across the stage, *upstage of another actor, group of actors, piece of furniture, etc. See CROSS BELOW.

**Cross below**. To pass *downstage of another actor, group of actors, piece of furniture, etc. The term eliminates the ambiguity of 'cross in front of'. If an actor or a chair, for example, is facing *upstage, then to cross 'in front of' could mean to move *upstage of the actor, i.e. before his face, rather than *downstage, between the actor and audience. 'Above' and 'below' assume a *raked stage, as do *upstage and *downstage. The terms continue to be used for unraked stages.

**Cross-cutting**. A term from film editing which refers to the process of replacing one image by another, generally from a different sequence of actions in another location. The *cut has a shock effect on the viewer which is different from the slow 'fade' or 'dissolve', in which images mingle. The obvious equivalent process in drama is a sudden *scene change, effected by a *transformation scene, *blackout or *lighting change. It is, however, the unlit, bare stage of *Elizabethan or *Jacobean drama, with its 'filmic' structure, and many changes of scene (over 40 in *Antony and Cleopatra* (1606–7)) to which the term is more appropriate. Cross-cutting between Egypt and Rome, as between Greece and Troy in *Troilus and Cressida* (1602), is fundamental to Shakespeare's method. It is also applicable to Middleton's method in *The Changeling* (1622) and Webster's in *The White Devil* (1612). The 'edginess' and tension created in the audience by these sudden shifts and ironic contrasts resemble the effect of an unexpected *metaphor, and remind us of the way Eisenstein developed cutting and *montage in *Battleship Potemkin* (1925).

**Cruelty**. Both *tragedy and *comedy contain elements of cruelty. In *tragedy, scenes may provoke *pity for the victim, and rejection of those responsible for his suffering — as in the blinding of Gloucester in *King Lear* (1605). In comedy it is often the spectator who is cruel. Characters hurt each other, fall off ladders, raise enormous bumps on craniums, suffer from appalling speech deficiencies, and so on. Yet we laugh. Only happiness at seeing a biter bit (like the bully in a Chaplin *farce) or a general awareness that the hurting is only a game, justifies the cruelty of our laughter. The closeness and the distance between tragedy and comedy relate to a consideration of such cruelty, and it raises the thorny question of *catharsis. See THEATRE of CRUELTY.
ARTAUD, A., 'The Theatre of Cruelty' (1932–3), Manifestos I and II, in *Le Théâtre et son Double*, Gallimard, 1964.

**Cue**. The line, phrase, word, sound or action which tells the actor it is his turn to speak.

Normally actors should enter smartly 'on cue'. Pausing even very briefly (as happens when a breath is taken as the cue is given) creates a slackness of *tempo which is characteristic of much inexperienced playing. Generally speaking, any pause on cue should be filled by a physical or facial response which reveals to an audience the impact a speech has made. This adds variety to essential rapid cueing.

**Cup and saucer dramas**. Nineteenth-century plays set in domestic interiors, whose dialogue was frequently accompanied by sips of tea. Tom Robertson's *Society* (1865) made them popular, and announced the early phases of *naturalism. Of such plays, Robertson's *Caste* (1867) is the best known.

ROWELL, G., *The Victorian Theatre: a survey*, Oxford University Press, 1956.

**Curtain**. Drapery which conceals the stage area from the audience. The 'front of house' curtain is usually drawn across the *proscenium arch on runners, or hung from it and hoisted in folds to reveal the stage. A 'roll curtain' is raised by a pulley wound round a pole. The *tabs are pulled upwards on diagonal lines. Other methods have been employed. In the Roman theatre the curtain lay in a trough on the *forestage. Raising it thus *concealed* the stage.

The curtain has various functions: it announces the beginning and end of the theatrical illusion; it conceals *scene changes, and machinery used to effect them; it emphasises the play's division into *acts and *scenes; and it often falls at moments of *climax to allow a period of relaxation before the tension 'builds' in the subsequent scene. A 'curtain' may also save time by doing away with the need for an *exit.

The curtain has only recently come to have such varied uses. Curtains to mark the end of acts did not appear in England until the 18th century, and scene-curtains were first used by Irving in 1881.

**Curtain music**. Introductory music played before the curtain rises, known also as the 'curtain tune'. The practice of playing at the start and between the *acts of a play goes back to the *Elizabethan theatre.

**Curtain-raiser**. A short play to 'warm up' the audience before the main drama. For examples see the full *playbills of eighteenth- and nineteenth-century theatres.

**Curtain set**. A simple *set, dressed in side and back curtains. It is very flexible and allows an audience to enter the dramatic fiction with a minimum of scene setting.

**Cut**. (a) The deletion of words, speeches or scenes from a playscript. Reasons for cutting vary. A play may need to be adapted to a new stage area, or to the medium of *film. Topical reference may become outdated; fashion and *censorship may require changes; the *director or author may wish to alter and exclude lines which do not work in rehearsal, and so on. Generally speaking, the better the play, the more a cut is likely to damage it. Tensions frequently arise between authors who insist on the presentation of their work in its full integrity, and *producers and directors who insist on change. (b) A cut is also a long slot in the stage floor in some nineteenth-century theatres. It runs at right angles to the *curtain, i.e. parallel to the *boards, and was probably used for lifting the wall of a *box-set from the basement. (c) It is also a *film and *television term for a change of image on the screen. The cut may show the same subject at a different angle, or a different subject (as when the editor cuts from speaker to listener), or it may remind the viewer of action happening elsewhere. For the similarity between this and certain dramatic techniques, see CROSSCUTTING; FOCUS.

**Cut cloth.** A piece of scenery consisting of a strengthened canvas into which openings have been cut.

**Cycle**. Term suggesting a series of episodes, loosely linked but forming a pattern of *recurrence or return. The subject-matter is generally mythological, as in Homeric and Wagnerian *epic. In drama, the term suggests the *mystery plays which re-enact in sequence the events of the Old and New Testaments.

**Cyclorama**. A rigid canvas or plaster structure built round the stage or upper stage and used to create effects of space, sky and distance whilst masking stage machinery.

# D

**Dada**. A movement in the arts, noted for its deliberate attempt to challenge and shock the art-loving bourgeoisie. It arose in Zurich in 1916 and was quickly absorbed into *surrealism and *constructivism. Robert Motherwell's *The Dada Painters and Poets* (1951) brought the movement back to public attention and it began to be seen as a forerunner of the *theatre of cruelty and *theatre of the absurd. The *happenings of the 1960s drew on Dadaism. Tom Stoppard (1937– ) used and satirized dadaist material in his 'philosophical *farce' *Travesties* (1974).

**Dame**. Female *pantomime character, played by a man. The mother of Aladdin or the Ugly Sisters in *Cinderella* are 'Dame' roles.

**Dance**. Art form, closely related to drama, based on rhythmical movements of the human body. It may be accompanied by music, and shares with drama the use of *gesture, *grouping, *costume, *lighting, *scenery, and so on. Though it does not use *dialogue, it often narrates a story.

**Dead areas**. Term used by performers to describe parts of the auditorium where the audience seems unresponsive. The size of the theatre, its shape and *acoustics, are often responsible.

**Deadly theatre**. Term coined by Peter Brook (1925– ), and explained in the opening section of his book *The Empty Space* (1968). It describes theatre in which the fewest risks are taken. Management selects plays which attract the customer; not too intense, not too boring, and generally respectable. They are treated with 'old formulae, old methods, old jokes, old effects, stock beginnings to scenes, stock ends'. Such productions do not disturb conditioned reflexes. They are, in Brook's view, reassuring, dull and *deadly*. His own practice opposes such theatre with all its strength, and seeks constantly for freshness of interpretation and treatment. See HOLY, ROUGH and IMMEDIATE THEATRE.

**Débat**. Poem in the form of a contest in *wit and debating skill, popular in the twelfth and thirteenth centuries. It derives from classical models, such as the *pastoral contests in the *Eclogues* of Theocritus (c.308–c.240 B.C.) and Virgil (70–19 B.C.). The thirteenth-century *Owl and the Nightingale* is an example. The stage *debates which are frequent in *Elizabethan drama may have been influenced by such models.

**Debate**. Highly formalized discussion in which opposing views are argued in turn. Drama has often employed the form. Examples are found in Aristophanes's *The Frogs* (405 B.C.) and in the morality play, *Castle of Perseverance* (early fifteenth-century), which incorporates a debate between the four Daughters of God — Mercy, Peace, Truth and Righteousness — for the soul of Mankind. Medwall's *Fulgens and Lucrece* (fifteenth-century) is a secular *debate.

A less formalized debate is often found in modern *political drama. George Bernard Shaw's *The Apple Cart* (1929), among other of his plays, contains much debating. Brecht's *The Caucasian Chalk Circle* (1948) has a debate in the opening scene and the debating tone of his plays has been both persuasive and influential. The philosophical *farce of Tom Stoppard (1937– ) uses much argument and counter-argument. Trevor Griffiths's *The Party* (1973) contains political debate of a semi-formalized kind.

**De casibus tragedy**. Tragedy based on the fall from prosperity to adversity of famous men and women. It derives its name from Boccaccio's *De Casibus Virorum et Feminarum Illustrum* (late fourteenth-century) which depicted such falls from grace.

**Declamation**. Rhythmical and emphatic *diction. A pejorative term when the *conventions are *naturalistic, but the 'natural' mode of verse-speaking in the *classical theatre.

**Deconstruction**. Method of critical analysis which treats a play or literary text as a 'construct'. It examines its processes of production and questions a text's unquestioned assumptions by using hidden contradictions within it to undermine each other. So far the method has mainly been applied to fiction. See Barthes's classic analysis of Balzac's *Sarrasine* in:
BARTHES, R., *S/Z* (1970), trs. R. Miller, Cape, 1975.

**Décor**. See SCENERY.

**Decorum**. *Neo-classical principle. It demands that the 'proprieties' be observed and that the speech and behaviour of dramatic characters be appropriate to their social status. The classical rules, stemming from Aristotle, forbade violence, death and sexuality on stage.

**Degree**. See GREAT CHAIN OF BEING; CORRESPONDENCE.

**Deixis**. Semiotic term for verbal indices, i.e. the act of *showing* in demonstrative words such as 'here', 'there', 'now', 'this', 'that', and other pronouns, including very importantly 'I' and 'you', 'he' and 'she'. In the theatre, which is a 'seeing place' (*theatron*), these words take on powerful meaning.

**Delivery**. Manner in which lines are spoken. See DICTION; PROJECTION.

**Denotation**. The 'core' or central meaning of a word, as compared with its *connotation or associative field. If a word be compared to a candle, the denotation is the flame, and the connotation the area it sheds light upon. The word 'rose', for example, has connotations of love, thorns, pain, gothic windows, and so on. Its denotation, however, is the flower itself. Denotational language tends to be more prosaic and functional.

In prose drama, a *character may often employ words in this way, but the context of the play may supply connotations of which the character is unaware. Gina Ekdal, in Ibsen's *The Wild Duck* (1884) is a prosaic person. She complains when her lodger lights a fire and fills his room with smoke. The language seems denotational, but the play's context makes us aware that the lodger is going to cause a mental conflagration which will fill many minds with confusion, including his own. The play adds a connotation and the audience hears *dialogue which is prosaic and poetic at the same time.

**Dénouement**. Literally the 'unknotting' or unravelling of the *plot. The play's final movement, when the ultimate *disclosures are made.

**Description**. The rendering of a scene or situation in language; one of several procedures in the *novel form. In drama, the *messenger and *chorus generally have descriptive and *narrative functions. In addition, the actor may render scene by word and *gesture. Stage *scenery, of course, normally takes the place of verbal description in *naturalistic plays.

The problem with verbal description is that it is of necessity sequential and thus temporal, whereas a scene is spatial. The theatrical impact of a scene is immediate, whereas in a novel, or a critic's verbal description of a play, one detail must follow another. It is diachronic, not synchronic, and encourages a listener or reader to seek for connections between the details, rather than experience the immediate spatial effect. However, the work of Charles Dickens (1812–70) serves to remind us that verbal rendering of *space and scene can constitute a powerful appeal to the imagination. *Radio drama, too, in the absence of visual means, must use language to create scene, though it has the advantage of *voice and *sound effects.

**Designer**. One who plans and designs *costumes and/or *scenery for stage productions. It is important that designer and *director work closely together. Stage designs can limit the freedom of a production, dictating *movement within a *set before the director and actors have worked out in *rehearsal their interpretation of a play. It must be remembered, however, that costume and set need careful preparatory work, and planning must often begin before rehearsals start. An understanding between director and designers should be established early on, to avoid clashes of creative intention.

**Detail scenery**. Small pieces of scenery, used within or in front of a permanent *setting to indicate *scene-changes.

**Deus ex machina**. The god who descends in a kind of crane, or *machina, at the end of a classical play, to rescue bewildered mortals and resolve complicated *plots. Hence it has come to mean any act of providential rescue.

Aristotle suggested that the *deus ex machina* should be used only to inform *protagonists of events they cannot know, or to predict events which the audience is aware happen later. Bertolt Brecht (1898–1956) inverts the device in *The Good Woman of Setzuan* (1938–41) by making the gods disappear without solving the problem. In his theatre the gods leave the problems to mortals.

**Deuteragonist**. Second of the three individual actors employed in Greek classical *tragedy. Like the other actors, he might have several *roles for which he would wear different *masks. See PROTAGONIST; TRITAGONIST.

**Deutsches Theater**. Famous theatrical enterprise, founded in 1883. In its early days it was associated with productions in the *Meininger style, then, from 1894, with the *Freie Bühne, and from 1905, with Max Reinhardt (1873–1943) the brilliant Austrian director.

**Dialect**. Form of a language whose pronunciation, phrasing and vocabulary identify it with a particular region.

The use of dialect in drama is interesting and complex, related as it is to the evolution of a common form of 'English', and an accompanying sense of the superiority of this form to the regional dialect. A brief survey of this growth is to be found in Section Four of Raymond Williams's *The Long Revolution* (1961).

Regional dramatic forms, such as the *mystery cycles, possess no sense of the inferiority of the dialectal language used. (God, in the York cycle, would naturally speak with a Yorkshire accent.) A common, written form of English developed, however, out of the growing power of the court in the Tudor period and the educational and business axis based on London, Oxford and Cambridge. The tension between this new standard and the dialectal forms is seen in *Elizabethan drama, where dialect is often associated with comic and humorous characters. Note Shakespeare's use of dialect in his *history plays, and the way Prince Hal, in the comic *sub-plot of *Henry IV* (1596–7) prepares for kingship by learning the various 'languages' of his subjects.

The mockery of dialectal speech was accompanied, in Shakespeare at least, by the mockery of attitudes of assumed superiority. The apparently comic Welshman, Fluellen, in *Henry V* (1599), makes Pistol eat his condescension with a Welsh leek. Congreve (1670–1729) effects a similar reversal a hundred years later. The country dialect of Sir Wilfule Witwoud in Congreve's *The Way of the World* (1700) conceals his value only from the foolish. This includes the fops in the play, who learn their mistake. Even in Congreve, however, dialect implies a form of limitation; its dramatic use can make an appeal to class prejudice, as well as subtly correct it.

In nineteenth-century *melodrama, written for a mainly lower-class audience, the use of dialect for the *comic man, and upper-class forms for the *villain, reversed the audience's sympathies. The nature and appeal of the language of *hero and *heroine varied with the locality of the theatre and the nature of its audience. By this time a common standard of *spoken* English was attracting both support and resentment.

The growth of a respect for dialect, and a diminishing of its 'comic' stigma, may be seen in the industrial and regional novels of some nineteenth century authors, notably Mrs Gaskell (1810–65) and Thomas Hardy (1840–1928). The London theatre, however, was less accessible. D.H. Lawrence's serious dialect plays, such as *The Daughter in Law* (1912), waited fifty years to be produced in London.

The strong link between dialect and comedy is self-evident in various forms of *stand-up comedy and, until Tony Harrison's version of *The Mystery Plays* at the *National Theatre (1983–5), God in productions of the York Cycle was likely to speak BBC English or 'Received Pronunciation'.

**Dialectic**. (a) Formal *rhetorical dispute, or (b) the theory of opposing principles underlying science (Kant (1724–1804)) or nature and history (Hegel (1770–1831) and then Marx (1818–83)). Both the latter developed a progressive theory, suggesting that the world evolved in triadic stages from 'thesis' to 'antithesis' and then to a 'synthesis' which became the first stage of a new triad. Marx, however, transformed Hegel's idealist view into a materialist dialectic, or economic determinism, which argued that recent history shows a development from feudalism to a mercantile capitalist stage, inevitably leading to a synthesis in socialism.

Dramatists and critics adhering to such a principle apply it to drama in various ways: (a) the structure of a play may be triadic, (b) there may be triadic patterns of relationship between characters who represent different stages of personal and social development, (c) the *protagonist's consciousness may develop in dialectical stages, or (d) there may be 'dialectical' oppositions of behaviour and response in individual scenes.

Brecht (1898–1956) attempted to coordinate Marxist theory and dramatic structure. In *Mother Courage* (1941), for example, there are dialectical oppositions of various kinds. The most famous is, perhaps, the contrasting of Kattrin, in scene 11, with the Peasants. As the army approaches the apparently doomed town, Kattrin beats a drum. The Peasants pray. Meanwhile the small capitalist, Mother Courage, is absent on business. Feudal passivity (thesis) seems to be contrasted with Mother Courage's active concern with family survival (antithesis) and Kattrin's behaviour, which serves a whole community (synthesis).

It is dangerous, of course, to equate three characteristic forms of human response with the feudalism/capitalism/socialism triad. Brecht is difficult to pin down, and the dramatic embodiment is likely to be more complex than a simple theoretical pattern. Nor can an audience be relied upon to respond to such a pattern. But Brecht's plays were meant to be *parables, and a study of his theory and practice illuminates the relation between Marxism and dramatic form. More recent English *political drama has built on Brecht's example. (See, for instance, Trevor Griffiths's *Occupations* (1970) and *The Party* (1973)). For a drama which mocks the dialectic, see *Travesties* by Tom Stoppard (1937– ).

LUKÁCS, G., *The Historical Novel*, Penguin, 1969, Ch. 2.
WILLIAMS, R., *Modern Tragedy*, Chatto and Windus, 1966.

**Dialectical form**. A term used in varying ways to mean: (a) the triadic form as above, (b) a dramatic form which invites the audience to answer the questions asked by a play, and (c) a formal rhetorical dispute.

**Dialogue**. Verbal exchange between two or more characters on stage. It occurs when characters speak on a common subject, when they suffer from the delusion that they speak of the same subject, when they do not desire to listen to the other person's thoughts (simultaneous *monologue) and sometimes when the character communes with himself or herself (internal dialogue or *soliloquy).

Good dialogue is usually highly individualized and immediately comprehensible. There is little time in performance for an audience to stop and ponder the meaning. Dialogue is thus more limited in vocabulary and less polysyllabic than *narrative and descriptive modes of expression. From the actor's point of view, dialogue should normally avoid awkward phrasing, the repetition of *cues and anything that gives the actor problems when memorizing, or in his *delivery. Sometimes, however, the actor welcomes difficult but purposeful dialogue since it offers an opportunity to test and reveal his or her skill.

Even comparatively simple dramatic language has a complex effect since dialogue is always spoken *in context*. The words are given meaning by *voice and *facial expression, and by the silent or spoken reactions of other characters; in short by everything happening on stage as the words are spoken. The effect of dramatic language is also intensified by the relation of the words to whatever precedes or follows them. (See DENOTATION.) Simple words gather resonance as a play proceeds, and form patterns of contrast, since each character handles them in an individual way.

Dialogue is ostensibly the spoken thought and feeling of a *character. Thus the creation of characters with strong feelings and interesting minds will produce good dialogue. The creation of inarticulate or introverted characters, as in, say, Pinter's plays, will require dialogue which points, in its silences, to what has not or cannot be said. Extremely restricted language, as Pinter and Beckett have shown, can be as powerful in the theatre as eloquence. Liv Ullman's comments on the way she handled Pinter's dialogue in *Old Times* are interesting: 'I do not have wonderful lines . . . they are very strange lines, so I think of the part as a dancer . . .'
BATES, B., *The Way of the Actor*, Century, 1986, p.200.

**Diction**. The actor's mode of delivery, both 'natural' and stylized. Acting, it is said, has three rules: 'to be heard, to be heard, and to be heard'. Where plays are very heavily dependent on *dialogue this is obviously true, and large theatres, in particular, require clarity of diction. Clear speech, however, as Marlon Brando and the *method school have reminded us, is not always *in character*, and excellent *elocution may be out of place if the emphasis lies on what an inarticulate character *does* rather than says. (The trick here is no doubt to give the impression of being inarticulate while still making oneself heard.) Where drama is less *naturalistic, and particularly in *verse drama, clear diction is obviously essential to the poetic and musical effect.

**Didactic theatre**. Theatre which aims to teach a moral lesson. See AGITPROP; COMMITMENT; LEHRSTÜCK; MORALITY PLAY; ALLEGORY; SATIRE; FUNCTION OF DRAMA.

**Diderot, Denis** (1713–84). French philosopher and dramatist, editor and major author of the *Encyclopedia* (1751–77). He placed emphasis on the dispassionate craftsmanship of acting:

> Fill the front of the theatre with tearful creatures, I will none of them on the boards.

See: ACTING; DRAME; PARADOX OF ACTING.
DIDEROT, D., *Paradox sur le comédien* (1830); *The Paradox of Acting* (together with Archer's *Masks or Faces*), Hall, 1957.

**Digby plays**. Three late *mystery plays: *Mary Magdalene, The Conversion of St Paul* and *The Killing of the Children of Isreal*. The first is probably the most theatrically interesting.
BAKER, MURPHY AND HALL (ed), *Early English Text Society O S 283*, 1982.

**Dilemma**. Situation causing perplexity. More precisely it is a *rhetorical term describing the situation of a debating opponent who must choose one of two unfavourable alternatives. In drama it describes a character who must decide between two opposing lines of action, between two opposed desires, between duty and love, morality and expediency, obedience to two masters, two codes of morality or two evils, and even between living or dying. To judge by the fame of Hamlet's 'To be or not to be' soliloquy, the expression of a dilemma makes for powerful theatre.

**Dimmers**. Form of stage *lighting, introduced to vary intensity and balance focused lights.
LOUNSBURY, W.C., *Theatre Backstage from A to Z*, Washington University Press, 1967, pp.37–40.

**Dionysiac**. Relating to the god Dionysos, son of Zeus by Semele, princess of Thebes. He was born again out of Zeus's thigh. Killed by Perseus, he then descended into Hades where he rescued his mother's spirit, and finally rose to Olympus.

His followers were the maenads and satyrs, sons of Silenus, who celebrated Dionysos's gift of wine in orgiastic 'dionysiac' rites. They appear in the *Bacchae* of Euripides (484–407/6 B.C.) and in the extant *satyr plays — Euripides's *Cyclops* and the incomplete *Ichneutae* of Sophocles (496–406 B.C.).

Dionysos was indeed the god of drama. According to Aristotle, *tragedy arose out of hymns in his praise, or *dithyrambs. His altar stood at the centre of the *orchestra of the Theatre of Dionysos, on the slopes of the acropolis in Athens, and the drama festivals were celebrated in his honour.

In 1872, F.W. Nietzsche (1844–1900) published his famous *Birth of Tragedy* in which he made a celebrated distinction between two principles — the 'dionysiac' and the 'apollonian'. The dionysiac he associated with natural and primitive energy, and the apollonian with order, visual beauty and self-knowledge. The first expressed itself in music and the *dances of the *chorus; the second was the 'individuating principle' which expressed itself in visual or scenic design and through the actors on stage. The combination of these two elements or principles, argued Nietzsche, was necessary for the production of *tragedy.

Nietzsche's distinction is related to other famous oppositions in German thought; for instance, Schiller's *Naive and Sentimental, Schopenhauer's *Will and Understanding, and Freud's Ego and Id. The concept is very important in dramatic theory. See UNCONSCIOUS; ORIGINS OF DRAMA.

**Dionysos.** See DIONYSIAC.

**Director.** Person responsible for guiding the performance of a play. The term has replaced the word *producer which is now used mainly of the organizer and money-raiser. Only in *radio drama (and occasionally for some reason in TV comedy) is the term producer used for director.

The director must envisage and create a dramatic text in *space. This he does by directing the actors and coordinating the work of *designers and technicians. Sometimes he must choose between an actors' theatre and a designer's, for it is often a question of giving more freedom to one or the other. He must select the period in which he wishes to place the play, choose whether to adapt his text, and what style, if any, to impose. A director has a coordinating function, and the modern director no doubt resembles his ancestors — the Greek author-actor-choreographer, the medieval 'superintendents' or *pageant-masters, the seventeenth-century actor-authors, such as Shakespeare and Molière (1622–73), and the famous *actor-managers, such as Garrick at Drury Lane, or Samuel Phelps at Sadler's Wells.

The modern conception of the director seems to have emerged in the later nineteenth century, out of a need to harmonize the craft of acting with the demands of pictorial staging. The Duke of Saxe-Meiningen is sometimes called the first 'modern' director. With his *Meininger Company, he sought rigorously for a unity between designed *sets, *costume and choreographed *movement. He imposed thorough *rehearsal schedules and placed heavy emphasis on *ensemble playing. Since then, a line of distinguished figures, including Antoine, Stanislavski, Reinhardt, Copeau, Meyerhold, Piscator, Jessner, Brecht, Brook, Grotowski, Bergman, and others, have demonstrated the enomous creative influence a director can have upon a production. In their sensitivity to actors' needs, in their capacity to channel the creative energies of others, in their will-power, determination, dedication and perfectionism, in their readiness to use whatever the rehearsal process brings to light, the great directors control the complex tensions which can exist between creative talents, be they *actors, *designers, or, indeed, authors.

COLE, T., and CHINOY, H.C., *Directors on Directing*, MacGibbon and Kee, 1963.

HUNT, H., *The Director in the Theatre*, Routledge, 1954.

MACGOWAN, K., *Continental Stagecraft*, Blom, NY, 1964.

**Disclosure**. The discovery or *revelation of fresh knowledge, changing a character's awareness, affecting his course of action and the play's direction. Disclosures tend especially to occur towards the end of a play, bringing about either *catastrophe — Emilia's disclosure of Desdemona's innocence in Shakespeare's *Othello* (1604) — or *reconciliation, as in the establishment of Perdita's identity in *The Winter's Tale* (1610).

**Discourse**. Linguistic term for the process of utterance or 'enunciation' rather than that which is 'enunciated'. Discourse is a term especially appropriate to *theatre language since it can be expressed verbally, scenically, through *movement and *gesture, and as a *'house style'. For the distinction between discourse and '*histoire*' see:

BENVENISTE, E., *Problems of General Linguistics*, Miami University Press, 1970.

**Discovery**. See REVELATION; DISCLOSURE.

**Discovery scene**. A scene upon which the curtain rises to discover the characters already on stage. At the start of such a scene, actors must endeavour to convey the illusion of a continuing action. Thus Turgenev (1818–83), in his play *A Month in the Country* (1850), has the curtain rise on characters in the middle of a card game.

**Disguise**. A change of *costume, facial appearance, gait etc., which aims to conceal the identity of a character, actor on stage or person in everyday life. On the stage such disguises need not be realistic. A token change will serve an audience accustomed to a theatrical *convention.

**Disguising**. An early form of *masque, and a medieval and Tudor name for any performance in *mask or *costume.

WICKHAM, G., *Early English Stages (1377–1660)*, Vol. I, Routledge and Kegan Paul, 1958, Ch. 6.

**Disorder**. State resulting from the failure of some ordering and controlling principle. Critics have especially applied the word to different kinds of breakdown portrayed in *Elizabethan and *Jacobean drama. Thus Shakespeare's plays generally begin with some suggestion of disorder. It may be a fight between brothers as in *As You Like It* (1599), or a ghost as in *Hamlet* (1601), or war as in

*Macbeth* (1606), or a storm as in *The Tempest* (1611). The disorder may be in nature, in the *hero's mind, within the family, within the state, or between states, or in all these, as in *King Lear* (1605). In Shakespeare's plays the moral, psychological, natural and political forms of disorder can generate one another. His vision reflects the breakdown of a unified Elizabethan world picture. (See CORRESPONDENCE.)

Disorder seems to lie at the centre of drama. It exists in *farce and *comedy as well as *tragedy. Indeed, a primary function of drama is to project and resolve it. An introductory text-book on the theme of disorder of Shakespeare is:

DUTHIE, G.I., *Shakespeare*, Hutchinson University Library, 1951, Ch. 2.

**Dissociation of sensibility**. A term coined by T.S. Eliot in his essay on the metaphysical poets (1921) and since used by literary critics to identify a change of sensibility 'setting in' after the early seventeenth-century 'metaphysical' period. This change Eliot identifies as a loss of 'a mechanism of sensibility that would devour any kind of experience'. It was 'aggravated by the influence of the two most powerful poets of the century, Milton and Dryden' and resulted, he claims, in a refinement in the *language* despite which 'the feeling became more crude'.

Such a generalization is stimulating but vast. Eliot seems to be talking about a decline which has been variously attributed to the rise of puritanism, the development of empiricism with Hobbes and Locke, the collapse of a poetic and mythologized picture of the natural world, the discoveries of Galileo (1564–1642) and Kepler (1571–1630), the growth of mercantilism, and the dominance of a new middle class. Linked with these is a change of sensibility between *Jacobean and later *Restoration theatre.

The questions raised are complex, but perhaps we can say that it is an absence of the *theatrical* that Eliot feels, an absence of ironic joking, of a capacity to energize and *play with opposed attitudes. He seems to identify a shift from a dramatic dynamism, produced by strongly competing possibilities of 'truth', which characterized the early seventeenth century, to a more secure and dogmatic tone which lasted until a resurgence of drama in the later nineteenth century. This new drama, it may be claimed, came out of cultural changes reminiscent of the early seventeenth century. The rise of empires and the decline of belief helped produce doubt, conflict, a new tragi-comic drama, the *modernist movement and the dramatic poetry and sardonic humour of Eliot's early work, in which he claims such affinity with the metaphysicals and Jacobeans.

That the above analysis is simplistic, if one comes to consider the parodistic, satirical and sardonic elements in Swift (1667–1745), Pope (1688–1744), Sterne (1713–68), Congreve (1670–1729) and

Sheridan (1751–1816) is obvious, and may be a reason for Eliot's later embarrassment at the term's popularity. Or it may be that the sensibilities of, say, Coleridge (1772–1834) and Keats (1795–1821) can scarcely be held to be 'dissociated'. Or again one may challenge Eliot's original claim that Milton and Dryden are guilty of fostering such a separation of thought and feeling.

Perhaps it is wisest to see the term as relating, not to the major writers of the *Enlightenment or of *romanticism, but to minor writers and a general cultural change. Again, however, the sense of a change, even in the major writers, and a general narrowing of the capacity to handle a vast range of experience (occurring some years before the Commonwealth) tells us that Eliot had supplied a phrase for a real cultural shift, and that this has something to do with the production of drama.

**Distance**. The physical distance between characters on stage, between stage and audience, and between spectators in the audience is very important. Closeness establishes intimacy and immediacy, whether it is between actors who really watch each other or between tightly packed spectators. The absence of arm-rests in the *auditorium can create the sense of togetherness on which the theatre thrives. The greater the distance between stage and audience, the greater the importance of group move-ment on stage. The closer an audience, the more artificial it seems to deny the audience's presence. See SPACE.

**Distancing**. See ALIENATION EFFECT; ESTRANGEMENT.

**Dithyramb**. According to the earliest account in Aristotle's *Poetics* (335–323 B.C.), *tragedy developed from improvisations by the leaders of *dithyrambs, which seem to have been hymns sung and danced in honour of *Dionysos, god of wine. They may originally have been songs with a refrain sung by a *chorus. Arion is credited with writing dithyrambs on heroic subjects and giving them titles, Thespis with adding lines and a spoken *prologue to elements of dance, song and lyric poetry.

The first day of the *City Dionysia in classical Athens was given over to the performance of dithyrambs. Episodes from the life of Dionysos, it seems, were mimed and narrated in a powerful chant.

The rhythmical form was used by Dryden (1631–1700) in his poem *Alexander's Feast* (1697).

**Doctor**. '*Il dottore*': a character from the *Commedia dell'Arte*. Crammed with classical quotations, he was a pedantic loquacious bore from the university city of Bologna and inevitably, like *Pantaloon, an enemy of the young. As he appeared in 1560, with his black gown and book, he wore a black or flesh-coloured half-mask, above red cheeks, bulbous nose and short beard. Magnificent platitudes and mountains of miscellaneous and curious information issued from his lips. His influence can perhaps be seen in Shakespeare's Holofernes, the pedagogue of *Love's Labour's Lost* (1595).

**Documentary drama**. This implies a drama which deals with contemporary social problems, usually in a direct and *naturalistic way. It is associated with the rise of left-wing theatre since the First World War. Piscator (1893–1966), in Weimar Germany, used film and complicated stage machinery to reflect contemporary events. In America in the 1930s, the Federal Theatre Project developed *The Living Newspaper, which dramatized public issues (until the government closed it down in 1939). More recently, with the impetus given by World War II to film documentary, and the subsequent growth of television, the term has come to suggest TV plays on contemporary social issues, but with fictional characters, such as Jeremy Sandford's *Cathy Come Home* (1966), and Alan Bleasdale's *Boys from the Black Stuff* (1985). *Fringe Theatre has also been very much concerned with such theatre — John McGrath's *The Cheviot, the Stag and the Black, Black Oil* (1981), for example, examines social and political problems associated with North Sea oil. The play, however, uses satirical and caricatural techniques which carry it beyond the *naturalism of TV documentary.

The attempt to convey in drama the 'reality' of contemporary issues raises problems concerning the dramatic form. How can a two-hour play do justice to the complexity of a political event? The brevity of the form, the need to select and the casting of actors, all change the nature of what is being represented. Drama *mediates* actuality and also fictionalizes it, hence the various means adopted by dramatists who wish to render 'reality': the use of the longer TV serial (Bleasdale); the use of *parable and *allegory (Brecht); the exposure of the conventions of the theatre illusion as part of the performance (Brecht and Pirandello); and the use of *farce, *comic heightening (Dario Fo) and the *happening.

Sartre's essay, *Myth and Reality in the Theatre* (1966), calls attention to how, in documentary theatre, or *'theatre of fact' as he calls it, the 'illusion may swallow the real', whereas in a happening 'the real swallows the illusion'. See REALISM.

**Domestic drama**. General term for plays concerned with family problems. Domestic drama developed with the growth of middle-class audiences in the early eighteenth century. This development reached its height with the domestic interiors of *naturalist drama in the later nineteenth century. More recently the range has extended to radio and TV serials reflecting middle- and working-class life.

One of the problems of this *genre is its confinement on stage to the family living-room, and methods have to be evolved of relating the family to the wider world. Work relationships, of course, can at least be discussed over meals. Neighbours and relations can introduce fresh material, and the entry of a stranger generates interest and disquiet. Properties, such as newspapers, may refer to contemporary events, and the play's past and the play's future encompass the enacted scene. Although the genre may appear narrow, Ibsen (1898–1906), Chekhov (1860–1904) and other important naturalist writers showed what could be done with domestic theatre.

An English play which illustrates the strengths of the genre is D.H. Lawrence's *The Daughter in Law* (1912). This play compares two homes in which there is family and class tension. A vivid impression of a working world is created, with attendant social problems (a miner's strike). The dialogue communicates a strong impression of a rich world outside. It is, however, the strong family tensions which impart power to the play, as they do to Lawrence's novel, *Sons and Lovers* (1913), to which it seems closely related.

BERNBAUM, E., *The Drama of Sensibility: a sketch of the history of English sentimental comedy and domestic tragedy*, Harvard University Press/ Oxford University Press, 1925.

**Domestic melodrama**. A category of nineteenth-century *melodrama, set in humble urban or rural homes and concerned with the sufferings of the family. The many 'temperance melodramas', sponsored by temperance organizations, in which heroes go to ruin, then reform and swear never to allow alcohol to pass their lips again, often belong to this genre. They derive, fairly clearly, from eighteenth-century *sentimental comedy, with its reforming dissolute rake.

**Domus**. *Mansion in *medieval drama.

**Doors of entrance**. Doors which opened onto the *forestages of *Restoration playhouses. See PROSCENIUM DOORS.

**Double**. Two parts, in a single play, written to be played by the same actor.

**Double act**. Entertainment in the form of a comic encounter between two performers, one of whom, the *straight man, 'feeds' the zany and illogical behaviour of the other. The pairing of Ernie Wise and Eric Morecambe is only one of the most recent of a long tradition of comic couples, found in *music hall entertainers and *circus clowns. The tradition stretches back through Shakespeare's Beatrice and Benedict, and Dogberry and Verges, to the older varieties of *fooling which always seem to emphasize the duality of man's nature and situation. In their chatter they seem to present a distorting mirror to one another and to their audience, in which, despite the distortion, some uncomfortable truths can be seen.

**Double masque**. Late and more complicated form of *masque in which there were two groups of characters. A performer could appear in each group under a different guise, instead of retaining the same *mask throughout.

**Double plot**. A plot in which two stories run side by side without either becoming dominant. A device used by Middleton in *Women Beware Women* (1621) where the Isabella-Hippolyte story is too strong to be described as a *sub-plot.

Sub-plots are more common than double plots because there is always a tendency for one plot to prove more interesting or popular. When equal time is given to the less popular plot, the audience can become impatient and the material seem unbalanced. This arguably happens in Shakespeare's *Much Ado about Nothing* (1598–9). The functions of a double plot are similar to those of a sub-plot.

EMPSON, W.H., *Some Versions of Pastoral*, Chatto and Windus, 1935, Ch. II.

**Downstage**. Area of stage close to the audience. The term derives from the period of the *raked stage. See UPSTAGE.

**Draft**. Part of the preliminary process of writing a play. Drafting a scene is an act of discovery. It explores the different ways in which characters respond and situations develop. Revisions are constantly required as ideas occur and the author struggles to reconcile their expression with the demands of the medium. He must, for example, take account of time needed for scene- and costume-changes, of the actor's or audience's need for a rest, and the maintenance of balance and *tempo. A play cannot afford lapses of interest, and only continual drafting and redrafting will ensure that they do not occur. To be sure, Ben Jonson said that Shakespeare never blotted a line. For apprentices, lesser mortals, and even a major dramatist such as Ibsen, the process is less miraculous.

**Drag**. Female apparel worn by male actor. See ROLE REVERSAL.

**Drama**. Art-form involving the physical embodiment of a story. Its requirements are a *space and a person pretending to be someone other than himself, who enacts a story in front of another person who accepts the pretence.

Drama derives from the Doric Greek '*dran*', to do, and may exist without *dialogue. It is a very broad art form and has different modes of expression, which it shares with *ballet, *opera, *music, painting, architecture, *poetry, fiction, and *film. The central basis, however, is the relationship between actor and actor, or actor and spectator. See MYTHOS; ORIGINS OF DRAMA; THEATRE LANGUAGE.

**Drama in education**. The importance of *drama as a means of learning has long been known, and determined efforts have been made to extend its use in educational institutions. See THEATRE IN EDUCATION; LEARNING AND DRAMA.
WAGNER, B.J., *Drama as a Teaching Medium*, Hutchinson, 1979.

**Dramatic criticism**. Criticism of drama responds to different aspects of the dramatic process. It may examine a play's cultural origins, its author's attitudes, the play's structure and content, the actor's performances, the style of production. The audience response takes different forms. It may be a response to performance, an analysis and evaluation of a production, an analysis of dramatic structure and/or content, or a concern with the value, purpose and potential impact of a play. It may also be concerned to place a play in a historical context.
PAVIS, P., *Languages of the Stage*, Performing Arts, NY, 1982, pp.97–107.

**Dramatic history**. See HISTORY OF DRAMA.

**Dramatic irony**. See IRONY.

**Dramatic monologue**. *Monologue within or even constituting a play. It is more particularly used of long poems in which a dramatic *character addresses a reader or listener. Robert Browning's *My Last Duchess* (1864) is a famous example. Listeners are addressed as if they belong to the world of the poem, so that they take on a role the monologue assumes.

A similar (but not identical) intimacy between speaker and reader is to be found in T.S. Eliot's dramatic monologue, *The Love Song of J. Alfred Prufrock* (1915), which begins, 'Let us go then, you and I . . .'. The relationship between author and speaking character, character and the listener addressed, the listener addressed and the reader, and the author and the reader, is complex, indirect and dramatic.
SINFIELD, A., *The Dramatic Monologue*, Critical Idiom Series, Methuen, 1977.

**Dramatic poetry**. See POETIC DRAMA.

**Dramatic prose**. See PROSE DRAMA.

**Dramatic verse**. Metrical language expressing heightened emotion in a dramatic situation. Most European drama, originating in *ritual, was written in metre up to the later seventeenth century, though dramatic *prose was increasingly used in the *Jacobean period, especially for *comedy. Verse was employed in much nineteenth-century *Romantic drama and Wordsworth, Coleridge, Keats, Shelley, Byron, Tennyson, Browning and others were drawn to its use. So too were Schiller and Goethe in Germany, Hugo in France and the earlier Ibsen in Norway among others. Prose, however, was the language of the *farce, *melodrama and social comedy of the popular theatres when they became the dominant modes in the eighteenth and nineteenth centuries. Attempts in the twentieth century to write in verse have been made by major poets including W.B. Yeats, W.H. Auden and T.S. Eliot. (See VERSE and POETIC DRAMA.)

Eliot's observations on the relation of poetry to the craft of drama are illuminating. He attempted, particularly in *The Family Reunion* (1938) and *The Cocktail Party* (1949), to find a flexible metre which at quieter dramatic moments could be heard as prose (for example, during the comic exchanges which open the latter play). Later the verse underpins a situation of greater intensity when the character's natural form of expression under emotional stress becomes poetic, as in Edward's duologue with the 'stranger'.

Within a play, therefore, dramatic verse, dramatic prose and dramatic poetry tend to shade into one another. It can also be argued that much *theatre language which is non-verbal, *stage imagery in particular, may be regarded as dramatic poetry, though this is a different use of a term normally restricted in its application to a text.

ELIOT, T.S., 'Rhetoric and Poetic Drama' (1919) and 'A Dialogue on Dramatic Poetry' (1928), in *Selected Essays*, Faber and Faber, 1932.

**Dramatis personae**. List of *characters in the play. A *cast list gives the names of actors.

**Dramatist**. Playwright; maker of drama. The dramatist is discoverable in the style, design and thematic concerns of a play. His presence, however, is often hard to define since he is only one part of a creative process.

**Dramatization**. The making of a play out of material originally presented in another form, as a diary, historical episode, short story or novel etc. Shakespeare converted prose romance and *chronicle history into drama. Medieval clerics and others gave the Bible dramatic form. Nineteenth-century melodramatists dramatized Scott and Dickens. Modern *fringe groups dramatize contemporary events — a strike, for example — by interviewing people involved. *Films and *television, of course, thrive on dramatizing many kinds of source material. See ADAPTATION.

**Dramaturg**. German term for a literary adviser, play-reader and press agent. He was attached to a professional theatre and his duties would include writing publicity for plays, actors and performances, *adapting texts, contributing to *rehearsals and selecting appropriate plays.

Lessing (1729–81) was the first *dramaturg* of the Hamburg National Theatre and his judicious reviewing, published in *Die Hamburgische Dramaturgie*, formed a critical basis on which German drama could develop.

Brecht became a *dramaturg* in Berlin in the early 1920s.

**Dramaturgy**. The art of writing for the theatre.

**Drame**. (a) Eighteenth-century French *domestic middle-class drama of a serious nature, which anticipated *sentimental comedy and includes the tearful or *weeping comedy of Nivelle de La Chaussée (1692–1754). Diderot used this term for his own plays. (b) A nineteenth-century French form of drama written both in prose and verse and described as 'romantic' ('*drame romantique*'). Victor Hugo discusses the term in his *Préface de Cromwell* (1827). The form is an expression of rebellion against the new classical *unities of *time and *space, retaining only unity of action. Where written in verse, it frees itself from stricter classical rules, allowing *enjambement* and displacement of the *caesura. Even such apparently mild adaptations of the rules provoked strong reactions when first introduced. Witness the riotous audience response to Hugo's *Hernani* (1830).

Generally, *drame* has melodramatic plots, high emotions and superficial characterization. It may thus be considered a form of *melodrama. Major English romantic poets, including Byron, Shelley and Keats, attempted this genre. Rostand's *Cyrano de Bergerac* (1897) is perhaps the last successful attempt at it.

**Drapes**. Side-curtains, whose function is to hide the sides of the picture-frame stage.

**Drawing-room comedy**. A kind of *domestic drama, akin to *farce, but perhaps with fuller characterization. It flourishes commercially in the *West End, as a source of mainly middle-class entertainment. Noel Coward's *Hay Fever* (1925) and the plays of William Douglas Home (1912–   ) are examples.

**Draws in, off, over**. Eighteenth-century stage directions. They refer to the practice of drawing *wings along grooves, either 'in' (i.e. onto) the stage, 'off' the stage or 'over' a wing belonging to a previous scene.

**Dream**. The characteristic structure of a dream, with its indirect symbolism, its illogicalities and anxieties, its dislocations in *time and *space, has been more closely associated with poetry, music, or film than with drama. A play normally needs causal, temporal and spatial coherence which is difficult to reconcile with the communciation of dream states. However, the desire to overthrow an expectation of *realism, and the querying of the nature of the 'real', has led major dramatists to incorporate forms of dreaming into their plays. Shakespeare, in *A Midsummer Night's Dream* (1595), was much concerned to study and create an atmosphere of dream. The late *Cymbeline* (1609), *The Winter's Tale* (1610) and *The Tempest* (1611) also have this quality. Characters sleep, dream, wake and find difficulty in separating the events of the play from dream. And audiences too, are invited to consider the imaginery events they witness to be a form of dream: 'These our actors, look you, are melted into air, into thin air . . .'.

Shakespeare's concern with dream was shared by other seventeenth-century dramatists, including Calderón (1600–81) who wrote the famous *La Vida es Sueño* ('Life is a Dream') in 1635. Between the later seventeenth and nineteenth centuries, however, drama was little concerned with dream states, despite the psychological interests of *romanticism and the connection between *gothic melodrama and nightmare. The exploration of obsession, fantasy and unconscious elements appears again, however, in the apparent *naturalism of Ibsen (1828–1906) and in the more revolutionary structures of the late Strindberg (*A Dream Play* (1902); *Ghost Sonata* (1907)).

The *expressionist and *surrealist movements were, of course, strongly preoccupied with dream. The *theatre of the absurd built on these movements and created fantastic situations which characters, like Ionesco's Béranger in *Rhinocéros* (1960), contemplate with the same lack of surprise as Kafka's characters confronting their nightmares. There has indeed been, in the twentieth century, a strong emphasis on dramatic situations which seem to be projections of subjective states. It is tempting to examine expressionist or absurdist plays as if they were dream material and interpret their 'latent meaning' by examining forms of displacement, *condensation and transference which Freud argues occur in the 'dream-work'. It is important to remember that the process of playwriting is highly conscious. As the playwright elaborates his material, the dream or fantasy is likely to be set against a more objective *'realism', as happens in Ibsen's *The Wild Duck* (1884).

Dream, fantasy and the processes of art are not identical, though obviously related. And if we agree that the dreamer, as well as the

lunatic, the lover and the poet, are 'of imagination all compact', we should remember that the speaker, Theseus in *A Midsummer Night's Dream*, was somewhat sceptical about the whole question.
FREUD, S., *The Interpretation of Dreams* (1900), Pelican, 1976.

**Drolls**. Short comic performances which developed during the Commonwealth period when long plays were banned from the stage. They generally involved *farce and *dance and were usually a crude rendering of popular material taken from a well-known play. *Bottom the Weaver*, abstracted from Shakespeare's *A Midsummer Night's Dream* (1595), or *The Gravedigger* from *Hamlet* (1601) are examples. They were played at inns and fairs, and were still being performed in England in 1800.

**Drop**. A back-drop or *backcloth lowered and raised, generally on rollers. It was introduced in the late seventeenth century, when its function was probably to conceal the back wall of the stage area, allowing actors off-stage passage behind in less well-equipped theatres. It also offered a large flat surface for *scene-painting, and came to be preferred to the earlier pair of *flats in *grooves which closed off the rear of the stage.

**Drum and shaft**. Former scene-shifting device which moved scenery attached by ropes to a turning shaft. The different pieces could be moved simultaneously, with economy of effort, and controlled effects were achieved by using a shaft of varying diameter to move scenery at varying speeds.

**Dry**. An actor who loses his lines in performance is said to dry. The reason may be anxiety, or some loss of *concentration caused by noise in the audience or some unexpected variation in performance. Equally, some irrelevant thought may have been permitted to enter the actor's mind. See CIRCLE OF ATTENTION.

**Dumb ballet**. A nineteenth-century form of theatre involving acrobatic use of the various kinds of *trap. *Ki-Ko-Kookeree* (1871) is an example.

**Dumb show**. A dramatic device whereby events in a play are mimed rather than acted out in *dialogue. They were used in the *interludes of Renaissance Italy and revived in England in *Gorboduc* (1560), the first full-length tragedy in English. The device was freely used by Elizabethan and Jacobean dramatists such as Webster (*c*.1580–1634) and Middleton (*c*.1570–1627). The most famous usage is no doubt in the 'play scene' of Shakespeare's *Hamlet* (1601).
The functions of a dumb show varied. It could, as in *Gorboduc*,

summarize the events of the following acts, and clarify a complex story for the audience. It also created suspense: 'first the music of the hautboys began to play, during which time they came forth, as though out of hell three furies ... Hereby was signified the unnatural murders to follow'. The three witches in *Macbeth* (1606), though not in dumb show, seem to be a refinement of this prophetic function.

The dumb show could accelerate the events of the *plot, like the dumb show in Middleton's *The Changeling* (1622) which enacts Beatrice's wedding. The device also provides variety of dramatic style, thereby sustaining dramatic interest.

In *Hamlet* the function of the dumb show is complex. It summarizes the action of Hamlet's 'Mousetrap', and in J. Dover Wilson's view is an 'extra' incorporated into the performance by the Players. It thus comes as a surprise to Hamlet, who is afraid it will give the game away to Claudius (who must not know what is to happen). Claudius, therefore, must not watch, says Wilson. Harley Granville-Barker disagrees. It seems likely, however, that the dumb show allows the audience to understand what the players are going to perform so that it can focus on the responses of Claudius, who is watching upstage.

MEHL, D., *The Elizabethan Dumb Show; the history of a dramatic convention*, Methuen, 1965.

**Duodrama**. A short theatrical entertainment, developed in Germany in the later eighteenth century as part of a triple bill. It involved a number of silent actors and two speaking roles (as compared with *monodrama, which has only one).

**Duologue**. A dialogue exchange between two characters. The *epeisodia* of *Greek tragedy were frequently duologues between the *protagonist and one other actor. Shakespeare often uses duologues to supply information, advance the action, and provide *contrast with fuller 'public' scenes. Chekhov's plays reveal many contrasting character relationships through duologue.

# E

**Eccentrism**. A term invented by Grigori Kozintsev, Georgy Kryzhitski and Leonid Trauberg to describe their experiments at the studio theatre which they opened in Petrograd in 1921 called the 'Factory of Eccentrism' (FEKS). The term describes a style which some have identified with Tolstoy's comedy, *The First Distiller*, produced by Annenkov in 1919. In it circus acrobats enact a scene in hell by means of a flying ballet.

Meyerhold's production in 1922 of Sukhovo-Kobylin's *Tarelskin's Death* is another antecedent. Acrobatics, knockabout comedy, surprise effects with collapsible tables and helter-skelter chases are a mark of its style.

BRAUN, E., ed., *Meyerhold on Theatre*, Hill and Wang/Methuen, 1969.

**Editing**. The process of joining together the various shots or *takes of a film in a particular narrative sequence.

**Effects man**. Man responsible for *sound effects.

**Egyptian drama**. The growth of Egyptian and Mesopotamian civilizations over 5000 years ago suggests the existence of important dramatic activity. It is likely that priests enacted rituals to ensure the continuity of life and the well-being of a dead pharaoh. Certain 'pyramid texts' have passages of dialogue which suggest dramatic performance (2800–2400 B.C.) though there is no definite evidence for this. A ritual called the 'Memphite Drama' seems to have been performed on the first day of spring every year, telling of the death and resurrection of Osiris and the crowning of Horus. It is possible that the pharaoh impersonated Horus on this occasion. For 2000 years, until 550 B.C., another annual ritual was performed at Akydos. It related to Osiris but no part of a text remains. The performance may have been an elaborate spectacle, performed over a long period, enacting the life and death of Osiris. Some historians argue that it was a spectacular funeral ceremony, rather than a kind of *passion play. Whatever the nature of the ritual performances, it seems that an independent theatre with new plays every year, such as became established in Greece, did not arise in Egypt. The rituals must have been repetitive, and their aim the preservation of a static society.

GASTER, T., *Thespis: Ritual Myth and Drama in the Ancient Near East*, Norton, NY, 1977.

**Eighteenth-century drama**. Congreve's *Way of the World* (1700) marked a time when audiences, and consequently public demand, were changing. The work of Vanbrugh (1664–1726) and Farquhar (1678–1707) reveal the forms and attitudes of the earlier, aristocratic Restoration drama, but a new and mixed audience, consequent on the 'bloodless revolution' of 1688, resulted in the rise of *sentimental comedy and *bourgeois tragedy, which, despite a certain loss of vitality, can be seen as a widening of sensibility.

As court patronage fell away, so the middle-class attacks on the theatre (inherent in Puritanism and expressed from the establishment of the first professional theatres onwards) had to be taken into account. Collier's *A Short View of the Immorality and Profaneness of the English Stage* (1698) provoked attack (by, for instance, Vanbrugh). It also encouraged an impulse towards reform, as in Farquhar's later work, and helped break the brittle aristocratic mould. The successful merchant class joined the 'fashionable' audience, and slowly influenced the offerings of playwrights of the new class.

The eighteenth-century was a confused period. An emphasis on spectacle, characteristic of aristocratic performances from the court *masque onwards, and the Restoration theatre's cult of actors and actresses, particularly the latter, continued side by side with a drama which mirrored the desire of the new middle class for flattering moral reflections.

Three interesting forms arose: *ballad opera, bourgeois tragedy and sentimental comedy. The first of these was a promising satirical form, best represented by Gay's *The Beggar's Opera* (1728) and its sequel *Polly* (1728). The *Licensing Act of 1737, however, cut short its life. Bourgeois tragedy, represented by Lillo's *The London Merchant* (1731) extended the range of dramatic sympathy beyond the traditional aristocratic hero and influenced the work of Lessing (1727–1781), in Germany, and Diderot (1713–1784), in France. In England, however, though the theatre expanded, the quality of dramatic writing was low. Only the revival of *high comedy in the work of Goldsmith (1730–1774), and Sheridan (1757–1816) stands out. Otherwise the eighteenth-century playgoer was provided with a diet of *farce, *pantomine, *burlesque and *melodrama.

BERNBAUM, E., *The Drama of Sensibility*, Harvard University Press/ Oxford University Press, 1925.

VAN LENNEP, W., *et al.* (eds.), *The London Stage*, Parts I–V, Southern Illinois University Press, 1960–8.

**Eiron**. 'Dissembler'. A comic character *type which Northrop Frye sets against the *Alazon or braggart in his interesting dramatic typology. Eirons may be of different kinds. They may dissemble so as to trap people into a recognition of the truth — like the Socrates

of Plato's *Dialogues*. Other dissemblers may wish to avoid responsibility and commitment (see Theophrastus's *Characters*). But whichever of these it is, an eiron's dissembling creates dramatic interest out of the *ironic contrast between two different worlds.
FRYE, N., *Anatomy of Criticism*, Princeton University Press, 1957.

**Ekkyklema**. Greek term for a stage device in the Greek theatre. The word suggests either a rotating stage or some kind of *tableau or stage-setting, 'wheeled out', perhaps, through the large central doors of the *skene. It may have been used to display the corpses of Agamemnon and Cassandra after their murder in Aeschylus's *Oresteia* (458 B.C.).
WEBSTER, T.B.L., *Greek Theatre Productions*, 2nd ed., Methuen, 1970.

**Electricity**. Electric lighting was introduced into the theatre in the 1880s, achieving a saving in manpower and a greater degree of safety after the many fires in the gas-lit theatres. The principles of stage *lighting changed gradually at first, then radically at the turn of the century when the work of Appia (1862–1978) and Craig (1872–1966) revealed how the growing sophistication of electrical equipment could make of stage lighting a very subtle instrument.

**Eliot, T.S.** (1888–1965). American poet, critic and dramatist. His plays employ a wide variety of styles and dramatic structures. They include the *pageant, the Greek *chorus, the thriller, *drawing-room comedy and *farce.

I say that prose drama is a slight by-product of verse drama.

The human soul in intense emotion strives to express itself in verse.

See: AGON; ALLEGORY; BUFFOON; CORRESPONDENCE; DISSOCIATION OF SENSIBILITY; DRAMATIC VERSE; OBJECTIVE CORRELATIVE; POETIC DRAMA; REORGANIZATION; TRADITION.
ELIOT, T.S., *Poetry and Drama*, Faber, 1951.

**Elizabethan Stage Society**. Society founded by William Poel in 1894 as a form of protest against performances of Shakespeare on encumbered Victorian stages. It sought conditions close to those for which the plays were written, i.e. with little scenery, on *thrust stages, without *proscenium arch, and with the emphasis on rapid *scene changes and a fast *tempo. It was a major influence on twentieth-century Shakespeare production.

**Elizabethan theatre.** (a) The drama of the late sixteenth and early seventeenth centuries. The term is often used to include *Jacobean drama, written after the death of Queen Elizabeth in 1603. (b) The building for which this drama was written. Evidence, especially visual evidence, is extremely meagre, but it indicates a circular

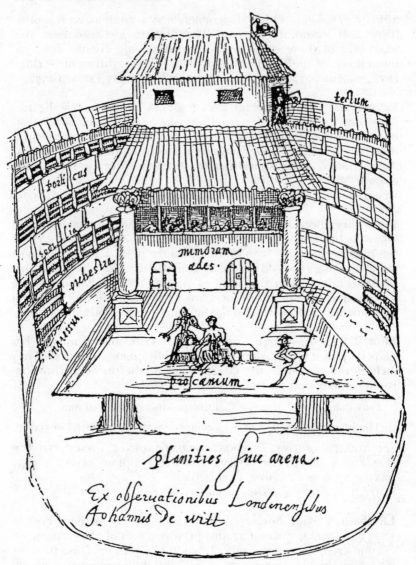

**6** *The famous copy of de Witt's drawing of the Swan Theatre in London about 1596. The most important piece of contemporary pictorial evidence regarding the interior of an Elizabethan playhouse.*

*auditorium with an audience in three tiers, on three sides of a very deep (8.4m), very wide (13m), *thrust stage, with at least two acting levels. There was little *scenery. Scene changes were fast and frequent. The large stage permitted sophisticated *grouping, with different characters and groups watching and commenting on each other. In addition, direct audience address from *downstage positions could be varied with *upstage performance which did not acknowledge the presence of an audience. Iago in *Othello* (1604) and Edmund in *King Lear* (1605) frequently inform the audience of their intentions and then move upstage to carry them out.

The fact that the audience was close, and roughly equidistant from the central downstage position, meant that it was more aware of changes in acting style than audiences containing spectators who were both close and distant. Iago and Edmund can quietly confide in the audience and then give a subtly changed performance for the benefit of the other characters. The thrust stage allows an actor to make clear the delicate distinction between characters who are 'natural' and characters who pretend. Such nuances in perform-ance probably paralleled the variously colloquial, ceremonial and highly artificial language of Hamlet, Claudius and the Player King in the famous 'play-scene' is *Hamlet*, where different styles of acting seem to be coordinated with different forms of human behaviour and speech.

In brief, the Elizabethan theatre allowed for the mingling of old styles, deriving from a formal and symbolic *medieval drama, and a new individualism and informality. It became a microcosm which reflected historical changes and made its appeal to all levels of society in as various and extraordinary an upsurge of dramatic expression as the world has seen. It is entirely appropriate that its most famous playhouse was called the Globe.

GURR, A., *Shakespeare's Theatre*, Cambridge University Press, 1970.

**Elocution**. The art of public speaking. The term has become less popular as views of what constitutes 'proper' English have widened. It now has a snobbish ring, and 'voice-training' is preferred. Whatever the name, clear articulation, training in breathing and *projection, and the control of *stress, *intonation and all verbal colouring, remain essential in all drama dependent on speech. See DICTION.

**Emotion**. Strong feeling. An aroused state which manifests itself differently according to the nature of the emotion felt. Emotions can be spontaneous responses to physical danger or personal threat. They may express themselves in flight or aggression (fear and *anger). They may tend to the appropriation of others, or to the sinking of the self in others (desire and love). They may equally arise out of attitudes of approval or disapproval of the self (pride and shame) or of other people (liking or disgust). The attraction or repulsion which emotions seem to manifest is often bound up in aesthetic as well as moral forms of response. The beautiful attracts; the ugly repels. Emotions thus tend to express themselves in *action*. They are fundamentally dramatic, and actors and writers, through introspection and *observation, study them carefully.

An *audience is made to feel emotion by sympathetic response to a *character's emotions. But this is not the only way. An audience can also feel repugnance for a character, or for what he or she stands for. In some plays the response may be a subtle mixture of the sympathetic and the disapproving. (See EMPATHY; IDENTIFICATION; PITY; FEAR; CATHARSIS.)

Emotional response is intensified by awareness of the dramatic situation. Emotions are felt not only for what is happening to a character in the present, but in terms of what has happened or might have happened in the past, and what will happen or might happen in the future. *Dramatic irony thus extends and complicates our feelings.

Plays also operate upon our basic responses through effects of *light, *colour, *rhythm and so on which again involve movements of attraction and repulsion. Indeed one might suggest that the greater the extremes of attraction and repulsion in a play the more powerful it will be as drama. Such a crude rule of thumb might apply to the heroism and monstrosity of the *Greek theatre and the extremes of *Jacobean tragedy — or for that matter of Ibsen and Strindberg. Perhaps, however, it applies more to *tragedy than to *comedy.

SARTRE, J.-P., *Sketch for a Theory of the Emotions*, Methuen, 1962.

JAMES, W., *Principles of Psychology* (1890), Encyclopaedia Britannica, 1952.

**Emotion memory**. Stanislavski's term (taken from the psychologist Ribot) for the process whereby the actor develops his capacity to recall personal experiences and emotions, and uses them in the creation of a *role: 'If the bird does not rise of its own accord . . ., you have to coax it, whistle to it, use various lures . . .'. One of Stanislavski's 'lures' was to ask an actor to rediscover his own past. If the past is seen as a number of houses, the actor was to focus on one 'house' in his past, then on a room, then on a cupboard within the room, then on a drawer within the cupboard, then a box within the drawer, then a bead lost from the tiniest box . . . In this way the actor might discover tiny details which could illuminate, and be incorporated into, a role. The effect of such work was to strengthen the role's emotional basis.

**Emotion of multitude**. See SUB-PLOT; PARALLELISM.

**Empathy**. Term often used loosely as a synonym for *identification or *sympathy. It is, however, worth making some distinctions. Empathy was originally a translation of the German '*Einfühlung*', which, as developed by Lotze in 1858, meant a physical or kinetic response to an object, or to the physical activity of animals, birds or

human beings. Thus, as applied to drama, it could imply a kind of
*physical* sympathy with the stage setting and dramatic activity. This
physical element is often forgotten in the common use of the term
to suggest participation in the feelings of another person.

The term, however, is more complex. The *Shorter Oxford
Dictionary* defines empathy as 'the power of projecting one's
personality into, and so fully comprehending the object of
contemplation'. This implies both a *movement towards*, which is
mental, or physical (or both) and a subsequent *standing off* or
'contemplation', leading to a process of *comprehension*. In this
double process there is both *sympathy and detachment.

An audience's response to a dramatic situation is always apt to be
more than simple identification with characters. It is true that
Brecht (1898–1956) spoke of *dramatic response as simple ('I weep
when they weep, I laugh when they laugh') and set against it *epic
response ('I weep when they laugh. I laugh when they weep'). But,
in practice, 'dramatic' and 'epic' overlap in complex ways. In the
theatre an audience sees a whole picture, and compares the
character response. It judges who is deserving of sympathy and
tends to weep for characters who refuse to weep for themselves but
weep for others. Empathy can spring from an audience's awareness
of a character's awareness of more than his or her own suffering.
Sympathy here is increased by a kind of distancing. See EMOTION;
ALIENATION; ESTRANGEMENT; IDENTIFICATION.

**Ending**. The action with which a writer concludes a story. It is not
easy to convince an audience that a story is fully told, and though
some writers aim to create a sense of dissatisfaction with the
ending, the normal expectation since Aristotle's *Poetics* has been
that an ending should satisfy. See CATHARSIS; BEGINNING, MIDDLE
AND END; EPIC DRAMA.

V. Shklovski, in an essay contributed to T. Todorov's *Théorie de la
Littérature* (Seuil, 1965, pp.170–96) argues that endings occur
when: (a) a relationship between characters shifts to its opposite;
(b) a prediction we fear is realised; (c) a problem posed has been
solved; and (d) a situation misrepresented or misunderstood at the
beginning is rectified. He adds that endings are also made evident
through the *epilogue to an episodic story, which shows us, for
example, the hero ten years on. 'Illusory endings' may also be
employed. These, he adds, are usually furnished by 'descriptions of
nature or the weather'. If we relate Shklovski's four types to the
four most famous plays of Shakespeare, we find they fall with some
qualification into these categories. In *Othello* (1604) the relation
between Othello and Iago shifts to its opposite, though the relation
between Othello and Desdemona has shifted earlier and now
reverts to a former state. (The shifting to an opposite state was not
conclusive in itself.) In *Macbeth* (1606) there is a realization of a

prediction, that the *hero 'shalt be king hereafter', but this again comes earlier, and further prophecies, together with the hero's realization of their full significance, are needed to provide an ending. In *Hamlet* (1601) a problem posed is solved finally with the recognition of Claudius's guilt, and his death. Hamlet's death, however, involves the death of others, and leaves unanswered questions: 'the rest is silence' are words which linger in the mind. *King Lear* falls into Shklovski's last category: a situation misunderstood. The rectification, however, of the king's misunderstanding, as he emerges from madness and is reconciled with Cordelia, occurs a little before the end. The ultimate conclusion of their mutual deaths comments ironically on the earlier 'rectification'.

Perhaps we can say that endings which recognize their own incompleteness leave a greater sense of satisfaction than those which pretend to completeness. This seems to be true of comic endings too. The audience is made accomplice to a *convention. A wedding is only an apparent ending. The audience knows it and the play, perhaps in an *epilogue, can acknowledge it.

Shklovski speaks of particular 'illusory' endings but in a way all endings are 'illusory'. Descriptions of nature and the weather may seem more illusory at the end of a novel (see D.H. Lawrence's *The Rainbow* (1915)) because a *metaphor or *symbol is being imposed upon a *'realist' form. It is a matter of shared convention and expectation. The endings of a play tend to acknowledge this. A stage picture; a dead prince high on a platform with an armoured figure beside him; an old woman pulling a waggon; the sound of an axe chopping down an orchard; these supply 'satisfactory' endings because they summarize, in some way, the scenes which have been presented.

Drama may also use musical means, a dance, a funeral march, or a *choral song, to impose a sense of conclusion, but whatever the means, something which tells the audience it is time to go home is necessary. Our need for patterns and solutions may arise because we seek solace in a world which denies the possibility of order. Or we may wish to assert the existence of order in the world which drama reflects. However this may be, a problem arises. 'Relations stop nowhere', as Henry James observed in the 1909 Preface to *Roderick Hudson* (1876). The artist must make 'relations' appear to cease, respecting, but at the same time ignoring, the continuity of things. For an interesting literary study see:
KERMODE, F., *The Sense of an Ending*, Oxford University Press, 1966.

**Ends and means**. The problem of whether good ends can be achieved by evil means, or whether good means always result in good ends, has been explored in *political and other theatre from the Greeks to the present day. The ethical problems involved are intensely dramatic, whether presented as a conflict between two powerful characters arguing opposed moralities (such as Antigone and Creon in Sophocles's play) or arousing sympathetic feelings for a character forced to make a difficult choice (Othello killing Desdemona as an act of 'justice'). In *Antigone* and *Othello*, the issues are relatively clear. Othello and Creon are wrong. But there are plays in which an evil means may lead to a 'good' end: for example, the killing of Claudius in *Hamlet* (1601) or of Clytemnestra in *The Oresteia* (458 B.C.).

In modern plays the problem has often emerged as a choice between the good of the individual and the good of the community. This is Kattrin's choice in Scene Eleven of *Mother Courage* (1941). Sartre's *Lucifer and the Lord* (1951) sardonically analyses a series of situations in which the means chosen to achieve a particular good fail to achieve the ends envisaged.

In English drama, Charles Morgan's *The River Line* (1952) is a simpler play in which an individual is forced to choose between the life of an individual and risking the lives of a whole group. The problem, as with Sartre, is that choices must be made half in ignorance of the circumstances which compel the choice.

Arthur Koestler's *The Yogi and the Commissar* (1945) is an attractive essay on this question. His novel, later dramatized, *Darkness at Noon* (1940), is a fuller exploration of the psychology of men in positions of political power, who believe, or cease to believe, that the end justifies the means.

**End-stage**. A stage which occupies the end of a theatre building, but which is not separated from the auditorium by a *proscenium arch. (See illustration overleaf.)
JOSEPH, S., *New Theatre Forms*, Pitman, NY, 1968.

**Energy**. The capacity of a physical system for doing work. Energy is very important in the theatre, where the intensity of a dramatic experience seems directly related to the energy generated by the performers. The process is mysterious but crucial.

**English Comedians**. A name given to a number of companies of English actors who travelled through Europe in the later sixteenth and seventeenth centuries.

In 1585 the Earl of Leicester took William Kempe (?–1603), the famous Elizabethan *clown, together with other actors, on a campaign in Holland. They played to the Danish court of Elsinore and were invited to Dresden. In 1592 Robert Browne took a company on a long tour abroad, performing *jigs, *interludes, comedies such as *Gammer Gurton's Needle* (1566) and mutilated versions of Marlowe's plays. Since they performed in English, the more difficult passages were cut. Farcical elements became more prominent, and music and dance were added, as can be seen from

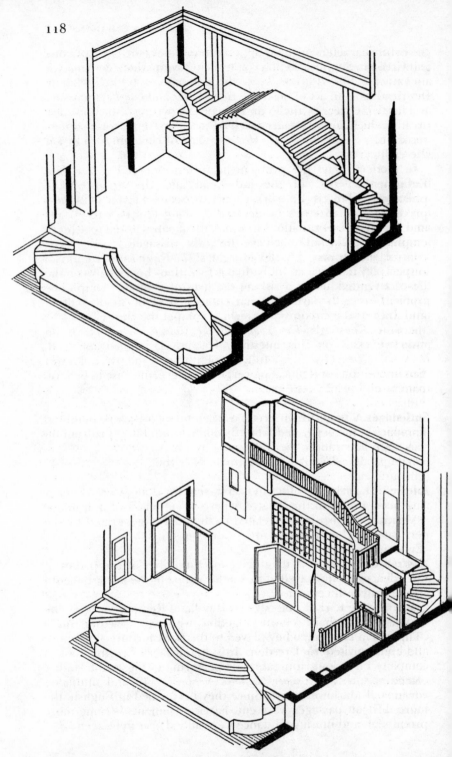

**7** *Copeau's end stage at the Théâtre du Vieux Colombier, showing how Louis Jouvet adapted it for a production of* The Brothers Karamazov

the collections of performed texts printed in 1620 and 1630. Native actors then joined the various troupes, which began to play wholly in German, instead of using low German only in the comic interludes.

Their emphasis on rumbustious and violent action can be seen as an influence in the *Haupt und Staatsaktionen*. The last authentic record of performance is 1659, though the name was still used in the eighteenth century, such was their fame and popularity.

**Enlightenment**. Name given to the period of development of philosophy and science which followed from the Renaissance and preceded *romanticism. In effect, this means the late seventeenth and eighteenth centuries. Works of this period tended to place emphasis on classical models; they were concerned with formal control, refinement of language, decorum and social polish, and a respect for reason and education. *Satire and *allegory were characteristic forms, and in the theatre the dominant mode was comic. Lessing (1729–81) in Germany, and Voltaire (1694–1778) and Diderot (1713–84) in France, were the important dramatic theorists of the period.
CARLSON, M., *Theories of the Theatre*, Cornell, 1984, pp.37–197.

**Ensemble**. Permanent acting company, working together with a community of aims and evolving its own style and techniques. The *Elizabethan and *Commedia dell'Arte troupes might be called ensembles. The term, however, is more readily applied to modern companies, including Brecht's *Berliner Ensemble. The ensemble has many advantages over the company which assembles only for a single production. The members develop an understanding which encourages mutual confidence in performance, fuller exploration of the text performed and more detailed and imaginative *grouping and *movement. This has been seen in ensembles from the *Meininger Company to the *Royal Shakespeare today.

**Entrance**. The emergence of an actor into the view of the audience. Entrances require careful timing and confidence. Actors must be 'in role' as they enter, giving the impression that they have just come from some other place within the fiction of the play — the garden or an adjoining room — rather than from the *wings or the dressing room. Good entrances establish the play's *continuity. They can also lend variety, create surprise and advance the *plot. Bad entrances weaken the 'suspension of disbelief'.

**Entremés**. A form of entertainment associated with the Spanish dramatists of the 'Golden Age', notably Cervantes (1547–1616), Lope de Vega (1562–1635) and Calderón (1606–81). The word originally suggested performances 'between courses' of a banquet, but came to refer to *interludes in religious processions and short entertainments between acts of plays in the public theatre.

**Entry**. Festive display to celebrate an important occasion, such as a military victory, a coronation, an accession to power or a wedding. They occurred in ancient Rome and in medieval cities. With the Renaissance they became extremely popular. The royal entry of Henry II of France into Rouen (1508) is one example. Richly costumed marchers and spectacular *tableaux would parade before the populace, or an important personage might himself parade before static platforms bearing *tableaux vivants*, and *dumb shows were performed.

The purpose of the entries was generally to demonstrate power and encourage loyalty and submission. They were the secular equivalents of the religious *pageants. The subjects, however, were classical and mythological. Displays often ended with a performance, banquet and dance in the ruler's palace. In this they anticipate the *court masque.

**Environmental theatre**. Term used to describe the experimental work of Richard Schechner (1934–   ), who founded the Performance Group in New York in 1967. Schechner believes in using theatre *space in original ways so as to intermingle actors and audience. Events occur which are not visible to the whole of the audience. Events can happen simultaneously so that an alternative *focus of attention is offered. Emphasis is placed on the sculptural elements of theatre: performers are treated as 'mass and volume, colour, texture and movement', and physicality and nudity play a large part. This was especially the case with *Dionysus in '69* which was developed from the orgiastic elements of Euripides's *Bacchae*. Influences include the *happening, Grotowski's *poor theatre techniques and the explorations of encounter groups.
SCHECHNER, R., *Environmental Theatre*, Hawthorn Books, NY, 1973.

**Epeisodia**. The episodes or *scenes in Greek drama, often consisting of confrontations between the major characters. They were separated from each other by *choral song and movement.

**Epic**. Narrative poem celebrating the exploits of some *hero of *myth, legend or history. Homer's *Odyssey* and *Iliad* (?8th century B.C.), Virgil's *Aeneid* (c.18 B.C.), *Beowulf* (10th century), the Finnish *Kalevala*, Dante's *Divina Commedia* (?1307–20), Milton's *Paradise Lost* and Wordsworth's *Prelude* are all examples. There is a comic epic tradition in prose which runs from Cervantes's *Don Quixote* (1605–15) to Fielding's *Tom Jones* (1749) and other 'picaresque' or 'quest' novels including James Joyce's *Ulysses* (1922).

The epic is long and spacious. It usually presents a journey in a number of self-contained *episodes which yet form a whole. Character does not change but there is a descent at some stage into a real or psychological underworld and it ends with a recovery and a return. All this is treated in a grand style which can communicate strong feelings of pride.

The length of epic, its *narrative elements and *episodic nature normally differentiate the *genre from drama. According to Northrop Frye the Bible is an epic of 'unsurpassed range, consistency and completeness'. For Eric Auerbach, however, a distinction is to be made between the epic style of Homer and the style of the *Old Testament*. Homer works by telling all; the Bible works by concealment: 'The Homeric style knows only a fore-ground, only a uniformly illuminated and uniformly objective present', whereas the Old Testament story of Abraham is 'like a silent progress through the indeterminate and the contingent'. In the first all is externalized. In the second only that which is necessary for the purpose of the narrative is there. All else remains mysterious and 'fraught with background'. If this seems a way of saying that the Bible is more dramatic it should be remembered how much Homer's episodes bequeathed to the Greek dramatists. The form of Homer's epics, however, contributed to Brecht's *epic drama and this was a theatre in rebellion against the form and idea of *tragedy.

AUERBACH, E., *Mimesis*, trs. W. Trask, Princeton University Press, 1957, Ch. 1.

CANDELARIA, F.H., and STRANGE, W.C., *Perspectives on Epic*, Allyn, 1965.

**Epic theatre**. A term closely associated with the work of Bertolt Brecht. It carries meanings deriving from German usage which suggest its episodic nature and concern with surface detail.

Epic theatre is not to be equated with the 'heroic'. Brecht's theatre is anti-heroic in the attitudes it takes to its *heroes. In his notes to the *opera *Aufstieg und Fall der Stadt Mahagonny* (*Rise and Fall of the City of Mahagonny*, 1929) Brecht defined his epic theatre in a series of antitheses. Epic, he says, focuses on *narrative rather than *plot. It forces a spectator to confront a world and take decisions about that world. It aims to send a spectator *active* into the world at the end of the play. This is diffrent from the effect of what Brecht calls 'Aristotelian drama'. Such plays 'implicated' spectators, involving them with the play's action, identifying them with individual characters, clouding with sensation their capacity for political judgement.

Brecht disapproved of plays which present the human being and human situation as unchangeable, where the plot is a kind of fate within which the character moves to an inevitable end. Caught in the *causality of events, the spectator, too, is unable to embrace the possibility that people both within and outside a play have some freedom to avert or control events. Brecht preferred a play to suggest more optimistic possibilities, *progressive and not deter-minist. He therefore structured his dramas as an appeal to the spectator's freedom, dividing his scenes from one another by gaps in time, so that the plays are, as the German suggests, *episodic, and the spectator has time to think. 'Each scene for itself', says Brecht, rather than 'one scene makes another'. The epic play uses *montage. It does not have a linear movement. It proceeds in 'jumps and curves' so as to avoid the spectator's absorption in a fiction, and the consequent *catharsis which in Brecht's view reduced the pressure to act in the world. In the gaps between and within the scenes, *alienation devices are used. Blocks of narrative are projected on screens. A *backcloth suggests the 'real' world outside the play (such as the nuclear explosion shown behind the playing of *Galileo*). In this way the connection between *story and history is emphasized. Epic drama and *allegory are thus related.

The distinction between epic and 'dramatic' theatre is useful, but too clear-cut. Brecht's theatre is an amalgam of many forms, including *morality and *chronicle plays. It uses techniques drawn from forms of *comedy and from *oriental theatre. Brecht also studied the structures of *Greek tragedy and the plays of Shakespeare, and knew that to label, say, Shakespeare, Sophocles, and Chekhov as 'dramatic' and his own plays as 'epic', was a simplification. These and other dramatists use what Brecht termed alienation devices and also possess epic elements. Brecht's theatre mingled the 'epic' and the 'dramatic'. In *Mother Courage* (1941) there is a tension between the *identifications of dramatic theatre and the *distancing or *estrangement of epic. This is both a source of power and a source of difficulty in the presentation. Mother Courage arouses *sympathy; like Oedipus and Lear she is stripped of almost all she possesses. The question for Brecht is, 'what has she learnt?', and the reply ('nothing') is meant to distance the spectator. In practice, however, much sympathy remains.

Brecht recognized this dramatic/epic tension. In 1953 he wrote, in *Kleines Organon für das Theater* (*A Short Organum for the Theatre*):

> . . . a sister lamenting that her brother is off to the war, and it is the peasant war: he is a peasant off to join the peasants. Are we to lose ourselves in her agony? Or not at all? We must be able to lose ourselves, and at the same time not to. Our mutual emotion will come from recognizing and feeling the *double process* [italics added].

Brecht's epic theatre, then, like Shakespeare's, mingles a variety of forms. Its originality lies in the nature of the mix. It also lies in Brecht's stress on the relation between *form and *ideology (see DIALECTIC) and, perhaps especially, on the invitation to spectators to 'write' their own *ending (Brecht's *Good Woman of Setzuan* (1938–41) makes this very clear.)

It is not correct to say that epic theatre is 'rational' and 'cold'. The visual presentation of, say, the ageing Galileo, or the decay of Mother Courage (and her waggon), encourages sympathy. It is true that the distancing techniques cut across this process. They administer shocks. But a shock has emotional impact. Brecht's *alienation effects have much to do with well-established comic devices, but in his theatre they are related to a deep human concern.

BRECHT, B., *Messingkauf Dialogues*, trs. J. Willett, Methuen, 1965.
WILLETT, J., *(ed.), Brecht on Theatre*, Methuen, 1964.

**Epilogue**. Speech addressed by an actor to the audience at the end of a play. It was used by Euripides (480–406 B.C.), and freely employed by the *Elizabethan and *Restoration dramatists. Its function is generally to confirm a harmonious relationship between play and audience. In *The Way of the World* (1700) Congreve gave the actress, Mrs Bracegirdle, an epilogue which assures the audience that his satire was not personal:

> Satire scorns to stoop so meanly low,
> As any one abstracted fop to show.

Rosalind is *As You Like It* (1599) disarms a different kind of anticipated criticism with a graceful mock apology for the lightness of the play. In *tragi-comedy and *tragedy the epilogue tends to be more fully integrated into the play. This is true of the final *monologue of Pandarus in Shakespeare's *Troilus and Cressida* (1601–2) and especially of Mark Antony's epilogue on Brutus in *Julius Caesar* (1599): 'This was the noblest Roman of them all'. Epilogue here becomes a kind of farewell. In *A Midsummer Night's Dream* (1595) Puck says 'Good night' to the audience, but Mark Antony's epilogue, like Ophelia's 'Good night, sweet ladies', and Horatio's 'Good night, sweet prince', says farewell to characters *on stage*, thus incorporating the convention into the play's fabric, making the artificial 'real'. Pandarus's epilogue is spoken, like Puck's, to the audience, but if, like Puck, he acknowledges a mutual game which he and the audience play, the epilogue is bitter and the game has lost its fun.

**Epirrema**. Speech delivered by one of the choral leaders in the *parabasis of Greek *old comedy.

**Episode**. An action which has its own *unity, but exists within a longer *narrative sequence. An 'episodic' play may be criticized for lacking unity, because its constituent episodes are too complete in themselves. This, however, may be a deliberate effect, as in Brecht's *epic drama, or medieval *pageant plays.

**Epitasis**. Section of a play, during which the action becomes more intense as it leads to the *catastrophe.

**Epode**. 'Additional song' sung by immobile Greek *chorus, after the preceding movements and songs of *strophe and *antistrophe. It is written in a different metrical form.

**Equestrian drama**. Spectator performance, normally in an *arena, involving the use of horses. It has existed since Roman times and finds its modern equivalent in the *circus turn. Plays with live horses became popular in the nineteenth century. Byron's narrative poem *Mazeppa* (1819), for instance, involving a man bound on the back of a wild horse, was made into an equestrian drama.

**Equity**. Trade union of theatre workers in Britain (founded as the British Actors' Association in 1929) and the American equivalent, founded earlier, in 1913. They are both responsible for the salaries, working conditions and terms of employment of their members (who also work in film, TV and radio).

In Britain, about two-thirds of the members are actors. Variety performers, stage managers, designers, broadcasters and others make up the rest. An 'equity card' constitutes valuable recognition of an actor's status within the profession. American Equity is principally for performers. It has pursued a non-racial policy since 1961.

**Establishing character**. The process of 'planting' a character firmly in the audience's, reader's or listener's mind. This is a problem for both actor and author. The author needs to make clear a character's name, function in the *plot, and relationship with other characters, as soon and as economically as possible. Vivid *dialogue and intriguing behaviour establish a character, and the actor's *voice, *presence and physical behaviour make an essential contribution.

Occasionally this rule is broken. *Suspense can be created by holding back information. The suppression of the name and identity of a single character in an otherwise 'known' scene, can, like the 'stranger' in Eliot's *The Cocktail Party* (1949), intensify dramatic interest.

**Estrangement**. A term sometimes used as a translation of Brecht's *verfremdungseffekt*. The emphasis it places on Brecht's concern to 'make things strange' (to make an audience see character and situation in a new light) recommend it as an alternative to the more familiar translation: *alienation effect. See STRANGENESS.

**Everyman**. The central figure in the most famous of the Christian *morality plays. Beset by temptation, and hoping for redemption, the figure walks along a road towards death. Equivalent figures in other plays, such as the early fifteenth-century *Castle of Perseverance*, are called Mankind or Humanum Genus. They may be besieged within a castle, competed for by Vices and Virtues, and arraigned before the Judgement Seat of God.

These patterns are incorporated into later drama, such as Marlowe's *Dr Faustus* (*c*.1589) and Shakespeare's *Macbeth* (1606) and *King Lear* (1605). The battle for Faustus's soul, the journeys of Lear and Gloucester, the siege of the castle, all these seem to be legacies of the Everyman morality pattern.

ROSSITER, A.P., *English Drama from Early Times to the Elizabethans*, Hutchinson, 1966.

POTTER, R., *The English Morality Play*, Routledge, 1975.

**Existential drama**. The philosophy of existentialism seems to have found as powerful an expression in drama and fiction as in philosophic discourse. This may well be because it lays such strong emphasis on the uniqueness of the individual in this world, and the painful choices which confront him there.

Atheist and, less obviously, Christian existentialism argue for the priority and reality of existence in this world over any transcendent 'essence'. In this it finds its antecedents in both classical *tragedy and in Christianity, though on the surface the movement is a reaction against the long 'essentialist' tradition. The nineteenth-century existential writers, Kierkegaard (1813–55), Dostoievski (1821–81), and Nietzsche (1844–1900) had a profound interest in drama, and much of the writing of the twentieth-century French existential philosophers, especially Sartre (1905–80) and Camus (1913–60), was for the theatre. In addition, existentialism has a strong kinship with the *theatre of the absurd, since it suggests we live in a world in which fundamental questions are never answered. Plays such as Beckett's *Endgame* (1957) communicate the anguish and absurdity of such a situation.

CAMUS, A., *Caligula* (1944), Gallimard, 1961.

SARTRE, J.-P., *The Theatre of Situations*, essay, (1947), in *Sartre on Theatre*, Quartet, 1976.

**Exit/Exeunt**. Latin: 'he or she leaves/they leave'. Points at which an actor or actors leave the stage. If the exit occurs in mid-scene, it often provides an opportunity for actor or writer to make a strong dramatic impression. Thus Lady Bracknell in Wilde's *The Importance of Being Earnest* (1895) makes a majestic exit, advising Ernest Worthing to acquire at least one parent before he can hope to marry her daughter. The *timing, the power of the 'punch line', the *silence left behind and the new situation to be coped with are all marks of a strong exit. The exit must sustain the audience's belief that the character is going *somewhere else* within the world of the play. Hurried escapes into the *wings demolish this essential illusion. Amateur actors in particular need to remember to continue acting until *a little after* they are out of sight. See ENTRANCE.

**Exodus**. The choral *exit from the *orchestra at the end of a Greek play.

**Exploration**. A creative *rehearsal process in which actors work not only on the play's text, but upon variants and extensions of it. The aim is to appreciate what lies 'beyond' and 'beneath' the play. Such activity may suggest possibilities not anticipated by the writer, and a writer-director like Brecht would *adapt the play as a result.

**Exposition**. The opening section of a play, also known as the *protasis*, in which the dramatist must supply essential background information while developing interest and creating *suspense. The experienced playwright allows information to emerge 'naturally'. Thus Shakespeare creates suspense in *Hamlet* (1601) by the early appearance of the Ghost. He then causes Horatio to seek for an explanation of the Ghost's appearance, and in so doing provides the audience with the 'background' of events preceding the play (which includes a description of the relations between Norway and Denmark). Horatio's explanation, once found, then helps the character to cope with the shock of the Ghost's appearance, and temporarily lowers the tension.

Horatio is a good example of a 'protatic character'. Since he has been absent from Denmark, and is new to the situation, he needs to be enlightened. His enlightenment, and his response, enlighten the audience. A simpler example of such a character is Jensen, the inquisitive hired waiter in the opening scene of Ibsen's *The Wild Duck* (1884).

One should add that, in Ibsen's case, exposition of 'expired events' (Irving's phrase) is not confined to the opening scenes. The suppression of information helps suspense to 'build', and Ibsen allows the audience's knowledge of the past to accumulate gradually. When exposition continues through much of the play it becomes more than the communication of basic information and approaches *discovery or *revelation.

**Expressionist drama**. Movement in drama, usually dated between 1910 and 1925. It is related to expressionist painting which aimed to express inner states by means of strong colours, powerful, gestural movement and heightened lighting. It also exhibited a strong interest in primitive and children's art, folk art and the art of the insane.

The forerunners in drama include the later plays of Ibsen (1898–1906), especially *When We Dead Awaken* (1905), Frank Wedekind's *Spring's Awakening* (1891, prod. 1906), Dostoievski's novels which were being translated and read in the 1880s and the later Strindberg of *Road to Damascus* (1898–1904) and *Dream Play* (1902). After 1910 the foremost dramatists were Georg Kaiser (1878–1945) and Ernst Toller (1893–1939). The young Brecht's early experimental plays *Baal* (1922) and *Drums in the Night* (1922) are also noteworthy.

The movement is important and complex and seemed to take two forms. The better known is the one which presented the fragmented and anguished individual, isolated and crying out like Edward Munch's nightmare figures in his painting 'The Cry'. The other, which Raymond Williams terms 'social' expressionism, examined moments of historical crisis — wars, revolutions, strikes — and led to the new social and political drama of Brecht and Piscator, in which the stress on anguish is replaced by a new concern with political action and an emphasis on the comic mode.

RICHARD, L., *Encyclopedia of Expressionism*, Phaidon, 1978, pp.156–213.

WILLETT, J., *Expressionism*, Weidenfeld, 1971.

**Extravaganza**. A form of *burlesque, based on a story from mythology and providing plentiful opportunity for music and spectacle. The names of Mme Vestris (1797–1856) and James Planché (1796–1880) are closely associated with extravaganza. Shaw suggested that his fantasia *Heartbreak House* (1920) was partly based on the form.

# F

**Fable**. (a) A prose narrative with a moral. The characters are frequently animals, birds or insects, as in the fables of Aesop, La Fontaine or the Russian, Krylov. Drama has no exact equivalent, though the *mimesis of animals seems to have been an important element in the Greek *chorus, and their imitation takes us back to the *origins of drama. *Pantomime and *puppet theatre, too, have animal characters, but it is satirical and *absurdist modern drama such as Capek's *Insect Play* (1921) or Ionesco's *Rhinocéros* (1960) which seem closest to fable. One might also mention the successful *adaptations of George Orwell's *Animal Farm* (National Theatre Company, 1985–7) and Kafka's *Metamorphosis* (by Steven Berkoff's London Theatre Group). A distinction, however, could be made between the tone of a La Fontaine fable in which animals behave as human beings, and the drama cited, which shows human beings behaving like animals. (See GROTESQUE.) (b) The word also translates the term *mythos, in Aristotle's *Poetics*. (c) The 'fable' is also the overall *story of a play, which includes the events referred to as happening before, between and after the enacted *scenes. (d) In *epic drama the 'fable' is a story which the actors explain and offer for our consideration. It is the *parable or *allegory they invite us to relate to the world we live in.

**Fabula**. General name for various types of Latin play, including rustic *farce (*fabula atellana*), urban comedy (*fabula togata*), historical and mythological drama (*fabula praetexta*) and the descendant of Menander's *new comedy (*fabula palliata*). 'Atellana' relates to Atella, a town in south Italy. (See ATELLAN FARCES.) The other names indicate the various kinds of costume worn: 'togata' from the Roman citizen's toga, 'praetexta' from the toga worn by magistrates and 'palliata' from *pallium* a Greek cloak.

**Facial expression**. An important means of dramatic communication, especially in modern 'head dominated' psychological theatre. Actors may obviously transmit what the character thinks and feels by means of the play of facial muscles and the use of eyes and mouth. Such expression is normally considered 'natural', though divergences exist between facial expression natural to the theatre, and natural expression in daily life. The sheer artificiality of communicating to people at a considerable distance, in a large theatre, means that the mouth, eyes and eyebrows work in ways which would seem extravagant in proximity.

Certain dramatic forms, such as *mime, *melodrama and kinds of *oriental theatre deliberately heighten and codify facial expression. (See CODE). The Elizabethan theatre, to judge from Hamlet's advice to a Player to 'cease his damnable faces', mixed the heightened and the more naturalistic styles. Probably it is only in intimate theatres, and in *film and *TV close-up, that 'theatrical' and 'natural' facial expression coincide. To watch Ingmar Bergman's actresses, say Liv Ullmann or Bibi Andersson in *Persona*, or Ingrid Bergman in *Autumn Sonata*, is to realize how subtly and powerfully the face can convey thought and feeling.

JOSEPH, B.L., *Elizabethan Acting*, Oxford University Press, 2nd ed., 1964.
BOOTH, M., *English Melodrama*, Jenkins, 1965.

**Facsimile stage**. Form of staging in which the *set, style of furniture, fittings and source of *light aim to represent in exact detail a particular place and time. Only a *fourth wall is missing, through which the audience watches as the action unfolds.

**Fade in/out**. Film term referring to the practice of gradually disclosing a photographic image on a dark screen (fade in) and removing the image leaving the screen blank (fade out). The fades are generally used to begin to build up interest, or to indicate a temporary close. They vary in speed according to the *rhythm a director wishes to establish. A close theatrical equivalent is the *blackout with the use of *dimmers.

**Fairground**. See POPULAR DRAMA and, for comments on the fairground booth:
BRAUN, E., *Meyerhold on Theatre*, Eyre Methuen, 1969, Section 3.

**Falling action**. G. Freytag's term for the descent after a play's *crisis or turning-point, towards a tragic *catastrophe. See RISING ACTION.
FREYTAG, G., *Die Technik des Dramas*, 1862.

**Falling flap**. A hinged piece of scenery, painted on both sides, which can fold and fall so that the hidden face is exposed and the exposed face hidden. It was employed in *transformation scenes.

**False proscenium**. *Border and *wings decorated with painted curtains and tassels to resemble the true *proscenium arch.

**Fan effect**. Synchronized *scene-change in which the *wings fall outwards, closing like fans to reveal, with spectacular effect, the scene to follow.

**Farce**. Probably the most consistently popular western form of drama. It has existed since the Greek and *Atellan modes, through the *Commedia dell'Arte, to nineteenth-century French farce and contemporary *West End comedy.

In farce, characters are subjected to various forms of indignity. They find themselves in compromising situations, lose items of clothing, suffer physical assault. They do not, however, suffer too heavily, either physically or from loss of face. The characters of farce often have a curious childish innocence, a lack of awareness of other people's concerns and a total obsession with their own. We laugh at them whilst envying their capacity to ignore the hurts of life. They overcome indignity and *chance, but chaos is close and the game is to avert its every threat. Thus a farce moves quickly. The characters are like jugglers. The situation grows ever more complicated and the actors juggle faster to keep the play, like a ball, in the air. The audience watches, holds its breath and laughs when a ball almost drops. There is no time for deep analysis, or complex characterization. No one is crushed. The characters preserve their youth. Even the old preserve their bounce. They survive sexual humiliation and the depredations on their power. If they do not, the play takes on a seriousness which farce cannot tolerate.

Farce depends on our awareness of problems of authority, sexuality and disorder, even whilst the play pretends to conjure them away. It is found as a component of serious plays because dramatists know that it touches something deep in our nature. Perhaps that is why Shakespeare, in *A Midsummer Night's Dream* (1595), shows us a stage audience responding to farce. The farcical characters attempt to present a serious play to Duke Theseus. The laughter of the watching lovers, Lysander, Demetrius, Helena and Hermia, sets aside the pain of the experience they have just gone through. They do not seem to recognize that the 'comical tragedy' of Pyramus and Thisbe presents them with a distorting mirror in which, if they wished, they could see themselves.

BERGSON, H., *Le Rire*, NY, 1956.

DAVIS, J., *Farce*, Methuen, 1979.

HUGHES, L., *A Century of English Farce*, Princeton University Press/Oxford University Press, 1957.

**Fastnachtsspiel**. German for Shrovetide or Carnival play. A sixteenth-century folk comedy which contained knockabout *farce and much lampooning of figures in the local community. The *Narr was a central figure (*Hanswurst in the south of Germany, *Pickelherring in the north). It placed the usual *carnivalesque emphasis on the body and its appetites. In its mock arraignment of greed, envy and other vices it is reminiscent of *morality plays.

At first acted by amateurs in local halls and village squares, the *Fastnachsspiel* was taken over by the guilds, who formed companies known as Mastersingers. Hans Sachs (1494–1576) is the best known author, famous on account of Wagner's opera *Die Meistersinger von Nürnberg* (1868). He seems to have written eighty-five such plays, and established for them in 1550, in a deserted church, the first German theatre. This burgeoning native drama was, however, destroyed by the religious and civil strife which led up to the Thirty Years War.

**Fate drama.** Early nineteenth-century German *suspense play in which fate (see CAUSALITY) and *chance drive a character inexorably toward some dreadful deed. See Grillparzer's *Die Ahnfrau* (1817), and *Die Schuld* (1816) by Mullner (1774–1829), who established the form.

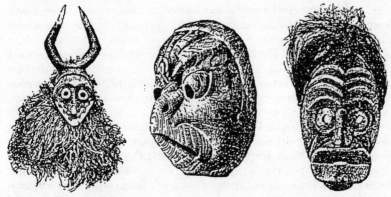

**8** *Fear-inspiring masks*

**Fear.** An important *emotion in drama. According to Aristotle, *tragedy achieves its effect of *catharsis, or purgation, through the emotions of *pity and fear. In the *mystery and *morality plays, where the question of man's salvation is apt to be central, fear is a sought effect, since fear of Hell or Death is an early step towards redemption. The play *Everyman* (1509–1519) brings this salutary fear to both character and audience.

Shakespeare, in *Macbeth* (1606), analyses the destructive effects of attempting to master, and stifle fear: 'The time has been my senses would have cooled/To hear a night shriek . . .'. Macbeth seems deliberately to test his capacity to conquer 'natural' fear. In the highly dramatic novels of Dostoievski, including *Crime and Punishment* (1860) and *The Possessed* (1872), characters also test themselves against their own fear, with the destructive results suggested by Macbeth's: 'I dare do all that may become a man. Who dares do more is none'. Fear, or terror, is thus important both as subject and effect in the western tragic and Christian tradition.

In tragedy, fear is a subject of analysis and a condition aroused in the audience. It is also important in other forms of drama, such as *melodrama. When Bill Sykes enraged the audience, dragging Nancy round the stage by her hair in adaptations of Dickens's *Oliver Twist* (1837–8), fear for Nancy, as well as pity, must have mingled with their response. In *farce, too, it is arguable that fear lies behind the *laughter which the chaotic and frenetic energy of the characters provokes. The psychological processes involved are, however, extremely complex. Fear shades into anxiety and terror, and raises questions of 'instinctual' and 'learned' behaviour. It seems to involve the impulse to flee and in this can be contrasted with more aggressive emotions such as *anger and hatred or with sympathetic feelings such as love, pity and compassion. Sometimes, of course, the fear is of the 'self', or of something within the self, and sometimes it seems to have no object. But however it manifests itself, and whatever theory seeks to define and explain it, fear is a feeling dramatists analyse, appeal to, and seek to provoke in an audience. See PHOBIA.

A complex book, concerned with fear in the western tragic and Christian tradition, is:

KIERKEGAARD, S., *Fear and Trembling* (1843), trs. W. Lowrie, Doubleday, 1954.

**Feast of Fools**. A celebration of the New Year in European churches during the middle ages. It consisted of a kind of holiday protest against church authority in which the younger and lower clergy would *burlesque the liturgy. It involved *roleplay, *role reversal and the appointment of a mock king, who later became *Lord of Misrule. The celebration raises questions about the nature and function of *comedy, and the complex and dramatic figure of the *fool.

WELFORD, E., *The Fool*, Faber and Faber, 1935, Ch. 9.

**Fedeli**. Troupe of *Commedia dell'Arte* actors formed at the turn of the seventeenth century.

**Federal Theatre Project**. The response of the American government in 1935 to the theatre's economic problems during the thirties. The project aimed to provide actors with employment and to generate cheap, high-quality theatre. It had high political ideals and was divided into five units: a Negro theatre, a *Living Newspaper, an experimental theatre, a unit collaborating with commercial theatre and another specializing in new plays at low cost. The Negro theatre encouraged serious black actors; Orson Welles (1915–85) produced an all-black *Macbeth* for it in 1936. The Living Newspaper proved the most contentious part of the project. It involved a number of companies, using documentary material to mount projects concerned — among other issues — with Mussolini's war in Ethiopia, with profiteering, farming conditions, judicial conditions, judicial corruption and government ownership. The Project as a whole was terminated in 1939.

**Female impersonation**. Men and boys have played female roles in ancient Greek, Elizabethan, Chinese, Japanese and other forms of drama. The primary reason, no doubt, has been the social exclusion of women from the theatre. But this does not explain the continuing interest audiences find in men, and now women, imitating the characteristic speech patterns, voice, physical mannerisms and dress of the opposite sex. In the past, Shakespeare's *As You Like It* (1599) and *Twelfth Night* (1601) (with one boy actor playing a girl who played a boy playing a girl) raised questions about sexual identity and the *mimetic process. In *music hall, *pantomime,*variety acts and now *TV comedy such *role reversals are an important part of the show.

The theatre then is a place where the sexually ambiguous nature of the self, whether 'natural', or constructed by social experience, or both, is often presented and sometimes explored. Carl Gustav Jung's poetic concepts of the 'animus' and 'anima', the male within the female, and the female within the male (which he believed 'should function as a bridge or a door leading to the images of the collective unconscious'), have been much drawn upon in explanation of sexual dualities.

JUNG, C.G., *Selected Writings*, Fontana, 1983.

**Feminist theatre**. This theatre developed as a genre in the United States and in Britain in the 1960s and early 1970s. A growing pressure for equal opportunities for women in society led to a demand in the theatre for equal earnings and greater opportunities for women in technical, artistic and creative fields, as opposed to the clerical, publicity and servicing fields which they dominated. Since most drama is written by men and contains more major and minor masculine roles, the average acting company has contained twice as many male actors as actresses. The present rise of women's *fringe groups and women writers such as Megan Terry (1932– ) and Caryl Churchill (1938– ) (*Cloud Nine*, 1979 and *Top Girls*, 1982) reveals a determination to rectify this imbalance by providing more female parts, by questioning the presentation of women in the various media, by heightening the political consciousness of theatre workers and focussing generally on female experience, which they feel is unrepresented or misrepresented. This has encouraged the development of original dramatic techniques, involving 'transformations' or *role reversal. Red Ladder (1972) and Monstrous Regiment (founded in 1975) are two important *fringe groups in this important social and artistic movement.

CHINOV, H., and JENKINS, L. (eds.), *Women in American Theatre*, Crown, NY, 1981.

KEYSAAR, H., *Feminist Theatre*, Macmillan, 1984.
TODD, S. (ed.), *Women and Theatre*, Faber, 1984.
WANDOR, M., *Understudies*, Methuen, 1981.

**Fiabe**. Plays in which Carlo Gozzi (1720–1806) attempted to recover the spontaneity of the *Commedia dell'Arte* within a written fairy-tale framework. *Turandot* (1762) is an example of the genre and it has been revived in the twentieth century.

**Fill in**. To 'fill in' is to cover a hiatus in performance, caused by a late *entrance, a wrong *cue, a *'dry', or any other threat to the theatrical illusion. The usual reaction is to *ad lib, but other means are available. A *movement or a *gesture may suffice, and even a long silence may be tolerable if the actors remain 'in character'.

A performer who, for reasons of illness or other temporary absence, replaces another at short notice, is also said to 'fill in'.

**Film**. Art form combining dramatic, photographic and musical elements. Film drama differs vitally from theatre in that it lacks a live relationship between actors and audience. Although, on occasions, an actor may address the camera directly, the process is artificial and film has generally remained within its *proscenium or *fourth wall. Since the advent of sound, acting has usually been *naturalistic. (The stylized performances of *mime, or of Brecht's *epic theatre, seem more effective when the actors are physically present, whereas film must first create the illusion of reality.)

Film, however, is an extremely flexible medium. Its realist content is allied with a *form which resembles, but is perhaps not recognized as, *dream. A film director can *cross-cut from one 'natural' scene to another with the rapidity of a dream sequence, creating the kind of excitement and surprise that a relatively cumbersome theatre *scene-change does not allow. The director can also create tension by constantly shifting the apparent distance between audience and scene, and by changing the angle of vision. *Pans, *zooms, *cuts, *fades and so on keep the viewer in constant illusory movement. The camera, too, with its deep, narrow field of vision, is constantly excluding things which the audience knows or suspects to be part of the dramatic scene. The audience's curiosity, then, about what is *out of shot*, and may come into shot, creates *suspense. Alfred Hitchcock did this in his 'thrillers', and he would also reveal to an audience what he concealed from a character, as in the opening scenes of *Psycho* (1958).

Change of *focus and the *zoom also control the audience's viewpoint in a very specific way. A director can select a detail, a bulge in a pocket, a sheet of paper, a forgotten cigarette lighter, and point it out to the film-goer. (See INDEX.) It is the camera here, not the actor, which 'speaks' directly to the audience.

The *sound track, too, allows for skilful use of *music to create an atmosphere, and also to comment on the performance — as a 'voice over' may more obviously do. Documentary films freely use this technique. Fiction films however, tend to hide their different forms of commentary. It is the images rather than the sound track or the camera techniques which occupy the attention. Film, like the naturalist theatre and unlike *epic theatre, does not often dare, or cannot afford, to call attention to its own artificiality. It concentrates attention on its powerful capacity to render real places or 'real' emotions, through the very detailed presentation of a town or landscape, a room or a face; its dream quality the viewer is usually encouraged to forget.

**Fit-up**. Temporary nineteenth-century theatre, offering a diet of popular plays, especially *melodramas, at low prices.

**Flat**. A flat piece of scenery, made of stretched canvas on a wooden frame. Flats were used as *wings in the *Restoration theatre, and could be moved backwards and forwards in *grooves to effect *scene changes. Since the advent of the *box-set, flats have been joined together in various ways by hinges or battens, usually to create the impression of a room. 'Backing flats' are set behind openings in the box-set, to give the impression of, for instance, further rooms, a hallway or a garden.

**Flies**. The space above the stage. It houses *scenery, suspended on ropes and pulleys so that it can be 'flown in' for changes of scene.

**Flipper**. A hinged addition to a *flat; it disguises a straight edge and gives it visual interest.

**Fluff**. A verbal slip in performance, generally due to nervousness or lack of concentration. Fluffs destroy the *suspension of disbelief and are especially to be avoided in television and film *takes. Not only are they very obvious to the viewer, but they may also necessitate costly re-runs.

**Fly-floor**. Platforms over the *wings giving the *flymen access to ropes, *lighting and *scenery in the *flies. (See Ill.13, p.166.)

**Flying effects**. Effects achieved by lifting actors into the air. The appeal is no doubt similar to that of watching *circus acrobats — a combination of admiration, *surprise and *fear. The harness and wire are still used for flying effects in *pantomimes such as J.M. Barrie's *Peter Pan* (1904). In the *court masque and in ancient Greek drama, actors were transported through the air by means of disguised platforms and the **machina*. Modern cinema, of course, employs special effects which the theatre cannot rival, unless one argues that *film cannot communicate the thrill which derives from the actual physical presence of a performer.

**Flymen**. Stage hands working in the *flies.

**Focus**. The centre of audience attention. On stage a variety of different actors, or *groupings of actors, may simultaneously compete for the audience's attention, and a director needs to establish a focus to prevent dispersal of interest. In *film and *TV drama he does this by selecting from different camera shots, each focusing on different aspects of the scene, so that the audience only sees the grouping, *facial expression or detail which the director wishes it to see. In the theatre other methods must be found to narrow the field of attention.

The most obvious means of doing this is by the use of *voice, and the *convention which allows only one person to speak or to be clearly heard at once. The person speaking, however, need not always be the dramatic centre of attention. A silent, isolated figure, watching or listening in a commanding stage position, dressed in a different colour or style, or lighted more obtrusively than other actors, may by the twitch of a feature, the movement of a foot, or by absolute stillness, become the central focus. One thinks of Shakespeare's black-clad Hamlet in the first court scene.

A commanding stage position is, of course, very important, and it varies with the kind of stage used. Proximity gives a natural advantage. With *theatre in the round the actor closest to the whole audience is in the centre. On a *thrust or *proscenium stage he or she is *downstage centre. A dominant position, however, may easily be established at the *upstage apex of a series of triangular groups. See:
FERNALD, J., *Sense of Direction: the director and his actors*, Secker, 1968.

**Folio**. An edition of a play printed on bound sheets, folded once only to provide two leaves and four pages. Shakespeare's famous First Folio of thirty-six plays was printed in this way in 1623.

**Folk drama**. Drama performed originally at folk festivals — notably May-day, Harvest Home or Christmas. Examples include the *mumming and *Plough Monday plays, and the *sword dance and *morris dance. Much folk drama seems to be related to ancient fertility rites and magical ceremonies connected with the migration of the sun, and its annual death and rebirth. Characters based on local figures and patron saints like St George often featured in the drama.

Interest in folk literature and drama has been growing ever since *romanticism supplied an initial stimulus. The part played by folk and *popular drama in Shakespeare's work, for example, has come under close scrutiny. See:

BARBER, C.L., *Shakespeare's Festive Comedy*, Princeton University Press, 1959.

BETHELL, S.L., *Shakespeare and the Popular Dramatic Tradition*, P. Staples, 1944.

CHAMBERS, E.K., *The Medieval Stage*, Vols. I and II, Oxford University Press, 1903.

WEIMANN, R., *Shakespeare and the Popular Tradition in the Theatre*, Johns Hopkins University Press, 1978.

**Follies**. A kind of *revue, associated particularly with Florenz Ziegfeld (1867–1932) who staged his 'Ziegfeld Follies' in New York annually from 1907. They involved song and dance, comic turns, and scenic display of a lavish kind.

**Fool**. A complex stage figure, especially associated with *Jacobean and *Elizabethan drama. He derives from such folk festivities as the medieval *Feast of Fools, from the court *jester, and from an associated literature ranging from Brandt's *Narrenschiff (Ship of Fools)* (1494), through Alexander Barclay's adaptation of Brandt in 1509, to the popular *Encomium Moriae (In Praise of Folly)* (1511) by Erasmus. These writers refined and analysed various kinds of fool and foolishness (Brandt found 112). They made of the fool an *Everyman figure who proclaimed a human condition: '*Numerus stultorum infinitus est*' (the number of fools is infinite).

In the Elizabethan theatre, and especially in Shakespeare's plays, the fool's symbolic complexity is subtly exhibited. The fool acts as a distorting mirror, mocking his betters, as Falstaff does in the *sub-plot to *Henry IV* Part I (1597). He may also be a reminder of death. The most famous, perhaps, of all fools — Yorick in *Hamlet* (1601) — appears on stage as a skull. The Fool appears frequently as the counterpart of a king, as in *King Lear* (1605). When he appears in the forest, like Touchstone in *As You Like It* (1599), or exchanges clothes with the Prince, as does Autolycus in *The Winter's Tale* (1610), the fool is exhibited in relation to complex *codes implicit and explicit in much medieval iconography.

The fool figure brings together ideas of youth and age, innocence and stupidity, sexuality and death, luck and misfortune, night and day, wisdom and foolishness, humility and pride. *Love, or *time, or *pride, or *chance make fools of everyone sooner or later. The fool presents us with a mirror in which we have an opportunity to see ourselves. Till Eulenspiegel ('owl in mirror') holds it up to us, and in it the wise man tends to see a fool and the fool a wise man. The fool, clown or jester constantly warns us of the way our bodies and desires, and our mental self-absorption, make fools of us. In the recognition of this lies health and wisdom. The

**9** *The fool and the Devil (from Barclay's* Ship of Fools*)*

tradition can be traced in the work of Rabelais (*c*.1494–*c*.1553) and Cervantes (1547–1616), in Swift's *Gulliver's Travels* (1726) and Sterne's *Tristram Shandy* (1759–65), in the *music hall and *circus, in the silent cinema and in Samuel Beckett's plays, with their clowns and double pairings.

KAISER, W., *Praisers of Folly: Erasmus, Rabelais and Shakespeare*, Gollancz, 1964.

WELSFORD, E., *The Fool*, Faber, 1935.

WILLEFORD, W., *The Fool and his Sceptre*, Arnold, 1969.

**Footlights**. Lights hidden from the audience on the front edge of the *forestage. They were introduced in the seventeenth century to strengthen the *light of the overhead chandeliers, and remained when gas and electricity replaced candlelight in the nineteenth century. They helped to establish the growing separation between audience and actors, and the heightened contrast of light and shadow on the actors' faces no doubt contributed to the effect of popular *melodrama. *Naturalism, however, required a less artificial light: Strindberg (1849–1912) criticized footlights in his Preface to *Miss Julie* (1888). With the development of sophisticated lighting techniques they became obsolete.

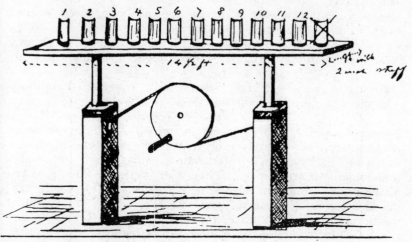

**10** *Moveable footlights*

**Footlights trap**. Long opening in the *forestage through which footlights could be lowered into the cellar, either to reduce the *lighting or for trimming.

**Footmen's gallery**. The upper gallery in the *Restoration theatres of Dorset Garden and Drury Lane. Footmen waiting for the aristocratic clientele were admitted to it free of charge at later stages of the performance.

**Foregrounding**. A literary term translating the Czech word '*actualisace*', a central concept of the Prague school of linguistics in the 1930s. Roman Jakobsen defined it as 'the set towards the language for its own sake', which implies a mental focusing on words as shape and sound, rather than on their content or reference. In other words, language is 'looked at' rather than 'seen through'.

The term needs to be handled with some care. When Yeats argues that a 'good' line in poetry should not have as good a line on either side of it, this might be described as a kind of foregrounding. Shakespeare foregrounds a word when Lady Macbeth puns: 'I'll gild the faces of the grooms withal, for it must seem their guilt'. Attention is called to the arbitrary similarity of sound between 'gild' and 'gilt'; this intensifies a fusion of meaning. The grooms are to be smeared with the blood which Macbeth is guilty of spilling. It is the king's blood, therefore 'golden', which will be the gilt which covers their innocence and the guilt of Macbeth. The line gains power by the way form and content reinforce each other. This is a more complex 'foregrounding' than a simple awareness of language 'for its own sake'.

'Foregrounding' words in the theatre can be achieved by the writer's skill, by the actor's use of *voice, or by changes of acting style. The word *focus is best used for other kinds of emphasis, created by *lighting changes, *sound effects, *movement and so on.

JAKOBSEN, R., article in T.E. Sebeok (ed.), *Language*, Linguistic Society of America, Cambridge Mass., 1960, pp.350–77.

**Foreshadowing**. A form of *dramatic irony of which the spectator is not always fully aware. Future events are suggested in *hints which are half recognized at the time, and perhaps only fully understood in retrospect. They can be very subtle, like Shakespeare's pun at the beginning of *The Winter's Tale*, where it is said the friendship between Leontes and Polixenes 'cannot choose but branch now'. The speaker intends to suggest a 'branching' in the sense of natural growth. The word foreshadows, however, the branching or division between the two which is shortly to come.

Foreshadowing creates a vague unease, which gradually grows more intense as the hints multiply. Ibsen is a master of the technique.

**Forestage**. The *downstage area; the area in front of the *proscenium arch, onto which an actor may step when he wishes to address an audience directly.

**Form**. As compared with *genre, which normally defines tone or content (*tragedy, *history, *comedy, and *pastoral, for example) the word 'form' may imply the obvious structure and shape of a work, as in 'three-act play'. Less obviously a play's form may consist of the elements which hold it together, the 'inner form'. This may consist of *story or *plot, or, in a more Platonic sense, the pressures and tensions which express themselves in character relationships, in recurrent *motifs or in patterns of *dialogue. The obvious 'form' of Shakespeare's *Antony and Cleopatra* (1606–7) is that of a five-act tragedy. Its 'inner form' seems to lie in the tension between the values of Rome and of Egypt, which is expressed as an opposition between Cleopatra and Octavius, and as a private struggle within Antony, the Roman who has 'gone native'. The 'surface forms' of the play — *diction and *imagery, verse and sentence structure — may be seen to express this central conflict.

A relation between the form of a dramatic work and all it

emerges from — the natural world, social culture, historical process, shared language, formal conventions, the individual mind — is generally assumed in the use of such terms as 'organic form', 'dialectical form', 'conventional form', 'mechanical form', 'original form', and so on. How far a play actually reflects, embodies, or recreates the patterns of the world it comes from is open to dispute, as is the question of whether Nature, History, Language or some transcendent or free Mind is the dominant force behind the process.

Such considerations appear even more complex in drama than in art forms which are the product of a single artist. In drama a transaction takes place between various minds. The writer *designers, *director, *actors, technicians and *audience all contribute to the varying form known as the performance. Even if one considers only the printed text of a play, its form has emerged from the writer's consideration of theatre conditions, size of company, the nature of the play's likely audience, its conventional expectations, the money available, and the individual talent available. These consideratioons and others, such as political *censorship and the attitudes of theatre management, must all be taken consciously into account. The difficulty lies in knowing *how* conscious (and how free) writers are when they mediate the natural, historical and/or linguistic patterns with which, and within which, they work. *Chance too may play a part in the creation of form. As for the writer's 'freedom', it may be there in the recognition, in both *comedy and *tragedy that the form is never, in a sense, final. (See ENDING.) Some uncomfortable ingredient – a Jaques in *As You Like It* perhaps – suggests the limitations of the form which attempts to contain him, and indicates a need to find a new one. With a Shakespeare, or Dostoievski, the form of the next play or novel seems to emerge from an awareness of the incompleteness of the previous one. See also TIME; CHRONOLOGY; SPACE; DIALECTIC; THEATRE LANGUAGE.

EFFNE, H., 'Towards a definition of form in drama', in *Classical Drama and its Influence*, edited by M. Anderson, Methuen, 1965.

**Formalism.** An influential school of literary criticism which grew up in St Petersburg and Moscow during and after World War I. Linguistic in its emphasis, it asserted the formal independence of the work of art, and came under fire from critics who adhered, under Stalin, to *socialist realist principles, and from others who felt that art was inseparable from the historical process.

In drama, formalism is associated in particular with *constructivism and the theatre of Meyerhold (1874–1940) and the early Tairov (1885–1950) in the years after the Russian Revolution. Its principle of 'estrangement' is interestingly related to Brecht's *alienation effect.

EHRLICH, V., *Russian Formalism*, Mouton, The Hague, 1955.
SHKLOVSKI, V., *Art as Device*, 1925.

**Fortune**. *Chance or accident; a concept personified as a goddess turning a wheel. It is very important in the *Elizabethan theatre, where Fortune is usually contrasted with Nature and linked with the figures of *King, *Fool and *Everyman, all of whom rise and fall on the wheel of life. King Lear's assertion, 'I am even the natural fool of fortune', or Rosalind and Celia in *As You Like It* (1599) debating as to whether Touchstone was sent by Nature or Fortune, remind us how this pervasive concept was still, in Shakespeare's day, highly pictorial. For a discussion of Nature and Fortune in *As You Like It*, see:
SHAW, J., *Shakespeare Quarterly*, vi, 1955, pp.45–50.

**Four-hander**. A play for four characters, usually two strongly contrasting couples, as in Edward Albee's *Who's Afraid of Virginia Woolf?* (1962). It is a popular form with theatre management, since production costs are low and the *rehearsal process is simplified by the small *cast.

**Fourth wall**. The invisible wall, assumed to exist across the *proscenium arch, through which an audience watches actors apparently oblivious of its presence. The fourth wall is more than just a *naturalist convention. Stanislavski would rehearse for a considerable time before deciding which wall should be opened up to the audience. It was at 'stage twenty-three' of the rehearsal process that he advised: 'Test the pattern of the stage business by opening arbitrarily any one of the four walls.' See:
STANISLAVSKI, C., *Creating a Role*, Methuen, 1981.

**Freedom**. See CAUSALITY; REALISM; SITUATION; WILL.

**Free theatre**. A movement which dates from the last decades of the nineteenth century. It was strong in France, Germany and England, where the dominant figures were André Antoine (1858–1943) at the Théâtre Libre (1887) in Paris, Otto Brahm (1856–1912) at the *Freie Bühne (1889) in Berlin, and J.T. Grein (1858–1943) who founded the *Independent Theatre Club in 1891 in London. These theatres resulted from a need to find a platform for the new naturalistic social drama which could not get an easy hearing in the commercial theatres. For the English background, see:
ORME, M., *J.T. Grein: The Story of a Pioneer, 1862–1935*, Murray, 1936.

**Freeze**. A sudden cessation of movement which transforms the flow of performance into a *tableau. Its effect is to shift the audience into a new mode of apprehension. Caught in the passage of *time, the audience cannot fully catch the *signs behind the action; in the freeze these are made explicit.

The effect of a freeze brings to mind Henri Bergson's famous definition of *comedy as 'the mechanical encrusted upon the living', and it is not surprising that freezes and tableaux have been much used in *farce and the closely related *genre of *melodrama. Here, *stereotypes are close to the surface and characters fight against becoming objects. In a freeze they become, in one synchronized moment, props at the mercy of the machine in which they play. Should an actor betray his human fallibility, and freeze too late, the effect is generally spoiled.

The effect is not always comic. The function of a freeze in Meyerhold's production of Erdman's *The Warrant* (1925) was to convey the characters' sudden realization of their dilemma. They did not become comic objects; rather the audience was made aware of the characters' awareness.

A further subtlety can be seen in Chekhov's *Three Sisters* (1901), where the freeze is 'naturalized'. A soldier takes a photograph, and the characters become immobile for a few seconds. 'You can move now', says the soldier, but the percipient spectator asks whether this is entirely true: the sisters are always talking of moving away to Moscow, but the audience remains poignantly aware that they are still 'frozen'.

Finally, the freeze is also a workshop or rehearsal device, used to find appropriate groupings, good visual contrast, and to make actors aware of the patterns they are making. The sudden shift from a temporal to a spatial mode heightens the awareness of actors as well as spectators. It seems to touch on something central to the nature of *theatricality. See COUP DE THEATRE.

**Freie Bühne.** A Berlin theatre group, established in 1889, by Otto Brahm, to pursue similar policies to André Antoine's Théâtre Libre in Paris, founded two years previously. This involved the promotion of the new *naturalism inspired by Ibsen (1828–1906). Performances of plays by Hauptmann (1862–1946), Holz (1863–1929), Strindberg (1849–1912), Zola (1840–1902) and Tolstoy (1828–1910) followed the initial production of Ibsen's *Ghosts*. It affiliated with the *Deutsches Theater in 1894.

**French flat.** *Flats battened together to form a back wall, normally for a *box-set.

**Freud, Sigmund** (1856–1939). Psychoanalyst and major thinker. He provides us with a theory of human behaviour and by extension of art. 'These are my masters', he declared to a visitor in Vienna, indicating texts of Greek *tragedy and of Shakespeare. The cornerstone of his theory of the Oedipus complex derives in part from a study of Sophocles's play, and his essays on Ibsen's *Rosmersholm* (1886) and Shakespeare's *Merchant of Venice* (1596–8)

apply his theories to dramatic character and structure.
See: AMBIVALENCE; CATHARSIS; COMEDY; CONDENSATION; DREAM;
PARAPRAXIS; UNCONSCIOUS.

FREUD, S., *The Interpretation of Dreams* (1900); *Psychopathic Characters on the Stage* (1905).

**Freytag's pyramid**. A model of the *action of a play, offered by G. Freytag in *Die Teknik des Dramas* (1862). As compared with the traditional four basic movements of a play — *protasis, *epitasis, *catastasis and *catastrophe — Freytag offered six: *introduction, *inciting moment, *rising action, *climax, *falling action and *catastrophe.

Since the movements of all plays differ in some degree from one another, such patterns are best seen as rough guides. All long plays have, arguably, many more movements than six, and what is considered a major movement is particularly subject to dispute, especially when plays are not divided by *acts or intervals.

**Fringe theatre**. A movement, normally assumed to have begun in 1968 in protest against 'establishment theatre'. It was preceded by the work of Joan Littlewood (1914– ) in London's East End; by the attempt of John Arden (1930– ) and his wife Margaretta D'Arcy to 'take theatre to the people'; and by a shift during the early 1960s towards the dramatic presentation of working-class experience, in the plays of Arnold Wesker (1932– ) and Edward Bond (1935– ).

Since 1968 the various kinds of fringe or 'alternative theatre' have included 'community theatre, *Theatre in Education, *feminist theatre and *gay theatre. With or without a strong political emphasis, fringe companies are concerned with new material and with formal experimentation. Their emphasis on individual and group creativity, their search for new venues and audiences, the opportunities they have offered for the development of acting, directing and writing talent, and perhaps above all their challenge to conservative views of the function of the theatre, have made an important contribution to British cultural life, both locally and nationally.

For the American equivalent see OFF OFF BROADWAY.

CRAIG, S. (ed.), *Dreams and Deconstructions: Alternative Theatre in Britain*, Amber Lane, 1980.

ITZEN, C., *Stages of the Revolution*, Eyre Methuen, 1980.

SHANK, T., *American Alternative Theatre*, Macmillan, 1982.

**Frons scaenae**. The large and impressive back wall to the Roman stage.

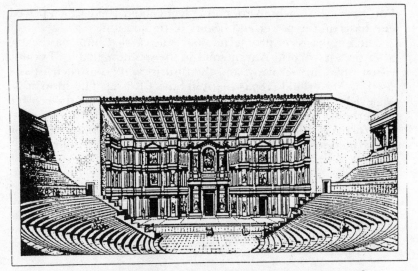

**11** *Reconstruction of the* Frons scaenae *of the Roman theatre at Orange (from* Caristie, Monuments Antique à Orange, *1856)*

**Front of house**. The *auditorium; the area in front of the stage in a theatre. It is an administrative term, used to define an area of responsibility including house lighting and seating arrangements.

**Full house**. A performance at which all seats are taken. The filling of an *auditorium usually creates a strong rapport between actors and audience.

**Full scenery**. A system of staging which involves a complete change of scenery for each change of scene. See DETAIL SCENERY.

**Funambulist**. A tight-rope walker.

**Function of drama**. Why do men and women engage in performances in which they pretend to be someone or something other than themselves? Why do they write plays? Why do audiences gather to watch such plays? No doubt the explanations differ according to the stage of development of a culture and the nature of the play performed.

The different needs of different members of different audiences in different cultures ensure that any one performance fulfils a variety of dramatic functions. A sense of their variety and complexity may be gained from consulting some of the more important entries in this book: see, for example: TRAGEDY; COMEDY; EMPATHY; CATHARSIS; IDENTIFICATION; RITUAL. One way of distinguishing between the various dramatic *genres is by attempting to define the *function* of each.

**Futurism**. Movement in art, dating from about 1909, which placed emphasis on the power and beauty of the machine.

The emphasis on new technology was carried into the theatre after the First World War, notably in the sets designed for Piscator (1893–1966) in Germany, and the futurist and *constructivist sets used by Meyerhold (1874–1940) in Soviet Russia. The futurist K. Malevich, for example, designed the costumes and sets for Meyerhold's revolutionary production of Mayakovski's *Mystery-Bouffe* (1918). Vladimir Verhaeren's *The Dawn* (1898), produced by Meyerhold in 1920, had sets designed by Vladimir Dimitriev.

# G

**Gaelic drama**. Drama written in Irish Gaelic. It developed during the 1890s, notably in Dublin and Galway, out of a growing desire for Irish national expression which resulted in the founding of the Gaelic Drama League and the Abbey Theatre.

**Gaff**. Makeshift, low-class nineteenth-century theatre. Its clients usually paid one penny for a diet of rough *melodrama; hence 'penny gaff'.

**Gag**. Originally, extra material introduced by the actor into a script; now a funny story or joke.

**Galanty show**. Nineteenth-century term for a street show in which the shadows of performing *puppets were projected onto a screen between them and the spectators.

**Gallery**. The cheapest seats, high in the *auditorium, traditionally containing the most vociferous members of the audience.

'Playing to the gallery' is, of course, a temptation for actors. Where there are major audience class divisions, sharpened by price divisions in the auditorium, 'playing to the gallery' has been used to create deliberate political tension in the house, as, for example, by Piscator (1893–1966) during the Weimar Republic.

For an actor the control of such response is important. It is less problematic, perhaps, when noisy spectators are in a distant gallery than when they are close to the stage, as must have occurred in Shakespeare's theatre, where the tiers of galleries were more expensive than the standing places for 'groundlings' around the *apron stage. If, as Hamlet says, the groundlings were 'for the most part capable of nothing but inexplicable dumbshows and noise', then, in a play which was 'caviare to the general', Elizabethan actors had the difficult task of appealing over their heads to the tiers of perhaps more appreciative galleries. One wonders how far actors were relieved when productions 'transferred' from the open air *Globe to the *private theatres, where the cheaper places were further away from the stage.

**Game**. A playful contest with rules, the outcome of which depends in varying degrees on skill, strength and luck.

Drama has been considered a kind of game. The actors engage in a contest, pitting themselves against each other, and struggling also to hoodwink an audience. In a sense, however, drama is a game which has *already been played*, since (except in *improvisations) the script is written and the actor has no freedom. Whether he loses or wins is already determined.

If drama is a game at all it is a very sophisticated one, since it can take up an attitude to itself by examining its own nature. Prince Hal in Shakespeare's *Henry IV* Part I (1597) plays games as part of his education. Then he abandons them (and his games-loving companion Falstaff) for the serious matters of kingship and social responsibility. The play places limits on the value of games. The holiday mood must be set aside. (But one should add that although the character, Prince Hal, becomes serious, the actor is only *playing* at being serious, and the seriousness remains a game. See PLAY.) Games, of course, have a vital function in training actors, and they are very important in general education.

BARKER, C., *Theatre Games*, Eyre Methuen, 1977.
HUIZINGA, J., *Homo Ludens: a study of the play element in culture*, Routledge, 1949.

**Gas lighting**. Form of stage *lighting introduced to British theatres at Drury Lane in 1817. It soon replaced candlelight and was general until later in the nineteenth century when *electricity took over.

The advantages of gas over candlelight were considerable. It could be intensified or lowered at will (and later it could be extinguished and relit automatically by electric spark). Such flexible lighting could emphasize changes of *mood and *atmosphere. Spectacular scenic effects, such as sunsets, also became possible.

**Gauze cloth**. A cloth which is opaque when lit from the front and transparent lit from behind. It may be used as a *backcloth for a scene performed on the *forestage. When the *upstage area is lit, a new setting is magically revealed and the action can continue without pause.

***Gebrauchsmusik***. German term for *incidental music.

**Gelosi**. Well-known early *Commedia dell'Arte* company which travelled extensively in Europe in the later sixteenth century and played at the French court. Francesco Andreini (1548–1624) and his wife Isabella (1562–1604) were famous members of the troupe.

**General utility**. A lesser member of a *stock company in the mid-nineteenth century. He performed various small *roles in the different plays within the company's *repertory.

**Genre**. Sub-category of an art form, with its own *codes and *conventions. According to Hegel (1770–1831) the two principal genres — *lyric and its antithesis *epic — combined to form their synthesis, *drama. (See DIALECTIC.) In practice these main categories can be split into subordinate genres: *tragedy, *comedy, *romance, *pastoral, *heroic, *melodrama, *gothic, *satire and so on. The categories often suggest a characteristic structure and content. They are also differentiated by a characteristic *tone*.

In practice the genres often overlap. 'Tragical, comical, historical, pastoral' is not only Polonius's description of the Players' repertoire in *Hamlet* (1601), but also of Shakespeare's own mingling of tone and subject matter in his plays. So, too, Shaw claims to mingle *melodrama with *extravaganza and *sentimental comedy in *Heartbreak House* (1919). Chekhov (1860–1904) also interweaves comedy and tragedy in his plays.

The *classical tradition, it is true, strove to keep the genre pure. Racine (1639–99) achieves immense power by remaining within the narrow codes of neo-classical tragedy. At the other extreme, writers of *farce rarely venture outside the genre. Dramatic forms, however, have tended, with the advent of Ibsen (1828–1906) and *naturalism, to become mixed. In Ibsen, Shaw, Chekhov and Brecht the genres challenge one another. A more recent example is Dario Fo's *Accidental Death of an Anarchist* (1970). Farce, here, is a component of a serious political satire.

Critical concern with genre has sought to explain how and when it arises. Russian *formalism has tried to link literary form and linguistic structure. Northrop Frye has assembled an impressive and systematic description of literary *form, genre and *archetype. Others look for explanations in the social and historical process. A consideration of genre thus raises important theoretical questions about the nature and origins of art form.

FRYE, N., *Anatomy of Criticism*, Princeton University Press, 1957.

TODOROV, T., 'The Origin of Genres', in *New Literary History*, Autumn, 1976.

**Georgian theatre**. Term describing the drama of the London *patent theatres, Drury Lane and Covent Garden, during the reigns of George I (1714–27), George II (1727–60) and George III (1760–1820). The adjective 'Georgian' is more usually applied to the architecture of the period. When applied to poetry, the term refers to the early part of the reign of George V (1910–36).

SOUTHERN, R., *The Georgian Playhouse*, Pleiades, 1948.

VAN LENNEP, W., *The London Playhouse*, Vols I–V, Southern Illinois University Press, 1960–8.

**Gesamtkunstwerk**. German for 'complete art work', a concept associated with Richard Wagner (1813–83) who envisaged a theatre in which music, language and setting would work together in harmony without any one of them becoming dominant He thus aimed at a *synaesthetic experience, which recent technical developments have rendered more attainable.

The work of Adolphe Appia (1862–1928) developed from Wagner. Appia argued that the actor, through his body, expresses the music of his text, within an architectural *space, suffused by *light and shadow. (Appia therefore abolished *scene-painting.) His aim was to express in the theatre an 'essence' which the representation of reality could not achieve. His work is close to that of Edward Gordon Craig (1872–1966) and related to *symbolism. Reactions against this kind of theatre aim at creating dissonances between forms, rather than fusion. (See EPIC THEATRE.)

APPIA, A., *Die Musik und die Inscenierung* (1899).
WAGNER, R., *Oper und Drama* (1851).

**Gestalt**. *Form or pattern. A term borrowed from one of the main schools of psychology, founded by Wertheimer, Koffka and Kohler around 1910. Its principal concern was with the nature of design or pattern as the expression of more than the sum of its parts. A disciple of *Gestalt* might assert that in music the melody is more than the sum of the individual notes. As applied to drama, it could be said that the overall form is more than the sum of the play's speeches or scenes. The consideration of *Gestalt* raises complex questions about *code and *convention, and the interplay between author, culture and spectator, as also more generally between Nature, History, Language and the individual mind.

KOFFKA, K., *Principles of Gestalt Psychology*, Routledge, London, NY, 1935.

**Gestures**. Movements of the arms or hands, fluent or jerky, tense or relaxed, fast or slow. They may be *mimetic, or exist in their own right as created movement and form. The work of Artaud (1896–1948) and Grotowski (1933–   ) has sought to create original gesture in this last sense, but most theatrical gesture is mimetic and calls attention to what it copies. This it may do either naturally or, as in various forms of *comedy, in a stylized and/or extravagant way. In *naturalist drama, gesture has various functions. It may reinforce the point being made in speech (this is known as an 'echo' gesture), or throw doubt on what is said. It may seem to deliberately disguise feeling — or involuntarily to reveal it. Gesture communicates unvoiced as well as voiced emotion.

Sometimes the visual gesture can cut across the *dialogue, with the momentary effect of a *freeze. It can also communicate the 'gist' or essence of an attitude or response, as in much *oriental theatre, or in *mime, or in Brecht's 'gestic' theatre (see GESTUS).

The language of gesture varies with the style of theatre. In naturalistic plays, where verbal language is dominant, it is often best cut to a minimum. Repeated gestures communicate an actor's tensions rather than a character's feelings. 'Natural' gesture generally comes of itself when an actor relaxes. It should not attract unwanted attention.

Gesture, however, may belong to a complex and precise system of *signs, as in forms of *dance. It may then call attention to whatever attitude or feeling it represents, and at the same time call for appreciation of the skill with which it is performed. In this case, as in *mime, the continuity of the natural movement may be broken down into separate movements for emphasis.

Sometimes different gestural *codes may be introduced into the same play. This is often a source of humour, as when, say, an exuberant Mediterranean character is introduced into an English middle-class drawing room. This may have the effect of mocking both an extravagant and an inhibited physical response. Such contrastive effects are the stuff of theatre. Shakespeare achieves such an effect when he introduces a 'fantastical Spaniard' (Armado) into *Love's Labour's Lost* (1595). Brecht uses gesture for contrastive *alienation effects in his *epic theatre. For comments on gestural coding in Shakespeare's theatre, and for hints on naturalistic techniques, see:

JOSEPH, B.L., *Elizabethan Acting*, Oxford University Press, 1951.
BARKWORTH, P., *More About Acting*, Secker and Warburg, 1984, pp.40–42.

**Gestus**. A term used by Lessing as long ago as 1767, but appropriated by Bertolt Brecht in about 1930. Brecht wished to ask questions about the situations in which he placed his dramatic characters in his *epic theatre. In an attempt to show the 'gist' or essence of situations he sought a cool objective acting style which isolated and clarified a character's emotions and social attitudes. He wanted his actors to communicate by demonstration, rather than by sympathetic *identification. To this end Brecht encouraged them to carry their bodies in ways which were identifiable with social attitudes: humble or dominant, meek or aggressive. He borrowed elements from the acting style of the famous Chinese actor, Mei Lan Fang (1894–1961) and added to this a caricatural quality, deriving in part from his work on Gay's *ballad opera. To this was added a new anti-romantic baroque emphasis, which could be seen at the time in Stravinski's work (and in Russian theatre in Meyerhold's *biomechanics). In Stravinski this may be defined as an emphasis on 'one passion at a time', with each key, instrument and rhythm having a specific effect. Brecht wished each speech and scene in his plays to do the same.

Gestus is thus broader than *gesture. It is an expression in words and movement of basic attitudes. It demonstrates a relationship cut to essentials, presenting it in a dry 'chopped off' manner. This style naturally tended towards caricature and the isolating effect of a *freeze. Brecht called it 'gestic' acting.

BRECHT, B., *Brecht on Theatre*, edited and translated by J. Willett, Methuen, 1964.

**Ghost glide**. A form of *trap which allowed the ghosts of *melodrama to move eerily across the whole width of the stage. Boucicault's *The Corsican Brothers* (1852) seems to have prompted this clever device. The ghost rose along a ramp through a narrow cut in the stage which closed behind it again instantaneously. It was also known as a 'Corsican trap'.

**Globe Theatre**. The theatre built for Shakespeare's company, the Lord *Chamberlain's Men, on Bankside, Southwark, in 1599. It was burned down after a performance of Shakespeare's *Henry VIII* in 1613, and rebuilt, remaining in use until the closure of the theatres in 1642. The name reflects an attitude expressed in Jaques's famous 'All the world's a stage' in *As You Like It* (1599). The circular theatre, or 'wooden "O"', as the Chorus in *Henry V* (1599) terms it, sustained the global metaphor.

**Gloss**. Marginal comment explaining a word, phrase, or section of text.

**Gods**. Slang name for the *gallery. The French is more picturesque — '*le paradis*' and also '*le poullailler*' (the hen-run).

**Goliard**. 'Glutton'. One of the various types of *jester, *buffoon or wandering entertainer of the twelfth and thirteenth centuries.

**Gothic melodrama**. A form of *melodrama, developing in the late eighteenth century and thriving in the early nineteenth. It is full of the trappings made popular by Horace Walpole's novel *Castle of Otranto* (1764). Bandits wander through dark forests and aid or oppress the rural poor. The *hero and *heroine suffer imprisonment in ancient castles, lose themselves in the forest, and escape death by the usual hair's breadth. Matthew Lewis, author of the notorious gothic novel *The Monk* (1796), wrote ten of these melodramas, including *The Castle Spectre* (1797). Like a *suspense film by Hitchcock, these dramas seek to produce effects of *fear. They also aim to create extreme *pathos. This reminds one of Aristotle's description of the tragic *catharsis: 'through pity and fear effecting the purgation of the emotions'. Melodrama is a crude descendant of *revenge tragedy as well as a precursor of the horror film.

**Gracioso**. Comic servant figure in seventeenth-century Spanish drama.

**Grand guignol**. Collective term for nineteenth-century *cabaret theatres in Montmartre and the plays they produced, which were short and highly melodramatic. Guignol was a French *puppet deriving from *Punch. *Grand guignol*, however, used live actors.

*Grand guignol* was also played in England for short seasons. Sybil Thorndyke and Lewis Casson played a season at the Little Theatre in 1920. For a discussion of its appeal, see MELODRAMA.

**Grand opera**. Spectacular lyric *opera with no spoken *dialogue.

**Great chain of being**. Phrase describing the ancient view that the world is planned as a hierarchy of beings. At the bottom are the minerals, which only exist. Above them are the plants which exist and grow; then the animal world which exists, grows and moves; then man, who adds the faculty of thought. This relates man to the beings of pure reason, the angels who stand only under God.

Within each of the levels there are further hierarchies: the cherubim standing higher than archangels, the nobleman above the commoner, the eagle above the sparrow, gold above lead, and so on. This scale of value, and model of the world, could not long survive the collapse of the Ptolemaic cosmology which followed on the discoveries of Copernicus (1473–1543), Galileo (1564–1642) and Kepler (1571–1630).

Shakespeare made considerable use of this system. It provided a common scale of moral reference, and the *correspondences between the various levels allowed a constant cross-referencing between the natural, supernatural and political orders. Psychological, theological and social concerns could thus be simultaneously invoked and particular dramatic situations could be made 'global'.

The fullest and most famous description of the system is found in Act I scene iii of Shakespeare's *Troilus and Cressida* (1601–2). The breakdown of 'order' which Ulysses there defines is relevant to the general tension between the 'old' and the 'new' which runs through the whole of *Elizabethan and *Jacobean tragedy.

LOVEJOY, A.O., *The Great Chain of Being, A Study of the History of an Idea*, Harvard, 1936.

TILLYARD, E.M.W., *The Elizabethan World Picture*, Chatto and Windus, 1943.

**Greek theatre**. Broad term embracing the various forms of *comedy and *tragedy performed in Athens and elsewhere in Greece between the sixth century B.C. and the rise of Rome. It generally implies the extant, mainly fifth-century B.C. drama played at religious festivals in honour of *Dionysos.

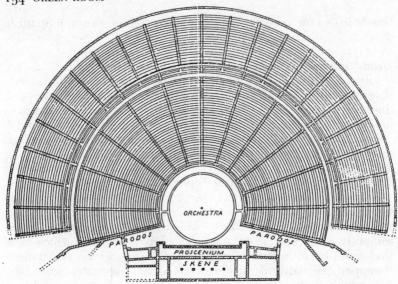

**12** *Plan of the theatre at Epidauros*

Greek theatres were large amphitheatres seating up to 18,000 spectators, who looked down on a circular dancing-place or *orchestra and a long narrow stage backed by the *skene. The *chorus had a very important function, since music, dance, song and group movement could make a powerful appeal to such huge audiences. Unfortunately, beyond the metrics of the text, little evidence of the operatic nature of Greek drama remains to us. Moreover, only about one-tenth of the plays written by Aeschylus (525–456 B.C.), Sophocles (496–406 B.C.) and Euripides (484–407/6 B.C.) are extant. About one-quarter of the plays of Aristophanes (c.448–c.380 B.C.) remain. Thus the extant proportion of the total dramatic output of this extraordinary culture is very small.

BIEBER, M., *The History of the Greek and Roman Theatre*, Oxford University Press, 1961.

JONES, J., *On Aristotle and Greek Tragedy*, Chatto, 1962.

NIETZSCHE, F.W., *The Birth of Tragedy*, trs. W. Kaufmann, Doubleday, 1956.

VICKERS, B., *Towards Greek Tragedy*, Longman, 1973.

**Green room**. Room for actors not required on stage, often used for receiving friends before and after the play.

**Groove**. A scene-setting device used in the *Restoration, *Georgian and *Victorian theatre. The *wings slid into place on grooves set (in Sheridan's Drury Lane) five feet apart. This created scenic and *perspective effects, and allowed quick *scene-changes, especially with the introduction of the *drum and shaft. The system was superseded by the *box-set (which masked the wings more effectively) and the more complex staging which nineteenth-century technology permitted. Henry Irving removed the last grooves from his Lyceum Theatre in 1880. (See Ill.30, p.432.)

**Grotesque**. A *genre in drama, music and the plastic arts. It presents strange, even hideous, incongruities and embodies a mocking attitude to aspiration after purity, beauty and all absolutes. The word originates in the discovery of bizarre sculpted forms, mingling human, plant and animal elements, in catacombs (*grotti*) in fifteenth-century Italy. These seem to assert the totality of life, and remind us of the connections we prefer not to recognize. They mock the 'individuating principle' to which Nietzsche gave the term 'apollonian'.

In the theatre it has obvious connections with the medieval spirit of *carnivalesque, as defined by M. Bakhtin in *The World of Rabelais*, and it runs through forms of *popular drama, such as *puppet theatre and the *Commedia dell'Arte*, to satirical and caricatural drama in the twentieth century.

V. Meyerhold (1874–1940) was especially interested in the grotesque. 'The basis of the grotesque,' he declared, 'is the artist's constant desire to switch the spectator from the point he has just reached to another which is totally unforeseen'. This reminds one of the comic and caricatural *alienation effects of Brecht. Meyerhold, however, was thinking of Aleksandr Blok (1880–1921) in *The Unknown Woman* and *The Fairground Booth* and of Sologub (1863–1927) and Frank Wedekind (1864–1918) in *Spring's Awakening* and *Pandora's Box*. They achieve, he says, unusual effects 'within the bounds of realistic drama, by resorting to the grotesque'. Unlike Brecht, Meyerhold's concerns seem to be with the *inclusiveness* of the genre, which was comic, but could easily, as in Goya's pictures or Edgar Allan Poe's stories, come close to *tragedy. He saw in it a search beneath the surfaces of life to 'vast unfathomed depths' and continues: 'In its search for the supernatural the grotesque synthesizes opposites, creates a picture of the incredible, and invites the spectator to solve the riddle of the inscrutable'. He goes on to argue that only in *dance can the grotesque be subordinated to a decorative task. The observation raises again the question of the function of choral dance in ancient drama. Consideration of the genre carries one back to the *folk and religious *origins of drama.

BRAUN, E. (ed.), *Meyerhold on Theatre*, Eyre Methuen, 1969.
SYMONS, J.M., *Meyerhold's Theatre of the Grotesque: The Post-revolutionary Productions 1920–32*, Rivers Press, 1973.
THOMSON, P., *The Grotesque*, Critical Idiom Series, Methuen, 1972.

**Grotowski, Jerzy** (1933–   ). Influential Polish director and founder of the *Theatre Laboratorium which sought to develop the powers of the *actor to the utmost:

> I am trying to create a theatre of participation, to rediscover factors which characterize the original of the theatre. Place actors and spectators close together, in a new scenic space which embraces the entire room, and you may create a living collaboration. Thanks to physical contact the spark can cross between them.

> No one since Stanislavski has investigated the nature of acting, its phenomenon, its meaning, the nature and science of its mental-physical-emotional processes, as deeply as Grotowski. (Peter Brook).

See: RICH THEATRE; POOR THEATRE; VOICE.
GROTOWSKI, J., *Towards a Poor Theatre*, edited by E. Barba, Methuen, 1969.
KUMIEGA, J., *The Theatre of Grotowski*, Methuen, 1985.

**Groundplan**. Plan of the lay-out of a stage set, showing position of doors, windows, furniture, *rostra, etc. It is of practical use to *carpenters and stagehands. It also helps readers to visualize stage *movement.

**Groundrow**. Long, low piece of *scenery representing, say, a hedge or any other appropriate scenic detail and designed to stand independently *upstage. It was originally used to mask the strips of gas lighting (also called groundrows) which lit upstage scenery.

**Grouping**. The placing of actors in relation to one another on stage. In *naturalistic theatre the grouping should normally be such as to focus unobtrusive attention on whatever is most important to the scene. This usually means avoiding placing the characters in flat lines, or in rectangular groups, but rather in triangles with the apex *upstage, so that the dominant character may face outwards, and the positions of subordinate figures may lead the eye towards him.

More stylized theatre, less dependent on spoken *dialogue, has a greater flexibility of formal composition. Whatever the dramatic *genre, however, the nature of the *space and the position of the spectators will determine the effective groupings. The main rule is to avoid *masking wherever possible, and to create groups of visual interest, with a clear dramatic *focus. Where the spectators are mainly looking down on the action the grouping will inevitably be more three-dimensional. Where they are on a single *level, and on one side only of the stage, the limitations are greater. The need then, especially in plays with large *casts, is to use different levels on stage. See POSTURE, MOVEMENT, FREEZE. For comments on naturalistic direction see:
FERNALD, J., *The Play Produced*, pp.50–61, Kenyon-Deane, 1933; *Sense of Direction: the director and his actors*, Secker, 1968.

**Group theatre**. Form of theatre in which drama is produced as a collaborative venture; the group researches, writes, improvises and finally creates the overall structure of performance. It often uses an extension of Stanislavski's *improvisation methods and is practised by *avant-garde, *community theatre and *fringe groups of various kinds. Julien Beck's *Living Theatre is an example. Such groups often possess a common social or political purpose and develop a great cohesion because they use techniques which make them aware of the problems, qualities and capacities of each member. This awareness is invaluable in production and in the creation of performances which express the group's aims. The tensions which arise in such groups are those which occur whenever creative individuals come together, gifted in different ways and to different degrees. Some unifying mind and dominant personality generally arises to provide direction and control. For a discussion of group working methods see:
CLARK, B., *Group Theatre*, Pitman, 1971.

**Group Theatre**. The Important American company which flourished artistically, and struggled financially, between 1931 and 1941 under Harold Clurman, Lee Strasberg and Cheryl Crawford, who later became associated with the *Actors' Studio of New York and the well-known *'method' school of acting. As with the later company, the principles of Stanislavski lay behind the Group Theatre. It was concerned with high standards of *ensemble acting and sought to stage serious social drama. Brecht's musical collaborator, Kurt Weill (1900–1950) settled in New York in 1935 and was involved in productions of Paul Green's *The House of Connolly* and *Johnny Johnson* (1936). *Waiting for Lefty* (1935) by Clifford Odets (1906–63), its major dramatist and a member of the company, is perhaps the best known of the Group Theatre's productions.
CLURMAN, H., *The Fervent Years*, Hill and Wang, 1957.

**Guignol**. French *puppet figure deriving from *Polichinelle and dating from the late eighteenth century. See GRAND GUIGNOL.

**Guild productions**. Medieval plays produced by the guilds in market-place and guildhall. After the church had banned the clergy from participation in Easter plays within church buildings the guilds took over responsibility for appropriate episodes of the *mystery cycles. They built the scenes, provided the actors and costumes and produced the plays. Records remain both of the moneys they disbursed and the seriousness of their concern. See:
WICKHAM, G., *Early English Stages*, 2 vols., Routledge, 1959 and 1963.

**Guiser/Guisard**. Performer in a *disguising.

# H

**Ham acting**. Acting which is exaggerated and unconvincing. The development of *naturalism called attention to the artificiality of nineteenth-century melodramatic and tragic acting, so that strong histrionic gestures came to be seen as 'ham'. The old serious *convention then became comic or *burlesque. *Melodrama, in particular, began to *parody itself, as audiences became more sophisticated.

The old style, however, may still be put to serious use. Brecht's notes on the performance of Peter Lorre in *Mann ist Mann* (1928) show an interest in heightened 'gestic' acting for caricatural purposes (see GESTUS). Pirandello's *Six Characters in Search of an Author* (1921) requires a contrast between heightened and more natural acting styles to distinguish the 'Characters' from the 'Actors' in the play. Samuel Beckett (1906–   ) has characters who alternate between pretence and 'ordinariness'. 'How was I?', says Pozzo in *Waiting for Godot* (1953), worried lest he has given a 'ham' performance. The central character in *Endgame* (1957) is even called Hamm.

Each of these authors in different ways calls attention to the element of artifice in life. The 'ham acting' mocks, or makes poignant, the human beings who become, wish to become, or fail to become, the *roles they play. Deliberately exaggerated styles can thus do more than appeal to accepted conventions; they may mock or illuminate our conventional attitudes. The style is only 'ham' where the acting is unskilled, or the actor unaware that the convention is no longer acceptable.

**Hamartia**. Greek for 'error'. The term occurs in Aristotle's discussion of the best kind of *protagonist in *tragedy. He concludes that the tragic *hero should be neither eminently virtuous nor deliberately wicked, but should suffer from hamartia — some human frailty, error of judgement, or ignorance which precipitates his fall. Since the *naturalist movement, the tendency has been to assume that the error is the fault of the individual, but in ancient forms of tragedy the error is imposed from above by the gods. The concept hovers between psychological and theological views of the world and raises the central tragic questions about freedom, responsibility and fate. The most famous expression and consideration of hamartia is found in Hamlet's introspective concern with the reasons why he cannot avenge his father's murder. Before he even meets the Ghost he is already reflecting on men who have 'some vicious mole of nature in them', whose virtues

> Shall in the general censure take corruption
> From that particular fault: the dram of eale
> Doth all the noble substance of a doubt,
> To his own scandal. (I.iv.35–8)

How far Hamlet was responsible for his situation and in what consists the 'dram of eale' not only puzzled Hamlet but has intrigued critics and audiences ever since.

**Hand-props**. The *properties an actor brings on stage with him, as opposed to those which are already there as part of the set.

**Hand-puppet**. A *puppet which is pulled on the hand like a glove, and manipulated by inserting fingers into the head and arms. *Punch and Judy are hand puppets.

**Hand-worked house**. A theatre in which the scenery is worked by ropes from a *fly-floor. See COUNTERWEIGHT HOUSE; HEMPHOUSE.

**Hans Stockfisch**. Stage name of John Spencer, who travelled the continent with the *English Comedians in the seventeenth century.

**Hanswurst**. Peasant character from Austrian folk-lore; *knock-about clown in early eighteenth-century Viennese comedy. He wore a red jacket with a blue heart on it, a green hat, leather belt, red braces, and yellow trousers. He was seen no more after the death of Gottfried Prehauser (1699–1769) who had taken over the part from the originator, Joseph Stranitsky (1676–1726).

The sausage, '*Wurst*', seems to play an essential role in this kind of comedy. Punch and Judy shows and the *Commedia dell'Arte* tradition frequently feature strings of sausages. The reason no doubt lies in the earthiness of the folk tradition.

**Happening**. Theatrical event, not generally staged in a theatre, in which, to quote J.-P. Sartre, 'the real swallows the illusion', destroying the comfort of the *suspension of disbelief.

Antecedents of the happening can be seen in *surrealism, *dadaism and in the *theatre of cruelty of Antonin Artaud (1896–1948). They are found more directly in the *synaesthetic experiments of Allan Kaprow at the Black Mountain College in North Carolina in the 1950s. Music, noise, movement, light, film, and so on, combined to assault the senses. Kaprow's original *Happening* (1959) encouraged many such performances in the 1960s. They generally consisted of a planned series of actions or signals which triggered responses from actors and spectators, leading to spontaneous improvising. The purpose, as defined by J.-J. Lebel, was 'to allow creativity to function freely without regard for market forces or social approval or disapproval.' The happening aimed, he said, 'to eliminate middlemen and ignore cultural watchdogs'.

One notorious happening *within* the theatre was the reputed burning of a real butterfly in Peter Brook's production of *US* (1966), about the cruelty of the Vietnam war. Such a break with theatrical pretence aims to arouse audience anger, but the problem then is how to direct it. If the intention is to call attention to the cruelty of war, then the butterfly is only a *symbol. But to burn a real butterfly is to call attention to the 'vehicle' or *signifier and divert attention from the 'tenor' or *signified. The butterfly is no longer a *metaphor. The burning arouses sympathy for the butterfly and anger against the perpetuators in the theatre. The shock of reality prevents the anger from being transferred. (The counter-argument is that the spectator is shocked into an awareness that the seriousness of events in Vietnam far outweighs the death of an insect. We interrogate the nature of our sympathies. The discomfort, arguably, remains.)

Happenings in the theatre seem to have been a passing phase. This may have been because such shock tactics inhibited the spectator's imagination. The emphasis, too, on spontaneity and freedom made it difficult to record and reproduce texts.

KAPROW, A., *Assemblage, Environments and Happenings*, NY, 1965.
KIRBY, M., *Happenings — an Illustrated Anthology*, Dutton, NY, 1965.
LEBEL, J.-J., 'On the Necessity of Violation', in *The Drama Review*, Fall, 1968.

**Harlequin**. The dreamy lover of *Columbine in the early English *pantomime and *harlequinade. He is the eternal child: open, trusting, always going forward. He 'acts horizontally' says the well-known *mime, David Glass. The name, but not the character, derives from *Arlecchino, one of the quick-witted *zanni of the *Commedia dell'Arte*.

**Harlequinade**. An important element of the early English *pantomime, deriving from the scenarios of the *Commedia dell'Arte*, and brought to London in the late seventeenth century, as *Italian Night Scenes*, by the Drury Lane dancing master, John Weaver (1673–1760). The transfer, together with some confusion in the doubling of roles, changed the quick-witted *Arlecchino into *Harlequin the persecuted lover, who, with the aid of a good fairy, a magic wand, and *transformation scenes, managed to elude Columbine's father *Pantaloon.

The Harlequinade changed in character in the early nineteenth century when Joseph Grimaldi (1778–1837) made Clown the chief figure. The dance element and the Harlequin story were then overpowered by *knockabout comedy and the folk and fairy-tale

elements of pantomime.
WILSON, A.E., *The Story of Pantomime*, Home and Van Thal, 1949.

**Hatred**. See ANGER.

***Haupt und Staatsactionen***. A form of vernacular historical
*melodrama, performed by the *English Comedians, and by native
travelling players, in Germany and Austria in the seventeenth and
eighteenth centuries. The clowning of *Pickelhering and later
*Hanswurst, cutting across the serious action, had strong comic
appeal, but the *farce and mingling of *genre led to condemnation
by *neo-classical dramatists such as Johann Gottsched (1700–66).

**Heavens**. See TIRING HOUSE.

**Heavy father**. A type role in Victorian *melodrama, played by one
specialist actor in the *stock company. A 'heavy' was an actor who
normally played serious rather than comic roles, for example,
Maria Marten's father in the anonymous *Maria Marten or Murder in
the Red Barn* (1830s).

**Hegel, G.W.F.**, (1770–1831). Major German philosopher who
attempted to unify the dualisms of Immanuel Kant within the
dialectical model which Karl Marx was to adapt to an economic
materialism. His influence on dramatic theorists such as Bertolt
Brecht and Jean-Paul Sartre is strong.

> Hegel taught us that drama emerges from a collision of possibilities.
> (Jean-Paul Sartre).

See: CAUSALITY; DIALECTIC; UNIVERSALS.
HEGEL, G.W.F., *Aesthetics: Lectures on Fine Art*, 2 Vols., Clarendon,
1975; *On Tragedy*, edited by H. and A. Paolucci, Harper, 1975.

**Hellenistic theatre**. The period of the *Greek theatre roughly
between the death of Alexander (323 B.C.) and that of Cleopatra
(31 B.C.). Information about the drama and its staging is very
scanty. We have the remains of theatres, such as that at Epidauros
(4th century B.C.) which tell us that drama was acted in a circular
*orchestra, and on a raised stage, before thousands of spectators.
Of the plays performed, apart from fifth-century *classical drama,
we have fragments and reconstructions of six plays by Menander
(c.342–292 B.C.). These indicate the continuing decline in the
importance of the *chorus, and a shift from the exuberant *satire
of Aristophanes's *old comedy to the urban love plots of *new
comedy. Apart from Menander, the Hellenistic period bequeathed
little drama to later ages.
BIEBER, M., *The History of the Greek and Roman Theatre*, Princeton
University Press, 1961.

**Hemistichomythia**. Verse *dialogue of alternating half-lines. See STICHOMYTHIA.

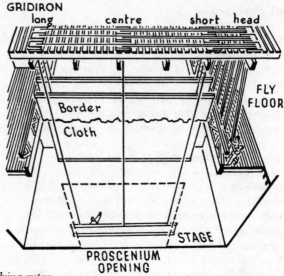

**13** *Hemp line flying system*

**Hemphouse**. A *hand-worked house using rope rigging for *flies, rather than wire-rope and counterweights. Originally hemp, the rope now used is manila.

**Hermeneutics**. A branch of study concerned with the revelation of biblical truth, or more generally with the essential meaning behind human behaviour and human institutions. Applied to drama it is concerned with the interpretation of essential meanings behind external *plot development. It is closely related to the *proairetic analysis of plot, and to the way an author suppresses, postpones and reveals *secrets. For a literary analysis, see:
BARTHES, R., *S/Z*, Seuil, 1970, trs. R. Miller, Cape, 1975.

**Hero/Heroine**. In early mythology, *epic heroes such as Achilles and Theseus were demi-gods endowed with supreme strength and courage. The later heroes of Greek drama, though still legendary, move more in the realm of history. As kings and queens, princes or princesses, they have special powers, and may, like Oedipus, have special wisdom. It is, however, their mortality and fallibility which begins to be emphasized. They break sacred laws and commit acts of *hubris. Heroes are thus gradually diminished and humanized. With Euripides (484–407/6 B.C.) they are often treated with ironic detachment and become smaller still. At this point the word 'hero' acquires its principal meaning: the *protagonist or central character in a play.

Heroes and heroines in Greek *tragedy thus move across the borderline between myth and history, and between theology and psychology, losing their god-like powers as they do so. In *Elizabethan drama, the nature of the hero's weakness and the limitations of human power continued to be scrutinized. In *King Lear* (1605) and *Othello* (1604), Shakespeare examined men who would be heroes to themselves. In *Antony and Cleopatra* (1606–7) a certain irony invests the heroic vision the protagonists have of one another. They aspire to immortality but in their poignant loss of power, the disparity between these heroes and the gods is clear.

With the rise of the European merchant and middle classes, heroes and heroines of lower rank began to appear. Men and women previously accorded comic treatment were now presented seriously as central figures. Lillo's *London Merchant* (1731) anticipates the *bourgeois figures of Ibsen (1828–1906) and Strindberg (1849–1912) in such plays as *The Master Builder* (1896) and *The Father* (1887). The hero's power is now localized. Supreme social power gives way to power in the family, or in business.

Loss of power is again a central concern, and interestingly it is often the woman who gains power. Whether this woman may be called a heroine is frequently dubious. The word has normally been applied to women in whom *moral value* is invested, such as Sophocles's Antigone or Shakespeare's Cordelia or Desdemona. Heroism with power has tended to be male, and it has probably always been more difficult to call women with power 'heroines' than men with power 'heroes'. Such figures as Clytemnestra, Phaedra, the Bacchae, and Ibsen's Hedda Gabler, challenge male dominance, but in the process they may seem, to many men and some women, immoral rather than heroic.

The idea of heroines thus changes with the rise of new social groups. Working-class *melodrama creates heroines who languish in the power of aristocratic *villains but compensates them with an almost magical power to escape their machinations. Chekhov has 'heroes' and 'heroines' who lack power in a paralysing social situation. His declared intention, however, is anti-heroic. We must see people as they are, he stated in his *Letters*, 'not outsize, and puffed up'.

Serious working-class heroes emerge in such plays as Arthur Miller's *Death of a Salesman* (1949). (See Miller's comments on 'mundane heroes' in the introduction to his *Collected Plays*.) It was Brecht, however, who warned us against needing or seeking heroes. The adulation of Hitler and the growth of twentieth-century personality cults created a new awareness of the dangers of admiring *power. Brecht's small heroes and heroines maintain human values within a power structure which threatens to destroy them. Unlike Antigone, they know compromise and capitulation. They struggle as much to exist *within* power structures as to resist them. The moment of moral choice comes, however, as for Kattrin in *Mother Courage* (1941), and the need for heroism is again revealed.

Discussions of the historical evolution of the hero owe much to Hegel, who distinguishes three types of hero corresponding to three historical phases: (a) the *epic hero who struggles with natural forces and is crushed by fate; (b) the *tragic hero who bears his fate within himself as *hamartia; (c) the dramatic hero who adapts to the world and avoids destructive passion. See DIALECTIC.

BRECHT, B., *Brecht on Theatre*, ed. J. Willett, Methuen, 1964.

HEGEL, G.W.F., *Aesthetics*, Clarendon, 1975; *On Tragedy*, Harper, 1975.

**Heroic comedy**. Play with happy ending involving conflict between characters of high rank. It was imported from Spain and the drama of Lope de Vega (1562–1635) by Pierre Corneille in his *Don Sancho d'Aragon* (1650).

**Heroic drama/tragedy**. A form which developed out of *Jacobean drama. It may be traced in the work of Beaumont (1584–1616), Fletcher (1579–1625), Richard Brome (1590–1652/3) and James Shirley (1596–1666). D'Avenant's *Love and Honour* (1634) may be taken as characteristic of this genre. Social intrigue takes the place of matters of national and general concern. Concepts such as 'innocence' and 'honour' are removed from the human situation and become conventions. The verse structure, too, loses flexibility.

After the *Restoration, with the strong influence of French drama and the observance of such *neo-classical principles as the *unities, heroic drama acquired an elaborate formalism. Dryden's *Conquest of Granada* (1670) reflects this influence as it exhibits the violence and rhetoric of the post-Senecan tradition. Buckingham (1628–1687) in *The Rehearsal* (1671) burlesqued the form to such effect that heroic drama virtually ceased to exist.

DRYDEN, J., *Of Heroic Plays* (1672).

**High comedy**. George Meredith's term for witty and sophisticated comedy, as compared with *slapstick and *farce, which are *low comedy.

MEREDITH, G., *The Idea of Comedy* (1877).

**Hilarody**. Form of low Greek *mime which seems to have involved a *parody of *tragedy. See LYSIODY; MAGODY; SIMODY.

**Himation**. A long mantle, usually hanging from the right shoulder, worn with a *mask and long-sleeved, yellow robe, by Greek actors portraying gods or *heroes in *classical tragedy. See CHLAMYS.

**Hints**. Clues, both obvious and subtle, deliberately placed so that a dramatic character, and/or the audience, may divine the *secrets hidden in a play. Hints advance or *foreshadow the *action, intensify *suspense and generally implicate the spectator in the web of ignorance and awareness normally known as dramatic *irony. Thus in Sophocles's *Oedipus Rex* (*c*.430 B.C.) the hints which Oedipus is given of his origins involve spectators in Oedipus's growth of awareness and remind them of the varying states of knowledge of the characters around him. A distinction should be made between this function of the 'hint', which creates *empathy (the audience is aware of the pain it will cause characters to learn facts which the audience already knows) and the 'whodunnit' hint, which comes to an audience in an exciting flash of *discovery.

**Historical drama**. Drama which deals with historical events. It includes: Aeschylus's *The Persae* (472 B.C.); the Elizabethan *chronicle plays; the Elizabethan history plays which followed from them, such as Marlowe's *Edward II* (1594) and Shakespeare's *Richard III* (1593); Dryden's *All for Love* (1678); Sheridan's (adapted) *Pizarro* (1799); Goethe's *Goetz von Berlichingen* (1773); Byron's *Manfred* (1817); Ibsen's *The Pretenders* (1864); Shaw's *St Joan*; and Brecht's *Galileo* (1937). Such examples illustrate the variety and extent of the *genre.

Historical material presents particular problems for a dramatist. The complexity of the historical process means that a writer must select and eliminate. Only a limited number of characters and events may be presented, and those chosen must fit a dramatic shape which will keep the audience's interest. This normally involves some falsification of the historical time sequence.

A dramatist may argue that the accurate representation of historical events does not lie in the rendering of detail, but in the discovery of *pattern*, and hence his selection is 'true'. Such truth, however, is always subject to dispute. In particular, it may be argued that drama personalizes history, giving too much freedom to individuals in positions of power. It cannot, by its very nature, suggest the operation of material trends over a substantial period. It works most effectively by selecting moments of crisis and private conflict. The moments drama can best present are not necessarily the moments when history is 'made'.

However, by focusing on 'nodal' conflicts, on moments of crucial decision, and by making characters represent the diversity of interests at stake, much can be vividly communicated. Social trends express themselves in human attitudes, and though, compared with the novel, or with written history, drama lacks room for comment and analysis, and though compared with *film it lacks a capacity for precise visual reconstruction, the form at its height, as in the history plays of Shakespeare, can vividly convey the amalgam of surface reality and social tendency which one may call history (especially when that drama adds a sense of what Schopenhauer (1788–1860) called 'the derisive mockery of *chance'). One may further argue that even if the play does not represent the 'actual' past it may present a *model of human and social interaction which reveals how the past was *seen*, and this itself becomes history.

LUKÁCS, G., *The Historical Novel*, Merlin Press, trs. 1962, Ch. 2.

RIBNER, I., *The English History Play in the Age of Shakespeare*, Princeton, 1957, rev. ed., Methuen, 1965.

**History of the theatre; History of drama**. The two terms are often used interchangeably. The first, however, generally implies a greater emphasis on the study of theatre buildings; the second, on the study of dramatic texts. Any study of the history of either, of course, involves study of its relation to cultural history. See:

BROCKETT, O., *The Theatre: an Introduction*, 2nd ed., Holt Reinhart, NY, 1969.

FREEDLEY, G., and REEVES, J.A., *A History of the Theatre*, 3rd ed., Crown, NY, 1968.

HARTNOLL, P., *A Concise History of the Theatre*, Thames and Hudson, 1968.

NAGLER, A.M., *Sources of Theatrical History*, Theatre Annual, 1952.

**Histrio**. A general medieval term for an actor.

**Hobby horse**. A performer dressed as a horseman with a wickerwork frame around him to represent a horse. He was commonly seen in *folk drama and festivals, and appeared with *morris dancers and *mummers from medieval to Elizabethan times.

**Hocktide Play**. Medieval game played at Hocktide, a holiday festival commemorating an English victory over the Danes in 1002. It seems to have consisted of obstructing the highway with ropes and extracting forfeits from passers-by of the opposite sex. The men played on the Monday and the women on Hockday itself, which was a Tuesday.

Sir Walter Scott's novel *Kenilworth* (1821) contains, in chapter 39, a description of revels put on for Queen Elizabeth I at Kenilworth, over Hocktide in 1575.

**Holograph**. A manuscript wholly in the author's handwriting.

**Holy theatre**. One of four categories of theatre that Peter Brook defines in his influential book *The Empty Space* (MacGibbon and Kee, 1968). He invokes the sacred origins of drama, and argues that theatre 'makes visible the Invisible', using *sound, *form, *rhythm, *colour, and *movement. Holy theatre breaks out of the ordinary world. It carries an actor, and perhaps the spectator, to some further reality where they become 'rapt' or 'possessed'. In doing so, Brook hints, it may bring back those problematic words — poetry, nobility, beauty, magic — to our ordinary lives. The term suggests what Brook attempted, and for many achieved, in his production of Shakespeare's *A Midsummer Night's Dream* (1970). For a critique see Kenneth Tynan 'On the moral neutrality of Peter Brook' in:

TRUSSLER, S. (ed.), *New Theatre Voices of the Seventies*, Eyre Methuen, 1981, Ch. 12.

**Horace** (65–8 B.C.). Latin poet and critic whose work greatly influenced *neo-classical critics in the seventeenth and eighteenth centuries. He was an advocate of *decorum and the 'rules' of the five-act play — off-stage action and a *chorus with a high moral tone, for example.

> You will not let Medea slay her boys before the audience.

> Neither should a god intervene unless a knot befalls worthy of his interference.

> For yourselves, do you thumb well by night and day Greek models.

See: ACT.
HORACE, 'On the Art of Poetry', in *Classical Literary Criticism*, Penguin, 1965.

**House**. (a) The 'domus' or *mansion of *medieval drama. (b) The theatre audience, as in the terms 'full house' or 'good house'. (c) Actor's parlance for the whole theatre, or playhouse; 'front of house' is the area in front of the stage.

**House curtain**. The front *curtain.

**House style**. A style of production associated with a particular theatre or group.

**Hubris**. A dominant idea in ancient Greek culture and in *classical *tragedy. Hubris is arrogance in word, deed or thought, deriving from complacency and success, and inevitably punished by the jealous gods. Agamemnon is guilty of hubris when he treads on the sacred carpet in Aeschylus's *Oresteia* (458 B.C.). Oedipus is hubristic in his ignorance of the limits of his knowledge. Shakespeare's King Lear is hubristic to imagine he had god-like power: 'They told me I was everything.' (See PRIDE.)

It is possible that a function of the tragic *catharsis was to purge the audience of complacency and hubris, by engendering *fear and presenting a spectacle of mortality.

DODDS, E.R., *The Greeks and the Irrational*, University of California Press, 1951, Ch. 2.

**Humour**. (a) Form of sympathetic *comedy, less biting than *wit, with which it is often compared. (b) One of the four fluids which, according to early psychological theory, constituted the human body, as the four elements constituted the natural world. Black bile, phlegm, blood, and yellow bile or choler, were the equivalent of earth, water, air, and fire. When mixed they formed the four human 'temperaments' — melancholic, phlegmatic, sanguine or choleric — depending on which humour was dominant. The types were recognizable and the Elizabethans used them in their drama both as a *code of reference and as a typology to question and redefine. Shakespeare's Hamlet, for example, is melancholy, but a primitive psychology, such as the 'theory of humours', is insufficient to account for his behaviour. Indeed the character himself uses his theoretical 'humour' as a *mask behind which to hide. Ben Jonson, in his *Everyman in his Humour* (1598) and *Everyman out of his Humour* (1599), uses the typology for comic and satirical purposes. See COMEDY OF HUMOURS.

BURTON, R., *Anatomy of Melancholy* (1621).

CAMPBELL, L.B., *Shakespeare's Tragic Heroes*, Cambridge, 1930, pp.52ff.

TILLYARD, E.M.W., *The Elizabethan World Picture*, Chatto and Windus, 1943, Ch. 5, Section 4.

**Hurry**. A kind of musical accompaniment in Victorian *melodrama, communicating the need for characters to hurry at anxious moments.

**Hut**. See TIRING HOUSE.

**Hypocrites**. Literally 'answerer'; the Greek term for an actor. It probably derives from the original speaker, who answered in part or full the questions asked by the chorus.

# I

**Icon**. The American logician, C.S. Pierce, defines three kinds of *sign: icon, *index and *symbol. The icon is 'a sign which refers to the object it denotes merely by virtue of characters of its own.' Thus a portrait or a photograph is an icon because it possesses *identifiable characteristics* of the person it represents.

The word is not widely used in drama criticism, though its obvious application is to *naturalism, which presents identifiable characteristics of a particular time and place. Even in naturalistic theatre, however, the sign may become index and symbol as well as icon. Shaw's St Joan is a case in point, or more obviously perhaps Chekhov's seagull. In the play of that name the stage prop represents a 'real' seagull, and is thus an icon. It also indicates off-stage 'realities', such as the lake, and is thus an index. Author and characters, however, use it symbolically: 'I'm a seagull,' says Nina.

A sign in the theatre varies between the condition of icon and the condition of symbol. It may be icon for one spectator, or for one character within the play, and it may be symbol for another spectator or character. The sign may be complex in itself and complex also in the ways it can be seen. The dramatic power of much naturalistic theatre, in fact, depends on the tension between different ways of seeing the sign. In Ibsen's *The Wild Duck* (1884) the duck is seen prosaically by pedestrian characters and symbolically by the neurotic. An adolescent girl lives at the point where these ways of seeing are not clearly differentiated. She has the common sense to know that a duck is only a duck, the attic only an attic. But under pressure this gives way to a symbolic way of seeing, with tragic results. The tension between icon and symbol is the central psychological concern of the play. For an application of these terms to theatre criticism see:

ELAM, K., *The Semiotics of Theatre and Drama*, Methuen, 1980, Ch. 2.

**Iconography**. Pictorial representation. The 'making' or 'writing' of *signs. The term may be applied to straightforward *scene-painting, but it is also applicable to those elements of dramatic *dialogue which refer to visual *codes shared by writer and audience. Thus Shakespeare makes iconographic references to 'Patience on a monument', or to 'Fortune's wheel' or 'Hell-gate'. Such phrases assume the audience's recognition of commonly available pictures — especially important in a culture where literacy was low.

A problem arises, of course, when these pictorial codes are no longer shared, as is the case now with the examples cited. We no longer have mental images of goddesses sitting patiently or turning fortune's wheel. We have no visual memory of the monstrous mouth from which the devils issued in a medieval *morality play. The pictorial codes have disappeared and some study of medieval iconography is necessary before such mental images can rise again from the words. Even then, the associated feelings will have largely gone, though a new sense of the alien nature of a past culture may replace them.

What then should *designers do when working on a new production of a play which appeals to iconographic conventions? The answer will vary according to whether a designer feels he should use and recover the old patterns, whether he should find some modern equivalent, or whether he should ignore the past altogether.

FRASER, R.A., *Shakespeare's Poetics: in Relation to King Lear*, Routledge, 1962.

CAWLEY, A.C., JONES, M., MACDONALD, P.F., MILLS, D. (eds.), *Revels History of Drama in English*, Vol. I, Methuen, 1983, pp.281–6.

**Ideal spectator**. (a) The average man or woman for whom a dramatist writes, e.g. Terence Rattigan's 'Aunt Edna'. (b) A character who is the 'audience's representative'. Horatio in *Hamlet* (1601) is an example of the latter. He is Hamlet's *confidant, a man who never acts or pretends; he remains himself, and not only Hamlet, but the audience, can be assured of his identity. His function is to give the audience, as well as the central character, a kind of security. With him we feel we know where we are, and who Hamlet is. Such a character is especially useful when a play is ambiguous, or difficult in other ways. There may be more things in heaven and earth than are dreamed of in his philosophy, but Horatio lends solidity to the nebulous scene. (c) The term may also be used of a character who seems to represent the author's viewpoint, such as the choral commentator in Arthur Miller's *A View from the Bridge* (1955) or the Stage-Manager in Thornton Wilder's *Our Town* (1938). Of course, a character who is too close to the author can easily become a bore. Omniscience is dramatically dangerous and it is wiser to disguise authorial views within characters who have obvious limitations. Thus the narrator, Henry Carr, in Tom Stoppard's *Travesties* (1974), steps entertainingly in and out of the play, sometimes ignorant and sometimes wise. Moreover his younger self within the play is sometimes wiser than the older choral commentator. Older is not necessarily wiser, and ideal observers, such as Eliot's Harcourt-Reilly in *The Cocktail Party* (1949) do not always make omniscience appealing. Where 'ideal spectator' means 'author's mouthpiece' it is often best to do without one.

SCHLEGEL, A.W., *Course of Dramatic Literature* (1814).

**Idée fixe**. A fixed idea or obsession. The character with an *idée fixe* may receive both comic and serious treatment. According to the theory of Henri Bergson (1859–1941) comedy depends on *stereotypes who have ceased to *live* and therefore change. Molière gives us the miser obsessed with money, or the hypochondriac obsessed with his own health, and these characters are objects of mirth. Their minds are literally fixed and our laughter betrays a healthy awareness of the narrowness of such states.

At a certain point, however, perhaps when an obsession is felt to be dangerous or harmful to either the possessor, or to other characters around him (i.e. when 'reality' enters the dramatic situation), obsession ceases to be comic. King Lear's obsession with his daughters' unkindness, or Timon's misanthropy, are too understandable and too powerful to be laughed away. The fixity approaches madness and a tragic condition.

The *idée fixe* is clearly related to neurotic and psychotic states. Valéry's theories on the condition (see his *Idée Fixe* (1932)) argue a relation with memory and creativity. It is certainly an important question for theorists of drama to consider.

BERGSON, H., *Le Rire: essai sur la signification du comique* (1900).

**Identification**. Process by which a writer, actor, spectator or reader extends or loses his own *identity and acquires, or merges with, a new one. The extent to which there is loss or gain of identity when performing, watching, writing, or reading about the activities and sufferings of dramatic and fictional characters cannot be precisely established. Coleridge remarked that in their *play, children never allow the *roles they assume to usurp their personalities. The same writer coined the phrase *'suspension of disbelief', but was careful to call it a 'wilful' suspension. This implies that part of the self always remains aware of the difference between the fiction it enacts and the reality it lives in. This awareness is arguably only fully lost in psychotic states, though people can often blur the difference between fiction and reality. *Soap opera seems to encourage very strong identifications, and it is not infrequent for people to send flowers on the death of a popular character. There is also the notorious occasion when a lady climbed on stage to tell Othello that Desdemona was innocent. Fortunately audiences do not normally identify to such a degree with a dramatic fiction.

W.B. Yeats in *The Trembling of the Veil* argues that 'at the height of tragedy all is lyricism'. Spectators and actors, he says, lose the sense of separate identity, and fuse in a trance-like state. This is only momentary, however, and at earlier and later points in the play, and especially in *comedy, which is 'built on the dykes which separate man from man', self-awareness may be strong.

Theories of acting vary in the emphasis they place on the degree of identification involved. Stanislavski (1863–1938) seems at times to advocate a total merging of actor and character with a complete loss of the actor's personality. Brecht, in his *epic theory of drama, aims at a dramatic presentation in which the actor indicates his *separateness* from the character. (See GESTUS; ALIENATION.)

Perhaps one can argue that the spectators' degrees of identification vary with *genre, and that there is pleasure both in the more extreme identification with characters in *tragedy and *naturalist drama, and in the awareness of difference, and perhaps superiority, that *comedy provides. (See LAUGHTER.)

Psychoanalysis defines four different forms of identification: 'primary', 'secondary', 'projective', and 'introjective'. Primary is the state in which separate identity is not recognized; secondary states recognize the separateness of the object identified with, as in identification with parents. Drama seems principally concerned with the third state, in which spectators and actors imagine they are inside, and have control over, some outside object. Introjective states are the opposite of this in that the subject imagines some outside object to be himself. For a specialist account see:

KOFF, R.H., 'A Definition of Identification', in *International Journal of Psychoanalysis*, 1937, 18, pp.269–293.

**Identity**. The sense of being a continuous self, different from all others. The dramatic process presents a mirror which both confirms and undermines this sense, since it encourages both *identification and loss of self-awareness. Actors attempt to lose themselves in a character, and a watching audience may do the same. Some plays are concerned with showing characters losing their sense of self: Shakespeare's *King Lear* and *Othello* are examples. In both plays, the main *protagonists regain their sense of self at the end. This process of loss and recovery, whether witnessed, or experienced, or both, can arguably create an awareness of self in relation to others and hence create a firmly based individual and communal sense of identity. See SUSPENSION OF DISBELIEF.

ERIKSON, E.H., *Childhood and Society*, 2nd ed., Norton, NY, 1963.
LAING, R.D., *The Self and Others*, Tavistock, 1960.

**Ideology**. Beliefs implicit or explicit in a play's form or content. In certain kinds of theatre, such as *agit-prop, or in the *morality play, these beliefs are comparatively easy to discover. Much drama, however, is concerned with a conflict between opposing ideologies, which it embodies in different characters or groups of characters. Moreover, the playwright may not see it as his responsibility to resolve the conflict. Thus Chekhov (1860–1904) declared, 'It is not my task to answer', and in *The Good Woman Of Setzuan* (1938–41) Brecht let his *epilogue tell the audience: 'It's for you to find a way'. Ideology here resides in a felt need to find a solution to human and social problems, rather than in any advocated line of action.

The matter is further complicated by questions of *intention. Writers may have attitudes which find their way into their work unconsciously. T.S. Eliot argued that this was true of Shakespeare's *Hamlet* (1601). The play possessed material which had 'not been drawn to consciousness'. If writing a play is an act of self-discovery, as Eliot implies, the process may not be complete. The surface ideology will not fully reveal the intentions an author hides from himself.

A further problem may be that a writer is struggling with other people's material. His sources, and the very language he is using, are in the public domain. His material may carry within it an ideology the author cannot fully subdue and make his own. Thus again in *Hamlet* there seem to be fundamental problems concerning the interpretation of the Ghost, and ideological conflicts not only between Christian and pagan elements, but between Catholic and Protestant interpretations. (Only a Catholic could accept that the Ghost had returned from purgatory, since purgatory is a Catholic concept.)

A further complication arises from the ideological contributions of *actors, *directors and *designers. Although the aim of performers may be to communicate the author's ideology and intentions, they can never fully achieve this, as interpretations will always differ. Each production adds or loses something; no performance is the same as any other, and even if the performers achieve an ideologically coherent production, the *audience's interpretation of it will still vary.

The ideology of a play may thus be considered to be dependent on the audience as well as on the performance, the writer's psyche, the source material and the form or language which the writer employs. It may also be said to arise from the social and cultural patterns which inform both the language of the play and the mind of the writer. Where a dramatist embodies the ideological conflicts of his time, the question of how far he is aware of the conditions which govern his writing and his existence, how far he is rebelling against a dominant ideology and how far he is mediating the prevailing mode of social relations, will remain debatable. See DECONSTRUCTION.

RIDLESS, R., *Ideology and Art*, Lang, NY, 1984.

**Illegitimate drama**. General term for the forms of *popular drama which grew up at *minor theatres in England in the eighteenth and early nineteenth centuries. The *legitimate, *patent theatres (Drury Lane, Covent Garden and later, after 1766, for short seasons, the Haymarket) had a monopoly on serious and 'classical' plays. Illegitimate theatre incorporated much music, spectacle and popular material.

**Image**. Term used for different kinds of 'likeness', whether mental, verbal, pictorial or sculptural.

(a) A sense impression held in the mind. Hence there may be visual, auditory, tactile, olfactory and even gustatory images. Such images impinge on the mind and mingle with each other to become a composite memory. (b) Memory images, besides incorporating sense impressions, are inevitably accompanied by vestiges of feeling, such as attend any experience. Since they belong to the past they are often accompanied by an awareness of the *pastness* of the past, which may express itself as nostalgia or relief. Such images are a source of emotional power in a writer's work. (c) *Dream images are more mysterious. They seem to draw on memories, and what Freud called the 'day's residues', but they are varied and complex and often appear emancipated from time. Perhaps this is because an awareness of the future, expressed in accompanying feelings of *fear and hope, anxiety and desire, often underlies the disguising of memory images in the 'dreamwork' process of 'transference' and 'condensation' which converts the memories to *symbol. (d) Images of the future may be more consciously formed. The sense of a personal past will be developed by reading and by social exchange into a more objective sense of history. This will project itself into a complex picture of one's own or the world's future. Hope and fear will often invest such images, thus Utopia and Doomsday, Paradise and Catastrophe are images of ultimate hope and fear. Most images of the future are more immediate and less extreme.

Drama, of course, is fundamentally concerned with an image of the present. But images of past and future underpin the dramatic *time process, whether in a *mystery play directed towards salvation, a political play directed towards social improvement, or a fatalistic *tragedy which sees the past as inescapable and the future as a trap. One should add that dramatic characters often have their own images of past and future. Chekhov's *Three Sisters* (1901) is full of ironic interplay between the visions of characters: Vershinin, for example, exhorts others to 'think of the world in two or three hundred years' time', but adds, 'when we'll all be dead'.

The words used in a play are all images of a kind. They represent something other than their own shape on the page or their sound in the theatre. The term is normally reserved, however, for those words which evoke mental pictures. (See SIMILE; METAPHOR; METONYMY.) *Stage imagery includes the visual images created by directors and actors, designers and lighting technicians. Any dramatic character is a stage image, most obviously when defined as a quality like 'Greed' or a function such as 'Doctor'. (See POSTURE; GROUPING; COSTUME; SET; LIGHTING.)

Samuel Beckett (1906–   ) is an expert at using theatre resources to leave a powerful memory image in the minds of spectators. He does this by force of repetition, using an extreme economy of means. The stage image of Pozzo and Lucky in *Waiting for Godot* (1953), tied by a rope, long in Act I, short in Act II, expresses one of the play's central concerns. 'We're not tied'? Gogo asks Didi. 'Tied to Godot? What an idea!' replies Didi.

BARTHES, R., *Image, Music, Text*, trs. S. Heath, Fontana, 1977, pp.32–51.

**Imagery**. Collective term for mental, verbal or other *images.

**Imagination**. The faculty which shapes and combines the various *images registered by our senses and held in our minds. It obviously plays a major part in the creation of dramatic characters and their combination in plays. (See UNCONSCIOUS.) Dramatic characters may also be endowed with this faculty, as has been the case with drama which is sceptical of the Romantic view that imagination is god-given: 'An echo in the finite mind of the infinite I AM' (S.T. Coleridge in *Biographia Literaria* (1817)). Ibsen, in *The Wild Duck* (1884) and elsewhere, shows imaginative characters who confound reality and dream. The gift of imagination may deceive as well as create. Chekhov, too, shows characters chained by images. In *The Cherry Orchard* (1904) characters fail to break with an image of the past. Images, says George Eliot, in her novel *Middlemarch* (1871–2), are 'the brood of desire', and the desires which underlie the imaginative process, already questioned in the nineteenth-century novel, are examined ironically in the *naturalistic drama which derived from it.

In the twentieth century, Pirandello (1867–1936), in *Six Characters in Search of an Author* (1921), dramatises the way mental images tap at the door of the writer's mind, presenting themselves as material for his imagination to work on. But the process had already been allegorized by Shakespeare. In *A Midsummer Night's Dream* (1595), Theseus speaks the famous lines: 'The lunatic, the lover and the poet/Are of imagination all compact.' His betrothed, Hippolyta, feels the imagination is not so deceptive as Theseus finds it. The audience is caught up in this ambivalence as it follows the mental changes of the characters who enter the mysterious wood, there to love and dream, wake and lose, and fall asleep to wake and find again. The uncertain nature of the imaginative faculty is made clear, yet Hippolyta's sense of 'something of great constancy' remains with us. See DREAM.

**Imitation**. Drama has been variously taken to be imitation or *mimesis of human behaviour; patterns of speech; historical events; dramatic and literary *models; particular scenes; or some *universal design.

**Immediacy**. Vividness; the quality of being present. See the fourth chapter of *The Empty Space* (1968) where Peter Brook argues that the theatre 'always asserts itself in the present'. 'Time in the theatre is always on the move', he argues, asserting that drama has an immediacy which film does not possess. The cinema is a record of past performances; in the theatre the actors are always present. *Film, however, has a different kind of immediacy. It operates directly on the spectator's sense of security by its constant shifts of *viewpoint and camera angle.

**Impersonality**. The absence of an identifiable personality. It is used as a term of praise for writers who can hide their own presence in a play and create a wide range of different characters. Shakespeare, of course, is usually regarded as the impersonal dramatist *par excellence*. In this context it is worth looking at Keats's definition of *negative capability and at the theories of James Joyce's character, Stephen Dedalus, in:
JOYCE, J., *Portrait of the Artist as a Young Man*, Cape, 1968.

**Impersonation**. Pretending to be someone else. The term is pejorative when applied to impersonators in life who seek personal gain. Inside the theatre impersonation is the dramatic process itself, and gains general approval.

Sometimes in the theatre, the process of actors impersonating characters is carried a stage further by having *characters* impersonate characters. In *comedy, a rogue or servant figure will often wear disguise to dupe another. Thus in Shakespeare's *Twelfth Night* (1601), Feste fools Malvolio by impersonating a priest (Sir Thopas), and in many of Shakespeare's comedies female characters impersonate men. In *tragedy, too, characters like Iago in *Othello* (1604) and Edmund in *King Lear* (1605) wear *disguise, emerging from impersonation to bring an audience 'in on' the act. This form of impersonation creates dramatic *irony, and in *tragedy the process seems to create both complicity and disapproval. The appreciation of an Iago's cleverness together with a disapproval of his actions, i.e. an aesthetic and a moral response, are set at odds within the spectator, involving him very directly in the dramatic conflict. In comedy, disapproval is less in evidence, presumably because comedy is more of an acknowledged *game.

**Improvisation**. The spontaneous reaction of actor or actors, in play or *rehearsal, to a new situation. In rehearsal, improvisation quickens, trains and tests responses, and helps an actor develop character and a 'natural' stage *movement. It may also be used by writers and actors to create a play. The process not only generates dramatic situations, but tests whether they work and how they relate to one another. (See MAGIC IF.)

Stanislavski (1863–1938) is well known for developing improvisational techniques. His main aim was to enable actors to 'become' a play's characters. Thus he would improvise the general outlines of a *story, including scenes which occur, or may occur, *off-stage before, between or after the staged action. Gradually this process unearths and builds up a *sub-text, so that the actor is able to carry with him a very full sense of the character's 'life'. This aids an actor's *concentration (see CIRCLE OF ATTENTION) and allows him or her to perform with conviction and complete *relaxation.

It is fairly clear that this creative process is a form of playwriting and it is not surprising that new plays have their origins in it. Mike Leigh (1943–   ), for example, built such plays as Nuts in May (1975) and Abigail's Party (1977) out of intensive improvisation. Tom Stoppard's Rosencrantz and Guildenstern are Dead (1967) also seems to have arisen out of a consideration of the Stanislavskian question: 'What do the characters do when they are not on stage?'

Improvisation is not a new idea. The *Commedia dell'Arte used similar techniques, improvising a story around varying sequences of set pieces, using practised stage *business, acrobatics and prepared *monologues which each actor had in his repertoire. The uncertainty of knowing which *lazzo was to come next probably generated the same kind of theatrical excitement, in both actors and spectators, as modern variations of the technique create.

'Improvs', as they are familiarly known, are also extremely valuable in *Theatre in Education. They can widen social and personal understanding, from a sense of what it feels like to be in a particular situation. The development of compassion, a sense of purpose and responsibility, and an awareness of real situations can arise out of their use, especially when allied to *role-playing techniques and followed by skilled analysis and discussion.

Whichever way it is used, improvisation constitutes an appeal to freedom and talent. The creative anxiety it arouses in those who participate can become a barrier and needs careful channeling, but the dramatic and educational potential is high.

HODGSON, J., and RICHARDS, E., Improvisation, Eyre Methuen, 1966.
SPOLIN, V., Improvisation for the Theatre, Pitman, 1963.
STANISLAVSKI, C., Creating a Role, Theatre Arts, NY, 1961.

**Incidental music.** Music especially written to accompany dramatic performance. It includes music written for song and dance, music for the opening and close of plays, and — as in *melodrama — for the entrance and accompaniment of characters at moments of *suspense. It is intensively used in *film. (See MUSIC AND THEATRE.)

Shakespeare, Dryden, and other seventeenth-century dramatists used incidental music, of which Purcell (1659–95) wrote a great deal. In nineteenth-century Germany, the availability of orchestras at ducal courts encouraged the use of music in drama. Elsewhere in

Europe, Bizet, Grieg, Fauré, Sibelius and Tchaikowski all wrote for dramatic performance, as have Vaughan Williams, Elgar and Benjamin Britten in England more recently. In 1982 Harrison Birtwistle's music made a powerful contribution to Peter Hall's National Theatre production of the *Oresteaia*. Incidental music of this order ceases to be incidental as drama approaches the nature of *opera and music becomes the dominant structure.

**Inciting moment**. See FREYTAG'S PYRAMID.

**Incongruity**. (a) A discrepancy between different ways in which a character or situation can be seen. (b) Logical incompatibility. (c) Incongruity of tone or *mood.

**Incorporated Stage Society**. A pioneer Sunday play-producing society, founded in 1899 for the purpose of staging plays of high merit but little apparent commercial appeal. It brought a number of Shaw's early plays to the stage including, for example, *Mrs Warren's Profession* (performed in 1898; published in 1902). It also put on plays by a number of important European dramatists, including Gorki (1868–1936), Wedekind (1864–1918), Kaiser (1878–1945) and Pirandello (1867–1936).

**Independent Theatre Club**. An organization founded in London in 1891 by a Dutchman, J.T. Grein, as an English equivalent of Antoine's *Théâtre Libre. He staged the notorious first English performance of Ibsen's *Ghosts*, condemned by one critic as an 'open sewer', and in 1892 the first London performance of Shaw's *Widowers' Houses*. See: N. Schoonderwoerd, *J.T. Grein, Ambassador of the Theatre 1862–1935*, Van Gorcum, 1963; and the biography by Grein's wife, M. Orme, *J.T. Grein, The Study of a Pioneer 1862–1935*, Murray, 1936.
GREIN, J.T., *Dramatic Criticism*, Vols. I–V, Blom, NY, 1968.

**Index**. One of three categories of *sign. (See ICON; SYMBOL.) According to C.S. Pierce, an index is 'a sign which refers to the object it denotes by virtue of being really affected by the object', i.e. it is a *symptom* or *effect*. Thus a cough is an index of an illness; smoke is an index of fire.

   In the theatre, as in life, there are many such signs. The way a character walks or moves may be an index of a profession or personality trait. A rigid backbone, a bowed head, an assertive walk, the colour of an actor's costume and the length of his hair may all be indices to some psychological or social attitude. *Properties and the *set itself may also act as indices. Verbal indices point both forwards and backwards, establishing continuity and linking the various parts of the *fable.

PIERCE, C.S., *Collected Papers 1931–58*, Harvard University Press, 1958.
GREENLEE, D., *Pearce's Concept of Sign*, Mouton, The Hague, 1973.

**Indian melodrama**. Colourful American *melodrama about Red Indians. It has the usual clear opposition betwen *heroes and *villains which makes it, together with the rich historical background, an obvious predecessor of the 'western' film. *Nick of the Woods* (1838), from the novel by R.M. Bird, is a good example of the *genre.

**Indian Theatre**. The term may imply: (a) Sanskrit drama which flourished from the third to the eighth century A.D. This seems to have borrowed from Greek *new comedy which reached India during successive invasions. The plays concern the loves and adventures of gods and princes, usually in five-act plays divided by *interludes. The emphasis is on coded gesture and physical movement. The best known author is Kalidasa (fourth century A.D., (b) Various kinds of classical dance, the only form of Indian Theatre between the 11th and the 18th centuries. (c) Modern, western-style Indian Theatre, not directly deriving from the old drama, and ushered in by the British, who opened a theatre called 'The Playhouse' in Calcutta in 1776. Indian companies began to use it at the beginning of the nineteenth century.
WELLS, H.W., *The Classical Drama of India*, Taplinger, NY, 1963.

**Induction**. The 'lead-in' to a play. The *prologue, or opening scene, in which the *exposition takes place.

More strictly, the term is used of an opening scene in which the dramatist uses *ideal spectators, i.e. characters who sit down to watch a play ostensibly put on for their benefit, as in the Christopher Sly scene in Shakespeare's *The Taming of the Shrew* (c.1592) or the opening debate in Brecht's *A Caucasian Chalk Circle* (1944).

**Information**. In order to establish the fiction of a play, a dramatist needs to convey such basic information as the names of characters, what they do, where they live and how they are related. He must also establish events which occurred before the play began: a crime, a last will and testament, or some other event which affects the action of the play. The author may also decide to hold some information back, in order to arouse *curiosity and create *suspense. How much to communicate, and when, is always a dramatic problem.

The most obvious method of providing information is to use a *prologue or *chorus — a narrator who stands outside the play — as in Shakespeare's *Henry V*. Alternatively, the dramatist may employ the *soliloquy or the *aside, particularly in *farce. The *messenger, the telephone call and the delivery of a letter to be read aloud are other devices which (rather more subtly than *conventions of direct address) enlighten the characters as well as the audience. One further means to this end is the introduction, usually in an early scene, of a character who is new to the situation, whose questions are answered by characters familiar with it. The hired servant at the beginning of Ibsen's *The Wild Duck* (1884) is an example.

Information may also be given obliquely, when the dramatist drops careful *hints. This method, which was perfected by Ibsen, maintains and increases suspense, while allowing an audience the excitement of *discovery. Usually, of course, hints heighten *dramatic irony, which depends on an audience having information or knowledge a character does not possess. Thus the skilful dramatist must distinguish between information given to *characters and information given to the *audience. See DISCLOSURE; RECOGNITION.

**Initiating action**. Early events in a play which create dramatic interest and *suspense.

**Inner creative state**. The state of mind necessary, according to Stanislavski (1863–1938), for a 'true performance'. It implies a complete understanding of the meaning of the play-text and a full marshalling of the actors' talent to express it. See CIRCLE OF ATTENTION; THROUGH-LINE.
STANISLAVSKI, C., *An Actor Prepares*, Theatre Arts, NY, 1936.

**Inner proscenium**. A *proscenium arch contained within and *upstage of the main proscenium. It may be used to create a separate stage area, in which a different style of acting, and a different 'reality', may be found.

A *play within a play, such as Nina's play in Chekhov's *The Seagull* (1896), could be played within this inner proscenium.

**Inner reality**. Rather old-fashioned critical term for (a) the inner workings of a character's mind; (b) the essential core or *form of a play.

Drama may not at first seem the best medium for the communication of a character's inner thoughts. The novel, in which a *persona or *narrator confides in a reader, or where an author can allow the reader directly into the most intimate thoughts of a *character, seems more appropriate. Drama is a *public* medium, heavily dependent on *dialogue, and therefore favours characters given to strong speech rather than those with quiet and introspective temperaments. How then is this 'inner reality' to be rendered within the active verbal interchange of the stage?

First of all, since dramatic tension often depends on this, the audience must be made aware of what one character keeps hidden from another. A *narrator or choral character may do this, or the *convention of the *soliloquy may be used. More 'natural' techniques, however, are possible. One character may reveal his thoughts to another and keep them from a third. Thus, early in *Othello* (1604), Iago reveals his mind to Roderigo but conceals it from Othello — his more important victim. He also, of course, reveals in soliloquy, thoughts which he conceals from Roderigo. The revealed thoughts of Iago are not, however, the full 'inner reality' of either Iago or the play, since Iago seems not fully to comprehend himself. His musings, and his multiple and confusing explanations of his own motives, suggest 'inner realities' which an audience can consider to be beyond the full knowledge of the most informed and intelligent character. Iago is, in fact, an unreliable narrator. The audience is left — as in *Hamlet* — with an impression of realities beyond the spoken or understood. Such realities, of course, may be clarified or complicated by the discussion of, or reference to, a character's behaviour or motives by other characters in other scenes, or by direct *asides to the audience in the same scene. In the case of Iago or Hamlet, however, other characters know *less* than the audience. The audience here must select from multiple possibilities, and find its own explanations.

At this point the phrase 'inner reality' becomes problematic. Where do these multiple possibilities cease to be the author's and become the readers or spectator's? How far does an audience create the reality it sees? And how far does the selection from a number of possibilities which constitute performance reveal the 'inner' or core meaning of a play? When actors embody a character, they may aim through *gesture, *facial expression and *movement to reveal that character's 'inner reality', but they also contribute aspects of themselves which are necessarily unique.

Similarly, *directors and *designers indicate by choice of *colour and *costume, and the specific *groupings of characters, *their* view of the central reality of a play. They need to have a broader view than an actor. Their sense of central relationships in the play not only works through the inner life of characters, but seeks visual unity — a total poetic impression expressed in such *stage images as the storm scenes in *King Lear* (1605) or the spectacular fairy scenes in *A Midsummer Night's Dream* (1595). These directly disturb the audience's security and involve it in the play through means other than the interpretation of character. Visual impact, *sound, music and *rhythm can communicate 'inner reality' as much as words.

Directors like Stanislavski or Peter Brook (1925– ) seek to

discover such an 'inner reality' in the text, but the words 'in' and 'inner' remain problematic. The freshness of performance arises from a transaction between the play, the audience and the various creative artists involved. The meaning is part revealed and part created. The endeavour of performers and directors may be to reveal an 'inner' meaning, but in performance there is always something new, brought to the play from outside, from a different culture, a different time, a different language, different bodies, different voices and different stage conditions. The seeking for 'inner reality' creates a *new* reality. Even *expressionist drama, which aims to communicate inner states in a direct and theatrical way, is a fusion of this kind.

**Inner stage**. A stage area supposedly let in to the stage wall between the two upstage doors of the *Elizabethan stage and beneath the gallery. That it ever existed is dubious. The strongest visual evidence we have of the appearance of an Elizabethan theatre — the de Witt drawing of the Swan — shows no inner stage. There must, however, have been some space where actors could be 'discovered'. Plays such as Middleton's *Women Beware Women* (1620–7) and Shakespeare's *The Tempest* (1601) evidently require this, while a curtained arbour would have had obvious uses for stage listeners such as Polonius in the 'closet scene' in *Hamlet* (1610). A 'discovery space', however, might well have been an independent stage *property brought on for a particular scene and placed further *downstage — as a wood-cut of Kyd's *The Spanish Tragedy* (1592) seems to suggest, or it might have been a removable, curtained platform placed against the back wall. Whatever form it took, it is unlikely that much dialogue or action would or could have taken place inside it. *Sight lines would have been poor, and sound likely to have been muffled. In a theatre which did not depend on *full scenery, and where the actor was generally relied on to create the nature of the *space around him, it must have been possible to create on the open stage, through *movement and *gesture (and even *mime) the impression of being in a confined inner room. It is only *naturalism which tries to persuade us that such a room must be a *visual* reality.

GURR, A., *Shakespeare's Theatre*, Cambridge University Press, 1970.

**Institute for Advanced Studies in the Theatre Arts**. An American association which brings eminent theatre professionals, especially directors, to New York in order to give American actors and theatre technicians the chance to work with them and study their approaches.

**Intention**. A dangerous word to use of any dramatic work, since what an author consciously 'intends' is tempered by his less conscious wishes, and by such external factors as the source material, the language he is writing in, the economic limitations of the theatre company, its size, available stage space and the nature of an audience's expectations. A play is always a *transaction between an author and cultural conditions.

In performance, of course, the author's intentions are mediated by *director, *designer and *actor, who may supplement, contradict or transform them. Their choices, and the playgoer's own predilections, oppose the author's claim to full control. Thus when a writer creates a character who represents the authorial voice very closely — a *raisonneur or *choral commentator — there is no guarantee the audience will think what that character thinks or feel what he feels, whatever the author's intention. T.S. Eliot's character, Harcourt-Reilly, in *The Cocktail Party* (1949), is perhaps a case in point.

The classic critical discussion of the 'intentional fallacy' is to be found in:
WIMSATT, W.K., and BEARDSLEY, M.C., *The Verbal Icon*, Kentucky University Press, 1954.

**Interlude**. A comic performance, probably first interpolated between courses at a banquet and later between *acts of a play. Interludes seem to have occurred first in the reign of Henry VII, as a development of the *morality plays. John Heywood first gave them form (1497–1580), notably in *The Playe Called the Four P.P.* (c.1520) — 'a newe and a very merry interlude of a palmer, a pardoner, a potecary and a pedlar'. Goneril, in Shakespeare's *King Lear*, makes sarcastic reference to her husband's intervention: 'O ho an interlude!'
CHAMBERS, E.K., *The Medieval Stage*, Vol. II, Book iv, Oxford University Press, 1903.

**Intermezzo**. Italian equivalent of the English *disguising or *interlude; performed on important occasions, between *acts of an *opera or a serious play.

**Interpretation**. The meaning of a text. In drama this may be taken to be (a) the author's *intention; (b) the *'inner meaning' of the play; (c) the impressions of the *actor or *director; (d) the response of the spectator; and (e) the appreciation of all these. 'To interpret a text is not to give it a sense but to appreciate its plural meanings' says Barthes. This has special importance for the novels of Franz Kafka (1883–1924) and the fiction and drama of Samuel Beckett (1906–    ). See:
BARTHES, R., *S/Z*, trs. R. Miller, Cape, 1975.

**Intertextuality**. A term from *semiotics which may be applied to drama. The interaction between the *conventions and *codes implied in the *text, and the codes and conventions of a reader or spectator. An actor or spectator may be affected by the 'intertextual history' of a *role or text, that is, by his or her awareness of past performances. Arguably, a text is only comprehensible when seen against a background of the texts which influence its production. A reader's or spectator's *interpretation must by extension be comprehensible only when seen against the texts (and personal experience) which influence his or her response.

BARTHES, R., *The Pleasure of the Text*, trs. Cape, 1976.

ELAM, K., *The Semiotics of Theatre Drama*, Methuen, 1980.

**Intonation**. The rise and fall in musical pitch of the voice. This is very important in *acting. A wide range of intonation gives variety and interest. Actors also learn not to lower the pitch at points where it destroys the continuity of a speech.

**Introduction**. The opening movement of a play. See FREYTAG'S PYRAMID.

***Introit* trope**. Liturgical music-drama, in particular the Easter Introit or *Quem Quaeritis* trope which celebrates the resurrection of Christ.

WICKHAM, G., *The Medieval Theatre*, Weidenfeld and Nicolson, 1973, pp.38–42.

**Irish Literary Theatre**. The theatre founded by Yeats (1865–1939) and Lady Gregory (1852–1932), together with George Moore (1852–1933) and Edward Martyn (1859–1923), for the performance of new Irish plays. Its aim was to accelerate the Irish national and cultural revival and it led to productions of Synge's plays, a merger with the Fay brothers and the establishment of the Abbey Theatre in Dublin in 1904.

KAVANAGH, P., *The Irish Theatre*, Blom, NY, 1969.

**Irony**. Many kinds have been defined, including Socratic, verbal, dramatic, cosmic and tragic irony. What links them all is an appeal to a reader, listener or spectator who is not only aware of the implications of a sentence or situation, but aware of the unawareness of *other* readers, listeners or spectators. Thus verbal irony, 'to say one thing and mean another', establishes complicity with the person able to understand, and at the same time deceives the person who accepts the surface meaning. This has obvious implications for drama, where words spoken can be interpreted differently depending on whether listeners, either on stage or in the audience, are aware of the hidden *secret or not. The irony may be *immediately* apparent, as in sarcasm, where the tone of voice generally constitutes an obvious attack on a listener's ignorance, or in the dramatic irony of Macbeth's 'Fail not our feast' for those who know Banquo is about to be killed (and know that Banquo does *not* know). On the other hand, irony may only become apparent *later*, as in Socratic irony, where the mask of innocence leads the listener unaware of his own limitations into a logical trap. This is also true of forms of dramatic irony, where the audience is deliberately kept in ignorance of certain facts — such as the survival of Hermione in Shakespeare's *The Winter's Tale* (1610).

In drama, of course, it is often important that the comprehension of hidden ironies should *not* be complete and immediate, since they create interest and *suspense. Tragic and comic irony is often more subtle in that it is frequently concerned with making character and audience aware of possibilities they prefer not to think of, involving guilt, suffering and death. *Oedipus Rex* is probably the prime example of ironic drama, in its appeal to an audience aware not only of what Oedipus himself is ignorant of, but of the dangers for himself of knowing it. Such irony may also be said to remind an audience of, and by *empathy *involve* an audience in, truths it 'knows' but allows to slip beneath everyday consciousness. Irony in tragedy thus makes knowledge 'real' again. The spectator becomes aware of a preference for ignorance.

In *comedy, and especially in *farce, the irony of a situation is often visual. The audience watches the approach of the deceived husband whilst wife and lover remain ignorant, or, as often in Brecht, the audience sees opposite *groupings on a 'split' stage, each unaware of the other's activity. In *melodrama, visual irony contributes to suspense. The audience watches as the *villain approaches the innocent *heroine. The tendency towards simple *identification in melodrama operates differently from the greater distancing of comedy and the complex identification and rejection of tragedy.

The study of irony carries one deep into theological and philosophical questions related to the Fall, to fate and the relation of the individual to the world. Existential writers have been fascinated by its nature and its problems. The concept of the *absurd, in particular, is relevant to a discussion of irony since it implies that man asks questions of a God who appears to be deaf ('*surdus*'), may not know, may not exist and in any case does not reply. See SECRET.

KIERKEGAARD, S.A., *The Concept of Irony* (1841).

**Isotopie**. Semiotic term, introduced by A. Greimas, to define the thread linking a whole dramatic *discourse.

# J

**Jacobean drama**. Drama written during the rule of James I (1603–25). The term is sometimes loosely used to include *Caroline theatre, since many Jacobean dramatists continued writing under Charles I. The major Jacobean dramatists include Webster (*c*.1580–1634), Tourneur (1575–1626), Middleton (*c*.1570–1627), Dekker (*c*.1572–*c*.1632), Massinger (1583–1616), and Ford (1586–1639), and the period covers the later work of Shakespeare (1564–1640), and Jonson (1572–1637).

Apart from denoting perhaps the most energetic period in the history of drama, the word 'Jacobean' implies a characteristic sombre and sardonic tone, which invests both tragedies and comedies. Highly individualized characters seek power and self-realization in a world of desperate appetites and sudden death. New men hasten the breakdown of old ideals, old *conventions and old forms of social behaviour.

For stage conditions and a study of the clear shift in tone from the *Elizabethan to the Jacobean period, perhaps first evident in Shakespeare's *Hamlet* and *Troilus and Cressida*, see:

BENTLEY, G.E., *The Jacobean and Caroline Stage*, 7 Vols., Oxford University Press, 1941–66.

CRUTTWELL, P., *The Shakespearean Moment*, Chatto, 1956.

MACK, M., 'The Jacobean Shakespeare', in *Jacobean Theatre*, edited by J.R. Brown and B. Harris, 1960.

**Jester**. An entertainer and permanent member of a royal or noble household. Will Somers, Henry VIII's jester, is an example.

Characters based on the court jester, wearing 'motley', i.e. parti-coloured costume, cap and bells, and carrying a 'bauble' (usually a replica of themselves), were introduced into Elizabethan plays. Shakespeare's jesters or court fools include Touchstone in *As You Like It* (1599) and the fool in *King Lear* (1605). They have a very important dramatic function as 'reflectors' of other characters in the play. (See FOOL). For the social background see:

WELSFORD, E., *The Fool*, Faber and Faber, 1935.

**Jesuit drama**. Form of *school drama, first written in Latin by teachers of *rhetoric for annual performance in Jesuit colleges. It flourished in Catholic Europe from the mid-sixteenth century until the suppression of the Jesuit order in 1773. The plays gradually came to be presented in the native language of the country of performance. They were extremely spectacular, even operatic, using large casts, big crowd scenes, elaborate *lighting effects, large orchestras and magnificent costumes. Calderón (1600–81), Corneille (1606–84), Molière (1622–73), Le Sage (1668–1747), Voltaire (1694–1798) and Goldoni (1709–93) must all, as pupils at Jesuit schools, have come into contact with such drama.

**Jeune premier.** Young actor who takes the *juvenile lead.

**Jig.** An Elizabethan stage play involving *song, balladry and *dance. In their fullest form, jigs were played as separate pieces after a longer play and seem to have involved improvised political and topical satire, and *knockabout farce. *Singing Simkin* was one example, based on the ancient comic situation in which an old husband catches a *clown making up to his wife.

Ned Tarleton (?–1588) was a great jig-maker and the first of the great jigging clowns. Will Kempe (?–1603) of Shakespeare's company and George Attewell of the Admiral's Men followed him. In Shakespeare's time, the fashion seems to have continued in the playhouses to the north of the city after the Bankside theatres had abandoned it. When the public theatres were closed down in 1642, jigs mainly survived as *street theatre. They returned to the stage, however, in Pepys's day and often contained a 'trailer' or announcement of a new play to be performed. In the eighteenth century they developed into musical *farce and condensed comedies called *afterpieces.

CHAMBERS, E.K., *The Elizabethan Stage*, 4 Vols., Oxford University Press, 1923.

GURR, A., *The Shakespearean Stage*, Cambridge University Press, 1970.

**Joculatores.** Medieval stage entertainers who seem to have sung of heroic deeds, the lives of saints and other such subjects.

WICKHAM, G., *Early English Stages*, 2 vols., Routledge/Columbia University Press, 1959 and 1963.

**Jocus.** The original Latin meaning was 'joke' or 'a play with words'. In the medieval period it acquired the meaning of *ludus, i.e. a play with physical movement, as in the French descendant word '*jeu*'. See:

WICKHAM, G., *The Medieval Theatre*, Weidenfeld and Nicolson, 1974.

**Jornada.** Spanish word for a major division in a play or *act.

**Juvenile drama.** Imitative games played in nineteenth-century toy theatres. They involved accurate and colourful paper cut-outs of scenery, and dramatic characters which children could make and move across the model stage on slides. They are based on the *pantomimes, *melodramas, operatic *extravaganzas and Shakespearean *revivals mounted by well-known nineteenth-century actor-managers such as Madame Vestris, Edmund Kean and the Kembles. Especially popular in the first half of the nineteenth century, they continued to make their appeal throughout the Victorian period. Ingmar Bergman's film *Fanny and Alexander* opens with a shot of a boy playing with such a model.

SPEAIGHT, G., *Juvenile Drama*, Macdonald, 1946.
WILSON, A.E., *Penny Plain, Twopence Coloured*, Harrap, 1932.

**Juvenile lead**. The actor or actress in a Victorian *stock company who took the part of the younger *hero or lover in the staple repertory of the Victorian theatre. The term went out of use in the 1880s, with the break-up of the resident London theatre companies.

**Juvenile tragedian**. The juvenile tragedian was the specialist actor in the Victorian *stock company. He took important younger parts secondary to the *juvenile lead, such as the part of Laertes in *Hamlet* (1601).

# K

**Kabuki**. Form of popular Japanese theatre involving song, dance and *mime. It dates from the mid-seventeenth century, as compared with the older aristocratic *Noh drama. It is highly formalized, and uses only male actors. Female impersonation is very skilled. Performances are given on a wide shallow stage with exits and entrances made on a narrow path along the left-hand side of the *auditorium. Musicians play behind a lattice. Two stage hands, one hooded and both by convention invisible, move the scenes. Kabuki can last for as long as twelve hours and the audience comes and goes between the dances and set-pieces around which a dramatic framework is fairly loosely constructed.
ARNOTT, P., *The Theatres of Japan*, Macmillan, 1969.

**Karagöz**. Well-known figure in Turkish *puppet theatre.

**Kasperle**. German *puppet character, rather like *Punch. He was translated onto the stage in 1764 by the Austrian actor Johann Laroche (1745–1806), and became a well-known figure in Viennese comedy.

**Katharsis**. See CATHARSIS.

**Kierkegaard, Soren**, (1813–55). Danish philosopher and early *existentialist who emphasized individual choice and freedom and the anxieties which stem from these. He wrote of

> …the dizziness of freedom, when freedom looks down into its own possibilities.

Such a condition is the dramatic subject of much *tragedy. See also: ABSURD; FEAR; IRONY; TENSION.
KIERKEGAARD, S., 'The Ancient Tragical Motif as reflected in the Modern', in *Either/Or*, translated by D. and L. Swenson, 2 Vols., Garden City, NY, 1959.

**King**. Serious drama, from *classical tragedy, through medieval *chronicle plays, to *Elizabethan drama and French *neo-classical tragedy, has generally had a monarch, or man with social *power, as *protagonist. The comic tradition, on the other hand, usually chooses its heroes from the 'little men' who lack such power. In certain dramatic forms, however, this obvious separation is deliberately blurred. Comedy and tragedy seem to meet where the king and little man confront each other, or merge in the same figure. All men are equal in death and it was a medieval commonplace that the king, like *Everyman, must also come before the Supreme Judge. The two figures often fuse in the *morality play.

The *fool figure, too, is intimately associated with the king whom he mirrors and parodies. Shakespeare's *Henry IV* Part I (1597–8) and *King Lear* (1605) juxtapose the two figures in ways which have their origins in the character of the court *jester and *Lord of Misrule. One is reminded, too, of the rituals described by James Frazer in *The Golden Bough* (1890–1915), where mock kings are allowed to reign for a certain period instead of the real monarch. Complex questions relating to the function of the *scapegoat, the guilt of authority and the function of *laughter derive from this. (Jacob Bronowski, in the preface to his play *The Face of Violence*, develops an interesting theory based on Frazer's anthropological work.) It is highly likely that the *hero king derives his dramatic status from his social power, his original closeness to the supernatural, and the danger which his sins and errors represent for those beneath him.

UBERSFELD, A., *Le Roi et le Bouffon*, Corti, 1974.

**'King' actor**. A term describing actors of powerful *presence, normally cast in authoritarian roles. Orson Welles described himself as such.

**King's Men**. See CHAMBERLAIN'S MEN.

**Kitchen-sink drama**. Form of *naturalism which used lower-class *sets rather than the middle-class drawing-room. The term came into common use with John Osborne's *Look Back in Anger* (1956). Arnold Wesker's *The Kitchen* (1959) is another example. The phrase, often used pejoratively, indicates the growth of the representation of working-class social experience in the drama of the later 1950s.

TAYLOR, J.R., *The Angry Theatre*, Methuen, 1969.

***Klucht***. Kind of short medieval Flemish play.

***Knockabout comedy***. Farcical rough and tumble in which *laughter is provoked by the infliction of physical misfortune. Custard pies, banana skins, black eyes, misplaced buckets of water and lumps on the cranium are standard ingredients of a form of entertainment which seems to have perennial appeal. Do we laugh because we enjoy the spectacle of human dignity brought low, or because as a Beckett character says: 'There is nothing funnier than suffering, I grant you that.'? Does the laughter recognize the potential childishness of every adult, or does the play situation allow us to laugh our fear of pain away? The questions raised are profound though the comedy may be superficial. The *genre is not entirely to be scorned, especially in the hands of Samuel Beckett (1906–    ). See, for example, *Act Without Words* (1956), in which the knockabout comedy ends with the victim refusing to play with the joker God (or joker playwright) in whose power he is. See FARCE; COMEDY.

**Komos**. A comic revel consisting of a company of men singing in a festive manner. It was a feature of the Greek *City Dionysia, and may be one origin of Greek *old comedy. The elements of song and dance, the mockery of spectators, and, in one form, the wearing of animal masks, seem to anticipate the comic *choruses of Aristophanes (*c*.448–*c*.380 B.C.).

**Kommos**. A kind of lyrical dialogue, often a lament, between *chorus and *protagonist in *Greek tragedy.

*Kuppelhorizont.* A 'sky-dome', made of silk, invented by Mariano Fortuny (1871–1949). It enclosed the upper stage, and achieved natural effects of daylight and distance by the diffusion of reflected light. Since it limited the position and number of stage *entrances the *cyclorama has come to be preferred.

*Kyogen*. Comic interludes of the *Noh play.

# L

**Laboratorium**. See THEATRE LABORATORY.

**Lady Elizabeth's Men**. A Jacobean theatre company founded in 1611.

**La Mama Experimental Theatre Club**. An *off-Broadway theatre; established by Ellen Stewart in 1961, it acquired a permanent company in 1961. The first rock musical, *Hair*, was produced for La Mama in 1967. The club housed *open theatre productions and experimented with dance and acrobatics, mingling rock with classical styles. Megan Terry (1932–   ) and Sam Shepard (1943–   ) were two of the dramatists sponsored by the club.

**Language**. From '*langue*', French for tongue; system of verbal communication. Recent usage extends the term to any *sign system; thus, *theatre language.

The 'language' of the theatre may be roughly separated into visual and acoustic sign systems. The visual signs are of different kinds, and include *facial expression, *movement and *posture, *colour and *set design and *lighting. The acoustic signs similarly divide into *dialogue, *sound effect and *voice.

A musical 'language' deriving from the above may be said to exist. This is the set of signals which emerge from the rhythm of stage movement and the speed, volume, intensity, tone, pitch and timbre of speech. Thus theatrical *discourse carries far richer meaning then the printed *text.

The importance which critics attribute to these two languages varies. Literary critics generally stress the flexibility of spoken language, its capacity to convey thought, and subtle nuances of feeling. Theatre critics tend to emphasize the *power of the visual, and argue that great subtlety can be conveyed by facial and physical movement. Drama can exist without words, they argue, but not without *action.

Nearly all theatrical performances, of course, with the notable exception of *mime, use both visual and acoustic languages. Compatibility between them, within the general musical flow, is what a director must discover. For reflections on one man's experience of how this may be achieved see:

BROOK, P., *The Empty Space*, MacGibbon and Kee, 1968, Ch. 4, 'The Immediate Theatre'.

**'langue' and 'parole'**. A celebrated distinction made by Ferdinand de Saussure (1857–1913) between the language system and the particular set of individual units, i.e. spoken utterances or written words, to which it gives meaning. Thus 'langue' is the system or 'field of possibility' within which 'parole' operates.

If the distinction is applied to drama, 'langue' is the set of theatrical *codes which give significance to individual acts of *theatre language: word, costume, prop, gesture and facial expression.
BARTHES, R., *Elements of Semiology*, Cape, 1967.

**Laughter**. Mysterious reflex reaction triggered by feelings of incongruity, superiority or relief. There seems to be a difference between laughter dependent on moral responses and that which, according to Baudelaire (1821–67), is absolute and Rabelaisian, of the whole body and arising from the *grotesque nature of existence. See COMEDY.

**Lazzo**. Element of comic fooling in the *Commedia dell'Arte*. The word was applied to various kinds of rapid stage *business. See BURLA.

**Lead**. Leading lady or leading man; the actress or actor in a Victorian *stock company who normally took the leading female or male role.

**Leap**. Spectacular effect in Victorian *melodrama, whereby an actor used trick scenery and *traps to intensify the dramatic impact of an acrobatic jump.

**Learning and drama**. Since the Greeks, drama has been appreciated as a means of learning. A training in *rhetoric was long a part of the European cultural tradition, and aimed at the development of vocal and physical control, personal confidence in public situations and the capacity to express thoughts and feelings.

Theorists have more recently grown aware of the social skills which can be acquired from forms of dramatic training such as *improvisation. To assume, if only in *play, an unaccustomed *role and situation, is a way to gain awareness of other people's lives and problems. From such an awareness it is possible to learn a sense of responsibility and the capacity to work in groups.

Drama may enhance physical confidence, encourage relaxation and develop a sense of movement and *rhythm. It trains the *voice, aids memorization and extends active vocabulary. It may also lead to increased confidence in the handling of the spoken language in unaccustomed situations.

One of the problems for those who advocate the extensive use of *drama in education is that the advantages are not immediately manifest or measurable. Involvement is probably the best method of testing the process. Unfortunately many sceptics are reluctant to engage in it.

WAGNER, B.J., and HEATHCOTE, D., *Drama as a Learning Medium*, Hutchinson, 1979.

MCGREGOR, L., TATE, M., and ROBINSON, K., *Learning through Drama*, Heinemann, 1977.

**Legitimate theatre**. Serious plays which, according to the Theatres Act of 1737, could only be performed at the *patent theatres — Drury Lane and Covent Garden. Their monopoly of serious drama was broken in 1843. 'Legitimate' plays included Shakespearean revivals and non-musical 'classical' plays. See ILLEGITIMATE.

**Legs**. Long extensions hanging at each end of a *border to form a kind of frame over the stage.

***Lehrstück.*** 'Didactic play'; Brecht's name for a group of plays he wrote in the early 1930s to combat the threat of fascism in Germany. They include the short opera *He Who Says Yes*, and *Measures Taken*. Both are concerned with problems of *ends and means, and involve situations in which a choice must be made as to whether an individual should be sacrificed in the interest of the community.

**Leicester's Men**. Early company of Elizabethan actors who performed under the patronage of the Earl of Leicester before his death in 1588.

***Leitmotif.*** Term derived from the operas of Richard Wagner (1813–83); a musical theme running through a work and associated with a particular character or dramatic situation.

Applied to drama, it implies some recurrent theme, word or *image. It may throw light on the character who uses it, and often constitutes an ironic commentary on the action. The repeated references to some hidden sickness 'mining all within' in *Hamlet* (1601) are a *leitmotif*. It connects the mental sickness of Ophelia, the deaths by poison, the strange behaviour of Hamlet and the general sense of 'something rotten in the state of Denmark'.

*Naturalistic dramatists sometimes use a *leitmotif* to unify a play and throw light on the nature of different characters. The wounded wild duck which lives in a dark attic in Ibsen's play of that name (1884) is an obvious example. It connects the various wounded characters who live in different kinds of mental darkness.

**Lessing, Gotthold** (1729–81). Liberal-minded German dramatist and theatre critic who applauded the freedom of Shakespeare and contested the narrowness of French *neo-classicism. He argued for naturalness, 'internal probability' and individual expression:

> The genius . . . has the proof of all rules within himself.

LESSING, G.E., *Hamburg Dramaturgy*, trs. H. Zimmern, Dover, 1962.

**Levels**. The different heights from which a dramatic character speaks to the audience.

A flat, or even *raked, stage can lack scenic variety. This can be provided by introducing platforms, stairs, pedestals or galleries from which actors can speak. In this way, the height of the stage space can be utilized as well as the width, and more interesting stage *groupings can be formed. The power relations between characters can also be emphasized, as when the gods appear 'above', or the angels descend, or when Shakespeare, inverting these relations, has the dying Antony hoisted onto a 'monument'. The most obvious difference of level is between ground and stage. Theatre, from the Greeks to modern street theatre, has used this to vary *actor/audience relations.

**Liberty**. See EXISTENTIALISM; CAUSALITY; SITUATION; WILL.

**Libretto**. The text of a musical and vocal composition such as an *opera or *oratorio. It is much shorter than the full text of a play, since words take more time to sing than speak and repetition is apt to occur in moments of intense lyricism. Eighteenth-century operas have frequent repetition.

A librettist must be aware of the singers' and composers' needs, and the musical difficulties presented by the language used. He must be careful of word-length, the quality of vowels and consonants, sentence *rhythm and the position of stress. In addition, the structure of a libretto is simpler than that of a play. *Sub- or *double-plots tend to be less complex. The result is that a libretto such as that of Boito for Verdi's *Otello* (1887) may seem melodramatic when *abstracted* from the music, and far less rewarding to read than Shakespeare's *Othello* (1604) from which it is taken. It was not written to be read, however, but to allow Verdi a basic but suggestive structure which he could develop musically.

The main difference between a play and a libretto lies in the lyrical elements. At the one extreme there are operas which rigorously separate action and lyricism (those of eighteenth-century *opera seria* and *opera buffa*); in these the librettist needs to be highly conversant with the musical conventions of his time. At the other extreme there are operas which integrate the two, such as Debussy's *Pelléas and Mélisande* (1902) and Berg's *Wozzeck* (1925); in these instances the composer can use the text of a play with little or no alteration.

W.H. Auden (1907–72) and Michael Tippett (1905–   ) are notable English librettists.

BLACK, J., *The Italian Romantic Libretto*, Edinburgh, 1984.

SMITH, P.J., *The Tenth Muse*, Gollancz, 1971.

**Licence**. Dramatic licence, like 'poetic licence' implies freedom to use the *conventions of the genre. See also LICENSING ACT.

**Licensing Act** (1737). This act defined the wide powers of the Lord Chamberlain in the theatre and made him responsible for all performances of new plays. In addition, licences for all places of entertainment, with the exception of the *patent theatres, had to be sought through him. The Licensing Act established strong political control of the theatre, one result of which was to cause Henry Fielding (1707–54) to turn his energies away from satirical drama towards fiction. See CENSORSHIP.

**Light**. A rich resource in the theatre. Its function is to illuminate *actor, *action and *set. It can be used to *focus attention on a main actor, or a *facial expression, or an important *entrance. Powerful effects can be obtained by 'sculpting' body movement in more formal theatre and *dance. It can create atmospheric effects in white or colour and its illumination or extinction, gradual or rapid, can communicate apprehension and excitement and a variety of other moods. It also coordinates stage *movement and individual *scenes. *Expressionist theatre used powerful, heightened lighting effects while *naturalism strove for effects of natural light. A *blackout, of course, provides an alternative to a *curtain.

Lighting is a comparatively recent addition to the theatre. Early drama from the Greeks to the Elizabethans was performed during the day in open air theatre or marketplace, and had no need of artificial light. One can assume, however, that torchlight was used for evening performances and when indoor theatres were established in sixteenth-century Italy, the use of candles replaced daylight illumination. Serlio (1475–1554) used tinted glass and bottled liquids to vary colour. Di Somi (1527–1592), theatrical advisor to the Montrian court, intensified light by using reflectors. Candelabra were later placed over the stage area and in the early seventeenth century *footlights began to be installed. In 1765 Garrick (1717–1779) removed candelabra to eliminate glare and replaced them with lights placed in the *wings. Footlights remained popular and the invention of *gas lighting and *limelight, which allowed light to be focused and controlled with much greater precision, did not eliminate them. Gas, of course, led to considerable fire-risk, and *electricity, used as early as 1846 for *spotlighting at the Paris Opéra, eventually replaced it. With the development of complex and sophisticated lighting systems and the emergence of theoreticians such as Adolphe Appia (1862–1928) and Edward Gordon Craig (1872–1966), lighting became a *theatre language in its own right. (See LIVING LIGHT.) Later developments have included the use of *dimmers to balance focused lights, and, in the 1960s, the use of controlled independent lighting.

BENTHAM, F., *The Art of Stage Lighting*, Pitman, 1970.
PILBROW, R., *Stage Lighting*, Cassell, 1970.

**Light batten**. Structure of wood or metal rods from which a row of lights is suspended, usually above the stage.

**Light opera**. Comic *opera; it often parodies the style of *grand opera and its characters and subject matter reflect a lower social class.

Sir William Gilbert (1836–1911) and Sir Arthur Sullivan (1842–1900) have made the most popular and extensive contribution to the *genre in the famous 'Savoy Operas' presented at the Savoy Theatre.

**Light tower**. Vertical steel structure designed for mounting *spotlights.

**Limelight**. A strong white light used in the first half of the nineteenth century for *spotlighting the main actors. Hence to be 'in the limelight' means to be the *focus of attention.

**Lincoln cycle**. A lost cycle of *mystery plays, now thought to be the *Coventry cycle or *Ludus Coventriae*.

**Lincoln's Men**. An Elizabethan troupe of *travelling players.

**Line ending**. The syllable ending a verse line, especially of *blank verse. Stressed endings are called 'masculine', and unstressed 'feminine'. Variation of line ending can help preserve flexible speech rhythms within the stricter verse form. Thus in Shakespeare's *Antony and Cleopatra* (1606–7) Scarus describes Cleopatra's flight:

> . . . Yon ribald-rid nag of Egypt —
> Whom leprosy o'ertake! — in the midst o' th' fight,
> When vantage like a pair of twins appeared,
> Both as the same, or rather ours the elder —
> The breeze upon her, like a cow in June!
> Hoists sails and flies.

The first and fourth lines have feminine, the others masculine, endings. In *verse speaking it is a common fault to drop the voice at the end of a line, and especial care should be taken with the unstressed feminine endings.

**Listening**. An acting skill requiring *relaxation and confidence. Actors unable to listen and react to one another on stage are unlikely to convince an audience. For a play to work well, the tensions arising from anxiety or egotism, or any reason which impels actors to concentrate on their own parts to the exclusion of others, must be dispelled.

**Little Theatre Movement**. A movement which began in England between the wars and resulted in the foundation of a number of amateur theatre groups and the establishment of the Little Theatre Guild in 1946. The groups own their own theatres and mount productions at frequent intervals. Some clubs, like the Questors in Ealing, run training schemes for their members, and their standards can be very high.

An equivalent movement began in the United States in the 1900s. The American 'little theatres' are now commonly called 'community theatres'.

**Liturgical drama**. Drama developing out of the *liturgy, and performed within the church. It had emerged by the twelfth century in the *Quem Quaeritis trope*. Gradually the whole of the Easter story came to be enacted. Dramatic *dialogue was invented to render the episodes more vivid, and the various episodes — including the preparations for the Last Supper, the betrayal, arrest, trial of Christ, denial of Peter, the stations of the cross, the crucifixion, deposition and entombment — were performed at various *mansions between the west door and the altar. It thus took the form of a procession and became the *passion play when performed outside.

The Christmas services similarly gave rise to the nativity play, which seems to have fused with the Epiphany story to provide sequences of episodes, varying from place to place but normally including the journey of the Magi, the meeting with the shepherds, the presentation of gifts, Herod's anger, the Massacre of the Innocents, and the Flight into Egypt. Wall-paintings of the period indicate the use of a variety of musical instruments.

Secular and comic elements inevitably emerged as the drama developed. These included the episode of Balaam's ass, the introduction of a comic spice-seller (from whom the three Marys buy spices for the embalming), the presentation of Herod, the behaviour of the devils and the fooling at the *Feast of Fools. The tone of these episodes, together no doubt with the cost of the spectacle, contributed to the disquiet with which church authorities came to view this drama, and it moved outside the church walls.

The *mystery cycles, of course, performed in medieval towns and cities at the feast of Corpus Christi, moved away from strictly liturgical drama when they began to intermingle its solemnity and power with secular elements.

CHAMBERS, E.K., *The Medieval Stage*, Vol. II, Oxford University Press, 1903.
WICKHAM, G., *The Medieval Theatre*, Weidenfeld and Nicholson, 1974.

**Liturgy**. (a) The service of the Holy Eucharist; (b) Greek term for a number of duties which the Athenian state, in the fifth and fourth centuries B.C., imposed on wealthy citizens. One of these duties was the 'choregia' — the production of a chorus at dramatic and musical festivals. See CHOREGUS.

**Living light**. Term used by Adolphe Appia (1862–1928), who saw light as a powerful means of relating the *movement, *grouping and *posture of the actors to the architecture of the stage *set and to musical accompaniment and sound effects, thus unifying the different dramatic elements.

APPIA, A., *Music and the Art of the Theatre*, Miami University Press, 1962.

**Living Newspaper**. See FEDERAL THEATRE PROJECT.

**Living Theatre**. Experimental theatre company founded in New York in 1951 by Julian Beck (1925–1985) and Judith Malina (1926–   ). It became especially influential in the 1960s when its anarchist and pacifist aims, and dedicated group life-style, offered a model to new groups both in America and in Europe. 'Life, revolution and theatre are three words for the same thing: an unconditional NO to the present society', said Julian Beck in 1968. The attitudes and theories of Antonin Artaud's *theatre of cruelty are clearly discernible behind the group's activities from the late 1950s onwards. A deliberate attempt to create audience hostility, strong visual effects, the use of nudity and *improvisation, together with an attack on political power structures, mark such famous (or notorious) productions as *Mysteries* (1964), *Frankenstein* (1965) and *Paradise Now* (1968).

BINER, P., *The Living Theatre*, trs. R. Meister, Avon, NY, 1972.

**Loa**. A *prologue used in sixteenth-century Spanish plays. Its function was to create a warm friendly atmosphere by paying initial compliments to the audience.

**Locus**. The fixed *mansion or station in medieval drama, erected on a scaffold and symbolizing a locality such as heaven or hell. The *loci* were set around an open space, or *platea*, and actors would perform on or around them in the sequence the play demanded. For a complex view of the relationship between *locus* and *platea* see:

WEIMANN, R., *Shakespeare and the Popular Tradition in the Theatre*, Johns Hopkins University Press, 1978, pp.73–85.

**London Theatre Studio**. School founded by Michel St Denis for the training of young actors. See:
SAINT-DENIS, M., *Training for the Theatre*, Heinemann, 1982.

**Long run**. A series of performances of the same play at the same theatre for an unusually long period. The celebrated *Mousetrap* by Agatha Christie (1890–1976) has now run for well over thirty years and looks likely to hold an unbeatable record.

The advantages of such runs are commercial. They make money and provide the actors with steady employment for as long as they can stand it, or until they are replaced. Staleness is the obvious threat. Where there is no *repertory system, and no variation of acting roles, performers often have to balance financial rewards against the need to broaden their experience, or simply to escape what has become a mechanical routine.

The problems of the long run have been known since the practice became widespread in the nineteenth century. Some of Stanislavski's work, especially his striving after *communion, is based on observation of the way the Italian actor Salvini preserved his freshness during such a run. A more recent actor, Simon Callow, observes: 'the last West End run I did was for nine months. It was Hell and I recommend it to everyone.' He then describes various phases of the experience, from the initial honeymoon to a period of increasingly mechanical playing, to forms of recovery or the achievement of spontaneity.
CALLOW, S., *Being an Actor*, Methuen, 1984, pp.196–214.

**Long shot**. A distant view of a scene. A camera shot whereby a *film or *TV director establishes location and enables the spectator to identify a setting and also to see the characters in relation to one another within that setting. Thus it unifies the more fragmentary and more closely focused shots by giving them a context.

The long shot often requires a 'bigger' performance from the actor than the *medium shot and especially the *close-up, since the audience cannot see *facial expressions very clearly.
BEAVER, F.E., *Dictionary of Film Terms*, McGraw Hill, 1983.

**Lord Admiral's Men**. Elizabethan acting company of Edward Alleyn (1566–1626).

**Lord Chamberlain**. See LICENSING LAWS; CENSORSHIP.

**Lord Chamberlain's Men**. See CHAMBERLAIN'S MEN.

**Lord of Misrule**. Man appointed to take the dominant role in the Christmas *revels which took place at court, at the Inns of Court and in certain Oxford and Cambridge colleges during the fifteenth and sixteenth centuries. The Lord of Misrule was a successor to the Boy Bishop or King of the early *Feast of Fools.

CHAMBERS, E.K., *The Mediaeval Stage*, 2 Vols., Oxford University Press, 1903.

**Lord Strange's Men**. See STRANGE'S MEN.

**Love**. One of the fundamental concerns of drama, whether it is considered as a religious principle, a biological drive, a source of illusion or the core of life. If *comedy arose out of the Greek 'gamos', which involved sexual union and fertility rites, love was bound to become a pervasive concern. A celebration of union between the sexes traditionally ended *old comedy and *new comedy presented a constant spectacle of young love winning through against the opposition of the old, wealthy and powerful.

In *tragedy, love has often been seen as a source of joy and anguish leading to *catastrophe, as in Euripides's *Hippolytus* (428 B.C.), Racine's *Phèdre* (1677), Shakespeare's *Romeo and Juliet* (1595), *Othello* (1604) and *Antony and Cleopatra* (1606–7). Other profound studies of love are Shakespeare's *Troilus and Cressida* (1602) and *Measure for Measure* (1604) in which the value of the emotion and the imaginative processes it engenders are questioned with a bitter and searching irony.

STENDHAL, H.B., *De L'Amour* (1822).

**Lovers**. Character parts in the *Commedia dell'Arte*, sometimes taken by the nobility when acting companies gave performances in their banqueting halls. The roles were generally passive, and the actors needed only to look young, attractive and beautifully dressed. One imagines the *zanni improvising around them in performance.

**Low comedian**. Leading comic player in the *farce and *melodrama of the Victorian *stock company. He took minor parts in other plays of the *repertory.

**Low comedy**. General term for comedy, especially *farce, which contains much physical by-play, bawdy reference and *slapstick. Such comedy began to be mingled with serious drama in the *mystery cycles and was developed in subsequent *morality plays, particularly in the portrayal of devils and vices. By the late *Elizabethan period, an astonishingly rich and mixed drama had incorporated many of the *knockabout elements of low comedy into *sub-plots centred on *fools and *clowns. During the *Restoration period, 'low' elements were still present in the drama. The tone of Wycherley (1640–1716), for instance, still drew on the bawdy and rumbustious energy of the early seventeenth century, but, gradually, a *neo-classical desire for order and unity of tone began to impose itself. 'Low' material was relegated from the *legitimate to the illegitimate theatres and in the nineteenth century the Victorian gentility took a disapproving and condescending attitude towards it, though it flourished as ever. In recent years, and especially since the abolition of theatrical censorship in England in 1968, the theatre has begun to experiment vigorously with material of the kind which links the *circus clown and Rabelais (*c.*1494–*c.*1553). Trevor Griffiths in *Comedians* (1974), Dario Fo in *Accidental Death of an Anarchist* (1970) and Tom Stoppard in *Jumpers* (1972) are among the writers who have used knockabout farce and clowning for complex and serious dramatic ends.

**Ludus** (plural *ludi*). Latin for 'game' or 'play'. The word survived into the Middle Ages, when it signified war-games, and animal or *circus entertainment, as well as drama. There were various kinds of *ludus*: '*ludus gladiatorum*', '*ludus scenicus*', '*ludus venalis*' and '*ludus circensis*'. All involved physical activity and pretence, however much their purposes may have differed.

WICKHAM, G., *The Medieval Theatre*, Weidenfeld and Nicolson, 1974.

**Lunch-time theatres**. Theatres which have grown up in London and elsewhere since 1968. They have provided new venues, opportunities and work for writers, directors and actors. Their material is frequently experimental, the audiences young and active, and the costs, in small theatre spaces, minimal. On the other hand, the audiences and *casts are small, long plays cannot be shown and there is little money to be earned. They provide, however, a welcome extension of the professional theatre. See FRINGE.

**Lyric**. Originally a song to be sung to the lyre. It has come to signify a short poem imbued with strong feelings, frequently a love poem.

'Dramatic lyric' was the term used by Robert Browning (1812–89) to describe his *dramatic monologues, including *Fra Lippo Lippi* and *My Last Duchess*. He also used it of long *narrative poems, such as *How They Brought The Good News from Aix to Ghent*.

**Lyric Players**. An amateur theatre group founded in Belfast in 1951, specialising in productions of Irish verse drama.

**Lysiody**. Farcical Greek *mime. Its characteristics are unclear, but the actor seems to have played female parts in male costume. See MAGODY.

# M

**Machiavel**. Elizabethan and Jacobean stage intriguer and *villain, named after the Florentine, Niccolò Machiavelli (1469–1527), writer of *Il Principe* (*The Prince*, 1513). In that book Machiavelli describes the political practices of rulers who wish to achieve and maintain political power. His name came to stand for such villainous and extraordinary power-seekers as Shakespeare's Richard III (1595), Iago in *Othello* (1604), Edmund in *King Lear* (1605), John Webster's Bosola in *The Duchess of Malfi* (1612–3) and Thomas Middleton's De Flores in *The Changeling* (1622).

**Machina**. Latin for 'mechani', a kind of crane used in the ancient Greek theatre for the *exits and *entrances of the gods. Hence the term *deus ex machina*.

**Machine**. Name given to a *workshop technique in which the workshop director tells a group of actors to interpret a word or feeling by making a *gesture or movement. One actor begins and repeats the action rhythmically. Other actors join him, each choosing to interpret the emotion in his or her own way. The 'machine' effect is often very interesting visually. Its function is to 'free' inexperienced actors so that they use the body to express an emotion rather than merely use *voice and words. It may also give a director ideas about possible *groupings. It further encourages *ensemble acting, since actors develop a sense of *rhythm and learn to synchronize their movements within an overall effect. In particularly stylized productions, such machines may be incorporated into performance.

The term 'machine' also more obviously refers to a piece of stage equipment. The theatre has always used machines to help create spectacular effects. The Greek theatre had its *machina and *ekkyklema, the medieval theatre its *tableaux. The *court masque, *opera, *ballet, *pantomime and *melodrama steadily developed methods of *scene-changing, and employed *flying effects, *traps and other paraphernalia which opera, *musical and pantomime still use, although the versatility of *film has rendered them mainly obsolete. The development of brilliant mechanical effects in the cinema has helped to throw the theatre back on its own natural resources. Thus the Polish *director, Grotowski (1933–   ), for example, has developed a *'poor' theatre in which the only 'machine' is composed of the bodies and voices of his actors.

**Machine play**. Play given over to the spectacular scenic effects which Torelli (1608–78) developed in Paris in the mid-seventeenth century. Corneille's *Andromède* (1650) and Molière's *Amphitryon* (1668) are examples.

**Maeterlinck, Maurice** (1862–1949). Belgian *symbolist dramatist and exponent of *static theatre.

> ... an old man sitting in his armchair, simply waiting by his lamp, listening unconsciously to all the eternal laws which reign around his house ... this unmoving old man is living in reality a deeper, more human and more universal life than the lover who strangles his mistress, the captain who wins a victory, or the husband who 'avenges his honour'.

> At the foundation of my dramas lies the idea of a Christian God, together with the ancient concept of fate.

> He aims to provoke a fearful yet reasoning acceptance of the inevitability of life, to move the spectator to tears and suffering and yet to soothe and console him. (Meyerhold).

MAETERLINCK, M., 'Le Théâtre', in *La Jeune Belgique*, 9 (1890).

**Magic if**. 'Much virtue in "if"', says Touchstone in Shakespeare's *As You Like It* (1599). Stanislavski (1863–1938) agreed, and used *improvisation methods which invited actors to consider a part *'as if' it extended beyond the limits of the play. 'Our work on a play begins with the use of "if" to lift us out of everyday life on to the plane of the imagination', said Stanislavski in *An Actor Prepares*. The 'magic if' allowed an actor to discover and create the play's *sub-text. Behind the *plot lies a *story, and this story can be enacted in *rehearsal so as to give a character a fuller past, and give the actor a greater confidence in the 'reality' of his role. If, for example, the death of the boy Grisha in Chekhov's *The Cherry Orchard* (1903), which has occurred some years before the play begins, is reenacted in rehearsal as if it had just happened, the improvised scene can strengthen the playing of the boy's tutor, Trofimov, and the boy's mother, Madame Ranyevski, when they meet and remember the tragedy in Act One. The 'magic if' aims to help actors to relax, concentrate and feel secure. (See CIRCLE OF ATTENTION.) The method has since been developed by Mike Leigh (1943–   ) and other writers, not only to strengthen an existing play but also to create new ones. See IMPROVISATION.

**Magody**. Form of low-class farcical Greek *mime. Its nature is uncertain, but the actor, accompanied by cymbals and kettledrum, may have played his roles in female clothing, as compared with the lysiody, where female roles were played in male *costume.

**Main plot**. The most important sequence of events in a play. The term implies the existence of a *double or *sub-plot.

*Maisonnette*. Unusual name for a *mansion, or fixed scenic place, used in productions of medieval plays. It is associated with performances at Mons in Belgium.

*Maître du jeu*. The *stage manager of a large scale medieval civic production. His job was to organize the host of amateur actors, ensure *scene-changes and direct scenic displays.

**Make-up**. Material used to disguise or enhance an actor's features. It may emphasize the *strangeness of theatrical performance by heightening stage appearance. On the other hand, it may retain a life-like appearance by recreating the light and shade which artificial stage *lighting eliminates. It may also serve to distinguish between different styles of acting as in, say, Pirandello's *Six Characters in Search of an Author* (1921) where the 'characters' and 'actors' form two groups who must be distinguished as 'real' (*naturalistic make-up) and 'artificial' (heightened make-up). Make-up thus heightens *contrast, enables facial expression to be seen more clearly and can be used to create effects of 'ageing'. It may also be useful to the actor as a *mask behind which he or she can shelter and allow their *characterizations to grow.

Laurence Olivier is a master of make-up. Many other contemporary actors, like Alec Guinness, rely on it less, and the modern tendency is to do without it if at all possible.

**Malapropism**. An 'inappropriate' (French '*mal à propos*') use of long words. The term is taken from Sheridan's Mrs Malaprop in *The Rivals* (1775), who was apt to say such things as: 'Illiterate him, I say, quite from your memory!'

Characters who misuse language in similar ways may be found as early as Dogberry in Shakespeare's *Much Ado about Nothing* (1598) and Fielding's Mrs Slipslop, in the novel *Joseph Andrews* (1742).

**Manager**. A person generally responsible for commercial arrangements in the theatre such as theatre receipts, paying and hiring staff, and managing the income from sales of food and drink. A large theatre would, of course, divide up these responsibilities. It is particularly inadvisable to combine such duties with those of *artistic director.

*Manet.* Stage direction. Latin for 'remains'. Used to warn an actor not to *exit*.

**Mannerist drama**. A term drawn from Italian art history and applied to exaggerated literary and dramatic styles such as the euphuistic writing of John Lyly (1554–1606) and the metaphysical poetry of the early seventeenth century. The term has also been applied to stylistic modes of other periods. James Joyce's *Ulysses* (1922), for example, has been called 'mannerist'.

According to J.L. Styan, 'Mannerism is very much aware it is playing a game of theatre, believing and not believing'. The style has also been defined as self-conscious, uncertain, grotesquely cynical and exploratory, and likely to be found where conventions are rapidly changing. Within such a broad definition the term has been applied to drama as different as Shakespeare's *Antony and Cleopatra* (1606–7), John Marston's *Antonio and Melida* (1599) and the plays of Ionesco (1912–   ) and Dürrenmatt (1921–   ).

**Manners**. The *comedy of manners is an elaborate game, played by characters who are aware to varying degrees of the gains and penalties involved in conforming or not conforming to a social *code. The term normally refers to *Restoration and *eighteenth-century drama. It may also be applied to a play such as Oscar Wilde's *The Importance of Being Earnest* (1895), in which a competition for respectability supplies much of the energy behind the plot.

**Mansion**. A medieval 'domus' or 'house', usually a booth or scaffold representing the location of a particular scene in the *mystery plays and other *medieval drama.

**Manuscript**. A text written by hand. The term is often wrongly applied to a typescript or typewritten document. A manuscript, of course, has much greater editorial authority.

**Marionette**. Shaped *puppet, operated by wires or strings attached to head, body and limbs.

**Marivaudage.** Affected dramatic *dialogue, in the style of the French writer of comedies, Pierre Marivaux (1688–1763).

**Marxist theatre**. Drama influenced by, and held to express the theories of, Karl Marx (1818–1883).

Theatre dubbed 'Marxist' tends to be preoccupied by the material conditions of the working-classes, and their relation to those in power. The subject-matter is social, historical and *'dialectical', with an emphasis on communal rather than private experience. Processes of eating, drinking, buying, selling and working are given prominence and economic need is stressed. Use may be made of popular *comedy, with its emphasis on the earthy and the physical, and its subversive attitudes to those in positions of social power. The *ending of such plays, however, need not be an assertion of Marxist dogma; it may, if Brecht's example is followed, invite spectators to resolve for themselves the contradictions presented in the drama. A solution to political disunity in the world is more important than artistic unity. Thus in Brecht's *The Good Woman of Setzuan* (1938–41), no *\*deus ex machina* solves the play's problem. Instead, the gods disappear, leaving the heroine (and audience) with the question: 'What then must we do?'

Marxist theatre is a twentieth-century phenomenon. It emerged after the First World War, partly as a form of resistance to the rise of fascism in the Weimar Republic (1918–33). Erwin Piscator (1893–1966) and Bertolt Brecht (1898–1956) were the leading figures at this time, and their example led to a variety of left-wing drama, from the sombre vision of the later Sartre in *Altona* (1960) to the *\*farce of the Italian actor and playwright, Dario Fo (1926–    ). In England, Brecht's later *\*parable plays have influenced a generation of socialist writers, including John Arden (1930–    ), Edward Bond (1935–    ), Howard Brenton (1942–    ) and Trevor Griffiths (1935–    ).

Trevor Griffiths's *The Party* (1974) dramatizes the opposed attitudes of several Marxist and post-Marxist activists and theoreticians. His play *Occupations* (1970) presents the tensions and problems of a revolutionary situation involving Antonio Gramsci, founder of the Italian Communist Party. See POLITICAL THEATRE.

ITZIN, C., *Stages in the Revolution: Political Theatre in Britain since 1968*, Eyre Methuen, 1980.

MCGRATH, J., *A Good Night Out*, Eyre Methuen, 1981.

**14** *Comedy masks* (from F. Ficaronius, *Dissertatio de Larvis Scenicis*)

**Mask.** Covering for the face. Masks have been in use since drama began. In primitive dramatic rituals, before and after a hunt, men donned animal masks and took the *\*roles of hunting and hunted animals. There is a famous Greek vase (*c*.550 B.C.) which shows a *\*chorus mounted on men masked as horses. A fourteenth-century illustration of dancers in animal masks and skins indicates that Shrovetide and other festival revels had existed since Roman times.

Both *comedy and *tragedy seem to have inherited the mask from such activities. Masks were used extensively by the Greeks, and also in forms of *medieval drama and in the *Commedia dell'Arte. The rise of humanism, however, led to a growth of *naturalism. The mask grew less popular since it restricted the *individual* expression a more individualistic culture demanded. The mask assigns formal and stereotyped *roles to the wearer and can therefore reflect the attitudes of a rigid and formal society. With the powerful social and economic changes which broke up the feudal system in Europe, medieval patterns of thought gave way to more complex views of human possibility. The inflexible mask was then removed to reveal the flexible human countenance.

Forms of masking continued, however, especially in *popular and *street theatre. In *oriental theatre and *dance, the tradition has been particularly strong. In the twentieth century, the established theatre found a political use for these forms. Brecht (1898–1956) drew on oriental and popular traditions, and used masks to represent men and women acting out stereotyped social roles. In his play *The Good Woman of Setzuan* (1938–41), the heroine dons a mask to emphasize the inhuman role forced on her by her economic situation. The mask is alternately donned and discarded, as the character responds to inner impulse and outer circumstance.

Other writers who employed masks were Meyerhold (1874–1940), who was interested in popular *street theatre and ideas of the *grotesque (see his article on the fairground booth), and W.B. Yeats (1864–1939) who, like Brecht, was interested in oriental theatre. For Yeats the mask represented an alternative personality: 'It was the mask engaged your mind/Not what's behind', he proclaimed in his poem *The Mask* (1910). The mask was a defence, a protection of the self. It was also an escape from the self, into a potentially passionate role.

The mask is profoundly connected with theories of personality, and for an art such as drama, which is so strongly concerned with the nature of *character, it is a central concept and a major practice. Jung's writings on the *persona are relevant, as is the whole *modernist fragmentation of the self, which finds expression in, say, T.S. Eliot's famous lines in Prufock, 'Prepare a face to meet the faces that you meet', or in the fiction and drama of Pirandello (1867–1936).

For a discussion of the way the donning of a mask can generate states of concentrated energy which are akin to trance or possession, see Keith Johnstone's interview with Zina Barniek, printed in *Discussions in Developmental Drama* (No. 47).

Tony Harrison, Britain's leading theatre poet, has an interesting comment on the use of masks in Peter Hall's 1981 production of the *Oresteia*, for which he provided the translation. Masks in drama, he says, have 'the same function as welder's masks . . . The mask and its language compel us to keep our eyes open in situations of extremity, when we might otherwise flinch away in horror and stop looking, and therefore stop feeling and thinking.'

Evidently the functions of the theatrical mask are important and diverse. They give the actor confidence and energy and allow one actor to play several roles. They create *character, and when a character dons a mask within a play it establishes *dramatic irony and *suspense (because the audience knows one character is disguising himself from another). Traditional masks are *signs or *indices of conventional *types which evoke an immediate and predictable audience response (see HARLEQUIN; PANTALOON).

The mask may also create an effect of *estrangement. This is true when the actors fix their own faces in a mask (as they are recommended to do in the *stage-directions to Eugene O'Neill's *Mourning Becomes Electra* (1931)). This can be comic, and fits exactly Henri Bergson's definition of *comedy: 'the mechanical encrusted upon the living'. It can also be disconcerting. When the mask is donned, or a mask-like expression adopted, even our laughter contains an unease. In *tragedy this unease may be intensified to the point of *fear or terror. It reminds us that one purpose of primitive masked rituals was the placation of the gods.

**Masking**. 'Masking' can mean the obstruction of an audience's clear view of the play's focal action. The problems of masking and of establishing *sight-lines increase with the number of actors on stage and the size of the *audience in front of, and in the same plane as, the actors. A steep *rake, and the use of varying stage *levels help to overcome such problems. With *thrust stages, or in *theatre in the round, some masking is bound to take place. It is important therefore that the stage *movement should be fluid enough to ensure that the masking is only momentary.

A 'mask' is a film shot in which the camera lens is masked in various ways to achieve an effect of concentration or distancing, or both.

**Masque**. A Renaissance court entertainment in which masked or disguised figures present a dramatic action interspersed with *dance and *song. The masque may have originated in a courtly gift-bearing ceremony, involving long and complimentary speeches with elaborate costuming and *masking. This developed into the court-shows of Italy, copied by the English court as early as 1512, when Henry VIII 'with 6 other, were disguised after the manner of Italie, called a masque, a thing not seen afore in England'. The form employed sophisticated settings designed by artists such as Brunelleschi (1377–1486) and Leonardo (1452–1519). In these, stage machinery spouted water-fountains and created cloud, sky and fire effects.

Characters were mythological and allegorical: Neptune and Diana, Reason and Love. Stages were filled with 'Satyres, Fools, Wildmen, Antiques, Ethiopes, Pygmires and Beasts'. Trained singers and dancers mingled with court and royalty in a lavish entertainment concluding with a mingling in dance of actors and audience.

In England the court masque became very ambitious. Inigo Jones (1573–1652) went to Italy in 1606 and 1613, bringing back designs by Giulio Parigi (1590–1636). Ben Jonson (1572–1637) wrote thirty masques including *The Masque of Queens* (1609) and *The Masque of Oberon* (1611). This latter cost £1500, three times the cost of building the Fortune Theatre.

Masques were used for complex dramatic purposes within longer *Elizabethan and *Jacobean plays. *A Midsummer Night's Dream* (1595) and Shakespeare's late plays *Cymbeline* (c.1609), *The Winter's Tale* (1610) and *The Tempest* (1611) contain elements of the masque. Middleton's *Women Beware Women* (1621) has a lavish and complex masque in its final act.

With the closing of the theatres, public and courtly, in 1642, the masque was incorporated into other forms such as *opera and *ballet. Inigo Jones's influence continued to be felt after the Restoration, in the use of *proscenium, *perspective, *wings, *grooves and general scenic display.

**Master of the Revels**. An officer first appointed in 1494 to serve under the Lord Chamberlain and supervise court entertainment.

The office became extinct in 1737 with the *Licensing Act, at which time the Lord Chamberlain took over responsibility for the supervision and *censorship of plays.

CHAMBERS, E.K., *The Elizabethan Stage*, Vol. I, Oxford University Press, 1923.

**Mastersingers**. Members of the dramatic or musical guilds of southern Germany in the fifteenth and sixteenth centuries. Wagner (1813–83) depicts such a group in *Die Meistersinger von Nürnberg* (1868).

**May-day, Maying**. Spring *folk festival involving dance, games and dramatic activity. The Queen of the May, Hobby Horse, Jack a Lantern, and the various characters of the *Robin Hood story are associated with the May-day games.

**Meaning**. There are varying degrees of emphasis in the critical use of this word. I.A. Richards, in *Practical Criticism* (1929), suggested that any text had four kinds of meaning: the 'sense' or intellectual content, the emotive content or 'feeling', the writer's attitude to the reader or 'tone', and the writer's 'intention'. More recent criticism has divided meaning between: (a) that which it was the *intention to express; (b) that which has been expressed 'in' the text; and (c) that which is communicated to an audience. The meaning may thus lie in the author's head, in what he creates, or in the receiver's mind. It may also lie in the public language used and in the general cultural patterns which inform a language. (See INTERPRETATION; THEORY OF DRAMA.) The debate about where the 'real meaning' of a play lies thus ranges from an insistence on the study of *sources, to the study of the text, to the study of *performance, to the examination of *audience response and the general study of language and culture.

Since drama fairly obviously involves a series of transactions between *dramatist, *actor, *director, *designer and *audience, and at a more abstract level between 'history', 'language', and 'nature', the question of where meaning lies will always be a source of dispute. Meaning lies in the relationships between what is within and what is outside, between individual writer or actor, the *genre, *codes and *conventions they employ, and the historical or other processes which inform them. Where theorists choose to place their emphases, however, will no doubt continue to vary.

**Mechanical acting**. Stanislavski's term for acting which is not informed by human feeling, but by conventions and clichés, or what Stanislavski calls 'worked-out stencils'. See:
STANISLAVSKI, C., *An Actor Prepares*, Eyre Methuen, 1980.

**Mechanism**. A dramatic device, especially of *plot, which heightens interest and *suspense. *Peripeteia is one example; the use of a *messenger is another.

Generally, the writer endeavours to conceal his mechanisms and trusts that the audience will not question a conventional device. Sometimes, however, dramatists engage in an elaborate game with the audience in which recognition of artifice is part of the pleasure. This often occurs in *farce. Occasionally, a writer will fail to master such devices and his dramatic means will work against his ends. Arguably, this occurs in T.S. Eliot's late plays, *The Confidential Clerk* (1954) and *The Elder Statesman* (1959) where comic mechanisms are employed for a religious purpose and the effect can lead to confusion.

**Medieval drama**. There are three main categories of medieval drama: (a) *folk play; (b) religious and *liturgical drama; and (c) court *revels. All three categories existed before the establishment of the permanent *professional theatre in 1576. They were usually communal enterprises linked with seasonal celebrations at Twelfth Night, Easter and Midsummer. Audience illiteracy meant a widespread dependence on the use of visual *sign, *colour and *costume. A sense of the natural world, the cycle of the seasons, of cold and hunger, and thanksgiving for the return of light and food, is strong. The stories were usually known, and their impact generally depended on a recognition of a shared situation in a world which repeats its patterns. *Fear of death, of nature and of damnation lie behind dramatic performance. Both *burlesque and *buffoonery in the comic drama, and the recognition of the power of God in the serious drama, seem strongly related to this primary emotion. Chaos, misrule, death, sin and the devil lurked beneath the world's harmony, and a main function of medieval drama seems to have been to express and control this polar opposition. See MYSTERY; MORALITY PLAY; DISGUISING; MASQUE.

WICKHAM, G., *The Medieval Theatre*, Weidenfeld and Nicolson, 1974.

**Medium close-up** (abbreviation MCU.) Camera shot showing the whole head and shoulders. See BIG CLOSE-UP.

**Meininger Company**. Famous and influential acting company founded by the Duke of Meiningen (1826–1914). He enforced a rigorous discipline, long *rehearsal schedules and meticulous attention to details of *costume, *property and *set design. The resulting unified style of performance impressed Henry Irving (1838–1905) in England, Antoine (1858–1943) in France and Stanislavski (1863–1938) in Russia. His *repertory was mainly classical and included plays by Shakespeare, Schiller, Kleist, Grillparzer, Lessing and Molière, as well as Ibsen's *The Pretenders* (1864) and *Ghosts* (1881). Crowd scenes in large historical plays were orchestrated by the careful placing of experienced professionals within various groups of *supernumeraries. Variety was also achieved by using different *levels and designing impressive three-dimensional sets (though these encumbered the flow of a Shakespeare play). The tours the company embarked upon, from 1874 onwards, were a major influence in the development of *naturalism.

**Melodrama**. Literally, 'music drama' (owing to the extensive use of musical accompaniment). Melodrama was a form of popular drama which grew up in the late eighteenth and early nineteenth centuries to satisfy the demands of the urban poor. It originated in the early plays of Goethe (1749–1832) and Schiller (1759–1805), especially his *Die Räuber* (1781), and in the eighteenth-century *pantomime and *gothic novel. *Elizabethan and *Senecan revenge drama also lie behind the tradition.

Melodrama, however, simplified its antecedents for a mainly illiterate population. Moral sympathies were clearly defined, and characters — *heroes, *heroines, *villains, the *comic man — were always immediately identifiable. These *stock characters engaged in a rapid action, enhanced by appropriate music, in which virtue was normally rescued in the nick of time and villainy came to a sticky end.

Different kinds of melodrama existed, from the early *gothic variety, full of brigands, ghosts and haunted castles, to more *domestic forms, often based, like the famous *Maria Marten or Murder in the Red Barn* (1830s), on contemporary and local crime. *Nautical, *Indian and various 'spectacle' or *sensation melodramas were written, and they lived on into the early cinema in 'horror' film, the 'western' and the crime story, where music continued to be extensively used.

Most nineteenth-century melodrama, written for the poor, played seriously, at first, on *fear, social resentment, and the need to escape from appalling living conditions. The heightened forms of the acting, however, with its grimaces and special gestures, and a peculiar enunciation of individual syllables, laid themselves open to *burlesque, and when a more sophisticated middle-class audience was introduced to melodrama, the form's basic naivety came to have comic appeal. In the theatre, soon after the First World War, it died.

Melodrama, in a general sense, has some basic appeal for all audiences. It can be found in the novels of Dickens (1812–70) and Dostoievski (1821–81) and it lurks beneath the subtle integument of drama from Euripides (484–407/6 B.C.) to Chekhov (1860–1904) and later. Its basic appeal to *pity and *fear raises Aristotelian questions of *catharsis and carries us to the centre of discussion about the nature of *comedy, *tragedy and the function of drama. The absence of subtle characterization and moral complexity may encourage us to dismiss it too easily.

BOOTH, M. (ed.), *Hiss The Villain: Six Melodramas*, Eyre and Spottiswoode, 1964.

BOOTH, M., *English Melodrama*, Jenkins, 1965.

DISHER, M.W., *Blood and Thunder*, Rockliff, 1949; *Melodrama*, Rockliff, 1954.

**Melodramma**. A musical play deriving from the *pastoral, developed in Italy by Apostolo Zeno (1668–1750) and Metastasio (1698–1782) in the late seventeenth and earlier eighteenth century.

**Melopoeia**. 'Song-making'; literary term popularized by Ezra Pound. It describes the musical appeal of the poetic line and, by extension, *poetic drama. See T.S. Eliot's essays 'The Music of Poetry' (1942) and 'Poetry and Drama' (1950) for his observations on how the dramatic verse line can have musical appeal. See also:
POUND, E., *ABC of Reading*, Faber, 1961, pp.197–206.

**Melpomene**. The muse of *tragedy.

**Memory**. Human faculty which preserves a sense of personal and communal continuity.

If memory is where *images of the past are in some way stored, then drama, like other art forms, is a kind of cultural memory, preserving the thoughts, the modes of thinking and feeling, and the images created by (and in some way characteristic of) a particular time, place and culture. A past is important for any culture or group wishing to retain its identity and traditions. Without shared memory an audience cannot understand dramatic representation. An actor, too, needs what Stanislavski called *'emotion memory' for the performance of his or her part, and the writer needs to work from memory to create recognizable characters.

Memory thus helps preserve communal and individual continuity. It is a desperate situation for Didi in Beckett's *Waiting for Godot* (1953) when Gogo either cannot or does not want to recognize that he has been in *this* place and worn *these* boots before. Didi needs to connect yesterday with today. The loss of memory in old age threatens that connection.

**Mesode**. 'Mid-ode'. Section of a Greek choral ode between *strophe and *anti-strophe.

**Message**. Semiotic term for a *signal, generally of a verbal or visual nature. Such signals are given meaning by *codes shared by the individuals who send and receive them. In drama, a word, *facial expression, *posture, *gesture or any other form of *theatre language is a message which invokes codes common to both audience and performer.

**Messenger**. Character who enters to report offstage events. Messengers are frequently used in *classical and *neo-classical tragedy and in the Elizabethan theatre. One of his functions in the former was to exclude violent, distasteful and/or potentially unconvincing stage action. But he has other uses: (a) he is a *narrator whose words may, like a novelist's, give the audience free rein to *imagine* rather than *watch* a scene; (b) the device may thus be used to vary direct dramatic action and increase *suspense; (c) his narrative also telescopes events which would take a long time to enact. Description *condenses* action (and incidentally avoids the necessity for *scene changes). The messenger can create the impression of *space around the stage action, fill in *time gaps and supply information necessary to the chosen main action. Shakespeare uses the device very economically in *Othello* (1604) to report both the gathering and dispersal of the Turkish battle fleet. Since the narration is in the present, or immediate past, the excitement of the enactment comes through the messenger's *voice. The messenger also focuses audience attention on the dramatic response of the characters he or she enlightens. The most famous instance is in Sophocles's *Oedipus Rex* (*c*.430 B.C.) where first the Messenger, then the Shepherd (who is also a messenger figure), enlighten the king on the circumstances of his birth.

Narrative, of course, can be tedious in the theatre. Delivery of information must often be broken up, perhaps by excited questioning, as in *Oedipus Rex* (*c*.430 B.C.). Sometimes it is better to use narrative to *reduce* the dramatic power of an event because dramatic action would lessen the impact of an onstage event which is to follow. Thus in *The Winter's Tale* (1610), Shakespeare has three Courtiers narrate the offstage reunion between Leontes and his daughter Perdita so as not to weaken the reunion between Leontes and his wife Hermione in the climactic 'statue scene'. These three bear a heavy dramatic responsibility. It is that of all messengers — to register the importance of their information in voice, word and physical response when the action has been elsewhere.

Skill in selecting from the *story events which are to be narrated by some form of messenger is basic to the art of playwriting.

**Metaphor**. Literally 'carrying over' — a figure of speech which compares two dissimilar things and implies that they are identical because they share one or more characteristics. Thus 'the man is a barrel' is a metaphor: it asserts the identity of two things which share a characteristic shape. 'The ship ploughed the seas' is a metaphor which asserts that a ship is a plough because the two share a characteristic movement.

The appeal of metaphor is different from that of *simile. Metaphor sets up a pretence of identity. The likeness is stated to be exact and not merely a resemblance. This entails a complicity between writer and reader or speaker and hearer. A simile acknowledges, by the words 'like' or 'as', that the things compared are not the same. It makes a rational appeal, whereas the metaphor invites complicity in a fiction.

This complicity may take different forms, as in the examples quoted. In the first the metaphor may provoke a smile, since the resemblance of shape between man and barrel is, presumably, exaggerated. In the second the movement of the ship through the water resembles the movement of the plough closely enough to prevent any sense of absurdity. In addition the comparison is so commonplace that the fictional and metaphorical element may not even be noticed. The effect of metaphor thus depends on how close and how fresh is the resemblance invoked. Far-fetched metaphors tend towards comedy. They invite the hearer to pretend that the resemblance is exact. More precise comparisons such as 'the ship ploughed the sea' invite a *suspension of disbelief.

This discussion is relevant to drama in a number of ways. First of all, an audience accepts, or pretends to accept, the fiction that an actor is a character. Actors behave as if they *were* Julius Caesar, or Greed, or Moonshine, or Mrs Alving, or whoever. The audience accepts the fiction and may almost forget that a fiction exists; this is the aim of *naturalist drama, and it also tends to occur in tragedy. This is akin to the effect of the metaphor, 'the ship ploughed the sea'. In *comedy the actor's relation to his role is more open. The audience only pretends to accept the fiction that the actor is Wall or Moonshine, though it must be physically obvious that he or she cannot be the thing they represent. This is closer to the effect of such a metaphor as 'the man is a barrel'.

The effect can also be more subtle. When an actor plays a character who pretends in the course of the play to be some other character, as Feste pretends to be 'Sir Thopas' in Shakespeare's *Twelfth Night* (1601–2), the pretence is evident to the audience but not always to the other characters in the play. The audience accepts that the actor 'is' Feste but 'is not' Sir Thopas. This simultaneous *identification and acceptance of difference is not dissimilar to the way metaphor makes its appeal.

There are more obvious ways in which metaphor relates to a discussion of drama. It is a vehicle for strong emotion; it not only defines and describes shapes and movements, but also communicates feeling. Thus characters, especially in *poetic drama, use metaphor when they are under strong emotional pressure. King Lear speaks, for instance, of his 'pelican daughters' and the figure conveys Lear's belief that his daughters, Goneril and Regan, are greedy and feed on his blood. While communicating the character's feeling, this metaphor also contains a kind of ironic commentary on it. A pelican was supposed to give its own life-blood to save its young, and was a symbol of the Redeemer. In this the pelican suggests Lear himself rather than his daughters. The metaphor carries two opposed charges, one condemnatory and the other evoking sympathy. Lear would like to apply the negative meaning to his daughters and the positive one to himslf. For a careful listener, however, the simple oppositions are not entirely accurate. Lear has not behaved with selfless generosity to the third of his daughters, and the metaphor can suggest a certain similarity between Lear, Goneril and Regan which the speaker did not intend. Lear has been an unkind, perhaps even 'pelican', father. The metaphor implies more to the listener than the speaker intends. A further ironic distancing resides in the *grotesque element in the metaphor. Lear's daughters certainly do not *look* like pelicans and for Lear to see them as such reveals further aspects of the speaker. The comparison strengthens the audience's awareness that Lear is going mad. The metaphor is both appropriate and inappropriate. An awareness of simultaneous fiction and truth separates the audience from the character, for whom the metaphor possesses only truth. The audience glimpses an element of comedy, or incongruity. It sees that Lear is ceasing to be aware of the fictional element in figurative language. In other words he is losing a sense of reality. Madness, which fuses unlike things and sees symbols as truths, is taking over. The speaker has lost an ironic awareness of self. In seeing only his own tragedy he loses his sanity.

Metaphor can thus be seen as a kind of invitation to be mad, a total rather than a partial suspension of disbelief, a loss of an awareness of the separateness of things. Lear's metaphor extends this invitation, but the play, like the audience, and the actor who plays the role, has to remain sane. Only the character takes metaphor for truth.

Metaphors may thus reveal the condition of a character's mind. They may also comm.unciate to an audience things the character does not suspect. This may give a character further depth, by creating the impression of an *unconscious mind which utters things the conscious mind is unaware of.

Metaphors may also signal to the audience the things that lie in wait. Thus in the opening scene of Shakespeare's The Winter's Tale (1610) Camillo says of the friendship between Leontes and Polixenes that it 'cannot choose but branch now.' Although he seems to mean 'give off branches' or grow, the other meaning of branch, 'to split', is soon seen to be more appropriate, since this is what happens to the friendship. The metaphor, like Lear's *image, has two opposite and contradictory characteristics. Whether or not the author placed the word 'split' in Camillo's mind so that it could emerge as a form of *parapraxis, cannot be known. What is certain is that the metaphor sets up the form of dramatic *irony known as *foreshadowing: a statement made by a character in one sense comes true in another.

In *poetic drama metaphors may become a *leitmotif within the general poetic organization of the play, as in The Winter's Tale where Camillo's words refer us to a strong pattern of images of growth. Metaphor in naturalistic drama is less frequent. Characters speak in more everyday terms. It may, however, enter the play as *stage image, as in Chekhov's The Cherry Orchard (1904) or Ibsen's The Wild Duck (1884). The central metaphor in these works is drawn from the world of the play. In one sense the orchard and the duck are everyday realities and not metaphors at all. But they are seen as metaphors or symbols by some of the characters and their function is to show the audience different ways of viewing reality. For Gina the wild duck is only a duck. For her daughter Hedwig, as for Gregers Werle, it becomes a symbol, and this precipitates the *catastrophe. As in King Lear the metaphor is an invitation to madness. It contains both a truth and a fiction. It implies the identity of different objects but assumes an awareness of their difference. Audiences, like the saner characters, recognize the dangers of embracing the fiction of identity. Drama which calls attention to this, is, like metaphor, a fiction and a truth. See METONYMY; STAGE IMAGERY.

**Metatheatre**. Drama which consciously scrutinizes the nature of *play and playing. This includes works as widely differing as Shakespeare's *Hamlet* (1601), Sheridan's *The Critic* (1779) and Beckett's *Waiting for Godot* (1953). See PLAY WITHIN THE PLAY.

ABEL, L., *Metatheatre: A New View of Dramatic Form*, Hill and Wang, NY, 1963.

RIGHTER, A., *Shakespeare and the Idea of the Play*, Penguin, 1967.

**Method, The**. An American school of acting associated with the *Group Theatre in the 1930s, under Lee Strasberg, Cheryl Campbell and Harold Clurman, and with the *Actors' Studio after World War II, under Elia Kazan (1909–85) and then Strasberg. Its most famous figure is Marlon Brando (1924–  ) and its greatest impact was felt in the 1950s in the films of Kazan and a series of productions of the plays of Tennessee Williams (1914–83). Both the Group Theatre and Actors' Studio took as their basis the *system of Stanislavski (1863–1938) as developed first in *My Life in Art* (1924) and expanded in *An Actor Prepares* (1936) and the postumous *Building a Character* (1950) and *Creating a Role* (1961). According to Eli Wallach the 'method' used Stanislavski's *naturalism 'in rebellion against posturing, singing orators, technically polished and emotionally empty actors'. He added, 'In the beginning the important stress was on having something to communicate, *then* came the study of means of communicating.' It thus had a reputation for encouraging roughness and incoherence. But it was a vigorous and important school of acting. In 1957, when its influence was at its height, Tyrone Guthrie described it as 'a valuable force for thought and discussion about the art of the theatre, about the craft of acting and the philosophy and technique of self-expression'.

HETHMON, R.H. (ed.), *Strasberg at the Actors' Studio*, Viking 1965, Cape, 1966.

**Metonymy**. Figure of speech in which an appurtenance of a thing is substituted for the thing itself. Thus to say 'crown' for 'monarchy' is metonymy. It is very close to synecdoche which substitutes a part of a thing for the whole, or a whole for a part. To say 'crown' instead of 'king' is synecdoche, and arguably the same figure as metonymy.

The term has gained in critical currency since Roman Jacobsen (1896–  ) differentiated the term from *metaphor, which he associated with *symbolism, and linked it with *realism. Previously metonymy had been considered a sub-category of metaphor.

Jacobsen's distinction is founded on observation of the linguistic behaviour of sufferers from aphasia. He noted that patients unable to remember individual words would substitute either metonyms or metaphors in their place, according to the type of aphasia they suffered from. One patient, unable to remember the word 'ship', might use the metaphor 'plough'. Another would use the metonym 'keel'. The first substitution involves a leap into another context. The second does not. 'Keel' is a part of and closely associated with a ship. 'Plough' only shares a characteristic movement.

Jacobsen came to see these processes as polar opposites, characteristic of different forms of mental activity, and he extended the distinction to a discussion of different cultural *genres. Drama he saw as metaphorical, *film as metonymic. Painting used both modes. A surrealist picture was symbolic and metaphoric. A realist or cubist painting was metonymic. Prose and *naturalism are metonymic, whereas poetry tends to the metaphoric.

How useful are these polar oppositions when one comes to examine a play in detail? Obviously, naturalistic drama tends to the metonymic, in that it substitutes a part for the whole: it shows one room of a house, one house in a town or village, one or two families of a community. The less naturalistic the play the more it approaches metaphor.

The two modes, however, do not work to their mutual exclusion. After all, drama, like the novel, represents different ways in which human beings think. If we think both metonymically and metaphorically both modes will be present whenever we attempt to present human complexity. It is reductive to argue that drama is only metaphorical. (See STAGE IMAGERY.)

To say that *film is metonymic is also to simplify. Film tends towards naturalism of setting. The *long-shot of a scene provides us with a context for the metonymic *close-up, which is part of the same scene. On the other hand the process of *cross-cutting and *montage can bring together with striking effect two different worlds. This is the process of metaphor. Dramatic structures are similarly both metonymic and metaphorical. They may use naturalistic settings and aspire to the *unities. They may also cross-cut between different worlds, as frequently in the *sub- and *double plots of *Jacobean tragedy.

We should remember too that as a work recedes from us in time, what may have been a contemporary world shared by writer, actor and audience becomes a world distantly removed. The metonymic becomes metaphorical as the world changes. For an interesting literary application of the term see:

LODGE, D., *The Modes of Modern Writing*, Edward Arnold, 1977.

JACOBSEN, R., and HALLE, M., 'Two Aspects of Language and Two

Types of Aphasic Disturbance', in *Fundamentals of Language*, The Hague, 1956.

**Meyerhold, Vsevolod**, (1874–1940?). Russian director whose concern for *stylized forms of theatre seemed directly to oppose the *naturalist theories of Stanislavski.

> How long will it be before they inscribe in the theatrical tables the following law: words in the theatre are only embellishments on the design of movement?

> Cannot the body sing as clearly as the voice?

See: BIOMECHANICS; CINEFICATION; CONSTRUCTIVISM; ECCENTRISM; FUTURISM; PARADOX OF ACTING; PRE-ACTING; THEATRE TRIANGLE; THEATRE OF THE STRAIGHT LINE.
MEYERHOLD, V., *Meyerhold on Theatre*, edited by E. Braun, Methuen, 1969.

**Mezzotino**. One of the wittier servant figures of the *Commedia dell'Arte*, elaborated in the 1680s by the Italian actor, Angelo Constantini (1655–1729).

**Miasma**. Sense of pollution or contamination resulting from some act of impiety, requiring purification or *catharsis. According to E.R. Dodds the development of a universal *fear of miasma contributed powerfully to the rise of *Greek tragedy. Its relevance to such tragic *heroes as Orestes and Oedipus seems clear. See TABOO; SCAPEGOAT.
DODDS, E.R., *The Greeks and the Irrational*, University of California Press, 1950.

**Middle**. The central part of an *action, according to Aristotle's definition in the *Poetics*, which established the critical assumption that a play without *beginning or *end is lacking in *unity. However, certain plays, for instance Shakespeare's *Troilus and Cressida* (1601–2) and Beckett's *Waiting for Godot* (1953), seem deliberately to challenge Aristotle:

>           . . . our play
> Leaps o'er the vaunt and firstlings of these broils,
> Beginning in the middle, starting thence away,
> To what may be digested in a play . . . [Prologue of *Troilus*]

These plays suggest that there is no *resolution of the situation presented and *parody the idea of formal *unity. Where the idea of unity in life or art is problematic, to present the continuing middle at the expense of the end may be more realistic and honest.

**Middle Comedy**. A category invented to define a type of comedy intermediate between Aristophanes's *old comedy and the *new comedy of Menander (342–292 B.C.). The late plays of Aristophanes (c.448–380 B.C.) such as *Ecclesiazusae* (392 B.C.) and *Plutus* (388 B.C.) are felt to initiate this transitional comedy, which lies between the festive and choral older comic drama and the new individualistic social comedy.

**Mime.** (a) A crude, farcical play, which appeared in Greece before the comedies of Aristophanes (c.448–380 B.C.), later influencing Roman comedy; (b) a silent performance in which the actor, generally working alone with a few simple *props, imitates human or animal behaviour by highly skilled and controlled movements of body and face; and (c) a term for the actors in both these *genres.

The *make-up of the mime actor today usually resembles that of the *circus clown, indicating common antecedents in the *pantomime, *Commedia dell'Arte*, medieval *fool, and Greek and Roman *farce.

The reasons why mime continues to have a strong appeal are intriguing. The performer attracts admiration for the skill and physical control which creates a *setting out of nothing. A table, a door or a flight of stairs is created by a *posture or a *movement. The performer gives one a sense of the texture, shape and weight of the imaginary objects handled. Laughter mingles with the admiration, since the performance exaggerates *gesture and *facial expression, breaking down the normal continuity of human *movement. Marcel Marceau (1923–   ) explains: 'When I am going to pick up a wallet I lift my hand. The audience looks at the hand. Then I pick up the wallet.' This causes the audience to *focus on operations which are often taken for granted — lighting a pipe, putting on a jacket or sitting in a chair, for example.

At the same time there is something *grotesque and disquieting about mime. Marceau walks from the cradle to the grave in a few brief minutes and recalls the proximity of *tragedy and the *absurd. Mime points up man's subjugation to the limits of his body and his resemblance to the rest of the animal kingdom — the ease with which he becomes an insect (as Camus said of Kafka's Gregor Samsa). A kind of horror lies behind the humour and the skill. Nola Rae's time-honoured clowning routine in which she finds a flea in the hair of a member of the audience; Steven Berkoff's production of Kafka's *Metamorphosis* in which the central character becomes a dung-beetle; the sea monsters mimed by David Glass; all these reveal in different ways the mime artist's fascination with the relations between the animal, insect and human worlds. See GROTESQUE.

DECROUX, E., *Paroles sur le Mime*, Gallimard, 1963.

LECOCQ, J., 'Le mouvement et le théâtre', in *ATAC – information* 13, December, 1967.

MAWER, I., *The Art of Mime*, Methuen, 1932.

**Mimesis**. Greek term which seems originally to have meant the imitation of a person, god or creature through *dance, *gesture and *facial expression. As used in Aristotle's *Poetics* it marks the difference between *rituals performed by a priest before a congregation, and 'imitations of an action' performed by actors before an audience.

Plato (*c*.428/7–348/7 B.C.) used the word to describe the relation of the world to the 'real' world of ideal forms which lay beyond it. Artists, he said, who imitate, as they must, the world we live in, merely 'imitate an imitation' of reality. He therefore excluded them from his ideal Republic.

Aristotle (384–322 B.C.) reinterpreted the term. Artists, he implied, imitate permanent not transient modes of thought, behaviour and feeling. They should represent the actions of men according to laws of 'plausibility' and prefer a 'plausible [probable] impossibility' to an improbable possibility. The truth was in the *form. For Aristotle the natural and human world was a world in movement. It exhibited dynamic forms moving from their *beginning to a *middle and *end. Flowers, animals, men and women are born, grow to maturity and die. Drama in its mimesis of life should possess the same pattern.

The term changed emphasis with the *neo-classical writers. For them it was the imitation of the supreme classical models which was important. The function of art was the mimesis of art. Then a new *realism appeared with the novel form. According to Stendhal (1788–1842) the novel was a kind of 'mirror on a highroad'. Its purpose was the imitation or mimesis of 'life'. This emphasis led, via Emile Zola (1840–1902), into *naturalism in drama and the mimesis of the surface of human behaviour, especially *costume, *setting and natural speech.

Modern theorists have grown sceptical of this idea of the function of art and have placed emphasis on the way art creates its own reality. Artistic means transform the reality they purport to mediate. Thus Antonin Artaud (1896–1948) claims: 'The theatre is not mimesis of an event, but the event itself, not a representation of life but a way of living'.

Twentieth-century *political theatre, however, is still very much concerned with the portrayal of the outside world. It emphasizes not the drama as an end in itself, like Artaud, or the representation of an unchanging pattern, as do many theorists of *tragedy since Aristotle, but the processes of social and historical change.

The term mimesis thus raises central theoretical questions. Is drama an imitative process, or does it create its own world? Or do both processes mingle? If drama is mimetic what should it imitate? Should it represent 'man' or 'nature' or 'history'? Should it show the 'surfaces' or the deeper 'trends'? Does the medium embody *reality in some sense, or is the means used quite 'unreal'? The

answers have varied as concepts of reality have changed. See:
AUERBACH, E., *Mimesis: The Representation of Reality in Western Literature*, trs. W. Trask, Princeton University Press, 1953.

**Mimus**. See PANTOMIMUS.

**Minor theatres**. Theatres without a *patent which grew up in the eighteenth century to satisfy a popular demand for *illegitimate musical and *pantomime shows.

**Minstrel**. Itinerant medieval musician and story-teller who earned a living entertaining in village marketplace or nobleman's hall. The term may be extended to *travelling players and acrobats, groups of whom had probably lived by their talents and wits ever since the demise of the Roman theatres. The term usually implies, however, a single entertainer.
CHAMBERS, E.K., *The Medieval Stage*, Vols. I and II, Oxford University Press, 1903.

**Minstrel show**. A popular form of family entertainment in America and England in the mid-nineteenth century. It originated in the song and dance acts of the negro impersonator T.D. Rice, known as Jim Crow, and raises interesting questions about the popularity of *role reversals. Groups of white entertainers corked their faces, sang sentimental songs, danced 'soft-shoe shuffles' and played banjo, tambourine, 'bones' and one-string fiddle. Authentic negro groups followed them. After World War II the Kentucky Minstrels successfully brought the show to television audiences.

**Miracle plays**. Medieval plays based on the stories of the Bible, the lives of the Saints and the Acts of the Apostles. The *mystery plays are play cycles based on the Old and New Testaments. (See illustration over page.)

**Mise en scène**. Standard French term for the *scenery and visual aspects of a dramatic production. Antonin Artaud's *theatre of cruelty put especial emphasis on *mise en scène*. This he defined very widely as 'a language in *space and *movement' which included all the resources of the theatre. See Artaud's lecture, given at the Sorbonne on 10 December, 1931: *La Mise en Scène et la Métaphysique*, contained in:
ARTAUD, A., *The Theatre and its Double*, trs. V. Corti, Calder, 1970.

**Misrule**. A holiday period involving the overturning of normal social roles. See LORD OF MISRULE; FEAST OF FOOLS; DISORDER.

**Mix**. (a) A 'dissolve' in a *film, effected by a *fade out of one scene and a simultaneous *fade in of another. Unlike the *cut, the mix is slow. It may announce a time shift or flashback. (b) The sound 'mix' which involves the editing together of film music, *sound effect and *dialogue from different recording tracks.

A rough theatrical equivalent of the visual mix is a *scene-change in which actors make their *entrance before the end of the previous *scene.

**15** *A scene in a miracle play depicting the martyrdom of St Apollonia. Note the booth stage in the background, with devils on the left or 'sinister' side of the king and angels on his right; also the superintendent or pageant master. (After a miniature by Jean Fouquet)*

**Model**. An aid to the understanding of a dynamic structure. It may take the form of a '*modellbuch*', the Brechtian term for a book containing suggestions for *directors, including dramatic analysis and notes on *characterization, with an accompanying maquette.

Theoreticians create models of dramatic structures, often in the form of a diagram, which can be more informative than a simple description since it aims to present the 'essential' impulses behind a process. Drama lends itself to such diagrammatic analysis. In a simple way, Richard Moulton in *Shakespeare as a Dramatic Artist* (1885) provided useful diagrams of dramatic patterns in Shakespeare. More recently *formalism, and subsequently *structuralism, have made ambitious attempts to establish a working model not only for individual plays but for the whole dramatic process. A.J. Greimas, for example, has sought a kind of 'grammar' beneath the surface action of *narrative, and has found three main pairs of dynamic forces: 'impulse' and 'beneficiary'; 'subject' and 'object'; 'auxiliary' and 'obstacle'. Such a grammar can be applied to plays as different as Molière's *Dom Juan* (1665) and Shakespeare's *Hamlet* (1601). In Molière's play the 'impulse' is sexual desire and the 'beneficiary' Dom Juan; the active 'subject' is Dom Juan and the passive 'object' is women in general; the 'auxiliary' who advances the primary impulse is the servant-figure Sganarelle, and the 'obstacle' or obstructing will is represented by Elvire, Pierrot and Sganarelle again.

In *Hamlet* the primary 'impulse' might be described as the 'will to knowledge' (the *existential writer Karl Jaspers has claimed that this is so). The 'beneficiary' is Hamlet and the people of Denmark. The 'subject' is Prince Hamlet, the 'object' is 'truth', the 'auxiliary' is the Ghost and possibly Horatio, and the 'obstacle' is Claudius, Rosencrantz and Guildenstern.

The labelling of such a model is, of course, a difficult business. A play as complex as *Hamlet* lends itself to many kinds of description. The 'impulse', for example, in the well-known psycho-analytic explanation of the play, might be sexual desire for the mother. In this case Gertrude becomes the 'object' and it is more difficult to see the Ghost as 'auxiliary'. The impulse might equally be seen as 'revenge', and the 'object' then becomes Claudius. It is even possible to argue that Prince Hamlet is too passive to be considered the 'subject'. In this case the 'subject' might be seen as the Ghost, the 'object' as Hamlet, the 'impulse' as 'escape from suffering' and the 'beneficiary' the Ghost. His 'auxiliary' then becomes Hamlet and the 'obstacle' Claudius. Since in *Hamlet* motivation is open to doubt, the identification of the different parts of the model will vary with interpretation. Furthermore, a new labelling will be necessary at different points in the play. As Prince Hamlet becomes less or more active, he might be seen as either 'object' or 'subject'.

The construction of such models is still a useful way of visualizing the dynamic structures and alternative interpretations of a play. They can also clarify definitions of the theatre process. See the complex models of *code, system and *performance in: ELAM, K., *The Semiotics of Theatre and Drama*, Ch. 3, Methuen, 1980.

**Modernism**. A general term describing the revolutionary period of cultural change often dated from 1890 to about 1930. The movement is generally considered to have been announced by such important forerunners as Kierkegaard (1813–55), Dostoievski (1821–81) and Nietzsche (1844–1900).

The roots of modernism lie in startling changes in attitude to the nature of 'history', the nature of 'nature' and the nature of human consciousness in the nineteenth century. Darwin's *Origin of the Species* (1859), Einstein's special theory of relativity (1905), Marx's 'dialectical materialism' and Freud's development of concepts of the unconscious mind, together with enormous social and historical changes associated with the various stages of the Industrial Revolution, led to radical revisions of the concept of 'reality' and to a flood of artistic activity comparable to that of the Renaissance. The historical accuracy of the Bible and Newton's concept of the 'ether' became suspect. Irrational areas of the human mind took on great importance, new concepts of *space and *time developed, and the securer models of *romanticism broke down.

Modernism is especially related to the cultural movements which followed impressionism, *symbolism and *naturalism. These include *expressionism, *existentialism, *surrealism and lesser movements such as *dada and *constructivism.

In the theatre, modernism meant first of all the revolutionary prose drama of Ibsen (1828–1906), productions of which stimulated the *free theatre movements in Paris, Berlin and London in the 1890s. This theatre, with its surface *naturalism and intimations of underlying personal and social breakdown, leads into the symbolic and expressionist drama of the later Strindberg. His *Dream Play* (1902) and *Ghost Sonata* (1907) announce in turn the anguished German expressionist drama which emerged from World War I. In the mid-1920s the *new objectivity established itself in Germany in reaction against the extreme subjectivity of expressionism. The *epic theatre of Piscator (1893–1966) and Brecht (1898–1956) is associated with this. A fourth strand of 'modernist theatre' is normally identified as the *theatre of the absurd and the plays of Beckett (1906–    ), Adamov (1908–70), Genet (1910–86) and Ionesco (1912–    ).

Modernist theatre is thus composed of such different elements that definitions are unlikely to be of much use. Attempts to find common characteristics usually insist on a general rebellion against complacent nineteenth-century middle-class attitudes, together with an ironic complexity and *tragi-comic tone. Modes of social and personal breakdown are expressed in variously fragmented forms, often highly self-conscious and analytical of their own processes — as in Pirandello (1867–1936) and Beckett. What most agree on is the extreme importance of this revolutionary movement. See:

BRADBURY, M., and MCFARLANE, J. (eds.), 'Modernist Drama', in *Modernism*, Pelican, 1976.

ELLMAN, R., and FEIDELSON, C. (eds.), *The Modern Tradition*, NY, 1965.

WILLIAMS, R., *Modern Tragedy*, Chatto and Windus, 1966.

**Momus**. The Greek god of *clowns. The fault-finder who makes fun of his fellow gods.

**Monodrama**. Short entertainment by one actor or actress. It was supported by music and silent choral figures. Invented by the German actor-playwright Johann Brandes (1735–99) it was used to fill a multiple bill. Brandes's *Ariadne auf Naxos* is the best known example.

In the twentieth century the term has been applied to the solo performances of actresses such as Ruth Draper (1884–1956).

**Monody**. Ode in *Greek tragedy, often a threnody or lament, sung by one actor.

**Monologue**. A long speech, usually reflective, lyrical or rhetorical. It may be spoken direct to the audience, like a *prologue or *epilogue, or within the play like Iago's speech at the end of Act I of Shakespeare's *Othello* (1604). It may also be spoken to other characters on stage, as in Mark Antony's oration in the forum in *Julius Caesar* (1599). Finally it may be spoken aloud as if voicing private thoughts, as in Hamlet's famous *soliloquy: 'To be or not to be . . .'

An *actor or *director may, of course, choose to mix these modes within the same monologue. The writer's intention is not always apparent. See also DRAMATIC MONOLOGUE.

**Monostich**. Greek term for single line of metrical verse.

**Montage**. A Brechtian term, taken principally from the photo-techniques of the German designer and painter, John Heartfield (1891–1968), and the cinematographic techniques of Eisenstein (1898–1948). What Brecht seems to mean by it, as he uses it, for example, in the notes to *Mahagonny* (1930), is a sequence of disparate scenes following quickly on one another, and representing a picaresque journey through life. It is a central principle of his *epic theatre and owes something to Shakespeare, Büchner (1813–37), *revue and *documentary drama as well as *film. The technique is highly developed in *Galileo* (1937–9) where the central character is seen in different ways in different scenes. Galileo is variously greedy, heroic, studious, pedagogic, cowardly, and cheating. He alters as circumstances alter, and Brecht superimposes a montage of different images of the character on the spectators' minds.

The process may be compared to the building up of a Heartfield 'photomontage' or to Eisenstein's 'montage of attractions', using the juxtaposition of apparently disparate *shots by *cutting, to achieve a shock effect. It is one of Brecht's *alienation effects; a visual technique, used to force the spectator to make comparisons, to contrast and think about the discrepancies between stage pictures, rather than become totally and uncritically absorbed in the play fiction.

For an analysis of various kinds of film montage see: EISENSTEIN, S., *The Film Sense*, Faber, 1986, pp.136–68.

**Mood**. (a) The feelings of a dramatic character; the attitude of a speaker to what he says. This relates to the grammatical sense of 'mood' which implies affirmation or negation, probability, doubt and questioning. Such moods are communicated not only by language but by the actor's *voice and the way he moves and stands. (b) Mood also suggests the general atmosphere of a scene or play, established by the different forms of *theatre language. Chekhov (1860–1904) was a master of these forms and established subtle changes of mood by *lighting, *sound effect, musical instruments, shifts of dramatic *pace, sudden *entrances and *exits, *colour and *costume changes, and other spatial and temporal effects.

**Moral interlude**. A title sometimes given to *morality plays with a strong comic element, such as *Lusty Juventus* (1550) or *Hyckescorner* (1512).

**Morality play**. Name given to a small number of late medieval religious plays, of which the most famous are *Everyman* (c.1495), *Mankind* (c.1465) and *Castle of Perseverance* (early fifteenth century). They are widely different from one another in tone, length, structure and size of *cast. The plays may be classified together, however, since they take as their subject the life and death of a central figure faced with the choices leading to damnation or salvation.

They do not portray a vast cosmic cycle of events like the *mystery plays. The morality pattern confronts the individual man with death. Thus Everyman, in the play of that name, moves from a state of indifference to fear of death, recognition of sin, repentance, penance, absolution and salvation in a seven-fold movement. *Castle of Perseverance*, on the other hand, has a four-fold movement consisting of contests for the soul of Humanum Genus, won firstly by the Seven Deadly Sins, then by their opposites the Seven Virtues, then by Covetousness, then finally by Mercy, in whose favour God gives judgement after a long *debate. This early play exhibits a complex and highly symmetrical dramatic and verse structure. Before any judgement is made about the relative crudity of morality plays (based perhaps on the *knockabout elements which travelling actors were apt to incorporate in performance) *Castle of Perseverance* should be carefully studied. It subtly places audiences in the position of both judge and accused. Humanum Genus is the audience's representative seen from the outside through the eyes of God. Such major plays as Marlowe's *Dr Faustus* (*c*.1589) and Shakespeare's *King Lear* (1605) and *Macbeth* (1606) employ morality patterns and establish a similar audience relationship.

**Moritat**. Moralizing horror ballads of the kind sung in German *cabaret by Frank Wedekind (1864–1918). They were adapted and incorporated by Bertolt Brecht (1898–1956) into his *ballad operas. The song 'Mack the Knife' in *Threepenny Opera* (1928) is an example.

**Morris dance**. English rustic dance associated especially with characters and episodes in the *Robin Hood legend. The use of castanets and costumes hung with bells may indicate a Moorish (Morris) origin, but in fifteenth-century England the dances were linked with spring-time, May-pole, harvest and Christmas festivities. Maid Marion, for example, often appears as Queen of the May.

**Moscow Art Theatre**. Leading Russian theatre, founded in 1898 by Stanislavski (1863–1938) and Nemirovitch-Danchenko (1859–1943). It was securely established by the famous and successful performance of Chekhov's *The Seagull* which caused the company to place the emblem of a seagull on its curtain. Productions of *Uncle Vanya* (1899), *Three Sisters* (1901) and *The Cherry Orchard* (1904) ensured a permanent connection with Chekhov's name.

The theatre was shaken by the 1917 Revolution but with the aid of Lunacharski (1875–1933) and the intervention of Lenin it adapted itself to the post-revolutionary world. It continued to tour performances of Chekhov and specialize in productions of *realist plays, especially those of Gorky (1868–1936).

**Motif**. A recurrent *image or other element in the total design of a dramatic, literary or musical work. Examples include the references to photography in Ibsen's *The Wild Duck* (1884), the 'disease images' in Shakespeare's *Hamlet* (1601) and the images of food in *Antony and Cleopatra* (1606–7). In the examples given, the motif is an *ironic commentary on the action of the play and the behaviour of the characters. Hjalmar, the photographer in Ibsen's play, for instance, is very fond of 'touching up' reality. Disease and food images in Shakespeare suggest forms of mental and social sickness. *Leitmotif* is the term applied to a dominant motif.

**Motion**. A puppet play based on a Biblical subject. It was performed in the sixteenth and seventeenth centuries by itinerant showmen. There is a reference in Act IV scene iii of Shakespeare's *The Winter's Tale* (1610) to 'a motion of the Prodigal Son'.

**Motivation**. See WILL.

**Movement**. Important form of *theatre language, both visual and auditory.

The movement of the human body on stage, whether in *silence or accompanied by the *rhythms of speech, helps to establish the general appeal of a play to eye and ear. Convincing stage movement in *naturalistic plays needs to be relaxed and unselfconscious, since physical stiffness, immobility or anxiety about the use of hands can embarrass an audience. Movement also needs to be convincingly in *character, so that actors must take on the stiffness of age or recover the liveliness of adolescence where necessary. More formal plays involve many of the skills of *dance, such as synchronization of body movement with a group or a *chorus.

Movement is also a musical term, as in 'movements' of a symphony, and may be applied in this way to the structure of a play. Successful plays seem to have a characteristic *tempo, with rhythmical variations of movement between and within the *acts and *scenes. The *director needs to become aware of this in pre-reading and *rehearsal, and may suggest to the actors certain individual 'moves' which point up the dramatic *contrast between individuals or groups. Moves are specific movements which a director is normally expected to *block. This involves the working out of stage positions and the *timing of *exits and *entrances. Actors, however, often prefer to work out their own moves. A famous anecdote recalls an unfortunate director asking Dame Edith Evans, 'What am I to do if I am not to give you your moves?'.'Oh, we'll find something for you to do,' was the reply.
LABAN, R., *The Mastery of Movement*, revised by L. Ullman, Macdonald and Evans, 1960.

**Multiple setting**. A stage on which stand at one and the same time all the different settings of the play's action. An early example occurs in *liturgical drama where different scenes were performed at different locations within the church.

The multiple setting remained when the drama emerged from the church. Medieval illustrations reveal that different settings, or *loci, were disposed in a semi-circle in the market place, or in a straight line on a stage. The actors would move from locus to locus as the action of the play required.

The flexible Elizabethan *open or *apron stage does not appear to have used multiple, fixed locations, except perhaps for occasional scenes, reminiscent of medieval staging, such as occur in Shakespeare's *Comedy of Errors* (1590–4). The same is true of the Italian *Renaissance stage. This pictorial theatre and its eighteenth-century descendants preferred to obtain scenic effects by use of *perspective and *scene-changes. Multiple settings were still used, however, in noblemen's halls and in seventeenth-century *masques.

In the nineteenth century the development of complex stage machinery allowed for the building of a whole house on stage, rather than a single room. With a *fourth wall opened up, activity could then be seen both *On the Ground Floor and on the Second Story*, to quote the title of a Nestroy play performed in the 1830s.

Prodigious use of vast multiple sets came with Erwin Piscator (1893–1966) in the 1920s. He showed the various activities of urban life — eating, cooking, talking, phoning — occurring simultaneously in different rooms and locations, on split stages and at different *levels. He could thus contrast different forms of individual and class behaviour and place the private room of the *naturalist box-set within a broader social setting. Brecht also developed split scenes, as in *Mother Courage* (1941) where the kitchen is set side by side with the dining room, and the attitudes of consumers and providers are ironically contrasted. Brecht, however, does not use the cumbersome technology of Piscator, and indeed the cinema was already proving a more subtle instrument for the juxtaposition of visual settings.

Large and complex sets, of course, require heavy investment, and are inappropriate for small theatres and poor companies. Large and wealthy theatres may use them to dramatic and spectacular effect. Eugene O'Neill's *Desire Under the Elms* (1921) and Tennessee Williams's *The Glass Menagerie* (1945) are examples.

The disadvantages of multiple sets include, besides cost and scene-shifting difficulties, the problem of establishing dramatic *focus. Careful *rehearsal of actors to synchronize dialogue with *lighting and *scene-changes are required for its successful use. Compensating advantages include the reduction of scene-changes and the dramatic *irony established by showing simultaneous or intercut stage action using groups of characters unaware of each other's behaviour or even existence.

PISCATOR, E., *The Political Theatre*, trs. H. Rorrison, Eyre Methuen, London, 1980.

**Mummers' play**. A \*folk ritual drama. Its early forms are uncertain since folklorists only began to record it in the eighteenth century. Its origin probably lies in fertility rituals and the celebration of the earth's annual regeneration. The play seems to have begun with a \*prologue introducing two champions, Saint George and 'Bold Slasher'. They boast, argue and fight. One is slain, often by beheading. A doctor appears and cures the fallen warrior. He revives. The actors dance and a collection of money is taken.

A.P. Rossiter remembers a Gloucestershire boyhood in which Saint George and the Turkish knight fought in fur hats with wooden swords. When Saint George is killed, the doctor resurrects him, saying:

> Ere come I, ole Dr Grub
> Under me arm I carry a club
> In my pocket I carry a bottle
> An a gr't big volume o' Harris tottle.

Rossiter recalls: 'the club was poked into the corpse in a way that struck me as improbable even in doctors'.

The ceremony was widespread in the British Isles, where it can be traced in over a thousand different localities. Such popularity points to a pre-Christian folk ritual which was very likely to have influenced the development of medieval drama. Traces of the ceremony can be found in the fifteenth-century \*morality play *Mankind* (*c*.1465) in which there is a magical, curative beheading and a collection. In the sixteenth-century play *Wit and Science*, by John Redford, there is also a miraculous revival and a beheading.

BASKERVILLE, C.R., *Dramatic Aspects of Mediaeval Folk Festivals in England*, SP XVII, 1920.

CHAMBERS, E.K., *The English Folk Play*, Oxford University Press, 1933.

ROSSITER, A.P., *English Drama from Early Times to the Elizabethans*, Hutchinson, 1966.

SOUTHERN, R., *Seven Ages of the Theatre*, 2nd edition, Faber, 1964.

**Muse**. One of the goddesses who inspire learning and the arts. Thalia is the muse of \*comedy; Terpsichore of \*dance; Melpomene of \*tragedy.

**Musical comedy**. Form of \*light opera which grew up in the late nineteenth century. Musical comedies, or 'musicals', are now the most popular and lucrative form of \*Broadway and \*West End theatre. They require large \*casts, highly rehearsed and choreographed \*chorus work, displays of physical charm, immense physical energy, star quality in the main performers, and popular and catchy tunes and \*numbers, spun on a dramatic thread which can be light-heartedly interrupted. George Edwardes, George

Gershwin, Rodgers and Hammerstein, Lerner and Loewe and Andrew Lloyd Webber are noted composers and writers of musical comedy.

GREEN, S., *The World of Musical Comedy*, Grosset and Dunlap, NY, 1962.

**Music and theatre**. Spoken drama is closely related to *dance and *opera. Its *rhythms, however, are usually established not by music but by *dialogue and *movement. At times drama has closely approached a fusion of the modes — as in ancient *Greek tragedy and forms of *oriental theatre, where *dance and *choral work is highly important — but in more modern European theatre music has generally had the subordinate function of varying or reinforcing *mood. The Elizabethans and Shakespeare used it in this way. (Feste's songs in *Twelfth Night* (1601) are an instance.)

The use of music in *legitimate eighteenth-century *prose drama was limited, though Sheridan's *School for Scandal* (1777) contains a song in the drinking scene in Act III. *Illegitimate theatre used music more extensively, as did nineteenth-century *melodrama. (The word means 'music drama'.) In these popular plays the music director would create a kind of musical sound-track to accompany words and reinforce character, situation and the general emotional atmosphere. Thus *hurries, *combat music, *storm music and 'soft music' would be used, often at moments of stillness on stage to render the feelings of a silent character. In the famous melodrama *Maria Marten* (1839) 'villain's music' would be heard as the villain approached off-stage. Such effects were to be emulated by the Hollywood film of the silent era with its live piano accompaniment. Later the sound film would supersede it and music would continue to be used to create atmosphere, arouse expectation and establish continuity.

*Realist theatre has resisted such uses, and music has tended to be employed in highly stylized drama where physical and rhythmical movement is very important. More recently, Brecht's *epic theatre, developing out of his *ballad opera, employed a kind of *cross-cutting in which music was used as an *alienation technique to interrupt stage realism. In this theatre music can function as an *ironic commentary on stage action, like jazz instruments in the 'blues'.

**Music-hall**. A nineteenth-century institution which developed after the *patent theatre monopoly ended in 1843. The *minor theatres turned to *legitimate drama and the music halls took over forms of popular *variety entertainment previously classified as *illegitimate. This included *song and dance, nationalist *extravaganza, *stand-up comedy, acrobatics and juggling. The atmosphere was often that of the public-house sing-song. The early music-halls were often housed in tavern annexes before such special halls as the Canterbury, the Alhambra and the Holborn Empire were built. Music-hall is now widely regarded as the voice of the urban working-class, and the vitality and comic brilliance of such performers as Marie Lloyd (1870–1922) and Little Tich (1868–1928) left a lasting legacy to silent and sound cinema and later forms of popular radio and television entertainment. In the theatre, John Osborne's *The Entertainer* (1957) and Joan Little-wood's production of *Oh What a Lovely War* (1963) incorporate the form and subject matter of music-hall.

The music-hall was undoubtedly an important cultural form. Marinetti (1876–1944), the Italian dramatist and *futurist, praised it as follows:

> Variety theatre is naturally anti-academic, primitive, and naive ... It destroys the solemn, sacred, serious and sublime in Art with a capital A. It co-operates in the destruction of immortal masterpieces, plagiarising them, parodying them, making them look commonplace by stripping them of their solemn apparatus.

With the rise of the cinema the old music-hall declined, but it lives on in various forms in *cabaret, *TV and *community and *street theatre.

BAILEY, P. (ed.), *Music Hall: The Business of Pleasure*, Open University Press, 1986.

FLINT, R.W. (ed.), *Marinetti: Selected Writings*, Secker, 1972.

MANDER, R., and MITCHENSON, J., *British Music Hall*, Studio Vista, 1965.

**Mystère/Mysterienspiel**. French and German equivalents of the English *mystery plays.

**Mystery plays/Mystery cycles**. Medieval epic dramas based on the Fall, the Redemption and the Final Judgement of God. They were played on the Feast of *Corpus Christi and generally took the form of a procession of pageant waggons which stopped at appropriate 'stations', such as a market cross or other open space, to perform episodes of the Bible story. In England the trade guilds normally took responsibility for episodes appropriate to their trade and would perform them a number of times during the day as the procession moved from station to station. As many as 48 pageant episodes were included in the *York Cycle and it has been suggested that each might have been performed once at each of the stations on the processional route in the course of a single day. The costs were high, the costuming and spectacle lavish. The overall pattern was also complex, since the Old Testament stories were seen as prefiguring the New. Adam parallels Christ, Eve parallels Mary, the Tree of Knowledge anticipates Calvary and Noah's Flood corresponds to Doomsday. The central events are those of the Easter story: the Entry into Jerusalem, the Trial before Pilate, the Crucifixion, Deposition, Harrowing of Hell and Resurrection. The players were principally male and amateur, though some payments were made and women seem to have played Eve or Bathsheba on occasion. They were performed from 1311, when the feast of Corpus Christi was instituted, and remained popular until the mid-sixteenth century. Only four complete English cycles survive: the Chester, York, Wakefield or Towneley, and Coventry or 'N-town', whose origin is obscure. A recent *promenade production by the British National Theatre company displayed the immense dramatic potential of these cycles.

KOLVE, V.A., *The Play called Corpus Christi*, Stanford University Press, 1966.

WOOLF, R.E., *The English Mystery Plays*, Routledge, 1972.

**16** *Hell as represented in a medieval fresco in the Chapel of the Holy Cross, Stratford-upon-Avon (from Sharp,* A Dissertation on the Pageants or Dramatic Mysteries, *1825)*

**Mythopoeia.** Mythopoeia is myth-making, the elaboration of a *story by an individual or a community — a process which often takes dramatic form. Myth-making is not necessarily conscious *fiction*-making. In the earlier stages of a civilization, myth is usually regarded as embodying religious and historical truth. The Trojan Wars, for example, and the stories of the Old and New Testaments, were celebrated in forms of drama whose function was the confirmation of a common core of belief. The stories might vary but they were, in an important sense, considered true. It is only later that a sceptical spirit, associated with the rise of science and empiricism, causes the great myths to be seen as *myth* rather than truth. Such a change of attitude can be detected in the plays of Euripides and, in modern times, in the eighteenth-century 'Age of Reason'.

Copernicus (1473–1543), Galileo (1564–1642) and finally Newton (1642–1727) undermined the myth of the *great chain of being. Poetry and drama based on myth became entertainment, acknowledging its own fiction. The Augustan emphasis on reason, and its concern with the social and the local, meant that poetic and mythical elements tended to be treated in a comic spirit, as in Pope's *Rape of the Lock* (1712).

*Romanticism brought a new insistence on the validity of myth. Blake (1757–1827) in his *Prophetic Books* (1789–1804) developed serious private myths and there was a general resurgence of interest in Greek mythology and folk-tale. Myths of Biblical origin were still accepted as true but the new geological discoveries of Charles Lyall (1797–1875), followed by Darwin's *Origin of the Species* (1859), threatened to reduce the Old Testament account of world history to the fictional status of myth.

With the growth of anthropology and psychology, however, it became possible to see myth as a kind of *metaphor: a fiction containing a truth. The old myths could have psychological validity, even if they were historically false. Attempts were still made to elaborate myths which were true in more than a metaphorical sense. Later Romantics, like W.B. Yeats in *A Vision* (1925) and D.H. Lawrence in *The Crown* (1915), created personal myths and poetic structures in ambitious attempts to explain the patterns of history. Unfortunately the private nature of their myths was an obstacle to their successful use in the theatre. Drama needs myth which has power for the *audience, and a work like Yeats's *The Herne's Egg* (1938), and even his more popular earlier plays based on Irish mythology, lacked the dynamic of a shared myth. Lawrence, on the other hand, concentrated on a powerful social realism in his drama, expressing his mythical concerns in the patterns of his fiction and poetry.

The use of well-known classical and Christian stories has been more successful in twentieth-century drama. The Orestes myth is particularly popular. Eugene O'Neill's *Mourning Becomes Electra* (1931), T.S. Eliot's *The Family Reunion* (1938) and Sartre's *The Flies* (1942) are variations on that theme. French theatre has used classical myth extensively. Claudel (1868–1955), Giraudoux (1882–1944), and Anouilh (1910–87) have all demonstrated the power the myths retain.

Where this power resides has been a subject of concern to major thinkers. Nietzsche declared in *The Birth of Tragedy* (1872) that the world was returning to myth. James Frazer's *Golden Bough* (1890–1915) aroused interest in primitive *ritual. Freud's theory of the 'Oedipus complex' and Jung's concern with *archetypes in the *unconscious mind stimulated deep interest. But the argument that myth-making was fundamental to man because he retained primitive elements in his psyche also aroused suspicion. Myths became a subject of analysis rather than, as in early drama, a form of worship. The fascist use of the myth of an Aryan master race made the study of mythopoeia very important, and myth-making became even more suspect. Myths, as Ibsen had shown, did not only reside in the *story and *plot. They operated within the psychology of the principal characters.

In part this was a reaction against naive elements in *Romanticism. In Ibsen's plays characters weave their personal myths and dreams to tragic effect. But we should add that suspicion of myth-making has long been a dramatic subject. Sophocles's Oedipus has a tendency to mythologize himself, as do Shakespeare's Othello and King Lear. Shakespeare's sombre *Troilus and Cressida* (1602) presents a sardonic satire on the human propensity to mythopoeia, especially under the influence of love — love of self, love of group, love of honour, love of power, love of the opposite and of the same sex. In this sense mythopoeia is still a truth to be investigated, and indeed modern literary theorists and philosophers such as Jacques Derrida (1930–   ) treat virtually all *narratives and *ideologies as fictions and myths.

KIRK, G.S., *The Nature of Greek Myths*, Penguin, 1974.
RUTHVEN, K.R., *Myth*, Methuen, 1976.

# N

**Naive *and* Sentimental**. A celebrated distinction made by Schiller (1759–1805) between the intuitive (naive) or natural poet and the conscious (sentimental) poet, who imitates not nature but an ideal. It occurs in his essay *Über naive und sentimentalische Dichtung* (1795) and anticipates further famous dichotomies in German philosophy, notably Schopenhauer's *will and understanding, Nietzsche's *apollonian and *dionysiac, and Freud's 'id' and 'ego'. According to Goethe (1749–1832), subsequent distinctions between *romantic and *classical poetry stem from Schiller's essay.

The distinction raises complex questions about unconscious and conscious processes in artistic and creative activity and the essay must be read in its entirety. Schiller, however, was speaking of a tension he found within himself, and which he also discerned between himself (as *'sentimentalisch'*) and Goethe, whom he saw as *'naiv'*. Schiller defined an important dualism which can be seen as a distinction between different styles, writers, cultures and individual minds; it can also be seen as a tension within a single mind. Its historical relevance is clear in relation to Schiller's early *Sturm und Drang* drama and the philosophy of Immanuel Kant (1724–1804).

**Narr**. The *fool or *clown of the German *carnival play of Hans Sachs (1491–1576) and the Meistersingers (see FASTNACHTSPIEL). He derives from the foolish characters in Sebastian Brandt's *Narrenschiff* (*Ship of Fools*, 1494).

**Narrative**. A story told in words, rather than by facial expression or body movement. It is usually associated with the *novel, *epic or *romance, rather than drama. Forms of narrative are often used, however, within the dramatic action, to relate events which occur offstage before and at the same time as the enacted events. The *prologue and *messenger have an obvious narrative function, as does any dramatic character who recounts offstage happenings to any other.

Narrative in drama provides essential information. It also expands the spatial and temporal dimensions of a play (see SPACE and TIME). It does so very economically since to recount an event takes far less stage time than dramatic embodiment. Violent battle or crowd scenes are expensive in terms of stage and *rehearsal time, as well as money, and are not always convincing. Verbal narration requires only one actor and avoids the problems posed by limited resources.

On the other hand, narrative lacks the vividness and simultaneity of dramatic embodiment and makes great demands on the listener's imagination and concentration. If the audience loses the narrative thread it cannot be recovered. A play is not a book with pages which can be turned back, for the performance cannot be arrested. Narrative is therefore best used as a device to retain interest by varying the dominant dramatic process.

Verbal and sung narratives seem to have been the original basis of the drama we know. Early *medieval drama emerged from the Easter *liturgy (see QUEM QUAERITIS), and *Greek tragedy developed out of Homer's epic narratives. Presumably, dramatic performance developed from a need to render the narrative more vivid, by physical demonstration. No doubt, however, *dance and *mime began to accompany some narrative accounts at a very early stage. It is even possible to imagine that primitive forms of dramatic *mimesis — the *ritual enactment of a hunt for example — preceded verbal narrative. Mime and dance may indeed be seen as alternative forms of narrative, if the definition is extended.

Analysis of the nature of narrative, in a more complex sense than the one so far used, has been a concern of linguists and *formalist critics since the 1920s. 'The narratives of the world are numberless', declares Roland Barthes, and he argues the need for *models which will bring order to this heterogeneity. Barthes (especially in S/Z), A.J. Greimas, T. Todorov and other well-known linguists have examined the different procedures of fictional narrative, paying special attention to questions of *space, *time and *chronology. Their insights extend into the study of narrative discourses in drama and *film.

Narrative, we have said, may be a component of dramatic *form. In forms of *self-reflexive drama it has itself been a subject of analysis. The *theatre of the absurd has shown a deep concern with language and with the nature of drama and fiction. Beckett (1906– ), particularly in Endgame (1957), parodies the process of story-telling and calls attention to its function. When Hamm bribes the reluctant character Nagg to listen to his story Beckett asks why some people tell tales and why others listen or refuse to listen. Such psychological questions are difficult to answer and are different from the questions which linguistic scientists address. Beckett asks what is behind the narrative process rather than how it is constituted. The motives seem to be ones of aggression and self-defence, but Beckett's *silences should make us wary of giving a confident reply.

BARTHES, R., Image, Music, Text, Fontana, 1977.

**Narrator**. In drama, any character who can narrate offstage action; but the term is more frequently used for a figure who acts as *chorus, commentator, *prologue or *epilogue.

Such a figure is useful where a play involves complex material which cannot be easily performed in the appropriate time-span and needs to be organised into a dramatic pattern. Thus *historical or *chronicle plays often use a narrator, such as the Chorus in Shakespeare's *Henry V* (1599). A narrator also avoids the problems of large *casts, small stages, and a shortage of money and resources. His normal function is to relate information which the audience needs to know but which lies outside the dramatic pattern. Father Time in Shakespeare's *A Winter's Tale* (1610) does this, but at the same time he creates a feeling of magic and a sense of the passage of time which the play at that point requires. Narrators also create the scene and generate atmosphere. It should not be forgotten that *song is a form of narration.

The narrator's function may be interpretative. He can act as an *ideal spectator and comment on the action. Like the Greek chorus, however, he may be more effective if he's not entirely omniscient. Narrators who speak direct to an audience need to enlist sympathy and they may be more human if they occasionally appear ignorant. Thus audiences are sometimes made aware of what narrators like Henry Carr in Tom Stoppard's *Travesties* (1974) do not know.

Vivid stage narrators include the Stage Manager in Thornton Wilder's *Our Town* (1938) and Arthur Miller's Lawyer in *A View from the Bridge* (1955). They express what the characters cannot express and their treatment follows John van Druten's advice: 'Once used [as prologue] the device must be used again. It must be made a part of the play'. Van Druten himself used a narrator in *I am a Camera* (1951). See NARRATIVE; MESSENGER.

**National Endowment for the Arts.** American equivalent of the *Arts Council of Great Britain, formed in 1965 to provide the first national support for the arts since the government discontinued funds for the *Federal Theatre Project in 1939. See:
AMERICAN ASSEMBLY, Columbia University, *The Performing Arts and American Society*, Prentice-Hall, 1978.

**National Theatre.** The idea of an English National Theatre, first proposed in the eighteenth century by Garrick and advocated by Irving, Shaw and others before World War I, was finally realized with the establishment, under Laurence Olivier, of a National Theatre Company at the Old Vic in 1963. It was followed by the completion of a theatre building containing three different kinds of *auditorium: the *proscenium arch Lyttleton (895 seats), opened in October 1976; the *open stage Olivier (October 1976); and the 200-seat Cottesloe (November 1977).

The arguments for a national state-subsidized theatre, which has an independent management, are strong. The establishment of a permanent company on regular salaries allows longer rehearsal schedules, a potentially higher quality of *ensemble acting and greater understanding and cooperation between *directors, *actors, *designers and technicians. A large company with high skills, which is salaried for a long period and is therefore less subject to commercial pressures, also permits a wider variety of programme, including the performance of new plays, of rarely seen *revivals, and of productions by the best foreign companies. It should also permit a policy of touring productions to encourage theatre in the provinces.

Arguments against a National Theatre tend to be financial and political. A radical critic, Sandy Craig, in *Dreams and Deconstructions* (1980), sees it as a product of 'a mindless utopian belief in technology' and objects to 'anonymous auditoria' and 'an atmosphere of airport transience in the foyers'. Others would argue that the cost is high and that the money should be spent elsewhere. Dependence on state funds means that risks are less likely to be taken with controversial and highly political material, and the audience, it is said, is not a representative cross-section of the population. Nonetheless, radical dramatists such as Howard Brenton (1942– ), Howard Barker (1946– ), Trevor Griffiths (1935– ) and David Hare (1947– ) have not refused to work within this structure. It supplies opportunities for staging plays with larger casts, and hence has a wider social scope than small cast, small budget, *fringe productions. It also reaches wider, and arguably more influential, audiences, attracts national attention, and acts as a platform for radical foreign playwrights such as the South African Athol Fugard (1932– ). One ought to add that some radical British writers, such as John Arden (1930– ) and John McGrath (1935– ), remain opposed to the concept of a national theatre because it involves compromise with an economic system which they condemn.

ARCHER, W., and GRANVILLE-BARKER, H., *A National Theatre: Scenes and Estimates*, Duckworth, 1907.

**Nativity play**. See LITURGICAL DRAMA.

**Natural acting**. A term which alters its meaning according to theatrical fashions. What seems 'natural' acting to one generation may seem artificial and contrived to the next. On the whole, however, it is the term associated with *naturalistic (or *'method') acting, and implies relaxed and unselfconscious stage performance.

**Naturalism**. (a) Nineteenth-century movement in art, drama and literature, placing emphasis on the careful study of natural causes. (b) More generally, an artistic method involving careful observation and realistic reproduction of the detailed surfaces of life. Hamlet's remark that 'the purpose of playing . . . was and is to hold as t'were the mirror up to nature' is naturalistic in this sense.

Dramatic naturalism normally implies the work of such theatre directors as Antoine (1858–1943), Otto Brahm (1856–1912) and Stanislavski (1863–1938) and particularly their productions of the prose drama of Ibsen (1828–1906) and the early Strindberg (1849–1912), as well as the work of Chekhov (1860–1904) and Hauptmann (1862–1946). The general tendency of such productions was to seek, by employing realistic *sets, *costumes and *dialogue, to reflect a convincing picture of individual people, living at a particular time, in a particular place. Naturalism also embodied the post-Darwinian assumption that the environment which determines human behaviour should be shown as fully as possible. The drama was thus attempting to perform on stage what Balzac and then Zola had developed in the novel: a detailed social *realism.

Problems, of course, arose out of the limitations of the medium. A two-hour play could not present a wide range of social worlds, particularly if realistic and cumbersome *box sets were to be used. The number of settings was restricted, as was the number of characters. A full dramatic environment thus meant a narrow environment. Historical plays, set like Shakespeare's in a variety of public places, could not use a heavy naturalistic set for each of up to forty scenes. Naturalistic dramatists, however, who were ambitious to reflect 'the very age and body of the time, his form and pressure' (*Hamlet* III.ii.23) and also wished to achieve the high degree of realism which new staging and lighting technology permitted, could not manipulate *time and *place with the same facility as a *Jacobean playwright. They had to be extremely selective and they frequently chose climactic moments in family life where social and sexual tensions received concentrated expression. The impact on contemporary audiences was often devastating. The various productions of Ibsen's *Ghosts* in the 1890s were particularly notable in this respect.

There are, of course, distinctions to be made between different kinds of naturalism. Chekhov chose to create plays of apparently ordinary, even desultory, behaviour, behind which the forces of change operate slowly. Ibsen and Strindberg were more highly and obviously dramatic, creating active characters — often dreamers close to the edge of madness. Chekhov's characters (and dreamers) are more passive.

One of the paradoxes of naturalistic drama is that a close study of the causes of human behaviour carried playwrights towards *expressionism, the presentation of the internal rather than the external. Naturalistic emphasis on social and historical analysis also led, paradoxically, to a non-naturalistic *realism which emphasized the theatre's artificiality and employed *allegory. This is characteristic of the *epic theatre of Brecht, which emphasized economic causality and moved away from the psychological naturalism of

Ibsen and the portrayal of middle-class drawing rooms.

Naturalism continued to have a powerful impact, however, especially in America and New York, where Lee Strasberg (1901–82) at the *Actors' Studio helped create the new style of screen and stage acting associated with the films of Elia Kazan (1909–85), the plays of Arthur Miller (1915–   ) and Tennessee Williams (1914–83), and the acting of Marlon Brando (1924–   ).

These names remind one again of the social concerns of naturalism. Emphasis on inner psychological pressures was not divorced from a consideration of the general social conditions that helped produce them. Naturalism, as Raymond Williams says, chose a 'middle-ground' where the 'economic pressures, the condition of the family and of marriage, the general complex of institutions and beliefs' could be shown as interacting.

FURST, L.R., and SKRINE, P.N., *Naturalism*, Methuen, 1971.

STRASBERG, L., and HETHMAN, R.H. (eds.), *Strasberg at the Actors' Studio*, Cape, 1966.

WILLIAMS, R., *Culture*, Fontana, 1981, pp.176–7.

ZOLA, E., 'Le naturalisme au théâtre', in *Oeuvres Complètes*, edited by H. Mittérand, Paris, 1968.

**Natya**. Indian dance drama based mainly on the epics *Ramayana* and *Mahabharata*.

**Naumachia**. Roman name for a water pageant or aquatic spectacle staged in a flooded arena.

**Nausea**. See EXISTENTIAL DRAMA.

**Nautical melodrama**. Late eighteenth- and nineteenth-century popular drama concerned with shipwreck, smuggling, piracy and wrecking. It was often imbued with patriotic sentiment and generally contained a *hero ready to die for king and country. According to M. Booth, this hero 'speaks with a peculiar vocabulary full of sea metaphors, and is liable to break without warning into a hornpipe or merry ballad.' *Black-eyed Susan* (1829) by G.W. Jerrold is an example, while Gilbert and Sullivan's *HMS Pinafore* (1878) is a *burlesque of the form.

BOOTH, M., *English Melodrama*, Jenkins, 1965.

**'negative capability'**. A famous phrase of John Keats (1795–1821). It means, according to the poet, a capacity to remain 'in uncertainties, Mysteries, doubts, without any irritable reaching after fact and reason' (letter to his brothers, December 1817). He goes on to reflect that 'with a great poet the sense of Beauty overcomes every other consideration, or rather obliterates all consideration' and feels that it would have been an advantage to

Coleridge if he could have remained 'content with half-knowledge'.

The term seems to define a psychological state very necessary to dramatic creativity and which, in Keats's view, Shakespeare supremely possessed — the capacity to allow other identities to take over one's own. The assumption is that both dramatist and actor must lose *identity in the act of writing or performance, and critics should remember that the question 'why' can often destroy such a state. Keats felt that this was an element of his own talent and contrasted his own tendency to be invaded by other personalities in a room, and that of a friend, Charles Dilke, who always knew who he was and always spoke as himself.

If certitude and logical analysis is sometimes destructive, however, it is unwise to assume that 'negative capability' is a full definition of the qualities needed to create a character or perform a role. Great actresses, as Pirandello (1867–1936) said of Eleanora Duse (1858–1924), are not chameleons who assimilate roles and shed them as easily. It is true some actors and actresses seem to possess in high degree an uncertainty about self-identity and enjoy acting, as the actress Fenella Fielding once remarked, 'because at least you know who you are supposed to be'. But Duse, said Pirandello, developed her own definite and strong personality. This, though it made acting more difficult for her, also strengthened it.

We may speculate that this capacity both to shed and develop the self is true to an even greater degree of the dramatist. He must be capable of remaining in doubt, and must be wary not to resolve uncertainties too soon. Resolution, however, must come. The danger lies in 'irritably reaching out' for it. This can destroy the creation of both *role and *play.

**Nemesis**. Greek term for retribution. It is usually incurred, as with Oedipus, by the sin of *hubris and an infringement of the laws of the gods.

**Neo-classical drama**. Drama which takes *classical plays as models, and admires the precepts of Greek and Latin critics such as *Horace (65–8 B.C.).

In France, the tragedies of Racine (1639–99) were often neo-classical in subject-matter and rigorously so in form. In England, neo-classicism flourished from Ben Jonson (1572–1637) through Dryden (1631–1700) and Congreve (1670–1729) to Goldsmith (1730–1774) and Sheridan (1751–1816). The tradition was mainly comic, the emphasis being on the study of classical *form and the observation of rigid rules (such as the *unities). It demanded respect for accuracy, *decorum, balance and *wit. The analysis of social vices and general truths about mankind was its particular concern. See RESTORATION DRAMA; COMEDY OF MANNERS.

**New comedy**. A term applied to the plays of Menander (342–292 B.C.) and Greek writers of the fourth and third centuries B.C. They tended to have an urban setting and a stereotyped plot in which the older generation (those with social power) attempt, but ultimately fail, to block the loves of the young. The rake, the old man and the witty slave are characteristic *stereotype characters and the mode descends through Plautus (254–184 B.C.) and Terence (159–90 B.C.) to the *Commedia dell'Arte and the *neo-classical comedy of Ben Jonson (1572–1637), Molière (1622–73) and their eighteenth-century successors.

Among Shakespeare's comedies, the *Comedy of Errors* (1590–4) and the *Merry Wives of Windsor* (1598) are set in the urban world of new comedy. Even here, however, Shakespeare invokes the natural world of *old comedy and adds elements of magic and enchantment which the new comedy, with its farcical and satirical tone, generally lacks.

**New Objectivity**. Translation of '*Neue Sachlichkeit*', a German movement of the mid-1920s which arose to counter the extreme subjectivism of the *expressionist movement. Its concern with social *realism is seen in the work of Bertolt Brecht (1898–1956) and Erwin Piscator (1893–1966).
WILLETT, J., *The New Sobriety 1917–33*, Thames and Hudson, 1978, pp. 111–17.

**Nietzsche, Friedrich** (1844–1900). German philosopher and major theoretician of *tragedy.

To suspend the emotions is to castrate the intellect.

Man would sooner have the void for his purpose than be void of purpose.

See: CHORUS; DIONYSIAC; SERENITY.
NIETZSCHE, F.W., *The Birth of Tragedy* (1872), Doubleday, 1956.

**Nigger minstrel**. See MINSTREL SHOW.

**Nineteenth-century theatre**. The European theatre in the nineteenth century underwent a series of changes. Eighteenth-century *neo-classicism and the *comedy of manners gave way to a *romanticism stimulated by the *Sturm und Drang movement of Goethe (1749–1832) and Schiller (1759–1805). This expressed itself in popular *melodrama and in the growth of serious national and historical drama, as in the work of Ibsen (1826–1906) and Strindberg (1849–1912). This led, in the last third of the century, to the powerful *naturalist movement.

Theatres grew smaller but increased considerably in number. The French Revolution broke the monopoly of the Comédie

Française, and gave France forty companies. The *Patent Theatres in London were abolished in 1843. A proliferation of French melodrama, *farce, *vaudeville and other forms of theatre supplied a wealth of material for plagiarists and translators alike. *Gas, *limelight and finally the incandescent bulb were installed in the search for more imaginative *lighting and staging techniques. This developed into the *Gesamtkunstwerk of Wagner (1813–1883) and the theory and practice of Adolphe Appia (1862–1928) (see LIVING LIGHT) and Edmund Gordon Craig (1872–1966) (see ÜBER-MARIONETTE). A search for stage realism, the development of *ensemble acting (notably with the *Meininger troupe) and the emergence of the *director, marked further general differences between European theatre at the beginning and at the end of the nineteenth century. For a fuller introduction see:

ROWELL, G., *The Victorian Theatre: a survey*, Oxford University Press, 1956.

SOUTHERN, R., *The Victorian Theatre: a pictorial survey*, David and Charles, 1970.

**Noh drama**. A traditional form of Japanese drama which draws on oriental mythology and Buddhist scriptures. It incorporates elements of sacred and folk dance such as the *Bugaku*, one of the pantomimic dances from which the Noh sprang. Over two hundred plays are extant, many written by Kwanami (1333–84), a priest, and his son Zeami (1363–1443). They were originally staged in cycles at the court of the Shogun. The cycles might include a play set in 'the Age of the Gods', then a battle, a study of women, a study of human weakness, a moralizing play and finally some celebratory play paying compliments to audience and court.

The Noh stage seems to have developed from the open-air scaffold stage, linked to a dressing room by a bridge which came to be used for stage action. It now has a square stage, placed in the audience's right hand corner, and backed by a wall painted with a fir-tree. It has a place for a *chorus stage left, four musicians upstage, a decorated roof, an unobtrusive *exit upstage left and the principal *entrance from a 'Mask House' across the railed '*hashi-gakari*', originally the bridge, leading in upper stage right. The stage is of polished wood with pebbles around it as a reminder of the original open-air location. The *costumes are rich and beautiful. *Masks are used by certain characters. Performances incorporate *dance and are highly stylized.

W.B. Yeats experimented with the Noh in his short, symbolic *Plays for Dancers*, of which *At the Hawk's Well* (1916) is an example. Michel Saint-Denis also tells us, in his book *Training for the Theatre*, that Jacques Copeau (1879–1949), in the acting group or 'labora-tory' he established in 1920, proposed that his actors should work on a Noh play in order to find a new style based on the expressiveness of the body. He chose *Kantan* which allowed the actors to experience its ceremonial nature as they sang and subtly mimed the formal rhythmical and poetic text. 'Our performance,' says Saint-Denis, 'was for me the incomparable summit of our work.'

ARNOTT, P., *The Theatres of Japan*, Macmillan, 1969.

FENELLOSA, E.F., and POUND, E., *Noh or Accomplishment*, 1917; republished as: *The Classic Noh Theatre of Japan*, New Directions, 1959.

YEATS, W.B., *Certain Noble Plays of Japan*, Cuala Press, Dondrun, Ireland, 1916.

**Noises off**. Off-stage *sound effects, especially those made by the actors themselves. An amusing *farce of this name by Michael Frayn (1933–   ) uses the *play within the play convention and reverses it in Act II to show *knockabout backstage activity and the making of 'noises off' which are somewhat unprofessional.

**Novel**. 'Prose fiction of a certain length', to take the broad definition of E.M. Forster (1879–1970). The novel differs from *drama in many ways. It contains written *narrative, which is usually performed in drama. It contains descriptions of scene and character, whereas in drama *set and *character are *embodied*. It describes or allows a reader to 'listen in to' a character's thought processes. In drama, thought and unconscious processes are not normally narrated. Both *genres, of course, use *dialogue.

Each mode has advantages. The novel, with its longer time-span and private appeal, has much greater freedom since it can be laid aside whenever the reader wishes and there is not the same essential need to keep up interest and concentration throughout. The range of characters is normally far more extensive and scenes can be changed at will. It also invites the reader imaginatively to construct a fictional world, whereas drama generally, and especially *naturalistic drama, represents the choices of the artists who direct and perform it. The scene is chosen, the actor is *cast, and the spectator is presented with interpretations of characters and their relationships, with the emphases which appear important to an *actor. The novel, however, presents itself to a reader as a play does to a director, although perhaps not with quite with the same freedom. When drama is read on the page, rather than performed, it makes heavier imaginative demands on the reader, who must create a fictional world out of dialogue and stage directions alone. Many of the scenes which a novel would contain are missing.

Drama is public performance. It has a kind of direct aggression (Artaud would say *cruelty) and the excitement which comes from simultaneous and direct visual and auditory impact. (See THEATRE LANGUAGE.) The novel, on the other hand, builds up slowly and consecutively to create its most powerful effects. See NARRATIVE.

**Nursery, The**. School for actors established by Thomas Killigrew (1612–83) during the *Restoration period.

# O

**Oberammergau**. Village where the Bavarian *Mysterienspiel* takes place every ten years.

**'objective correlative'**. A phrase invented by T.S. Eliot in his essay on *Hamlet* (1919). It defines his view of how drama communicates an emotion. 'The only way', he declares, 'is by finding an objective correlative; in other words a set of objects, a situation, a chain of events which shall be the formula of that particular emotion'. This seems to imply that an emotion is communicated by involving the reader or spectator in a process of *identification with the characters who engage in a sequence of events. Thus if an author wishes to communicate feelings of *pity and *anger he may invent a situation in which a young man attacks an old lady. Pity arises out of sympathy for the victim and anger from repudiation of the aggressor. One may argue, however, that other methods of communicating emotion exist, including the use of *rhythm, *description and *metaphor or *simile. These may also be regarded as 'objective correlatives' since the 'formula for an emotion' may be a set of sounds, a particular scene or a compared object. Happiness, for example, can be communicated rhythmically by a lively tune, descriptively by a sunlit landscape and figuratively by the phrase 'I am as happy as a sandboy'; the dramatic objective correlative may be two lovers finding each other again after a long absence. Eliot's objective correlative, in fact, sees a dramatic situation as a kind of simile or metaphor, in that it is a 'vehicle' for the transmission of the feeling or 'tenor'.

A writer who intends to communicate an emotion, however, may experience other emotions in the process of transmission. The vehicle employed to communicate the emotion will almost inevitably arouse other feelings besides the ones intended, including the enjoyment of the process of communication. It often seems the case that the correlative itself — an invented character, or a developing story — takes over a writer's imagination. W.B. Yeats's famous late poem 'The Circus Animals' Desertion' records such a process:

> Players and painted stage took all my love
> And not those things that they were emblems of.

Instead of love of the woman for whom he created his 'painted stage' it is the dramatic vehicle itself which engrosses him.

In drama, of course, the process of transmission involves creative activity of a further kind. It is not only the author's choice of vehicle, but the contributions of *actors, *directors and *designers which further transform the author's original conception. In other words 'objective correlatives' escape the writer's full control.

Ultimately it becomes difficult for any person but the writer to know what emotions existed prior to the writing of a play, and what emerges in the processes of composition and then performance. Biographical evidence does not always exist, and if it does it may not be reliable. The writer may not remember, may not want to divulge, may not even *know* out of what subtle emotions the work came. Thus for a reader to speak at all of the 'objective correlative' is perhaps unwise.

In his essay, Eliot compares the unsatisfactory language and behaviour of Hamlet with the responses of Macbeth when he hears of his wife's death. Macbeth's words and reactions, says Eliot, appear 'completely adequate to the state of mind'. In other words the objective correlative is fully satisfactory. But the state of mind referred to is the character's not the author's, and there is no real way of testing a character's state of mind, since it is a projection of the author and an impression created in a listener's or actor's mind by the language the author chooses. Only the author can make an estimate of the correlation between primary impulse and vehicle — and the author may be dead, or have left no evidence, or may not himself know.

The term, in short, must be used with as much caution as the word *'intention'. Eliot himself would probably have welcomed its decline in popularity since he was clearly aware that a writer has, as he puts it, 'a medium to express' as well as an emotion.
ELIOT, T.S., *Selected Essays*, Faber and Faber, 1932, pp.141–6.

**Obstacle**. That which hinders the *will of the *hero. This may take the form of an outer situation, another person, lack of resources or *power, or some inner obstacle. An obstacle of some kind is a key dramatic element. See HAMARTIA.

**Off Broadway**. Term describing the avant-garde theatres which developed in New York to provide a serious alternative to commercial *Broadway productions after World War II. The European *theatre of the absurd played an important early role. New American plays continued to be performed, however, and these included Edward Albee's *Zoo Shocker* (1960). The *Living Theatre of Julian Beck (1925–85) and Judith Malina (1926–  ), founded in 1947, was the most radical company. After the closing of *The Brig* (1963) by the tax authorities the company was driven into exile in Europe. By the mid-1960s Off Broadway had become sufficiently established and conservative to prompt a new avant-garde movement. See OFF-OFF BROADWAY.

**Off-off Broadway**. New radical theatre which took shape in the early 1960s in New York with the founding of the *La Mama Experimental Theatre Club, the Café Cino and others. Initiators included theatre professionals and politically committed individuals from outside the theatre. Groups were formed with a bias towards the exploration both of deeply private experience and of contemporary social and political issues. Aims were artistic and political rather than commercial, and the focus was on creative group activity rather than on the staging of a script produced by writers in private rooms. Joseph Chaikin's *Open Theatre provides a well-known example of a dedicated acting *ensemble which created plays from group *improvisation. For texts of off-off Broadway plays by such authors as Sam Shepard, Ronald Tavel and Jean-Claude van Itallie, see:
SCHROEDER, R.L. (ed.), *The New Underground Theatre*, Bantam, 1968.

**Offstage**. In the *wings. Out of sight of the audience but not out of earshot. The offstage area must be silent during a performance.

**Old Comedy**. A term normally applied to the earlier plays of Aristophanes (448–380 B.C.) to distinguish them from *middle and especially *new comedy. These plays, which include *The Wasps* (422 B.C.), *The Clouds* (423 B.C.) and *The Frogs* (405 B.C.), have prominent festive and *choral elements, a cast of characters which includes gods and *heroes, very little plot, and a great deal of *farce, personal invective, *parody and political propaganda. As compared with the urban new comedy, these plays have a much stronger feeling of the natural world.

**Old man; old woman**. Stereotype roles for specialist actors in the *farces and *melodramas of the Victorian *stock company. The old man, traditionally a power figure who obstructs young love, may be traced back through the figure of *Pantaloon in the *Commedia dell'Arte* to Roman and Greek *new comedy. Polonius in *Hamlet* (1601) and Sir Peter Teazle in Sheridan's *School for Scandal* (1777) seem to be complex variations on the 'old man' stereotype. Dame Marten in *Maria Marten, or Murder in the Red Barn* (c.1839) is an 'old woman' role.

***Ombres Chinoises***. Shadow plays in which flat *puppets are manipulated in front of a light source so as to throw moving silhouettes on a screen. They derive from the Far East and were popular in Paris in the eighteenth and nineteenth centuries.

**One-act play**. A short 20–50 minute play, generally with few characters and no change of *scene. Its dramatic coherence distinguishes it from the short entertainments or *interludes which were performed before, after and even between the *acts of the longer plays on eighteenth- and nineteenth- century bills. It became a respected form in the late nineteenth century. Chekhov (1860–1904) wrote several one-act plays and they have been used since on 'double bills' and in *lunch-time theatre, or on any occasion where brevity is an advantage. Strindberg (1849–1912) also wrote 'one acters', as did the Irish dramatists, W.B. Yeats (1865–1939) and J.M. Synge (1871–1909). Expressionist and *absurdist writers, including Beckett (1906–   ), Ionesco (1912–   ) and Pinter (1930–   ) have since made considerable use of the form.

The qualities of the one-act play resemble those of the short story. There is no room for *sub-plots, excess words or broad treatment of a character's relationship with the wider social world. The emphasis tends to be on pairs of characters or on the lonely individual. The action is often hallucinatory and emblematic. Ionesco's *The Lesson* (1951) and *The Chairs* (1952), which can form a double bill, are fine examples of more extended one-act plays. One-act plays generally begin late in the *story, observe *unity of place and require very economical and skilful exposition. One-act plays for television, performed in a 'half-hour slot', can use the *film medium to offer a greater flexibility of location.

**One-liner**. A single brief remark, usually comic or sardonic.

**Onkos**. Hairdress of the Greek *mask which gave height and dignity to the tragic actor.

**Ontological-hysteric theatre**. American *alternative theatre. See SELF-REFLEXIVE.

**Open stage**. A *thrust or *arena stage. It resembles Shakespeare's *apron stage in that the audience is placed on three sides of it and there is no *curtain or *proscenium arch. The Chichester Festival Theatre is an example.

The open stage poses problems of *grouping and *projection, since actors can never face the whole audience at once and are always likely to *mask other actors from certain sections of it. Good *acoustics, and precise *movement and *diction are essential. A steep *rake in the *auditorium helps avoid *masking problems.

This kind of stage grew in popularity early in the century when William Poel (1852–1934) and Harley Granville-Barker (1877–1946) encouraged a return to more flexible methods of staging Shakespeare. Partly as a result, the *National Theatre and *Royal Shakespeare Company now use open stages. The proximity of the audience helps to establish a close *actor-audience relationship and this leads to an emphasis on *acting and grouping rather than

scenic display.
JOSEPH, S., *New Theatre Forms*, Pitman, London, NY, 1968.

**Open Theatre**. Group formed by Joseph Chaikin (1935– ) in 1963. Early productions were short pieces which developed from exploratory *improvisations. The first long play, *Viet Rock* (1966), was provoked by the Vietnam war. It used *dance, *mime and *chorus techniques to emphasize violence and terror. The following production, *The Serpent* (1967), included images of the deaths of President Kennedy and Martin Luther King. These were intermingled with scenes from the Book of Genesis, such as the tasting of the apple and the killing of Abel. Death was the principal concern of *Terminal* (1969); human adaptability was the concern of *The Mutation Show* (1971), and sleep and *dream the concern of *Nightwalk* (1973), the group's last production.

Influences on the style of the Open Theatre included Stanislavski and the *'method' school, Artaud's *theatre of cruelty, the Living Theatre and Grotowski's *theatre laboratorium. Its emphasis was increasingly on group activity and the theatrical presence of the group.
CHAIKIN, J., *The Presence of the Actor*, Atheneum, NY, 1972.

**Opera**. Highly developed musical form closely related to drama. Opera-lovers may indeed consider it the dominant dramatic form. It is normally divided into *acts, with their appropriate *climaxes and *curtains. Like *Greek tragedy it has individual *characters, a *chorus and sometimes employs *dance. It inherits the *Italian theatre's strong emphasis on spectacle. *Costume and *scenery are usually lavish, and there is a frequent emphasis on spectacular *lighting and other *stage effects. However, the fundamental dominance of orchestral music, the limitations placed on physical movement when words are sung rather than spoken, and the relative simplicity of plot and *libretto make opera a different form from spoken theatre, though the connection with *melodrama and with ancient choral *tragedy is very close.
GROUT, D.J., *A Short History of the Opera*, Columbia, 1966.
KERMAN, J., *Opera as Drama*, Knopf, 1956.

**Opera bouffe; opera buffa**. French and Italian names for *operetta, which became fashionable in Paris in the mid-eighteenth century.

**Operetta**. Light opera which varies in length, is generally satirical and uses dramatic *dialogue as well as song and *chorus. The 'Savoy operas' of Gilbert (1836–1971) and Sullivan (1842–1900), John Gay's *The Beggar's Opera* (1728), Offenbach's *Orpheus* (1858) and *La Belle Hélène* (1864) all come under this heading.

**Opposite prompt**. Usually marked 'O.P.'; *stage direction indicating the side of the theatre opposite the prompt corner (i.e. stage right since the *prompter is usually placed stage left).

*Orateur*. An important function for an actor in one of the French seventeenth-century acting companies. It was the responsibility of the *orateur* to publicize the next production at the end of a performance and gain the goodwill of the spectators in a carefully phrased speech. He had other responsibilities, too, such as the composition of the posters advertising new performances, chairing meetings of actors, calling *rehearsals and organizing play-readings. A contemporary account of his function is to be found in: CHAPPUZEAU, S., *Théâtre Français* (1671).

**Oratorio**. Semi-dramatic musical composition written for voices, and generally for instruments, but not acted. The religious tone and the continuing importance of the *chorus distinguish it from *opera. In England Handel (1685–1759) made important use of this form and introduced secular subject-matter. His *Messiah* (1742) is the most famous of all oratorios. His *Samson* (1743) based on Milton's *Samson Agonistes* (1671) has a much stronger dramatic element.

**Oratory**. The art of public speaking. See RHETORIC; SPEECH; PERORATION.

**Orchestra**. The 'dancing-place' of the Greek and Roman theatres. It was originally circular and had an altar to *Dionysos, the god of dramatic festivals, at its centre. It was flat, very large (78 feet (24m) across in Athens when it first appeared), and was usually placed in a convenient hollow where two slopes met. At some stage it came to be placed lower than the *skene. The later, paved orchestras tended to be smaller. The first stone theatre on the south-eastern slope of the Acropolis in Athens was 64 feet across.

It is interesting to speculate on how the *chorus performed in the orchestra. When did the dancers align themselves with the audience to face the actors and when did they align themselves with the actors to face the audience? Did they move always in straight lines or did they adapt their figures to the circular shape? Certainly, the huge audiences must have looked down on a varied and powerful choral *movement, suited to the different rhythms and metres of the choral songs.

In later Graeco-Roman theatres, the *skene began to encroach on the orchestra, and in Roman times it had become semi-circular. No doubt this indicated an increased emphasis on stage performance.

ARNOTT, P., *An Introduction to the Greek Theatre*, Macmillan, 1959.

BIEBER, M., *The History of the Greek and Roman Theatre*, Oxford University Press, 1961.

**Ordinary**. See PAGEANT MASTER.

**Organic**. Term implying life and growth, as compared with 'mechanical' which implies something fixed and dead. The term began to be used of literary *form when the biological sciences started to challenge the mechanical patterns of natural process established by Newtonian physics. It became a basis for Coleridge's celebrated distinction between *imagination and fancy and is still a term of approval for 'vital' literary and dramatic works which are seen to 'evolve' rather than copy dead or conventional forms. *Farce, for example, is often seen as 'mechanical', and thus the opposite of organic, since manipulation and calculation seem to play a large part in its making. However, if *laughter arises, as Henri Bergson (1859–1941) says, from 'the mechanical encrusted upon the living', *comedy depends upon a perceived tension between the mechanical and the organic. For a longer discussion of the term's relation to 'organ' and 'organization' see: WILLIAMS, R., *Keywords*, Fontana, 1976, pp.189–192.

**Originality**. Term of praise for that which is not copied or derivative, but grows spontaneously from some *organic principle. It is singular, unique, and originates in itself.

The strong sense of approval in this word has been qualified in the twentieth century. T.S. Eliot, for example, has asserted: 'That which is absolutely original is absolutely bad.' The artist, writer or dramatist, he implies, is dependent on the past — on a community or a *tradition which nourishes his art. Originality is a reshaping of materials held in common, bringing these into relation with 'something new in the writer's own time'. A new art for T.S. Eliot was *reorganization, not something which originates entirely in itself.

A similar attitude is evinced by the painter Paul Klee (1879–1940), who sees the artist as resembling the trunk of a tree and his art as the foliage. A tree, however, has roots, which for an artist are the language, its *forms and *conventions, and the social and literary experience he inherits or acquires. Originality lies not in novelty, but in the nature of the process of assimilation and transformation. In these ways, the positive stress on the 'organic' creative principle of growth is kept, but incorporated into a sense of historical and cultural flow. This replaces the implicit romantic stress on self-origination which may be seen as too individualistic or too mystical, or both.

**Origins of drama**. The most persistent theories of the origin of drama argue that it developed from early religious *ritual. From a basis of observation of primitive tribes, and on the assumption that all cultures develop in similar stages, early anthropologists led by Sir James Frazer (1854–1941) identified ways in which early peoples sought control of their food supply by developing certain rites which they perform for a supernatural power — rather like actors hoping to charm and control an audience. Stories or *myths containing human and supernatural characters developed from these simple rites and were impersonated in associated ceremonies. Gradually, as a people becomes less primitive, these ceremonies split off from the religious rite and become the first independently acted secular drama. In line with the views of 'social Darwinism', such dramatic forms evolve from the simple to the complex.

Such theorizing came to be regarded with suspicion by later 'functionalist' anthropologists, led by Malinowski (1884–1942), who made no axiomatic assumptions about the similarity of evolutionary patterns. Applying rigorous empirical methods, Malinovski suggested that individual cultures developed in different ways. Hence drama has many origins.

More recently, universal solutions to the problems of how drama arose have been encouraged by the work of Claude Lévi-Strauss (1908– ) who has investigated myths as modes of thought which differ from but are not necessarily inferior to (or more 'primitive' than) the logical processes of scientific method. He argues that the savage mind works with *signs rather then concepts. *Mythopoeia embodies this form of thinking, which is holistic and works on several levels at once, rather than logically and sequentially. Early drama which expresses itself through myth may be seen as the natural expression of such forms of consciousness.

A rather different view finds the origins of drama in the active impersonation of *narratives. In other words, verbal expression precedes physical enactment. Drama may also have emerged from primitive *dance and the *mimesis, or imitation, of animal behaviour and sound. In this case drama could be thought to arise from aesthetic rather than religious or social needs and functions. One may speculate too, that other motives played their part. Man writes, performs and creates for many reasons: (a) to record and fix time passing; (b) to escape 'reality'; (c) to protect the self against violence and threat; (d) to retain 'sanity'; (e) to affirm the values of a group; (f) to impose the values of a community; and (g) to reaffirm these values.

The authority nearest the source, Aristotle (384–322 B.C.), affirmed that the origin of European drama, in particular of *tragedy, was the *dithyramb. But this, too, remains in doubt. Gerald Else, for instance, contends that dramatic readings of the Iliad and the Odyssey at religious festivals were transformed into full drama by deliberately wedding them to *choral dance and song when the *City Dionysia were reorganized in 534 B.C. The association with *Dionysos is established by the official recognition of drama at state-sponsored festivals from that year onward. What fragmentary evidence we have of the nature of this earliest of European drama suggests that a single actor played all parts, using different costumes and *masks. The subject matter seems to have been primarily mythological, with much formal experimentation and strong *choral and lyrical elements. It seems likely that the origins were religious and ritualistic but the absence of strong evidence will ensure that speculation continues.

**Orta dyunu**. Turkish folk play consisting mainly of routines involving the comic figure Kavuklu and the main character Pisekar, who carries a club and, like Punch, spends much of his time hitting the minor characters, who are Turkish regional *stereotypes.

**Ostension**. 'Holding out'. A philosophic term for the most primitive form of *sign, whereby a thing is signified by the thing itself. Thus a cup is signified by holding up a cup; a tree by showing or touching a tree. In life this most frequently happens in answer to two questions. The question 'what is a cup?' addressed to a child or language learner, may result in the ostension of the object in question, meaning '*this* is a cup'. The question, 'what do you want?' addressed to a thirsty speaker may result in the expression of a desire — the ostension of a cup, meaning 'I want a cup of . . .'
    Swift satirizes forms of ostension in *Gulliver's Travels* (1726). His Laputans carried sacks around on their backs, full of objects they might need in conversation, so that they could hold them up as required. It may be argued that Brecht's *epic theatre is a form of ostension since it 'shows' the audience a character and a situation, rather than inviting it to participate in a fiction. In epic theatre, however, the play 'held out' to the audience represents a parallel situation, rather than the thing itself. If epic drama is 'ostension' it is of a more complex nature than is indicated by our definition.
    It might seem that *naturalist drama fulfils the definition more satisfactorily since it offers a direct rather than an allegorical image. It says: 'This is life as I conceive it.' It may also, no doubt, be offered to spectators as a desire, involving them in the author's wishes and dreams. But naturalism, like all theatre, uses substitute objects rather than the object itself. The stage may be a facsimile and the character an apparently exact representation, but *props and *characterization are still imitations, though more exact than, say, as the candle which conventionally represents a star in a *nativity play or the boy playing Cleopatra. Such ostension is *symbolic and presupposes an audience's capacity to play, to join in and to accept the *as if. It is not 'representation of the thing by the

thing itself'. Perhaps, however, one may say that naturalist plays (and other forms of theatre) are like the second kind of ostension. They express a wish. They hold out an empty cup and invite the audience to fill it (like the *chorus in Shakespeare's *Henry V* (1599)).

Drama then is not simple ostension, but expressive of a wish which it may also invite. It may be useful to consider whether its appeal often lies in a tension between the two kinds of ostension: between the showing of what 'is', and the holding out of what might be or might have been. In the conflict between these two, between actuality and desire, dramatic action grows.

**Outdoor theatre**. Theatre in the open air was normal practice until the development of architectural techniques allowing large spaces to be roofed over and the space therein to be adequately lit.

The Greek amphitheatres, medieval market places, *Cornish rounds, *Elizabethan theatres and the *Commedia dell'Arte* all used the light of the sun — and braved the weather. But the problems posed by rain, fading light and extraneous noise, together with the difficulty of voice *projection in open spaces and the problem of establishing *silence and *suspense, have meant that although forms of *street theatre continue to entertain and attract custom at city festivals and elsewhere, a warm, roofed, well-lit, comfortable interior has generally been preferred since the seventeenth century.

**Overhearer**. Character who listens and is seen by the audience but not by other characters. The overhearer is a dramatic device which advances the *plot. It allows *secrets to become known and gives the overhearer a new basis on which to act. It is frequently used in *melodrama to produce a crude *dramatic irony and induce *suspense: the audience knows that the listening *villain knows what the *heroine does not know he knows; perhaps there is even someone on stage who knows the villain knows that the heroine does not know, and knows the villain does not know he knows what the villain knows ... The effect is subtler still if the overhearer misconstrues what he hears. Thus in Shakespeare's *Othello* (1604) the *hero listens to Iago and Cassio and assumes they speak of Desdemona not Bianca. The suspense this engenders is more complex since the audience is aware of the false basis on which Othello acts.

**Overplot**. Term suggested by the American critic Harry Levin for festivities and ceremonials of which the play is only a part, or to which it makes reference. Thus, for instance, the 'overplot' of Shakespeare's *Merry Wives of Windsor* (1597) is the ceremony to which it refers: the Order of the Garter, performed at Windsor in that year. *A Midsummer Night's Dream* (1595), too, has an overplot, since it seems to make reference to an actual wedding and may well have been performed as part of the marriage festivities.

An overplot thus exists as an appeal in the text to knowledge existing in the minds of the play's early audiences. Later audiences lose that knowledge. Who Shakespeare's betrothed couple, Duke Theseus and Hippolyta, were meant to represent is uncertain, and when Jan Kott in his book *Shakespeare Our Contemporary* suggests that the play contains sly *hints at the former amatory activities of a married couple in the first audience (and hence in the overplot) this is unlikely to be corroborated by documentary evidence. The overplot, however, continues to exist as a suspicion that a *code exists which time has hidden.

LEVIN, H., *The Overreacher*, Harvard University Press, Cambridge, Mass., 1952.

**Over the top**. Colloquial expression describing an exaggerated and unconvincing performance. What is 'exaggerated', of course, depends on the norms and expectations of an audience at a particular time. The performances of Henry Irving (1838–1905) or Ellen Terry (1847–1928), not to mention Richard Burbage (*c.*1567–1619) would probably now seem to us, with our *naturalistic expectations, to be exaggerated. On the other hand, we should remember that the expression of emotions which may seem extreme and 'over the top' when the audience is 'cold' can become acceptable after a careful build-up. It is the intention of much powerful drama, especially *tragedy, to move us away from our conventional expectations. (See HAM ACTING.)

Exaggerated performance is, of course, something we expect of *comedy. Comics and clowns break normal conventions to provoke laughter yet they do not go 'over the top' because they act deliberately and within the *codes of comedy. The term, nonetheless, is pejorative when applied to serious acting and it generally occurs when actors lose a sense of their audience and attempt to impose or force an interpretation on both spectator and *role.

**Oxford's Men**. A sixteenth-century company of actors patronized by successive Dukes of Oxford.

# P

**Pace**. See RHYTHM; TEMPO.

**Pace-egging play**. Mumming play associated with the old practice of rolling Easter eggs on Easter Monday. 'Pace' relates to the French *'pâques'* meaning Easter.

CHAMBERS, E.K., *The Medieval Stage*, Oxford University Press, 1933.

**Pageant**. Waggon on which episodes of the *mystery plays were performed, or which carried the displays of the secular *triumphs. It came to mean a stationary stage, set up perhaps for royal visits, and hence the canvas or wooden structure used for Tudor *masques. The word then came to apply to any spectacular procession in which a secular or religious organization displays scenes from its own history.

CAWLEY, A.C., et al. (eds.), *Revels History of Drama in English*, Vol. I, Methuen, 1983, pp.23–31.

**17** *A pageant car (etching by Jacques Callot)*

**Pageant master**. Central coordinator of large medieval productions such as those taking place at the feast of Corpus Christi. He is to be seen in a famous miniature by Jean Fouquet, wearing ecclesiastical robes and carrying a prompt book and conductor's baton. Other names for figures with similar functions are 'superintendant' or 'ordinary'. (See Ill.15, p.228.)

WICKHAM, G., *Medieval Theatre*, Weidenfeld and Nicolson, 1974, pp.81–3.

**Palliata**. Latin name for Roman plays deriving from Greek *new comedy. One of their main preoccupations was the contrast between the attitudes of the older and younger generations (see the *Adelphae* (160 B.C.) of Terence (*c*.190–159 B.C.)). The term derives from '*pallium*', a Greek cloak worn by the actors.

**Palsgrave's Men**. Name given to the important *Jacobean company *Prince Henry's Men, formerly Lord Admiral's Men, when Prince Henry died in 1612.

**Pan**. Short for 'panorama'. A camera movement from right to left or vice versa. Such a movement, especially a 'slow pan', places spectators at the centre of a circle, allowing them to *focus in turn on objects or faces arranged around a wide arc of that circle. The camera can bring the audience within a scene in a way normally impossible with a conventional stage. The spectator in the *stalls is further from the stage action, which therefore takes place within a narrower arc of the spectator's vision. A theatrical equivalent is occasionally found when an *auditorium is part encircled by the stage, and spectators swivel their seats (or the whole auditorium rotates) to face the action. A *promenade performance provides a rough equivalent. Another approximation may be obtained on an *end or *proscenium stage by focusing the audience's attention on an actor as he moves slowly across it. The theatre, however, cannot vary the distance between spectator and action as the camera can.

**Pantaloon**. The 'lean and slippered pantaloon' of Jaques's famous 'All the world's a stage' speech in Shakespeare's *As You Like It* (1599) is a *stereotype character from the *Commedia dell'Arte and the English *Harlequinade. Dressed in long black coat, red suit and skull cap, he is old, stupid, suspicious, greedy and an obstacle to young love, especially to Columbine, his young wife or daughter. He is thus an object of ridicule to the various servant and *clown figures who surround him.

**Pantomime**. A silent play using *mime, music and spectacle to communicate a mythical story. The term derives from the Greek 'pantomimos', meaning a man who imitates everything. The form was very popular under the Roman Empire. Apuleius describes one such production in *The Golden Ass* (*c*.A.D. 150).
 A second form of pantomime was created by John Weaver in 1716. It was further developed by the actor-manager of Lincoln's Inn Fields Theatre, John Rich (*c*.1692–1761), in order to compete commercially with the other *patent theatre, Drury Lane. He interwove comic, mimed episodes from a *Harlequin story with a serious *fable, such as the Orpheus and Eurydice or Perseus and Andromeda stories, and spiced the result with spectacular stage tricks and *'transformation scenes'. The mixture continued to

appeal throughout his long career.

Meyerhold (1874–1940), who was much influenced by the pantomime tradition, declared: 'Pantomime excites not through what is concealed within it, but by how it is created'. By this he seems to imply that dramatic *tension derives from admiration of the skill of the performers rather than *plot or intrigue.

Nowadays, the term usually refers to the Christmas entertainment which derives from the *Harlequinade, but whose nineteenth-century accretions have eliminated the Harlequin story completely. It consists of fairy tale and *burlesque elements, with strong emphasis on spectacle, *dance and song. It has two popular *role reversals: an actress as *principal boy and the comic *dame played by an actor in *drag. For an account of its complicated evolution see:

WILSON, A.E., *The Story of Pantomime*, Home and Van Thal, 1949.

**Pantomimus**. A silent performer in a sung *pantomime, popular in Imperial Rome. He wore a *tragic costume and a *mask with no mouth aperture. He was accompanied by a *chorus, wind instruments and percussion. The stories were taken both from history and *myth. Emphasis was placed on beauty and skill of performance.

**Papposilenus**. The leader of the satyr *chorus in the Greek *satyr plays which followed the tragic performances at the *city dionysia in the fifth century B.C.

**Parabasis**. Greek for 'digression'. A direct choral address in Greek *Old Comedy. In the parabasis the *chorus abandoned the dramatic *role for which it was costumed (as 'wasps' or 'birds', for example). The *chorus leader would don the author's mask, satirize well-known citizens and comment on current events. Aristophanes's *Wasps* (422 B.C.) contains a traditional parabasis (lines 1032–1121). It was divided into seven sections: prelude; opening audience address in anapaests; a rapid comic exchange; the *strophe: the *epirrhema, usually in trochaic metre and addressed to the audience; the *antistrophe and the final antepirrhema.

**Parable play**. Dramatic *allegory which invites a spectator to set the story in parallel with another set of events and act accordingly. Unlike the New Testament parable — 'Hear ye therefore the parable of the sower' (Matt.xiii 18) — a dramatic parable does not always offer clear solutions. Drama needs to maintain *suspense and it thrives on divisions of sympathy. A dramatic parable with a clear moral is probably best presented in a short *one-act form. Ionesco's three-act *Rhinocéros* (1960), a parable about the growth of fascism in which characters turn into rhinoceroses, is unusually long for a play whose sympathies are clear. It is notable that Ionesco (1912– ), along with other dramatists of the *absurd, frequently employs parable, and favours a shorter form. This is not to say that brief dramatic parables always make a clear moral statement. Beckett's plays, long or short, have no clear moral. They invite interpretation as parables and mock the attempt to see them as such.

The term 'parable play' is often applied to Brecht's later *epic drama which uses historical and fictional situations to present a contemporary problem which the audience is invited to solve. Brecht (1898–1956) does not mock the attempt, nor does he suggest easy solutions. *The Life of Galileo* (1937–9) is a parable play about the political value of scientific knowledge. It asks to whom a scientist should entrust his discoveries and when he should put the truth above expediency. A play about Galileo's problems with the Inquisition becomes a parable about the political responsibilities of scientists in the twentieth century.

**Parade.** Short sketch performed outside fairground booths to encourage customers to see the performance within. Some appear to derive from the *Commedia dell'Arte* and medieval *farce.

**Paradiso.** Piece of stage machinery, invented by Brunelleschi (1377–1446) for the play of the Annunciation in the Church of San Felice in Florence. It consisted of a copper dome containing an actor representing St Gabriel and a number of choirboys representing cherubim. The dome was suspended from the roof. It was lowered to allow Gabriel to make his *entrance, then raised again to heaven.

**Paradox.** The reconciliation of apparent contradictions or the apparent reconciliation of contradictions. Paradox may have a serious or comic effect, or both. Bertolt Brecht (1898–1956) in *Mother Courage* (1941) uses it as a form of *alienation effect to attack conventional attitudes and persuade the audience to see things from an unusual angle. When, at the beginning of the play, the Recruiting Officer says, 'And they're so friendly around here, I'm scared to go out at night', the paradox is only an apparent contradiction since for the Recruiting Officer everyone is a potential enemy and friendliness must therefore be a *mask. The effect is comic though a serious point is made. Similarly, Mother Courage uses paradox to explain her name: 'They call me Mother Courage 'cause I was afraid I'd be ruined.' Mother Courage braves the bullets to save her business. An unheroic self-preserving instinct creates a reputation for heroism. Brecht uses the paradox to mock our conventional judgements about *heroes and ask how close *fear, heroism and self-interest often are.

Serious paradox has received much attention from literary

critics, especially from the American 'new critic', Cleanth Brooks (see *The Well Wrought Urn*). Brooks makes it the centre of his poetics and analyses various uses of it in Shakespeare and other major poets. His interest derives in part from the growth of interest in dramatic and metaphysical poetry stimulated by the work of T.S. Eliot (1888–1965). Eliot's use of paradox, however, is especially notable in his later poetry, where the comic note is absent. In the first line of *Little Gidding* (1942), for example — 'Midwinter spring is its own season' — Eliot presents an image of a world paradoxically rescued from the flow of *time: 'This is the spring time/But not in time's covenant'. The paradoxical image attempts a reconciliation between time and the idea of eternity. Similarly, in his drama Eliot uses paradox to resolve such fundamental questions as the relation of human suffering to the idea of a benevolent God. The paradox is not so much verbal as an intrinsic part of the play's action and assumptions. In *The Cocktail Party* (1949) the intense suffering of Celia Coplestone is presented as a road to salvation. The play's Christian *ideology attempts a resolution of the deep contradictions inherent in a *tragic view of the world.

Paradox may thus project an ideology. In Eliot it implies the possibility of reconciliation between time and a world beyond time, between idealism and the way of the world or between a benevolent creator and the existence of suffering. How far paradox is merely a consolatory image, and how far the contradictions of the world are apparent or real, is a matter of personal faith. See PARADOX OF ACTING.

**Paradox of acting.** According to Henry Irving (1838–1905), 'it is necessary that the mind should have, as it were, a double consciousness in which all the emotion proper to the occasion should have full sway, while the actor is all the time alert for every detail of his method'. Two main, and apparently contradictory, theories of acting have developed since Irving's time, stressing differing relations between an *actor and his *role. Stanislavski (1863–1938) in his theory of acting laid stress on full *identification, whereas Brecht (1898–1956) laid stress on the actor's independence of the character played. In practice, however, both theoreticians were well aware that actors must, as Irving suggests, identify with their characters yet remain somehow separate. They must be simultaneously hot and cold. If an actor is not to some degree dispassionate, aware of his craft and watching his own processes, he will not communicate passion. The best proof of this is perhaps when a character labours under such intense emotion that he or she *appears* to lose complete control; the actor, nonetheless, must remain in control. If this is lost there is a danger of *'drying'; the audience loses confidence in the actor and the dramatic illusion is destroyed.

Such problems were familiar to earlier theoreticians. They find expression in the famous book of Denis Diderot (1713–84), *The Paradox of Acting* (1773–8), where he declares: 'The extravagant creature who loses his self-control has no effect on us . . . Fill the front of the theatre with tearful creatures. I will none of them on the boards.'

Diderot's was a *classical rather than a *romantic view. It emphasized regulation and control rather than intense self-expression. But the process of acting, as Irving suggests, works on two levels and within it these two opposites are reconcilable. One is reminded of Wordsworth's famous description of poetry, 'emotion recollected in tranquillity', which seems equally applicable to acting. An actor builds up a role in *rehearsal. There he can engage in intense emotional experiments, in which he can allow himself to lose control. The violent emotions of rehearsal, however, may be 'recollected' or assimilated into a relaxed or even 'tranquil' stage performance in which the control achieved by the actor allows the character's emotional loss of control to be mediated.

This control is important in *naturalistic drama and *tragedy, but it is of even more importance in *comedy. Loss of control, one should remember, can provoke *laughter or embarrassment. The actor who plays a comic character in a furious passion must take care that it is the character who is laughed at, not himself. The actor's timing and precision will establish confidence and avoid any embarrassment. When the character is 'hot', the actor must be several degrees cooler.

For a reprint of Diderot's essay and a considered reply, based on the views of nineteenth-century actors see:
ARCHER, W., *Masks or Faces* (1888), Hill and Wang, 1957.

**Parallelism.** An echo or *repetition of one element by another; a form of *correspondence. It occurs in drama when two characters are placed in similar situations, as are Gloucester and King Lear in Shakespeare's play. The *double or *sub-plot gives rise to a series of comparisons: Lear and Gloucester are both old, both are cast out, both suffer loss and betrayal, both are foolish and mistake good for evil. Verbal echoes reinforce this outstanding example of parallel action and character.

Strindberg (1849–1912) asserted, in the important preface to *Miss Julie* (1888), that all effective plays should contain a parallelism. Certainly the device has important dramatic functions. It keeps the audience aware of what has happened elsewhere in the play, thus ensuring dramatic concentration, and if W.B. Yeats was right, a sub-plot parallel ensures a kind of poetic reverberation which, in his essay *Trembling of the Veil* he called 'emotion of multitude'. The spectator, Yeats suggested, becomes aware that the dramatic situation is about more than the suffering of one character. The echo or parallel reveals similar cases, breaking down 'the dykes that separate man and man'. This universalizes the situation and draws the spectator into the play.

On the other hand, parallel situations can point a *contrast between characters who react differently to similar trials. Such juxtapositions often reveal the human or moral superiority of one over the other and recall the processes of *comedy, which Yeats declared is built *on* the 'dykes' which divide us. *King Lear* (1605), of course, establishes in its parallels both similarities and differences between the characters, bringing tragedy and comedy uncomfortably and powerfully close. See SIMILE; ALLEGORY; METAPHOR; PARABLE; PARODY; BURLESQUE.

**Paraphrase.** Language which summarizes the general meaning of a passage. Paraphrase clarifies understanding and can be a useful tool in the early stages of *rehearsal when actors have difficulty in following the sequences of thought or feeling in a *speech or *scene. Directors, including Stanislavski (1863–1938), have encouraged the use of paraphrase, especially in *improvisation exercises. The practice seems to free actors from the tyranny of the text and allows them to discover more 'natural' *movements which can be incorporated into a *role when the precise words of a play have been learnt.

**Parapraxis.** Mistakes such as slips of the tongue, hearing incorrectly and misplacing objects. According to Sigmund Freud (1856–1939), although they appear to be accidental, many 'slips' reveal a deep-seated wish in the *unconscious mind. Freud discovered instances of parapraxis not only in everyday speech but in dramatic *dialogue. Thus he cites Portia in Shakespeare's *The Merchant of Venice* (c.1597):

> One half of me is yours, the other half yours,
> Mine own I would say . . .

Portia reveals by her verbal slip a wish wholly to belong to Bassanio her lover. Dialogue of such subtlety is rare, however.
FREUD, S., *Introductory Lectures*, Pelican Books, 1973.

**Paraskenia.** 'Side-scenes'; the equivalent of *wings on the classical Greek stage.

**Parodos.** The side entrances between *skene and amphitheatre in the classical *Greek theatre. Also, by extension, the opening song of the *chorus.

**Parody.** A mocking imitation of an author's style and work. Dramatic parody began with the *satyr play and *old comedy. Aristophanes's *Frogs* (405 B.C.), for example, compares and parodies the styles of Aeschylus (525–456 B.C.) and Euripides

(484–407/6 B.C.). In *medieval drama, parody of the Christmas story is found in the *Second Wakefield Shepherd's Play*. Shakespeare parodies fellow writers in *Love's Labour's Lost* (1595). Buckingham parodies *heroic tragedy in his *burlesque *The Rehearsal* (1671). These are but a few examples among many.

If drama is a form of *mimesis then dramatic parody mocks the seriousness with which we take it and reminds us of the artificiality of the means we employ. Parody works like the *fool in Shakespeare, holding up a mocking mirror, as Touchstone does to Jaques in Act II of *As You Like It* (1599). Parody ridicules our postures and makes us beware of taking ourselves and our modes of communication too seriously. Indeed it causes us to revise our tone and style, and our ways of seeing and presenting *character and *situation.

Parody takes on great importance in Russian *formalist theory, which argues that *genres develop as successive parodies attack the automated procedures of earlier forms of expression.

**Paso**. Short sixteenth-century Spanish *interlude; predecessor of the *entremés*.
SHERGOLD, N.D., *A History of the Spanish Stage*, Oxford University Press, 1967.

**Pasquino**. A minor servant role in the *Commedia dell'Arte*, later assimilated into French comedy.

**Passion play**. Religious play which concentrates on the biblical events of Good Friday and Easter Sunday: the Entry into Jerusalem, the Trials before Herod and Pilate, the Crucifixion, Deposition, Harrowing of Hell and the Resurrection.

Versions of the Passion seem to have arisen in both Latin and the vernacular in the thirteenth century, based on the *liturgical treatment of the *Visitatio Sepulchri* and the *Victimae Paschali*. They became part of the Feast of Corpus Christi and developed into the central movement of the English *mystery cycles. In France and Germany, sophisticated and separate plays arose. The medieval concept of 'All the world's a stage' is evident in their spectacular staging and use of *loca, as can be seen in famous illustrations of the Valenciennes Passion Play (1547).
CHAMBERS, E.K., *The Medieval Stage*, Oxford University Press, 1903.

**Pastiche**. A work made up of borrowings from other writers, either as a kind of literary game or as deliberate *parody. The term is generally applied to works of literature, unlike *burlesque and *travesty which are usually theatrical terms.

**Pastoral**. Literary mode deriving from Theocritus (c.308–c.240 B.C.) and the Greek myth of the Golden Age. Pastoral poetry is a nostalgic urban dream of a spring-time Arcadia where shepherds and shepherdesses play games of love in a golden world of peace and natural plenty. Behind the dream is an awareness of a decline from this paradisal state through a silver and bronze to an iron-age world from which justice has departed, and relations have declined to those of property and strife.

The Italian Renaissance saw a strong revival of this lyrical mode, and pastoral drama began to appear. Tasso's *L'Aminta* (1573) and Gnarini's *Il Pastor Fido* (1590), together with the *Pastorale Amoureuse* (1569) of Belleforest (1530–83), encouraged a vogue for the pastoral in England, practised in particular by John Lyly (1554–1606) and John Fletcher (1579–1623), and in France, practised by Racan (1589–1670) in *Les Bergeries* (1625). Shakespeare made powerful dramatic use of the psychological and moral implications of pastoral in his comedies and *romance plays, where he uses it to counterpoint more realistic modes of behaviour and expression. Silvius in *As You Like It* (1599), for example, is a pastoral shepherd whose attitudes to love are gently mocked. On the other hand, the pastoral elements in *Pericles* (1608), *Cymbeline* (1609), *The Winter's Tale* (1610) and *The Tempest* (1611) have a strong positive emphasis and the idealized dream seems to hint at realities above the 'realistic' behaviour of those who live after the Fall. Nostalgic arcadianism seems to have given way in these late plays to a different and more energetic feeling, related to Christian ideas of the shepherd, crystallizing around the female characters such as Perdita, the shepherdess/princess in the long pastoral scene in *The Winter's Tale* (1610).

Pastoral is thus an important lyrical mode with moral and psychological implications. It was, of course, to resurface in Wordsworth's treatment of shepherd figures in his epic poem *The Prelude* (1805) and in other *Romantic poetry.

GREG, W.W., *Pastoral Poetry and Pastoral Drama*, A.H. Bullen, 1906.
LEVIN, H., *The Myth of the Golden Age in the Renaissance*, Indiana, 1969.
MARINELLI, P.V., *Pastoral*, Methuen, 1971.

**Pataphysics**. Mock philosophy of Alfred Jarry (1873–1907), a parody of logic, language and learning which he developed in his novel *Gestes et Opinions du Docteur Faustroll* (1911). It has been regarded as a primary source of the *theatre of the absurd, along with his early surrealistic play *Ubu Roi* (1888).

**Patent Theatres**. Drury Lane and Lincoln's Inn Fields were the two theatres to be given royal charters by Charles II on his restoration to the throne. Thomas Killigrew (1612–1683) and William D'Avenant (1606–1668) obtained by this means a virtual monopoly of serious, or *legitimate, drama and this monopoly was confirmed by the terms of the Licensing Act of 1737. Drury Lane and Covent

Garden (to which theatre the Lincoln's Inn patent passed via Dorset Garden in 1732) retained the patent until 1843. The London Theatre obtained a patent in 1766, valid only for the summer season.

The effect of such a monopoly meant a great restriction in the production of serious plays and an encouragement of spectacle, song and dance in the *illegitimate theatres.

**Pater Noster play.** John Wyclif (c.1330–84) is the first to refer to a Pater Noster play, of which a number were performed over a period of at least two hundred years in York, Lincoln and elsewhere. The texts disappeared during the period of suppression of religious drama after the dissolution of the monasteries (1537). We know from Wyclif's remarks that production of the York play lay in secular hands. A guild was founded to perpetuate the tradition 'for the health and amendment of the souls of the upholders as the hearers of it', as officials of the Guilds explained in a compotus roll in 1389. This document gives a general account which allows us to assume that the play dramatized the seven deadly sins and the seven petitions of the Lord's Prayer from 'hallowed be thy name' to 'deliver us from evil'. Its function was to assert and confirm basic Christian doctrine, and to represent them visually and orally for a non-literate community. It is related to the medieval *morality play in its emphasis on repentance and confession, and clearly anticipates the battle between the seven virtues and seven vices in *The Castle of Perseverance* (early fifteenth century).
POTTER, R., *The English Morality Play*, Routledge, 1975, pp.22–9.

**Pathos.** Greek for 'feeling' or 'suffering'; the quality in a work which arouses *pity or compassion. For Hegel (1770–1831) there were two kinds of pathos: 'objective' and 'subjective'. The first encourages activity and the second passivity. It is 'objective pity' which *epic and *political drama must appeal to if an audience is to be politicized.
HEGEL, G.W., *Aesthetik* (1832).

**Pause.** A temporary and deliberate halt in the *dialogue or dramatic flow. It concentrates attention on a character's facial or physical reaction and gives an audience time to reflect on what remains unsaid. It provides variety and *contrast, and acts as a form of relief whilst remaining intensely dramatic. Pauses and longer *silences need to be carefully orchestrated, and actors can pause too frequently. A pause also applies to the action as a whole. All the actors must have a reason for pausing, not just the actor who is speaking at that moment.

According to Peter Hall, when directing Harold Pinter 'A pause is a bridge where the audience think you are this side of the river;

then when you speak again you're the other side'. It reminds one of Edith Evans's view that a pause must be more interesting than the author's next line. Hall also distinguishes between different lengths of pause: 'Three dots is a very tiny hesitation, but it is there, and it is different from a semi-colon, and it is different from a comma.' See TIMING.

**Pedrolino**. *Commedia dell'Arte* servant figure and ancestor of *Pierrot.

**Peking Opera**. The traditional Chinese theatre based on Chinese legend, *myth and history. Besides orchestral music, *song and speech, it employs spectacular *dance and acrobatics in a highly formal and symbolic setting. Social rank and character are defined by colour: for example, red for high officials, black for suspicious characters, white make-up to indicate treachery, yellow to indicate strength, gold for immortals and grey for old men. Until recently, the cast was all-male with a little highly skilled female *impersonation. The Chinese and Cultural Revolutions, however, have brought about changes in this respect.

Its influence upon the West came mainly from tours of Europe and America by the Chinese actor Mei Lan Feng (1894–1961). Brecht's theories of *epic or *gestic acting cite his methods and example.

SCOTT, A.C., *The Classical Theatre of China*, Barnes and Noble, NY, 1957.

**Pembroke's Men**. Elizabethan acting company for which Shakespeare may have written in the early 1590s before joining the Lord *Chamberlain's Men.

CHAMBERS, E.K., *The Elizabethan Stage*, Vol. II, Oxford University Press, 1923.

**Penny gaff**. Cheap gaff or ramshackle nineteenth-century theatre specializing in *melodrama in poorer urban areas.

**'penny plain, twopence coloured.'** A phrase used to describe the sheets from which cut-outs were made for nineteenth-century toy theatres. (See JUVENILE DRAMA.)

**Pepper's ghost**. A device with mirrors, used in a number of nineteenth-century *melodramas to create the stage effect of a transparent ghost.

**Performance art**. Form of fine art which employs live actors, dancers, lighting etc. in a variety of ways to create striking visual effects. It is a kind of rebellion against the stillness of paint.

GOLDBERG, R.L., *Performance. Live Art 1909 to the Present*, Thames and Hudson, 1979.

**Performance Group**. Name of Richard Schechner's *environmental theatre group.

**Periaktoi**. Triangular prisms bearing scene painting on each of their three sides so that scenes could be changed by revolving them. Vitruvius's *De Architectura* (first century B.C.) describes the device as used in the *Roman theatre. After Vitruvius's treatise was published again in 1511, Italian Renaissance architects began to use periaktoi as *wings, placing them *stage left and *right behind one another. Additional panels could also be placed on the sides hidden from the audience to increase the number of scenes. Inigo Jones (1573–1652) brought the device to England and used it in his *masques. (See TELARI.)

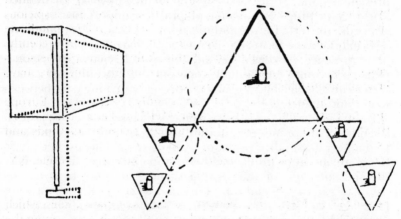

**18** *Italian use of periaktoi. Sometimes as many as six of these prisms were used on each side, with a larger one at the back; here we see a simple arrangement recorded in 1583 (from Sabbatini,* Practica di fabricar Scene e Machine ne' Teatri*)*

**Period**. Convenient but arbitrary division of historical time whereby cultural historians give shape to the past and define the patterns they believe exist in it.

**Peripeteia**. An unexpected *reversal of fortune. A term used by Aristotle (384–322 B.C.) in his *Poetics*. It is an important element in the tragic *fable, and usually, but not always, implies a change in the *hero's situation from prosperity to adversity. Its dramatic effectiveness, says Aristotle, is highest when the reversal coincides with *anagnorisis, such as Oedipus's *recognition in *Oedipus Rex* (c.430 B.C.) of the truth about his parenthood. In this famous instance, the expectations of both Oedipus and the *messenger are reversed. The reversal of *fortune and the reversal of the character's ignorance combine in a painful revelation of the truth. As in *King Lear* (1605), the painful descent in fortune involves a painful growth of awareness. The reversal may thus be a simultaneous rise and fall.

When the audience is ignorant of the outcome, peripeteia also has the effect of *surprise. With an audience which is aware of both the situation and the hero's ignorance, as in *Oedipus Rex*, peripeteia constitutes a complex *dramatic irony.

**Peroration**. Technically, the conclusion of a speech; more generally a highly rhetorical and exhortatory utterance without the quieter introductory passages on which a speech normally builds. See RHETORIC; SPEECH.

**Persona**. Jungian term for the face or mask a human being presents to the world. 'To present an unequivocal face to the world,' says Jung, 'is a matter of practical importance.' Literary critics use the term for the author's presence in a work of literature. This may take the form of a *character or *narrator, but it may also be a presence perceived behind the overall *narrative. Such a persona becomes increasingly apparent the more the narrator is seen as unreliable. The persona is a presence inviting trust between writer and reader.

Drama generally lacks the personae which seem most reliable in the novel. Author and narrator are usually missing. We sometimes find a narrator in the *prologue, *epilogue or *chorus, but where these are absent or unreliable the persona must be constructed by the spectator out of the *conflicts and *contrasts between the characters of a play and out of a general feeling that *this* style of language, *this* structural pattern is that of an *individual and trustworthy author. Of course, the identification of a persona in drama is made even more difficult by the mediation of the actors and director. Their interpretations tend further to conceal the authorial presence.

However, authorial personae may still be said to exist. In Pirandello's *Six Characters in Search of an Author* (1921) one character, the Father, seems to speak with more of the author's authority than the others, although other characters, especially the Daughter, with her conflicting view of the Father, prevent any full confidence being placed in what the Father says. It is out of the conflicts between the Father and the Daughter, and out of the style, method and general concerns of the play that the spectator constructs the persona.

Audiences seem to need such a persona even though it is impossible to determine how far it is reliable. An author reconstructs his own persona constantly; the spectator partly invents it; general historical and linguistic processes may be said to produce it; directors, actors and designers (although their intent may be to render what is 'there' in the text) complicate the author/spectator relationship by their own creative contributions. Impressions of authorial persona thus vary with performance.

JUNG, C.G., *Selected Writings*, ed. A. Storr, Fontana, 1983, pp.93–103.

**Personification**. (a) A figure of speech which attributes human qualities to animals, plants, natural forces, abstract qualities and so on. (b) The representation of such things by human beings on a stage.

The two processes are related but opposed, since in the first the non-human is humanized and in the second the human pretends to be non-human. Both processes, however, raise questions about the close link between man and the natural world, and remind us that drama may have originated out of *choruses dressed as animals. The personification in medieval plays of angels, devils, virtues and vices, not to mention the personification of Lion, Wall, and Moonshine in Shakespeare's *A Midsummer Night's Dream* (1595), raises questions about the *grotesque, the functions of *play and *games, and the nature of human *identity. Shakespeare's play is about *fear of the natural or supernatural forces in the forest, as they exist inside or outside ourselves. Personification, especially *comic personification, may be a way of controlling this threat to identity.

**Perspective**. The art of depicting objects on a flat surface to give these objects a three-dimensional appearance when viewed from a fixed point.

The use of perspective was dominant in *scenic design, from the publication of Serlio's *Architettura* (1545) to the brilliant use made of it by the Bibiena family (1680–1780) and by Philip de Loutherbourg (1740–1812) at Drury Lane. Scenic perspective had a number of effects on the construction of *stage and *auditorium. It placed emphasis on the pictorial scene, on spectacle, *colour and *costume, rather than on the physical *movement and grouping of a company of players (as in open-air theatre or on Shakespeare's *apron stage). The playhouse needed a frame, or *proscenium arch, and since pictorial designs on flat surfaces could best be appreciated from the front, seats began to be placed in straight lines, on one side of the stage only. This encouraged the building of rectangular theatres in which, unlike *arena theatres, some members of the audience were near the stage and others could be very distant. Perspective design thus changed the *actor/audience relationship and created special problems for the actor.

The term 'perspective' is also used to mean *viewpoint or visual angle. The most interesting consideration here lies in the way a dramatic perspective can change or shift — as when a *film cuts from one camera shot to another. In the theatre, of course, a spectator cannot suddenly change his actual angle of vision, but viewpoint can be intellectual as well as visual and a sudden shift in

**19** *Perspective scene for tragedy from Serlio's famous* Architettura *of 1545*

the way a character or situation is *mentally* perceived has been part of theatrical practice since the Greeks. It is a stock-in-trade of Chekhov (1860–1904), for example, and when Bertold Brecht (1898–1956) developed his *epic theatre he experimented further with a *montage technique, most obviously in the *Life of Galileo* (1937–39). In this play he placed his characters in a multiple perspective, showing different aspects of Galileo in successive scenes. The Jacobean theatre also employed 'double perspectives', a term for a pictorial scene which changed dramatically when viewed from different angles (the figure of Venus might become the figure of Death when the spectator changed position). Theatrical effects of this kind are achieved in Webster's *The Duchess of Malfi* (1614), in Middleton's *The Changeling* (1621) and in Shakespeare's *Othello* (1604) and *Troilus and Cressida* (1601–2). In all of these plays a double image of woman as either angel or beast is fixed within the characters' psychological make-up.

EWBANK, I.-S., 'Double Perspective in the Jacobean Theatre'.

SERLIO, S., *Tutte l'opere d'architettura e prospettiva, Il secondo libro,* (1545).

SOUTHERN, R., *Changeable Scenery: its origin and development in the British Theatre, Faber, 1952.*

**Petrushka**. Russian *puppet figure, descended from the *Commedia dell'Arte* Pulcinella.

**Phallus**. Enlarged representation of male genitalia, worn traditionally by comic actors in Greek and Roman times, and even by *Pantaloon in the earlier *Commedia dell'Arte*. The practice suggests that the origins of *comedy lie in forms of fertility *ritual.

**Phatic communion**. Malinowski's term for language which, rather than communicating ideas, acknowledges or establishes a basis for a relationship. Observations on the weather, or such phrases as 'How do you do?', fall into this category.

As dramatic *dialogue, phatic communion might be thought to have no value. Recent theatre, however, especially the so-called *theatre of the absurd, has called attention to the process. By imposing a dramatic *tempo, and punctuating apparently commonplace language with *pauses and *silences, Samuel Beckett (1906–   ), Harold Pinter (1930–   ) and Ionesco (1912–   ), for example, have made a kind of poetry out of phatic communion. Placing this language in dramatic *focus causes the listener to seek what lies behind it. The effect can be an ironic and strangely moving *tragi-comedy. See Harold Pinter's revue sketch *Last to Go* (1959).

**Phlyax**. Kind of play which flourished in the Greek colonies in southern Italy in the fourth century B.C. The evidence of vase paintings indicates that it involved *mime, *burlesque of classical Greek *tragedy and the enactment of comic scenes from everyday life.

**Phobia**. An irrational and obsessive *fear of an object which is a symbolic substitute for some real and more threatening cause. Fear, of course, with *pity, is the emotion Aristotle identified as inducing the tragic *catharsis. Phobia, however, perhaps since it seems excessive and absurd to the outsider, frequently receives comic treatment, as in Molière's *Le Malade Imaginaire* (1673). Molière's play deals with the common phobia of hypochondria and provides support for the theory of Henri Bergson (1859–1941) that comedy is concerned with human beings whose living impulses have become in some way *fixed*. The 'mechanical', he said, becomes 'encrusted upon the living'. Hypochondria may thus be seen as an unhealthy and mechanical reaction, which the comic spirit mocks.

A list of phobias, however, such as claustrophobia (fear of enclosed spaces), acrophobia (of heights), agoraphobia (of open spaces), nyctophobia (of the night), pathophobia (of disease), microphobia (of insects), zoophobia (of animals) reveals a varying comic appeal. Fear of mice or ants (the large lady on the grand piano) may seem ridiculous and can be dealt with in *farce. The phobia of claustrophobia seems closer to us and it is therefore harder to laugh at. Pathophobia is perhaps too painful to be funny and invites tragic treatment. Sometimes, of course, a phobia can be *tragi-comic. In Pinter's *The Caretaker* (1960) the tramp Davies has an irrational fear of a disconnected gas-stove. It is *absurd, yet *pathos mingles with the comedy. The phobia is real and our laughter is uneasy. When tragic and comic responses come so close we enter the realm of Franz Kafka (1883–1924).

**Phoenix Society**. Society formed for the performance of neglected English drama, especially *Restoration and *Jacobean plays, of which it produced 26 during its lifetime (1919–1925).

**Piccolo Teatro della Cittá di Milano**. 'Little Theatre of the City of Milan'; important Italian theatre founded in 1947 and associated with the director Giorgio Strehler. It has toured extensively with various contemporary productions and a number of highly imaginative *revivals, including Strehler's famous *King Lear* (1972) which transformed the upper stage into a kind of marsh through which characters waded, from which they emerged, and on which as on a 'ship of fools' they were afloat at the height of the storm.

**Pickelhering**. An early *clown figure in seventeenth-century German comedy, popularized by the *English Comedians under Robert Browne, John Green and the player of Pickelhering, Robert Reynolds.

**Picture-frame stage**. Stage framed by a *proscenium arch. It focuses attention on scenic and *perspective effects, creates a *fourth wall and allows the use of a *curtain. See THEATRE OF ILLUSION; NATURALISM.

**20** *Pierrot (drawn by Maurice Sand, from his* **Masques et Bouffons** *1859)*

**Pierrot**. Character deriving from Pedrolino of the *Commedia dell'Arte*. He has remained popular in his various transformations. These range from the simple and awkward servant of the seventeenth-century *Comédie Italienne*, with his familiar loose, white garment, long sleeves, floppy hat and white face, to the pale and disappointed lover of the early nineteenth century then came the late nineteenth- and early twentieth-century seaside pierrot-troupes in which men and girls in dunces' caps and loose white and black costumes, with large ruffs and buttons, engaged in song and dance and various kinds of banter.

**Piscator, Erwin** (1893–1966). German Marxist theatre director who developed *epic theatre as a political weapon during the Weimar Republic.

> A proletarian state cannot adopt bourgeois art and the bourgeois mode of enjoying art.

> You often don't know whether you are in a theatre or a public meeting.

> What an imposition! Hundreds must hold their breath, just to allow one egocentric actor to air his soul!

See: POLITICAL THEATRE; VOLKSBÜHNE.
PISCATOR, E., *The Political Theatre* (1929), edited by H. Rorrison, Methuen, 1980.

**Pit**. Term for the area in older playhouses below the level of stage and ground floor boxes. The introduction of seats in the *stalls first pushed the pit backwards beneath the *circle, then replaced it altogether. The word derives from 'cock-pit'.

**Pity**. Since Aristotle (384–322 B.C.) stated in his *Poetics*: '*tragedy effects through pity and *fear the *catharsis of the emotions', the nature of pity has remained central to dramatic theory. The feeling is usually felt to imply strong *sympathy or compassion for the sufferings of others. Some critics stress, however, that sympathy is never complete and insist that pity, like *empathy, has an element of detachment. The novelist Joseph Conrad (1857–1924) even suggested it was a form of contempt. Most assume, however, that Aristotle implies a positive sympathetic feeling. James Joyce (1882–1941) takes it that way in *A Portrait of the Artist as a Young Man* (1914) when his character Stephen Dedalus declares: 'Pity unites us with the secret sufferer, terror with the secret cause.' Brecht's view, in *The Messingkauf Dialogues* (trs. 1965), is similar; he suggests that we identify with suffering and fear those who cause it:

> The ancients thought that the object of tragedy was to arouse pity and terror. That could still be a desirable object if pity were taken to mean pity for people, and terror, terror of people.

'For whom does one feel pity?' is a crucial question in *political theatre. Is it to be for an aristocratic, middle-class or working-class *hero, or for some universal representative of mankind? And does pity incite one to action, or is it a *substitute* for action? (Hegel defined two kinds of pity. See PATHOS.) Is it true that 'a little help is better than a lot of pity', as popular usage has it, or does pity actually encourage help? Some writers, including Joyce and I.A. Richards (1893–1979), argue that pity and terror are balancing opposites which create a cathartic and tranquillizing stasis. Joyce's Stephen Dedalus implies that this stasis is a 'pure' response, unlike that invoked by 'kinetic' writing, such as propaganda and pornography, which lead to action. Brecht, however, has a different view of the function of art and sees in pity a stimulus to activity. An awareness of suffering, together with the detachment which allows clear-sighted action, is what Brecht recommends if we are to change the pitiable situations in which people make other people suffer.

HENN, T.R., *The Harvest of Tragedy*, Methuen, 1956.

**Plague**. Usually implies bubonic plague or the 'Black Death', the contagious and agonizing disease which ravaged Europe in the fourteenth century and later.

In literature, plagues have been used as a basis for fiction and *allegory, notably in Defoe's *Journal of The Plague Year* (1722) and in Camus's *La Peste* (1948). Plague has also received dramatic treatment. In Sophocles's *Oedipus Rex* (c.430 B.C.) it is seen as the vengeance of the gods visited on the city of Thebes because of Oedipus's parricide and incest. In much other *tragedy, including Shakespeare's *Hamlet* (1601), there is a *leitmotif of hidden sickness for which plague is an apt analogy.

Antonin Artaud (1896–1948) devoted a whole chapter of his very influential *The Theatre and its Double* (1938) to the analogy between theatre and plague. The plague represents 'the conflicts, struggles and cataclysms' that life brings. It is also the latent cruelty within the individual which the theatre brings into *focus, and *foregrounds (or perhaps fore*stages*). Plague, says Artaud, acts upon individuals, as a 'contagious delirium' which transforms the sufferer's personality, and 'pushes towards extreme gestures'. In this it resembles the acting process.

Artaud thus sees the theatre as concentrating and localizing 'the perverse possibilities of the mind', mediating the great *myths ('all the great myths are black') and creating 'a sort of strange sun — an abnormal intensity in which the difficult and impossible become normal'. One play cited by Artaud is John Ford's *'Tis Pity She's a Whore* (1628), a drama involving both incest and murder. The theatre, then, mediates 'plague'. It also reacts against it. The theatre is prophylactic or *cathartic, and induces a 'redemptory epidemic', a purification through delirium, a 'crisis unknotted by death or healing'. Actor and audience are gripped by a gratuitous contagion which prompts the discovery of other personalities within the self. When acted out to extremes of intensity, the state resembles the delirium of the plague carrier infected by visions of hell. Such visions, Artaud argues, may be redemptory. There is in the theatre *une épidémie salvatrice* (a redemptory epidemic), acting on brain and lungs. The *crisis of play or illness, unknotted by death, embodies a kind of healing in which profound changes take place without destruction of the organs. Theatre, like the plague, is 'made for the collective draining of a huge moral and social abscess'.

Artaud's eloquent exposition won many converts, especially in the 1960s. *Happenings, as well as Peter Brook's *Marat/Sade* (1962) and *US* (1966) show his strong influence. Artaud's obvious debt to *Greek and Elizabethan tragedy, and his clear connections with *modernist thinkers and novelists such as Dostoievski (1821–1881), Nietzsche (1844–1900) and Thomas Mann (1875–1955) — all concerned with the creative aspects of disease — strengthened his appeal.

Artaud's opponents would, with Brecht, stress the importance of rational discourse and distancing. It is possible to see Artaud as a revolutionary seeking a form of demonic and explosive break-through. His opponents question whether this can create a basis on which discourse can begin. The impact of his theories on his contemporaries and successors is to a large extent due to his brilliant handling of unexpected and extended analogies. It is paradoxical, perhaps, that a theorist who wished to reduce the role of words in drama, and substitute for them a kind of total theatre, should owe such a profound debt to his own brilliant handling of the written language.

ESSLIN, M., *Artaud*, Fontana, 1976.

**Plant.** See POINTER.

**Platea.** Open space in front of the locus or *mansion of *medieval drama. Unlike the locus, which signified a particular locality such as Hell, Heaven, Jerusalem or the Temple, the platea was a space which the actor shared with the audience. (It was no doubt often the market-place.)

Moving from locus to platea established a different *actor/audience relationship and it may be argued that Shakespeare's *apron stage inherited this flexibility. In other words, actors could break through the *fourth wall, as it were, of an *upstage performance, to take the audience into their confidence *downstage. Shakespeare's *villains do this frequently. For a detailed treatment of the platea see:

WEIMANN, R., *Shakespeare and the Popular Dramatic Tradition*, Johns Hopkins University Press, 1978, pp.73–85.

**Platonism**. A belief in a transcendental reality which is 'more real' than the world we live in. Such a belief raises questions about the function of drama. If drama, as Plato suggested, is *mimesis, then what kind of reality does it imitate or mediate? And does the value of drama depend on the value of the world it chooses to portray?

**Platt**. Elizabethan term for a listing of events in a play, including *entrances and *exits, and *prop requirements. It existed for the use of the *prompter or *stage manager.

**Play**. Behaviour outside the sphere of use or material necessity; it obeys certain rules, normally in an established sequence, generating tension and excitement followed by *relaxation.

Play has a variety of functions which may clearly be seen in children's behaviour: (a) they learn how to use the body in physical *games; (b) they learn how to use words in language games; (c) they learn how to relate to others in social games; and (d) they learn how to discover and create the self in these and other forms of self-expression. Play is also a protest against adult social power (ringing doorbells and running away) and it can help to test and establish the limits of that power. Children's play is also a reflection of the way they see the world.

The idea that play has meaning is a relatively modern notion which has been with us since Jean-Jacques Rousseau (1712–78). He and subsequent writers, including Dickens (1812–70) in *Hard Times* (1854), argued that play has a positive value and does not merely undermine the Puritan ethic of hard work. ('He who plays as a child will play as a man,' said Charles Wesley disapprovingly.) As its origins indicate ('*illudere*' in Latin means 'play within'), play and drama allow one to 'play inside' a set of rules which enable various forms of learning. These have a civilizing function, and the scholar J. Huizinga has even claimed: 'A civilization does not come from play. It arises in and as play and never leaves it!' To this statement creative artists bear witness. When Ingmar Bergman (1918–   ) speaks of making a film he asserts: 'It's a game like everything else. When we get together to make a film, I have the feeling I had as a child when I took my toys out of the cupboard. It is exactly the same thing'.

Such play generates high excitement. It is a form of discovery, the recreation of life or the creation of something which has not previously existed. It generates a sense of freedom and power and we are tempted to assign to it a very high value. One should mention, however, that drama has in the twentieth century frequently examined the nature of its own processes and has taken a sardonic view of them. Beckett (1906– ) in particular creates dramatic characters who play to escape the non-play world. In a world in which, as a Bergman character in *The Silence* (1960) asserts, we are in the grip of political and natural forces which we cannot control, it may be that the invention of a play-world which we *are* able to control is a necessary form of therapy.

COURTNEY, R., *Play, Drama and Thought*, Cassell, 1974.
HUIZINGA, J., *Homo Ludens*, Routledge, 1949.

**Playbill**. Single sheet detailing the evening's entertainment in the theatre. It can be used as a *poster, unlike the modern theatre programme which generally carries advertisements and information about actors in the form of a booklet.

**Play within a play**. Performance which characters on stage put on for other characters. In a sense, whenever one character conceals something from another, and pretends to be other than what he 'is', there is an element of play within the play. Iago's pretence of honesty in Shakespeare' *Othello* (1604) is an obvious example. The expression normally refers, however, to acknowledged *roleplay within a brief and separate dramatic structure. This normally takes up one scene in a whole play.

The play within a play was a frequent device in *Elizabethan and Jacobean theatre. It can be seen in Beaumont's *The Knight of the Burning Pestle* (1607), Middleton's *Women Beware Women* (1621) and in Shakespeare's *A Midsummer Night's Dream* (1595) and *Hamlet* (1601). More recent plays have staged 'rehearsals as a play within a play. Pinero does so in *Trelawny of the Wells* (1898), and in a more complex way, so does Pirandello in *Six Characters in Search of an Author* (1921). Tom Stoppard (1937– ) frequently uses the device.

One value of the device lies in its blurring of the division between *actor and audience. If actors sit down on stage to watch other actors, they become an extension of the audience and it is no longer clear that they are part of a fictional world. In addition, these spectators within the play can present the theatre audience with a mirror image which it may or may not recognize. Dramatic *irony may arise out of the audience's recognition that the *stage* audience does not at once recognize itself. This occurs in different ways in *Hamlet* and *A Midsummer Night's Dream*, where Claudius and Gertrude in the former, and the lovers in the latter, seem to be ignorant of what the play within the play implies. Claudius learns what Hamlet and the audience know; Gertrude does not. The lovers simply forget their experience in the wood when they laugh at Bottom's 'comical tragedy'.

The play within a play also allows for comment from the watching actors. Pirandello, for instance, is interested in discussing the way people play *roles in everyday life, and his characters frequently debate the relation between life and drama. Shakespeare uses the device in another way, when his character Hamlet shocks Claudius out of his *role as king. The device also draws the audience into the play by creating various levels of 'reality'. Several kinds of 'acting' are presented, from the exaggerated *dumbshow, to the stylized 'Mousetrap'; from the more natural but still ceremonious behaviour of king and court, to the unconventional, direct and apparently 'real' behaviour of Prince Hamlet. In this way different levels of language and reality are established and the audience associates with the level which seems most 'real'.

One should add that a play within the play is often a climactic scene. It makes a heavy demand on theatrical resources since it usually requires a large *cast. It also calls for careful *direction and control of *focus.

NELSON, R., *Play within the Play*, Yale University Press, 1958.

**Playwright**. Maker of plays. Some critics prefer the term to 'dramatist' because it places emphasis, like the terms 'shipwright', 'wheelwright' and 'ploughwright', on craftsmanship.

**Plot**. Causal *narrative sequence of events which forms the basis of a play. It normally involves a *hero faced by an *obstacle which he surmounts or fails to surmount.

Aristotle, in the *Poetics*, makes plot or *mythos the centre of his discussion of *tragedy. A plot, he says, has a *beginning, middle and end. It has a certain length and the events are all related. It produces an emotional effect which varies according to the chosen *form, *epic, *tragedy or *comedy. In tragedy this is a combination of *pity and *fear which leads to a *catharsis or purging of the emotions. To achieve this catharsis certain combinations of events are preferable to others. Reversals of *fortune, discoveries and *recognitions are particularly valuable, and Aristotle finds a model of the ideal plot or *action in Sophocles's *Oedipus Rex* (c.430 B.C.). (See PERIPETEIA; ANAGNORISIS.)

Aristotle's reflections in the *Poetics* formed the basis of most later dramatic theory. With the recent growth of the disciplines of anthropology, psychology and linguistics the study of plot and narrative has received considerable attention. Anthropological studies lie behind Northrop Frye's influential *Anatomy of Criticism* (1957) which defines four basic kinds of plot each relating to a different season. There are 'mythoi', he argues, of Spring and Autumn, which are opposites. The 'Spring plot' exhibits a comic pattern expressed as a movement from restriction to freedom, with love triumphant. In the Autumn mythos obstacles triumph, opponents gain revenge and reconciliations are for another world. The Summer plot is the opposite of Winter. It involves a quest, a perilous journey, a struggle and the exaltation of a *hero. The Winter quest is unsuccessful, with no escape from the situation except through death or madness. Frye's patterns thus assume that plot is derived from the natural year.

Others have seen plot, like Aristotle, in terms of the psychological satisfaction it affords to spectators. The Russian *formalist critic, Victor Shklovski, defines plots which have different movements: (a) from one relation between characters to its opposite; (b) from a prediction of *fear to a realization of that prediction; (c) from a problem to its solution; and (d) from a false accusation or misrepresentation to its rectification. He adds that the reader's need for a solution or closure may be satisfied by an *epilogue which differentiates itself from the main narrative by, say, presenting the hero ten years later or by closing with a description of the weather, 'inscribed as a parallel to the preceding story', which gives a feeling of completion.

The emphasis here on the satisfaction of the reader's needs points to the work of the French critic Roland Barthes (1915–70) who proposes what he calls a 'hermeneutic programme'. Plots, he argues, contain a 'statement' followed by 'stages of arrest'; the basis of the narrative sequence is first established and then the problems it poses are kept open in various ways. In the extraordinary *S/Z*, his work on Balzac's *Sarrasine*, Barthes divides the primary statement into: (a) 'thematization' (mentioning the object of an enigma); (b) 'position' (indicating the existence of an enigma); and (c) 'formulation' (making this explicit). The secondary 'phases of arrest' then hint that the problem is not insoluble; they open possible false trails, supply ambiguous explanations, offer an admission of defeat and apparent insolubility before the partial and then full *disclosure. Such a description, despite the terminology, does not seem too distant from Aristotle's analysis of the plot of *Oedipus Rex*. Nor does Aristotle's theory of *catharsis seem far from Barthes's conception of plot as the creation of a form of disturbance to which a solution is then offered.

Other theorists have viewed plot particularly in relation to the structures of language. The Russian linguist T. Todorov, for example, has used the parts of speech to define the various fictional elements. He identifies *character with proper nouns; adjectives are associated with the establishment of emotional states, moral properties and social and physical conditions; verbs modify situation, embodying the movement or the plot. More specifically, verbs express: (a) direct action; (b) obligation or necessity; (c) wish or desire; (d) condition ('if x then y'); and (e) a prediction. Such a pattern can easily be applied to the different movements of a dramatic action. Todorov's theory implies, since the verb has grammatical primacy in the sentence, that action or plot is, as Aristotle says, of primary importance to the play.

There have been a number of other attempts to provide basic models of plot forms. In 1895 G. Polti defined 36 dramatic situations. E. Souriau, in 1950, offered a *model of six dramatic functions in a book entitled *Two-hundred Thousand Dramatic Situations*. The plot involved: a force desiring action; the good desired; the one who benefits; the *obstacle; the judge; and finally the helper. To these Souriau gave the colourful names Lion, Sun, Earth, Mars, Scales, and Moon. W. Propp, in a book on the morphology of fiction, defined seven active forces or *'actants'* in seven spheres of dramatic action. These are the *hero and 'false hero' (who usurps the hero for a time); the 'sender' who sends the hero on a mission and the 'helper' who aids him; a *villain; a 'princess' who requires an exploit from the hero; and a 'giver' who provides a magic object. The French critic Julia Kristeva has developed a theory based on eight different linguistic structures. A.J. Greimas works from a 'four term homology' composed of: (a) movement in (b) time; and the (c) posing and (d) resolution of a problem. (See MODEL.)

An investigation of the nature of plot leads into an investigation of language, nature, the *dialectic of history and the relation between these and the human mind. Theorists are divided over which of these is primary, but whichever they choose they all tend to seek a unifying source behind the diversity of *narrative form. The fact that many plots have remarkable similarities suggests the existence of basic patterns. Whether their identification will explain how plots come to diversify is another matter. Dramatists of note tend to complicate and mix familiar patterns in their individual endeavour for *original expression. The search for basic plot patterns, whether they derive from historical, linguistic or natural processes, tends to assume that the writer is 'chosen' by these processes. Whilst this is evidently to some extent true, it is also possible that the writer himself has some freedom to choose.

BARTHES, R., *Image, Music, Text*, Fontana, 1977, pp.79–124.

OLSEN, E., 'The Elements of Drama and Plot', in *Perspectives in Drama*, edited by J. Calderwood, Oxford University Press, 1968.

**Plough Monday play**. Early festive play performed on the Monday after Epiphany. The fragments which remain show that the dramatic characters were farmworkers and that the main action involved the accidental death of one of them. There is a likely connection with the *mumming play.

CHAMBERS, E.K., *The English Folk Play*, Oxford University Press, 1933.

**Plug**. 'Plugging a line' means forcing it through the laughter of the audience in order to get an additional laugh which caps the preceding one. The more common slang usage, 'to plug a show' or 'put in a plug for it', means to refer to something in which one has an interest, for purposes of publicity.

**Poetic drama**. In one sense all drama is potentially poetic since it communicates strong feeling and emotion. Not all drama, however, uses highly figured language and a rhythmic verse line. *Comedy and *naturalistic drama in particular tend to use the common rhythms and language of everyday speech. Most serious drama, however, from *Greek tragedy to the *Sturm und Drang drama of Goethe (1749–1832) and Schiller (1759–1805) was written in poetic form. In the twentieth century a new *verse drama, developed in a reaction against naturalism, has provided us with a critical theory of the genre.

According to T.S. Eliot in his essay *Poetry and Drama* (1950), poetry can communicate states which it is not possible to deal with in prose drama. These Eliot defines as qualities 'which we can only detect . . . out of the corner of the eye and can never completely focus'. Poetic drama, he suggests, 'without losing that contact with the everyday world with which drama must come to terms', should approach 'the border of those feelings which only music can express.'

The use of a musical beat in the verse line is the basic distinction between prose and poetic drama and the function of music may be as Eliot says. However, other theorists, notably Bertolt Brecht (1898–1956) have maintained that a musical beat tends to induce a suspect communal state of receptivity. Brecht had no wish to encourage the loss of individual detachment which he witnessed in the 1920s during the rise of fascism. Other German theorists from Schopenhauer (1788–1860) to Nietzsche (1844–1900) and Thomas Mann (1875–1955) have emphasized the power of music. All drama is inherently musical in structure, whether or not it is written in verse. The comic tradition, however, to which Brecht is drawn, has a critical and ironic appeal which expresses itself in colloquial dialogue and prose.

There are thus two traditional tendencies which often merged in major drama. *Jacobean drama, for example, exists on the knife-edge between poetry and prose. Taking the Jacobeans as a model, Eliot sought for a flexible verse line which can be heard as prose but which underpins the more passionate poetic language natural to more intense dramatic situations. The opening scene of *The Cocktail Party* (1949) works in this way, beginning with light comedy and building to the powerful speech of the Stranger.

Brecht, on the other hand, sought to create a dramatic medium which would work in alternating 'blocks', using verse and music to cut across the prose scenes, without merging with them. Both Eliot and Brecht, however, were aware of the way the Jacobean drama created dramatic tensions out of different forms of speech, plotting poetry against prose, *tragedy against *comedy and *main-plot against *sub-plot, with a flexible blank verse which incorporates colloquial speech yet remains capable of high poetic expression. See:

ELIOT, T.S., *Selected Essays*, Faber and Faber, 1932, 3rd ed. 1951, pp.37–58.

**Pointer**. Oblique clue to the motivation of a character or the dynamics of a dramatic situation. Clues intensify an audience's awareness of *secrets and thus establish *dramatic irony and *suspense. A 'plant' is a clue placed well in advance of where it will be useful in making a scene plausible and effective; it is 'planted' for later recognition. A pointer, on the other hand, is liable to be recognized at once as a clue, rather than retrospectively. There is, however, no absolute distinction between the two. Any reader of 'whodunits' knows that the point at which such hints are picked up varies with each reader. The plays of Henrik Ibsen (1828–1906) are full of such obliquities.

MACGOWAN, K., *A Primer of Playwriting*, Doubleday, NY, 1962.

**Polichinelle**. A *puppet figure deriving from the Pulcinella of the *Commedia dell'Arte*. See PUNCH.

**Political theatre**. Drama which deals with public events and the historical process. In a sense all theatre is political because it arises out of relationships between an individual writer and a group of theatre workers within a social situation. The degree, however, to which the dramatist consciously analyses the social process, as opposed to mediating it in the play, varies considerably. One may distinguish between: (a) plays in which the political *ideology is obvious and deliberate, as when the drama directly attacks contemporary social attitudes and institutions; (b) political theatre which uses *allegory and *parable, inviting audiences to draw parallels between the *fable and the contemporary scene (the method Brecht normally adopted); and (c) forms of religious, 'private' and *'bourgeois' drama which are not normally seen as political, though they contain certain implicit assumptions, often of a conservative nature.

Overtly political theatre in the twentieth century usually reveals a strong Marxist influence. Its immediate origins are in the left-wing theatre of the Weimar Republic (1919–33) and the *epic theatre of Piscator (1893–1966) and Brecht (1898–1956). Their antecedents lie in the less obviously political *history and *chronicle tradition which goes back through Goethe (1749–1832) and Schiller (1759–1805) to Shakespeare and the Greeks. *Henry IV* Parts I and II (1597) and *Antony and Cleopatra* (1606–7), by Shakespeare, and the *Persians* (472 B.C.) of Aeschylus (525–456 B.C.) are early examples of political plays.

Many offshoots of Piscator and Brecht are to be found in American and British drama. They include the workers' theatre groups which grew up after the Wall Street Crash and Great Depression. In the last thirty years the political consciousness engendered by the nuclear bomb, the Suez crisis, the invasions of Hungary and Czechoslavakia and perhaps especially the Vietnam War have led writers and groups to make considerable use of *epic theatre. Brecht's use of song and episodic structure can be seen in British plays as different as John Arden's *Sergeant Musgrave's Dance* (1960) and David Hare's *Plenty* (1978). *Fringe groups frequently have political leanings and American *alternative theatre contains many radical theatre groups which aim to break down audience preconceptions about social behaviour. There are also more specifically political groups such as the San Francisco Mime Group which draws on the popular traditions of *circus, the *carnivalesque and the *Commedia dell'Arte* in open-air performances in the parks of San Francisco. The history of this group is instructive since it developed from a director-dominated group into a white collective, and then into a multi-racial company. (In 1980 it had seven white, five latin and three black members, playing equally to black, Mexican, white and mixed audiences.) Joan Holden, the principal script-writer for the company, declares: 'The basic theme of all our plays is the same: there is a class-system in this country that is not run in your interest. It is run in the interest of rich people and they fool you about your interest.'

Other American groups to have been influenced by the San Francisco Mime Group include the Chicano (American Indian and Spanish) farmworker group, El Teatro Campesino, which itself became a powerful influence under Luis Valdez (1940– ). See:

SHANK, T., *American Alternative Theatre*, Methuen, 1982, pp.50–91.
BULL, J., *New British Political Dramatists*, Methuen, 1984.
ITZIN, C., *Stages in the Revolution. Political Theatre in Britain since 1968*, Methuen, 1980.
KEYSSAR, H., *Feminist Theatre*, Macmillan, 1984.
PISCATOR, E., *The Political Theatre*, Eyre Methuen, 1980.

**Poor theatre**. A term associated with the Polish director Jerzy Grotowski (1933– ). It may be defined by its opposite, *'rich' theatre, which employs the technological resources of the theatre to create powerful effects of *light and *sound, using spectacular *costume, *make-up and *mask. Poor theatre, on the contrary, eliminates all technology and rejects the idea of theatre as *Gesamtkunstwerk or *total theatre — the synthesis of forms which Wagner (1813–83), Appia (1862–1928), Craig (1872–1966) and Artaud (1896–1948) all encouraged. Poor theatre is centred on the *actor, concentrating on the direct live involvement of actor and audience. It eliminates the barriers separating *stage and *auditorium. The actors play among the spectators, either with them or ignoring them, using the entire hall. They employ only stationary light sources and become themselves a source of light. The only masks are their own faces and they create a scene using nondescript costume, occasional *props and the resources of their own bodies and those of their fellow actors. The actor's *voice alone produces the 'music' of the drama, which is an orchestration of words and vocal sounds.

Grotowski worked in his 'laboratory' to develop the actors' physical, vocal and emotional resources, aiming to produce an immediacy of response in which 'impulse and action are concurrent'. In doing so he moved beyond the *naturalism which Stanislavski's *system encouraged, towards the realization of a stylized and ritualistic intensity. At a moment of shock or terror or joy, human beings, says Grotowski, do not behave 'naturally'; they use 'rhythmically articulated signs' and begin to dance and sing. 'A sign', asserted Grotowski, 'not a common gesture, is the elementary integer of expression for us.'

Grotowski's search for extreme moments drew him towards 'archaic situations' involving *taboo and *myth. Although living in the present century makes identification with myth difficult, myth must still be confronted 'in the attempt to put on its ill-fitting skin'. The confrontation of brutal situations, he suggests, enables the actor 'to touch an extraordinary intimate layer' when 'the life-mask cracks and falls away'. The exposure of this 'intimate layer' returns us to 'an experience of common human truth'.

Grotowski's ideas are reminiscent of those of Artaud, though he claims his own are based on different premisses. Critics see the influence of Nietzsche (1844–1900), Durkheim (1858–1917) and Jung (1875–1961). Grotowski claims, however, that his work is based on practice, on 'an articulation of the particular psychophysiology of the actor' and it is on the very close relation between the actor and director that he insists: 'The actor is reborn, not only as an actor, but as a man, and with him I am reborn.' Among English directors Peter Brook (1925–   ) has been strongly influenced by Grotowski.

GROTOWSKI, J., *Towards a Poor Theatre*, Methuen, 1969.

**Popular theatre**. The theatre of the common people. This can include: *folk plays such as the *mumming play; urban and mixed forms such as the nineteenth-century *melodrama and *music-hall; and *circus turns and various kinds of fairground and *street theatre. The term has been used disparagingly to imply a drama which is crude and undeveloped. Although it is true that popular theatre places strong emphasis on the *body* rather than the head, on physical activity rather than words and cerebration, this is not necessarily a limitation. Recent studies have treated popular theatre with respect, as a form made by the people *for* the people. Studies of the use made of popular festive forms by Shakespeare (1564–1616), notably in his *fool figures, and by Ben Jonson (1572–1637) have increased this respect, and the use of popular forms in modern *political theatre is considerable. One may cite the *fooling and *farce in Dario Fo's *Accidental Death of an Anarchist* (1969) or the serious analysis of popular *comedy in Trevor Griffiths's *Comedians* (1974).

Diverging views of popular theatre can clearly be seen in the debate over how the media, and *television in particular, serve the people. Does television debase its audience, or can it function as a sharp critical instrument? Trevor Griffiths's play demonstrates how popular theatre can do both.

BRADBY, D., JAMES, L., and SHARRATT, B., *Performance and Politics in Popular Drama*, Cambridge University Press, 1960.

BRADBY, D., and MCCORMICK, J., *People's Theatre*, Croom Helm, 1978.

MCGRATH, J., *A Good Night Out*, Methuen, 1981.

**Portable theatres**. Temporary stages erected at fairs and country wakes, in fields and market places, wherever *travelling players could find an audience. The name also applies to the whole company, its *properties and the theatrical fare it provided. Its repertoire may have been improvised *melodrama in the nineteenth-century 'fit-ups', Biblical stories and historical episodes in the days before permanent theatres, or acrobatics and *puppet shows in the fairground tradition. The name 'Portable' has been adopted by a well-known *fringe theatre company.

**Poster**. Bill originally hung on posts to advertise the evening's fare in the theatre. Posters varied in size, were often used as handbills or *playbills, and until the nineteenth century contained only lettering. French designers extended its attractiveness, however, and the work of Toulouse-Lautrec (1864–1901) confirmed the poster's status as an art form.

**Postponement**. A holding or temporary diminishing of *suspense. This is usually achieved by interpolating material which the audience does not expect. This relieves a created tension whilst allowing the subsequent *climax to build up again at a greater length and intensity. An obvious instance is Shakespeare's insertion of the Laertes farewell scene in *Hamlet* (Act I, scene iii) between Hamlet's being informed in Act I, scene ii that his father's Ghost 'walks' and his confrontation with it in Act I, scene iv.

**Post-structuralism**. See STRUCTURALISM.

**Posture**. The position of an actor's body on stage. Posture communicates many things: age or youth, athleticism or physical weakness, intense emotion or relaxed equilibrium, interest or boredom, resolution or weakness. Through posture, as through *facial expression, a silent actor continues to communicate even when others are speaking. By means of the *tableau, which is a *grouping of postures, directors can achieve a variety of effects, *comic and *tragic, which create a general mood and define individual character.

**Power**. The capacity to affect the world. This may derive from personal strength of character, social position, political or legal authority, or a combination of these. If drama is action, it must be about power. This normally takes the form of a competition of *wills, either in personal relations between people of the same or opposite sex, or between parent and child; in social relations between king and nobility, or between social classes; in political relations between countries or between imperial power and colony; between institution and institution, or between institution and individual. Shakespeare's *Antony and Cleopatra* (1606–7), for example, presents the relationship between a man and woman in love, each in positions of power, against a background of political ambition, civil war and conflict between rival powers. Drama may also be about 'aesthetic power', about the way people attempt to keep power over their own lives by *play, by creating fictional games which compensate for lack of power in the 'real world'.

Loss of power is a central dramatic theme, perhaps because we are jealous of those with power and rejoice in their fall. It may be that *pity is foremost in us when the *tragic or *comic hero struggles to control forces which threaten from without — the powers above, the gods, *fate, *chance, state power — or from within — illness, hunger, obsession, secret knowledge or sexual drive. As a character in Ingmar Bergman's film *Silence* (1960) declares, 'We are in the grip of forces . . . .'. (See CAUSALITY; PLAY.)

The struggle to control such forces raises questions of value. If human beings have any freedom to act, what principles do they act by? Can Might be reconciled with Right? Pascal asserted that 'instead of making Right mighty we have made Might right'. The conflict is a central dilemma in European tragedy but it found supreme expression in Sophocles's *Antigone* (*c*.441 B.C.).
DE JOUVENAL, B., *Power*, trs. J.F. Huntington, Beacon Press, 1962.

**Practice**. The methods employed by a writer, performer or other worker in the theatre. It is also a more specific Marxist *dialectical term; 'theatre practice' in this sense implies that drama is the 'product' of a social view and the 'transformation' of social relations.

**Praetexta**. *Fabula praetexta*; a Latin play based on Roman history or legend.

**Praxis**. Action; what a man *does*, as compared with *pathos, which is what happens to him. Aristotle, in the *Poetics*, defines praxis more widely to include pathos and the whole of a man's life. It may thus mean: 'the whole working out of a motive to its end in success or failure'. The critic Francis Fergusson has related it to Stanislavski's *superobjective.

**Pre-acting**. The preliminary performance in *mime of what is to ensue in speech. Thus the *dumb-show in *Hamlet* is the pre-acting of the famous 'Mousetrap' or *play within the play. In the drama of Shakespeare its function is debatable and complex. The critic Dover Wilson, in *What Happens in Hamlet* (1935), argues that this pre-acting prepares the audience for what is coming, and allows it to *focus on the characters' reactions to the 'Mousetrap' rather than on the Player King and Queen. Granville Barker (1877–1946), in his *Prefaces to Shakespeare* (third series, 1937), argues that pre-acting the scene is a double test of Claudius's nerve and is necessary to precipitate his loss of control.

More recently, Vsevolod Meyerhold (1874–1940) borrowed the device from the Chinese and Japanese theatres and used it to achieve what Bertolt Brecht (1898–1956) called *alienation effects. The 'actor tribune', as he calls the 'pre-actor', needs to convey to the spectator his attitude to the lines he is speaking and the situations he is enacting; he wants the spectator to react in a particular way to the action which is unfolding before him. Meyerhold saw pre-acting as a method of commenting on the political realities behind the dramatic situation. It was one of the methods, he says, which the theatre lost 'during the period of reaction when it slid into the quagmire of apolitical chit-chat.'
BRAUN, E. (ed.), *Meyerhold on Theatre*, Eyre Methuen, 1969.

**Presence**. The capacity of an actor to attract attention. A striking physical appearance, *relaxation, confidence, talent, animal magnetism, even the accidental possession of a bent nose, all contribute to the command of stage and audience exhibited by actors of presence. Further explanation is perhaps impossible. As Glenda Jackson said of Marlon Brando and Greta Garbo: 'That kind of talent is like an act of God'. See KING ACTOR.

**Presentational theatre**. Theatre which acknowledges the audience's presence and uses direct *audience address. It is to be contrasted with the *theatre of illusion. See FOURTH WALL.

**Pride**. Important in both *comedy and *tragedy, pride is an emotion which encourages characters to build their self-approval on their real or imagined achievements. A high self-estimate is potentially more dramatic than a low self-estimate since it leads to *action. It can also create blindness to outside opinion and a resentment or unawareness of social disapproval. This increases the shock of the dramatic collision.

As *hubris, the Greeks saw pride as a loss of a sense of inferiority to the gods: in *tragedy the gods punish this as they punished Oedipus. Hubris particularly menaces men in positions of *power, and Shakespeare's Othello and King Lear, who both take ideal views of themselves, leading to wrong action and suffering, suffer from it. In these characters, hubris takes the form of a loss of a sense of reality, of a capacity to see the self from the outside. It creates a powerful *dramatic irony in which an audience recognizes a character's ignorance of himself and of his situation, and experiences a painful kind of *sympathy.

Pride is also important in comedy. The vain or proud comic character is the object of laughter. 'Pride comes before a fall' is the recipe for much *knockabout comedy with ladders and buckets and banana skins. It also lies behind the more subtle psychological comedy of Malvolio's yellow stockings in *Twelfth Night* (1601).

Pride or self-approval, and the self-condemnatory emotion shame, have received far less attention from the critics than Aristotle's *catharsis of *pity and *fear. Pride, however, may also have its relevance to *catharsis, since the audience's self-recognition in a proud *hero may lead to a possible chastening of its own ignorance and pride. The analysis of pride in *Jacobean tragedy, where villainy is often associated with a lack of social recognition, is very important. A study of Dostoievski's heroes and *villains also helps to emphasize the importance of pride and shame, as does the study of other *existenialist writers such as Franz Kafka (1883–1924) and Jean-Paul Sartre (1905–80). Pride is the sin of Lucifer and forms of extreme pride can issue as madness and megalomania, just as low self-estimation can lead to forms of madness. Feelings of pride, however, seem to be more dramatic than those of shame in so far as they tend to action and encourage a projection, rather than a hiding, of self.

CAMPBELL, L.B., *Shakespeare's Heroes, Slaves of Passion*, Cambridge University Press, 1930.
JAMES, W., *Psychology*, Fawcett, 1963, Ch. 12.

**Prince Charles's Men.** Jacobean theatre company formed by the actor Edward Alleyn (1566–1626) in 1616.
BENTLEY, G.E., *The Jacobean and Caroline Stage*, Vols. I, II and VII, Oxford University Press, 1941–66.

**Prince Henry's Men.** New name for *the Lord Admiral's Men on the death of Queen Elizabeth in 1603. See G. BENTLEY, as above.

**Principal boy**. Main role for an actress in English *pantomime; examples include Aladdin and Prince Charming. See DAME; ROLE REVERSAL.

**Private theatres**. Indoor theatres such as *Blackfriars, St Paul's and, later, Whitefriars, which developed in competition with the Elizabethan *public theatres from about 1576. They were mainly used by *boy companies such as the Children of the Chapel Royal. The staging was probably similar to that of the open-air theatres, but the *auditorium was rectangular and smaller. Entrance costs were higher and the audience more select. The whole theatre was roofed and lit by artificial light so that more spectacular evening performances became possible.

The term also refers to theatres erected in private houses for amateur theatricals at such places as Blenheim Palace, Richmond House and Brandenburgh House. The vogue, which Jane Austen illustrates in *Mansfield Park* (1814), flourished in the houses of the English nobility during the later eighteenth and early nineteenth centuries.

GURR, A., *The Shakespearean Stage: 1574–1642*, Cambridge University Press, 1970.

**Proairetic**. Relating to the reader's interpretation of, and response to, *plot development. The term concerns the way in which audiences resolve events into a meaningful sequence, by applying their experience of theatrical conventions. It has so far been used mainly in semiotic literary analysis.

BARTHES, R., *S/Z*, trs. R. Miller, Cape, 1975.

**Problem play**. A play dealing with social problems, such as Shaw's *The Apple Cart* (1929) or Ibsen's *The Doll's House* (1879). The term is also used for several plays by Shakespeare which are difficult to assign to a genre, and whose handling of dramatic *conventions is puzzling. *Troilus and Cressida* (1601/2), *Measure for Measure* (1604) and *All's Well That Ends Well* (1603/4) have been so described, as have *Antony and Cleopatra* (1607/8) and even *Hamlet* (1601). The diversity of these demonstrates that 'problem play' is not a genre or form. What the plays seem to share is a jesting and sardonic awareness of dramatic convention and a denial of secure values.

SCHANZER, E., *The Problem Plays of Shakespeare: A Study of 'Julius Caesar', 'Measure for Measure' and 'Antony and Cleopatra'*, Routledge, 1963.

TILLYARD, E.M.W., *Shakespeare's Problem Plays*, Chatto, 1950.

**Producer**. A synonym in England for *director, now falling out of use. In the cinema the producer is responsible for the organization and financial side of film-making, whereas the director *makes* the film.

**Production**. A play which has been or is being produced. The term emphasizes the performance which emerges from the collaboration of *director, *designer, *actors, technicians and others.

**Professional players**. Late medieval term for actors who earned their living by performance. They are to be distinguished from the *amateur players who performed at New Year, spring and midsummer or harvest *festivals, who earned their livelihoods in other ways during the rest of the year.

There must have been professional actors before the establishment of the first permanent European theatres in the sixteenth century. The collapse of the Roman Empire released across Europe crowds of entertainers who travelled the countryside endeavouring to make a living. Their numbers were no doubt swollen in medieval times by actors in the Guild plays, the Herods and Christs and Lucifers, who could not bear to go back to ploughshare or loom. Such men formed groups of *travelling players 'with their apt houses of painted canvas and properties incident' and their 'sundry tragedies, plays, masques and sports'. Some of them attracted aristocratic patronage, finding a permanent base in the *Elizabethan theatre.

Professionalism, of course, means a relationship of economic dependence. Whoever pays the piper expects to call the tune and the professional theatre has always struggled with commercial and political pressures which do not beset the amateur. The Fool's lament in *King Lear* (1605) that the king will have him whipped for lying, his daughters for telling the truth, 'and sometimes I am whipped for holding my peace' still applies to professional groups not disposed to compromise with whoever can withdraw their livelihood or subsidy.

**Programme**. Playbill or booklet containing a *cast list, details of actors' careers and other information about a production. Copious advertisements and a high price offer a tempting source of extra revenue.

**Progress; progression**. A movement forward in time; the purely chronological sequence of events constituting a *plot. The terms can also apply to an improvement in quality or condition, as, for instance, in the *protagonist's fortunes.

Plays must progress in the first sense, but variations in *chronology, such as *flashbacks, are also possible and can achieve interesting effects, as in J.B. Priestley's *Time and the Conways* (1937). Interruptions of this kind are less easy in drama than in fiction due to the short time-span of a play and the need for a clear narrative line. In *naturalist theatre, practical problems also arise, since flashbacks require *make-up and *scene-changes which can interrupt the natural time-flow of the play. As regards the second sense of the term, a play's movement often oscillates between an improvement in fortune and a decline. A progression in fortune is unlikely to be dramatic unless it is threatened in some way. Equally, a simple decline in fortune lacks *conflict and *suspense unless the possibility of progression is suggested.

A play's *ideology has been said to depend on its 'progressive' form. J.-P. Sartre, for example, has criticized J.M. Barrie's *The Admirable Crichton* (1902) for confirming a *bourgeois social structure. Though it contains a disturbance of the normal relation between master and servant (the valet takes control in the second act) bourgeois order is restored by the play's end. The play, says Sartre, has a *beginning, middle and beginning. There is thus no progression, but a confirmation of the *status quo*, which is what the audience wants.

In a different way, the universal and recurrent patterns of *tragedy have been held to challenge the idea of progress and meaningful change. This is why left-wing theatre has aimed to use progressive and open-ended *epic forms which look to a better future and reject tragedy.

In practice, of course, a play will normally have both progressive and static elements. The *mystery plays, for example, envisage a blissful future for the saved, and hell for the damned, even though they assume a universal and static view of the human social condition. *Tragedy, though its heroes are caught in a deadly trap, often shows growth of human awareness, as in *Oedipus Rex* (*c*.430 B.C.) and *King Lear* (1605). The progression, nonetheless, is generally personal rather than social.

Aeschylus's *Oresteia* (458 B.C.) could be described as a progressive tragedy, since the old Gods are appeased and a future secured for Orestes and Athens. On the other hand, if it shows a transition between a matriarchal and a patriarchal society (as George Thomson argues) the play's *ideology can be challenged and its movement seen as change or even regression. Drama, however, cannot dispense with ideas of progress. The strong emotions of *fear and *hope are closely linked with images of the future, whether immediate or distant, and dramatic conflict arises out of attempts to avert or attain such images. Both high idealism and self-interest play their part in this.

For a Marxist view of the importance of progressive form see the *anti-Aristotelian ideas of Bertolt Brecht (1898–1956) in *The Short Organum for the Theatre* (1948), or the comments of Georg Lukács (1885–1971) on Samuel Beckett (1906–    ) in the opening chapter of *The Meaning of Contemporary Realism* (trs. 1963) or of Jean-Paul Sartre in his essay *Epic Theatre and Dramatic Theatre* (1960).

BURY, J.B., *The Idea of Progress*, Macmillan, London and NY, 1920.
GINSBERG, M., *The Idea of Progress: a Revaluation*, Methuen, 1953.

**Projection**. The use of the *voice to fill, but not overfill, a *space. It can take years of practice and exercise to achieve the *relaxation, lung capacity and breath control necessary for perfect projection. Actors must be heard by an audience even when they are pretending only to speak to one another. Edith Evans (1888–1976) used to imagine she was stringing her syllables on a thread, stretching from the tip of her front teeth to the back of the *gallery. The term also applies to the throwing of *light of different colours and intensities onto a stage by means of 'projectors'. A *movement or a *grouping can also be 'projected' by heightening the style of performance and creating a dramatic *focus.

BERRY, C., *Voice and the Actor*, Harrap, 1973.

**Proletcult Theatre**. Soviet theatre founded in Moscow in 1917 by Eisenstein (1898–1948), the film director, to educate the working class and serve the Russian Revolution. It became the Trades Unions Theatre in 1932.

PAUL, M.E. and C., *Proletarian Culture*, New Era, 1921.

THOMSON, B., *The Premature Revolution*, Weidenfeld, London, 1972.

**Prologue**. 'Foreword'; a speech which precedes the dramatic action, often spoken by a *narrator who reappears later in the play. In *Greek tragedy it at first implied the early action before the entry of the *chorus; Euripides (484–407/6 B.C.) then made this into a *monologue. The prologue seems to have been spoken by a master of ceremonies in *medieval drama. It was extensively employed by the *Elizabethans and retained by *neo-classical dramatists. *Naturalist drama does not employ the device but twentieth-century *epic and other forms of theatre have returned to it. The prologue's functions are various: it creates atmosphere, provides essential information and eases an audience into a play by creating a direct and intimate relationship between spectator and spectacle. The Chorus in *Henry V* (1599) is an example.

A prologue can also set up a false expectation. Note the ironic contrast between the warlike Prologue in Shakespeare's *Troilus and Cressida* (1602) and the tone and style of the opening scene, which begins:

Call here my varlet, I'll unarm again.
Why should I war without the walls of Troy,
Which find such bitter battle here within?

Properly speaking, the prologue stands outside the stage action and creates a feeling of omniscience since he or she already knows the ending. Characters can perform a similar function, and create more dramatic tension since they are caught up in the action of the play. The Watchman in Aeschylus's *Oresteia* (458 B.C.) is such a 'character prologue'. Modern writers have sought to incorporate the prologue into the play, while retaining his overall vision. The Stage Manager in Thornton Wilder's *Our Town* (1938), for example, links a disjointed action and looks back at the play from its own future. His function is to make the audience aware that the action of the play takes place in the past and not the present; a painful nostalgia arises from this distancing. A complex use of a semi-ignorant narrator/prologue/*epilogue is found in Tom Stoppard's *Travesties* (1974), where an old and unreliable character called Henry Carr comments on events in which he plays his younger self.

**Promenade performance**. A performance during which the audience, usually at specific points during the play's action, can move around. This requires very flexible staging. Some scenes can be presented in the *round, with the use of, say, medieval *mansions, or their equivalent. Other scenes can be spectacular and *end-staged. Others still may incorporate the use of a balcony round the *auditorium. Bill Bryden and Tony Harrison's *adaptation of *The Mystery Plays* at the Cottesloe Theatre (1985) was a particularly successful example of promenade methods. It offered intimacy, immediacy and scenic splendour, arousing in the audience a feeling of almost child-like wonderment at the theatrical game being played in its midst.

**Prompt book**. Copy of a play prepared for the *prompter.

**Prompter**. The man or woman, usually seated stage left, whose job is to whisper lines to actors who *dry. Prompters need to know the *rhythms and *pauses of a production, so as not to prompt unnecessarily, and will attend at least the final *rehearsals in order to grow accustomed to these. They may also be called upon to make quick decisions as to the best line to give when an actor has 'jumped' sections of text. On *open stages, where a prompter cannot be hidden, actors are often left to prompt one another.

**Pro-ode**. A *strophe without *anti-strophe which precedes a *choral ode in Greek drama. See EPODE.

**Property**. Usually shortened to 'prop'. Stage object necessary to the dramatic action — a gun, a decanter or a packet of cigarettes for example. Props have proliferated on stage since Stanislavski (1863–1938) and André Antoine (1858–1943) put a particular emphasis on social *realism. The handling of props helped actors achieve a natural, relaxed behaviour on stage, and this practice was subsequently developed in naturalistic *film acting. Stanislavski's influence on the *Actors' Studio and the *'method' school of acting can be seen in the work of Elia Kazan (1909–85) and the performances of Marlon Brando (1924–   ).

The encouragement of natural behaviour and the achievement of greater realism is not the only function of props. In nineteenth-century *farce a prop could take on a life of its own, as in *The Italian Straw Hat* by Labiche (1815–88) and in the films of Charles Chaplin. Props become a source of humour when they cease to be the tools of man and threaten to take over control. This happens in *circus clowning and in absurdist drama, perhaps especially in the plays of Ionesco (1912–    ).

The plays of Brecht (1898–1956) call for props related to *work and other physical activity. (Shifting props between scenes in *epic theatre can resemble a military operation.) The washing-line, the cannon, the Chaplain's axe as he chops wood violently (asserting he is a man of peace) 'speak' in *Mother Courage* (1941) more strongly than the normal stage object, and comment on the social situation. (See INDEX; OSTENSION.)

The properties in Beckett's plays, the handbag and parasol of Winnie in *Happy Days* (1961), for example, are also very important. They raise psychological questions concerning the nature of *play and the relationship between *time and consciousness. They 'prop up' *amour propre* and distract the characters from disquieting thoughts. The stage objects are few and the audience of *Waiting for Godot* (1953) is likely to look at Lucky's hat, Pozzo's watch and Gogo's boots with more than usual attention. The characters clown with these stage props, focus attention on them and call up associations of, respectively, 'thinking caps', the passage of time and the journey of life.

Props play an important part in the stage *symbolism of naturalism, though the symbolic element is not made evident. The dead bird in Chekhov's *Seagull* (1896) is an instance. It needs to look *real* and not wooden or artificial if it is to function within the naturalistic illusion of the play. This is essential because the audience needs to see characters making a symbol out of the apparently real. The seagull is an *icon for an audience which is aware that it becomes a *symbol for the disturbed Nina: 'I'm a seagull' she says. The audience must be aware of the different ways in which the object can be seen. This is different from the direct use of caricatural props by Beckett and Brecht: the obviously artificial tree, the stagey moon in *Waiting for Godot*, the enormous bandolier which Peter Lorre wore in *Man Equals Man* (1926). Gogo's boots and the Chaplain's axe are more realistic, but within *absurd or *epic play structures the prop is *foregrounded as a theatrical object. In Chekhov the seagull must exist as a dead bird within a natural context.

Such an effect, one should add, is not always easy to achieve. Real dead seagulls would not make pleasant companions on a *long run, and a stock of them is not easy to procure. With dummies, as with stage babies, it is best to keep the audience at a distance, so that the artifice is not perceived. It was wise of Ibsen to keep his bird in *The Wild Duck* (1881) *offstage. In naturalist drama, the closer the audience the more realistic the prop needs to be.

Props are thus very important in recent drama and in the farce tradition. Different kinds of drama use props in different ways but they often provide a dramatic *focus bringing great interest to a performance and to the lines an actor delivers as he handles them.

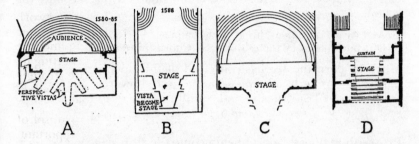

**21** *The evolution of the picture-frame stage, showing how the stage wall of the classic theatre became the modern proscenium arch. In the last the stage has retreated behind a proscenium arch and curtain*

a. *Vicenza 1580–85*
b. *Sapionetta 1588*

c. *Inigo Jones design about 1610*
d. *Parma 1618–19*

**Proscenium arch.** Permanent or temporary structure framing the stage. It was brought to England from Italy by Inigo Jones (1573–1652), who erected such an arch for his court *masques. *The proscenium arch has come to be associated with *naturalistic, *fourth wall plays, in which arch and *curtain separate the *auditorium from the acting area. This constitutes an imaginary barrier behind which the actors can pretend that no audience is watching. The arch conceals curtain lines, *flies, and other stage machinery, thus promoting the illusion that the setting which it frames extends beyond the visible stage area. By clever use of *lighting, *scenery, *sound effect and *movement, actors and dramatists can create houses around a room or a whole countryside around a garden. The *farces of Feydeau (1862–1921) show particular expertise in this creation of imaginary *space.

The term probably originated in the Greek *proskenion, and the early practice of placing a framed picture behind the dramatic action. The Italians detached the frame from the picture, advancing it to gain powerful *perspective effects through the use of *wings and *borders. In *Restoration theatres the actors would perform on a *forestage in front of the picture, but gradually stage action retreated within the arch until, in nineteenth-century fourth-wall plays using the *box-set, the scene enclosed the action.

The proscenium arch has limitations: it restricts *sight-lines and may obstruct clear views from side or *gallery. A play seen from the front only has a two-dimensional effect, which produces problems of *masking; it also limits the kind and number of sets which can be built on stage (*film and *television can frame a more convincing naturalist picture). These limitations have encouraged a return to more flexible *open stages where an appeal can be made to an audience to create its own imaginary frame around the action:

> And let us, ciphers to this great accompt,
> On your imaginary forces work . . . (Chorus in *Henry V*).

Much modern theatre has conceived of this openness as drama's particular strength. The proscenium arch, however, continues to frame much of our theatre and constitutes one of its major forms. SOUTHERN, R., *Proscenium and Sight Lines*, Faber, 1964.

**Proscenium doors**. Doors opening onto the *forestage in *Restoration drama. As many as three doors on either side were found in front of the *proscenium arch. These were gradually reduced as *entrances were made from the *wings, then eliminated in the nineteenth century when actors began to enter from doors in a *box-set entirely behind the arch.

**Prose**. Form of written language, distinguished from poetry by the absence of regular metre, verse pattern and rhyme. It is normally the language of everyday usage and logical argument but it has its own rhythms and can convey powerful feeling. Poetic prose is not to be fully differentiated from poetry. See PROSE DRAMA.

**Prose drama**. Prose drama seems to have developed naturally out of the comic spirit and the desire to express through colloquial speech a kind of opposition to, or *parody of, the *ritual, *music and *dance of early religious and *poetic drama. This spirit was seen in the Tudor *interludes and it led into the rich and mixed forms of the *Jacobean period, thence into the *Restoration and eighteenth-century *comedy of manners and nineteenth-century *farce. *Verse was retained for *heroic tragedy and the late eighteenth- and early nineteenth-century drama inspired by Shakespeare and the *Sturm und Drang* movement. This evolved into a prose *melodrama. The natural medium for drama, ever since the *naturalist plays of Ibsen (1828–1906), has been prose.

Advocating a new *poetic drama in the twentieth century, T.S. Eliot (1888–1965) argued that there are forms of reality which prose cannot mediate. Prose drama, however, is not necessarily prosaic. The handling of dramatic situation, the *rhythm of performance, vivid *stage imagery and powerful *dialogue can create effective dramatic poetry, even when the dialogue is ostensibly in prose.

**Proskenion**. Term from classical Greek theatre whose meaning is somewhat unclear. It may refer to the wall of the *skene (scene building) erected at the edge of the *orchestra, or to the acting space in front of this.

BIEBER, M., *History of the Greek and Roman Theatre*, Oxford University Press, 1961.

**Protagonist**. Literally the 'first actor' in ancient Greek drama, as compared with the less important *deuteragonist and *tritagonist. According to tradition he was introduced by Thespis of Icaria in the sixth century B.C. It is likely that a singer in the narrative *chorus separated from the group and began to *impersonate a *character in the song. Quite possibly this was the leader of the *dithyramb and the original protagonist. In the classical drama of Aeschylus, Sophocles, and Euripides in the fifth century B.C. the protagonist played several *roles, using *masks and changes of *costume. Nowadays the term is applied to any major character.

**Protasis**. Greek for 'reaching forward'. Opening movement of a play which is followed by epitasis, catastasis and *catastrophe.

***Proverbe dramatique***. French dramatic form deriving from a parlour game resembling charades in which a story was enacted to illustrate a proverb which then had to be guessed. It evolved from brief sketches into such skilful *one-act plays as *On ne badine pas avec l'amour* (*Love is not to be trifled with*) by Alfred de Musset (1810–57).

**Proxemics**. Semiotic term for the study of the organization of *space.

HALL, T.F., *The Silent Language*, Doubleday, 1959; *The Hidden Dimension*, Doubleday, 1966.

**Psychodrama**. A psychotherapeutic method which encourages patients to improvise *roles in dramatic situations. The director of the process observes the way the patient reacts in order to gain an insight into his or her condition. The aim of psychodrama is also to reveal the patients to themselves. Thus it resembles theatre *workshop improvisations in which actors test their responses, often in extreme situations, in order to gain personal insight. Both processes need expert direction. Only the first is psychodrama proper, since it is not aimed at public performance.

CZAPOW, G. and C., *Psychodrama*, Proba Oceny, Warsaw, 1969.

MORENO, J.L., *Psychodrama*, Part I, Beacon House, NY, 1946; Part II, Beacon House, NY, 1959.

**Psychology**. The scientific study of the mind has an obvious relevance to drama. It may be applied to the study of individual dramatic characters; to dramatic relationships between characters; and to the behaviour of groups of characters. The pattern of relationships and the evolution of events in a play may be taken as indicative of the author's psychology or of the state of mind and attitudes of a broader cultural group, defined as, for example, 'male', *bourgeois, *Elizabethan, *Romantic. Other subjects for psychological study include variations in *audience reaction and relationships between audience and writer. Actors influenced by Stanislavski's methods sometimes apply *psychotechniques in order to prepare themselves for performance. Thus a further psychological concern is the relationship between the actor and his *role.

The psychological study of Shakespeare's Prince Hamlet may therefore take a number of forms. Hamlet the prince can be studied in his own right. He may also be seen as part of a relationship (formed with characters such as Ophelia, Gertrude and Laertes). He may be seen as an extension of Shakespeare, or as a representative 'Renaissance Man'; he can even be seen as a focus of cultural attitudes. Different dramatic and critical interpretations of Hamlet arguably throw more light on the psychology of actor, critic or audience, and on their cultural period and nationality, than on the Prince himself. Psychological approaches to a play are thus not limited to *character analysis but involve questions about the ways in which author, director, actor, text, performance and audience relate to their own time, to each other and to their past and future.

**Psychotechnique**. Stanislavski's term for 'the inner work of the actor upon himself'. It is a principal element in a system which demanded also 'the outer work of an actor upon himself' and 'the inner and outer work of an actor upon his role'. Stanislavski (1863–1938) aimed to create, by methods involving the *magic if, *circle of attention, *emotion memory and *superobjective, a creative and relaxed *concentration in which the actor could call on his own unconscious processes, and play a part with utter conviction, night after night.

STANISLAVSKI, C., *An Actor Prepares*, Theatre Arts, NY, 1936.

**Public theatres**. A name for the *open-air theatres of Shakespeare's day, as compared with the smaller *private theatres, such as the *Blackfriars.

**Puff**. To overpraise in the manner of Sheridan's Mr Puff in *The Critic* (1779). The term suggests a deliberate favouring by a literary coterie of its members' own work.

**Pulcinella**. Rough, hump-backed, comic servant in the *Commedia dell'Arte*; the ancester of *Punch.

**Pulitzer Prize for Drama**. Prestigious American drama prize, first awarded in 1918.

**Pun**. See AMBIGUITY.

**Punch**. Famous bullying *puppet, descendent of the *Commedia dell'Arte *Pulcinella. He was noted by Samuel Pepys in 1662, and has appeared in puppet theatres ever since. He always exhibits aggressive traits, beating and killing his wife Judy and attacking all characters — Priest, Policeman, Doctor or Hangman — who try to correct his excesses. Frequently he is defeated, or carried off and eaten by the Crocodile or Devil, though sometimes he triumphs over all.

His popularity poses questions about the nature of *comedy. How far, for instance, does comedy appeal, as Enid Welsford suggested in her book *The Fool*, 'to the suppressed instincts of the bully'? Punch's bullying certainly makes an appeal. The appeal, however, may vary for children or adults, and men or women.

**Punch line**. Line of greatest dramatic impact, which needs to be delivered with careful *timing.

**Puppet**. Doll given the appearance of life by human manipulation. There are two principal types: (a) the marionette, to the head and limbs of which strings are attached, so that the puppet is worked from above; and (b) the glove puppet, such as *Punch, worked by placing a hand inside and moving head and arms with the thumb and first two fingers. Other forms may be worked by rods from below, or by machinery, like the ventriloquist's dummy.

**Puppet theatre**. An ancient form of theatre, going back at least to the very early shadow plays of India in which the principal figure was a tricky servant, always causing trouble for a rich master, and from whom *Harlequin, *Punch, the German *Hanswurst and the *Russian *Petrushka are probably descended. The central puppet figure is usually a kind of *Everyman with whose contradictory moods an audience finds it easy to identify. Frequently, of course, the audience is composed of children, and the characters seem to enact strong aggressions which invite *identification and rejection. Punch and the Crocodile are examples. The grotesque figures in the satirical *Spitting Image* television show invite, in a similar way, aggressive laughter. This seems to arise out of the humiliating reduction of authority figures to the status of manipulated puppets.

Puppet shows frequently have a *grotesque quality, deriving perhaps from the way a dead object can be made to live. This no doubt mixes with more attractive feelings: admiration for the skill of the puppeteer and perhaps sympathetic feelings for the less powerful puppet characters. Walt Disney works in this way, in, say, *Bambi* or *Pinocchio*. Here again, however, threatening elements are always present and they seem to have a primitive and continuing appeal.

**Purgation**. See CATHARSIS.

**Purim plays**. Short improvised plays incorporating song and *dance. They seem to have arisen in medieval times, at the Jewish festival of Purim, and originally represented events in the Book of Esther. The plays spread across Europe, taking in other Biblical stories and comedic *folk elements, remaining popular in the Yiddish communities of eastern Europe until the twentieth century. The plays deal with battles a man can win with God's help against great odds.

**Puritanism**. Religious movement which became a serious social force under Queen Elizabeth I. As it spread amongst those who felt the Anglican reformation had not gone far enough, a moral fervour and sabbatarianism developed which directed itself against all lapses from standards of behaviour adopted by the Children of Israel. Inevitably the theatre became an object of disapproval, and a conflict began which ended with the closure of the theatres in 1642, under the Commonwealth (1640–60).

# Q

**Quart d'heure**. (French for 'quarter of an hour'.) Short French play used as a *curtain-raiser.

**Quarto**. An edition of a play, printed on bound sheets, each folded twice to form four leaves and eight pages. Half of Shakespeare's plays were printed in this way. 'First quarto' and 'second quarto' indicate successive editions of the same play. See FOLIO.

**Queen Anne's Men**. Theatre company formed on the accession of James I in 1603 and named after the new queen.
BENTLEY, G.E., *The Jacobean and Caroline Stage*, Vols. I, II and VII, Oxford University Press, 1941–66.

**Queen of Bohemia's Men**. Little known Jacobean theatre company, formed in 1628. (See BENTLEY, G.E. above.)

**Queen Elizabeth's Men**. Elizabethan theatre company (1583–94) associated especially with Richard Tarleton (?–1588), the famous *clown.

**Queen Henrietta's Men**. Jacobean theatre company formed in 1625 by Christopher Beeston (?1570–1638), known generally as 'the Queen's Men' after Charles I's queen. (See BENTLEY, G.E., above.)

**Quem quaeritis**. Latin for 'Whom do you seek?' These are the words addressed to the Three Marys in the dramatic *trope which elaborates the Easter *liturgy and is generally thought to be the starting-point of medieval *religious drama.

**Quid pro quo**. The deliberate, fraudulent or accidental substitution of one thing for another. It is a frequent source of *comedy. In Tom Stoppard's *Travesties* (1974) there is a quid pro quo in which manuscripts by James Joyce and Lenin are accidentally exchanged. The play deliberately borrows a more famous quid pro quo – that of the absent-minded Miss Prism in Oscar Wilde's *The Importance of Being Earnest* (1895), who placed a manuscript in a perambulator and a baby in a handbag.

**Quotation**. The extraction of a text from one context to place it in another, thus *foregrounding it. This is a deliberate technique with

Samuel Beckett (1906– ) who incorporates half-quotation or misquotation into the *dialogue: 'The sun will set, the moon will rise and we away from here' says Didi. Pozzo is crying for help, like Marlowe's Dr Faustus from whose final speech the first half of this line is taken. Beckett substitutes a weak ending 'we away from here' for Marlowe's 'And Faustus will be damned'. The omission of the words may be *parapraxis. Didi does not want to think of damnation and so forgets the reference. It more obviously constitutes a direct invitation to the audience to fill in the *sub-text and relate the quote to earlier discussions of salvation in the play. The dialogue creates many such tempting echoes. Another is Didi's half-remembered quote: '"Hope deferred maketh the something sick," who said that?' The omitted half of the quotation is also particularly relevant to the play: 'but when the desire cometh, it is a tree of life'. The fact that the characters perform in front of an apparently dead tree gives the implied words a powerful dramatic *irony. Few writers use quotations with the subtlety of Beckett. Tom Stoppard (1937– ) makes clever but more overt use of the device.

The term is sometimes used pejoratively for an unconscious or deliberate 'lifting' of someone else's work, as when a writer borrows some other writer's style or an actor from another actor's interpretation. Antony Sher, playing Shakespeare's Richard III, has said that he was particularly anxious not to 'quote' from Olivier's famous film version.

Quotation may also be a form of *burlesque, as when Shakespeare mocks Marlowe and Elizabethan *rhetoric by giving alliterated lines to a comic character such as Pistol in *Henry IV* and *V* (1597–9).

# R

**Radio drama.** Non-visual form of drama using *voice and *sound effect. It involves no changes of heavy *scenery, no *blocking or *movement and no *costume or *lighting. *Lines need not be learned by heart, characters' thought processes can be rendered very easily and *narrative can be mingled with *dialogue as in a *novel. The medium, in short, is extremely flexible and the production process relatively simple. To write and perform radio drama, however, is not easy. Nuances of feeling, the social register, changes of location and a sense of *space must be communicated by sound and tone of voice. Banality and looseness in the writing is at once apparent, and the listener must be clear about who is speaking, where and at what time. There is much fine writing in the medium, as is shown by the work of Louis MacNeice (1907–63), Dylan Thomas (1914–53) and Samuel Beckett (1906– ). The relative simplicity of the medium is perhaps the reason why it has less prestige than theatre or *film. But it has great potential, especially perhaps for *poetic drama, as Thomas and MacNeice have shown. T.S. Eliot's famous poem, *The Waste Land* (1922), is a 'play for voices', and thus a kind of radio play. Major contributions to radio drama include Dylan Thomas's *Under Milk Wood* (1954) and Samuel Beckett's *All That Fall* (1957). See:
ARNHEIM, R., *Film as Art*, University of California Press, 1957, pp. 214–27.
*Radio Plays* (New English Dramatists 12), introduction by I. Wardle, Penguin, 1968.

**Rain machine.** *Sound effect device consisting of a drum filled with dried peas or beans which gives the effect, when rotated, of rain-drops falling.

**Raisonneur.** *Ideal spectator; a detached character who presents a point of view close to the author's own.

**Rake.** Slope, either of the stage or of the *auditorium. The terms *upstage and *downstage derive from the practice of raking the stage upwards from the front edge in order to enhance the illusions of *perspective scenery. It was first developed by Renaissance designers such as Sebastiano Serlio (1479–1554) and Vincenzo Scamozzi (1552–1616).
   A steeply raked auditorium can establish an intimacy between actor and audience. The steepness of the rake will also determine

how much of the audience will be above the action. This affects decisions about *grouping and *movement.

**Raking piece.** A *groundrow used to conceal the *rake on a stage.

**Range.** The variety of *roles within an actor's compass. The limits are imposed by age, sex, quality of *voice, general physical appearance and quality of personality, and so on. The range of roles actors are offered may be narrower than their actual range. This can occur because success in a particular role type-casts an actor. Antony Perkins's success in Hitchcock's film *Psycho*, for example, has perhaps prevented a fine actor from exploring his full range and potential.

**Reading.** A particular *interpretration given by an actor in performance.

**Realism.** The *mimesis of 'reality'. Men's assumptions about the nature of the real, and their attempts in art to represent that reality, have changed considerably from age to age and from culture to culture. Art which aspires to mimesis changes as concepts of reality change. Reality may be taken as the concrete world we perceive in *time and *space around us. Alternatively, we may take the reality of consciousness as central — a subjectivity which exists and yet is not to be weighed and measured. Again, transcendental essences may be conceived of, which exist beyond space and time, like Plato's ideal forms and Christian or other conceptions of a godhead. Some have taken 'the real' to be a *dialectical or other view of the processes of historical change, while others have viewed nothingness as the ultimate reality. ('Nothing is more real than nothing' is Beckett's favourite aphorism.) A popular recent view places a central emphasis on language, since it embodies the 'real' and is seen as the central organizing principle of the mind.

Different assumptions about 'reality' determine the kind of 'realism' a dramatist embraces. These range from extreme *naturalism which is concerned to render in detail the surface of life, to a 'critical realism' which presents a *model of the world, to more stylized or highly simplified forms of realism. The terms 'naturalism' and 'realism' cause confusion and are often used interchangeably. A useful way of separating them is to see naturalism as one *kind* of realism. According to Bertolt Brecht (1898–1956) naturalists see objects differently and less analytically than realists. 'The naturalists depict men as if they were showing a tree to a passer-by. The realists depict men as if they were showing it to a gardener.' Brecht's form of realism acknowledges the unreality of theatre and seeks to define how things *grow* rather than what they look like.

The naturalist attempts the illusion of full imitation.

These categories are helpful, but important drama cannot easily be assigned to a single category. 'Realism' today usually implies the form which grew up in opposition to the *Romantic movement and which aspired to present an accurate social picture of the time. It is represented by the novels of Balzac (1799–1850) and Zola (1840–1902), and emerged in drama in the *naturalism of Tolstoy (1828–1910), Hauptmann (1862–1946), Ibsen (1828–1906), Chekhov (1860–1904) and Strindberg (1849–1912). This tradition developed in the United States in the work of Arthur Miller (1915–   ) and Tennessee Williams (1911–83). The realism of such writers, however, cannot be taken as a mere representation of the material surfaces of life. They may emphasize the concrete world, but they invoke psychological, historical and, in the case of Strindberg, religious principles which compete as realities with the material world and generally form a source of dramatic tension. Their 'realism' may thus be seen as a competition between possible 'realities'. Ibsen, for example, presents recognizable people living in a particular place, speaking the language and wearing the clothes of a particular time. Yet the characters are dominated by *images of the past or future which compete with, and often repudiate, the present. The present is what is real, but the past is also real within them.

Ibsen's characters are produced by 'real' historical processes; a social causality lies behind the surface picture. By showing characters caught in a causal process, Ibsen's plays raise questions about the possibility of freedom. This is a 'reality' audiences find hard to abandon, since without freedom there is no responsibility. Fatalistic plays project the possibility of the reality of freedom even as they apparently deny it. Ibsen's *Ghosts* (1881) shows characters who are in a trap. It is possible, however, that they have in part created the trap themselves. The dramatic conflict depends on the spectator's inveterate wish to see them establish some control. A belief in freedom is thus a reality to which plays make appeal. Absolute freedom, on the other hand, is a romantic concept, a *dream which the plays sardonically attack. Ibsen's realism distinguishes between dreams and the real. The plays respect the world of here and now, and counsel wariness of dreams — however real they may seem to the individual.

Perhaps one may say that the various realisms of the past share this wariness. Scepticism of a dominant ideal, whether in Euripides (480–406 B.C), in *Jacobean drama, in *naturalism or in the rise of the *novel, seems to be a common attribute. The classic study of realism, ranging from Homer to modern realists, emphasizing the 'everyday reality' of the life of Christ in modern culture, is by Auerbach. See:

AUERBACH, E., *Mimesis and the Representation of Reality in Western*

*Literature*, trs. W. Trask, Doubleday, 1953.
HEMMINGS, F.J. (ed), *The Age of Realism*, Harmondsworth, 1974.

**Reception.** The response of spectators or critics to a particular work. The analysis of the psychological and social determinants of this response, and in particular of the *codes and *conventions which a *text or a performance invokes, is termed 'reception theory'.

**Recognition.** A growth of awareness, often sudden, which takes place in a dramatic character, or in the spectator, or in both. The process can give rise to both *laughter and tears. In *comedy, the recognition of characteristic behaviour on stage — the gait of a policeman, the voice of a politician, the eccentric posture of a known personality — seems to afford a pleasure which is often expressed as laughter, perhaps especially because the spectator is aware of the skilful mimicry involved. Comedy seems to encourage recognition by isolating characteristics. To *focus on a phrase, an expression, a movement or an accent is to see them abstracted from the normal flow of living. Like a *freeze, this can produce a kind of delighted surprise.

On the other hand, the more critical use of the term relates to *tragedy and the *anagnorisis of Aristotle's *Poetics*. There it is defined as 'a movement from ignorance to awareness' and Aristotle cites as a model Oedipus's recognition of the truth that he had killed his father and married his mother. The process is painful, both for character and spectator, though perhaps for different reasons. The character is faced with the pain of *knowing*. The spectator already knows and recognizes that the character himself does not know the truth — and perhaps does not want to know. Nevertheless the spectator waits for the character to move from ignorance to awareness and he seems to share in anticipating the pain that comes with knowledge.

In tragedy the situation is generally too painful for this recognition to bring laughter. Possibly, however, it brings some solace. An audience which recognizes the ignorance of even the wisest of men (Oedipus defeated the Sphinx) may realize that ignorance is a general condition, and experience a kind of relief and perhaps even *catharsis.

A follower of Freud would no doubt argue that recognition of Oedipal impulses deep in the self is part of a *cure*. To bring our desires to light is to recognize and effect the catharsis or purgation. More recent theorists see the theatre as a place of cultural recognition, where we recognize our collective rather than our private selves.

Whatever the truth of this, recognition is a crucial part of the dramatic process. The expansion of consciousness it brings is an important source of pleasure, as the pain it brings, when we would have preferred not to know, is an important source of learning.

**Reconciliation.** A term promoted by Andrew Bradley, in his influential *Shakespearean Tragedy* (1904), to define the effect of the *tragic ending. The word implies that some form of healing takes place at the close of a tragedy which comforts the spectator. Certainly, this can occur. One character, for example, may be reconciled with another, as Lear is reconciled with Cordelia. Or the protagonist may be reconciled to his fate, as in Sophocles's *Oedipus Coloneus* (*c.* 406 B.C.), or with the gods, as in Aeschylus's *Oresteia* (458 B.C.), or with society, as in Euripides's *Philoctetes* (432 B.C.). No doubt the audience participates to some degree in this sense of reconciliation, which Bradley saw as a desired effect.

Reconciliation, however, has not been universally seen as the proper end of drama. Brecht (1896–1956), for example, attempted to create plays which would send a theatre audience back into the world unreconciled and active, because the world needs to be changed, and he saw reconciliation with 'the tragic condition' as a kind of quietism.

Comfort and reconciliation are not always dominant in the tragic ending, as when unanswered questions leave a certain sense of unease. The solace of Lear's lines to Cordelia, beginning 'We'll sing together like birds i'th' cage', and Horatio's 'Flights of angels sing thee to thy rest', must be balanced against the final spectacle of Lear unable to accept the cruelty of Cordelia's death, or against Hamlet's flat 'The rest is silence'. It is tempting to sentimentalize tragedy, and the term 'reconciliation' has religious suggestions which many tragedies implicitly deny. The reconciliation offered remains as a possibility and a longing. As such, like all utopias, it brings a kind of anguish. Perhaps that is why modern *tragi-comedy — Beckett's *Waiting for Godot* (1953) for example — both mocks the need and sympathizes with it.

**Red Bull.** London theatre, built early in the seventeenth century and used by *Queen Anne's Men and other companies.

**Rederijkers.** Members of the Flemish chambers of *rhetoric in the sixteenth century, who mounted open-air productions on stages which may have influenced the architecture of the *Elizabethan stage.

**Reflector lights.** Lamps or candles with mirrors behind them to intensify the light. They were first advocated by the Italian scenic designers, Serlio (1475–1554) and di Somi (1527–92).

**Regional drama.** Drama representative of, or identifiable with, a particular region. Such drama has long existed. *Atellan farce, *folk drama, *mystery plays such as the Chester, York and Wakefield cycles, and indeed any play produced at local festivals before the coming of the more centralized *professional theatre, are examples of drama with strong regional characteristics. These might be of style, as in the use of dialect or the wearing of characteristic local dress; alternatively the regionalism might show in a natural concern with local problems. The establishment of permanent theatres in the capital, however, and the creation of theatre monopolies by royal charter in 1660 (see PATENT THEATRES), meant that plays staged in London tended to treat regional themes and characteristics as a source of *comedy. The 'country cousin' was a popular figure whose lack of London polish was mocked. At the same time his honesty often shamed the more devious metropolitans.

Regionalism, of course, had already become a component of *Elizabethan and *Jacobean drama. Shakespeare's *Henry IV* (1597), for example, travels widely across England and presents a range of regional characters and accents. But London remained the central location of early seventeenth-century *city comedy, as in Jonson's *Bartholomew Fair* (1614), and while London drama used mythological and classical material, it was unlikely to venture far from the domiciles of its spectators for its *comedies of manners. This preference lasted well into the eighteenth century and only began to change with the advent of the *Romantic period, which encouraged regionalism at the expense of the capital. One of its products, *melodrama, exploited local colour, crime and brigandage in particular, both in the country and in the bigger cities.

The development of regional poetry and the 'regional novel' in the early nineteenth century, however, did not find its full dramatic counterpart until the rise of *naturalism, and even there, in the provincial towns of Ibsen (1828–1906) and the country estates of Chekhov (1860–1904), the local setting was subordinate to more general psychological and social concerns. Drama does not have the same flexibility as the *novel or *film for detailed topographic presentation and the full analysis of regional characteristics. Its limitations of time and space restrict the use of *narrative or frequent *set changes.

Although serious treatment of regional subjects developed in nineteenth-century provincial 'rep' it was still unpopular with *West End audiences in the mid-twentieth century. The fine regional plays of D.H. Lawrence, such as *The Daughter in Law* (1912), only made their impact in London in the late 1960s, thirty years after his death. Regional British drama began to flourish, in fact, in the third quarter of the twentieth century. The success of Arnold Wesker (1932–   ), the opening of provincial theatres — with resident dramatists, such as Peter Terson (1932–   ) at the

Victoria Theatre, Stoke-on-Trent — and the post–1968 development of *fringe theatre, encouraged research and writing on local
themes. Since this time there has been a proliferation of regional
drama dealing with local issues. An outstanding example is John
McGrath's *The Cheviot, the Stag and the Black Black Oil* (1973), which
deals with the exploitation of the Scottish Highlands.

*Community and *feminist theatres in both Britain and the
United States have also done much work involving local and
regional problems. In Britain *television and *film have presented
popular dramatizations of such regional novels as Hardy's *Far from
the Madding Crowd*, and encouraged the writing of single and serial
material on regional issues, such as Alan Bleasdale's *Boys from the
Blackstuff* (1984). No doubt the camera's ability to record scenic
detail is an important factor in this, but it must also be remembered
that London is now subordinate to the national audience of
millions to which television appeals. Regional audiences are
interested in their own problems and regional drama has become
as serious and important as the metropolitan variety.

In America regional theatre has flourished in the twentieth
century, developing at first in reaction against the *Theatrical
Syndicate and the mounting of purely commercial drama. The
establishment in New York of such early groups as the Washington
Square Players heralded the growth of independent theatres. This
was seen in the expansion of the *little theatre movement, the
founding of university campus theatres and the vigorous growth of
civic theatres in Dallas, Houston, Washington D.C., Los Angeles
and elsewhere. By 1977 non-commercial theatres had been
established in 34 states.

**Régisseur.** French term, deriving from the medieval theatre, for a
*director or *stage-manager of large-scale performances.

**Rehearsal.** The period of practice and preparation for a play's
performance. There have been, and still are, great variations in the
length of time given to rehearsal and in the methods employed. We
can only speculate about the methods used in *classical drama, but
rehearsal of *choral movement must have taken considerable time.
We know more of the preparations for medieval plays. The actors,
being amateur, had to rehearse in their spare time, which meant in
the available daylight before work began in the morning.
Sixteenth-century guild account books record sums spent on
breakfasts for the players. Fines were levied for misbehaviour and
lack of punctuality. Where festival plays were repeated more or less
exactly from year to year, fewer rehearsals were necessary. Glynne
Wickham, in *The Medieval Theatre* (1974), suggests that one
rehearsal was given over to *blocking, then 'two or three sufficed to
ensure that the actors were word perfect and had memorized their

moves successfully. The dress-rehearsal brought the actors into contact with their costumes, stage-properties, music and machinery.' The practice of using a *regisseur* who prompted on the stage in the actual performance (as in the famous Fouquet miniature showing a scene from a play about St Apollonia) meant there was less need for learning *cues. (See Ill.15, p.228.)

From the *Elizabethan period we have in Shakespeare's *A Midsummer Night's Dream* (1595) a *parody of amateur actors in rehearsal and performance. In *Hamlet* (1601) we have a flavour of the methods of *travelling players and the kind of recommendations that Shakespeare was likely to have made to the *Lord Chamberlain's Men. From the seventeenth century onwards, we have more detailed information about both rehearsal and performance. The view of Denis Diderot (1713–1784) was that rehearsals 'strike a balance between the different talents of the actors so as to establish a general unity in the playing.' However, though Diderot seems here to be aware of the virtues of ensemble playing, the brief rehearsals allowed by the *star system did not encourage it. The growth of present standards of polished *ensemble playing, seen in such *repertory companies as the *Royal Shakespeare, depend on a long, rigorous, experimental and exhilarating rehearsal process (the most interesting and exciting part of an actor's work, in the opinion of Alec Guinness (1914–    )). It is a period during which actors experiment and make their mistakes, undergoing a process of self–discovery and at the same time discovering their *role. A line of strong *directors has encouraged and developed this. This line includes Madame Vestris (1797–1856), the Duke of Saxe-Meiningen (1826–1914), André Antoine (1856–1943), Stanislavski (1863–1938), Bertolt Brecht (1898–1956) and Jerzy Grotowski (1933–    ), and many others.

COLE, T., and CRICH CHINOY, (eds.), *Directors on Directing*, Bobbs-Merrill, 1963.

**Relaxation.** The essential capacity to release muscular tension whilst retaining maximum *concentration on the stage. According to Stanislavski (1863–1938) no inner creative work, or truth in performance, is possible without it. His methods of physical preparation are detailed in:

STANISLAVSKI, C., *Building a Character*, Theatre Arts, NY, 1949.

**Relief.** The lowering or variation of dramatic tension. Its purpose is to keep the audience's attention when the play is making heavy demands. It is affected in many ways: (a) by the entry of a new character; (b) by a change of setting or scene; (c) by a change of tone and a lowering of emotional intensity; (d) by some variation or unexpected twist in the *action; or (e) by a switch of viewpoint, or *alienation effect.

Such variations maintain tension while providing temporary relief. Witness the scenes between Cassio and Desdemona which cut across Othello's mounting rage in Shakespeare's play; the 'willow song' of Desdemona which provides a moment of lyricism before the death-bed scene; the 'porter scene' in *Macbeth* (1606) with its dramatic *ironies about Hell-gate; Ophelia's poignant mad scenes in *Hamlet*; the 'grave-digger scene' which opens up the play and provides a new viewpoint on the death of Ophelia:

> *Second Clown*: Will you ha' the truth on't? If this had not been a gentlewoman she should have been buried out of Christian burial.
> *First Clown*: Why there thou sayest. . . (V.i. 25–7)

Such scenes provide variation but maintain dramatic tension. The gravedigger's joking about 'pocky corses' which will not keep out water remind one that a death by water has just occurred. The scene makes the tension more bearable. It eases without diffusing, and if there is laughter, it provides only a stronger basis for the *climax to follow.

A 'relief' is also a *flat, attached at an angle to painted scenery in order to heighten the illusion of reality. There are also 'practicable reliefs' which were used on a 'relief stage' behind the *proscenium opening. The actor could touch them and they served a similar purpose to pedestals for sculpture. They brought a three-dimensional quality to two-dimensional *scene-painting, incorporating the actor, or singer in Wagnerian *opera, more fully into the scene.

**Religious drama.** (a) Drama which functions as part of a religious *ritual (see LITURGICAL DRAMA); (b) religious festival drama, such as Greek tragedy or the *mystery cycles; (c) secular drama with a religious intention, such as T.S. Eliot's *Murder in the Cathedral* (1935) and *The Cocktail Party* (1949); (d) plays with a religious subject, such as Shaw's *St Joan* (1923).

Much powerful drama, especially *tragedy, seems to express a conflict between religious belief and secular attitudes. Whether this is described as religious drama or not usually depends on the way in which the drama is resolved.

WICKHAM, G., *Medieval Drama*, Weidenfeld and Nicolson, 1974.

**Renaissance stage.** The form of *proscenium stage which developed out of the Renaissance concern with *perspective scenic effects. The actor is seen from the front in relation to a painted scene. There remains, however, a projecting *forestage with *proscenium doors in front of the proscenium arch. English *Restoration theatres had Renaissance stages.

**22** *The perspective scene for comedy, from Serlio's* Architettura *(1545) which had a strong influence on Renaissance staging*

**Renaissance theatre.** The permanent theatres which developed during the Italian Renaissance out of the rediscovery of the laws of *perspective and in an attempt to imitate the *classical theatre. The first such theatre was the Teatro Olimpico, built at Vicenza in 1580–4.

The term also suggests the forms of secular European drama that grew up in the fifteenth and sixteenth centuries. These varied considerably from the *carnival play comedies of Hans Sachs (1494–1576) in Germany, to English *Elizabethan and *Jacobean drama, to the spectacular Italian pictorial theatre which the term is most frequently taken to suggest.

CAMPBELL, L.B., *Scenes and Machines on the English Stage during the Renaissance*, 1923.

NICOLL, A., *The Development of the Theatre*, Harrap, 1966, Ch 7.

**Reorganization.** Critical term used in a special sense by T.S. Eliot to define his conception of the process of creativity. This he sees as possessing three stages; (a) *response* — the capacity to react emotionally to works of art; (b) *organization* — the faculty which

relates these responses to each other to create a sense of *tradition
and of the past; and (c) *reorganization* — when 'the artist meets with
something new in his own time' and finds 'a new pattern of poetry
arranging itself in consequence'. Eliot's definition is probably
drawn from his own experience and from a consideration of the
way Shakespeare combined old forms of drama and literature in
new ways, bringing them into relation with the present. See:
ELIOT, T.S., *The Use of Poetry and the Use of Criticism*, Faber and Faber,
1933.

**Repertory.** (a) The system whereby a permanent company develops a repertoire of plays, constantly varying its programme
instead of mounting one production at a time. (b) The repertoire
of plays which a theatre company can perform at short notice.

The *Lord Chamberlain's Men and other Elizabethan and
Jacobean troupes were repertory companies, as were the old
nineteenth-century *stock companies. These were eventually
ousted by the commercial success of the *long run. A new
repertory movement in the twentieth century resulted in a
compromise system of short weekly or longer runs which became
known as 'weekly', 'fortnightly' or 'monthly rep'.

The advantage of real repertory, as it is practised in England by
the large *national theatres such as the Royal Shakespeare and The
National are many. A permanent company provides financial
security, a training ground for young actors and a fine basis for
*ensemble playing. Actors have long rehearsal periods in which
they can adapt to their fellow actors. Where the financial basis is
strong, the experience and skill which actors can gain in a variety of
quickly changing roles, in varying theatre spaces, amongst talented
professionals, is immense.

The disadvantages become apparent when the financial structure is threatened. Actors can become too familiar to audiences.
Small companies may be unable to mount a sufficient variety of
plays, and miscasting and hasty production are sometimes inevitable.

CHISHOLM, C., *Repertory*, Davies, 1934.
RUSSELL, G. and JACKSON, A., *The Repertory Movement: A History of
Regional Theatre in Britain*, Cambridge University Press, 1934.

**Repetition.** Recurrence; using or doing something more than
once. An important formal component of drama where the
repeating of a word, phrase, action, sound, *grouping, *gesture or
situation has a variety of functions. It is, first of all, part of the basic
dramatic process. *Rehearsal ('*répétition*' in French,) fixes lines,
movements and scenes in the memory and helps the achievement
of precise performance.

Repetition is built into human experience in particularly profound ways. Dramatic performances are repeated night after night in a pattern which recalls the repetitions of *nature and the human need of *ritual. Religious ceremonies are repeated day after day, Sunday after Sunday, year after year, and the daily, monthly and yearly rounds of the sun, moon and earth, of night and day and seasons, are repetitions which are rediscovered in the *mythoi of early drama and literature, which were taken to embody permanent cyclical and religious truths.

Study of processes of history, however, has challenged the idea of repetition as basic to human experience. History can be seen as a process of continuing *change*; instead of 'being' we have 'becoming', a sense that nothing is the same from day to day. The world always moves on.

It is interesting to note that much drama embodies the conflict between these two attitudes to *time. *Comedy seems always to have mocked the search for harmony and repeated pattern. In comedy people are fooled by *chance and by events. The comic spirit mocks habit and the refusal to see change. Henri Bergson (1859–1941) built his theory of *laughter on a recognition of this. Comic characters, fixed in their habits and obsessions, need to be laughed out of their mechanical states of mind, which resemble the ticking of a clock. The catch-word, the slogan phrase, the blinkered view, deny the idea of flow and change and 'subjective time' on which life depends. *Tragedy, too, in a more painful way, can mock our expectations. The world does not go on as men and women expect. The idea that it will repeat itself is both comforting and dangerous. Tragic heroes such as King Lear and Othello find themselves mocked. Tragedy tends to flourish at times when set beliefs, which a particular social structure has created or appropriated to subserve its own continuity, give way to new beliefs and attitudes. This happened as feudalism gave way to the new mercantilism, giving rise to *Elizabethan and *Jacobean tragedy. Old feudal values embodying ideas of repetition give way to a new individualism which denied them.

Repetition does, of course fulfil a human need. It develops skills and stabilizes social forms. At the same time it can deny vitality and change. This duality is central to drama. It is present both in tragedy and in the mechanisms of *farce. It is crucial to the highly repetitious *tragi-comedy of Samuel Beckett (1906–    ), whose characters crave for coherence and pattern. Krapp in *Krapp's Last Tape* (1959) tries to hold his life together by listening to tape recordings. Didi, in *Waiting for Godot* (1953) endeavours to prove to Gogo that life has a pattern, that they were in the same place yesterday, and here are Gogo's boots to prove it. But the patterns may not be meaningful, and the progress of *chronological time mocks the desire to escape from it.

Thus our need of repetition is both essential and problematic.

as a confirmation of a pattern in life and the play. But when an actor at the end of a *long run begins to say, with Eliot's Prufrock, 'I have measured out my life in coffee spoons' it is time to stop.

**Repoussoir.** A contrastive figure; a French painting term applied to colours which bring out another colour by *contrast. It is employed by Henry James (1843–1916) to define characters who have a contrastive function. Henrietta Stackpole, in *Portrait of a Lady* (1881) is so described, and the term may be applied to such figures in drama as Fortinbras, and even Laertes, in *Hamlet* (1601). They sharpen our awareness of the central *hero. Like Prince Hamlet they have lost their fathers, but they respond to the event very differently. The term, it must be said, is unusual and literary.

**Representation.** The recurrent act of presenting, or 'making present'. An appropriate term for dramatic performance.

**Resolution.** The phase of a play in which discords and conflicts are resolved.

Art traditionally aims to achieve *unity but not all *endings are resolved. *Epic theatre does not aim at resolution; *tragedy often leaves an uncomfortable sense of the impossibility of fully resolving conflicts, and *comedy, too, has discords which linger after the play is over. To take examples from Shakespeare, both Hamlet and Iago leave troubled silences behind them, and after the comic resolutions of *As You Like It* (1599) and *Twelfth Night* (1600) the melancholy of Jaques and the pride and hatred of Malvolio linger in the mind. Such instances suggest that drama can do more than achieve a resolved *unity: it can question its own resolved form.

Out of unresolved material, a writer's later works often develop. This seems to be true of Shakespeare, if we can trust the established chronology of the plays. The melancholy of Jaques, for example, may have fed into the far fuller analysis of melancholia in *Hamlet* a year or two later. The hypothesis may be supported by examining such autobiographical material as Dostoievski's *Notebooks* which seem to show his later novels emerging from a failure fully to resolve the previous ones. Incompleteness seems to be a fertile source of artistic inspiration.

**Restoration theatre.** Drama written after 1660, mainly for the two *patent theatres which Charles II authorized upon the restoration of the monarchy. D'Avenant (1606–1668) and Killigrew (1612–83) were the dominant theatrical figures of the time, and Etherege (1634–91), Wycherley (1640–1716) and Dryden (1631–1700) the major writers. As compared with *Jacobean and *Caroline drama, which preceded the closure of the theatres under the Commonwealth, Restoration drama came under fuller court patronage and appealed to a narrower, aristocratic audience. Women were introduced to the stage, since there were no trained boy actors to take female roles, and Charles's experience of Parisian theatre during his exile encouraged an emphasis on the spectacular Italian operatic tradition. Thus D'Avenant used a *Renaissance stage with *perspective effects. Orchestras were housed at the side and, at the Duke's Theatre, over the stage. *Scenery was changed in full view of the audience and music punctuated the action. To intensify the lighting of the *forestage, which was illuminated by overhead candelabra, *footlights were installed. Candles and oil lamps, coloured by the use of stained glass, enhanced the scenic effect.

Restoration theatre did not provide an entirely Italian spectacle. The earthiness and vigour of the pre-Commonwealth theatre, together with its emphasis on a stage picture created by the *groupings of actors rather than by perspective scenery, showed for a short time in the work of Killigrew. The world of Wycherley and Etherege, and even the early Farquhar (1678–1707) and Vanbrugh (1664–1726), is recognizably related in tone to the *Caroline period, and *heroic tragedy lingered on from the earlier period until it was killed by *burlesque.

The influence of Molière (1622–73) on Etherege, however, and the *wit and polish of Congreve's plays Love for Love (1695) and The Way of the World (1700) indicated a shift, which a growing middle-class audience encouraged, towards the *comedy of manners and the *sentimental comedy of Goldsmith (1730–74) and Sheridan (1751–1816). The transition can perhaps best be seen in the short career of George Farquhar. Compare, for instance, his Love and a Bottle (1698) with The Beaux Stratagem (1707).

HOTSON, L., The Commonwealth and Restoration Stage, Harvard University Press, 1928; Russell, 1962.

**Retardation.** Musical term for the slackening of *tempo. Hence it can be applied to the deliberate slowing down of a scene to achieve a particular affect, usually one of *focus. The *freeze is an extreme example of retardation.

In Samuel Beckett's plays, retardation is used to force audiences to consider the nature of time's passage, not as an abstraction but as an effect upon themselves. The *tempo moves alternately fast and slow. Characters fill time with *play. When they cease to play, characters and audience together experience a passage of time unfilled by activity. Time and its effect then become a subject for discussion. Gogo in Waiting for Godot (1953) can remark 'How time passes when one has fun!' The laughter which results arises out of the spectator's disengagement from the play's own time process. In this play, as in Happy Days (1961) or Endgame (1958), spectators are continually deprived of dramatic games and 'pas(s)times'. At the very edge of boredom they experience a painful exposure to time.

The nature and function of the theatre, and the nature and meaning of a world subject to temporal process, are put in question. 'Slower, *slower*', one can hear Beckett say.

**Return.** A 'set-back' used to strengthen the wall of *flat or *box-set.

**Reveals.** Pieces attached to *flats forming the doors and windows of a *box-set to give the natural appearance of solid walls.

**Revelation.** The *discovery or *disclosure of a *secret. See ANAGNORISIS; RECOGNITION.

**Revels Office.** Office run by the *Master of the Revels. It dealt with court entertainments and was established in the early *Tudor period.

**Revenge tragedy.** *Tragedy whose action pivots on the desire of a *hero or *villain to avenge a wrong. Revenge tragedy is important from Aeschylus (525–456 B.C.) onwards, but the term usually describes *Elizabethan and *Jacobean plays influenced by the *closet plays of Seneca (*c*.4 B.C.–A.D. 65). These include Thomas Kyd's *Spanish Tragedy* (1586), Marlowe's *Jew of Malta* (*c*. 1589), Shakespeare's *Titus Andronicus* (1594), Chapman's *Bussy D'Ambois* (*c*. 1604) and Tourneur's (or Middleton's) *The Revenger's Tragedy* (1606).

These plays appeal to and invoke the various social and religious *codes which justify or condemn acts of revenge. The avenging of a wrong or tort has been taken variously as the responsibility of the wronged individual, of the wronged family or clan, of the state, or of God in an after-life. 'Vengeance is mine, sayeth the Lord' is the crucial Biblical text which condemns most of the Jacobean revenge characters. On the other hand, secular and more primitive codes require and justify acts of revenge. This contradiction between codes is often a source of powerful dramatic conflict.

It is possible to distinguish two kinds of revenge plays: (a) those which see revenge as personal and voluntary, and contain an energetic and atheist avenger who experiences no hesitation or pangs of conscience, as in Marlowe's *The Jew of Malta*; and (b) the plays in which revenge is seen as a sacred duty, as in Kyd's *Spanish Tragedy* (published in 1592). The subtlest of all revenge plays, Shakespeare's *Hamlet*, is different from both kinds. It presents a *hero who seems not to know why he cannot carry out a revenge which the ghost of his father commands. This incapacity raises fundamental questions about the psychological responses of the revenger, about the way moral forces operate in the world, and about how revenge can be reconciled with justice. Indeed it is possible to see two contradictory revenge ethics at work in it. In his standard book on *Elizabethan Revenge Tragedy* (1940), Fredson Bowers argues for an 'aristocratic' ethic: 'Few Elizabethans would condemn the son's blood revenge on a treacherous murderer whom the law could not apprehend for lack of proper legal evidence.' On the other hand, Eleanor Prosser in *Hamlet and Revenge* (1967) cites Bacon: 'Revenge is a kind of wild justice which the more man's nature runs to, the more ought law to weed it out'. She argues for the great importance of Christian and 'establishment' codes: 'For Elizabethan moralists revenge was illegal, blasphemous, immoral, irrational, unnatural and unhealthy — also unsafe'. *Hamlet*, however, is based on an old story which has primitive elements and its highly ambiguous Ghost seems to advocate a revenge murder in order to obtain its release from a Christian purgatory. The contradictory impulses within the characters seem to have existed already in the play's source material.

The avenging of a wrong is one of the standard ingredients of tragic drama. Shakespeare's *Othello* (1604) and *King Lear* (1605) have *protagonists who suffer at the hands of others, and in both cases the protagonist seeks to justify his desire for revenge by calling it a form of justice. Justice, however, must be publicly tested. For an individual to assume that he can right his wrong in private, while speaking of public punishment, is an act of *hubris. The individual may err, like Othello, or Leontes in Shakespeare's *The Winter's Tale* (1610), but when Leontes assumes he can use a public court merely to corroborate his private belief he discovers his mistake. In Shakespeare the revenge motive is subject to the most complex dramatic scrutiny.

The descendents of Elizabethan and Jacobean revenge plays are cruder. They include *gothic melodrama and, in recent times, 'western' films, which often use basic revenge plots.

**Revesby play.** English *folk drama, akin to the *mumming play, from the Lincolnshire village of Revesby. The action involves a *fool who is killed by his four sons and then revives. After a *sword dance they join together in wooing a young girl called Cicely. The play has obvious origins in fertility rites. There are comic echoes of the 'rebirth' notion in Shakespeare's *Henry IV* Part I (1596–7) where the fool figure, Sir John Falstaff, 'rises from the dead' on the battlefield.

CHAMBERS, E.K., *The Medieval Stage*, 2 vols, Oxford University Press, 1903.

**Revival.** A new production of a previously performed play.

**Revolving stage.** A turntable generally occupying most of the stage area. The mounting upon it of several *box-sets, only one of which can be seen by the audience at a time, enables rapid scene changes to be made. The 'revolve' usually moves when a new set is required for the next scene and the actors perform on it when it has stopped. A more open staging and the use of a revolve *during* the stage action can achieve highly imaginative effects. It may for example, allow scene-changes with no pause at all. Characters may *exit and others *enter simultaneously as they move into lighted or darkened areas. Long distances can be suggested if the stage revolves as characters walk, and so on. A brilliant use of the revolving stage was seen in the *Royal Shakespeare Company's 1985 production of Victor Hugo's *Les Misérables*. The stage turned to carry off the drowned Inspector Javert into the darkness, and as it revolved it placed the audience inside or outside the garden of Jean Valjean or behind or in front of the street barricades.

**Revue.** A mixed programme of entertainment dating from the late nineteenth century and containing readings, comic sketches, song and dance, and contemporary comment. Unlike *vaudeville and *music hall, performers appear in different 'turns' throughout the programme. Revues range from the spectacular to the intimate. The form has considerable satirical potential as was proved by the successful Cambridge Footlights revue, *Beyond the Fringe* (1961). It has been an established American form since Ziegfeld's *Follies (1907).

**Rhetoric.** The art of persuading people by oratory or the written word. It is based on such classical works as Aristotle's *Rhetoric* (329–323 B.C.) and Cicero's *De Oratore* (55 B.C.) which provide a general body of rules concerning: (a) the location of good material; (b) the organization of this material; (c) the manner or style of presentation; (d) the memorizing of speeches; and (e) the techniques of delivery.

Rhetoric was a very important subject in the *Renaissance school curriculum and its rules had a strong impact on sixteenth-century dramatists and actors. This may be seen in public speeches written for characters in *history and *chronicle plays. Thus Shakespeare's kings and statesmen, like Brutus and Mark Antony in *Julius Caesar* (1599), demonstrate rhetorical devices and styles. So, too, do more private characters, such as Falstaff in his speech on 'honour' in *Henry IV* Part I (1596–7). Rhetorical utterance is often counterpointed against the colloquial in Shakespeare's subtle interweaving of 'public' and 'private' languages.

Shakespeare probably also counterpointed rhetorical *gesture and heightened *facial expression against a more *naturalistic and less artificial behaviour on stage. As rhetoric has ceased to be taught, and as European drama has come to dwell on the examination of private experience, so our awareness of the rhetorical *codes which *Elizabethan and *Jacobean writers employed and parodied has declined. Our understanding, too, of Greek drama, in which characters are so concerned with arguing a public case, would benefit from a deeper knowledge of their rhetorical codes and practices.

The modern critical use of the word 'rhetoric', as in Wayne Booth's *Rhetoric of Fiction* (1961), no longer places a traditional stress on persuasive language and linguistic device, but emphasizes the handling of writer/reader relationships. Theatre remains a more public art than the novel, however, and it is unwise in the discussion of drama to apply only the recent literary use of the term.

**Rhythm.** (a) Regular *tempo or pace; (b) the variations on it within a work of music, literature or drama.

In drama, rhythm is determined by the speed of the actors' *movements and their delivery of the lines, as well as the relation between speeches in a scene, the relation of scenes and acts to one another and the general rise and fall of dramatic intensity.

Rhythm is very important in drama since the continued attention of the audience depends on it. The main responsibility lies with the *director, who must organize his *rehearsals in such a way that the individual sections of a play fit together rhythmically. A *run-through, for example, allows the actors to get a feel for the broader rhythms of a play and to distinguish between the minor and major *crises and *climaxes.

A notation in the script to suggest length of *pause, rapidity of speech and the nature and speed of movement required by the author at particular times, or even throughout the play, is not used in spoken drama and would not be popular with actors and *directors accustomed to making up their own minds about these matters. In *opera and other musical drama, of course, the actor/singer must adhere to the score. There have, nonetheless, been forms of spoken drama which use rhythmical notation. P. Pavis illustrates the notation of one such sixteenth-century playwright (G. de Vire) in:

PAVIS, P., *Languages of the Stage*, Performing Arts Journal, NY, 1982, pp. 116–124.

**Rich theatre.** Term used by Jerzy Grotowski (1933– ) to define the kind of theatre he works in reaction against: i.e. 'the idea of theatre as a synthesis of disparate creative disciplines — literature, sculpture, painting, architecture, lighting, acting (under a *metteur en scène)*'. He identifies this with *total theatre and argues that the technological superiority of *television and *film is such that it is best for the theatre to cease competition with the film media, concentrating instead on the *actor-audience relationship and excluding all technology. In short, he recommends a *poor theatre.

GROTOWSKI, J., *Towards a Poor Theatre*, Methuen, 1969.

**Rise and sink.** Form of spectacular *scene-change in which the upper part of a scene rises rapidly into the *flies and the lower sinks into the *cellar, revealing another scene behind.

**Rising action.** The first half of the play, according to *Freytag's pyramid, in which the *hero exerts his will and desires, and the mounting excitement leads to a central *climax.

**Ritterdrama.** Melodramatic Bavarian plays of the late eighteenth century, specializing in battles, jousting, and scenes of knight errantry.

They satisfied a theatrical taste for feudal warfare, aroused by Goethe's *Goetz von Berlichingen* (1773) and the *Sturm und Drang*. Von Torring's *Kasper der Thorringer* (1785) is an example.

**Ritual.** Ceremonial closely related to drama. The social functions of ritual have been defined in different ways as: (a) a form of knowledge – a society's understanding of its world; (b) a means of cultural transmission; (c) an expression of a desire to control nature and the future — a prayer for rain or success in battle, for example; (d) a means to create and confirm community pride (and energy); (e) an appeal to, and celebration of, the supernatural beings thought to have special care of the group; (f) a connection with the past and with the dead who enacted those same rituals; and (g) a safety valve, or expression of rebellious and suppressed feeling.

**23** *Ritual dance in which performers wear antelope masks or heads, while a chorus or audience of men and women apparently clap their hands (rock painting by African Bushmen)*

Ritual has strong preservation functions, and drama in its earlier stages, whether in *liturgical or *folk play, *comedy or *tragedy is highly ritualistic. This is obvious from the use of *costume, *mask, *dance, *choral movement, *music and heightened forms of speech. Gradually, however, with a growing post-feudal emphasis on personal and private experience, and an increasing emphasis on entertainment in the new *professional theatre, ritualistic elements became less obvious. Drama began to be performed for an audience and was no longer part of a community celebration. It still has a strong tendency to reflect and reinforce communal attitudes, but inevitably the mingling of social groups within a wider urban audience provides a conflict of attitudes and beliefs which works against the sharing of a common ritual.

In some modern drama, notably that of Samuel Beckett (1906–   ), the human need for ritual and *repetition becomes a subject of *parody as his drama examines and mocks its own rituals and conventions.

**Robin Hood.** Hero of legend, possibly based on a historical personage, associated with festive seasons. Robin Hood, who may be a survival of 'green men' legends, appears in lost plays by playwright Antony Munday (1553–1633). Later, the hero's story was taken up in *pantomime.

**Role.** (a) The part an actor plays; (b) the part a person plays in life; the set of attitudes associated with a position and a social function.

Erving Goffman has developed two concepts of particular relevance to drama. 'Role distance' defines how far a person may improvise around his role and the behaviour expected of him. (In drama this might be applied to Shakespeare's Hamlet, who frequently confounds the expectations others have of him as 'son' or 'prince'.) 'Role conflict' occurs when an individual finds himself playing two roles simultaneously. Again Hamlet can be cited: he is both prince and son. As son he has responsibilities to a murdered father. As prince he has responsibilities to the state and to the head of it, Claudius, his father's murderer. There is role conflict in Claudius too, since he must play the role of king whilst remaining aware that he has betrayed the role of brother. In a somewhat similar way, Shakespeare's Othello has to reconcile the roles of general, governor, lover and betrayed husband. In both *Hamlet* and *Othello* (1604) *irony and dramatic *tension derive from the audience's awareness of the conflict, while subordinate characters remain in ignorance of it.

The concept of role conflict raises fundamental questions about ethical values since it involves choices between different *codes of behaviour. It is highly dramatic and can be located in the work of dramatists as different as Sophocles (496–406 B.C.), Ibsen (1828–1906), Pirandello (1867–1936) and Brecht (1898–1956).

The phrase 'in role' is also common. It means 'to act as if one were another person'. The process may involve the actor's close emotional *identification with a role which has developed over a long *rehearsal period and cannot immediately be discarded. It may mean only a light appropriation of the externals of a role, such as accent, posture and gait. The term is frequently used in educational *roleplay, where students assume the identity of another person to explore a social or historical situation.

BIDDLE, B. and THOMAS, E., *Role Theory*, J. Wiley, NY, 1966.

GOFFMANN, E., *The Presentation of Self in Everyday Life*, Allen Lane, 1969.

JACKSON, J.A. (ed.) *Role*, Cambridge University Press, 1972.

**Roleplay.** (a) The activity of an actor; (b) the activity in which we all engage in our everyday lives — the assumption of a social function and behaviour consonant with that function, whether it is that of king or civil servant, mother or bus conductor. This normally means behaving according to the expectations of others within the social order. See ROLE.

**Role reversal.** The exchange of *roles, normally involving a change of *power relations as between man and woman, servant and master, and parent and child. The process seems to relate to *festive behaviour at *carnivals and other celebrations. The reasons why pleasure should arise from a change of identity, and from experiencing a playful loss or gain of *power, are highly problematic. (See CATHARSIS; LAUGHTER.) The process is important in drama, where exchanges of power are frequent, whether in *comedy, where *fool and servant figures take over from their masters, as for example in J.M. Barrie's *The Admirable Crichton* (1902), or in *tragedy, where characters with power lose it to social inferiors, as does King Lear to his daughters in Shakespeare's play.

In the above cases, characters do not actually *dress up* as one another, as might occur on festive occasions, but power passes from one character to another. Mock disguisings do sometimes occur, however, as when Falstaff and Prince Hal in *Henry IV* Part I (1597–8) don the crown and play at being king. The sudden playful shift out of personal identity provokes laughter and pleasure. It also makes an audience aware of the realities of power, an awareness which seems to connect in complex ways with the production of laughter. Perhaps Freud was right to suggest that in such circumstances we experience 'the innocent return of repressed desires'.

**Roll-out.** A flap in the base of a piece of hanging *scenery which allowed a Victorian actor to make a sudden appearance.

**Romance.** Term most frequently applied in drama to Shakespeare's late plays: *Pericles, Prince of Tyre* (1606–8), *The Winter's Tale* (1610), *Cymbeline* (1609) and *The Tempest* (1611). The plays draw on legendary material and use exotic settings and strange happenings to create a sense of wonderment and enchantment. Characteristic words are 'rare', 'rich' and 'strange'. The romance atmosphere, which is theatrically very real, is often plotted against the rougher words and behaviour of the characters who do not understand or share this magical world, such as Cloten in *Cymbeline* (1609) and Sebastian and Antonio in *The Tempest* (1611). Thus the 'romances' are not entirely *romantic. Realistic behaviour is a component of these plays as it is of other *Jacobean romances, such as those of Sir Francis Beaumont (1584–1616) and John Fletcher (1579–1625). A more complete *romanticism is to be found in the Greek and other *pastoral tales on which they drew, and in the more spectacular Italian tradition which emerged in England in the court *masque.

NICOLL, A. (ed.), *Shakespeare Survey No. 11*, Cambridge University Press, 1958.

TILLYARD, E.M.W., *Shakespeare's Last Plays*, Chatto, 1938.

WILSON KNIGHT, G., *The Crown of Life*, Methuen, 1948.

**Roman theatre.** The Roman theatre ensured the continuity of the *Greek theatre in the modern world. The comedies of Plautus (*c.* 254–184 B.C.) and Terence (*c.* 195–159 B.C.) mediated the tradition of *new comedy. The *closet drama of Seneca (*c.* 4 B.C.–A.D 65)

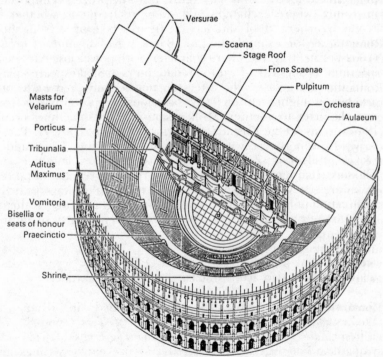

**24** *Theatre of Marcellus, Rome, 13–11 BC.*

helped transmit the mythological subject-matter of *Greek tragedy. Fragments and titles of plays by other Roman dramatists such as Livius Andronicus and Naevius (dates uncertain), Ennius (239–169 B.C.), Pacuvius (220–c. 130 B.C.) and Accius (170–c. 89 B.C.) remain. Much of their drama was based on the plays of Sophocles (496–406 B.C.) and Euripides (484–407/6 B.C.).

The Roman theatre building was, equally, adapted from the Greeks. It consisted of a semi-circular *auditorium and *orchestra, facing a long stage backed by an impressive *frons scenae with three to five doorways. The type was established in Rome's Marcellus playhouse and preserved at Orange and elsewhere. Stage right represented the direction of the town and stage left was an *exit to harbour or countryside. Larger theatres were open to the sky but smaller ones, as at Pompeii, had a wooden roof.

The theatrical fare included spectacle, such as gladatorial combat and *naumachia. *Farce, usually played by *mimes in portable *booths, was also performed in the big theatres. Since *masks were worn *gesture must have been very important.

BIEBER, M., *History of the Greek and Roman Theatre*, Oxford University Press, 1961.

BEARE, W., *The Roman Stage*, Methuen, 1964.

**Romantic comedy.** A general term for a light play about love between the sexes.

**Romantic drama.** The term has a variety of meanings including: (a) plays such as Noel Coward's *Bitter Sweet* (1929) about a 'romantic' or loving relationship; (b) drama written during the Romantic period, beginning with *Sturm und Drang* and *gothic melodrama, and leading into the 'national romantic drama' of, for example, the Norwegian patriotic dramatist Bjørnstjerne Bjørnson (1832–1910); (c) drama written in the 'romantic tradition', which derives from medieval romance and incorporates *pastoral. Thus the late plays of Shakespeare, based in part on such material, are included in this last tradition, as Jonson's *neo-classical and urban plays are excluded. Shakespeare incorporates natural settings, storms and mystery into such 'classical' comedies as *The Merry Wives of Windsor* (1598) and *A Comedy of Errors* (1590–3). Romantic drama places emphasis on emotion, dream-states, the exotic and the unusual. Shakespeare's *romance plays also contrast such states with waking consciousness and contain a high degree of psychological *realism.

**Romantic irony.** Form of generalized *irony in which the author takes a playful view of his own work, as of the *genre in which it is written and its function in the world. Romantic irony invites a sympathetic response to the writer. It is easiest to establish in fiction since the author is more obviously present as *narrator and can address the reader directly. Henry Fielding's novels illustrate its use, as does Sterne's *Tristram Shandy* (1759–67).

In drama, despite the lack of an established narrator, romantic irony may still be present. Certain authors such as Genet (1909–86), Pirandello (1867–1963) and Beckett (1906–    ) reveal a playful attitude to their own material. Their tone, however, is more sardonic than romantic. Shakespeare's romantic comedies have a warmer playfulness which acknowledges the game being played, differing from the *realism of comedy in a *classical and urban tradition. In the absence of a narrator, however, it is perhaps best to limit the use of the term to fiction.

**Romanticism.** The Romantic movement arising in the later eighteenth century and continuing in different ways to find expression throughout the nineteenth century.

'Romanticism' is a general term identifying qualities in a work which are the opposite of *classical, including an emphasis on content rather than *form; on emotion rather than *reason; on the 'natural' world rather than the urban and social; on the past and distant rather than the present and immediate; on life as a 'flow' rather than a succession of discrete units; on imagination rather than observation; on *dream and associative processes rather than on logic and causality; on the mental processes of children as much as of mature adults; and on hero-worship and idealizing tendencies rather than on *satire, *irony and *realism.

Frequently, in drama where characters are given to idealisation or dream, the tendency to romanticism is handled both with sympathy and a distancing *irony. In modern drama since the rise of *naturalism, romanticism has often been a quality of the characters rather than the play.

**Rope house.** Theatre in which scenery is controlled by hand from a *fly floor; *hemphouse or hand-worked house.

**Rose Theatre.** Early Elizabethan theatre built around 1587.

**Rostrum.** A moveable stage platform of varying size. The height of rostra is in multiples of six inches, the height of a step or 'riser'. They fit together and are used on large scenic stages to establish location and three-dimensionality. They create different acting *levels, enhance *grouping and *lighting effects, and can be used to emphasize power and dominance in group and character relationships.

The architectural sets of such directors and designers as Max Reinhardt (1893–1943), Leopold Jessner (1878–1945) and the American Norman Bel Geddes (1893–1958), make highly imaginative use of such stage-platforms.

**Rough theatre.** Peter Brook's term for the opposite of *holy theatre. By 'rough' he means the element of imperfection which marks all living human activity. For example, when an orchestra plays there lies behind its purity of sound the impure noise of breathing, scraping and shuffling, which imperceptibly gives it a rough 'body'. This roughness and human activity, he suggests, is what people miss in machine-made music. Roughness in the theatre, according to Brook, is similar to dung. It fertilizes; it mocks style, order and rule; it is energetic; it is like Jarry's *Ubu Roi* (1896), joyous and angry, preferring a belch to a prayer.

Brook is thus talking of a *popular theatre containing elements of the *grotesque and the *comic tradition, an anti-authoritarian theatre which reinvigorates the 'holy' and, as in the *Elizabethan theatre, may be wedded to it. Without 'roughness', he argues, theatre is dead.

BROOK, P., *The Empty Space*, McGibbon and Kee, 1968, Ch. 3.

**Round.** See CORNISH ROUND; THEATRE IN THE ROUND.

**Roundhouse.** Converted theatre, formerly a nineteenth-century locomotive shed and warehouse, at Chalk Farm in London. Arnold Wesker (1932–  ) took it over in 1964 for his *Centre 42, with the purpose of creating a working-class venue. Support from the trade unions was insufficient, however, and it became an entertainment centre. The episode was an interesting and gallant attempt to challenge the conventional commercial structure of the theatre.

**Royal Court.** Theatre in Sloane Square, London, of great importance in the development of twentieth-century English drama. In 1904–7 Harley Granville-Barker (1877–1946) and J.C. Vedrenne (1867–1930) used the theatre to mount an influential programme of European drama, including plays by Ibsen (1828–1906), Hauptmann (1862–1946), Maeterlinck (1862–1949) and Shaw (1856–1950). Granville–Barker's advocacy of a subsidized *National Theatre was a result of this experience.

The period of management of actor and director George Devine from 1956–65 was probably of even greater importance. The English Stage Company was founded to perform new English and European plays and encourage new writing. The success of John Osborne's *Look Back in Anger* (1956) provided a financial base for good but commercially less successful plays, notably those of John Arden (1930–  ) which included *Sergeant Musgrave's Dance* (1959). Productions of Ionesco's plays, including *The Chairs* and *The Lesson*, mingled *theatre of the absurd with more political and Brechtian drama. Writers' workshops encouraged experimental theatre. Edward Bond (1935–  ) emerged as a powerful and controversial writer and his play *Saved* (1965) led to the abolition in 1968 of the

Lord Chancellor's right to censor new plays. *Fringe and touring companies have been encouraged, and the Theatre Upstairs, housed since 1969 in the attic, has offered a new *theatre in the round to experimental writers. In short, the varied work done by writers, directors and actors at the Royal Court has been a powerful influence in the development of drama in England since 1956.

WARDLE, I., *The Theatres of George Devine*, Eyre Methuen, 1978, pp. 167–285.

**Royal Shakespeare Company.** Renowned *repertory company. It received its name when the Shakespeare Memorial Theatre in Stratford was reorganized in 1960. It performs at the Barbican in London and uses a small experimental theatre, The Pit, in the same building. In Stratford it has at present the main theatre, a refurbished theatre, the Swan and a small theatre, the Other Place. These extend considerably the variety of plays shown. Peter Hall (1930– ) and Trevor Nunn (1940– ) have been artistic directors, and, amongst many others, Peter Brook (1925– ) and Michel Saint-Denis (1897–1971) have been co-directors.

**Royalty.** The 'cut' or proportion of the proceeds an author is allowed on the performance or publication of his plays.

**Rules of drama.** (a) The *codes or *conventions tacitly agreed between writer, performer and public at different times and in different places; (b) prescriptive standards of construction, such as the *unities, based on the example of classical, or other, writers.

All drama is based on rules, but when they become restrictive and routine, dramatists of determined originality find ways to break, bend or vary them. (See ORIGINALITY; TRADITION.)

**Run.** A series of consecutive performances of a play. The commercial theatre still prefers the run to the *repertory system. It has financial rather than artistic advantages, especially in capital cities and tourist centres.

***Rundhorizont.*** German word for *cyclorama.

**Run-through.** A preliminary attempt in *rehearsal to perform a whole *act or play. One of the problems of rehearsing scenes separately is that a *rhythm and intensity may be achieved in a particular scene which is not consistent with earlier or later scenes. An early scene may need to be slower and quieter than at first realized, since a *climax may be required in the scene to follow. The run-through is necessary at later stages of rehearsal to allow actors to adjust their playing in order to achieve continuity and the correct *tempo. This can only be done by placing scenes in relation to one another within the whole play.

# S

**Sacra rapresentazione.** Italian version of the English medieval *mystery play.

**Sacrifice.** The offering of a victim, animal or human, to propitiate a deity. Out of such a *ritual, according to one hypothesis, *tragedy was born. The word 'tragedy' derives from the Greek for 'goat song' which may imply a song sung at the sacrifice of a goat. This has given rise to speculation that a tragic *hero is a kind of *scapegoat, a sacrificial victim who redeems the community and brings about a *reconciliation between God and Man.

In tragedy, however, the death of hero or heroine cannot be regarded with the same equanimity as the sacrifice of an animal. Feelings of reconciliation and *catharsis seem to be central to the tragic response, but tragedy emphasizes that sacrifice involves loss and suffering as well as redemption, and the loss may be deeply felt. Tragedy, indeed, seems to arise when established beliefs are subject to a growing scepticism, so that the propitiation of the god is balanced against a questioning of the value of the sacrifice. The supreme example of Christ, whose sacrificial death was to redeem mankind, is not normally seen as tragic. His death is not a waste but a triumph. For a believer his death is *positive*. Only a sceptic sees the pattern of Christ's death as negative. But the death of the tragic hero seems to combine both a negative and a positive response. A sense of redemption and a sense of waste seem to exist side by side.

Tragic sacrifice, then, invites a double response and this seems to relate to the degree to which the tragic victim chooses his or her own  fate. The more *power the victim has, the greater the possibility of redemption. The weaker the victim, the smaller that possibility becomes. The tragic hero operates between two extremes, neither fully in control of his fate (or triumphing over it like Christ) nor a passive sufferer who arouses *pity but little respect. The tragic response seems to lie in the audience's desire to see a hero struggle against the tragic situation. The victim may lack Christ's strength, but the struggle reveals his or her desire to control the fate that threatens.

Sometimes this assertion of control takes the form of self-sacrifice. If redemption lies in the struggle against fate, individuals who sacrifice themselves for a cause, or for the community, who make, for example, 'the supreme sacrifice' in war, assert their power and are valued and mourned. The *situation has chosen them, and they make a choice within it. Tragedy in this sense is *existential.

The contradiction then, between freedom and fate, as between the valuing and the waste, seems to lie close to the heart of tragedy. Where the contradiction is seen as *paradox, and the emphasis placed on value, as in the death of Christ or the self-sacrificial martyrdom of Celia Coplestone in T.S. Eliot's *The Cocktail Party* (1949), one of the tragic elements, the sense of waste, is rejected. Eliot's play aspires to show a Christian sacrifice which rises above tragedy (though against the author's intentions a sense of unnecessary waste may well remain). The martyrdom of Thomas à Becket as shown in Eliot's *Murder in the Cathedral* (1935) is also relevant to this discussion.

Too strong a sense of waste and futility can cause a play to fall below the pitch of tragedy, as arguably happens in Shakespeare's *problem plays, especially *Troilus and Cressida* (1602). Here futility and waste dominate the play and seem to deny all positive values. Men, the Trojans in particular, sacrifice themselves to create an *image which future generations will admire. There is self-regard at the centre of their apparent heroism and the result is a sardonic tragi-comedy.

The tragic balance of sacrifice and waste is strongly present in Shakespeare's *Othello* (1604), which explores similar psychological areas to *Troilus and Cressida*. Othello exclaims, when Desdemona denies having given the handkerchief to Cassio:

> O perjur'd woman! Thou dost stone my heart,
> And make me call what I intend to do
> A murder, which I thought a sacrifice . . . (V.ii.63–5)

The famous speech which contains the words 'Put out the light, and then put out the light' creates a remarkable sense of ritual slaughter, and suggests that Othello is trying to transform a private *revenge into public justice, sealed with divine approval. Shakespeare's compassionate scepticism probes Othello's motives in seeking to perform a sacrifice and the tragedy emerges both from a sense of waste, when Othello kills Desdemona, and a kind of redemption, when Othello redeems his error and retains his sense of value by executing vengeance upon himself. His self-sacrifice embodies both the waste and the existence of high value.

Self-sacrifice implies a belief in the existence of values higher than the self. It has high importance in tragedy — and also in drama which theoretically rejects the tragic pattern, like Brecht's *epic theatre. Brecht (1898–1956) may be suspicious of heroics, yet in *Mother Courage* (1941) he presents sacrifice as a virtue. Kattrin, in Scene Eleven, asserts her freedom to control a situation. She sacrifices herself for others and affirms the existence of human value in the face of apparent waste.

Sacrifice, of course, is measured by what it is made for, and its value will always be contested. Perhaps one may say, however, that even where the sacrifice seems vain a tragic value can be found in acts which rise above self-concern.

MANDEL, O., *A Definition of Tragedy*, New York University Press, 1961, pp.113–16.

WILLIAMS, R., *Modern Tragedy*, Chatto and Windus, 1966, pp. 156–173.

**Safety curtain.** Fireproof curtain which can be lowered from the *proscenium arch to separate *stage and *auditorium in case of fire.

*Sainete.* Eighteenth-century Spanish satirical *interlude, performed, like the earlier *entremes*, between the *acts of a play.

**San Francisco Mime Troupe.** Radical American alternative theatre group. See POLITICAL THEATRE.

**Sartre, Jean-Paul** (1905–80). French *existentialist and Marxist philosopher, dramatist, journalist, novelist and biographer. Sartre's drama and dramatic theory explore human situations in a mainly *naturalistic way:

> What the theatre can show which is most moving is a character making itself, the moment of choice of a free decision which calls forth a morality and commits a whole life.

> Hell is other people.

See: ABSURD; COMMITMENT; ENDS AND MEANS; SITUATION.

SARTRE, J.-P., *Forging Myths* (1946); *A Theatre of Situations* (1947); *Epic Theatre and Dramatic Theatre* (1960).

**Satire.** Literary form which ridicules the weaknesses of individuals and social groups. It employs verbal *irony and often tells an allegorical *story or *fable which traps the reader into false sympathies. Thus in Swift's *Gulliver's Travels* (1726) the reader tends to identify with Gulliver in Book I, laughing at the excesses of the Lilliputians, only to find in Book II that Gulliver has become a Lilliputian and is mocked in his turn by the King of Brobdingnag. When the king, after hearing Gulliver's 'admirable panegyric' upon his country, judiciously asserts that Gulliver belongs to 'a pernicious race of little odious vermin' the reader hastens to dissociate himself from Gulliver.

This sudden switch of viewpoint is very similar to what Brecht (1898–1956) called *estrangement or *alienation, and Brecht's *parable plays are very close to satire. Instead of operating through an ironic author/*narrator, however, satirical drama works through stage presentation and *dialogue.

The tradition of dramatic satire is long. It descends from

Aristophanes (c. 448 B.C.–c. 380 B.C.) through Roman *comedy, to Ben Jonson (1572–1637) to Molière (1622–73) and Oscar Wilde (1854–1900). In the twentieth century, the *theatre of the absurd, from Jarry's *Ubu Roi* (1888) to the work of Eugène Ionesco (1912–  ). has strong satirical elements. Ionesco's *Rhinocéros* (1960) is a political satire which employs *allegory to depict a world in which people herd together and are transformed into rhinoceroses. The seriousness of its real subject (the conversion of people to fascism) makes itself felt behind the gaiety of the allegorical story. One of the main characteristics of satire is the creation of a disquieting discrepancy between the playfulness of the fiction and the harsh *realism of its subject. Satire censures and protests, but it also entertains.

**Satyr plays.** Parodic plays which followed the performances of *tragedy at the *City Dionysia. They employed a *chorus of satyrs, followers of Dionysos, headed by Silenus. The only extant plays of this kind are Euripides's *Cyclops* (438 B.C.) and parts of Sophocles's *Ichneutae* (date unknown). The satyr play may have sprung from such primitive forms of drama as the dance on the threshing-floor, which celebrated harvest and offered thanksgiving to Demeter, goddess of fertility. Such dances may have developed into a *dithyramb and then into the satyr play.

Silenus started as a water-spirit in Asia Minor. His job was to see that the vines were well-watered. Later he took to drink, replacing the contents of his water-skin with wine. He was joined by the satyrs and recognized as their father. The god Pan seems to be a close ancestor of the satyr chorus. They wore tails, snub-nosed *masks, pointed ears and goat-skins, but they were never goat-legged. Amoral, indulging their appetites freely, child-like and acquisitive, they prefigure the *clown and *fool.

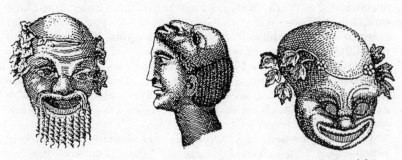

**25** *Masks for satyr-plays (from F. Ficaronius,* Dissertatio de Larvis Scenicis)

The two extant plays employ a heroic theme and tragic diction but mingle this with *burlesque elements and even *farce. The characters of Silenus and the satyrs, in their strong allegiance to the person in power and in their will to be on the winning side, are the precursors of the tricky servant of the *comic tradition.

**Scaffolds.** Raised platform stages used in the performance of *mystery and other medieval plays. They were erected on *Corpus Christi day, and at other festivals, along a processional route through a city or in market squares and round the edges of spaces such as the one in which the early fifteenth-century *morality play *Castle of Perseverance* was performed. (See Ill.28, p.394.)

**Scapegoat.** Chosen victim; person made to suffer for the sins of others. In the original Mosaic ritual on the Day of Atonement two goats were chosen and assigned by lot to the Lord or to Azazel (Satan). The goat which was 'for the Lord' was sacrificed; the other (the scapegoat) was allowed to go free into the wilderness. This and other rituals, described in Frazer's *The Golden Bough*, seem to be related to the central preoccupation with sin and guilt, and with *miasma and *catharsis, in Greek *tragedy. The word 'tragedy' comes from the Greek for 'goat-song' and a pattern of major tragedy from *Oedipus Rex* (*c.* 430 B.C.) to *King Lear* (1605) is that of the wanderer who sets himself beyond the pale by infringing grave rules such as the *taboo on incest, patricide or murder. He then goes forth into the wilderness, where he atones and dies. In different ways the scapegoat pattern can be applied to Lear, Gloucester, Othello, Macbeth, Hamlet, Antony and Coriolanus, who like their Greek forebears, are cut off from normal relations and, either literally or metaphorically, are set, or set themselves, outside the walls of society. They may even in their suffering enter a pattern of *sacrifice and, like Oedipus or Cordelia and King Lear, become in some way holy:

> Upon such sacrifices my Cordelia,
> The Gods themselves throw incense. (*King Lear* V.iii.20).

Sartre's *The Flies* (1942), based on the Orestes story, subjects the scapegoat ritual to psychological scrutiny. According to Sartre, scapegoating can be a way of evading social, political and personal responsibility. In this dramatic *allegory it is a form of 'bad faith' which allows *bourgeois groups to escape the guilt of living in occupied Paris during World War II. (To resist or do nothing both entail guilt.) In *The Flies* Orestes chooses to be the scapegoat and leaves the citizens of Argos/Paris to their unacknowledged crime. Again the scapegoat hero is shown as both sacrifice and wanderer, both polluted and holy. Perhaps, as Edmund Wilson suggests, he carries a terrible truth which the group fears to face. For further discussion of such highly speculative questions, see:

BRONOWSKI, J., *The Face of Violence*, Turnstile, 1954.
FRAZER, SIR JAMES, *The Golden Bough*, Macmillan, 1922.

SARTRE, J.-P., *The Flies*, Hamish Hamilton, 1946.
WATTS, C.T., 'King Oedipus', in *Reconstructing Literature*, edited by L. Lerner, Blackwell, 1983.
WILSON, E., *The Wound and the Bow*, Methuen, 1961.

**Scapino.** A servant figure in the *Commedia dell'Arte*.

**Scaramucchio.** A servant or *zanni figure in the *Commedia dell'Arte* who became Scaramouche in France and has points of resemblance with the *stereotype of boastful soldier, or '*miles gloriosus*'. See CAPITANO.)

**Scenario.** A brief outline of a *plot, indicating situation and changes of setting. The actors of the *Commedia dell'Arte* used scenarios as a common basis for their *improvisations. A *film scenario contains more detailed scenic directions.

**Scene.** Sub-division of an *act. It is divided from other scenes by brief breaks in the action when the stage momentarily empties, or by a *curtain or *blackout.

Variety of scene is essential to dramatic interest. A scene may be enacted in a public or private *space and the number of actors can vary from two to a crowd. *Rhythm, *tone and atmosphere vary both between and within scenes. A scene with great internal variety is the famous 'closet scene' in Shakespeare's *Hamlet*. It has its own subdivisions and points of *climax. Polonius is killed early in the scene and the Ghost appears late. These events give a different colouring to the exchanges which precede and follow them. The whole, however, is a single scene, being a confrontation in one place between mother and son. It is important within the total action of the play because it changes the Queen's attitude to the King and advances our awareness of Hamlet's feelings for his mother. Above all, it contains the action which gives Claudius a reason to banish Hamlet and have him murdered. It is a powerful example of the way a scene plays an integral part in the overall dramatic structure.

***Scène à faire.*** A scene towards which other scenes build and which the audience awaits so keenly that it cannot be omitted.

**Scene-change.** Change in dramatic location, usually involving change of *scenery. Until the later nineteenth century, scene-changing was done in full view of the audience; devices for the speedy and simultaneous changing of *wings and *shutters contributed to the audience's enjoyment of the spectacular visual and *perspective effects. With the development of *box-sets, and the use of heavy *properties in *naturalist plays, it became more difficult to effect rapid changes of scene and the dramatic action was restricted to few locations or, indeed, to only one.

On *open stages, of course, since the location of the scene is created by the actors' movements and words, scene-changes need not involve shifting of scenery and need cause no interruption of the play's *rhythm. Shakespeare's Antony and Cleopatra (1606–7) has over forty changes of scene. As it moves between Rome and Egypt *mood, atmosphere, *light, *time, locality and temperature alter almost instantaneously and the scene-change must be created by the actors with facial expression, *voice and *body. The nature of a scene-change thus depends on the nature of the play and the *stage on which it is played.

**Scene-dock.** Scene-room; the area of a theatre where *scenery is constructed and stored.

**Scene-painting.** The elaborate decoration of stage *scenery. It grew in the Italian scenic theatre with the work of Giacomo Torelli (1608–1678). Torelli brought it with him from Venice to Paris in 1645, whence Charles II took the fashion to England where the *court masques of Inigo Jones (1573–1652) had already introduced the *picture-frame stage and a taste for spectacle. It was not until a hundred years after the *Restoration, however, that the work of English designers began to compare in brilliance with that of such continental artists as the Bibbiena family. Scene-painting of such a standard was only achieved when Philip de Loutherbourg (1740–1812) became scenic director at Drury Lane, producing for Garrick (1717–79) and Sheridan (1751–1816) spectacular and strikingly realistic *lighting, scenic and *sound effects.
JOSEPH, S., Scene-Painting and Design, Pitman, 1964.

**Scene-room.** Room where scenery is stored. Also an alternative word for *'green room'.

**Scenery.** Stage decoration usually suggesting the location of a dramatic action. *Naturalistic scenery attempts to create a full illusion of location, but realistic items of scenery may also be used as an *index of place, as when a scenic *prop indicates the location. This occurs in *epic theatre where a waggon, door or bath-tub can indicate where a scene is set. Scenery may also be abstract or *symbolic, evoking an atmosphere or, as in *expressionist drama, suggesting states of mind.

Drama does not always require scenery since location can be suggested by words and established by the actors alone. In addition, when action is in the *round, or on an *apron stage, scenery can cause problems of *masking and simple props are often sufficient.

Scenery may be considered a recent development, since the unchanging back walls of the Greek, Roman or Elizabethan theatres were permanent, not created as *backdrop for a particular play. *Periaktoi carried scenic decoration, but three-dimensional scenery first appeared with the locus or *mansion of the medieval theatre. Set in church, then in market-place or hall, the dramatic action would move from one mansion to the next. On a stage, as shown in a famous design for the Valenciennes Passion Play (1547), this system was less flexible, and the basic perspective settings of Serlio (1475–1554) for *tragedy, *comedy and *satyr play superseded it. For interior and rural settings, painted backdrops were subsequently extended by *wings and *cloudings. Then a growing concern with historical accuracy and *realism in the eighteenth century led to the nineteenth-century development of the *box-set. This provoked in its turn a reaction against the rigidity of *facsimile staging and a realization that *film could create more convincingly 'real' sets. The early twentieth century saw more symbolic and expressionist theatrical designs, and a partial return to the *open stage. Nonetheless, the commercial theatre still employs much conventional and naturalistic stage scenery.

JOSEPH, S., *Scene-Painting and Design*, Pitman, 1964.

SOUTHERN, R., *Changeable scenery: its origin and development in the British Theatre*, Faber, 1952.

**Schiller, Friedrich von** (1759–1805). German Romantic poet, and tragic and historical dramatist, whose *Sturm und Drang* play *Die Räuber* (1771) helped create the vogue of *melodrama.

> The history of the world is the world's judgement. '*Die Weltgeschichte ist das Weltgericht.*'

> The depiction of suffering, as suffering alone, is never the end of art, though it is of the highest importance as a means of achieving that end. The highest aim of art is to represent the supersensuous, and this is achieved in particular by tragedy.

See: CHORUS; NAIVE AND SENTIMENTAL.

VON SCHILLER, F., *On Pathos* (1793); *On the Sublime* (1801); *Naive and Sentimental Poetry*, edited by J. Elias, Ungar, 1966.

**Schlegel, August Wilhelm von** (1767–1845). German Romantic dramatist, translator of Shakespeare, Dante and Calderón, and historian of drama. As a critic he insisted on the need for action in drama. His romanticism can be seen in his insistence on a poetic dimension in a play. This must

> bring bodily before us ideas, that is to say necessary and eternally true thoughts and feelings which soar above this earthly existence.

VON SCHLEGEL, A.W., *Uber Dramatische Kunst und Literatur* (1809–11).

**School.** A group of writers who proclaim a common programme. It is rare to speak of dramatists as belonging to a particular school. There are schools of painters and poets but dramatists rarely form such coherent groups: a *manifesto for a particular school of drama is almost unknown. On the other hand, there are many instances of writers collaborating. *Jacobean dramatists often worked together and modern *fringe writers frequently do the same. The recent emergence in England and America of *feminist and other groups has come close to the establishment of a school, but the groups are perhaps too fragmented and the formulation of common aims insufficiently precise to describe this as more than a general movement.

**School drama.** (a) Any play performed in a school; (b) drama which developed in European schools in the sixteenth century. The latter encouraged the study of Terence (c. 190–157 B.C.), Plautus (c. 254–184 B.C.) and the classics, and was often written to promote protestantism or catholicism during the Reformation and Counter-Reformation. It had other purposes too. Queen Elizabeth in 1560 decreed that scholars of Westminster should perform a Latin play 'that the young may spend Christmas with greater benefit and become better acquainted with proper action and pronunciation.' See JESUIT DRAMA.

**Scissor cross.** Two characters moving in opposite directions and *crossing on stage. It is normally considered an ugly move.

**Scissor stage.** This consists of two platforms, each pivoted at one corner *downstage left and right in such a way that they can be loaded with scenery offstage, then swung onstage together to effect a rapid and complete *scene-change.

**Scrim.** Gauze-like material used for *transparency effects in *box-sets. Scenes painted in dye on scrim give an illusion of solidity. They are opaque when the light source is in front but when the light source is behind, the scrim is transparent.

**Script.** Professional term for the *dialogue and *stage directions of a particular *role, or of a whole play or film. Critics tend to speak of a *text; there is something less definite about a script. Film-scripts in particular can be changed at the last minute, and improvised upon in performance.

**Scruto.** Material formerly used to effect rapid *scene-changes. It consisted of strips of wood on canvas which could be rolled and unrolled with great rapidity to cover *traps, for example.

**Secrets.** An important element in the creation of dramatic *suspense. All forms of *irony depend on two audiences, one ignorant and the other aware of a secret. In dramatic irony, the awareness both of a secret and of another party's ignorance of it is like an unresolved chord which impels a listener to go on listening until the *resolution.

The audience can be made aware of a secret early or late in a play. If it is early, the spectators enjoy watching the actors in what Strindberg calls 'their game of blindman's buff'. If it is late, the spectators are themselves kept in the dark. This is exciting and at the same time *uncomfortable* enough to create a strong desire for light.

The presentation of reality always involves secrets. Two people can rarely exist together and tell each other 'everything'. Few people, if any, know the entire truth about events in their own lives, and the less people know one another, the more secrets they keep. Three people together inevitably hesitate to talk of things important to them. The situation in which such things are revealed is of course highly dramatic for it is no accident that our greatest plays, *Oedipus Rex* (*c.* 430 B.C.), for instance, or *Hamlet* (1601), are about the discovery of secrets which people hesitate even to think of and whose revelation leads to catastrophe. Happiness may well depend on thinking we *know*, when we do not, and drama gains excitement from challenging assumptions of knowledge in both characters and spectators. The *hubris of Oedipus is a false assumption of knowledge.

It is thus not surprising that in *workshop practice, when *improvisation methods are used, a dynamic source of excitement lies in assigning 'secrets' to the various participants. Out of this, drama seems naturally to develop.

**Security.** A feeling of safety, to be distinguished from *serenity. To believe in oneself, in the future, in a group, a nation, a creed or a god is to have a sense of security. Audiences carry this with them into the theatre, and one of the functions of drama seems to be to threaten this feeling. Thus it often presents characters who suffer from the delusion of security or shows us characters seeking to recover a certainty or equilibrium which they have lost. The *hubris of Oedipus or King Lear, the everyday complacency of *Everyman, the unwitting *heroine of *melodrama and the unsuspecting figures of *farce all present an image of unjustified security. The plays present the image only to threaten or destroy it. Later, the play's *ending may suggest a new composure. *Comedy may even reconstitute the old security in the serene figure of the amazing, unruffled *fool.

In his celebrated first book *The Birth of Tragedy* (1872), Nietzsche (1844–1900) points to states of equilibrium which are of higher quality than a security which depends on the evasion of certain truths. Such states as those which he defines are less easily shaken than our more naive securities and are, one may argue, new forms of composure which art helps us to achieve.

**Sedes.** A *mansion, *locus or fixed scenic unit in the *medieval theatre. It was also called the domus or tentus.

**Self-reflexive.** Critical phrase for a work which is conscious of its own articifice and does not pretend to *realism. Catherine Belsey, in her influential book *Critical Practice* (Methuen, 1980), analyzes Shakespeare's *The Winter's Tale* (1610) as such a work.

The term is also used to mean 'self-focused'. In this sense much American *alternative theatre is self-reflexive. Actors draw upon incidents in their own lives and perform as themselves rather than as dramatic characters. Nudity is often employed to shock the audience into an awareness of the performers' physical reality. Individual directors and writers also make their own thought processes the subject of the drama. Richard Foreman's *Ontological-Hysteric Theatre (founded in New York in 1968) is an extreme case. *Le Livre des Splendeurs*, performed in Paris in 1976, enacts sequences of fragmented *stage images which represent Foreman's thought processes as he wrote the script.

ABEL, L., *Metatheatre: a new view of dramatic form*, Hill and Wang, 1961.

FOREMAN, R., 'How I write my (Self: Plays)', in *The Drama Review* XXI, December 1977, pp. 5–24.

SHANK, T., *American Alternative Theatre*, Methuen, 1982, pp. 155–190.

**Semiology/Semiotics.** The science of signs, hence the study of the means of human communication. Words and sounds, *gestures and other visual signals come under this heading. Drama, communicating through *theatre language in so many different ways, has special importance in this recently developed subject. The complexity of analysis required can be seen in:

BARTHES, R., *Elements of Semiology*, Cape 1967.

ELAM, K., *The Semiotics of Theatre and Drama*, Methuen, 1980.

**Send-up.** Colloquial term for *parody or burlesque.

**Senecan tragedy.** (a) Tragedies written by the Roman dramatist, Seneca (4 B.C.–A.D. 65); (b) plays highly influenced by these, especially Elizabethan *revenge tragedy.

Seneca's plays are *closet dramas. They are divided into five *acts with *choruses between, their subjects drawn from Greek drama and *mythology. They are static, containing long rhetorical *monologues and blood-thirsty descriptions (as of the death of Hippolytus in the *Phaedra*). They also make extensive use of ghosts and witches. The Elizabethans borrowed the ghosts and the gore and transformed the plays into highly effective theatre. The early *Gorboduc* (1562) by Norton (1532–84) and Sackville (1531–1608), *The Spanish Tragedy* by Thomas Kyd (1558–94) and Shakespeare's *Titus Andronicus* (*c.* 1590) all reveal a strong Senecan influence. Two important essays on Seneca — 'Seneca in Elizabethan translation' (1927) and 'Shakespeare and the Stoicism of Seneca' (1927) — are to be found in T.S. Eliot's *Selected Essays* (1932). See also:

BOWERS, F., *Elizabethan Revenge Tragedy*, Smith, 1940.
CHARLTON, H.B., *The Senecan Tradition in Renaissance Tragedy*, The University of Manchester, 1946.

**Sensation drama.** A term invented by Dion Boucicault (1822–90) to describe a kind of popular *melodrama which used the newly available heavy stage-machinery to mount spectacular scenes. When the machinery worked, and it sometimes did not, earthquakes, shipwrecks or train crashes heightened the dramatic excitement. Plays employing such effects proved so popular that instead of one sensation per play, sensations occurred in every act, each more sensational than the last. They were, of course, expensive, and productions were mounted only at the large London theatres. The 'disaster movie' is an obvious descendent of sensation drama.

BOOTH, M., *English Melodrama*, Jenkins, 1965.

**Sensation memory.** The retention in the memory of sense impressions, not only of sight and sound but also of touch, smell and taste. Stanislavski (1865–1938) employed the term, and stressed the way an actor can associate such memories with lines he speaks, or actions he performs. Sense impressions such as the feel of velvet or the taste of a particular food can be used by the actor to prompt facial, vocal and physical responses appropriate to the text and dramatic situation. This helps to keep a performance fresh night after night.

STANISLAVSKI, C., *An Actor Prepares*, Theatre Arts, NY, 1936; *Building a Character*, Theatre Arts, NY, 1949.

**Sense *and* Significance.** These terms differ in emphasis. 'Sense' suggests meaning 'contained' in a *text, whereas 'significance' suggests meaning within a framework of relations. Thus a 'significant remark' refers us to some meaning beyond its apparent sense.

**Sensibility.** Sensitiveness; the capacity to feel and respond.

Obviously important as a human attribute, it has been seen as inimical to the actor's need for detachment and technical control. Denis Diderot (1713–84), for example, asserts in his *Paradox of Acting* (1773–78): 'Sensibility cripples the intelligence at the very moment when a man needs all his self-possession.' It is, he adds, 'the disposition which accompanies organic weakness'. The word as employed by Diderot has a close relation to *sentimantality and to the effusions of feeling which Jane Austen gently mocks in her novel *Sense and Sensibility* (1811).

In the twentieth century the word has come to have the more positive sense of 'an interplay of thought and feeling', as in T.S. Eliot's famous phrase, *'dissociation of sensibility.' This usage, however, is to be found more in discussions of literature than of drama, and although the sensibility Eliot says was 'dissociated' in the seventeenth century is 'dramatic' (John Donne (1572–1631) is said to have had a sensibility which lent itself to theatrical gesture and dramatic expression) the use of the term has waned.

EMPSON, W., *The Structure of Complex Words*, Chatto and Windus, 1951, pp. 250–310.

WILLIAMS, R., *Keywords*, Fontana, 1976, pp. 250–8.

**Sentimental comedy.** An eighteenth-century theatrical form, traceable to Colley Cibber (1671–1757) and Richard Steele (1672–1729). What was new, after the licentiousness and vitality of *Restoration comedy, was a note of *pathos along with a conscious moralizing in the form of a fifth act in which the dissolute central figure underwent moral reform. (See Steele's *The Lying Lover* (1703) and his conscious statement of intent in the preface). At the heart of sentimental comedy lies a similar kind of hypocrisy to that which has been located in the eighteenth-century novel, and in particular in the work of Samuel Richardson (1689–1761); arguably, the old forms of comedy and licentiousness were retained so that they could be 'consumed' and enjoyed as much as the moralizing which was approved and applauded. Sentimental comedy can be traced in the novels of Dickens (1812–70) and anticipates nineteenth-century *melodrama and the Hollywood 'weepie' in its naive appeal.

Goldsmith's *The Good-Natured Man* (1768) seems to belong to the genre but the same writer attacked such sentimental drama in his *Essay on The Theatre* (1773). His comments might still apply to forms of *soap opera today:

> It is only necessary to raise the characters a little; to deck out the hero with a riband, or give the heroine a title; then to put an insipid dialogue, without character or humour, into their mouths, give them mighty fine hearts, very fine clothes, furnish a new set of scenes, make a pathetic scene or two, with a sprinkling of tender melancholy conversation throughout the whole, and there is no doubt but all the ladies will cry, and all the gentlemen applaud.

Goldsmith's *She Stoops to Conquer* (1773) confirms the writer's disapproval.

Sheridan (1751–1816) also attacked sentimental drama, through his *parody of the 'man of sentiment', Joseph Surface, in *The School for Scandal* (1777) and his *burlesque, *The Critic* (1779), in which Richard Cumberland (1732–1811), the dominant practitioner of sentimental comedy, is presented as Sir Fretful Plagiary. Despite the mockery of hypocritical exhibitions of surface sentiment in the former play, Sheridan yet presents us with Charles Surface, the reforming rake, whose warm heart and heroic status indicate that he belongs to the new sentimental comedy and that the writer found his moral centre in benevolence.

BERNBAUM, E., *The Drama of Sensibility; a sketch of the history of English sentimental comedy and domestic tragedy*, Harvard University Press/Oxford University Press, 1925.

**Sentimentality.** A strong, simple emotional response ungoverned by *irony or intellectual control; a kind of unthinking participation in the experiences and sufferings of living people or fictional characters. Writers can invite it; characters can both invite and demonstrate it; readers or spectators can seek it out and enjoy it.

It is found in extreme form in the nineteenth-century *melodrama and in the Hollywood 'weepie' which derives from it. Such forms are apt to make a clear differentiation between good and evil, and between *hero and *villain. They have often been condemned as 'escapist' or 'self-indulgent' and are strongly disliked by those with a taste for psychological subtlety. However, the tapping of a direct and deep sentimental response seems to be a characteristic not only of relatively crude and primitive forms, but of some of the greatest European writing. Simplicity and virtue exist in the *mystery cycles and *morality plays which lie behind Shakespearean *tragedy, especially *King Lear* (1605) and *Macbeth* (1606). Dostoievski and Dickens drew on popular *melodrama and presented the *pathos of suffering innocence. Sometimes simplicity can be so rendered that we are brought to suspect complex minds which express themselves ironically, as with Shakespeare's Cordelia, or Miranda in *The Tempest* (1611) or Dostoievski's saintly Sonia Marmeladov in his novel *Crime and Punishment* (1866). A powerful and simple response seems in these cases a necessary basis of our humanity and of our response to art.

At the same time, of course, *laughter lurks wherever too simple an appeal is made to our sentimental needs. It is a laughter which reasserts our independence and selfhood when the pull of sentiment has threatened to overcome them. Thus with some audiences melodrama can make a naive and serious appeal but with a more sophisticated audience it can appear as comic *burlesque. See NAIVE AND SENTIMENTAL; SENSIBILITY.

**Serenity.** Composure or tranquillity; one of the effects sought but not always found in art. F. Nietzsche (1844–1900) makes some intriguing distinctions in his seminal *Birth of Tragedy* (1872) between different kinds of serenity. He points to the chaotic and orgiastic elements in life which he calls the *dionysiac and associates with *music, dance and physical activity. The serenity induced by *tragedy emerges, he seems to argue, from the contemplation of these elements and their transformation into visual *image. This he calls the *apollonian principle. The wedding of Dionysus with Apollo, of music with painting, of choral dance in the *orchestra with the individual actor on the *skene or stage — these result in a kind of serenity. This, he further suggests, is a higher state of apprehension than the serenity achieved by the purely philosophic 'post-tragic' contemplation of Socrates or the 'pre-tragic' *epic serenity.

Nietzsche's ideas are based on a study of the elements of Greek *tragedy and also on an awareness of the nature of creativity, as is apparent when he quotes Schiller's observation:

> With me emotion is at the beginning without clear and definite ideas; these ideas do not arise until later on. A certain musical disposition of mind comes first, and after follows the poetical idea.

By exploring the complex relations between emotion and thought, action and dream, and what Schopenhauer termed 'will' and 'understanding', Nietzsche arrived at his distinction between the 'apollonian' and 'dionysiac' — which anticipates the duality of Freud's 'ego' and 'id'. When he says that tragedy achieves a serene synthesis of profoundly contradictory elements in life and in man himself, Nietzsche seems to argue that tragedy reconciles not only the visual with the musical, but the conscious with the unconscious.

NIETZSCHE, F., *The Birth of Tragedy* (1872), trs. F. Golffing, Doubleday Anchor, 1956.

**Sesame.** An organization which encourages the therapeutic use of drama for the handicapped.

**Set.** The environment within which the actor performs. The term refers especially to the three-dimensional element of this — the *rostrum, furniture of the *box-set — as opposed to 'flown' and two-dimensional scenery.

A set, being heavier, is more costly and can take longer to shift than *wings and painted scenery. *Waggon, *scissors and *revolving stages, with built sets on them, can effect rapid changes, but require large spaces and involve great expense.

A set can make a considerable contribution to the dramatic effect of a play by: (a) helping the actor to feel the 'reality' of the stage illusion; (b) providing a source of additional visual interest; and (c) relieving the actor and writer of the need to 'create' in actions and words the scene around them. The scene is already there and the actor need only perform appropriately.

The stage set has disadvantages, of course. It takes time to build and costs money; it can limit the actors by restricting them to one appropriate style of behaviour and delivery; it can be heavy, difficult to change, and may thus restrict the number of locations a writer can use. The *naturalistic set fixes a play in *time and *space, and fails to draw on the spectator's willingness to participate in the imaginative creation of the stage space.

**Set speech.** The equivalent of an aria in *opera; lines which have a special dramatic appeal and give actors a chance to demonstrate their skill. The 'All the world's a stage' speech by Jaques in Act II Scene vii of Shakespeare's *As You Like It* (1599–1600), is a famous example.

**Setting.** See SET.

**Shadow-show.** Popular show, originating in China, Java and Bali in which shadows are projected onto a lighted screen by puppets moving behind it. It came to western Europe via Turkey and Greece in the eighteenth century. Known as *ombres chinoises* in Paris, and as the galanty show on the London streets, the shadow-show was popular through much of the nineteenth century.

**Shame.** See PRIDE.

**Shaw, George Bernard** (1856–1950). Irish dramatist and critic, promotor of the *naturalist drama of Henrik Ibsen, socialist and advocate of the discussion play:

> Formerly you had, in what was called a well-made play, an exposition in the first act, a situation in the second, an unravelling in the third. Now you have exposition, situation and discussion; and the discussion is the test of the playwright.

In his concern with the discussion of social and political issues, and in his optimistic resistance to tragic attitudes, Shaw is an important forerunner of Piscator and Brecht.

> Now to me as a realist playwright, the applause of the conscious hardy pessimist is more exasperating than the abuse of the unconscious, fearful one. I am not a pessimist at all.

SHAW, G.B., *The Quintessence of Ibsenism* (1891), *Prefaces* (1934).

**Shutters.** A device deriving from the Italian *Renaissance stage. The shutters, as opposed to the *wings, shut completely to establish the back of the scene.

At scene-changes, shutters would either be drawn back *stage left and *stage right to reveal the 'backing' behind or were closed to conceal it. Inigo Jones introduced this device into the *court masques he designed for James I.

CAMPBELL, L.B., *Scenes and Machines on the English Stage*, Barnes, 1960.

SOUTHERN, R., *The Georgian Playhouse*, Pleiades Books, 1948.

**Sight lines.** Lines drawn between the eyes of spectators and the stage action. The general rule is that all members of the audience should clearly see all important stage activities. Actors' movements must therefore be carefully *blocked to take into account the view of the least privileged spectators — those seated extreme left, extreme right or in the highest row of the *gallery for whom the *proscenium arch threatens to *mask activity *upstage.

**Sign.** That which signifies something other than itself. Everything in the theatre is 'sign': the gun on the wall in Chekhov's *The Three Sisters* (1901), the portrait in Ibsen's *Hedda Gabler* (1890), even the tree in Beckett's *Waiting for Godot* (1953), which parodies the spectator's desire to see a sign; all *props, all *gestures, *colours, *costumes, *lighting changes, *facial expressions, *groupings and *movements. In short, all *theatre language, because it receives dramatic *focus on a stage, invites the audience to see it as sign. Characters too are signs, yet it is dangerous to see them purely as such. The director William Gaskill suggests that an actor's creative interpretation of character may be damaged if he begins to think in terms of what the character *represents* rather than of what he is. Yet audiences seem inveterately to transform the fluidity of perform-ance into the fixity of sign and message. It is a paradox which has itself become the subject of drama. Samuel Beckett's characters, for example, in *Waiting for Godot*, invite the audience to consider what they signify, and what Godot is. The play invites and parodies the desire to see signs everywhere, yet it provides a multitude of them and asks the profounder question: 'What is the reality which renders these signs intelligible?' Such a question returns one to the fluidity and vitality of the theatrical process which actors are generally so anxious to retain. This is as important as the signs at which we catch in the attempt to make sense of it all. (See INDEX; ICON; IMAGE; SYMBOL.) For an essay which applies the basic Prague School principles to the matter, see:

KOWZAN, T., 'The Sign in the Theatre', in *Diogène*, vol.61, 1968.

**Signifier/Signified.** The two aspects of a *sign according to the principles of the linguistic theorist Ferdinand de Saussure (1857–1913). The *signifier* is the material vehicle, and the *signified* the mental concept to which it refers. A play is thus a signifier containing many smaller semiotic units. The signified is what is retained in the individual and collective mind of the audience.

**Silence.** The absence of noise; a sudden break in the *dialogue lasting longer than a *pause.

Complete silence in the theatre is highly dramatic. When the words cease, all *movement and all *facial expressions have a heightened meaning. This creates a tension which must be held, not dissipated. Usually the silence resonates with the significance of the unsaid. Action is imminent, and its suspension is painful. Other silences allow the past to surface in the present. These tend to slow the action down. Both kinds of silence expand a character's and an audience's sense of *time. Thoughts of the past and future, bringing happiness and sadness, *fear and hope, intensify the drama of the situation, or relieve its tension.

The *theatre of the absurd, especially the work of Samuel Beckett (1906–   ) and Harold Pinter (1930–   ), makes brilliant use of silence, *Silence* (1969) is the title of a Pinter play which contains in its silences the rediscovery of its own past. As the play develops, certain phrases of the previous dialogue are repeated, accompanied by *pauses which prompt us to recall words in the dialogue which are *not* repeated. The play thus fills its own silences with its own half-remembered words. The result is a poetic but rather static drama.

Beckett also uses silences which focus on the past and lead towards nostalgia and inaction, but sometimes they look towards a future which promises little:

> *Vladimir*: What are you waiting for?
> *Estragon*: I'm waiting for Godot.
> (*Silence*.)

The silences invite us to reflect on what the characters prefer to leave unsaid. Gogo and Didi are caught between past and future, between inaction and action. They want to move and do not. The silences reveal their quandary, creating a powerful tension and cutting patterns in time which have the power of music.

Silence is dramatic because, like a rest in music, it is essential to a play's *rhythm and because it leaves a vacuum which needs to be filled. The audience fills it by discovering the author's *sub-text or by imagining things the author did not intend — or by mixing the two. There is a further possibility: the mystery a silence leaves, which according to T.S. Eliot (1888–1965), nobody likes to be left with, may hint at indefinable truths and a meaning which in Eliot's words 'reveals itself gradually'. See THEATRE OF SILENCE.

**Sill-irons.** Metal supports used to strengthen the base of an opening in a *box-set.

**Simile.** Verbal comparison indicated by the words 'as' or 'like'. Compared with *metaphor the simile is overt, not tacit. It calls attention to itself as a figure of speech, especially when it is worked out at length, as in Miltonic or Homeric simile. It thus tends to be a figure used in *narrative more than in drama, where the pithy metaphor can be accommodated more easily to the urgency of dramatic exchange. Simile is most likely to occur in drama where characters are in a reflective mood, speaking at length, concerned to describe rather than act. The consequent pause in the dramatic action varies the *tempo. Chekhov (1860–1904) supplies many examples of this. Gayev looks out of the window in *The Cherry Orchard* (1903) and reflects:

> How straight this long avenue is — quite straight, *just like a ribbon that's been stretched taut.* It glitters on moonlit nights. Do you remember?

The effect of such a comparison is to invite a spectator to travel with the character, into the past perhaps, or at least out of the immediate world of the play. Its effect is poetic. It introduces elements normally perceived 'out of the corner of the eye', as T.S. Eliot (1888–1965) says of *verse drama. It cuts across the flow of action in the immediate present and can afford the kind of relief that Homer or Milton offer in their *epic writing.

The dramatic simile tends, as in the example above, to be brief, and the world of the play is still close. Chekhov's simile moves us into the past but it also expands the immediate *space of the play. Gayev gives us a sense of the view he has from the window, before he moves off in memory. The simile has a descriptive function. But it does more than this. The taut ribbon suggests something that may snap, and refers us to subtle *sound effects in Act II, and at the end of the play, which also suggest something breaking: the snapping of a violin string, a break with the past, the breaking of a heart and the snapping of the thread of life as old Feers lies down just before the final curtain. Simile here is bound in with the poetic organization of the whole play.

Chekhov's simile connects the present with the past, what is seen with what is remembered or dreamed of. It is descriptive of scene and evokes feelings which cut across time. It is thus highly effective in the theatre where the spectator cannot be carried away as easily as a listener or reader. Unless he closes his eyes, the spectator remains in the present, in the often ironic context of the scene where the words are spoken. (The listener to *radio drama travels more easily away from the present scene in his imagination.) When in the theatre a character uses simile, therefore, and offers an invitation to identify with his imaginative world, the invitation is likely to be tempered by the spectator's awareness of the stage setting.

Where the dramatic simile is more extended than in the example given it can call attention to the way language is being used. We

watch the simile operate on other characters, and this distances us.
In Shakespeare's *Othello* (1604), for example, the Moor has a strong
pictorial imagination, and a special and dangerous habit of
self-projection which expresses itself naturally in extended
metaphor and simile:

> Like to the Pontic Sea
> Whose icy current and compulsive course
> Ne'er feels retiring ebb, but keeps due on
> To the Propontic and the Hellespont:
> Even so my bloody thoughts, with violent pace
> Will ne'er look back ... (III.iii.454–461)

The magnificent *rhetoric of this can, in the theatre, be shown to
be a form of self-delusion. Certainly when Othello ceases to speak,
the stage listener, Iago, distances the audience by his feigned
responses and calls attention to Othello's use of language with his
own mock rhetoric:

> Witness you ever-burning lights above!
> You elements that clip us round about!
> Witness that here Iago doth give up
> The execution of his wit, hands, heart,
> To wrong'd Othello's service! (III.iii.464–8.)

On the other hand, of course, powerful rhetoric easily arouses
group sympathy; the audience's awareness of Othello's sincerity
may cause the critical distancing to lapse.

The theatre, however, affords the *director a strong opportunity
for ironic distancing. The extended dramatic simile can carry the
audience into a character's mind and away from the present scene;
the audience focuses with the character on the content or 'tenor' of
the simile (i.e. on what is *signified). But when attention is drawn to
the *signifier or 'vehicle', as it is by Iago in the instance given, the
simile reveals something of the psychology of the character
employing language in such a way. Othello's poetic imagination is a
weakness as well as a strength.

The point is reinforced by another vivid Shakespearean simile,
in *Antony and Cleopatra* (1606–7). Cleopatra imagines Antony:

> ... realms and islands were
> *As plates dropped from his pocket.* (V.ii.91–2)

Again, here, Shakespeare seems to question the validity of the
pictorial imagination:

> Think you there was or might be such a man
> As this I dreamed of?

Dolabella's reply is: 'Gentle madam, no ...'. Cleopatra reasserts the
validity of her vision, but Shakespeare employs the stage situation
to *focus on Cleopatra's use of simile. He distances us and
simultaneously establishes sympathy for her mode of perception.

Similes are often used by Shakespeare as a way of defining the mental processes of his *fools and *villains. The villains demean others by comparing them with things of inferior status, thus raising their own. Iago in *Othello* does this constantly. Pairs of characters, like Beatrice and Benedict in *Much Ado about Nothing* (1600), use odious comparisons in a power game between the sexes. The emphasis here, however, as in the 'vile comparisons' of Shakespeare's Falstaff in *Henry IV* Parts I and II (1597–8), is on the fertility of imagination with which the author endowed these characters. This fertility has its own value. The capacity to find similes is a talent which renders language and human interchange vivid. Where the comparison is apt and clever it establishes a sympathy for the user, however much the author may make us ironically aware of the motivation behind such linguistic play.

**Simody.** Lower-class Greek *mime.

***Singspiel.*** Eighteenth-century German, popular, comic, *ballad opera, deriving from fairground theatre, French comic opera and Italian *opera buffa*. J.A. Hiller (1728–1804) was the earliest exponent of the form. It led towards the establishment of a German operatic style and the work of Mozart (1756–91).

**Situation.** The set of circumstances which the characters of a play must govern or submit to; the conditions which are established by money, power, influence and the *will to combat or control the will of others. These conditions may be seen as social, historical, natural, theological or a combination of these. The individual combats others. He also combats, or affirms, the laws of society, nature, history or the gods.

A well-known essay on the subject is Jean-Paul Sartre's *A Theatre of Situations* (1947). Sartre argues:

> If it is true that man is free in a given situation, chooses himself by and through that situation, one must show in the theatre simple human situations, and liberties chosen in those situations.

The view proposed is *existentialist, and in a sense optimistic since it implies that man is free and therefore responsible for his actions. The situation most strongly in Sartre's mind was no doubt that of war-time France, when the question of resisting or accepting the German occupation was fundamental:

> The situation rings us round, proposes solutions. The choice is ours. If one of the choices is death, liberty reveals itself in choosing self-destruction as self-affirmation.

Sartre later changed his mind about the degree of freedom man possesses. Nonetheless, he raised fundamental questions about the way man works upon his situation in the world, and how he allows such situations to work on him. When a choice must be made '*au pied du mur*', which will issue in pain and perhaps death, values are tested and the drama is intense. Sophocles's *Antigone* (441 B.C.), like Shakespeare's *Hamlet* (1601) and Brecht's *Galileo* (1937–9), presents the situation especially clearly, perhaps because the *protagonists are so aware of being '*en situation*'. Sartre's plays, such as *The Flies* (1943) or *Men without Shadows* (1946), provide a modern commentary on the situation.

**Skene.** The Greek stage building, originally the wooden hut or tent which was placed on the edge of the *orchestra, facing the amphitheatre. This skene, probably first used as the actors' dressing-room, became a permanent stage background, with three doors and entrances at the side. It also acquired one or even two additional storeys to provide entry for the gods, but the date of these changes is uncertain. We know, however, that in classical times the skene was on much the same level as the orchestra, so that actors and *chorus could relate easily and directly to each other. In *Hellenistic times the skene may have been raised as much as twelve feet above the orchestra. In Roman times it was about five feet higher. A standard work on classical stage conditions is:

BIEBER, M., *History of the Greek and Roman Theatre*, Oxford University Press, 1961.

**Sketch.** Short dramatic entertainment lasting about five to ten minutes and forming perhaps one 'turn' in a *revue. Harold Pinter (1930–   ) has written several revue sketches of this kind, including *Last to Go* and *Trouble in the Works* (both 1959). They are short dialogues, the first extremely slow and composed of *silences and forms of *phatic communion. The second makes play with specialized technical vocabulary and is spoken very fast.

**Sky-dome.** A device invented by Mariano Fortuny (1871–1949) who suspended a dome of silk over the stage to achieve impressive naturalistic effects of diffused daylight. The use of a *cyclorama has proved more popular, as it is less expensive and allows greater ease of *entrance and *exit.

**Slapstick.** Originally the wand used by *Harlequin in *pantomime to beat his enemies. The term now means *knockabout comedy.

**'Slice of life' drama.** Extremely *naturalistic drama which aims to create the illusion of real people behaving and speaking 'naturally' in a convincing *setting at a recognizable moment in time.

Such drama has its limitations. Public settings in, say, church or market-place, stock exchange or factory, demand large stages and are both difficult to make and expensive to build. Slice of life drama thus tends to limit its locations to relatively small rooms and has few *scene-changes. The slice of life it offers is therefore narrow. Paradoxically, however, this narrowness means that the dramatist must extend the play in *space and *time by referring to what has happened elsewhere at another time, and this constitutes an appeal to the imagination. As the naturalistic plays of Ibsen (1828–1906), Chekhov (1860–1904) and Strindberg (1849–1912) prove, the *genre has a great deal more poetry than its prosaic title suggests. A fine example of the type is Gerhard Hauptmann's *The Weaver* (1892).

**Sloat (slote).** Popular nineteenth-century device for dropping actors onto the stage from above, or for carrying them rapidly up into the *flies.

**Soap opera.** Long-running *radio or *television serial. Soap opera attracts a strong following and of all dramatic forms it seems to set up the strongest *identification between characters and audience. This may be because the *genre tries to present the 'people down the street' as realistically as possible, and because the story continues over months and years. The characters show 'ordinary life' from the inside, with the gossip and scandal and rows that we perhaps enjoy seeing in other people's lives, rather than our own. In British 'soaps', the Archers and Dales, the East Enders and the people of Coronation Street, come to seem so real that flowers are sent to their funerals.

Soap opera may also appeal through the generation of envy. American soap operas like *Dallas* create, not an ordinary world, but a world of power, where riches are yet no protection from disaster. Strong identifications are mixed with strong hatreds in a modern form of *melodrama which contrasts quite sharply with the *naturalism of the other principal brand of 'soap'. Each type, nonetheless, seems to exert a fascination. Its audiences become addicted to the genre. Perhaps this reveals a universal need both to see ourselves represented as images, and at the same time to escape from the narrowness of our own worlds.

**Social history of dramatic forms.** The study of changes in social and class-based attitudes within and towards the theatre, together with changes in theatre audiences, places of performance and the nature and structure of the drama performed. A useful condensed history of this kind is to be found in:
WILLIAMS, R., *The Long Revolution*, Chatto and Windus, 1961; Pelican, 1965, pp. 254–299.

**Socialist realism.** Theory of art evolved in post-revolutionary Russia in the 1920s and 1930s. It is associated in particular with

Lunacharski (1875–1933) and with Gorki (1868–1936) — who coined the phrase in 1934. The term defined the kind of art thought best able to advance the interests of the Soviet Union: a late nineteenth-century *realism which was didactic, propagandist and conservative in method, portraying working-class heroes striving to create a socialist future.

ARAGON, L., *Pour un Réalisme Socialiste*, Soviet Writers' Congress, 1935.

ZHDANOV, A., *Problems of Soviet Literature*, Lawrence and Wishart, 1977.

**Social tragedy.** A form of *tragedy which presents the fate of *hero and *heroine as determined by class background, social circumstance, parental attitude and childhood experience. The *genre emerged in the later nineteenth century out of a deterministic social Darwinism. The *naturalism of Ibsen (1828–1906) and Strindberg (1849–1912), and the novels of Thomas Hardy (1840–1928), have strong elements of social tragedy. They tend to deal with characters whose aspirations to personal freedom and control are blocked from without by public attitudes, and from within by acquired or inherited tendencies. See CAUSALITY; WILL.

**Society for Theatre Research.** Body founded in London in 1948 to preserve records of theatre activity and to promote research. An equivalent body was founded in New York in 1956. They publish, respectively, the *Theatre Notebook* (Quarterly) and *Theatre Survey* (Annual).

**Sociodrama.** Improvised drama whose aim is the exploration of social relations. Participants take on the *roles of representatives of particular social groups: a negro, a Jew, a waiter or an army officer, for example. The nature of their responses is observed and even sociometrically plotted. The process is not aimed at public performance but at group study and the development of social awareness. For a discussion of group interaction and behaviour, and for the early development of sociometry, see:

LEWIN, K., *Resolving Group Conflicts*, Harper, 1948.

MORENO, J.L., *Who Shall Survive?*, 1953.

**Sociology of the theatre.** The study of the theatre as an institution within the wider social process; the study of its resources, its audiences, of social attitudes towards it and its view of its own development and function. The study of the *social history of dramatic forms, and their relation to cultural and economic movements, is a natural extension of the sociology of theatre.

DUVIGNAUD, J., *Sociologie du Théâtre*, Presses Univ. de France, 1963.

SINFIELD, A., *Society and Literature 1945–70*, Methuen, 1983.

WILLIAMS, R., *The Long Revolution*, Chatto and Windus, 1961; *Culture*, Fontana, 1983.

**Sock.** Archaic term for *comedy, from the latin '*soccus*', meaning the shoe worn by the Roman comic actor. Milton makes a famous reference in his poem *L'Allegro* (1631–2) to Ben Jonson's 'learned sock'.

**Soft music.** *Stage direction indicating appropriate musical accompaniment to scenes in Victorian *melodrama.

**Soggetto.** Earlier term for the *Commedia dell'Arte *scenario.

**Soliloquy.** A monologue delivered by a character who either is — or assumes he is, alone on stage. Early soliloquies merely convey information about *plot or *characters, but during the Elizabethan period the device became very sophisticated and was used in various ways. The soliloquy could be spoken as if the actor were unconscious of the audience. The audience listened in, as it were, to the character's uttered thoughts. The actor could also address a soliloquy directly to the audience, taking it into his confidence. Iago in Shakespeare's *Othello* (1604) and Edmund in *King Lear* (1605) are characters given to this. The character may also impart in soliloquy what he *believes* to be the truth but which is in fact false. Thus Leontes in Shakespeare's *The Winter's Tale* (1610) reveals his own false suspicions of his wife to an audience which repudiates the assumed complicity. The speaker may of course mix the above kinds of soliloquy.

Whatever form it takes, however, the soliloquy is usually a pause in the action, gaining dramatic urgency, especially in *Jacobean drama, from the contemplation of immediate action to follow. If the device is directed towards the past it can prompt a passive mood and weaken the dramatic energy of a play.

**Song.** An arrangement of words set to music.

Colloquial *prose dialogue has not always been the language of drama. Classical drama may have arisen from *choral song and the *dithyramb, just as medieval religious theatre arose from the *liturgy. *Opera and *oratorio have continued to employ song, and it is often used in drama to vary colloquial speech. It may be used naturalistically, as by entertainers within a play, such as the *fool, or in drinking scenes, as in *Othello* (1604), or by men working, like the Gravedigger in *Hamlet* (1601). Alternatively, song may be appropriate to a character's mood, as when Desdemona expresses her sadness in *Othello*. Ophelia, in *Hamlet*, sings because of her unbalanced state of mind. Songs are lyrical and often satirical and they can lend great variety of mood to a play. This can be seen in Shakespeare's *As You Like It* (1599), which progresses from winter songs to songs of spring.

Songs occur in *naturalistic drama wherever it seems 'natural' to use them, but they are not always naturalistic. Brecht (1898–1956) often incorporates song into his plays as an *alienation effect, in order to break the *suspension of disbelief and to sum up the gist or *gestus of a scene or situation. Such is the use in *Mother Courage* (1941) of the 'Song of the Great Capitulation'. Brecht also uses song as a *narrative device to link his *episodes, as in *The Caucasian Chalk Circle* (1948), where it also marks and makes acceptable the narrative time-lapse between scenes.

Song thus has many functions. It may take the form of *choral commentary, or individual or group *narrative. It creates atmosphere, lends variety and accelerates time. It may also express strong individual feelings, whether mocking or deeply poignant, and when it is introduced in a *play within a play to entertain characters as well as audience it can establish a connection between stage listeners and auditorium which is part of a wider *realism.

**Sotie (sottie).** A *fool play, related to the *morality play and *farce, found in France in the late fifteenth and sixteenth centuries. Soties are associated wth festive occasions such as Shrove Tuesday and contain much mockery of officers of Church and State. Professional groups as well as amateurs may have performed them. The characters represent trades, vocations and social positions. Priest, Doctor, Councillor and Peasant mingle with more recognizable morality-play figures such as Abuse and World. Some of the action is spectacular enough to suggest a connection with the early *masque or masquerade, but the principle lies in the final reduction of all humanity, including the supposed wise man, to the condition of fool.

It is interesting to speculate on how far Shakespeare took the simple pattern of the sotie and transformed it into the subtle patterns of *As You Like It* (1599), *Troilus and Cressida* (1602) and *King Lear* (1605). All are plays concerned with ideas of fooling and foolishness, and all their characters are fooled or foolish at some stage of the action.

WELSFORD, E., *The Fool*, Faber and Faber, 1936, pp. 218–229.

**Soubrette.** The actress specializing in pert and coquettish maidservant roles, especially in *neo-classical comedy or *opera.

The soubrette's function is to add comic variety, act as *repoussoir* to the comic *heroine, advance the *plot with her clever scheming and encourage the confidences of her mistress. Dorine in Molière's *Tartuffe* (1664) is a notable example.

**Sound effect.** Also known as 'noises off', sound effects are especially important in *radio drama where the chink of a glass, a splash or a creaking door can create in the listener's imagination a whole pictorial scene. In stage drama, noises off, such as the sound of thunder or raindrops, can help extend the stage *space. Chekhov (1860–1904) is an expert handler of such effects. There is a very moving sequence of sounds at the end of *The Cherry Orchard* (1903). The family departs to the sound of an axe chopping down the trees. This is followed by the rattle of the horses' harness outside, a *silence and then the slow footsteps of the old serf Feers who has been left behind. The mysterious sound of a string breaking in Act II is then repeated at the play's end. This sound is never explained. It causes anxiety and uncertainty when it is first heard and provokes different reactions as the various characters try to explain it away. Its function is to disquieten the audience and illuminate character. The sound effects of *The Cherry Orchard*, together, say, with Beckett's radio play *All that Fall* (1958), repay careful study.

Less subtle plays, such as *sensation melodramas, may use sound to impress an audience with effects of great technical complexity. In *The Wrecker*, a train-wreck thriller of the 1920s, a crew of twenty men under the direction of the effects director created the impression of an express train rushing past a signal box, earning vociferous applause. Violent sound effects were also envisaged by Antonin Artaud (1896–1948) in his *theatre of cruelty. His purpose, however, was less to impress than to break down conventional audience responses.

*Film, of course, employs subtle use of sound. It does not always reinforce naturalistically the visual image it accompanies. The sound track may be musical and atmospheric, or it may comment ironically on the action. It may convey the sounds heard or remembered by a character on screen. It may also communicate the thoughts of an observer of the scene, as when in Polanski's *Tess of the D'Urbervilles* Angel Clare looks over a gate at an empty field and the sound track plays the music of the dance he remembers taking place there.

COLLISON, D., *Stage Sound*, Studio Vista, London, 1976.

**Source.** The oral, visual or documentary material out of which drama and other art is made. Every play has sources, though they may have been so disguised as to be unrecognizable. Fragments of conversation, old songs, forgotten plays and novels and well-known classics may be welded with other material and transformed in the process of creation. Material is often used whose origins are unknown. The rediscovery of such sources can be exciting and instructive, since the nature of the transformation throws light on a writer's methods, creative processes and primary *intentions. The identification of the material a writer borrows is of little value if a writer lacks the originality to make this material his own. The best authors, as Brecht says, do not borrow. They steal.

BULLOUGH, G., *Narrative and Dramatic Sources of Shakespeare*, Vols. I-VII, Oxford University Press, 1957–72.

**Source-book.** A work which an author has used as a *source.

**Space.** The use and organization of theatre space, and the way an illusion of space beyond the visible stage can be created, are both important subjects for study. The theatre architect, the *director, *writer, *designer, *sound and *lighting technicians, and of course, the *actor, must all make decisions about the use of the space they work in and the kind of space they create within the dramatic illusion. The architect establishes the relationship between *audience and *stage by shaping and organizing space within the building. The director, actors and designers between them organize the stage space by fixing precise *movement through it, *grouping and *posture within it, and *scenery around it. Effects of lighting can reduce the space or extend it. Sound effects, such as traffic noise, can create the illusion of a world outside the stage walls. The comportment of the actors, too, can give an illusion of rooms, or places they enter from or exit to. Within the stage space, *mime artistes can create the illusion of a room, a door, a fireplace or a cooking stove by simple precise movements of the hand and body. A *naturalistic play creates space by using solid *sets and *properties. This heightens the illusion of a 'real' place but loses perhaps the excitement and flexibility of forms which invite an audience to create the space in its own imagination. Naturalism may still, however, communicate 'interior space', a sense of what is occurring inside a character's head, even though, unlike certain forms of *expressionist or *symbolic drama, it does not do so by the use of setting.

Space then is organized and created in different ways, and the dramatist needs to be very clear about how this may be done, even though director, designer, actor and others may change or extend his *stage directions. A space can work very directly upon an audience. It can confine or expose, welcome or repel, and an audience responds to the way characters feel in a space, whether it be the claustrophobic set of Beckett's *Endgame* (1956), the exposed stage across which Oedipus journeys or the *offstage auction room where Chekhov's cherry orchard is to be sold. For recent experiments in the use of theatre space, see:
GROTOWSKI, J., *Towards a Poor Theatre*, Methuen, 1969, pp. 157–164.

**Spear-carrier.** A non-speaking *walk-on part in a play; by extension an undemanding and unrewarding role. Its function is usually to give the appearance of historical authenticity to a scene by swelling a crowd or a number of attendants. Actors playing such parts must take them seriously if they are not to destroy the scenic effect. For a discussion of the theatrical importance of careful preparation for a non-speaking role, see:

STANISLAVSKI, C., *On Producing Othello* (1948), contained in *Creating a Role*, Eyre Methuen, 1981.

**Spectacle theatres.** Theatres equipped to mount lavish spectacles. A term generally applied to the early, ornate and well-equipped permanent playhouses of Italy, such as the sixteenth-century Teatro Farnese at Parma which provided a model for European opera houses. Their emphasis on spectacle derives from *Roman theatre and lies at the opposite extreme from the Aristotelian tradition which runs through Shakespeare to Grotowski (1933–   ) and emphasizes *action, the importance of the *actor and the value of a bare stage. See POOR THEATRE.
KENNARD, J.S., *The Italian Theatre*, Vol. I, Blom, 1964.
NICOLL, A., *The Development of the Theatre*, Harrap, 1966.

**Spectatory.** Early word for auditorium.

**Speech.** (a) Spoken language; (b) a longer passage of a more formal nature; a 'set piece' amid the more fluid surrounding *dialogue. See DICTION; RHETORIC.

*Spieltreppe.* A staircase connecting various stage *levels, developed by Leopold Jessner (1878–1945) during the *expressionist period of German drama after World War I. It allowed impressive effects of *light and shadow, and of *movement and *grouping, in crowd scenes. The ideas and practice of Adolphe Appia (1862–1928) and Edward Gordon Craig (1872–1966) lie behind its development.

**Spoof.** Hoax. Game invented by the comedian Arthur Roberts Hoax (1852–1933).
ROBERTS, A., *Fifty Years of Spoof*, John Lane, 1927.

**Spot.** A strong, narrow beam of light used to *focus on a stage area, an actor or a face. Also the lamp which projects this beam.

**Stage.** Platform or space used for the performance of plays. There are various kinds: *arena, *thrust, *apron, *picture-frame or *fourth-wall, and *end-stage, amongst others.
  Stages vary in shape, size and height above the ground and they may be located indoors or out. Their *sight-lines and *actor-audience relations vary with the position of the audience, which may be above, below, in front of, around, or even *upon* the stage. A dramatist normally writes with a particular stage in mind. To mount a production on a different kind of stage may involve radical changes to the play. A good historical introduction to the development of stage spaces is:
SOUTHERN, R., *Seven Ages of the Theatre*, Faber, 1964.

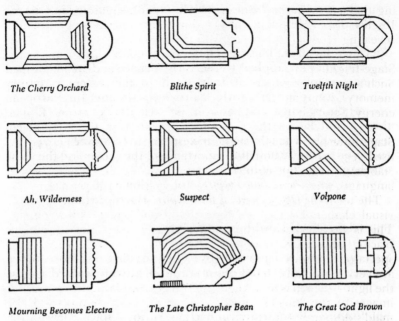

The Cherry Orchard · Blithe Spirit · Twelfth Night

Ah, Wilderness · Suspect · Volpone

Mourning Becomes Electra · The Late Christopher Bean · The Great God Brown

**26** *A very flexible playhouse was developed at the University of California by Ralph Freud between 1943 and 1947. Moveable risers for the seats permit the stage area to be rebuilt to suit each play. Above are plans for nine productions*

**Stage-business.** See BUSINESS.

**Stage-brace.** Rod supporting a *flat from the back.

**Stage-cloth.** Painted canvas serving as covering for stage floor.

**Stage design.** See DESIGNER.

**Stage directions.** Information give in the text of a play to clarify for *actor and *director the visual and auditory aspects of production. They are usually brief and indicate *movement on stage, *exits and *entrances, stage positions (*downstage, *upstage left and right), *sound effects, *lighting effects, *pauses and *scene changes. Stage right and left mean *actor's*, not audience's right and left. Sometimes directions indicate at greater length the *style of performance, the nature of the *set, the time of day or of year, or the temperature. Occasionally, as with G.B. Shaw (1856–1950), there is a lengthy physical and psychological description of the character, written for the general reader rather than the *director who, in any case, usually feels free to change any stage direction at his discretion. Imaginative directors, indeed, may transform the play by rearranging the set, as Ingmar Bergman did when he placed the attic in Ibsen's *The Wild Duck* (1884) downstage instead of upstage, revealing Hedwig's movements to the audience.

**Stage-fright.** Extreme nervousness before appearing on stage. Such a state induces physical tension and may affect the *voice or memory. Experienced actors learn, however, to harness such energy. See TENSION.

**Stage imagery.** Visual *imagery in the theatre. The term may be used very broadly to include *set, *props, *movements, *gestures, *tableaux and *groupings, in other words all visual *theatre language, where images impinge on the spectator's retina.

The term may, however, be used more selectively to mean those visual elements which are more heavily charged with meaning. This is always likely to happen in the theatre because the simple placing of objects, people and scenery on a stage causes the spectator to *focus on them and heightens their significance. Some are very powerfully charged: the noose held up — perhaps against the light — which is to strangle the Duchess of Malfi; the contrasted images of the Duchess meeting her death with dignity, and her maid's desperate effort to avoid it; the posture of King Lear as he kneels in ironic mockery to one daughter and in contrition to another. These are powerful stage images, heightened by *contrast, by the intensity of the dramatic moment and by their Christian context.

Stage imagery may perhaps be divided into Roman Jakobsen's categories of *metonym and *metaphor, with *naturalistic drama containing more metonymic images and *expressionistic drama more given to the metaphoric and symbolic. In the former, people and objects may be taken to represent the category to which they belong: father, mother, child, valet, landowner or peasant. In expressionist drama, characters and props exist more in the world of dream, where objects may often be symbolic substitutes for something else. (See ICON; INDEX; SYMBOL.)

This distinction, however, is too simple. A stage object, such as Chekhov's dead seagull, can be both naturalistic and symbolic; although part of the world of the play, it is treated as symbolic by the characters. Thus Nina's 'I'm a seagull . . .' causes an audience which sees the bird as a natural object (as metonym) to consider how Nina sees it as a symbol or metaphor. In this way the audience compares two *modes of imaging*. Similarly, a play can establish a stage image as metonym before a sudden cessation of movement heightens and emphasizes it. A *tableau, or a stilled movement (like Lear's kneeling) then takes on the power of symbol and remains in the memory after the play is over.

**Stage-keeper.** Principal stage-hand. Assistant to the *bookholder in the *Elizabethan theatre. See the induction to Ben Jonson's *Bartholomew Fair*, (1614), where Stage-keeper and Book-holder engage in a dialogue.

**Stage Society (Incorporated).** Important, pioneering society founded in London in 1899. It provided a platform for plays of high quality, both English and foreign, which the *West End would not stage. The first production was Shaw's *You Never Can Tell* (1899). The last was Lorca's *Blood Wedding* (1939).

**Stage-struck.** Obsessed by the theatre; smitten by the desire to be an actor.

**Staging.** (a) A temporary stage structure; (b) the process of putting a play on stage, taking into account the kind of stage to be used, the *lighting, costume, scenery and all aspects of production.

**Stagy.** Overtly theatrical and unconvincing. Used of a performance which calls attention to the means employed, to the acting and the *set, at the expense of the 'reality' of the play.

**Stalls.** Seats nearest the stage. Placed in front of the *pit in the 1830s, they gradually extended backwards under the circle. They are now usually divided into front, or orchestra, centre and back stalls.

**Stand-in.** Understudy; an actor who studies the part of another in order to take over in an emergency.

**Stand-up comedy.** Form of entertainment usually involving one or a pair of comedians. They work in different ways on different audiences but often get their laughs from mimicking *stereotypes and mocking (or flattering) rigid social, sexual or racial attitudes. Such 'light' entertainment has recently been used as a basis for powerful *absurdist and *political drama by, for example, Samuel Beckett (1906– ), Trevor Griffiths (1935– ) and the Italian, Dario Fo (1926– ). See LAUGHTER.
GRIFFITHS, T., *Comedians*, 1974, Faber and Faber, 1976.

**Stanislavski, Constantin** (1863–1938). Russian actor and director of the Moscow Arts Theatre who developed the most important and influential modern theory of *acting. His methods are very much based on his experience of producing the work of Ibsen, Shakespeare and, especially, Anton Chekhov, the *silences of whose plays provide so much material for actors to explore. Of the visit of the Moscow Arts to Paris in 1922 Michel Saint Denis says:

'Their performances were an enchantment. At once so moving and so comic, the dominant impression was poetic'. He adds that they displayed 'a freedom of acting I have never seen equalled'. It is as well to remember that although Stanislavski was concerned with 'inner states' – 'the sensing of the life of a role imparts an inner warmth' — he was very much concerned with external appearances: 'without an external form your inner characterisations will not reach the audience'.

> Here is a circle [running a finger round the edge of a glass]. In the centre is a superobjective. It is the circle of your life — the role. Life begins here and death . . .

See: ACTING; AS IF; CIRCLES OF ATTENTION; COMMUNION; CONCENTRATION; CONTINUITY; EMOTION; MEMORY; FOURTH WALL; IMPROVISATION; MAGIC IF; NATURALISM; PSYCHOTECHNIQUE; SENSATION MEMORY; SUB-TEXT; SUPEROBJECTIVE; SYSTEM; TENDENCY; THROUGH LINE; UNIT.
STANISLAVSKI, C., *My Life in Art* (1924); *An Actor Prepares* (1936); *Building a Character* (1950); *Creating a Role* (1961).

**Star-system.** Policy which bases commercial success in the theatre on the attraction of star actors and actresses, rather than on the reputation or quality of author, play or acting company. The term implies an absence of *ensemble playing, brief *rehearsals in which stars ensure than they will not be *upstaged and the deliberate creation and exploitation of 'big names'. The *staging usually focuses full attention on the star. One critic averred that the stage seemed to light up as Sarah Bernhardt entered. It did. The *lighting technician had been given specific instructions.

The system was prominent in the nineteenth century and, of course, in Hollywood. It evokes the names of a line of brilliant European and American actors which includes Deburau (1796–1846), Sarah Bernhardt (1845–1923), Eleanora Duse (1858–1924), Tommaso Salvini (1829–1916), Henry Irving (1838–1905) and Edwin Booth (1833–1893).

**Star-trap.** Opening with hinged flaps cut in stage floor. A counterweight system allowed such characters as the Demon King in *pantomime to be projected through it at speed.

**Stasimon.** A choral ode in *Greek tragedy.

**Static theatre.** Term used by Maurice Maeterlinck (1862–1949) to describe his *symbolist and *stylized theatre which eschewed extreme dramatic action and employed immobile forms and quiet words. Such a theatre was fundamentally religious. It provided consolation and reconciled the spectator to the inevitability of fate.

Meyerhold (1874–1940), who was much influenced by Maeterlinck in his reaction against *naturalism, makes the following comment:

> If an actor of the old school wished to move the audience deeply, he would cry out, weep, groan, and beat his breast with his fists. Let the new actor express the highest point of tragedy, just as the grief and joy of Mary were expressed: with an outward repose, almost coldly, without shouting or lamentation.

BRAUN, E. (ed.), *Meyerhold on Theatre*, Eyre Methuen, 1969, pp. 53–55.
MAETERLINCK, M., Preface to *Le Trésor des Humbles* (1896).

**Steal the thunder.** To steal applause from another actor. It is a phrase which originated with the writer John Dennis (1657–1734), whose invention of thunder for a play of his which failed was used in another play with a storm scene a few months later. Dennis complained that they had stolen his thunder. See THUNDER RUN.

**Stereotype.** Technical term for a casting in printing which can be used repeatedly. Hence in drama it is a type of character found in play after play: the tricky servant, the foolish old man, the absent-minded professor, the pert maidservant, the moustache-twirling *villain or the innocent young *heroine. Language, *gesture, and dramatic *situation may also be stereotypical.

The use of stereotypes is not necessarily a weakness in a dramatist. Stereotypes fulfil an audience's need for pattern and *repetition and it is not surprising that they recur in such dramatic forms as classical *farce, *morality play, neo-classical *comedy and *epic theatre. Nor is it surprising that stereotypes can be discerned behind some of the most complex characters in our drama: King Lear, the foolish old man; Macbeth, the fearful soldier; even Hamlet, the 'antick' or *fool. Stereotypes provide a base to build on, and dramatists may deliberately use a type and then depart from it to disturb an audience's automatic responses. If drama is *mimesis, in some sense a copy of the world, then the familiar and stereotypical can help us to represent it. One danger is that familiar patterns will *limit* our view of the world, and perhaps for that reason audiences and authors prefer them. As Nietzsche (1844–1900) observed, the copyist will paint only what he likes in the world: 'What does he like? He likes what he can paint!' But some authors can galvanize the stereotypes. They question the human need for them, and create the sense of *strangeness or *alienation which is close to the heart of both *comedy and *tragedy. (See LAUGHTER.)

The stereotype is not only to be found in literature and drama. The art critic E.H. Gombrich observes that artists need a vocabulary before they can embark on a study of *reality. Stereotypes provide such a vocabulary.

BERGSON, H., *Laughter* (1900), Macmillan, 1911.
GOMBRICH, E.H., *Art and Illusion*, Phaidon, 1960, pp. 55–78.

**Stichomythia.** A rapid exchange of single alternating lines of dialogue, usually between two characters. It is a rhetorical device of *classical drama, often used in disputations. The rhythmic balancing of equal lines can create both dramatic *suspense and comic effects of *repetition. Harold Pinter (1930–  ) and Samuel Beckett (1906–  ) have used stichomythia in these ways with colloquial dialogue. Pinter, in particular, has employed it to create a feeling of menace in situations where characters are seeking dominance. Shakespeare rarely uses it. When he does so as, say, in Act V of *As You Like It* (1599), it is to create an impression of playfulness and at the same time of utter control of theme and language:

> Phoebe:   And so am I for Ganymede.
> Orlando:  And so am I for Rosalind.
> Rosalind: And so am I for no woman.        (V.ii.90–118)

**Stock character.** See STEREOTYPE; STOCK COMPANY.

**Stock company.** A company that regularly acts together and performs a *repertory of plays at the same theatre. The term was used as early as 1761 and is usually applied to the nineteenth-century London theatres which became extinct in the 1880s (when Irving's company at the Lyceum was put out of business by competition from the *touring companies and the *long run).

A company of this kind can be a fine training ground for less experienced actors. It can cultivate the virtues of *ensemble acting. Actors who work together habitually can work fast and in great detail. A corporate sense can develop which sustains group energy and may impart a particular style and dynamic to production.

On the other hand, the word 'stock' retains a pejorative sense, suggesting the commonplace or conventional, as in the term 'stock character'. Economic pressures forced stock companies to develop a stock or *repertory of plays which could easily lose lustre on repeated performance. In addition, the Victorian practice of assigning stock or *stereotype roles to individual members of the company restricted both actors and writers. (See LEADING MAN; LEADING LADY; OLD MAN; OLD WOMAN; HEAVY FATHER; HEAVY WOMAN; JUVENILE TRAGEDIAN; WALKING GENT; WALKING LADY; UTILITY MAN; SUPERNUMERARY.) It also tended to encourage the cultivation of an actor's personality at the expense of character portrayal. By the 1880s acting styles promoted by the stock companies were becoming outmoded. Ibsen's new *naturalist drama created complex characters who no longer fitted the stock types. They required, as Shaw pointed out in *The Quintessence of Ibsenism* (1891), a new breed of actor, including *'heavies' who could tolerate being laughed at.

**Stock situation.** A pattern of relationships and events commonly found in drama; examples include the old father or husband blocking young love; variations on the 'eternal triangle'; the ambitious, poor man seeking power; or the couple parted by circumstances and mutual misunderstanding.

Such patterns often form the basic framework of major as well as minor drama; we may note for instance the love triangles in Chekhov's *Three Sisters* (1901) and the 'men on the make' in *Jacobean drama. They no doubt relate to the cultures from which they spring. They also raise questions about *universality; in this respect it is possible to see them as Jungian *archetypal patterns.

**Storm music.** A musical accompaniment to the frequent storms required by *Romantic and Victorian *melodrama.

**Storm and Stress.** See STURM UND DRANG.

**Story *and* Plot.** There is a famous definition in E.M. Forster's *Aspects of the Novel* (1927): 'The king died and the queen died. That's story. The king died and then the queen died of grief. That's plot.' The neatness of the distinction has its appeal. 'Story' is episodic. The various events are separate, linked by 'and' rather than 'because'. Thus Brecht's *epic drama is story, since its episodes are loosely connected. They may be added to, subtracted from, and even moved around within the play. Ibsen's *naturalistic drama, however, has plots, tight *causal *unities in which it is impossible to change the sequence of events.

The terms are not always used in this way. The Russian *formalists, on whom much modern literary analysis is based, make a rather different distinction. For them story ('*fabula*') is the *chronological sequence of all the events to which the plot ('*sjuzet*') refers. The author develops his *sjuzet* by selecting the events to be narrated, and if necessary changes their order. The plot re-arranges, interrupts, and moves backwards and forwards in time, giving greater emphasis to some events than others.

Drama normally retains a chronological sequence in the interests of clarity, and the formalist distinction may seem more relevant to literature than drama, since *flashbacks are more easily handled and therefore more frequent in fiction. However, drama is highly selective and if onstage action is defined as plot, and the term story or *fabula* is applied to a chronological sequence of all the events from which the play is taken, the definition is clear and useful. In Brecht's *Mother Courage*, (1941), for instance, the 'plot' consists of the trials of a small shopkeeper and is a very small part of a 'story' which includes the events of the Peasants' War narrated or flashed on screen at the beginning of each scene. In Ibsen's and Chekhov's plays, the enacted 'plot' is part of a story which includes many events which have occurred before the play begins. The audience must reconstruct the full story in order to interpret the events it witnesses. The formalist distinction could be interpreted as the difference between the embodied structure of the work and the mental reconstruction it invites. Forster's distinction is between two kinds of structure.

The formalist usage makes it easier to handle questions of causality. According to Forster, Brecht's plays would be 'story' because they are episodic and the scenes are connected by 'and' — like a compound sentence. Ibsen's scenes are 'plot' and linked by 'because'. Yet both Brecht and Ibsen are concerned with causality. In Brecht's case the looser sequence of *epic drama is meant to allow the spectator to question and even supply the *causality. (The 'story' for Brecht is not fully written though Marx supplies the causal pattern.) Ibsen invites the spectator to discover hidden motivations which he has worked out in detail and then concealed. *Rosmersholm* (1886) is an instance of such a hidden story. (Consider Freud's essay on Rebecca West's concealed relations with her father.)

Since drama is concerned with causality, whether it is in the 'plot', 'story' or in the audience's head, it is probably wiser to employ the more subtle formalist definition.

EHRLICH, V., *Russian Formalism*, Mouton, The Hague, 1980.

**Straight man.** The more serious of the two members of a *stand-up comedy 'double act'. The figure has a long ancestry and relates, like the *circus clown, to medieval conceptions of *Everyman. He is the 'ordinary' person who is often shown up as more foolish than the *fool or comic he appears on stage with. The old 'wise man/fool' pairing lies behind the modern comic television duo. Ernie Wise, the straight man of the former Morecambe and Wise double act, could not have been better named.

WILLEFORD, W., *The Fool and his Sceptre*, Arnold, 1969.

**Strangeness.** A feeling of *alienation or *estrangement. It is an important effect in the theatre. *Tragedy and *comedy both defamiliarize the world, as when Death takes *Everyman by the arm, or when a joke surprises us into a new perception of a person or situation. We see the world made strange for Oedipus upon the revelation of his birth, and comprehend why Hamlet finds it odd that others should be so much at home in the world. Drama, by its very nature, makes things strange by placing them in a new light on stage, often working by *revelation and *anagnorisis to confront character and audience with the crime of *hubris and the dangers of feeling secure within familiar and habitual surroundings. See FOREGROUNDING.

SHKLOVSKI, V., in T. Todorov (ed.), *Théorie de la Littérature: textes des formalistes russes*, Seuil, 1965.

**Strange's Men.** Elizabethan theatre company for whom Shakespeare may have acted and written his first play — *Henry VI Parts I–III* (1590–2). The company amalgamated for a time with the *Lord Admiral's Men, separated again in 1594, and left London for the provinces.

CHAMBERS, E.K., *The Elizabethan Stage*, Vol. II, Oxford University Press, 1923.

**Street theatre.** Theatrical entertainment which takes place in street or market-place. It often involves *clowning, busking, acrobatics, juggling and comic turns. Entertainment of this kind is one of the oldest forms of theatre, and groups of street performers seem to have a perennial attraction. The collapse of the Roman Empire must have released large numbers of *professional players across Europe to earn their living in such ways. Their descendents, the Elizabethan *travelling players, the *Commedia dell'Arte*, and some of the present-day *fringe theatre groups belong to an important, though underdocumented, theatrical tradition.

**Stress.** The amount of force, or breath, with which a vowel or syllable is uttered. In the spoken English language the breath is always expelled with more force on certain syllables than others. Thus Shakespeare's *Richard III* (1595) opens with:

> *Now* is the *win*ter of our *discon*tent
> Made *glor*ious *sum*mer by this *sun* of *York*.

The regular stress of the iambic pentameter $(-/-/-/-/-/)$ has been varied by inverting the stress in the first foot of the first line, and eliminating the stress in the third foot of each line (which should fall on 'of' and 'by'). Such variation brings the movement closer to that of everyday speech, whilst retaining the beat which arouses a certain expectation and excitement. In Shakespeare it is important to keep such a rhythm. At the same time monotony must be avoided and the speeches made clear by stressing the words of greatest importance. The selection of these is not always easy. Some of the stressed words need weaker stress than others and in the example given the very strongest stress could be made to fall on 'Now' or 'winter' or 'discontent', and on any one of four words in the second line. Listening to a highly skilled actor speaking Shakespeare's lines is very instructive. Further hints on discovering appropriate stess may be found in:

BARKER, C., *Theatre Games*, Eyre Methuen, 1977, Ch. 14.

**Striptease.** Entertainment in which a performer works up sexual excitement in an audience by discarding items of clothing. The dramatic tension this creates is sometimes used for effect in a film or play, as, for instance, in Tom Sheppard's *Travesties* (1974).

Bertolt Brecht once sarcastically compared the effect of *tragedy to striptease. The audience of *Oedipus Rex* (*c.* 430 B.C.), he says, become 'a lot of little Oedipuses' shouting 'take it off' as the tragic *hero is gradually stripped of all he possesses. One might argue that the pattern of his own *Mother Courage* (1941) is not dissimilar. How far one may compare the response of the audiences at a striptease with a serious theatre audience is another matter. Voyeurism and *Schadenfreude* may sometimes be elements of the tragic response, but this is debatable.

**Stroller.** Vagabond or itinerant actor. The term was used in the seventeenth century.

**Strophe.** Greek for 'turning'. Verse chanted by the Greek *chorus while it performed one movement of the choral dance. See ANTISTROPHE.

**Structuralism.** Intellectual movement which was developed out of the linguistic theories of Ferdinand de Saussure (1857–1913), and subsequent social anthropological theories, especially those of Claude Lévi-Strauss (1908–   ). It has widely affected literary and, recently, dramatic criticism. Briefly, structuralism seeks to define: (a) the structural relation between different parts of a play; (b) the relationship between play and audience; and (c) the dynamic social and historical *'structures' which generate drama. The structures may be considered *synchronic*, existing spatially, as it were, at a given moment in time, or *diachronic*, as patterns moving through time. The early emphasis was synchronic and tended to hypostatize the material it was applied to. A play is thus seen as a pattern in itself, or as part of a pattern linking it with its own, or the audience's, immediate present. Historical structuralism, on the other hand, may see a play as part of a 'flow' from the past into the future. Linguistic structuralism tends toward the former kind. It descends from Russian *formalism and seeks to apply linguistic *models to the play's organization. The relation between linguistic, historical and 'natural' structures is a matter of complex debate. 'Post-structuralism' is a recent development which shifts emphasis from the analysis of structures 'in' the *text to modes of perceiving it.

Structuralism has formed the conscious basis of live American theatre in the 'Structuralist Workshop' of Michael Kirby. His highly *formalist *Photoanalysis* (1976) and *Double Gothic* (1978) deliberately draw attention to their own structure by a series of careful repetitions of phrase, action grouping and movements which seem to relate to a narrative that yet remains incomplete. *Double Gothic* invites two audiences, seated on opposite sides of a central stage, and each invisible to the other, to complete two narratives which are shown simultaneously at a different distance and differently lit for each audience. As the performance progresses so the narratives intermingle, growing and fading or fading and growing, always remaining incomplete, so that the emphasis on *form rather than content is maintained.

EHRMANN, J., (ed.), *Structuralism*, Yale French Studies, 1970.

ELAM, K., *The Semiotics of Theatre and Drama*, Methuen, 1980, pp. 5–19.

GOLDMANN, L., *Le Dieu Caché*, Gallimard, 1955.

HORNBY, R., *Script into Performance: A Structuralist View of Play Production*, University of Texas Press, 1977.

KIRBY, M., 'Structural Analysis/Structural Theory', in *The Drama Review*, (T72), XX, 4 December 1976, pp. 51–68.

**Structuralist theatre.** See STRUCTURALISM.

**Structure.** A system or pattern. A complex term meaning originally (a) the process of making or building something, rather than (b) the completed product, which is the common meaning. It also implies (c) the relations between the parts of anything, and (d) its inner design.

In the first sense it might thus mean 'structuring' a play or performance. Much more commonly, the term defines the dramatic *genre: a one- or five-act play, an *epic, *chronicle or other form. It may also mean the network of relationships established between characters, events, verbal images or *theatre images, or between all these. It can also refer to *codes and *conventions to which a play makes appeal. These include the historical, psychological and linguistic patterns or processes to which it relates.

WILLIAMS, R., *Keywords*, Fontana, 1976, pp. 253–9.

**Sturm und Drang.** 'Storm and Stress'; a late eighteenth-century German movement, influenced strongly by Shakespeare, which produced the *Romantic drama of Goethe, including *Goetz von Berlichingen* (1773), and Schiller's *Die Räuber* (1781). These created a vogue for *melodrama, which lasted throughout the nineteenth century.

BRUFORD, W.H., *Theatre, Drama and Audience in Goethe's Germany*, Routledge, 1950.

**Style.** A set of characteristics associated with an individual author, a literary movement, a theatre company, a *genre or a historical period. In the theatre it may find expression in a characteristic language, syntax, range of vocabulary or form of speech. In visual terms it may be identified by a characteristic use of *colour, *lighting, *grouping or *gesture, or by any other special way of treating the dramatic material.

RUSSEL, D., *Theatrical Style*, Mayfield, 1976.

**Stylized theatre.** Any form of non-*naturalistic drama in which speech, scenic representation and/or *movement has a formal quality. The term is particularly associated with V. Meyerhold (1874–1940). In his published early theory, especially in *Teatr, kniga o novom teatr* (1907), he advocated a theatre which: (a) avoided detailed and complex *scenery; (b) put the emphasis on the plasticity of the actors' movements; (c) involved exaggeration and caricature; (d) used background music; and (e) avoided any pretence of not being in a theatre.

In this he was in rebellion against the *fourth wall convention and the *theatre of illusion. The influence of Wagner (1813–1883) and Maeterlinck (1862–1949) is strong. Meyerhold did not seek surface *realism but a method which revealed 'inner features which are to be found deeply embedded in the style of any work of art'. To represent this 'inner dialogue', which did not necessarily accord with the words, he sought a pattern of *movement. (In this he came close to Brecht's later emphasis on *gestus, and his often comic exploration of the discrepancy between verbal and visual language in the theatre.) He also had in mind the stylized and operatic Greek classical theatre, which invited much fuller audience participation. Extracts from Meyerhold's articles on *Don Juan* and *The Fairground Booth* in his *O Teatr* are available in:
BRAUN, E., *Meyerhold on Theatre*, Eyre Methuen/Hill and Wang, 1969.

**Subconscious.** An alternative term for the *unconscious — the area of the mind hidden from consciousness. According to Stanislavski (1863–1938) it is the source of an actor's creativity and a reservoir of energy. His famous *system and *psychotechnique developed out of his search for ways of tapping this energy.
STANISLAVSKI, C., *An Actor Prepares*, Theatre Arts, 1936, Ch. 16.

**Subject.,** (a) The theme of a play; (b) the *persona behind the play. See NARRATOR; IDEAL SPECTATOR.

**Sub-plot.** A sequence of actions within a play, involving a group of characters which is subordinate in dramatic and often social importance to the main group. Sub-plots vary in function, but generally they mirror and reinforce, or *contrast with and define, the main action. In subtle plays, such as Middleton and Rowley's *The Changeling* (1622) or Shakespeare's *King Lear* (1605), they do both. The famous 'Gloucester' sub-plot in *King Lear*, for example, with its old, foolish father, physically blinded, dispossessed by his wicked son Edmund, and accompanied by his good son Edgar, reflects the *main plot in which the old, foolish, mentally blind Lear, dispossessed and wandering, is oppressed by two wicked daughters and supported by the good Cordelia whom he has cast out (as Gloucester has cast out Edgar). The effect of a mirroring sub-plot, according to W.B. Yeats, is the creation of what he calls 'emotion of multitude'. By this he seems to mean an extension of the sense of suffering. The *protagonist does not suffer alone. At the height of the play, says-Yeats, awareness of distinctions between characters, or between audience and characters, melts and 'all is lyricism'. The sub-plot therefore brings about an intense and complete sharing in the characters' experience. This does not, however, occur throughout the play. The extraordinary intensity of Lear's responses is emphasized by the greater ordinariness of Gloucester, so that the audience does retain for much of the play a sense of the intense individuality of Lear. Gloucester acts as a kind of *chorus, a 'bridge' between audience and protagonist; but he is also a wall (if Nietzsche is right) to keep the audience out. He makes Lear human, but also superhuman.

The argument that sub-plots have a contrastive function is less obvious in *King Lear,* where the characters belong to the same suffering world, than in plays where a serious main plot has a comic and parodic parallel. It is evident in Shakespeare's *Henry IV* (1596–8) where the comic robberies of Falstaff and his gang reflect and *parody the serious political upheavals of the main action — just as the main action indicates the limitations of Falstaff's irresponsible 'holiday' view of the world.

The sub-plot thus comments on, repeats, varies and distances the main plot. It can supply an alternative mood and a *viewpoint which can define and extend, limit and/or intensify the play. It can also work less contrastively, as in *King Lear,* though still with the effect of 'setting off' the protagonists. This happens, too, in the Laertes/Fortinbras scenes in *Hamlet* (1601) and the Cassio/Bianca scenes in *Othello* (1604). See DOUBLE PLOT.

EMPSON, W.H., *Some Versions of Pastoral,* Chatto and Windus, 1935, Ch. 2.

YEATS, W.B., 'The Trembling of the Veil', in *Essays and Introductions,* Macmillan, 1961.

**Sub-text.** That which is 'hidden' or assumed to be hidden beneath the surface of the dramatic *dialogue; a felt pressure behind the words. It is a Stanislavskian (1863–1938) term, derived in particular from his work on Chekhov (1860–1904), Ibsen (1828–1906) and Shakespeare (1564–1616).

A writer may create characters who suppress thought and feelings, and all characters can be assumed to have a life beyond the play, which is not directly presented within the stage action. Stanislavski sought to create a sense of this hidden life through the actor's performance. He trained the actor to discover, or create, this hidden text so that he could communicate a sense of the unsaid through inflections of *voice, *facial expression, bodily *movement, *posture and *gesture. He used, in particular, methods of *improvisation to provide actors with a kind of *memory so that the actor as he moved and spoke would communicate a sense of his past, and of his hidden thoughts.

The sub-text, of course, may have been carefully worked out and disguised by the writer so that it is 'there' to be discovered. On the other hand, a writer who works more superficially gives the director and actors the task the writer should have performed — that of creating a sub-text to make a performance more convincing.

One should add that a writer's unspoken *intention can never be fully assumed. The 'sub-text' is usually generated by a complex transaction, in *rehearsal and on stage, between *text, *actor, *director and *audience, each of whom may discover what is there and create something which is not. See THROUGH-LINE; SUPEROBJEC-TIVE.

**Superintendent.** See PAGEANT MASTER.

**Super-marionette.** See ÜBER-MARIONETTE.

**Supernumerary.** Also known as the 'super'; a performer engaged by the Victorian *stock company for *walk-on parts.

**Superobjective.** The central purpose or ruling idea of a play. According to Stanislavski (1869–1938) actors must discover and define for themselves a play's superobjective. This will help them to find a *through-line, a shared direction in which all the perform-ances complement one another, and no scene, speech or piece of *business disperses the play's energy by throwing it off course.

To discover a superobjective, Stanislavski recommended that the actor should define his objectives at any point in performance by saying 'I want to' followed by an active verb. He should thus programme his role as a succession of desires. The actor playing Hamlet, for example, must decide when 'I want to kill Claudius' must take precedence over 'I want to prove Claudius's guilt'.

The actor of Hamlet may not find the approach simple. Stanislavski's technique raises large issues, such as the possibility of a subconscious desire opposing the conscious desire. Hamlet may *wish* to kill Claudius but at the same time he seems unable to will it. Nonetheless, Hamlet is a case of extreme difficulty, and it is possible to see the role as a sequence of alternating desires as one wish gains dominance over another. The same could be said of Macbeth and Lady Macbeth, as the will to power grows in the former, and an unconscious desire to cleanse herself of the deed grows in the latter. The case of Raskolnikov, too, in Dostoievski's novel, *Crime and Punishment* (1866) would yield to such an approach. The character wills murder, then wills to confess and conceal in alternation. The wills in these complex cases conflict within characters as well as between them. Stanislavski's method does at least offer a way of imposing a coherence on such conflicts of desire, and this may lead to the unity of performance that the director sought.

STANISLAVSKI, C., *An Actor Prepares*, Theatre Arts, NY, 1936.

**Surprise.** The reversal of the expectations of an *audience or a *character or both. Surprise appears to be an essential component of drama. Audiences may go to the theatre for confirmation of their attitudes and beliefs. (See BOURGEOIS THEATRE; STEREOTYPE.) They also go to be refreshed by the unexpected, to be reminded what they have forgotten, or told what they do not know. *Repetition fulfils a need, and so does surprise.

Drama surprises an audience in several ways. It does so firstly by *story and *plot. An unknown sequence of events communicates novelty. A known sequence, as when a play has been seen before or is based on a common *myth or known historical episode, must provide a different source of interest. This may come out of the further discovery of a play's richness which a second performance reveals. Again, a new production and new interpretation may contradict expectations. The dramatist may make slight and cunning adjustments to a well-known story by the creation of new languages and fresh characterization.

Such are the more obvious sources of surprise. A more subtle means derives from the audience's *identification or *empathy with a character such as Oedipus who is ignorant of what is about to happen. In this case the reversal of ignorance (see PERIPETEIA; DISCLOSURE; RECOGNITION; ANAGNORISIS; IRONY) comes as a surprise, not to the audience, but to the character. The audience, however, participates in some sympathetic way with the character's shock.

A spectator can thus be surprised by events, by the interpretation of events, by high skills of performance and by participating in the vicissitudes of a play's action through some degree of identification with a character. Other forms of surprise tend to occur in *farce and *comedy, where unexpected and *absurd turns of phrase, farcical pieces of business, the loss of a false moustache, or the sudden or *chance happening can reverse expectations. Nor should one forget Brecht's famous *alienation effect, which is fundamentally a sudden shift of perspective. One example Brecht gives is of a 'school-master hounded out by the bailiffs': a man with social prestige is placed in an undignified and unexpected situation which surprises us into a new view of him. Such a reversal can lead us to mock or to sympathize, but it points to a central way in which drama works — by setting up expectations in audience and character and then demolishing them in a shock of comic or tragic surprise.

**Surrealism.** Important literary and artistic movement of the 1920s which developed out of *symbolism and *dadaism in Paris. In its attack on *realism and *bourgeois art and attitudes, in its concern with the world of *dream and the *unconscious mind, it had a powerful impact on drama and *film. Artaud's *theatre of cruelty and the so-called *theatre of the absurd have their roots in surrealism.

NADEAU, M., *The History of Surrealism*, trs. R Howard, Cape, 1968.

**Suspense.** The condition of being kept waiting, experienced in a variety of ways by character and audience. It takes different forms which one may call: (a) sympathetic suspense; (b) suspense of ignorance; (c) performance suspense; and (d) musical suspense.

A theatre audience may *identify with characters in a painful *situation, often intensified by dramatic *irony. (The audience is aware of things the character is not aware of, knows what will or might happen to, say, the unsuspecting innocent of stage *melodrama or the Hitchcock thriller.) This is sympathetic suspense. The audience may also be in suspense because, like the characters, it is ignorant and needs to resolve anxieties, satisfy its interest or perhaps retain self-esteem. The whodunit appeals in this way. A third form of audience suspense may be created by the performance of something very skilled and difficult like a *circus act, *mime or any form of stylized drama which requires absolute physical control. Suspense grows out of the awareness of how easy it is to make a slip. Finally, musical elements in a play also create suspense. The *rhythm of the *verse line, for example, seems to create an expectation and a tension which is the common element in all forms of suspense. To obtain an awareness of how to induce, intensify, lighten and vary dramatic suspense, there is no better model than Shakespeare's *Hamlet* (1601). See SURPRISE; SUSPENSION OF DISBELIEF.

**Suspension of disbelief.** Temporary acceptance of the 'truth' of a dramatic or other fiction. The phrase originates in Chapter 14 of Coleridge's *Biographia Literaria* (1817). It is important to remember that Coleridge prefaced the phrase with the word 'willing' which indicates a double level of response in reader or spectator. One part of the mind momentarily wills to believe. It accepts the 'truth' of what is recounted or performed but at the same time it is aware of the fiction. When Othello kills Desdemona no one (usually) interferes because everyone knows the act occurs in the world of play. This awareness is important, and represents a desire to believe which, as Coleridge says, 'constitutes poetic faith'. It helps to account for the operation of certain forms of *comedy, *surprise and *suspense. See METAPHOR; SIMILE.

**Sussex's Men.** Elizabethan acting company, 1569–1618.

**Swan.** Elizabethan theatre built on Bankside in 1594. It is best known from the famous copy of de Witt's drawing of the theatre in 1596. Apart from two fragmentary pictures of stages this is the only contemporary visual representation we have of the inside of an Elizabethan theatre.

**Sword dance.** Ancient dramatic ritual still performed in parts of Europe. Its variations usually include a symbolic death and revival, as in the *mummers' play of which it is probably an antecedent.

**Symbol.** A mark or *sign or something other than itself, especially of some transcendent reality. A cross is thus the symbol of Christianity and the suffering of Christ. According to C.S. Pierce, a symbol is to be distinguished from an *icon or *index by its distance from what it represents. An icon is a direct representation, and an index is causally related to its reference as a symptom or effect. A symbol tends to have a richer *connotation than other signs, having accumulated meaning, often over centuries of use. Thus the moon, a rose and an eagle are rich literary symbols, existing within folk-lore and an elaborate context of *myth and legend.

The term also has a wider and less literary sense. A letter, or mark on a page, such as 'M' or 'R', or any word written or spoken, is a symbol of something other than itself, as are the utilitarian ways of marking a *script to represent movements or pauses: 'DL' for 'downstage left', 'acc.' for 'speed up tempo', 'RC' for 'right centre of stage' and 'Xs R' for 'crosses to stage right'.

*Theatre language, of course, is a system of visual and verbal signs, which may be regarded as less or more symbolic according to their distance from their reference. *Naturalist drama, in its close *mimesis, or imitation of *reality, tends towards the iconic. Symbols in such drama work by *contrast with other signs and are in danger of becoming intrusive. Where the emphasis is on *dream or other subjective states, as in *expressionist drama or *surrealism, the symbol is likely to be dominant. The danger here is that the spectators will rebel against an attempt to remove them too far from the 'real world'.

With the passage of time, of course, what was close to one audience becomes distant to another. Icon may become symbol. A *costume or *property which is icon at one moment in time (a sword, for example) may easily take on richer significance when it belongs to the past and not to the spectator's normal world. The reverse can also happen. A rich symbol at one moment in time becomes flattened, losing its rich overtones as cultures change and decline. Whether drama is seen as icon or symbol depends to some extent, therefore, on the audience and the time of performance. There is still a distinction to be made between *documentary forms of drama which tend to the iconic, and poetic forms which were originally intended to symbolize transcendental or other realities.

Perhaps one may say of a symbol, as of *metaphor and *simile, that it has a double tendency. It carries the mind elsewhere, but in the theatre one is conscious of the context in which the symbol operates, and this distances the spectator from the process of symbolizing. (The audience watches the character talk, and notices the way others respond.) Symbolism is most apt to be anchored to the ground in the theatre and the spectator today is as liable to be aware of the symbolic process as of what the symbol refers him to.

**Symbolism.** The practice of representation by *symbols.

**Symbolist drama.** Drama written in conformance with the beliefs and attitudes of the late nineteenth-century symbolist movement. It postulates the existence of a reality beyond everyday experience, which can be glimpsed through *symbols, as suggested in Baudelaire's famous poem, *Correspondances* (1840). Such symbols are fragments of a transcendental reality to which the writer must give *unity. Swedenborg (1688–1772) was an important source of symbolist thought, and the principal dramatists associated with the movement are Maurice Maeterlinck (1862–1949), W.B. Yeats (1865–1939) and the later Strindberg (1849–1912). The twentieth-century *verse drama of T.S. Eliot (1888–1965) and Christopher Fry (1907–   ) also has symbolist elements. Eliot, for instance, sought a dramatic poetry which would communicate realities not seen directly but perceived 'at the corner of the eye'.

LEHMANN, A.G., *The Symbolist Aesthetic in France 1885–95*, Oxford University Press, 1968.

MAETERLINCK, M., *The Bluebird* (1909).

SYMONS, A., *The Symbolist Movement in Literature* (1899).

**Sympathy.** Literally 'suffering with'; sharing a person's, or a *character's feelings. See EMPATHY.

**Synaesthesia.** (a) An aesthetic appeal to more than one sense. Drama, since it constantly appeals to both eye and ear, and occasionally to other senses, is naturally synaesthetic. (b) A deliberate mixing of terms which appeal to different senses. Such a phrase as 'a dark brown voice' is synaesthetic, as is Rimbaud's famous sonnet *Voyelles* (1870) which defines the vowels in terms of colour.

**Synecdoche.** Figure of speech in which the part stands for the whole, as in 'all hands on deck'. See METONYMY.

**System.** A word associated above all with Stanislavski (1863–1938), whose rigorous and influential methods of acting are set forth in *An Actor Prepares* (trs. 1936), *Building a Character* (trs. 1949) and *Creating a Role* (trs. 1961). (See SUPEROBJECTIVE; MAGIC IF; THROUGH LINE; CIRCLE OF ATTENTION; IMPROVISATION; EMOTION MEMORY; SUBCONSCIOUS; NATURALISM.) For a critique of Stanislavski see Brecht's remarks on the aims of *epic theatre and T. Komissarzhevski's *The Actor's Creative Work and Stanislavski's System*. See also: BRAUN, E. (ed.), *Meyerhold on Theatre*, Eyre Methuen, 1969.

# T

**Tableau.** A *scene, especially in French drama. The derivation of the word (meaning 'picture' in French) places emphasis on the visual and scenic rather than on stage action. By extension the word means a stage picture composed of actors in frozen dramatic attitudes (see FREEZE). *Melodrama and *farce often make use of tableaux just before a *curtain, as when illicit lovers are about to kiss and a husband or wife enters the room. The action is suspended in a tableau and the audience left with an image of the situation to be confronted in the next *act. A tableau may also make a final statement or comment on the characters. The film *Butch Cassidy and the Sundance Kid* borrows this technique; when the heroes charge to their deaths, their last technicolour moments are frozen in a sepia 'still'.

**Tableau vivant.** A silent and motionless representation by a single actor, or group, of a well-known picture or piece of statuary.

**Taboo.** An absolute prohibition, in primitive societies, against touching a particular person or thing. A strong taboo, for instance, attached to the holy man, the priest or king, his sacred vessels and the food he touched.

Primitive ritual behaviour involved strong prohibitions and if it is true that drama originates in *ritual, it is not surprising that it frequently treats the infringement of taboo. Matricide, patricide, infanticide, incest, pollution and regicide are characteristic crimes in *Greek, *Jacobean and *neo-classical tragedies, as they are in the tragic novels of Dostoievski (1821–81). In the twentieth century, where to a great extent the holy law has been replaced by social prohibitions, it might be felt that *terror of the monstrous — the incest of Oedipus or the matricide of Orestes — has been largely lost. Vestiges of such ancient terrors remain, however, and psychoanalysis has emphasized them. Disease and genocide are still realities and tragic drama and literature — one thinks of Thomas Mann's novel *Dr Faustus* (1947) and Artaud's *theatre of cruelty — still draw on such sources of *fear. (See PLAGUE.) If Freud is to be believed, *comedy, too, gains its power from the existence of social prohibition and from taboo subjects such as racism, sex, death and disease. Our primary responses are perhaps still primitive enough for the word 'taboo' to be meaningful. See LAUGHTER; SCAPEGOAT.
DODDS, E.R., *The Greeks and the Irrational*, University of California Press, 1951.

FREUD, S., *Jokes and their Relation to the Unconscious* and *Totem and Taboo*, in *The Complete Psychological Works of S. Freud*, trs. J. Strachey, Routledge and Kegan Paul, 1960.
STEINER, F., *Taboo*, Cohen, 1956.

**Tabs.** *Tableau curtain. Tabs were usually hung from the top corners of the *proscenium arch and gathered so that they could lift upwards and sideways at the beginning of acts and drop downwards and inwards at the end.

***Tafelspel.*** Dutch for 'table game'. A form of Dutch *interlude popular on festive occasions from the medieval period to the eighteenth century.

**Tails.** Long strips of canvas attached to the ends of a *border; they act as a frame to a scene.

**Take.** Section of *film taken in one continuous shot by a single cine-camera. The equivalent in the theatre is a uninterrupted *scene or *act. Film actors can make several attempts to get a 'take' right, but on stage it must be correct first time.

**Technique.** Skills. The dramatist, *director and *actor all learn techniques, though these in themselves will not guarantee excellence. The writer learns, among other skills, to select material and present it in an appropriate order. The director needs to understand the effect of *grouping, *movement and other forms of *theatre language. 'Technique', however, is a term usually applied to acting.

Acting technique involves the acquisition of vocal skills, such as clear *diction and *voice projection, physical skills involving control of hands and body movement, and mental skills involving development of *concentration and observation. It also entails learning how to use the stage, how to work with other actors, how to approach a part and how to 'reach' an audience. There comes a point, no doubt, where technique cannot be separated from the gifts and personal qualities of the actor. Self-awareness, sensitivity, experience of life and comprehension of the art of drama are not externals to be quickly acquired. For this reason *naturalistic schools of acting have encouraged a suspicion of 'mere' technique by placing emphasis on inner states of mind which govern external physical behaviour. This in turn has given rise to the rather naive view that actors need only be 'natural' to be convincing. Technique, however, is essential in all forms of drama — obviously so in the most artificial forms like *mime, which approach the condition of *dance and involve highly developed physical, and perhaps musical, skills; it is less obviously the case in naturalist drama where the art of concealing art is very important. Actors must still learn to speak their lines and eat a sandwich, smoke a cigarette, drink a cup of coffee, project the voice, handle their nervous energy and appear relaxed. The suspicion of 'technical actors', to use Lee Strasberg's phrase, is justified where actors use *only* their external skills in plays which require the exploration of human depth. Technique, however, remains very important. The term implies essential methods of concentration and control, as well as clever but mechanical stage *business. What appears rapid, intuitive and 'natural' may well be the result of long training.

BARKWORTH, P., *About Acting*, Secker and Warburg, 1980; *More About Acting*, Secker and Warburg, 1984.

STANISLAVSKI, C., *Stanislavski on the Act of the Stage*, trs. D. Magarshack, Faber and Faber, 1950.

**Teichoscopy.** From the Greek for 'looking through the wall'; from an incident in Homer where Helen describes a scene happening *offstage which she alone can see. It is the dramatic device of describing off-stage events as they occur from a vantage point on stage such as a door or platform. An example is the description of the sea-battle in Shakespeare's *Antony and Cleopatra* (1606–7) or the arrival in Cyprus of the fleet from Venice in *Othello* (1604).

**Telari.** Standing prisms carrying scene-paintings. *Scene-changes were effected by turning different sides to the audience. They were developed in Italy in the sixteenth century and were more sophisticated than the Roman *periaktoi* on which they are based, having removable scenic panels on each of the three sides in order to multiply the number of possible scenes.

**Television drama.** Filmed drama with technical advantages over live theatre. It can: (a) manipulate the distance between *image and spectator/viewer by *cuts from *long shot to *midshot or *close-up; and (b) vary the angle from which the spectator sees the dramatic action by cutting from one camera to another. This appears to shift the viewer rapidly from left to right, or from stalls to circle, or even from the gallery or stalls to an *upstage position amongst or behind the actors. The *zoom lens on a single camera can appear to move the spectator slowly or rapidly towards or away from the stage. Such changes of angle and *focus generate excitement and surprise. The theatre director cannot move his audience about in this flexible way and he focuses attention by means of *grouping and *lighting techniques (such as the use of *spots).

Television also has more general advantages over live theatre. It is relatively cheap (for the viewer), it has ease of access and it affords the opportunity to serialize. A sixteen-hour film such as Reisz's *Heimat* (1985) can be broadcast in episodes; long novels can be converted to the film medium without sacrificing too much of their slow and powerfully accumulated detail. Serial drama considerably extends the normal *time span of film and theatre. Its potential has been demonstrated many times, not least by Dennis Potter in *The Singing Detective* (1986). This brilliant serial centred on a sick novelist and *cross-cut from present to past, from the actual to the fictional and from exterior setting to interior thoughts, with the flexibility shared by the film and *novel forms. Such serials have the further advantage of access to an audience which is both large and socially varied. A television play can reach more people in one showing than can a stage play in a life-time.

The last thirty years have seen the recognition of television as a valid dramatic medium, and specialist television dramatists such as Denis Potter (1935– ), David Mercer (1928–80), Alan Plater (1935– ) and Peter Watkins (19 – ) have emerged. Successful stage dramatists, including Samuel Beckett (1906– ), Peter Nichols (1927– ), Mike Leigh (1943– ) and Trevor Griffiths (1935– ), have also created powerful television drama. With the development of video, the permanence of what was once regarded as an ephemeral medium has been established.

Television, of course, has its detractors. They point to: (a) its lack of excitement compared with live theatre; (b) the high cost of production; (c) the danger of trivialization; and (d) the economic pressure to produce bland material for an uncritical audience which does not wish to be disturbed in its own living room. Institutional pressures tend to prevent experimentation with *avant-garde dramatic forms; these also work to inhibit critical social comment. Nor are the established *naturalistic conventions easily broken. This may be true of much television drama but inferior use does not condemn the medium itself. Television drama is now an established art form.

BRANDT, G.W. (ed.), *British Television Drama*, Cambridge University Press, 1981.

**Tempo.** The pace or *rhythm of a performance. Arguably the most important aspect of any production since only by careful control of tempo can the attention of an audience be held. Too slow a tempo will cause boredom; too rapid a tempo will cause confusion. An unvarying tempo will become tedious, but too rapid a variation will prove a strain. See SILENCE; CLIMAX; CUEING; TIME.

**Tendency.** Stanislavski's term for any distraction from the general movement or *through-line of a play. 'Tendencies' are ideas imposed from the outside by *director or *actor either deliberately or without careful study of a play or a part. The introduction of 'slanted' local and/or propagandist issues is to be resisted, says Stanislavski, for 'tendentiousness and art are incompatible'.

STANISLAVSKI, C., *An Actor Prepares,* Theatre Arts, NY, 1936, p. 276.

**Tennis-court theatres.** The conversion of tennis courts to use as theatres in seventeenth-century Paris was introduced in England after Charles II's return from exile in France. Killigrew (1612–1683) and Davenant (1601–1668) — the two possessors of royal *patents — established such theatres in Vere Street and Lincoln's Inn Fields.

The rectangular shape of tennis-courts (and possibly the 'penthouse' for spectators round two sides) may have recommended their use. The smallness of the building and problems of stage construction and scene-building are among reasons why the practice was discontinued.

**Tension.** (a) A state of anxiety created in the audience by dramatic performance. (See SUSPENSE.) (b) The damaging or productive anxiety created in the actor before and during performance. Søren Kierkegaard (1813–55), speaking of a famous contemporary actress, Fru Heiberg, describes this state as follows:

> Her indefinable possession signifies finally that she is in the right rapport with the tension of the stage. Every tension can have two different effects. It can reveal the strain that it creates, but it can also do the opposite; it can conceal the strain, and not only conceal it, but constantly transform it, change and transfigure it into lightness. Thus the lightness is invisibly grounded in the strain produced by the tension, but this strain is neither seen nor suspected; only the lightness is revealed . . .

Kierkegaard argues that the weight of audience expectation allows the actress to 'swing up free and high'. The anxiety known as stage-fright can find its release in the freedom of the stage, especially when the actor has 'too great an elasticity' in the little world in which he or she lives. The weight of anxiety produces a release.

This reminds one of Fenella Fielding's comment that there is a sense of release in acting because 'in a play at least you know who you are supposed to be.' Certainly Fru Heiberg was astonished at Kierkegaard's percipience and said he described the state exactly.

KIERKEGAARD, S., *Crisis in the Life of an Actress and other essays on drama*, Collins, 1967.

**Tentus.** Term used in Lucerne for a *mansion or locus in the *medieval theatre.

BLAKEMORE EVANS, M., *The Passion Play of Lucerne*, NY, 1943.

**Terence-stage.** The stage portrayed in woodcuts in Renaissance editions of the plays of Terence (c. 190–159 B.C.), notably the Trechsel 1493 editions. The staging seems to have varied, but use appears to have been made of a *mansion, of a projecting

In image labels: Proscænium, ædiles, Theatrum, Fornices

**27** 'Terence-stage' for revival of the Roman classics, fifteenth century. Note the musician on a corner of the stage. The illustration fancifully sets the theatre over a bordello. (From the Trechsel edition of Terence's plays 1493) forestage, of a curtained recess in a *frons scaenae*, and of structures projecting onto the stage. The Terence-stage appears to have anticipated the development of the permanent Italian theatres of the late sixteenth century.

**Terpsichore.** The muse of *dance.

**Tetralogy.** Set of four plays, related in theme and structure, such as Shakespeare's two chronological sequences of *history plays: *Richard II* (1595), *Henry IV*, Parts I and II, (1596–8) and *Henry V* (1599); and his early *Henry VI*, Parts I, II and III (*c.* 1590–2) and *Richard III* (*c.* 1591).

**Text.** The printed *dialogue and *stage directions on which a performance is normally based. Actors usually refer to it as a *script and different *directors view it in different ways. Some see the text as a rich mine whose meanings are available to be discovered. Thus Peter Brook (1925–  ) stated that in his famous production of Shakespeare's *A Midsummer Night's Dream* (1970) he sought a *form which was 'hidden' within the text and which the memories of other men's interpretations had disguised. Other directors seek not so much a form as hidden material. A two-hour play necessarily omits many of the actions and much of the history of the men and women it portrays. According to Stanislavski (1863–1938), directors and actors must rediscover such omissions from *hints and dramatic references to events which occur before the play begins, between its scenes, and even after it ends. For Stanislavski all texts had a *sub-text. Nonetheless, the question of to what degree a text 'contains' a sub-text is problematic. Full confirmation of what lies behind a text is never possible and a hunt for meaning 'in' the text can lead to the creation in performance of a meaning which the text cannot corroborate.

All plays, of course, have some degree of 'openness' and the cruder the play the more necessary will it prove for actors to enlarge it by their own creative interpretations. No text is complete. One should add that some dramatic texts deliberately leave themselves open to a variety of interpretations, enabling the actor and spectator to project meanings which the text only partly confirms. This is particularly true of the plays of Samuel Beckett (1906–  ).

One may distinguish, perhaps, four basic 'texts': (a) the ostensibly 'closed' work which is a rich mine for the discovery of meaning, such as an Ibsen or a Shakespeare play; (b) the 'naive' or superficial plays which need to be 'added to' (actors sometimes speak of Agatha Christie whodunits in this way); (c) 'open' texts such as Beckett's *Waiting for Godot* (1953) whose meaning partly resides in its invitation to interpret it, together with its denial of full interpretation; and (d) a type of open text which invites an audience to write the *ending, of which Brecht's *epic drama is an example.

One should add that in the theatre the speaking of printed lines, the actors' embodiment of *character, together with elements of design and *production, form creative contributions often stimulated by the printed word but never entirely 'contained' within it. A printed play assumes a stage space or an available cast, and appeals to acting conventions, social *codes and verbal meanings which constantly shift and change. Any *revival of a play appeals to a new audience with changing conventions. It uses new actors in a different social, historical and theatrical setting. This makes dramatic performance a *transaction between past and present, between the *text and the creative subjectivities of *actor, *director and *designer.

BARTHES, R., *Image, Music, Text,* trs. S. Heath, Fontana, 1977.

**Thaddädl.** Childish and clumsy *fool figure created by the Austrian actor Anton Hasenhut (1766–1841). See Kringsterner's *Der Zwirnhandler* (1801).

**Thalia.** The muse of *comedy.

**Theatre.** From the Greek 'theatron' or 'seeing place'. (a) A building where *drama is performed; (b) *drama or dramatic performance.

The term 'theatre' suggests a permanent building and visual *spectacle, whereas 'drama' derives from the doric Greek 'dran' and suggests *action. Perhaps 'drama' has more primitive implications since in its *origins it was communal and festive; all participated and there was not the separation between actors and audience which a theatre implies. 'Theatre' suggests a public, shared activity arising out of the creative contributions of writers, *directors, *actors, *designers, technicians and *audience. Its collective and public form has indeed made it especially subject to political, social and economic pressures.

The 'theatre space' in which drama is now performed has become more flexible and many modern theatre buildings incorporate different kinds of *stage. Some modern companies also choose to mount plays in buildings not originally meant for drama, and seek to break down the old actor-audience relations, as in the work of Peter Brook (1925–    ) and the Théâtre du Soleil in Paris.

**Theatre architecture.** Theatre buildings have varied in size, shape and location. New building techniques develop, new materials become available, cultural *traditions evolve, social attitudes change and economic demands fluctuate. As they do so, the nature of the theatre *space, the position of the *stage, the nature of the *audience, its distance from or proximity to the actor, and the construction of the *auditorium, all influence the forms of drama which are presented. See STAGE.

**Théâtre des Nations.** Annual drama festival, held in Paris since 1954, at which foreign companies are invited to perform in their own languages.

**Theatre Guild.** New York society formed in 1919 to provide a platform for plays unacceptable to American commercial management. It did especially important work in the 1920s, bringing many European dramatists before the New York public and mounting many plays by G.B. Shaw (1856–1950).

**Theatre in education (T.I.E.).** Theatre considered as a means of learning, especially as used in schools. Dramatic methods have much to teach, as Plato recognized long ago, and *school drama has a long history. Conservatism in educational training and syllabus design, however, has restricted the numbers of teachers confident enough to employ dramatic methods in schools, other than by putting on the traditional school play. Drama has wide educational value in the class-room. Its use develops role-skills, observation, social confidence, sensitivity, and awareness of human and social interaction. *Improvisation techniques, simulation and *role-play can explore the nature of past, present and even future human situations. The study of history, psychology, human geography, literature, politics and the social sciences can be greatly enhanced by the employment of dramatic methods, and experts regret the infrequency of its use. Visits of professional theatre groups to schools, or the performance of school plays tend to be extra-curricular and, though valuable, are far from being the only forms of theatre-in-education. See:

WAGNER, B.J. and HEATHCOTE, D., *Drama as a Learning Medium*, Hutchinson, 1979.

HODGSON, J. and BANHAM, M. (eds.), *Drama in Education I: The Annual Survey*, Pitman, 1972.

SLADE, P., *Child Drama*, University of London Press, 1954.

**Theatre in the round.** Theatre performed with the audience on all sides of an acting area which can be round, oval, square, rectangular or irregular.

Its popularity has grown in the twentieth century as the *proscenium arch has declined in favour. Some *medieval drama, such as the *morality play *The Castle of Perseverance*, seems to have been in the round. Evidence suggests that Mankind, the *Everyman figure, stood at the centre of a circle with God in the east and the World, Flesh and the Devil at the other points of the compass.

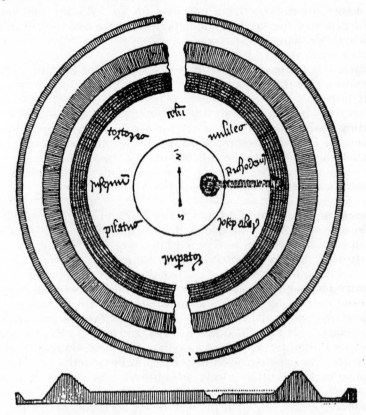

**28** *From the manuscript of the morality play* The Castle of Perseverance, *produced between 1461 and 1483, we learn that the castle stood in the middle with the Bed of Mankind below, and that the outer circle may have been 'strongly barred all about' to keep out the audience. There were 'skaffolds' for God, the World, Belial, and others. These theatres, or 'rounds' in Cornwall were 100 to 300 feet in diameter*

Modern *circus entertainment, of course, takes place in an arena, as did the Roman games, and there have no doubt always been forms of *popular or *street theatre in which entertainers perform for an audience ringed about them. Some recent theatre buildings in Britain have taken account of this. The Cottesloe Theatre on the South Bank, for example, has mounted *promenade productions in the round.

If the theatre building is large, theatre in the round may cause more problems with *sight-lines and *sound than the *open stage. Actors and directors have extended their techniques accordingly to allow for the different actor/audience relationships. Only one section of an audience can be directly addressed at any one time, and actors are continually being *masked except where the audience is raised above the stage area. In a small space, however, the actors' voices are always likely to be audible and there is little problem with masking since the audience can take in much from back and side views and from the general physical responses of the actors to each other.

Theatre in the round can be very stimulating since it extends to spectators a frank invitation to enter a *game and create a scene in their own imaginations. Adapting plays written for the *proscenium arch stage to a space surrounded by spectators can also be an exciting challenge.

JOSEPH, S., *Theatre in the Round*, Barrie and Rockcliff, 1967.
VILLIERS, A., *La Scène Centrale*, Klincksieck, Paris, 1977.

**Theatre Laboratory.** Experimental Polish theatre associated with Jerzy Grotowski (1933–   ). It shuns lavish spectacle and concentrates on the development of powerful physical and vocal acting skills. (See POOR THEATRE; VOICE.) The later work of Peter Brook (1925–   ) has been much influenced by Grotowski's methods.
GROTOWSKI, J., *Towards a Poor Theatre*, Methuen, 1969.

**Theatre language.** All verbal and non-verbal forms of dramatic communication come under this heading. A play uses words. It also employs *voice, *facial expression, *movement, *posture, *grouping, *colour, *costume, *scenery, *lighting, *sound effects — in short everything seen, heard, sensed, touched or smelled by an audience. Theatre language intensifies, supplies a context for and comments on the words found on the printed page.
STYAN, J.L., *The Dramatic Experience*, Cambridge University Press, 1965.

**Théâtre Libre.** Small independent theatre, founded in Montmartre by André Antoine (1858–1943) in 1887. It was the first of the *free theatres and was very important in the development of *naturalism.

**Théâtre Nationale Populaire.** French National Theatre, founded in 1920 by F. Gémier (1869–1933) as a theatre for the masses. It was based from 1937 onwards at the Palais de Chaillot in Paris. The appointment of Jean Vilar (1912–71) as its director was the start of a very fruitful period which saw many notable productions, including Brecht's *The Good Woman of Setzuan* (1938–41) and *The Resistible Rise and Fall of Arturo Ui* (1941) in which Vilar played the title role. After Vilar's retirement in 1963 the company continued to flourish under the actor Georges Wilson until the Gaullist government found its attitudes too much of a threat. In 1972 Roger Planchon (1931–   ), the new director, created an extensive touring programme in provincial France.

**Theatre of cruelty.** A term coined by Antonin Artaud

(1896–1948). His *First Manifesto*, (1932) argues for a new kind of theatre which works directly on the senses to create in an audience a feeling of 'metaphysical realities'. He was in rebellion against a 'psychological theatre', dependent on language, which appealed to the understanding. This he saw as having existed since Racine (1639–99). Its effect had been to make people unaccustomed to immediacy and violence. Artaud wanted 'a theatre that wakes us up ... nerves and heart ...', a theatre 'the burning magnetism of whose images' will provide 'a therapy of the soul'. And this it would do, as he was to explain in his *Second Manifesto* (1933), by resisting the modern materialist and technical revolution. The 'essential passions' were to be discovered in the recovery of ancient *myth, in old cosmogonies and in the 'actualizing' of *heroes and monsters. The theatre was to attack the spectator's whole organism and achieve, through a kind of *dionysiac breakdown, a more profound state of perception. For this, an element of cruelty was essential. See PLAGUE.

ESSLIN, M., *Artaud*, Fontana, 1976.

**Theatre of fact.** Term sometimes applied to drama of the 1950s and 1960s which represents historical events on stage. Joan Littlewood's *Oh What A Lovely War* (1963) and Peter Brook's *US* (1966) have been taken as examples. The term is in a way misleading. Such a theatre must select from complex material susceptible of varying interpretations. Where factual evidence does not exist, speculation must fill the gaps. An entirely factual theatre, if it were possible, would be very dull. The plays which have been mentioned communicate a strong sense of political and *personal* outrage, and, like Kipphardt's *In The Matter of J. Robert Oppenheimer* (1964), they are only 'factual' in so far as they dramatize actual events and encourage political involvement. The term's value lies in its insistence that the drama to which it refers is not wholly fictional or 'untrue'. Actors, directors and writers may select and condense actuality, but they still attempt to mediate it.

Erwin Piscator's theatrical methods, developed during the period of the Weimar Republic, are closely related. See DOCUMENTARY; CHRONICLE; HISTORY PLAY.

**Theatre of illusion.** A term usually applied to *fourth wall drama in which the actors pretend to be unaware of the audience and strive to create the *naturalist illusion of real people living in a real place at a precise moment in *time. It is to be contrasted with forms of drama which call attention to their own *conventions and often use direct audience address.

**Theatre of panic.** '*Théâtre panique*' was a term coined in 1962 by Fernando Arrabal (1932–  ) to describe a theatre which aimed at creating effects similar to those supposedly inspired by the Great God Pan, a mixture of awe, terror and a kind of orgiastic *farce. Arrabal published a manifesto in which he argues that the artist should 'unite the mechanics of memory and the rules of chance. The more the work is governed by chance, confusion and the unexpected the richer it will be'. The Mexican dramatist Alexandro Jodorowski (1930–  ) argues for a theatre which embraces its own ephemeral nature and improvises freely from performance to performance. The theatre of panic relates strongly to the work of Antonin Artaud (1896–1948) and his *theatre of cruelty. See:

ARRABAL, F., *The Emperor and the Architect of Assyria*, 1967; *And They Handcuffed the Flowers*, 1969.
ARRABAL, F., *Le Panique*, Christian Bourgeois, 1967.

**Theatre of silence.** Weak translation of *'théâtre de l'inexprimé'* or 'theatre of the unexpressed', a term associated with J.J. Bernard (1888–1972) who tried to call attention to the suffering of inarticulate people, such as the peasant girl Martine in the play of that name, revived at the *National Theatre in 1985 and first produced in 1922. It is especially concerned with tragedies of unrequited love and derives from the *'école intimiste'* founded by Maurice Maeterlinck (1862–1949).

**Theatre of situations.** A term employed by Jean-Paul Sartre (1905–80), who argue that in the theatre a dramatist should depict situations common to actors and audience, in which characters are forced to choose between painful alternatives. (See SITUATION.) Sartre moved steadily from an *existentialist philosophy which placed emphasis on freedom and responsibility towards a more determinist and less individualistic Marxist view of the world which saw a man's actions as determined by class, family and history. This evolution in Sartre's thought may be clearly seen by comparing *The Flies* (1942) with *Altona* (1960). His best play is probably *In Camera* (1944), an apparently deterministic play which Sartre argues was about characters who chose not to be free.

**Theatre of the absurd.** Theatrical movement which flourished in the 1950s; it is associated particularly with the names of Samuel Beckett (1906–  ), Jean Genet (1909–86), Eugène Ionesco (1912–  ), Fernando Arrabal (1932–  ), Arthur Adamov (1908–70) and Harold Pinter (1930–  ). It derives fairly clearly from the *dada and *surrealist art movements. Its originator was reputedly Alfred Jarry (1873–1907), author of *Ubu Roi* (1896).

The name '*absurd' derives from one of the central feelings of French *existentialism: a painful awareness of the absence of verifiable absolutes in the world. We ask questions of a god who is deaf ('*surdus*' in Latin) and does not answer. Thus in *Waiting for*

*Godot* (1953), Godot never arrives, or if he does (as the first powerful then impotent Pozzo) he is not recognised. The effect is to leave the central characters in anguish and uncertainty. Similarly, in Ionesco's *The Chairs* (1952), two characters wait for a message which, then delivered at the end of the play, is incomprehensible. The audience is left with strange and often *grotesque images which demand and deny explanation; the result is *tragi-comedy, arising out of the absurd situation and the way characters fail to recognize unpalatable truths. Ironical mockery mixes with sympathy for characters who are victims and perpetrators of situations which they create or in which they find themselves, or both.

Jean-Paul Sartre (1905–80), author of *In Camera* (1944) and *The Flies* (1942) gives us in the latter play a definition and description of absurd feelings in the character of Orestes — amounting to a sense of being superfluous in the world. Sartre, however, always insisted on the necessity for taking human responsibility. This led to his later Marxism, his repudiation of the tragic and passive implications of the absurd and indeed his eventual rejection of the term itself. Thus he declares that the term 'theatre of the absurd' is itself absurd 'since none of the writers believe the world or human life to be an absurdity, not Genet who considers the relation between reality and fantasy — nor Adamov who is a Marxist and has written "no theatre without *ideology" nor even Beckett.'

The term nevertheless has its value and helps to define the sense of *estrangement which these writers seem to share.

ESSLIN, M., *The Theatre of the Absurd*, Eyre and Spottiswood, 1962; Doubleday, NY, 1961.

IONESCO, E., *Notes and Counternotes*, Grove 1964; Calder, 1965.

**Theatre of the ridiculous.** American theatre movement which derives from 'pop' and psychedelic art and from the theories of Antonin Artaud (1896–1948). It rejects *naturalism and the *theatre of the absurd and seeks to use associative processes to escape 'the trap of words'. See:

TAVEL, R., 'The Theatre of the Ridiculous', in *Tri-Quarterly* 6, 1966, pp. 94–5.

**Theatre of the straight line.** Term used by V. Meyerhold (1874–1940) to define a relationship between author, director, *actor and *audience which he contrasts with what he calls the *'theatre triangle'. In the theatre of the straight line the director assimilates the author's vision and conveys his sense of it to the actor, who is then not tied by the director's conception, but communicates it freely to the audience. Above all, says Meyerhold, drama is the art of the *actor*, and his 'new' or *stylized theatre emphasized this form of theatre relationship. See THEATRE TRIANGLE.

BRAUN, E., *Meyerhold on Theatre*, Eyre Methuen/Hill and Wang, 1969, p. 50.

**Theatre triangle.** Term employed by V. Meyerhold (1874–1940) to describe a form of production dominated by the interpretation of an autocratic director. According to Meyerhold, the actors depersonalize themselves and submit to the director's vision as completely as does an orchestral musician to his conductor. Meyerhold is critical of the method. In the theatre, he says, it deprives both actor and spectator of creative freedom. It is a theatre he associated with *naturalism and the Duke of *Meiningen. See THEATRE OF THE STRAIGHT LINE.

**Theatre Upstairs.** Small theatre founded in 1969 at the *Royal Court Theatre in Sloane Square for the production of experimental plays.

**Theatre Workshop.** Touring company which settled at the Theatre Royal in Stratford, East London, in 1953, under the direction of Joan Littlewood. It mounted a series of important productions, including two plays by Brendan Behan (1923–64) — *The Quare Fellow* (1959) and *The Hostage* (1958) — as well as the Brechtian musical *satire *Oh What a Lovely War* (1963), which contributed to the growth of *political theatre in England.
GOORNEY, H., *The Theatre Workshop Story*, Eyre Methuen, 1981.

**Theatricality.** A mixture of expectation, uncertainty, *surprise, *action, *colour, and *suspense which is not necessarily limited to drama. There are elements of theatricality in any ceremonial public occasion. A public trial is theatrical, having an uncertain outcome, an audience, an action and a principal actor, as well as elements of horror and perhaps *pity. Sporting and political contests are also theatrical. They have an audience which identifies *heroes and *villains, and feels anxiety about the outcome. Religious *rituals, too, with their *costume and formal pageantry, may be so described.

**Theatrical Syndicate.** Group of American businessmen which established a powerful monopoly of New York theatres in the years leading up to World War I.

**Theory of drama.** Body of ideas concerned: (a) with methods of dramatic composition and production; (b) with the value and social function of drama; and (c) with the relation between these. Since drama combines elements of music, literature, sculpture and architecture — and more particularly of *dance, *song and *film — descriptive emphases vary. Attitudes also change with the cultural climate. Ideas range from the early *classical theories of

Aristotle (384–322 B.C.) and Horace (65–8 B.C.) to the *neo-classical theory of Denis Diderot (1713–84), and from the *Romantic emphasis of Schiller (1759–1805) to the *modernism of Bertolt Brecht (1898–1956).

Dramatic theory raises aesthetic, psychological, social and religious questions which relate to why people write, watch and perform the various dramatic *genres. It asks what relation plays have to the audiences before whom they are performed and how they mediate the historical period about and in which they were written. The most influential and pervasive theory of drama has been that contained in Aristotle's *Poetics* (See CATHARSIS; PERIPETEIA; HAMARTIA; TRAGEDY.) Recent western theories which have influenced acting, writing and directing methods include Stanislavski's *system, Artaud's *theatre of cruelty and Bertolt Brecht's *epic theatre. For a historical and critical survey see: CARLSON, M., *Theories of the Theatre*, Cornell University Press, 1984.

**Thesis play.** Translation of '*pièce à thèse*'; a play whose end is to communicate the social and political, or other views, of a writer or group. Much of the work of Shaw (1856–1950) and Ibsen (1828–1906) has been assigned to this category, as has a great deal of *political drama since Brecht (1898–1956). Such a classification, however, can do scant justice to the conflict between values which these writers' plays embody. Dramatic sympathies do not always coincide with moral attitudes, and powerful drama seems rather to explore moral conflict than to offer a simple 'thesis'. 'It is not my task to answer', said Chekhov (1860–1904) and many political dramatists would agree that the offering of doctrinaire solutions is neither their function nor their aim. Drama does not always embody the conscious *intention of the writer, and a thesis without antithesis — where dramatic sympathies are wholly on one side — rarely carries dramatic conviction. Perhaps this is because such a play endeavours to destroy an audience's freedom to make its own decisions. Plays can make their point, as Ibsen and Shaw demonstrate, without losing a sense of the humanity of the opposition and of what Henry James called 'the possible other case'. Even where moral judgements are clear, as in, say, a battle in a *morality play between Virtues and Vices, the dramatic sympathies are less obvious. Blake's comment on Milton to the effect that he was on the devil's side without knowing it, or D.H. Lawrence's famous adjuration: 'Never trust the artist, trust the tale', remind one of the limitations of doctrinaire art.

**Thought.** Mental process, especially, but not exclusively, conscious and analytical. Thought is rarely, if ever, 'purely rational' and both induction and deduction may be influenced by feeling. When logic defends a value system, or a prejudice, it arouses emotion, and the development of an argument often depends on *unconscious preferences which involve personal pride and make contradiction a source of potential conflict.

In the theatre one may study the thought processes of: (a) the characters; (b) the audience; and (c) the dramatist (see INTENTION). Thought in the form of *ideology may also be seen as a component of the more impersonal social and linguistic processes which dramatic *form mediates.

The conscious thoughts of a character may be expressed in *dialogue or in direct audience address, in *soliloquy or *aside. Thoughts which are less organized, and perhaps less conscious, are often communicated by *facial expression or movements of the hand and body. Such thoughts, however, are likely to be momentary. A sudden glance communicates an attitude and a feeling rather than a logical argument. Organized thought requires verbal language.

An audience can be stimulated to think by the development of an argument between the characters, by direct address or by the creation of situations towards which it needs to formulate an attitude. By its very nature, however, theatre provokes a *reaction*, creating sympathies and antipathies but giving an audience little time to reflect. Only after a play ends, or during the pauses and intervals, do spectators normally have time to develop individual lines of thought.

With regard to authors' intentions, a distinction may be made between plays which deliberately appeal to a reasoning process and those which seek to make a direct and powerful emotional impact. The *epic theatre of Bertolt Brecht (1898–1956) intends to make an audience think, and does so by the use of *parable, *paradox and various kinds of interruption and *alienation effect which break continuity and stimulate thought. The *theatre of cruelty of Artaud (1896–1948), on the other hand, tends to obliterate immediate thought. The overwhelming sensory impact which Artaud sought allows time for cogent analysis only after a performance is over.

The author's thoughts and intentions do not always find direct expression in a play, and the dramatic process may subtly transform them. The dramatist may use characters as mouthpieces, or allow them to be seen behind a *dialectic of opposed positions, each of which may gain a certain sympathy (sometimes in spite of the dramatist's intentions). Nor can a writer fully control the language, *structure, *codes and *conventions of a play. These partly mediate the thought processes of a class or a culture and it is difficult for any author to establish a personal independence. Sometimes he may not wish to. The author may no more have examined his attitudes and prejudices than some members of his audience have.

A few writers like Shaw (1856–1950) have an enormous thirst for intellectual exchange and deliberately attack conventional attitudes. The majority avoid material which is too challenging, and which poses a threat to the box-office. Developed argument is not, however, infrequent in major drama. Debates between opposed protagonists are characteristic of Greek *tragedy, and when the dramatic situation compels an Oedipus or a Hamlet to analyse and ponder, the spectacle of a man thinking seems to confirm the existence of a humanity which links the age of Sophocles and of Shakespeare with our own.

**Through-line.** Stanislavski's term for: (a) the principle which unites the scenes of a play; (b) the line of development which connects the series of appearances on stage which constitute a dramatic *role.

The central aim of an actor, said Stanislavski (1863–1938), is to find the organic unity which links his scenes and appearances. This he sees as an unbroken line leading towards a goal which he calls the *superobjective. The actor must explore a play's *sub-text and formulate a sentence which expresses his character's general *will. In the case of Shakespeare's Macbeth, such a sentence might be: 'I will become and remain king'. If a character's words and actions are all related to such an intention then the performance will achieve coherence — a 'through-line'.

STANISLAVSKI, C., *An Actor Prepares,* Theatre Arts, NY, 1936, Ch. 13.

**Thrust stage.** A stage which projects into the *auditorium and encourages direct audience address in the form of *monologue, *soliloquy or *aside. In comparison with the *proscenium or *fourth wall stage, it can create *acoustic and *masking problems, especially in a large theatre, since an audience will be to the side of, and sometimes behind, the actor speaking. A thrust stage, however, brings even large audiences closer to the action and this proximity creates an intimate awareness of actors' responses, that masking, acoustics and back- and side-views cease to be a problem.

**Thunder run.** See THUNDER SHEET.

**Thunder sheet.** Sound effect device consisting of a hanging strip of metal which when shaken makes a noise like thunder. In the *Georgian theatre such a noise had earlier been created by the rolling of iron balls down a wooden incline called a 'thunder run'.

**Thymele.** Altar to *Dionysos, situated at the centre of the *orchestra, or dancing place, in the *Greek theatre.

**Tilt.** Vertical up or down movement of the film or *television camera. It can create a feeling of dominance or threat when the viewer surveys objects from above or below. Orson Welles (1915–86) was a master of such shots. The theatre has no full equivalent. One might, however, consider the difference it makes to the *actor/audience relationship when the audience is above or below the actor and the way in which a production varies the *levels from which actors speak to each other on stage.

**Time.** The director William Gaskill has observed that the theatre is engaged in showing a moment in time. 'So you look at that moment in time and it's amazing how much you know backwards and forwards if you choose the right moment.' The rendering of the passage of time in drama raises a number of questions. (a) How does a play which assumes an audience attention span of two or three hours simulate the period of time which the play's fiction covers, which may be one day, several months or thirty years? (b) How should time be shown to move? Aeschylus has been said to present 'great swathes of time' in *The Oresteia* (458 B.C.); Sophocles's plays have been said to present a double movement forwards and back; the *Jacobeans were fascinated by the impact of the 'bewildering minute' which transforms a character's life. A play, like music, moves through time, and its *rhythm will raise the question of the dramatist's attitudes to the movement of *history. (c) There is also the question of how time affects the individual characters. What is their individual relation to the past, present and future, and what is the tempo of their lives? (d) How, too, does an audience respond to the time sequence presented in a play, given that events have occurred since the play was written? An audience has its own consciousness of time, formed by the age in which it lives.

We can thus distinguish 'theatre time', which relates to a play's rhythm and *tempo, from 'character time', 'audience time' and 'dramatic time'. The latter can be subdivided into '*plot time' and '*story time'. An examination of the time-structure or plot will reveal variations of *tempo between individual *scenes and *acts. It will involve scrutiny of why certain actions are included and others omitted. It will look at time–gaps between scenes, and at the parallel representation of events in *sub-plots or *double plots. It may also examine the way a dramatic action moves quickly while convincingly suggesting a long lapse of time. Shakespeare's *Othello* (1604) and *Macbeth* (1606), for example, have this subtle 'double time'. 'What! Keep a week away?' says Bianca to Cassio. In this economical way Shakespeare gives the impression of time having passed without interrupting the dramatic tempo. The plot cuts a pattern in time. The story to which the play refers may have a different pattern.

The presentation of the way time affects character is of perennial interest. As Rosalind says in Shakespeare's *As You Like It* (c. 1599):

> Time travels in divers paces with divers persons. I'll tell you who Time
> ambles withal, who Time trots withal, who time gallops withal, and who
> he stands still withal. (III.ii.288–93)

Attitudes to time are an interesting way to compare and contrast
dramatis personae. In *As You Like It* some characters, like
Touchstone and Rosalind, live 'through time' in the present whilst
others, like the melancholy Jaques, stand back and watch time pass.
Jaques seems to laugh only once in the play and this is when
Touchstone presents him with a mirror of a melancholy man:

> And so, from hour to hour we ripe and ripe,
> And then from hour to hour we rot and rot,
> And thereby hangs a tale.

Jaques, of course, does not recognize his image in the mirror.

Another play which presents and contrasts different attitudes to
time is Shakespeare's *Troilus and Cressida* (1602). It contains
characters like old Nestor who live in the past; another, the
politician Ulysses, attempts to effect change in the present; others
still, the Trojans, seem to live for an image of themselves projected
into the future. Interestingly similar, in a very different play, is the
contrast in Chekhov's *The Cherry Orchard* (1903) between Gaev the
landowner, who lives in the past, Lopakhin the active business man,
who lives in the present, and Trofimov the student, who lives for
the future. Samuel Beckett (1906–   ) is another playwright whose
characters are powerfully conscious of time. In their case the
consciousness is painful and it prompts them to play compensatory
games, or 'pass-times', which enable them momentarily to forget
time.

The way characters respond to time has a *universal appeal. All
individuals are aware of its passage, and for each it ends in death.
But attitudes to time and death vary between epochs and
individuals, and the dominant dramatic *genres — whether
*religious or *liturgical drama, *comedy or *tragedy — see time
differently. Tragedy shows the pattern of an individual's life in
time, normally ending in death. The emphasis of comedy is on the
flow of life and it ends in the group's celebration of life in the here
and now. 'What is love? Tis not hereafter', sings Feste in
Shakespeare's *Twelfth Night* (1600), 'Youth's a stuff will not endure.'
(II.iii.50). Religious drama sees man's time as of less account than
God's time and absorbs the individual time-sense in community
worship. The cosmic *mystery cycles again have a different sense
of time from the *morality play in which the individual *Everyman
begins to play a stronger role. In *Everyman* (*c.* 1509–19) the
movement towards a concentration on the individual character, the
isolated moment and the pastness of the past, which is to be found
in much *existential and *modernist drama, had begun. Such a
movement, one should add, has produced a counter-movement in

the swing towards the sense of community and the broader historical time-structures of much twentieth-century *political drama.

This brief consideration might end with the suggestion that dramatic *form gains power from a tension between different attitudes to time. The idea of permanence, of realizing and perfecting a temporal pattern, whether musical or dramatic, arises out of a form of rebellion against time, 'the dialectic that comes from without' (Kierkegaard). 'Perfectibility and potentiation', said Kierkegaard, 'are resistances to the power of the years.'

**Timing.** The selection of the moment to move or speak and the speed at which this is done. Drama is very dependent upon how actors time their lines, moving quickly or slowly, selecting the exact length of *pause for a line, or a movement of head or hand, to create maximum effect. Certain actors seem to have natural timing. Others labour to acquire it. Inexperienced actors learn not to defuse the tension built up by a phrase or a situation, but to allow it to subside gradually. The *pause must be carefully timed, since it affects the pitch of excitement to which the scene is allowed to drop. This, in its turn, affects the pitch at which the next scene, or movement within a scene, begins. As a general rule, the pause is longest when the *climax it immediately precedes is highest, and shortest where the rise is smallest. Where there is an emotional rise, there should be a consequent drop; an increase in *pace requires an equivalent slowing down. A failure to judge pace can produce *bathos, and provoke undesired laughter.

A further point derives from this. In comic acting deliberate *bathos can be used to call attention to the convention the actor is using, or to the comic nature of the character he plays. Good *comic timing often involves a deliberate interruption of a musical flow, or of a *suspension of disbelief. (See COMEDY.) The audience is hoodwinked by the actor into some momentary *identification. This is then broken by an *alienation effect and the audience laughs. In serious plays good timing maintains or modulates *suspense and assumes audience involvement in the dramatic situation. Comic timing seems to appeal to an audience more aware that it is an accomplice in the dramatic illusion.

Timing is perhaps at its most subtle in the *play within the play where a character adopts a disguise to trick other characters in the play, establishing a *dramatic irony which his sense of timing exploits. Thus he makes an appeal to an audience 'in the know' whilst concealing the situation from a character who is ignorant. In these cases *pauses and *silences indicate what passes in the 'knower's' mind. Edmund in *King Lear* (1605) and Iago in *Othello* (1604) share a joke (and their superiority) with the audience in this way and at the same time maintain credibility with the ignorant Gloucester or Othello.

Sometimes, of course, the joker gets his come-uppance. In Shakespeare's *Henry IV* Part I (1597) Falstaff is asked how he knew he was beset by 'eleven men in Kendal green' when he has already said it was so dark he could not see his hand before his face. The actor's timing of the pause to capture Falstaff's brilliant recovery from an awkward situation is crucial. In this situation the timing of the lines of Poins and Prince Hal intensifies the comedy. The occasional pause and glance communicate their awareness of things that Falstaff does not know.

In practice, there is often a quick pause *before* a line intended to get a laugh, and a longer breath often follows to allow for the audience's laughter. The actor waits for the laugh but not for too long — nor should he allow it to continue too long. The audience's response must be interrupted as it starts to die, at the point where the new dialogue can be clearly heard. New lines must not be lost; nor should the *pace sag through poor *cueing.

In *farce, it is a rule not to start too fast in Act I. Otherwise laughter cannot be sustained and built upon in subsequent acts. Timing of individual lines in this case is affected by the general *tempo. For valuable hints on timing, see:

BARKWORTH, P., *About Acting*, Secker and Warburg, 1980.

FERNALD, J., *The Play Produced*, Kenyon–Keane, 1933, PP. 100–121.

**Tirade.** A long and violent speech, such as the king's curse on his daughter Goneril in Shakespeare's *King Lear* (1605).

**Tireman.** Wardrobe manager in the *tiring house. He also supervised the stage seating and candles in the *private theatres.

**Tiring-house.** Dressing room associated principally with the *public *Elizabethan theatres. *Entrances and *exits were probably made directly to and from it, and it gave players access to an upper stage. The front of the tiring-house formed the back wall of the stage and could be used for drapes of various kinds. The *stage direction 'musicians within' indicates that music could be played there. It also contained the wardrobe, which was in the charge of the *tireman. In the top of the tiring house was the 'hut', with a room for cannon and sound machines. This provided entry to the 'heavens' above the stage from whence actors could descend as gods (as Jupiter descends in Shakespeare's *Cymbeline* (1609)).

According to John Florio's Elizabethan dictionary, the tiring house was 'a skaffold, a pavillion, or fore part of a theatre where players make them readie, being trimmed with hangings, out of which they enter upon the stage'.

Elizabethan and Jacobean dramatists used the tiring house to represent many different locations. The actors who entered from it were accustomed to suggesting that they had arrived from a banqueting hall or private room, from the street or from a blasted heath. See SPACE.

**Toby.** The dog in the *Punch and Judy* show.

*Togata.* Roman urban comedy, as compared with *Atellan farce which had a country background.

**Topping.** The term usually suggests the use of *voice — the strong, clear stressing of the opening syllables of a speech to 'top' a previous speech. This asserts a character's presence, creates a dramatic *focus, and gains the audience's confidence.

**Tormentors.** Fixed *flats covered in black material, used as *wings in modern *proscenium arch theatres.

*Totaltheater.* 'Total Theatre'; a project initiated in 1926 by the *Bauhaus architect Walter Gropius, for the Weimar theatre director Erwin Piscator (1893–1966). It was never completed.

It involved rotating a section of the auditorium to create three different stage spaces: *end stage; *theatre in the round; and a circular *thrust stage. Four machines placed at strategic points were to provide for the back projection of film round the entire auditorium. In John Willett's view, 'a more radical theatre structure has yet to be built'. The flexible stage space was intended for the ideal Bauhaus actor, who was to be master of the laws of 'movement and repose, optics and acoustics'. *Movement, *form, *light and *colour, together with verbal and musical *sound and the use of organic and mechanical bodies, were to unite in a total theatre clearly derived from the work of Adolphe Appia (1862–1928) and the *gesamtkunstwerk of Richard Wagner (1813–83).

The term has also been applied to such related forms as the *theatre of cruelty of Antonin Artaud (1896–1948) which aimed at a general or total impact on the audience through use of powerful sound, movement, colour and light.

WILLETT, J., *The New Sobriety: Art and Politics of the Weimar Republic Period (1917–33)*, Thames and Hudson, 1978, p. 155.

**Touring company.** A theatrical *troupe, normally with a *repertory of plays, which travels from place to place. Groups of *travelling players have existed at least since the closing of the *Roman theatres and the consequent release of groups of impoverished actors, who took to the road. The use of the word 'tour', however, seems to date from the later eighteenth century. Dion Boucicault (1822–90) is credited with sending out the first real touring company when the rapid nineteenth-century development of British and American railways opened up new commercial markets. Tom Robertson's *Caste* is an example of a play which toured the provinces at the same time as its London run in 1867. Companies of this kind travelled in search of profit, rather than out of personal necessity.

Further motives for travelling can be advanced: new audiences and unusual theatre spaces can restore freshness to a jaded production; reputations can be extended and enhanced; important plays can be shown outside the capital cities; and touring groups with specific *ideologies, such as Marxist or *feminist groups, may tour in order to politicize audiences.

The demands of touring are heavy. Constant travel, *rehearsal and adaptation to new venues can be exhausting as well as exhilarating. Transport difficulties mean that companies are small and travel light. Steve Gooch, a man with wide experience of touring, says productions should ideally be 'small-scale, light and punchy'. The plays which a touring company mounts tend to lack the scope of plays with large casts, written for large venues with huge resources. Courageous and committed groups nevertheless continue to tour, bringing the excitement of their physical presence to places where live theatre may rarely be seen.

**Towneley Cycle.** The Wakefield Cycle of *mystery plays which contains the famous *Second Shepherd's Play*.

**Toy theatre.** See JUVENILE DRAMA.

**Tracking shot.** Any moving camera shot; especially one in which the camera moves towards or away from the subject during shooting. To 'crab' is to move it sideways. The *zoom, which distances, or brings the subject nearer without the camera moving, has a less intimate effect.

**Tractor play.** Type of *socialist realist play developed in the Soviet Union.

**Trades union theatre.** See PROLETCULT THEATRE.

**Tradition.** Statement, belief or practice handed down from generation to generation and generally felt to embody some kind of truth. In the theatre this includes the body of *myth, legend and history on which so much drama has been based. It also includes devices or *conventions whereby such subjects are communicated.

T.S. Eliot, in his famous essay *Tradition and the Individual Talent* (1920), observes that tradition 'cannot be inherited, and if you want it you must obtain it by great labour.' He recommends a conscious and concentrated study of the past and suggests that a sense of tradition 'invokes the . . . historical sense . . . and the historical sense involves the perception, not only of the pastness of the past but of its presence.' Tradition meant for him an awareness of connection and continuity, something that as an American he had felt the lack of, and something he felt he needed to acquire in order to write:

> The historical sense compels a man to write not only with his own generation in his bones, but with a feeling that the whole of the literature of Europe from Homer, and within it the whole of the literature of his own country, has a simultaneous existence.

Eliot saw a sense of tradition as necessary to creativity. His view can be supported by examining the way he himself used traditional patterns, as in his employment of the Orestes story in *The Family Reunion* (1939). His practice relates to that of major dramatists, from the Greeks to Jean Giraudoux (1882–1944), who studied and reworked such traditional subject matter as the Orpheus legends and the Trojan wars.

**Traditionalism.** (a) A respect for *tradition. (b) A method of production developed by Vsevolod Meyerhold (1874–1940) in about 1910. Plays were revived and presented with elements of their original staging. Calderón's *Adoration of the Cross*, set in thirteenth-century Siena, was not given a thirteenth-century *naturalistic setting but staged in a seventeenth-century style. A contemporary *pantomime, *The Veil of Pierrette* by Arthur Schnitzler (1862–1931), was reworked in the *grotesque style of E.T.A. Hoffmann (1776–1822). Such 'traditionalism' achieved distancing effects, and recovered a sense of pre-naturalistic styles.

**Tragedian.** (a) Any player or writer of *tragedy; (b) Leading man in the nineteenth-century *stock company.

**Tragedy.** Plays predominantly concerned with human suffering, usually involving the decline and death of a *hero. Brief definitions normally compare it with *comedy. W.B. Yeats (1865–1939) defines them by distinguishing their effects. Tragedy induces a loss of individual identity in the spectator: 'At the height of tragedy all is lyricism'; comedy, on the other hand, 'is built on the dykes that separate man from man'. John Arden (1930–   ) neatly defines their contrasting subject-matter. Comedy is about 'the indestructibility of the little man' whereas tragedy is about 'the necessary destruction of the great'. J-L. Barrault (1910–   ) contrasts their differing strategies. We are all of us on a tightrope, he says, and sooner or later we all fall off. Both comedy and tragedy depend on our knowing this but comedy 'looks away' whereas tragedy 'confronts' the situation.

Such brief definitions, though valuable, cannot hope to suggest

**29.** *Greek statuette of a tragic actor.*
*Note the mask and the rich costume*

the complexity of the form, or cover the differences between *classical, *medieval, Elizabethan, *neo-classical, *Romantic, *absurdist and nineteenth-century *social tragedy. Philosophers from Aristotle to modern *existentialist writers have built up a formidable body of theory on the subject. The analysis of tragedy involves discussion of fundamental concepts such as fate, *chance, *causality and free will. It involves, too, a consideration of why and how the representation of suffering makes an appeal to an audience. Aristotle's *Poetics* still provides a vocabulary of basic terms, such as *hamartia, *peripeteia, *disclosure, and *beginning, middle and end. Discussion of tragedy involves a consideration of *taboo and *sacrifice, and the *origins of drama. It leads one into historical considerations of why tragedy occurs at particular periods, and whether its expression in, say, fifth-century B.C. Athens, late Elizabethan England, seventeenth-century France or nineteenth-century Scandinavia, shares common elements.

The collapse or weakening of a strong system of belief and its sudden or gradual replacement by a different set of values (associated with the rise to *power of a new social group) seems to relate to the value conflicts in much tragedy. The growth of national feeling and national and imperial power, together with the simultaneous rise of a deep pessimism, seems to link the worlds of

Sophocles (496–406 B.C.) and Shakespeare (1564–1616), Racine (1639–99) and Ibsen (1828–1906). The subject has long been felt to lie at the centre of fundamental human problems and tempts thinkers into making vast generalizations. See:

GOLDMANN, L., *Le Dieu Caché*, Gallimard, 1955.

HEGEL, G.W.F., *Vorlesungen über die Aesthetik*, 1835.

HENN, T.R., *The Harvest of Tragedy*, Methuen, 1956.

JASPERS, K., *Tragedy is not Enough*, trs. Reiche, Moore and Deutsch, Gollancz, 1953.

NIETZSCHE, F., *Die Geburt der Tragoedie*, (1872).

**Tragic carpet.** Green carpet spread on seventeenth-century stages to protect the valuable costumes of actors who must 'die' on stage.

**Tragi-comedy.** Mixed *genre in which a tragic tone or atmosphere mingles with comic patterns. Tragi-comedy did not have *classical approval. Cicero (106–43 B.C.) argued that to mix opposite qualities was folly. Plato (*c*. 428/7–348/7 B.C.) believed that an artist was unlikely to have success in both genres (though Socrates argues at the end of the *Symposium* (384 B.C.) that they are interconnected and that an ability to write one entails an ability to write the other). Aristotle (384–322 B.C.) was also in favour of keeping genre pure.

In more recent times the mixing of comedy with serious matter began when *folk elements entered the *religious drama, as in the *Second Shepherd's Play* in the *Wakefield cycle. In the sixteenth century, Renaissance writers began to advocate a mixed genre. Battista Guarini (1538–1612), author of the tragi-comic *pastoral play *Il Pastor Fido* (1590) argued against the classical view. Comedy and tragedy mix in nature; why not therefore in art? The practice of Shakespeare illustrates the wisdom of such a view.

Tragi-comedy has neither the light-heartedness of comedy nor the intense seriousness of tragedy. A sardonic attitude is frequently taken to painful subjects. The spectator is unsettled by the alternation of comedy and seriousness and the mixing of laughter with forms of *realism. Shakespeare's *problem plays, *Troilus and Cressida* (1602), *All's Well that Ends Well* (1603–4) and *Measure for Measure* (1604), though structurally different from one another, are sometimes termed tragi-comedies. So too are the plays of Chekhov (1860–1904) and much *theatre of the absurd. These are again very different in terms of *form both from each other and from Shakespeare's plays. This indicates that tragi-comedy is to be defined more by its disturbing tonal effects than by a particular dramatic *structure. See BLACK COMEDY; TRAGEDY; COMEDY; LAUGHTER; SATYR PLAY.

STYAN, J.L., *The Dark Comedy: the development of modern tragi-comedy*, Cambridge University Press, 1962.

**Tranche de vie.** See SLICE OF LIFE.

**Translation.** (a) The transference of a written or spoken text from one language to another; and (b) the text produced by such a process.

The possibility of full and accurate translation is a subject much discussed. Languages differ in grammatical structure, range of vocabulary, cultural reference, rhythmical effect and variety of sound. Poetry, which exploits all such linguistic resources, has been defined as 'that which gets lost in translation'. *Prose is usually easier to find an equivalent for, and drama, since the text is only one of its means of communication, and since its vocabulary is generally narrower than poetry (and even narrative prose), usually lends itself easily to the process. The enacted dramatic situation with its visual languages, scenic, facial, gestural, and choreographic, together with the use of *music, *sound effect and *voice quality, allows considerable communication of meaning over and above the words. Of course, *theatre language is also governed by its cultural context and by shared *codes. Even so, drama, together with *film, seems the most *international* of the spoken arts, perhaps because its speakers can be seen and heard.

In another sense, drama is a medium which is transformed by performance. The dramatic script is 'translated' by the director and actors into a 'language' that will change with each production. In this sense drama is written to be translated, and some translations will be more faithful than others. Adherence to the text, however, is not the only test of fidelity. The success of film translations of Shakespeare — Grigori Kozintsev's *Hamlet* and *King Lear* or Akira Kurosawa's *Throne of Blood (Macbeth)* and *Ran (King Lear)* — indicates the power and authenticity that can be achieved by the use of visual image, sound effect and music, even where Shakespeare's supposedly sacred text has been considerably changed. These *adaptations can be seen as translations of the spirit rather than the letter. For a discussion of literary problems of translation, see:

BENJAMIN, W., *Illuminations*, Jonathan Cape, 1970, pp. 69–83.

**Transparency.** A *cloth painted on its back and its front in such a way that a change in the intensity or direction of the *lighting reveals or highlights different subjects. It thus achieves effects of visual surprise and can be used for transformation scenes, as, for example, when an apparently empty rural scene is suddenly filled with figures, or a barn is seen to be ablaze.

**Transpontine melodrama.** Sarcastic phrase for crude *melodrama, offered in the Victorian period at such theatres as the Elephant and Castle, south of the Thames, and thus transpontine — 'across the bridges'.

**Trap.** Aperture in *scenery or stage floor through which *props or characters could appear, usually with extreme rapidity. The industrial revolution brought developments in technology which encouraged spectacular use of traps in *pantomime, *melodrama and the *dumb ballet in the nineteenth century. See GHOST GLIDE; SLOAT; BRISTLE TRAP; VAMP TRAP; ROLL-OUT.

**Travelling players.** Companies of *professional actors who travelled from place to place to make a living, both before, during and after the establishment of permanent European theatres in the late sixteenth century.

**Travesty.** A 'low' imitation of serious work. It is similar to, but inverts, *burlesque, which normally uses a high style for less serious subjects. Tom Stoppard's play *Travesties* (1974) is in part a low-style imitation of James Joyce and Lenin, seen through the failing memory of an English consular official (who has reason for disliking them both). Its characters, however, acquire a persuasiveness which makes the play a very superior form of travesty, if it remains one at all.

**Tree-border.** A *border, cut in the shape of foliage, masking the top of the stage area.

**Trilogy.** A chronological sequence of three plays containing characters common to each. Aeschylus's *Oresteia* (458 B.C.) and Shakespeare's *Henry VI* Parts 1, 2 and 3 (1590–2) are examples. Trilogies are usually composed of *tragedies or *historical plays. It was the practice to present such trilogies in the drama competitions in Athens in the fifth century B.C., and the trilogy, followed by a *satyr play, was the dramatic fare for a whole day. Of these ancient trilogies only the *Oresteia* is extant.

The form is not dead and the twentieth century has seen trilogies written in a number of dramatic *genres. Eugene O'Neill composed *Mourning Becomes Electra*, a version of the *Oresteia*, in 1931; Arnold Wesker (1932–   ) wrote, in 1960, a well-known trilogy of *naturalist plays — *Chicken Soup with Barley, Roots* and *Talking about Jerusalem*; Alan Ayckbourn (1939–   ) composed a *farce trilogy, *The Norman Conquests*, in 1974. A trilogy adapted from the *mystery cycles, entitled *The Nativity, Crucifixion* and *Doomsday*, was performed by *The National Theatre at The Cottesloe and Lyric Theatres in 1985; this divided the Old and the New Testament material into three movements, ending at the birth of Jesus, the death of Christ and the end of the world respectively.

The advantage of a trilogy is the extensive time-sweep it allows. Characters can more easily be seen at different stages of development and may be set against varying backgrounds (as in Wesker's plays). The trilogy has something of the appeal of the *novel or the *soap opera in that it can create a more detailed world and involve the playgoer for a longer period than is otherwise possible.

Disadvantages tend to be practical; the amount of *rehearsal time needed, high production costs, and the difficulty of staging three plays on the same day — or finding an audience prepared or able to come to all three on different occasions (and in the right order). These problems, and the heavy demands made on the writer's and the theatre's creative resources, explain why the form is rarely attempted. These disadvantages do not apply to *television drama, but even in this medium trilogies are rare, being less popular than serial drama.

**Triumph.** A spectacular *entry into a city; usually a procession or *pageant celebrating some victory. The practice was common in Roman and late medieval times.

**Trope.** From Latin '*tropus*' meaning 'added melody'. The term was extended to short Latin poems which comment on and enact in dialogue a liturgical story and text. They are first mentioned by the Benedictine St Ethelwold in the *Regularis Concordia* between 968 and 975. A well-known trope was the *Dies Irae*; another, the *Victimae Paschali*, led to the growth of the new drama. See QUEM QUAERITIS.

WICKHAM, G., *The Medieval Theatre*, Weidenfeld and Nicolson, 1974, pp. 32–3

**Troupe.** Theatrical company. An 'old trouper' (not 'trooper') is an experienced actor or actress.

**Trust exercise.** Exercise which encourages mutual confidence in members of a group. It generally involves one or more group members relaxing completely in a situation involving full physical dependence on others. Carrying, catching, falling and playing a blind person are often involved.

**Tudor drama.** The Tudors reigned from 1485 to 1603. The term *Elizabethan, however, is usually employed to describe the extraordinary and prolific output of plays which followed the building of the first permanent *public theatre in 1576. The term Tudor tends thus to refer to forms of drama which predate this, such as the *interlude, *morality and *chronicle plays of the early and middle sixteenth century.

BOAS, F.S., *Introduction to Tudor Drama*, Oxford University Press, 1933.

WICKHAM, G., *Early English Stages*, Vol. II, Routledge, 1963.

WILSON, F.P., *The English Drama 1485–1585*, Oxford University Press, 1969.

**Turning-point.** A strong *crisis. An action, an event, a choice or a recognition which marks a powerful change in *plot, in a character's consciousness or in atmosphere — or in all of these.

An outstanding example is Leontes's declaration in Act III of Shakespeare's *The Winter's Tale* (1610): 'There is no truth at all in the Oracle!'. His denial of Apollo precipitates the immediate death of his son, and apparently of his wife. This forces Leontes's recognition of the falsehood of his accusation of her and marks a new feeling of humility. It also heralds a change in tone from a tragic *realism to the *tragi-comedy of 'Exit pursued by bear' and the clown's description of the death of Antigonus in the storm. These in turn establish a dramatic basis for the *pastoral and *romance elements of the subsequent acts.

A turning-point can thus precede a *rising as well as a *falling action. It can change the speed as well as the direction of events, and by affecting the state of mind of the *protagonist it can change the emotional responses of the audience. A play may have more than one crisis, but the single turning-point is the fulcrum of the play.

**Two-hander.** A play, often short, written for two characters. Ionesco's *The Lesson* (1951) is an example. The longer the two-hander, the greater the expertise required. What seems crucial to this form is a strong relationship between two contrasting characters who adopt a variety of moods and (possibly) *roles. The form evidently appeals to Samuel Beckett (1906–  ) who often uses pairs of characters, drawing upon the *double act of the *music-hall tradition, as well as upon common human pairings such as husband and wife, and mother and son. The form is economical in both senses of the term.

**Twopenny gaff.** Extemporized nineteenth-century theatre specializing in cheap *melodrama.

**Two-shot.** A *television camera shot framing two people. It is used to link *close-ups of individual characters speaking and reacting to one another.

The camera, of course, selects an area to *focus on. Stage actors and directors must direct the audience's attention by other means. A possible stage equivalent of a 'two-shot' would be two actors in a central or prominent position, watched by the other actors, or alone.

**Typology/Type.** See STEREOTYPE.

# U

**Überbrettl**. The German Uberbrettl or Buntes Theater was a literary *cabaret, founded in 1901 by Ernst von Wolzogen (1885–1934) in Berlin. For its manifesto, see Karl von Levetzow, *Ernst von Wolzogen's Offizielles Repertoir*, Erster Band, Buntes Theater, Berlin, 1902.

According to Meyerhold (1874–1940), the manifesto is an apologia for the fairground booth. It opposed 'plays which last the whole evening' with their 'ponderous bombastic expression of depressing events'. It advocated a return to the expertise of the variety acts and stylized performances of street entertainers, tumblers and the like, in an age where *naturalism was in vogue.

'We seek conciseness and precision in everything. We oppose decadence with its inherent diffuseness and obsession with detail,' says the manifesto, and the qualities it advocates are brevity, clarity, depth and contrast. Like Meyerhold, von Wolzogen was also attracted to the *grotesque.

**Über-Marionette**. Concept associated with Edward Gordon Craig (1872–1966). Craig began to make notes on it in 1905, after publishing *On the Art of the Theatre*. The pertinent essay is 'The Actor and the Über-Marionette', written in Florence and published in the second issue of *The Mask* in April 1908. There he asserted: 'The actor must go, and in his place comes the inanimate figure, the "Über-Marionette" we may call him . . .' (or 'super-puppet').

Craig seems to have felt that the actor was not an artist because too much in his performance was fortuitous. He also had doubts about the emotional impact an actor had on an audience. He repudiated *naturalistic assumptions that actors should get into the skin of a part and argued that they should remain outside their *roles, controlling emotion with imagination and intelligence.

This led him to the idea of the Über-Marionette. He had a collection of Javanese, Burnese and other oriental marionettes for which he wrote plays. He saw them as descendents of the stone images of the old temples and he admired their symbolic expression, untouched by the actor's personality and personal emotions. However, Craig did not want to *replace* actors with marionettes. As he explained in the 1925 edition of *On the Art of the Theatre*: 'The Über-Marionette is the actor, plus fire, minus egoism, the fire of the gods and demons, without the smoke and steam of mortality.' In other words, the Über-Marionette was a new, non-naturalistic, highly stylized actor who must not imitate but 'indicate' and whose acting must be impersonal and symbolic. For this reason Craig was drawn to the use of *mask because it concealed .the changing of a personal *facial expression and focused attention on *gesture and stylised *movement. His theatre in this way approached the condition of *dance.

Craig anticipated developments in the Soviet and German theatre after World War I, including the *biomechanics of Meyerhold (1874–1940), German *expressionism and Brecht's theories of gestic acting (see GESTUS). His theories closely resemble those of his older contemporary Adolphe Appia (1862–1928).

BABLET, D., *The Theatre of Edward Gordon Craig*, trs. D. Woodward, Eyre Methuen, 1981.

**Unconscious**. The area of the mind hidden from consciousness. Recent research threatens to superannuate the traditional division of the mind into unconscious and conscious areas and replace it with a division between 'right and left hand brains', each with specific functions. For the time being, however, the old model is still in common use.

Since Freud and fellow psychoanalysts developed the concept of the 'unconscious', of an area of the mind which the consciousness will not at once acknowledge, the question of how to represent this reality in art has frequently been asked. A play on the printed page appears as *dialogue, and since dialogue normally expresses the conscious *thought of dramatic characters, drama would appear to be at a disadvantage compared with forms of fiction where less organized mental processes can — as in Virginia Woolf's novels — be directly presented to the reader in interior monologue.

Drama, however, cannot be said to present only the conscious mind to an audience. In the first place, dramatic language has behind it the pressures of less organized parts of the mind and dramatists may create characters who do not fully understand the implications of what they are saying. The author creates a sense in the spectator of depths behind the dialogue, of desires which a character hides not only from others but from his or her own consciousness. Powerful dramatic characters such as Hamlet, Oedipus, Iago, Rebecca West and Hedda Gabler seem to carry behind their words a secret, a problem which they cannot or do not fully voice. The actor through *facial expression, *gesture, *movement and *intonation can create a sense of these hidden thoughts and feelings.

According to Freud the 'royal high road' leading to discovery of the unconscious was the *dream, and the strangeness of dream can sometimes be achieved in the theatre by creating an *identification with characters who suddenly see the world as strange. This can be done even in a *realist play. A dramatist can also employ symbolic *scenery and *surrealist *stage images to appeal to less conscious processes, as in German *expressionism and Artaud's *theatre of cruelty. Some element of dream exists in all drama, and the sensory effect of *colour, *sound effect, *silence, *lighting change, and the overall variations in a play's *rhythm, have the power to shake an audience out of a clearly conscious state. The feeling of intensification which comes to listeners in close physical proximity to one another seems to strengthen this sense of *strangeness in which the stage images and the power of the actor's presence and *voice communicate a meaning behind the words. It was this direct sensory appeal to unconscious forces which Bertolt Brecht (1898–1956) was suspicious of; it lay too near the hypnotic performances of demagogues like Hitler for his liking, and *epic theatre insisted on an appeal to reason and consciousness.

All plays, nonetheless, contain 'unconscious' elements, and writing, directing or acting in a play involves the analysis of material which lies not only 'in' the characters — if indeed one can consider a character to be more than marks on a page — but in the minds of the writer, director and actors who give the impression that the character 'lives'. Characters, one can argue, have no unconscious; they only leave silences for the spectator to fill.

Plays, again, may be seen as expressions of a *tradition which lies outside the mind of the individual artist — another kind of 'unconscious'. A play may be seen as a transaction between material which comes from the cultural background, and the individual who assimilates it 'unconsciously'. The individual may then strive to bring this material to consciousness to realize his own individuality. The act of composition is one way of exploring these unconscious realms.

Freud's central interest in drama lay in the examination of character relations and the relationship between the writer and his work. This has encouraged us to assume that the tensions of the dramatic situation express the writer's conscious and less conscious concerns. One should not forget, however, that the theatre is a place of collaborative activity. The dramatist's psyche has not been created in a vacuum. Nor does he write in one, though he may need solitude to clarify what he has been given. See THOUGHT.

ELIOT, T.S., *Selected Essays*, Faber and Faber, 1932.

FREUD, S., *The Interpretation of Dreams* (1900); *The Theme of the Three Caskets* (1913); *Some Character Types met with in Psychoanalytic Work* (1915). In the standard edition of Freud's works published by the Hogarth Press, Vols. 4, 5, 13, 14, 1955–7.

**Underground theatre.** A form of *alternative theatre which is associated with the 1960s in America and particularly the 'beat' and 'hippy' movements. It is to be distinguished from *avant-garde theatre by its direct attack on the conventional and legal restrictions on stage expression. Nudity, audience involvement and obscenity are among the tools it uses. It developed in New York and San Francisco, playing in warehouses and cellars, exploring fantasies and attacking American, and particularly Hollywood, cliché images.

ROSZAK, T., *The Making of a Counter-Culture*, Garden City, NY, 1969.
SCHROEDER, R. (ed.), *The New Underground Theatre*, Bantam, 1968.

**Units**. Stanislavski's term for the sections or movements into which an *actor divides a *role, and the *director divides a play, when preparing for performance. Having defined a *superobjective, the role or play is broken up into large sections, which in turn are regarded as containing smaller 'units'. Shakespeare's *Hamlet* could thus be broken into three sections: the opening *act dominated by the Ghost; the longer central 'unit' in which Hamlet puts on his 'antic disposition' and which ends with his departure for England; and the final movement which lasts from his return until his death. Each of these 'units' may obviously be subdivided. Thus the final 'unit' has within it: Hamlet's encounter with the gravedigger; his conversations with Horatio; his reaction to the burial of Ophelia; his encounter with Osric; his verbal exchange with Laertes; the duel; the final speeches to Horatio; the interchange between Horatio and Fortinbras; and the final funeral march. Each of these 'sub-units' may then be further subdivided. This process enables actor and director to gain a sense of the overall movement of a role and a play and thereafter cope with them in gradually increasing detail, instead of beginning with the detail and finding a *through-line difficult to acquire.

STANISLAVSKI, C., *An Actor Prepares*, Theatre Arts, NY, 1936; Methuen Paperback, 1980, Ch. 7.

**Unities**. The unities of *time, *place and *action are *neo-classical principles, defined by Boileau in his *Art Poétique* (1674) and introduced by Jean Mairet (1604–86) in his tragedy *Sophonisbe* (1634). They require that a play should possess a *single action*, without *double or *sub-plot. It should also be enacted in a *single place* during a period of no more than *24 hours*. Aristotle (384–322 B.C.), often cited as authority for the unities, was, in his *Poetics*, less emphatic. Unity of action was his main concern.

Observance of the unities can yield plays of economy, intensity and formal strength, as the tragedies of Racine (1639–1699) demonstrate. Such economy and power, however, is arguably obtained at the expense of the variety of mood and change of *perspective achieved by the English *Jacobean dramatists, or for that matter by Aeschylus (525–456 B.C.) and Brecht (1898–1956).

**Unity**. Aristotle (384–322 B.C.) in his *Poetics* advocated the writing of plays which were 'serious, complete and of a certain magnitude', possessing a *beginning, middle and end. His main emphasis was thus on an organic unity of *plot. *Neo-classical theorists added to this the greater rigour of the unities of *time and *place. This rigour was observed not only by Racine (1639–1699) but by many nineteenth-century practitioners of the *well-made play and by *naturalist dramatists confining themselves to a single *box-set. The *unities of action, time and place, however, are not the only forms of unity. Formal control can be achieved by the establishment of a dominant *mood or atmosphere and by subtle verbal and visual patterns. Chekhov (1860–1904), who frequently varies his dramatic location and employs a wide time-span, achieves formal unity in this way.

**Universal patterns *and* theatre**. That which, to cite Longinus, *On the Sublime* (c.1st Century A.D.), 'pleases all men in all times'. The concept of some sublime universal reality which exists beyond space and time in a work of art has been of comfort throughout the ages. The concept derives from Aristotle (384–322 B.C.) who saw poetry as a more universal thing than history (since poetry concerned itself with general truths and history with the particular). Plato (c. 428–348 B.C.), who believed in a transcendent reality, did not find his universals in art (see MIMESIS).

Those who argue for the existence of universals in drama may point, like C.G. Jung (1875–1961), to *archetypal patterns which appeal to individuals in all cultures because they form the content of the 'collective *unconscious', made up of the collective experience of past species. Jung's theory suggests that such patterns are expressed in the art forms of a culture. In drama they appear in such typological characters as the wanderer, the wise man, the *fool and various demonic figures, which are familiar to us in Shakespeare's *King Lear* (1605) and *Macbeth* (1606) to mention only the most familiar.

A Freudian might argue for the universality of family relationships in all cultures, and hence for the universality of the Oedipal patterns which he and others have seen in Sophocles's *Oedipus Rex* (c.430 B.C.), Shakespeare's *Hamlet* (1601) and Ibsen's *Rosmersholm* (1886), as well as in the works of Dostoievski (1821–81) and Eugene O'Neill (1888–1953).

Linguistic scientists, excited by the arguments of Noam Chomsky (1928–   ) in such works as *Reflections on Language* (1975) might seek for universals in the 'deep structures' lying beneath the semantic surface, whereby Chomsky seeks to explain language acquisition.

Others would argue for the biological similarity of human beings across the ages, and their sharing of mental and physical needs and characteristics — pride and shame, love and hate, greed, lust or hypocrisy. They also point to a 'permanent' human situation: all must face death and loneliness, and all feel a need for fellowship and love. Such universals appear banal when so described but when they are embodied in drama the common responses they call forth argue for their existence.

Universal patterns can be seen in art and in the human mind. It can also be argued that they exist in languages, and in historical and natural processes. A general acceptance of universals in nature, embodied in the cycles of the seasons and in the alternation of night and day, existed, no doubt, in primitive man. Dynamic and static patterns of the cosmos were formulated by the Greek philosophers Heraclitus (c.500 B.C.) and Parmenides (6–5th B.C.). Heraclitus saw nature as in a state of dynamic flux, whereas Parmenides saw change as illusory. The two opposed views were fused in the *idealism of Plato, who saw permanent pattern in transcendent, ideal forms, while the world in which we live remained transient, subject to *time and change. Ideas of change and flux were contained within a general belief in a patterned universe until the breakdown of feudalism and the rise of empirical science in the sixteenth century. The work of Copernicus (1473–1543), followed by Galileo (1564–1642) and others, undermined the belief in a geocentric 'world picture'. 'The new philosophy calls all in doubt' said John Donne (1572–1631) and this scepticism led to a breakdown of belief in universal patterns which is closely related to the development of *tragedy in Shakespeare's day. *Neo-classicism reasserted the importance of patterns and universal models, but in the nineteenth century the growth of the biological sciences and the development of ideas of randomness, chance and uncertainty, together with the challenging of the universality of Biblical truth by German philologists, and Darwin's implied attack on the book of Genesis in *Origin of the Species* (1859), engendered a further scepticism about universal patterns of any kind. Interestingly, this breakdown seemed to coincide with a new upsurge of *tragic feeling, found in the work of Thomas Hardy (1840–1928), Henrik Ibsen (1828–1906) and August Strindberg (1849–1912).

Ben Jonson said of Shakespeare that he was 'for all time' but such statements are rarely made nowadays. They are seen as a mere palliative in a changing world. The idea of universal dynamic patterns, however, remains. The *dialectic of Hegel lives on in Marxist thought, and when applied to drama, dramatic conflicts are seen as a reflection of the patterns of history. Georg Lukács (1885–1971), the Marxist critic, sees in Shakespeare's plays a pattern of conflict between feudalism and mercantilism, which is an early stage of the present conflict between capitalism and socialism. (See Lukács's *The Historical Novel*, published by P. Martin, 1962.) The relationship between such conflicts gives a historical play its apparently 'universal' appeal.

Those who locate universals not in history but in the human mind still put their trust in Freud's theory of the Oedipus complex, derived not only from case-studies but also from an examination of Greek tragedy and the plays of Shakespeare. Opponents of Freud see his theories as a function of the cultural patterns of his own society and thus not universal. Supporters find confirmation of his patterns in the 'modern' works of past cultures such as Euripides's *Medea* (431 B.C.), *Bacchae* (*c*.405 B.C.) or *Hippolytus* (428 B.C.).

Though universal truths may be impossible to verify, drama frequently represents men and women who seek to assert and live by permanent values. If it were proved that no such universals existed, drama would lose a principal source of *tension and the outlook would be bleak indeed. See PARADOX.

**University Wits**. A group of Elizabethan dramatists educated at Oxford and Cambridge and including Christopher Marlowe (1564–93), Robert Greene (1560–92), Thomas Nashe (1567–1601), George Peele (1558–97) and Thomas Lodge (1557–1625).

**Upstage**. The rear part of the stage, so-called because of the former *rake on the *proscenium or 'picture-frame' stage. The actor engaged in dialogue with another actor *downstage of him can, since his face is more fully visible, command the audience's attention. An actor who deliberately steals attention in this way is said to 'upstage' another.

**Utility man/lady**. A member of a Victorian *stock company whose function was to play the minor roles. Also known as 'General utility'.

# V

**Values**. See MEANING; IDEOLOGY; UNIVERSALS.

**Vamp trap**. A spring-leaved *trap in stage scenery through which an actor could make sudden apparitions. It was so-called after Planché's *melodrama *The Vampire* (1820), in which it was first used.

**Variety**. A name give to *music-hall and *vaudeville entertainment during the later nineteenth century, when specially built 'Theatres of Variety' replaced the public houses in which music-hall was formerly performed. These new theatres encouraged the introduction of a greater variety of 'twice nightly' performance including comic sketches, ballet and acts by well-known actors and actresses from the 'straight' theatre. This changed the rough and direct working-class nature of the original music-hall before the coming of the cinema helped to destroy it. Nonetheless, a few of the variety performers, especially the *double acts such as Abbot and Costello, managed to find their way way onto the screen, and forms of variety persist in *television today.

**Variorum edition**. A dramatic or literary text which assembles the notes and comments of previous editors and gives details of variants between successive editions.

**Vaudeville**. (a) Comic opera developing out of satirical urban ballads and unlicensed musical drama at Paris fairs in the seventeenth and eighteenth centuries. (b) American *variety theatres with their more respectable form of *music-hall entertainment; they acquired the name in the 1880s.
DOUGLAS, G., *American Vaudeville*, Constable/Dover, NY, 1963.

***Verfremdungseffekt/V effekt***. Brechtian term normally translated as *alienation or 'A' effect, and sometimes by the word *estrangement.

**Verismo**. Extreme *naturalism; a term applied in Italy to the work of Giovanni Verga (1840–1922) and his concern with social squalor and the life of the poor in his native Sicily. He dramatized his short story *Cavalleria Rusticana* (1880) and it became the *libretto for Mascagni's *opera (1890). The term *verismo* then came to be widely applied to the low-life opera of Mascagni (1863–1945) and Puccini (1858–1924).

**Verse drama**. Drama written in verse. The term in the English theatre refers especially to the work of T.S. Eliot (1888–1965), W.H. Auden (1907–72) and Christopher Fry (1907–  ). It also suggests the work of W.B. Yeats (1865–1939) and J.M. Synge (1871–1909) during the *Irish dramatic movement.

Generally speaking, verse drama aims at the communication of realities thought to be beyond the reach of *prose drama. For a discussion of Eliot's dramatic concerns, see POETIC DRAMA.

MARTIN BROWNE, E., *The Making of T.S. Eliot's Plays*, Cambridge University Press, 1969.

**Verse-speaking**. Skill which involves 'shaping' a speech, selecting the most important words to stress, developing clarity of *diction, and relating particular speeches to the *rhythm of the play. At the same time the actor must express his sense of the individual character whose words he speaks.

**Vice**. 'Old Vice' appears first as a buffoon and servant to the Devil in the *morality play. He wore the cap and bells of the court *fool and relates to the long tradition of fooling which goes back to *folk festivals and Roman *farce. His descendents include the servant figures of the *Commedia dell'Arte* and Shakespeare's Sir John Falstaff, whom Prince Hal calls 'that reverend Vice' in *Henry IV Part I* (1597).

CHAMBERS, E.K., *The Medieval Stage*, 2 Vols., Oxford University Press, 1903.

**Victorian period**. Queen Victoria's reign was not notable for important drama until the 1890s, when the work of Shaw (1856–1950) and Wilde (1854–1900) emerged from the welter of *farce, *melodrama and popular *revivals that constituted the principal dramatic fare. Exception here should be made for the work of Tom Taylor (1817–80) and Tom Robertson (1829–71) whose skill and, in Robertson's case, his attempt at early realism, mark them as above the common run.

A large number of Victorian novels, of course, including those of Dickens, were highly dramatic and many were adapted for the popular theatre. The financial rewards, however, were very small and major literary talents committed themselves to fiction or poetry. Only with the early productions of Ibsen's new *naturalist plays and the foundation of J.T. Grein's (1862–1935) *Independent Theatre Club in 1891 did the London theatre begin to produce new plays of importance — such as Shaw's *Widowers' Houses* (1892).

The plays of the *Irish dramatic movement began at the end of Queen's reign; the Abbey Theatre was not opened until after her death.

GLASSTONE, V., *Victorian and Edwardian Theatres*, Thames and Hudson, 1975.

ROWELL, G., *The Victorian Theatre: a survey, 1792–1914*, Cambridge University Press, 1978.

SOUTHERN, R., *The Victorian Theatre: a pictorial survey*, David and Charles, 1970.

**Viewpoint**. In the theatre a member of the audience cannot vary his physical vantage-point except by changing seats. He always watches an action from the same angle. This is a disadvantage when compared with *television or *film, which with their various cameras and techniques of *cutting can continually change the spectator's angle of vision. Nor does drama normally have *narrators who can, as in certain *novels, supply a variety of views on the action. Nonetheless, there are ways in which plays can vary our emotional and sympathetic responses so that we change our attitude to a character as the action develops. The usual dramatic application of the term is in this context. Drama may indeed be said to depend on a 'tension of viewpoints' whereby spectators both *identify with certain characters and see through their eyes, and at the same time manage to view them dispassionately from the outside. The emotions aroused by drama, such as admiration, respect, pity, compassion, fear, dislike and hatred, may be seen as viewpoints which the dramatist persuades the spectator to take up, even though his physical angle of vision does not change. See NARRATOR; IDEAL SPECTATOR; EPIC THEATRE; ALIENATION EFFECT.

**Villain**. Major dramatic character; antagonist of the *hero and *heroine, and deliberate perpetrator of the play's evil.

Villains are very powerful figures, arousing strong and ambivalent feelings. Disapproval of their actions is often mixed with admiration. The villain's sense of injustice, his resentment of power and his frequent intelligence, vitality and sense of humour seem to establish complicity with an audience. *Elizabethan and *Jacobean drama provide a number of complex villains of this kind. Shakespeare's Richard III, Iago in *Othello* (1604), Edmund in *King Lear* (1605), Webster's Flamineo in *The White Devil* (1612) and Bosola in *The Duchess of Malfi* (1614), together with Middleton's De Flores in *The Changeling* (1622), are perhaps the best known. Their dramatic ancestors include the tricky servant figure in classical *farce, and the devil and *Vice figures in the *morality plays. Their descendents include the simple but attractive moustache-twirling 'Sir Jasper' of Victorian *melodrama.

Major villains can become almost heroic in their challenge to goodness and authority. The attraction and repulsion they create and the strange enjoyment we feel when hissing the villain carry us into the major ambiguities which *tragedy explores. This is in part why the villain, like the *fool, occupies a *downstage position as an intermediary between audience and heroic action. He is an interpreter, and we listen half-willing to Iago, Edmund and the rest as they initiate us into their plans.

With the rise of *naturalism in the plays of Ibsen (1828–1906) and especially Chekhov (1860–1904) we move away from *stereotypes of villainy into the convincing psychological portrayal of human weakness. Heroes and villains are mixed and cease to be, in Chekhov's phrase, 'puffed up'. They become ordinary human beings. This is arguably achieved at some cost: we lose the sense of evil which emerges from the villain's relation to complexity and the Devil. The naturalization of the villain is, however, important. The stereotype figure normally reflects and appeals to simple social responses. Villains in Victorian melodrama for lower-class audiences generally possessed social rank, offering the opportunity for the spectators to express class resentment. Ibsen's 'villains' are often middle-class, like their principal audience, and therefore more disturbing. Jacobean villains also have a complex appeal since they generally lack social standing and seek to acquire it. They tend to be the 'new men' standing outside the social structure, lacking money and position but hungry for both. Their fascination lies in the challenge they represent to traditional attitudes to *power and evil, might and right. The Jacobean villain treads the borderline between politics and theology. See MACHIAVELLIAN.

**Visor**. Name for the black mask worn by the *guisers in the *disguising or early form of *masque.

**Visual symbolism**. See STAGE IMAGERY.

**Voice**. In 'spoken' rather than 'visual' theatre, voice is the most important part of an actor's 'equipment'. If the three rules of acting are 'to be heard, to be heard, and to be heard', this takes skill and training. Heavy roles in big theatres can make exceptional demands. They require not only strength of voice. Quality, timbre, variety of *intonation and clarity of *diction are also important. Since the basis of this is *relaxation and correct breathing, exercises such as Tai Chi or the Alexander Technique are often recommended.

Some of the most interesting work on voice has been carried out in the *Theatre Laboratorium of Jerzy Grotowski (1933–  ) who prescribes yoga and Chinese theatre exercises. The actor, he says, must 'produce sounds and intonations that the spectator is incapable of producing'; 'the very walls must speak with the voice of the actor'. Grotowski seeks to remove all barriers to the amplification of sound, to achieve 'total respiration' using both upper thoracic and abdominal areas, as well as 'resonators' — the upper thoracic and abdominal areas, as well as 'resonators' — the head, chest, larynx and occiput, employing the abdominal wall to create a 'base' for columns of air to be expelled. Actors aim at complete control of the voice, and must learn to produce natural and mechanical noises such as birdsong or humming engines, as well as multiple forms of verbal diction. The voice may be used as 'an axe, a pair of scissors, a drill, a broom, a hammer, a hand, a sheet of paper' and so on. Learning to breathe in the natural silences of speech is very important and the skills Grotowski advocates are only, he says, artificial in the sense that natural gifts and resources are being used to the full. 'The body must work first. Afterwards comes the voice.'

BERRY, C., *Voice and the Actor*, Harrap, 1973.

GROTOWSKI, J., *Towards a Poor Theatre*, Methuen, 1969, pp.147–185.

**Volksbühne**. German for 'People's Stage'; a drama association founded in 1890 by Bruno Wille. It split early over the issue of whether to align with the socialists. Reunited, it opened again in 1914, with 70,000 members. The association was suppressed by the Nazis in 1933. After World War II it was reborn in both East and West Germany. Erwin Piscator (1893–1966), who had been chief director in 1924, became director again in 1962, staging a spectacular production of Gerhard Hauptmann's *House of Atreus* and plays by R. Hochhuth (1931–   ) and Peter Weiss (1916–   ).

GARTEN, H.F., *Modern German Drama*, Methuen, 1959, NY, 1962.

*Volkstheater*. General term for the popular tradition in German drama. It includes the work of Hans Sachs (1494–1576) and later improvised theatre, influenced by the \*Commedia dell'Arte, which contained folk figures like Hanswurst. There is much \*clowning and \*slapstick, \*song and direct audience address.

*Volkstück*. Popular Austrian play, thought to have developed out of Viennese eighteenth-century theatre as an alternative to the court or \*Burgtheater. Under the pressures of censorship and commercialization the *Volkstück* became an uncritical form of popular entertainment, though elements of \*satire and social criticism are to be found, as in the prolific work of Nestroy (1801–61). When the \*operetta split off from the form it became small-town \*comedy, employing \*stock situations and dialect, dealing with love, marriage and the problems of inheritance and small businesses: to quote Bertolt Brecht (1898–1956), 'The bad get punished, the good get married, the industrious inherit and the lazy face the consequences.' According to Brecht it was irrelevant to the real '*Volk*' and their economic circumstances.

MCGOWAN, M., 'Comedy and the Volkstück', in *Brecht in Perspective*, edited by Bartram and Waine, Longman, 1982.

**Waggon stage**. A platform on which full *scenery can be assembled offstage, in order to effect rapid *scene-changes when rolled in from the *wings or lifted from the *cellar.

**Wagner, Richard** (1813–83). Major operatic composer, critic and theatre designer. With the architect Gottfried Semper he planned the Bayreuth Festspielhaus which opened in 1876. Its wedge-shaped *auditorium and fine *acoustics made it ideal for his operas. Deeply influenced by Greek *choral drama, he stands behind the 'synthetic movement' of Adolphe Appia (1862–1928) and Edward Gordon Craig (1872–1966) which sought to express the 'inner' and 'universal' man.

> A means of expression [music] has been made the end, while the end of expression [drama] has been made a means.

> In drama, therefore, an action can only be explained when it is completely justified by the feeling: and it is thus the dramatic poet's task not to invent actions but to make an action so intelligible through its emotional necessity that we may altogether dispense with the intellect's assistance in its justification.

See: GESAMTKUNSTWERK; LEITMOTIF.
WAGNER, R., *Das Kunstwerk der Zukunft* (1850); *Oper und Drama* (1851).

**Waits**. Medieval musicians, formerly watchmen, who were probably resident in noble households and played when required at dramatic performances. They also entered the service of town corporations and in London were probably hired from the corporation by the *Elizabethan theatres when they needed musicians.

**Wakefield Cycle**. One of the four surviving English cycles of *mystery plays, otherwise known as the Towneley Cycle. It contains the famous, farcical *Second Shepherd's Play* in which Mak the sheep-stealer and his wife disguise a stolen sheep as a child.

**Walking Gent/Lady**. Specialist actor or actress in Victorian *stock company who took secondary comic roles, such as that of Pharos Lee in *Maria Marten* (1830).

**Walk(ing)-on part**. A part involving no *dialogue, in which the performer is required to stand on stage as a soldier or attendant or another passive character. Such parts, though low in prestige, are not always unrewarding and can help establish a scene's credibility. See Stanislavski's discussion of the function and preparation of the 'walk-on' gondolier in his production of *Othello*:

STANISLAVSKI, C., *Creating a Role*, Methuen, 1961, Part II, Ch. 7.

**Warburton's cook**. Betsy, the cook of the well-known antiquary John Warburton (1682–1759), who 'burned, or put under pie bottoms' 55 manuscripts of rare Elizabethan and Jacobean plays. See:

GREG, W.W., 'The Bakings of Betsy', in *The Library*, 1911.

**Warm-up**. A short period of physical exercise preceding a *workshop or performance. Its aims are: (a) to relax the performers, in part by giving them something to do; (b) to prepare the muscles (especially necessary for physically arduous role); (c) to increase blood-flow and overcome self-consciousness and nervousness; and (d) to accustom beginners to physical as well as verbal expression. Its general aim is to prepare the mind as well as the muscles and generate the energy necessary for acting.

**Weeping**. To weep 'spontaneously' in a stage situation is something not all actors can achieve. Some, however, including, by repute, Michael Redgrave (1908–85), have achieved such control that they can command the number of drops and even the eye they fall from. In *film and *television acting, control of this kind is very useful and avoids the placing of fake drops of glycerine in the eye before the *take. The best way of learning how to weep on stage, some actors say, is to try not to.

**Weeping comedy**. Also known as 'tearful comedy'. It translates the French term *'comédie larmoyante'*, and is associated with the name of Pierre Claude Nivelle de La Chaussée (1692–1754) whose best-known play is *Le Préjuge à la Mode* (1735). The genre is related to *sentimental comedy.

**Well-made play**. English translation of *'pièce bien faite'*, a phrase coined by the prolific French writer Eugène Scribe (1791–1861) for his own highly contrived *farces and *melodramas, with their *surprises and *curtains, their formulaic *climaxes and the essential *scène à faire. In fact, the plays of Scribe and those of Eugène Labiche (1815–1888) and Victorien Sardou (1831–1908), who used similar formulae, were less 'well-made' than the plays of Ibsen (1828–1906) and the new *naturalists, who achieved close integration of *plot and *character portrayal. When the new naturalism appeared, the 'well-made play' became a term to be used — as it was by G.B. Shaw (1856–1950) — with opprobrium, signifying shallow characterization and ingenious, over-elaborate and empty plotting.

ARCHER, W., *Play-making: a manual of craftsmanship*, Chapman and Hall, 1913; Dover, NY, 1960.

CRAIK, T.W., HUNT, H., RICHARDS, KENNETH and TAYLOR, J.R. (eds.), *The Revels History of Drama in English*, Vol. VII, *1880 to the Present Day*, Methuen/Barnes and Noble, 1978, pp.161–70.

**Wen *and* Win**. *Chinese classical theatre using civil (Wen) and military (Win) subject-matter.

**West End theatre**. The commercial theatre of London's West End, centred on the district around Shaftesbury Avenue and the Aldwych. It is the equivalent of New York's *Broadway. The term connotes success, glamour and professional expertise. For those who advocate an *alternative theatre, it also suggests a theatre concerned with cash profits which places emphasis on the production of popular *musicals and *farce at the expense of more serious, high quality drama.

**Will**. Faculty which prompts action. Hence it can mean wish, intention, desire, resolution. As these four synonyms indicate, wills vary in intensity. Where there is an opposition of strong wills there is dramatic conflict. This can take the form of: (a) a competition between individual wills; (b) a conflict between individual will and the will of the group; (c) a conflict between conscious and unconscious desires within an individual; and (d) a conflict between *fate or the gods and some personal desire.

Any attempt by an individual to impose his or her will in order to change a *situation is potentially dramatic and may involve all the forms above. The will can manifest itself as a powerful drive in whose grip a person is helpless, as is the case with Phaedra in Euripides's *Hippolytus* (428 B.C.). It can express itself as pride, ambition and egotism, as it frequently does in *Jacobean drama, where the 'competition of wills', which Thomas Hobbes (1588–1679) saw as the human condition, is powerfully expressed. It can also take the form of a desire for freedom or for the achievement of an ideal, as often, however ironically, in the drama of Ibsen (1828–1906).

The relation of the individual will to the nature of human values is a common subject of drama. For the Greeks, the will needed to be harnessed and controlled. 'Will' and 'Appetite' were like horses, supplying energy, but only under the control of 'Reason' the charioteer. This was still the conventional view of Elizabethan England. The plays of Shakespeare and others, however, throw doubt on the capacity of reason to control the new individualism which threatened the social structure. *Troilus and Cressida* (1602) is a play in which the concept of will is carefully examined. The picture it paints is of a world out of control:

> Then everything includes itself in power,
> Power into will, will into appetite:
> And appetite an universal wolf
> So doubly seconded with will and power
> Must make perforce an universal prey,
> And last eat up himself. (I.iii.119–124)

Though the view expressed here by Ulysses supports Plato's view of the necessity of controlling the will, the play as a whole provides a picture of will dominating reason.

The sovereignty of the reason was re-established in the *neo-classical eighteenth century, but with the rise of *romanticism the will took over as the central principle of natural energy, especially after the publication of Arthur Schopenhauer's *The World as Will and Idea* (1819). The growth of the biological sciences also gave rise to a sense of a universal will which was seen by writers of *tragedy as a fate or destiny against which man struggles in vain. This feeling is strong in Ibsen (1828–1906) and Strindberg (1849–1912) as in Thomas Hardy (1840–1928). It led to a strange optimism about a 'Life Force' which was expressed by George Bernard Shaw (1856–1950) and to a political rebellion against deterministic views and a sense that man must struggle to control his destiny.

Such a sketch can do no more than hint at the importance of the concept of 'will'. It is, however, central to a discussion of drama, since a play, through its action, reveals the interplay of human wills and in the working out of this competition reveals its assumptions about the way things happen in the world.

**Willing suspension of disbelief**. See SUSPENSION OF DISBELIEF.

**Wind machine**. *Sound effect device consisting of heavy canvas attached to a drum which whistles like the wind when rotated.

**Wings**. Either: (a) *flats carrying *scene-painting, placed parallel to the *proscenium arch and masking the sides of the stage; or (b) the hidden stage area behind them where actors wait 'in the wings' to go on stage.

Wings were developed in sixteenth-century Italian theatres. They could be angled (see *Practica di fabricar scene e machine ne teatri* (1638) by Sabbattini (1574–1654)). They could also be 'nested', which involved placing wings on top of one another, or removing the exposed wing to reveal the one beneath, at each *scene-change. A speedier change could be effected by a system of flat wings set in *grooves. The front wing of each group had only to be pulled out of sight to reveal the wing behind it which set the following scene.

To get a speedier, simultaneous change of scene, the wings were set on trolleys or 'chariots' beneath the stage. A system of pulleys would transform the scene before the spectators' eyes — a method which continued to be used until the late nineteenth century. Wings are still employed occasionally, as for instance in traditional *pantomime.

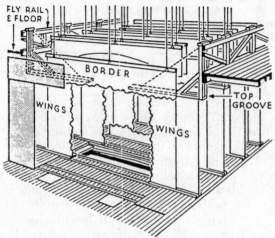

**30.** *Wings*

Inigo Jones (1573–1652), the architect and stage designer, introduced these procedures and others from Italy to England when he designed James I's court *masques. See:
CAMPBELL, L.B., *Scenes and Machines on the English Stage*, Barnes, 1960.

**Wise man**. See FOOL.

**Wit**. Play with language and ideas. The word has been used with a number of meanings including 'sense', 'common sense', 'judgement' and 'verbal ingenuity'. A 'wit' is a person who handles language cleverly and entertainingly. He was a frequent character in the eighteenth-century *comedy of manners where skill with words was admired and incompetence derided. Wits had allegorical names such as Truewit or Sir Wilfull Witwoud, the latter in Congreve's *The Way of the World* (1700). Discussion of the differences between 'true' and 'false' wit engaged an audience interested in the presentation of correct social surface. Congreve (1670–1729) was also concerned with the quality of feeling, self-centred or benevolent, which lay behind the wit.

The dramatic analysis of wit goes back to Shakespeare's comedies, where witty characters like Rosalind and Touchstone in *As You Like It* (1599) or Beatrice and Benedict in *Much Ado about Nothing* (1598–9) use it to establish dominance and control. Wit, in this tradition, is a powerful instrument — a way of handling situations, of relating to others and of controlling and distancing whatever threatens one's own life. The witty characters are aware of what is happening, and enlist sympathy, especially if they jest in adversity. The growth of *romanticism lowered the value set on wit, and much *melodrama, *sentimental comedy and perhaps especially the *historical drama which followed the *Sturm und Drang movement, was marked by an absence of wit and a ponderous high seriousness. Many of the mainly unsuccessful theatrical ventures of the major Romantic poets may be included here.

Wit, however, was not dead. It was subdued in nineteenth-century *farce, which set a premium on rapid plotting, but it returned to English drama with the Irish playwrights Shaw (1856–1950) and Wilde (1854–1900) in the 1890s, and emerged as a quality in the early dramatic poetry of T.S. Eliot (1888–1965) and the *ironic tone of the modern movement.

**Workshop**. Normally more experimental than a *rehearsal, a workshop aims to explore a text, situation, idea or feeling. Participants often use *improvisation techniques to discover areas of a character's (or of their own) personality. Workshop methods assume that we learn by acting out, experimenting and making mistakes. Such activity naturally gives rise to discussion, and, if carefully prepared and handled, it is a fine learning and general teaching method. See THEATRE IN EDUCATION.

**Wrath**. A *stereotype character (one of the seven deadly sins) in the medieval *morality play. See, for example, *The Castle of Perseverance* (early fifteenth century).

**'Writerly'**. Translation of R. Barthes's term *'scriptible'*, a word describing texts which invite the reader to 'write' them, or project interpretations into them, rather than to abstract their meaning from them (as do 'readerly' or 'classical' texts). The writerly text is plural; its meanings are never complete because it stimulates a process of continuing definition.

Barthes emphasized the importance of the reader and spectator in the artistic process. The nature of the audience/text relationship he sought to define might best be illustrated by the novels of Kafka (1883–1924) which seem to involve readers in a quest for explanation. They are 'writerly' because they invite readers to write the novel themselves.

In drama the example of Beckett is relevant. In *Waiting for Godot*, as in Kafka's *The Castle* (1926) or *The Trial* (1925), the audience or reader is invited to construct and define a 'meaning' which constantly changes. Gogo and Didi, the two tramps, seem to represent many different things. They are in turn 'sense and intellect', 'body and mind', 'poet and philosopher', 'man and wife', 'mother and child', two friends, a pair of tramps and a *music-hall duo, and so on. They are protean, like the relationships in Kafka's novels. They invite interpretation but the author never allows us to settle on a single explanation. The result is a dramatic world which confounds a full solution. In this it is *mimesis, not of the world, but of our doomed attempts to comprehend it.

The *ideology of such a *text is the repudiation of ideologies and a celebration of multiplicity. It parodies the search for a single meaning. In drama, more than fiction, the distinction is clear. There are plays which allow the spectator to join in and to answer; they are written for a space which both writer and spectator share. There are others which keep the spectator out, allowing him only to watch and understand. The former are open-ended and do not posit answers; the latter ask the audience to accept the writer's answer. The first are 'scriptible'; the latter 'lisible' — or perhaps one should say 'watcherly'.

BARTHES, R., S/Z, Seuil, 1970; Image, Music, Text, trs. S. Heath, Fontana, 1977.

# Y

**Yeats, William Butler** (1865–1939). Major Irish poet, dramatist, essayist and important figure in the development of the *Abbey Theatre and Irish national drama. His early plays are strongly influenced by the *Elizabethan drama. His later symbolic plays take the *Noh drama as a model. He rejected *naturalism, which he saw as 'photography', and sought to communicate a sense of other worlds in a drama centred on poetry.

I wanted to get rid of irrelevant movement, the stage must become still that words keep all their vividness — and I wanted vivid words.

See: TRAGEDY; VERSE DRAMA.
YEATS, W.B., *Essays and Introductions*, Macmillan, 1961.

**York Cycle**. One of the four extant cycles of the medieval *MYSTERY plays.

**Youth theatre**. Drama developed by and for young adults, often encouraged for social reasons. See:
COURTNEY, R., *Drama for Youth*, Pitman, 1964.

# Z

**Zany/Zanni**. A pejorative term in Elizabethan times for a poor imitator. The word derives from the Venetian form of Giovanni or John, and was given to servant figures of the *Commedia dell'Arte*. Thus Ben Jonson: 'He's like a Zani to a Tumbler,/That tries tricks after him to make men laugh.'

**Zarzuela**. Spanish musical play which has flourished in different forms at different times. In the later work of Calderón (1600–81) it was a court entertainment with a mythological subject. Later it acquired elements of lower-class realism in the work of Ramón de la Cruz (1731–94). In the twentieth century the form has undergone the strong influence of non-Spanish musicals.
SHERGOLD, N.D., *A History of the Spanish Stage*, Oxford University Press, 1967.

***Zauberstück***. German for 'magic play'. Play in which the mortal *hero is given a chance to live a different life by fairies who effect a magic change in his situation. Thus in one *Zauberstück* of 1826 a peasant was transformed into a millionaire. For left-wing dramatists such as Brecht the consolatory hope it offered was a form of *bourgeois propaganda, and its message was 'accept your social lot'.

**Zola, Emile** (1840–1902). French novelist, dramatist and theorist of drama who promoted the new *naturalism.

> Every winter at the beginning of the theatre season I fall prey to the same thoughts. A hope springs up in me, and I tell myself before the first warmth of summer has emptied the playhouses, a dramatist of genius will be discovered. Our theatre desperately needs a new man who will scour the debased boards and bring about a rebirth in art . . .

ZOLA, E., *Le Naturalisme au Théâtre* (1878); *Nos Auteurs Dramatiques* (1881).

**Zoom**. Cinematic device which allows rapid amplification or diminution of the object under the camera lens. To 'zoom in' means to move towards; to 'zoom out' means to move away, usually from a *close-up.

Its function is dramatic. The spectator is involved physiologically and mentally in the apparent change of viewing position. The cameraman may vary the impact by the speed at which the zoom takes place. The sudden shock of a fast zoom and the sustained *tension of a slow zoom are very different. The slow movements are often used to signal a beginning or an ending, whilst the rapid zooms are most appropriately used at critical moments during a *film.

As compared with the *tracking shot the effect of a zoom is strangely distancing. The relationships between objects in different planes remains the same and there is no full sense of entering the scene. In the tracking shot, spatial relationships between objects do change and we have a sense of entry. The zoom is like using opera glasses from the gallery. In the tracking shot we walk down the gangway. See VIEWPOINT.